PRAISE FOR *ISRAEL*

"Despite the billions that have been spent on·pro-Israel programs, there's a lack of approachable, popular histories that avoid polemics and actually teach you something. This is what Daniel Gordis aims to supply with *Israel*, which narrates the story of Israel from the origins of the Zionist movement in the late 19th century until today. Though written as a chronological narrative, Mr. Gordis's purpose is more poetic than historical. The author does not revise previous accounts of Israeli history. . . . He rather wishes to tell the story of the Jewish return to political sovereignty after two millennia of exile, and, despite its flaws, the stunning success of the enterprise so far. . . . The author loves his adopted homeland without ignoring its blemishes. He treats the most contested episodes in Israeli history, such as the plight of both Arab and Jewish refugees during the 1948 War of Independence, honestly and fairly." —*Wall Street Journal*

"Gordis is both open in his love for Israel and unsparing in his rejection of those who resist admitting that there are important criticisms of her that can't—and shouldn't—be waved aside. . . . [He] not only is unconcerned about an open discussion of Israel's flaws, including serious ones, but welcomes it. He embraces without citing it, Louis Brandeis' famous observation that sunlight is the best disinfectant. Knowledge doesn't hurt, either, and Gordis is determined to do his best to provide some to those who don't know as much about Israel as they think they know, or as much as they need to know." —*New York Observer*

"On the threshold of the hundred year anniversary since the Balfour Declaration, you will find volumes of material detailing Israel's creation and history; however, none of them is as succinct as Gordis's most recent contribution. You will appreciate the organization, maps, glossary of 'non-English terms,' and the mini-biographies of key figures. More critically, you will enjoy the fluid motion of Gordis's writing style, which somehow condenses thousands of details into memorable, thought-provoking passages. . . . Gordis grants us more than a peek at the past and present." —San Francisco Book Review

"Gordis is not in the camp of revisionist historians who find fault with every Israeli action. Nor is he the type to hide or deny Israel's mistakes. As the title promises, he delivers a concise, readable history that celebrates its subject without idealizing it. It's a book that belongs on the shelf of every believer in the Zionist dream." —*Atlanta Jewish Times*

"A welcome new primer, just in time for a new generation of English-speakers who are interested in Israel, to learn about the country and its struggles." —*Jerusalem Post*

"In *Israel: A Concise History of a Nation Reborn*, Daniel Gordis, an American-born Israeli, gives Israel its due. . . . He traces the country's origins to the Jewish people's traditional religious longings to return to their ancient homeland and to the grim political necessities Jews faced in late-19th- and early-20th-century Europe. He chronicles Zionism's heroic building against all odds of a Jewish and democratic state. And he captures the clamorous freedom, cultural effervescence, and economic prosperity that mark Israel today." —Hoover Institution

"Gordis shows how Israel has battled the odds for decades." —American Thinker

"Gordis describes how Israel grew into a flourishing country with the largest Jewish population in the world using a revived language that even the founder of Zionism believed could not be resuscitated. . . . Gordis has an ability to get to the core of issues and to discuss them in straightforward language that nevertheless conveys sophisticated analysis. . . . One of the best features of this book is the way Gordis weaves into his narrative literature, music—even dance—that capture, and sometimes shape, the emotions of the people at a pivotal point. . . . Gordis's concise history of Israel so well fills an urgent need." —Washington Free Beacon

"Like Israel itself, Daniel Gordis's *Israel: A Concise History of a Nation Reborn* is audacious, intensive, and unique. It tells the breathtaking story of the third Jewish commonwealth from the very beginning to today. Anyone interested in the history of Zionism will find profound insight in this much-needed, fair, and balanced book."

—Ari Shavit, author of
My Promised Land: The Triumph and Tragedy of Israel

"Daniel Gordis has written a luminous history that tells the story of Israel not only through its statesmen and warriors but also through its artists and writers and poets. Gordis gives us the soul of Israel, and helps explain why the most hated country on the planet is also among the most beloved."   —Yossi Klein Halevi, author of *Like Dreamers: The Story of the Israeli Paratroopers Who Reunited Jerusalem and Divided a Nation*

"A fascinating, accessible, nuanced, and smart account of a complex story, this book should be required reading for anyone who wants to understand this complicated corner of the world."

—Deborah E. Lipstadt, Dorot Professor of Modern Jewish History and Holocaust Studies at Emory University and author of *Denial: Holocaust History on Trial*

"Gordis captures the essence of who Israel is, where it has come from, and why the Jewish state will—and must—continue to exist. When I am asked, 'Is there one book to read about Israel?' I now have an answer."   —Ambassador Dennis Ross, Special Middle East Coordinator under President Bill Clinton and author of *The Missing Peace: The Inside Story of the Fight for Middle East Peace*

"The history of Israel is arguably the greatest story of modern times and telling it in a compact and compelling manner is an outstanding achievement. Daniel Gordis has accomplished this and more, rendering Israel's history in rich prose, fascinating insights, and passion. A riveting read for anyone interested in the Jewish State, his book will become an essential resource for scholars, students, and policy-makers."

—Michael Oren, Former Israeli Ambassador to the United States and author of *Six Days of War: June 1967 and the Making of the Modern Middle East*

"From near annihilation to resurrection, in the rich tapestry of Israel's concise—yet dense and painful—history, Daniel Gordis weaves awe into the complexity of constructing a new kind of Jewish society. Out of a dream that would not die, the new nation is self-reflective, spiritual, and intellectual, yet one that has conquered swamps and desert and taken arms time and again because there was never the option of turning back. *Israel* the book is an extraordinary reminder that Israel the country, with its new language, secular culture, and unparalleled achievements, is nothing short of a man-made miracle."

—Talia Carner, author of *Hotel Moscow* and *Jerusalem Maiden*

"Here it is at last—a sensitive, elegantly written, and fair account of the triumph and tribulations of the State of Israel."

—David Wolpe, rabbi of Sinai Temple, Los Angeles, and author of *David: The Divided Heart* and *Making Loss Matter*

"Daniel Gordis combines encyclopedic knowledge with the writing talent of a novelist. He makes complex historical events accessible as he spans the whole sweep of Israel's history, explaining how and why the rebuilding of the Jewish state in the twentieth century has transformed Jewish history forever. *Israel: A Concise History of a Nation Reborn* is a book that genuinely matters."

—Rabbi Joseph Telushkin, author of *Jewish Literacy, A Code of Jewish Ethics,* and *Rebbe*

"Gordis weaves anecdote with historic judgment, and effectively uses both literary sources and introductions to Israel's formative personalities to reflect on Israel's history, its politics, and especially its soul. *Israel: A Concise History of a Nation Reborn* is vibrant, articulate, and replete with wisdom."

—Ilan Troen, president of the Association for Israel Studies

ISRAEL

ALSO BY DANIEL GORDIS

God Was Not in the Fire:
The Search for a Spiritual Judaism

Does the World Need the Jews?
Rethinking Chosenness and American Jewish Identity

Becoming a Jewish Parent:
How to Explore Spirituality and Tradition with Your Children

If a Place Can Make You Cry:
Dispatches from an Anxious State

Home to Stay:
One American Family's Chronicle of Miracles and
Struggles in Contemporary Israel

Coming Together, Coming Apart:
A Memoir of Heartbreak and Promise in Israel

Saving Israel:
How the Jewish People Can Win a War That May Never End

Pledges of Jewish Allegiance:
Conversion, Law, and Policy-Making in Nineteenth- and Twentieth-Century
Orthodox Responsa (coauthored with David Ellenson)

The Promise of Israel:
Why Its Seemingly Greatest Weakness Is Actually Its Greatest Strength

Menachem Begin:
The Battle for Israel's Soul

ISRAEL

A CONCISE HISTORY

OF A NATION REBORN

DANIEL GORDIS

An Imprint of HarperCollinsPublishers

ISRAEL. Copyright © 2016 by Daniel Gordis. All rights reserved.
Printed in the United States of America. No part of this book may
be used or reproduced in any manner whatsoever without written permission except in the case of brief quotations embodied
in critical articles and reviews. For information address Harper-
Collins Publishers, 195 Broadway, New York, NY 10007.

HarperCollins books may be purchased for educational, business, or sales promotional use. For information please e-mail the
Special Markets Department at SPsales@harpercollins.com.

A hardcover edition of this book was published in 2016 by Ecco, an
imprint of HarperCollins Publishers.

FIRST ECCO PAPERBACK EDITION PUBLISHED 2017.

Designed by Suet Yee Chong
Maps courtesy of Joe LeMonnier

Library of Congress Cataloging-in-Publication Data has been
applied for.

ISBN 978-0-06-236875-1

17 18 19 20 21   LSC/RS   10 9 8 7 6 5 4 3 2 1

For

Ella Sara Ben Sasson-Gordis
רָנִּי וְשִׂמְחִי, בַּת-צִיּוֹן
(Zechariah 2:14)

and for

Bayla Chaikof,
whose lifelong passion for Israel and dedication to Jewish education
continue to inspire her children and grandchildren

Restrain your voice from weeping,
Your eyes from shedding tears;
For there is reward for your labor . . .
And there is hope for your future—
Your children shall return to their land.

—Jeremiah 31:16–17

A human life, I think, should be well rooted in some spot of
a native land, where it may get the love of tender kinship
for the face of earth, for the labours men go forth to, for the
sounds and accents that haunt it, for whatever will give that
early home a familiar unmistakable difference amidst the fu-
ture widening of knowledge . . . a spot where the definiteness
of early memories may be inwrought with affection.

—George Eliot, *Daniel Deronda*

CONTENTS

A GRAND HUMAN STORY

In Israel, in order to be a realist you must believe in miracles.
—David Ben-Gurion, Israel's first prime minister[1]

The Jew is being legislated out of Russia," Mark Twain wrote in *Harper's Magazine* in 1898.[2] "Spain [decided] to banish him four hundred years ago, and Austria about a couple of centuries later. In all the ages Christian Europe has . . . curtail[ed] his activities. Trade after trade was taken away from the Jew by statute till practically none was left. He was forbidden to engage in agriculture; he was forbidden to practice law; he was forbidden to practice medicine, except among Jews; he was forbidden the handicrafts. Even the seats of learning and the schools of science had to be closed against this tremendous antagonist."

Yet one Jewish man, Twain noted, had a strategy for ensuring that the Jews would have a future better than that past. "Have you heard of [Theodor Herzl's] plan? He wishes to gather the Jews of the world together in Palestine, with a government of their own— under the suzerainty of the Sultan, I suppose. At the [First Zionist Congress] last year . . . there were delegates from everywhere, and the proposal was received with decided favor."

Twain spoke with admiration for what Jews had accomplished,

with sympathy for their predicament in Europe, and even with some understanding of their renewed desire to create a state in Palestine. Yet Twain also had his reservations. "I am not the Sultan, and I am not objecting; but if that concentration of the cunningest brains in the world were going to be made in a free country . . . I think it would be politic to stop it. It will not be well to let the race find out its strength. If the horses knew theirs, we should not ride anymore."

TWAIN WAS MORE PRESCIENT than even he might have expected. The State of Israel was created exactly fifty years after his article was published in *Harper's,* and is, in many ways, one of the most extraordinary human stories of all time. It would be hard to name a single other people that had been through such a calamitous period and that, in the space of a few short decades, accomplished so much and rose to such heights. Though very real, what has unfolded in Israel over the last century sometimes sounds like a fairy tale.

Israel is a story of a homeless people that kept a dream alive for millennia, of a people's redemption from the edge of the abyss, of a nation forging a future when none seemed possible. Exiled from Judea by the Romans in 70 CE, Jews had dreamed for two thousand years of returning to their ancestral homeland. Their daily liturgy was replete with references to Jerusalem and with pleas that God restore them to Zion. When they prayed, wherever they were, they faced Jerusalem. They concluded the Passover Seder with the words *Next year in Jerusalem.* Never had the Jews left Zion willingly, and never had they ceased believing that they would one day return.

Toward the end of the nineteenth century and at the beginning of the twentieth, small numbers of Jews began to move to Palestine, some because they were certain that Europe would soon erupt in violence against Jews, but others out of sheer ideology. In an era of European nationalism, they felt that the Jews, too, should have a state. Sadly, though, it was not the Jews' prayers but the horrors of the twentieth century that transformed their dream into a reality.

Though the British had declared their support for the idea of a Jewish state in the 1917 Balfour Declaration, progress was slow. They turned from ambivalent to hostile; in the 1930s, the British began blocking Jews from immigrating to Palestine, frustrating Zionism's fledgling hope that it could create a viable state. Then, between 1939 and 1945, the Nazis murdered 90 percent of Poland's 3.3 million Jews—the most substantial Jewish community on Earth. All told, they killed one-third of the world's Jewish population.

Partially because of that unprecedented genocide, international consensus slowly began to shift. The Jews, it became clear, simply needed a place to go. The Zionists continued to build their prestate institutions and, eventually, forced the British to leave. In May 1948, the State of Israel was born.

The early years were desperately difficult. The new state, with no financial reserves and very little infrastructure, suddenly had to absorb masses of immigrants much larger than its own population. Jews from North Africa, Iran, Iraq, and elsewhere came to Israel by the hundreds of thousands when their host countries expelled them after the Jewish state was created; another one hundred and fifty thousand refugees from the Holocaust, bearing all the traumas of their horrific experience, also arrived at Israel's borders. Formerly swamp-ridden and still uncultivated in some areas and a largely barren desert in others, bereft of natural resources, and almost completely out of cash, the state had few options for feeding and offering shelter to all these people and began to ration food. Just a few years after its creation, the country was in danger of financial collapse.

Israelis did not give up, though, in part because they had nowhere to go. American Jews, long ambivalent about the very idea of a Jewish state, sent Israel desperately needed financial resources. Then Germany paid Holocaust reparations, and Israel began its slow climb out of poverty and weakness. With time, it built an infrastructure of roads and manufacturing, a national water carrier, and much more housing. It flexed its muscles and emerged as a player even beyond its own region, collaborating with the United

States, England, and France in complex international intrigue. Two
decades after the creation of Israel, its successes and the different
image of what it meant to be a Jew inspired Soviet Jews to demand
permission to emigrate. A few decades later, Israel became an economic and technological powerhouse; the envy of much of the
West, it had more companies listed on the NASDAQ than the entire
European continent combined.

Everywhere, there were signs of Israel's surprising flourishing. A country that had instituted food rationing in the 1950s was,
by 2000, producing internationally award-winning wines by the
dozens. A country that had had but one (government-controlled)
television station for decades now had numerous channels and
was producing films that competed for Oscars. A country home
to many Holocaust survivors, the very picture of helplessness and
passivity to some, became a military power. A people that had long
sanctified learning brought that tradition to their newborn country, with extraordinary results, winning Nobel Prizes and setting
international standards for research in numerous fields.

THOUGH IT IS A STORY of a country, the story of Israel is also the
story of a revolution. Zionism was the national liberation movement of the Jewish people, a movement committed to transforming
the existential condition of the Jew. It was time, Zionists insisted,
for the Jewish people to be reborn.

In many ways, Zionism was a rebellion against the Judaism of old.
As European Jews were attacked repeatedly and marginalized constantly, Zionist leaders began to argue that while Europe was obviously
to blame, so, too, were the Jews. It was time for the Jews to refuse to be
victims on call, living wherever they might call home until their host
country decided to evict or murder its Jews. England evicted Jews in
1290; Spain, in 1492. And then came violent European anti-Semitism.
Meanwhile, complained Zionist leaders, Jews remained passive, weak,
fearful, and huddled over ancient, sacred texts instead of defending
themselves and taking history into their own hands.

That, said many early Zionist thinkers, was what had to change. It would be hard to overstate the revolutionary zeal of these early Zionists. Zionism was in many ways about severing their connections to what had come before them. So desperate were the Jewish people to fashion a new kind of Jew that they even changed their names. Israel's first four prime ministers were a case in point. David Ben-Gurion had been born David Gruen. Moshe Sharett was born Moshe Shertok; Levi Eshkol was originally Levi Shkolnik. Golda Meir (Israel's first female prime minister) had been Golda Meyerson. Altering their names was a way of saying "no more"—it was time for a new Jewish worldview, a new Jewish physique, a new Jewish home, new Jewish names. It was time for a "new Jew," a Jewish people reborn.

In the State of Israel, that new Jew has emerged. In fact, many forms of the new Jew have emerged. Part of what makes Israel fascinating is the ongoing conversation about what Judaism and Jews should be and become. Sometimes that conversation is polite and restrained; at other times, it erupts into heated battles on Israel's many political fronts. All the vitriol notwithstanding, on that front Zionism succeeded—and admirably. Jews today are not the cowering, fearful Europeans of yesteryear. That Zionism succeeded in creating a new Jew is beyond doubt.

Zionism was also a revolution against the very possibility that there could be Jews who would have no place on Earth to call home. When mid-twentieth-century Europe erupted in a paroxysm of genocidal hatred, many Jews had nowhere to flee to. The United States closed its borders. So, too, did Canada. The British blocked Jews who sought to go to Palestine. Boats loaded with hundreds of Jews sailed the seas, desperately seeking a place to dock, often unsuccessfully. On occasion, ships that set sail from Europe loaded with Jews fleeing the Holocaust had to return to Europe, or were purposely sunk by enemy ships, simply because no one wanted "surplus Jews." Zionism was determined to change that; it was committed to a world in which Jews would never again be homeless. On that front, too, the creation of Israel brought a dream to fruition.

After centuries of Jews languishing in exile, Zionism was about restoring the Jewish people to the cultural richness that a people has when it lives in its ancestral homeland, speaks its own language, charts the course of its own future. If the Jews had been scattered to what their liturgy called the "four corners of the earth," Zionists hoped to gather them back together once again. If millennia of exile had reduced Hebrew, once spoken and vibrant, to a language used only for sacred and liturgical texts, Zionism would breathe new life into that ancient tongue. The Jewish people would produce music, art, literature, and poetry like all other peoples. There would be high culture and popular culture. Jews would live in the cities that their ancestors had known, would walk the same paths that had been home to their biblical forebears. Jewish leaders would make policy on war and peace, economics, health care, and immigration. Zionism succeeded in all that, and more. How Israel reflects this rebirth of the Jewish people is part of the story that this book tells.

Not all of Zionism's aspirations have been realized, of course. People like Theodor Herzl and Israel Zangwill believed that the Jews would bring such progress to the Middle East that they would be welcomed by the people already living there. A Jewish state could be established, they hoped and thought, entirely without conflict. That dream, tragically, was naive. Israel has been locked in a bitter and painful conflict since even decades before it was established, a conflict that sadly shows no signs of subsiding.

Theodor Herzl, in many ways the architect of the modern State of Israel, also believed that once the Jews had a country of their own, anti-Semitism in Europe and elsewhere in the world would be a thing of the past. That hope, too, was naive. In some ways, Israel has actually complicated the world's view of Jews and the condition of Jews in Europe. The rise and fall, the ebb and flow, of Israel's stock in the international community is a critical part of Israel's story, and this volume will examine that, as well.

Israel is a complex and dynamic place. It is a country filled with sacred places but also a secular (some would say profane) thriving bar and music scene. It is a deeply traditional society in some ways, and hypermodern in others. It is home to ultra-Orthodox Jews who shun much of modernity and one of the world's high-tech capitals. It is home to Jews of different colors, Jews of different ethnic backgrounds, Jews who speak different languages, Jews both secular and religious—and many non-Jews, as well. Most of the many immigrants that Israel absorbed (and per capita, Israel has absorbed more immigrants than any country in the world) came from countries without a democratic tradition; yet Israel has always been a democracy, and a thriving one, at that. And though a tiny country in terms of both size and population, Israel and its story are constantly at the center of the world's attention. It is essentially impossible to understand today's world without understanding the Jewish state—with all its vibrancy but also its complexity.

AS MUCH AS ISRAEL has captured the world's attention, there has been, until now, no single historically rigorous and balanced volume to tell Israel's story to a broad audience the way that this book does. There are, to be sure, several excellent one-volume histories of Israel. But many of them are two or even three times as long as this book, if not longer, and unlikely to appeal to general readers. And while the greater length of those books affords them the opportunity to delve deeper into some of the issues only touched on here, or to discuss issues and events not addressed in these pages, that often obfuscates the overall "story" that this book tells.

Many of those books tell *what* happened without providing adequate explanation of *why* it happened or how all the various components of the story add up to a coherent whole. Yet Israel figures too centrally in world affairs for us not to understand it. So this book tells the story of the *idea* of a Jewish state—where that notion originated, how it was preserved, and how the dream was transformed into reality.

As it tells the story of *what* happened, this book focuses especially on *why* things happened. Where did Jews get the idea of going to Palestine and building a country there? Why did the Zionists insist that their country had to be in Palestine, of all places? When and why did the world get behind the idea? How did people who came from mostly nondemocratic countries build a democracy that has chugged along admirably since its inception? Why do Israelis seem so hopelessly and vehemently divided on so many issues? Why have the Israeli and American Jewish communities long been so split on many critical issues? What lies in Israel's future?

This book also recounts many of the stories that are central to how Israelis understand themselves and their country. Just as the stories of Paul Revere's nighttime ride, George Washington against all odds crossing the frozen Delaware River, and the courageous fight to the end at the Alamo are central to the story that Americans tell about themselves, so too are the stories Israelis tell about their own history. These memories are key to understanding Israelis' mind-set, the way they view their history, their state, and how the world sees them; so this book tells the most important of those stories, as well.

Also introduced here are the formidable, passionate, and quirky people behind all this history. In the aim of being relatively brief, though, this book covers many events in Israel's history from a bird's-eye view. When it comes to Israel's wars, for example, this book focuses on why Israel was drawn into particular wars, the essentials of what transpired, and what happened to both Israel's society and its international standing because of a specific war. There are other books that document the military exploits of each of Israel's wars; that is not our purpose.

Some other issues remain virtually untouched. The economic history of Israel, for example, is fascinating, but with the exception of moments such as German reparations, which saved Israel economically, or Israel's improbable high-tech boom, this book does not devote much attention to Israel's economy. Of necessity, many events and personalities are not included in a brief history such as this.

ANY RELATIVELY BRIEF BOOK about a country as complex and fraught as Israel is, by nature, a work of interpretation. Even some seemingly "objective" facts are still the subjects of passionate disagreement, and to be sure, the motivations and intentions of key players are even more difficult to determine.

Beyond debates over facts, however, there is the larger matter of which "narrative" about Israel is the most fair. No two people would write a book of this sort in quite the same way. How much to celebrate the accomplishments, when and how to spotlight the mistakes and the disappointments, what to include and what to omit, what to assume about *why* certain people took the decisions and made the choices that they did, and how to put it all into a single, coherent perspective are the kinds of issues about which many readers will invariably disagree.

I have tried to be sensitive to these many positions, and at the same time, to tell the story in a way that I believe the facts support. By focusing on both the accomplishments and the missteps, the extraordinary history and the worrisome future, the well intentioned as well as the malevolent, I have sought to convey the history of Israel not as an amalgam of facts, but as a story. As in any great story, there are characters who develop and fade away, who make mistakes but also reach for greatness. The characters in this story are people, movements, political parties, states, and more. I have sought to tell the story in both as compelling and as fair a manner as I could.

Israel: A Concise History of a Nation Reborn tells the history of a tiny country and the ancient idea from which it springs. It tells the story of a country that has long beaten the odds, but which still faces frightening—some say insurmountable—enemies and hurdles. It is the story of a people reborn, but at great cost. Israel's story is a complicated one, both dramatic and sad. It is a wondrous and inspiring story, one that affects our world almost everywhere we turn.

Now is the time to tell the story, to understand what has transpired, and even more important, why.

POETRY AND POLITICS

The Jewish Nation Seeks a Home

In that warm and beautiful land, does evil reign and do calamities happen, too?

—Chaim Nachman Bialik, "To the Bird"

He would become the voice of a generation, a poet whose aching soul was a window into the pain of his entire people. Only nineteen years old when he published his poem *"El Hatzippor"* ("To the Bird"), Chaim Nachman Bialik would soon be recognized as one of the greatest Hebrew poets of all time, certainly the greatest of his era. Bialik's poetry captured both the desperation and sadness that the Jewish people felt at the end of the nineteenth century, as well as their longing for a place they thought of as home even though they had never seen it.

"How my soul longed to hear your voice," the poet says to a bird just returning from Zion, then known as Palestine. He asks the bird what life is like in the idyllic place that he imagines. "Does God have mercy on Zion?" "Does the dew fall like pearls upon Mount Hermon?" "In that warm and beautiful land, does evil reign and do calamities happen, too?" Not really questions, these musings were more wistful dreams of a place across the ocean that had once been home to the Jewish people, and that—Bialik and others of his generation thought—might be home once again.

WHEN BIALIK PUBLISHED "To the Bird" in 1892, Jewish life in eastern Europe was miserable in many ways. Russia's Jews were largely allowed to live only in a specific region called the Pale of Settlement. Violence against Jews was rampant, either encouraged or ignored by the government and local authorities. Pogroms, as these attacks on Jews were called, had happened before, but toward the close of the nineteenth century, they took on a new intensity over a wider area. There were pogroms in Romania in the 1860s, in Odessa in 1871; the Jews knew that they were confronting an utterly irrational hatred that reason could not undo.

European anti-Jewishness was becoming more complex. In eastern Europe, much of it was fueled by theological claims or the accusation that the Jews had killed Jesus.* In central and western Europe, though, which was now infatuated with science, race theory developed. Now, said European racists, the problem with the Jews was their race, not their religion. Even conversion to Christianity could no longer "fix" the Jew. In 1879, a German by the name of Wilhelm Marr, who rejected the notion that Jews could assimilate into general society, even coined a term for the modern incarnation of Jew hatred, which he himself shared. He called it "anti-Semitism."[1]

Violence was hardly the only expression of Europe's disdain for Jews. In the 1880s, the Russian government placed strict limits on the numbers of Jews who could be admitted to schools and universities. The authorities sought—and found—almost endless ways to harass the Jews; in 1891–1892, Russian police expelled no less than twenty thousand Jews from Moscow.[2] Everywhere they turned, Jews faced a continent that despised and harassed them.

Many Jews had expected that matters would be different, that

---

* That accusation is first suggested in Matthew 27:24–25: "When Pilate saw that he could prevail nothing, but that rather a tumult was made, he took water, and washed his hands before the multitude, saying, I am innocent of the blood of this just person: see ye to it. Then answered all the people, and said, His blood be on us, and on our children." (King James Version) modernity would herald a new era of reason and tolerance. But that hope was rapidly fading. Peretz (Peter) Smolenskin (1842–1885), a Russian Jewish novelist, warned the Jews that they ought to be realists. "Do not believe those who say that this is an age of wisdom and an age of love for mankind; do not turn to the words of those who praise this time as a time for human justice and honesty; it is a lie!"[3]

With time, it became clear to many that as bad as Jewish life in eastern Europe already was, it was going to become infinitely worse. A mass exodus began. Between 1882 and 1914, some 2.5 million Jews departed eastern Europe, primarily from Austria, Poland, and Romania. During the fifteen years that preceded World War I, approximately 1.3 million Jews left Russia.[4] A huge portion of them went to America, where they created what would become the thriving American Jewish community of the twentieth century. A small fraction of them went to Palestine.

IT WAS INTO THIS ATMOSPHERE of despair that Chaim Nachman Bialik had been born in 1873. After his father died when he was six years old, he was raised by his strictly religious grandfather. He received a classic Jewish education, learning in *heder* (a traditional Jewish schoolhouse) until he was thirteen and then studying in the Zhitomir Yeshiva until he was seventeen. Like many young Jews of his era (and as would soon be the case with many of his fellow Zionist writers and leaders), however, Bialik was fascinated by the worlds of Western culture and the Jewish Enlightenment (the *haskalah*). A movement that began in the 1770s and lasted until the 1880s, the *haskalah* sought to reform the Jewish emphasis on tradition and collectivism and to import into Jewish society a more rational, analytical, intellectual, and individualistic way of life.

The *haskalah*, though, was more than an intellectual movement—it also had social and national agendas. To the exponents of the *haskalah*, the challenge facing the Jew was to transcend the narrowness of ghetto life, "to bolster the self-confidence of the Jew-ish people, restore its dignity, reawaken its emotional life, quicken its aesthetic sense and generally counteract the stultifying conse-quences of long isolation and confinement."[5]

Bialik's encounter with the *haskalah* came after he transferred to a new yeshiva. Seeking a more modern approach to the study of traditional Judaism, Bialik transferred to the world-renowned yeshiva in Volozhin, Lithuania. It was there that he encountered the *haskalah* and soon became involved with *Netzach Israel* ("The Eternity of Israel"), an underground Zionist student group com-mitted to integrating Jewish nationalism, the Enlightenment, and Orthodox Judaism.

In 1891, Bialik left Volozhin for Odessa, which was at that time the center of modern Jewish culture in southern Russia.* It was then, largely under the influence of that intellectual circle, that he published "To the Bird," in 1892.

Not long thereafter, Bialik returned to Zhitomir to make sure his grandfather did not learn of his "escape" to Odessa. When he arrived home, he discovered that his grandfather and older brother were both dying. The desperate atmosphere at home seemed to mirror the condition of the Jews around him. After their deaths, he found a job teaching Hebrew in Sosnowiec, a small village in southern Poland, but the job made him miser-able. Yet the misery paid off. He wrote almost incessantly, and not long thereafter acquired a reputation as one of the world's most gifted Jewish poets.

Not all of Bialik's poetry dealt with Jewish anguish. In 1898, Bi-

---

* The word *Zionism*—referring to the movement to re-create a national Jewish home in the Land of Israel—was coined by Nathan Birnbaum, a well-known public intellectual at the time. He first used it on April 1, 1890, for an article he wrote for his journal, *Self-Emancipation*. He used the term in a public address for the first time in January 1892. (Lawrence Epstein, *The Dream of Zion: The Story of the First Zionist Congress* [Lanham, MD: Rowman and Littlefield, 2016], p. 13.)

alik wrote a poem not about Jewish despair, but about Jewish hope. Entitled *"Mikra'ei Zion"* ("The Assemblies of Zion"), the poem was written in honor of the First Zionist Congress that had been held in Basel in 1897. "Even if salvation has not yet come, our Redeemer still lives; the great hour has arisen and is coming," Bialik wrote in a poem brimming with hope and expectation.

Where had that hope suddenly come from? What was that "great hour" that Bialik saw growing ever closer? Why had what had happened in Basel been so important? And who was this Redeemer?

THE DELEGATES TO the First Zionist Congress had come to Basel from across the globe. From Britain and America, from Palestine and from Arab lands, from Russia, Germany, France, and more, the 197 delegates had gathered in Switzerland with the sense that they were making history.

It was August 1897, and for the first time in nearly two thousand years, since the Romans had destroyed the Second Temple and exiled a large portion of the Jews living in Judea, Jews from around the world gathered in one place to take history back into their own hands. No longer merely pods of disconnected Jews scattered around the globe, thanks to Herzl's call they were now, for the first time in millennia, reasserting their ancient claim that they were a single people determined to make Jews agents rather than bystanders on the stage of world history.

Elegantly dressed, they entered the hall under a large sign with a Star of David and two simple words: ZIONISTEN-KONGRESS. They chatted in their native languages, mostly men but some women as well, some rich and others poor. The energy in the air was palpable. When they finally took their seats, the First Zionist Congress began with three bangs of the gavel. There were some pro forma compliments to the sultan, since the Ottoman Empire then controlled Palestine. Then, Dr. Karl Lippe of Jassy, Romania, a longtime member of the

organization *Hovevei Zion* ("Lovers of Zion"),* and the most senior
delegate of the congress, stood. He covered his head in accordance
with Jewish tradition, and as many of those in attendance wept, ut-
tered the traditional Jewish *shehecheyanu* prayer: "Blessed are You,
Lord our God, who has kept us alive, preserved us, and enabled us
to reach this moment."

And then, Theodor Herzl, who had convened the congress,
stood to speak. "We are here," he opened in German, "to lay the
foundation stone of the house which is to shelter the Jewish nation."[6]

IN THE WESTERN EUROPEAN world in which Herzl lived and
worked, the mere idea that the Jewish nation needed a house to
shelter it was more controversial than it was in the east. Western
European Jews, unlike the eastern Europeans of Bialik's world, still
held on to some hope that anti-Jewish movements were a relic of
the past. After all, the walls of the old ghettos—neighborhoods in
which Jews had been forced to live—had come down, and Jews had
flocked to the continent's urban centers. They had quickly become
part of the very fabric of Europe's elite. They had climbed the ladder of European society educationally, culturally, and economically. On the surface, life seemed much better for them than it had
been a century earlier.

In 1800, the history of Central and Western European culture
could have been written without reference to the Jews or any
specific Jewish person . . . nor had there been a single Jewish figure in European politics, intellectual life, research or science. . . .
As 1900 approached, the picture was entirely different. Jews, or

---

* Technically, the organization's name was *Hibat Zion* ("Love of Zion") and
its members were known as *hovevei Zion* ("Lovers of Zion"). With time,
though, *Hibat Zion* and *Hovevei Zion* were used interchangeably as the
names for the organization itself.

people of Jewish origin, now played critical roles in economics, politics, science and the arts.[7]

Despite centuries of restrictions and anti-Semitism, what the Jews had accomplished in a relatively short period was astounding. They became professionals and intellectuals, leading scientists and leaders of significant intellectual and social movements.

Yet despite the progress, even western European Jews could not escape the continent's hatred. If Jews in eastern Europe were often scapegoated as disruptive revolutionaries, in western Europe, they were blamed for society's financial ills. Though they constituted less than 1 percent of Germany's population, Jews had quickly assumed high-profile and elite positions in all of society's professions, particularly in finance and politics.

But many Germans grew resentful. Almost everywhere one turned, there was an air of anti-Jewish sentiment. Newspapers, books, and magazines railed against the stereotypical greedy, capitalist, and corrupt Jew, a motif that informed genocidal regimes that would follow in the mid-twentieth century. In the wake of a financial crisis in 1873, much of the German bourgeoisie blamed the Jews for its newfound financial woes. Although the "[a]ristocrats were . . . as greedy as anyone else . . . in the prevailing myth . . . aristocrats remained great statesmen, valiant soldiers, and devoted public servants. In the aftermath of the crash, popular fury was directed not at them and the government they dominated but at the Jews."[8]

In western Europe, it was precisely the Jews' embrace of modernity and their professional and intellectual achievements that reawakened Europe's antipathy. The Jews hoped that they had put European resentments behind them, but Europe, it seemed, had an unlimited reservoir of Jew hatred that was on the verge of spilling over. There was nothing the Jews could do to change that.

IT WAS IN THIS promising, alluring, and yet increasingly despairing world that Theodor Herzl came of age. Born in Pest (one of the two cities that would eventually combine to create Budapest) in 1860, Herzl moved at eighteen with his family to Vienna. There, he was exposed to the intellectual and cultural riches of European society and—just as had happened with Bialik—he quickly became enamored. He read voraciously and aspired to attain the same level of fame of those authors he so avidly read. Like Bialik, he wrote almost constantly. Yet though the arts—and particularly the theater—were his real love, his parents and his other mentors worried about his ability to make a living and encouraged him to study law. So Herzl enrolled in the University of Vienna.

Early in his university career, Herzl picked up a book by Eugen Karl Dühring, one of the period's leading intellectuals. Entitled *The Jewish Problem as a Problem of Race, Morals and Culture* (1882), the book argued that the emancipation of the Jews in Europe and their integration into European society had been detrimental to Europe. Dühring advocated reversing much of the emancipation; some of his followers began to speak of returning the Jews to ghettos.

What was as disturbing to Herzl as Dühring's ideas was the fact that Dühring was hardly an uneducated thug. "If Dühring, who unites so much undeniable intelligence with so much universality of knowledge, can write like this," Herzl wondered, "what are we to expect from the ignorant masses?"[9]

Ironically, it was Dühring—both a celebrated European intellectual and also a vicious anti-Semite—who played a significant role in Theodor Herzl's dedication to the "Jewish question." He later mused on the origins of his interest in the Jews and their future in Europe, writing in his diary, "certainly from the time that I read Dühring's book."[10]

In truth, though, the seeds had been planted much earlier. He would later recall that as a young boy, when one of his teachers had sought to explain what the word *heathen* meant, the teacher had said, "Idolaters, Mohammedans and Jews."[11] At the University of Vienna, Herzl had applied to join the *Lesehalle,* a student association devoted to intellectual conversation and debate. But in March 1881, the *Lesehalle* was dissolved when a "discussion" devolved into a viciously anti-Semitic event. Undeterred, Herzl joined one of Vienna's German nationalist student fraternities, Albia, instead. Yet here, too, the university—the seat of Europe's intellectual elite—proved fundamentally hostile to Jews. Two years after he joined, several of his fraternity brothers attended a Richard Wagner memorial, which, again, turned into an anti-Semitic rally.[12] Herzl resigned from the fraternity in protest, but the members rejected his resignation, and then threw him out on their own terms.

Herzl's first encounter with the central idea that would consume his life—the need for a Jewish state—may well have been in the Hungarian Parliament. Győző Istóczy, a Hungarian nationalist and founder of the National Anti-Semitic Party, is said to have proposed that to solve Hungary's "Jewish problem," Jews ought to establish a state of their own and go there.[13] "Jew, Go to Palestine!" became a slogan of the Hungarian anti-Semitic movement. Ironically, Istóczy's motto would eventually become Herzl's, too.

Whether or not Istóczy's hate-filled calls for Jews to go to Palestine really influenced Herzl very much, we do not know. What is certain is that as his career progressed, Herzl encountered anti-Semitism at every turn. When he departed Vienna, he moved to Paris, working as a writer for the *Neue Freie Presse,* a leading European newspaper based in Vienna. Herzl was becoming a writer of note. While in Paris, he covered a scandal involving the financing of the Panama Canal, a project in which several Jewish financiers were accused of bribery and corruption. More than the scandal itself, though, what struck Herzl was how the Jews who were involved, whose families were all prominent figures in France's political and military circles, were characterized as archetypal cosmopolitan Jews who had speculated with the hard-earned money of simple, loyal French citizens.[14]

In Austria, he had seen the rise of an intellectually based anti-Semitism, which even leading minds at Europe's great universities did not reject. And now, in France, Herzl saw that even democracy and republican government were no solution.

Like Bialik, Herzl poured his heart into his writing. In the fall of

1894, in the space of just over two intense weeks, Herzl developed his play *The New Ghetto,* the first of his scripts to have distinctly Jewish characters and to deal openly with the "Jewish question." The point of the play, made rather transparently and not terribly artistically, was that though Europe had emancipated the Jew, Jews still effectively lived in a social and economic ghetto, under relentless pressure to prove themselves.[15] Even in ostensibly emancipated western Europe, Jews were presumed guilty until proven innocent.

But matters would soon grow worse. As Herzl was occupied with *The New Ghetto,* a new scandal erupted in France. Captain Alfred Dreyfus, a French artillery officer of Jewish descent, was charged with sharing French secrets with the Germans. With France in the grip of political and social turmoil, the trial was actually a foil for battles between the still competing parties. So obvious was the miscarriage of justice that when Dreyfus was found guilty and unceremoniously stripped of his rank, Émile Zola (the famed French novelist, journalist, and public intellectual) wrote his now classic letter, *J'Accuse,* accusing the government of both flagrant anti-Semitism and of unfairly jailing Dreyfus.

Though it is commonly said that it was the Dreyfus trial that spurred Herzl's engagement with the "Jewish question" in Europe, historians now believe that that was not the case. Herzl had, indeed, mentioned in one of his columns Dreyfus's comment to a prison guard, "You see, I am a victim of a personal vendetta. I am being persecuted because I am a Jew,"[16] but Dreyfus's Jewishness was not a central focus of his writing.

IRONICALLY, IT WAS HERZL'S utter failure in a meeting that led to his greatest success. He had gone to Baron Maurice de Hirsch, a financier and philanthropist, to ask for support for his radical idea of creating a Jewish state. But Hirsch, who feared for the Jews' future in eastern Europe, had an alternate solution to the "Jewish problem" in mind. The baron, who had earlier written off Palestine as an impractical option, had already helped finance the relocation of some of Russia's Jews to Argentina. Herzl tried to push back, but his response to Hirsch was amateurish and he left the meeting empty-handed. Determined to do better the next time, he decided to put his thoughts into writing to clarify precisely what he wanted to communicate to Hirsch.

Not easily dissuaded, and with his improved argument in hand, Herzl turned to another Jewish philanthropic family, the well-known Rothschilds. For them, he composed a much more detailed and well-organized exposition of the plan he had already begun writing. It was this version that would become the foundation of his best-known book, *The Jewish State*.

His case was quite straightforward. A Jewish state—in a location yet to be determined, either Argentina or Palestine—would solve the "Jewish problem." In contrast to what Hirsch believed, Herzl was convinced that the goal was eminently attainable. In fact, he argued, it was in everyone's best interest that the Jews should secure themselves a state.

Not only would Jews in a Jewish state not suffer from anti-Semitism, he believed, but the existence of a Jewish state would usher in an end to anti-Semitism everywhere. "The withdrawal of the Jews would not lead to any economic disruption, crises or persecutions," argued Herzl. "The countries they abandon would enter into a period of prosperity," he said. As for the creation of a Jewish state, "its very beginning means the end of anti-Semitism."[17] Nor was the task a mere flight of fancy. The Jews, he said unabashedly, were far more educated than many other peoples who had created sovereign states for themselves. If those other peoples had successfully undertaken revolutions, the Jews could certainly do so as well.

For similar reasons, Herzl argued, the Jews would not encounter much opposition to their movement; the international community would support the idea since those countries, too, "suffered" from the "Jewish problem." He wrote:

The creation of a new State is neither ridiculous nor impossible. We have in our day witnessed the process in connection with nations which were not largely members of the middle class, but poorer, less educated, and consequently weaker than ourselves. The Governments of all countries scourged by Anti-Semitism will be keenly interested in assisting us to obtain the sovereignty we want.[18]

The problem that the world had with the Jews, he argued, was neither social nor religious; it was political, and therefore, it required a political solution that the international community would accept.

I believe that I understand Anti-Semitism, which is a highly complex movement. I consider it from a Jewish standpoint, yet without fear or hatred. . . . I think the Jewish question is no more a social than a religious one, notwithstanding that it sometimes takes these and other forms. It is a national question, which can only be solved by making it a political world-question to be discussed and settled by the civilized nations of the world in council.[19]

But what about the fact that the Jews were spread across Europe and around the world and seemingly fragmented? That dispersion, Herzl said, should not mislead anyone. "We are a people—one people."[20] Since other peoples had states, he insisted, so, too, should the Jews.

Herzl wrote his book in a state of feverish excitement. "For some time past," he said when describing his writing the book, "I have been occupied with a work of infinite grandeur. At the moment I do not know whether I shall carry it through. It looks like a mighty dream. But for days and weeks it has possessed me."[21]

It possessed those who read it no less. A short book of approximately one hundred pages, The Jewish State made Herzl a household name across the Jewish world. Published in February 1896, it caused a stir worldwide. It was printed, translated, and read more quickly and more widely than any other Jewish work of the modern era. "In 1896 alone, it appeared in English, Hebrew, Yiddish,

Romanian, Bulgarian, Russian and French. Students, in particular, were enthused by his proposal; almost overnight, the appearance of *The Jewish State* transformed Herzl from a lone voice into the leader of an international movement."[22]

The movement's central idea—though it now sounds commonplace—was then a stunning proposal. And now, much of the Jewish world had been convinced: the Jewish people needed a state, and they could create one.

ALTHOUGH IT WAS THEODOR HERZL who launched Zionism as a political movement, others had begun to express similar ideas long before him. In 1853, some forty years before Herzl's *Jewish State* appeared, Avraham Mapu had published the first modern Hebrew novel. Like Bialik, Mapu had been born into a traditional family but grew enthralled with European culture. Mapu's novel, *The Love of Zion,* was set in ancient biblical Israel, during the period of the prophet Isaiah. The novel was more than a mere story; it breathed new life into memories of the Jews in their ancestral homeland, and "gave open expression to the mute longings . . . of a whole people [for] a fuller and richer life."[23] The book touched a nerve with the Jewish people and sold extremely well. With Mapu, the first stirrings of modern Zionism emerged.

Even more dramatic, though, was the work of Moses Hess (1812–1875). Born in Germany, raised in part (again like Bialik) by his traditional rabbi grandfather, Hess was a devotee of the renegade pantheist Dutch Jewish philosopher, Baruch Spinoza. Later, his radical inclinations led him to socialism. Distancing himself even further from traditional Judaism, he married a working-class Catholic woman.[24]

But Hess soon learned that even abandoning Judaism, embracing socialism, and marrying a Catholic woman could not protect him from Europe's anti-Semitism. "Even an act of conversion cannot relieve the Jew of the enormous pressure of German anti-Semitism," he wrote. "The Germans hate the religion of the Jews less than they hate their race—they hate the peculiar faith of the Jews less than their peculiar noses."[25]

So in 1862, Hess wrote *Rome and Jerusalem*,[26] in which he argued that for Jews, Europe's welcome would forever be tenuous. "We shall always remain strangers among the nations. They may tolerate us and even grant us emancipation, but they will never respect us as long as we place the principle *ubi bene ibi patria* [wherever things go well, there is one's homeland] above our own great national memories," he wrote.[27] Jews should return to Palestine, he said—the ancestral homeland of which they had dreamed and spoken for millennia—where they should work the land and create a socialist society.

Though now considered a critical text in the history of political Zionism, *Rome and Jerusalem* was virtually ignored while Hess was alive; Jews then were not concerned enough about the future of Jewish life in Europe to take him seriously.[28] When Herzl finally did read *Rome and Jerusalem*—only after he had written *The Jewish State*—he wrote, "Everything we tried is already there in his book."[29] Zionism was, as one of the great historians of the movement notes, a "twice-born movement."[30]

Hess's *Rome and Jerusalem* was hardly the only Zionist work that preceded Herzl's that was destined to become a classic. Yet another was written by Leon Pinsker, born in 1821 to a Russian family deeply informed by the *haskalah*. One of the first Jews to attend university in Odessa, Pinsker studied law but soon realized that quotas on Jews meant he would never get a job, so he became a physician.

As with others, it was violence against Jews that drew Pinsker into public life. In his case, the pogroms in Odessa in 1871 and wider attacks in 1881 shook him to his core. He eventually came to the conclusion that Jews would never be accepted in host countries. "For the living, the Jew is a dead man; for the natives, an alien and a vagrant; for property holders, a beggar; for the poor, an exploiter and a millionaire; for patriots, a man without a country; for all classes, a hated rival," he wrote.[31] A year after the 1881 pogroms he wrote *Auto-Emancipation*, which he subtitled "A Warning to His

Fellow People, from a Russian Jew" and in which he urged Jews to seek a national rebirth and independence.

Unlike Hess's work, which languished in relative obscurity, Pinsker's received some attention; and two years after it appeared, he was involved in the establishment of *Hovevei Zion,* one of the first European organizations created to foster Jewish immigration to Palestine. Yet he sensed that the organization alone would not suffice; the Jews needed a leader. "We probably lack a leader of the genius of Moses—history does not grant a people such guides repeatedly," he wrote. "But a clear recognition of what we need most, a recognition of the absolute necessity of a home of our own, would arouse among us a number of energetic, honorable, and distinguished friends of the people, who would undertake the leadership, and would, perhaps, be no less able than that one man to deliver us from disgrace and persecution."[32]

It was as if Pinsker were imagining a Herzl.

AGAINST THIS SLOWLY UNFOLDING background of early Zionist stirrings, Herzl's book, unlike those that had been written earlier, took the world by storm. So profound was the excitement generated by *The Jewish State* that by early March 1896, just weeks after the book was published, someone proposed to Herzl the idea of a Zionist congress, and he seized on it. In fact, it consumed him. As one person who helped in the early stages of the planning reported, "The whole world outside of the Congress had actually ceased to exist for him. He gave his attention to all the minutiae of the work. He let nothing slip past him. He issued the instructions, and supervised the carrying out of the instructions. And all this in a gentle voice, with a friendly smile, and yet so categorically that it simply occurred to no one to disobey or contradict."[33]

After almost eighteen months of planning, Herzl had made sure that the congress would be a stately affair. He wanted the congress's magnificence to announce the launch of a grand new political movement when it opened on August 29, 1897. He insisted that all the men in attendance (there were women delegates, as well) wear suits and white ties. When Max Nordau, possibly Herzl's closest ally and the only one of the early Zionists who had an international intellectual reputation even before his Zionist involvements, dressed in ordinary clothes, Herzl demanded that he go back to the hotel and dress as he had been instructed.

Some observers found his tendency to the theatrical excessive and even amusing, but Herzl was motivated by much more than a flair for the dramatic. "Something was needed to symbolize both to the delegates and to the world the break with the ordinary, the proclamation of the something great and beautiful [about] the dream which had brought them together."[34]

The First Zionist Congress, with all its pomp and circumstance, disparate ideologies, and unpolished ideas, was a resounding success. The audience was so enthralled—and so committed to an intellectually serious project—that they would sit for speeches that went on for hours.[35]

One of the crowning achievements of the congress was a clear definition of the goals of the newly organized movement. The Zionist program, which was drafted after days of impassioned debate about its exact wording, eventually read as follows:

Zionism seeks to secure for the Jewish people a publicly recognized, legally secured homeland in Palestine. . . .

To achieve this goal, the Congress envisages the following methods:

1. By fostering the settlement of Palestine with farmers, laborers, and artisans.

2. By organizing the whole of Jewry in suitable local and general bodies, in accordance with the laws of their respective countries.

3. By strengthening the national Jewish feeling and national consciousness.

4. By taking preparatory steps to attain any Governmental consent which may be necessary to reach the aim of Zionism.[36]

Given the degree to which Europe's emancipated Jews had availed themselves of Europe's educational opportunities, it is not surprising that one of the delegates present, Professor Zvi Hermann Shapira, urged that integral to the launching of political Zionism should be the creation of a "Hebrew University" in Palestine. Zionism was, from its very outset, a lettered movement—born of the encounter between traditional Judaism and European Enlightenment, Jewish desperation coupled with a Jewish sense of eternity—as committed to education and writing as it was to political goals.

The congress also adopted an anthem. Written in 1878, "Hatikvah" (in a version much briefer than the original) is a simple anthem, composed of but one sentence:

> As long as deep in the heart,
> the soul of a Jew yearns,
> and onwards, towards the end of the East,
> an eye still gazes towards Zion,
> our hope is not yet lost;
> the hope of two thousand years,
> to be a free nation in our land,
> the land of Zion and Jerusalem.*

The congress took on many additional issues. It was at the First Zionist Congress that the idea of the Jewish National Fund (whose original mission was to purchase and develop land in Ottoman

---

* "Hatikvah" is different from many other national anthems. Most such anthems ("The Star-Spangled Banner," "La Marseillaise," and even "The Internationale," plus many others) discuss battle and conflict, but "Hatikvah" does not. "Hatikvah" is also the rare anthem in a minor key; its lyrical, mournful melody makes it impossible to march to Israel's national anthem.

Palestine) was first raised. The congress also put into place many of the committees and administrative bodies that later made the movement so effective.

Herzl, who had so meticulously planned every detail, and who had dedicated so much of his energy to ensuring its realization, left the congress euphoric. Weeks later, he wrote in his diary: "Were I to sum up the Basel Congress in a word—which I shall be very careful not to do publicly—it would be this: 'At Basel I founded the Jewish state.' If I said this out loud today, I would be answered by universal laughter. Perhaps in five years, and certainly in fifty, everyone will admit it."[37]

Newly invigorated, Herzl was now even more determined than he had been before. He traveled to Palestine for the first time. Fittingly, he traveled not to see the Jewish people's ancestral land (and one of the places in which he thought a Jewish state might eventually be created*), but to play to the politics of the hour. Kaiser Wilhelm II and a number of the sultan's representatives were visiting the Holy Land during that period, and Herzl felt that the easiest way for him to curry their favor would be by meeting them there.[38]

The kaiser was hardly a natural ally. One of the German participants at the First Zionist Congress had written to the kaiser after the congress, detailing its aims. Upon receiving the note, the kaiser wrote in the margins: "Let the kikes go to Palestine, the sooner the better. I am not about to put obstacles in their way."[39] But the kaiser's antipathy for the Jews did not dissuade Herzl from trying to see him. If anti-Semites shared his goals, Herzl was willing to collaborate even with them, as long as he was advancing the goal of establishing a Jewish state.

---

* In 1896, when Herzl wrote *The Jewish State,* he was unsure where the country he imagined should be founded. "Two territories come under consideration," he wrote, "Palestine and Argentine" (see Theodor Herzl, *The Jewish State* [New York: Dover Publications, 1989], p. 64). In *Altneuland,* however, which he wrote six years later in 1902, Herzl clearly imagines the Jewish state in Palestine.

Many of his impressions of the barren country, in which he saw virtually limitless potential, made their way into Herzl's most well-known work of fiction, a utopian novel entitled *Altneuland,* or "Old-New Land." Published in 1902, *Altneuland* envisions the future Jewish state in a style similar to other utopian novels of Herzl's day. At the center of the book's plot are an assimilated Jew and his non-Jewish traveling companion who, after having been isolated on a remote island for a number of years, discover the newly reconstituted Jewish state in Palestine. The society Herzl describes is idyllic. The desert land has been made to bloom, modern cities have replaced the ramshackle neighborhoods Herzl had seen when he got there. People of all faiths live in harmony, all worshipping in their own way, without even a hint of tension in the air. Palestine is filled with intellectuals and inventors, writers and noble politicians.

It was an utterly utopian vision of a future Palestine, but perhaps precisely because life in Europe was becoming so desperate, it was also a vision that many of his readers found deeply compelling:

> The spell of the Sabbath was over the Holy City, now freed from the filth, noise and vile odors that had so often revolted devout pilgrims of all creeds, when after long and trying journeys, they reach their goal. In the old days they had had to endure many disgusting sights before they could reach their shrines. All was different now. . . . The lands and the streets were beautifully paved and cared for. . . . Moslem, Jewish and Christian welfare institutions, hospitals and clinics stood side by side. In the middle of a great square was the splendid Peace Palace, where international congresses of peace-lovers and scientists were held, for Jerusalem was now a home for all the best strivings of the human spirit: for Faith, Love, Knowledge.[40]

Nor was it only Jerusalem that had been repaired. The creation of a Jewish homeland had solved the problem of Jews in Europe, no less:

Dr. Walter . . . launched on a description of the effects of Jewish
mass migration upon the Jews who had remained in Europe.
He was bound to say for himself, it had always been clear to
him that Zionism was bound to be as salutary for the Jews who
remained in Europe as for those who emigrated.[41]

IT WAS A BOLD DREAM, and a fanciful one in many ways. But it
quickly became exceedingly practical, as well. The more desperate the Jews in Europe became, the more amenable they grew to
imagining a very different world. Hess had. Pinsker had. Then Bialik did. Theodor Herzl transformed all that passion into a political
movement. He was under no illusion that it was going to be easy,
but neither did he doubt that it could happen. His message to his
readers, as he pithily stated it in the epigraph to *Altneuland*, was
simple: "If you will it, it is no dream."[42]

SOME SPOT OF A NATIVE LAND

When the Lord restored the fortunes of Zion,
we were like those who dreamed.

—Psalm 126

Though it is commonly said that those delegates from around the world who gathered in Basel for the First Zionist Congress in 1897 were the people who created the Zionist movement, that is not entirely true. The participants in the First Zionist Congress launched Zionism as a *political* movement. But the dream at the core of their movement, the yearning to return to their ancestral home in the Land of Israel, had originated much earlier. It was a dream as old as the Jewish people itself.

The Jews were not the only ones who understood that on one's ancestral land, one could flourish in ways that were possible in no other place. More than twenty years before the First Zionist Congress, George Eliot (the pen name for Mary Ann Evans), wrote—without even mentioning the Jews—about the power of the love a people can feel for a land.

A human life, I think, should be well rooted in some spot of a native land, where it may get the love of tender kinship for the face of earth, for the labours men go forth to, for the sounds and

accents that haunt it, for whatever will give that early home a
familiar unmistakable difference amidst the future widening of
knowledge: a spot where the definiteness of early memories may
be inwrought with affection.[1]

To understand today's Israel—its dreams, its successes and disappointments, and the ways its citizens respond to the challenges
it faces—one needs to understand the ancient story that the Jews
have long told about themselves, and the centrality of the Land of
Israel in that story.

For Jews, memories of Zion were "inwrought with affection"
because of the Bible, the book they had seen as a kind of "national
diary." To be sure, for religious Jews, the Bible was God's revealed
word, filled with commandments about how they were to live their
lives. For secular Jews, the Bible was one of the greatest works of literature of all time. For all, though, the Bible was the book that told
the story of their people: what they had loved, where they had lived,
how they had succeeded, and when they had failed. It was the story
of their family. And central to the story of that family was the Land
of Israel, the land to which Theodor Herzl was now urging them to
return. There could be no Jewish nation, and no Jewish family, their
"diary" intimated, without their land at the center of the story.

THE LAND OF ISRAEL is part of the Jewish people's story from its
very first moments. When the Bible describes the moment at which
the Jewish people was born, it states: "The Lord said to Abram,* 'Go
forth from your native land . . . to the place that I will show you.'"[2]
Abram obeys, and shortly later, God says to him, "I will assign
this land to your offspring."[3] The notion of the "Promised Land"
emerges precisely at the moment that the Jews' story begins.

---

* His name is changed to Abraham in Genesis 17:15: "No longer will you be
called Abram; your name will be Abraham, for I have made you a father
of many nations."

That land will remain central to the people's story, throughout. Abraham makes Canaan (as it was then known) his home, but occasionally (especially during famines), he and his offspring have to travel to neighboring lands to ensure their survival. The book of Genesis (the first of the five Books of Moses, collectively called the Torah) is, in many ways, about the land. It is about building cities and digging wells, purchasing burial caves and dividing the land among the family. It is about leaving the land and returning to it. Genesis is fundamentally the story of Abraham's complex family, but central to that story is the land on which they have been told to live.

When the Book of Genesis has concluded and the curtain rises on the Book of Exodus, Abraham's descendants are no longer merely a family—they are now a people. Now called the Israelites, they are trapped in Egypt, slaves to Pharaoh. Pharaoh intuits, though, that keeping the Israelites as slaves is going to be impossible, for at their first opportunity, they will seek to return to their land. Pharaoh says to his people, "Look, the Israelite people are much too numerous for us. Let us deal shrewdly with them so that they may not increase; otherwise, in the event of war, they may join our enemies in fighting against us, and they will go up from the land."[4] At their first opportunity, Pharaoh understands, the Israelites will rebel not so that they can take his throne, but so that they can go home. There is, Pharaoh senses, a magnetic attraction between a people and its land. And peoples will always struggle to return to their ancient homelands.

That is precisely what happens. A new leader arises, determined to end their enslavement. Moses frees the people from bondage and leads them out of Egypt. The rest of the Torah unfolds as the Israelites make their long trek to the Promised Land. It was, as the Bible tells the story, a forty-year journey through the desert, punctuated by thirst and battles, doubt and rebellion. Thousands of years later, the Zionists understood what the Torah was saying—the road to true freedom would be long and difficult. In the Book of Joshua, the Israelites finally reach the land to which Abraham himself had journeyed, but the essential point—that getting home would never be easy—had been made eminently clear.

The biblical narrative had another point to make about establishing a national home: even after the Israelites arrived, remaining in their homeland would be no simple task. According to the biblical account, the land was occupied by seven different nations, and others menaced from the outside.[5] Wars were frequent, and several models of Israelite political leadership failed. Eventually, weary from the never-ending struggle to stay secure in the land, the Israelites—composed of twelve different tribes—demanded a king.

The Israelites' first king, Saul, was deeply flawed, and the young David soon replaced him. Seemingly small and self-effacing at first, David became a skilled military commander and established a stable monarchy and vast kingdom. (See Map 1.) Though David, too, was flawed (he could be ruthless, for example), the Bible tells a story in which he embodied vision, power, spiritual sensitivity—he was described as a leader as close to the ideal of perfection as a person of flesh and blood could be. Is it then any wonder that at the First Zionist Congress, when one of the delegates sought to express the grandeur that they felt in Herzl's presence, he wrote:

> Before us rose a marvelous and exalted figure, kingly in bearing and stature, with deep eyes in which could be read quiet majesty and unuttered sorrow. . . . [I]t is a royal scion of the House of David, risen from among the dead, clothed in legend and fantasy and beauty.[6]

Part of the magic and the power of the First Zionist Congress was that it seemed to its participants the beginning of the restoration of a previous glory, a glory the Jews had experienced thousands of years earlier, a flourishing that they had known before—in the Land of Israel.

David passed the kingdom on to his son, Solomon, who built the First Temple in Jerusalem in the tenth century BCE. The Temple became the epicenter of Israelite religious life. It was there that sacrifices were offered and to there that Israelites made pilgrimages three times a year. Jerusalem and the Temple also served, for all intents and purposes, as the capital of the Israelite world. The Temple Mount, on which the Temple was situated, would become sacred not only to Jews, because both the First and Second Temples stood there, but to Christians and Muslims, as well. To Christians, it was the place where Jesus preached against corruption in the Temple and expelled moneychangers. To Muslims, the Temple Mount's sanctity would stem from the Al Aqsa Mosque and the Dome of the Rock, which would be completed there in 691–692 CE to commemorate the site from which Muslim tradition asserts that Mohammed ascended to heaven.

Solomon's building projects came with steep costs, though, and in order to finance them, he raised taxes. As a result, the tribes grew restless; those in the north, in particular, felt neglected by Solomon, whom they perceived as favoring the southern tribes. Despite the political unrest, Solomon managed to keep his coalition together. His son, Rehoboam, however, was not as skilled a politician as his father, and in 928 BCE the monarchy disintegrated into two often-quarreling states: a kingdom in the north, the Kingdom of Israel (composed of ten of the twelve Israelite tribes), and a kingdom in the south, Judea (composed of two of the twelve tribes).

Thus entered yet another theme in the narrative that the Jews told about themselves—the danger of disunity. In the case of the two Israelite kingdoms, the split spelled disaster. Power struggles devoured the northern kingdom; in the space of two centuries, no less than nineteen different dynasties ruled the kingdom. Worse, the two separated kingdoms also often battled each other viciously.

Still another central dimension of Israeli life today was introduced thousands of years earlier in the Bible. As had always been the case in that region, and still is—the kingdoms were surrounded by powerful enemies. To the north lay the Assyrian Empire, situated in what today is northern Iraq. (See Map 1.) A brutal military power, it threatened many of the states to the west of the Euphrates River,

Israel and Judea among them. In addition to Assyria, the north was home to yet another menacing power: Aram. Due east lay Babylonia, an empire that also often joined the warring fray. Complicating matters even further was the massive Egyptian empire to the south. Any power that sought to control the region needed to conquer the land on which the kingdoms of Israel and Judea were situated. In many ways, the Jewish kingdoms were damned no matter what the outcome: whichever power triumphed would eventually subjugate them.

That, too, is a lens through which contemporary Israel sees its own challenges. Even then, the Middle East was a complicated region. Even then, survival was a constant struggle.

DESPERATE, THE ISRAELITE KINGDOMS did whatever they could to hold on. They forged alliances and paid tribute. In the long run, though, none of those tactics worked. In a story filled with numerous twists and turns, treaties and rivalries abounded, and the two kingdoms grew continually weaker. It was only a matter of time before they could no longer survive, both because of their own infighting and because of the massive threatening armies surrounding them.

From 733 to 732 BCE, the Assyrian king Tiglath-Pileser III annexed the Galilee and Transjordan, deporting a large portion of the inhabitants. In so doing, he introduced a new tactic into the Middle East—and one that would be repeated even in the modern era—the forced deportation of masses of people. In the case of the Israelites, this deportation had several effects on their religious life. Until then, Israelite identity had been tied in large measure to the particular tribe to which one belonged. But tribes' identities were derivative of the land they inhabited. Once Israelites were exiled from their land, tribal identity was almost impossible to sustain.

Suddenly, because of circumstances not of their own choosing, the Israelites would have to reimagine what it meant to be part of their people. On more than one occasion in the millennia that followed, that would be the very challenge that Jews (and Zionists) would face in an ever-changing world.

The Bible does not tell us what happened to the ten tribes of the northern kingdom who were dispersed. The story of the exile highlights the dangers—to any people—of forced migration, which both Jews and Arabs would endure again in the twentieth century. Whatever had happened to those lost biblical tribes, as the Bible tells the story, Judea's two tribes were all that remained of the Israelites and the eventual Jewish people.

BECAUSE THE SOUTHERN KINGDOM still faced massive powers to both the north and the south, the challenge of survival was far from over even for the remaining two tribes. Assyria's military strength declined, but Babylonia rushed in to fill the vacuum. In the south, the still powerful Egyptian Empire menaced. Judea's leaders then made a series of costly mistakes that significantly worsened their position. Believing, incorrectly, that the Babylonians were weakened, the king of Judea decided to stop paying tribute to the king of Babylon. Outraged, Babylon invaded Judea in 598 BCE, killed the Judean king, and soon thereafter, plundered the Temple and took some ten thousand people (mostly soldiers and craftsmen) captive. Taking a page from the Assyrian king before him, the king of Babylon used the power of dispersing a people to attempt to break the Judeans' national will.

A new Babylonian king, Nebuchadnezzar, then invaded Judea once again after the Judeans proved rebellious and refused to acquiesce to Babylonian rule. This time, to squelch the Jewish rebellion once and for all, the Babylonians decided not just to expel and disperse the population, but also to destroy the symbol of Jewish life in the land of Israel. In 586 BCE, they burned Solomon's Temple to the ground.

Now, Judea, too, was gone. Jewish independence had ended. The Babylonian exile had begun. And never again would the entire Jewish people live in the land of Israel.

GIVEN THE CENTRALITY OF the sacrificial cult and priestly leadership to Israelite religion, the destruction of the Temple, and with it the sacrificial rite and the power of the priests, might well have meant the end of Israelite life. With sociological and religious genius, however, the Israelites' leaders begged their followers not to see this loss as the end, but to maintain hope even in the face of catastrophe.

Jeremiah, a prophet who witnessed the fall of Jerusalem and who then prophesied during the exile, insisted that the brutal turn of events did not have to spell the end of their people. "Build houses, and dwell in them; and plant gardens, and eat the fruit of them; take wives and beget sons and daughters; and take wives for your sons, and give your daughters to husbands, that they may bear sons and daughters; that you may be increased there, and not diminished."[7] Jeremiah was advocating both hope and patience; the covenant between the Jews and their God, he insisted, was not over, but they had to wait until powers greater than themselves returned them to Zion.

Yet there was a very different view, as well, represented in the Bible by the prophet Hananiah. He insisted that the Babylonians would rule for only two years—and not seventy. The Israelites need not get accustomed to exile, he intimated. They could go home much sooner than Jeremiah thought.

This debate between the figures of Jeremiah and Hananiah—should the Jews become accustomed to life in exile, or insist on getting back to their land as quickly as they possibly could—would persist in Jewish life for centuries. It raged between Herzl, who desperately sought to create a Jewish state, and his religious opponents, who wanted to leave their fate in the hands of God. It was reflected in the later debates between Israel's early leadership, who hoped that Jews from around the world would make their way to Israel, and the leadership of American Jewry, who insisted that in the United States—outside the Jews' ancestral land—American Jews had found their ideal home.

Ultimately, the exile lasted for a few decades. But the dream of returning to Zion, their ancestral home, did not dim. The exiled Israelites focused their collective memory on the land from which they had left, the land they still considered home. The Book of Psalms offers glimpses into what must have been the worldview of many. "By the waters of Babylon, we sat and wept, as we remembered you, Zion," says Psalm 137.[8] They wept, but they also dreamed of returning to the land they had lost. Another psalm spoke not of tears at the memories of Zion, but of dreams of a much better day still to come:

> When the Lord restored the fortunes of Zion,
> we were like those who dreamed.
> Our mouths were filled with laughter,
> our tongues with songs of joy.
> Then it was said among the nations,
> "The Lord has done great things for them."
> The Lord has done great things for us,
> and we are filled with joy.
> Restore our fortunes, Lord,
> like streams in the Negev.
> Those who sow with tears
> will reap with songs of joy.
> Those who go out weeping,
> carrying seed to sow,
> will return with songs of joy,
> carrying sheaves with them.[9]

For centuries, Jews would sing this psalm. They had never seen the land, and knew that they, themselves, might not live to go back. They knew not much about the place to which they hoped to return, but deep in their souls lay a promise that they were sure would be fulfilled—one day, they would go home. And until they did, dreams of Zion would remain a central pillar of their spiritual and national lives.

IN THE CLOSING WORDS of the Hebrew Bible, Cyrus, King of Persia, who defeated the Babylonians in 539 BCE, informed the exiles that they could return home and rebuild the Temple. "Any of you of all [God's] people . . . let him go up [to Jerusalem]."[10] We do not know precisely what portion of the exiled community chose to return to Zion and to rebuild the Temple, but it was apparently a small percentage.[11]

The story that the Bible weaves, however, focuses not on those who chose to remain in exile, but on Cyrus's exhortation that it was time to go home. The Jews' national story that had opened with God telling Abram to go to the "place that I will show you" (the Land of Israel)—concludes with the Bible's very last words, "Let him go up [to Jerusalem]."

Instructively, the biblical story begins with the promise of home and concludes with the Jews returning to the Land of Israel. The Bible tells the story of a people always yearning, never giving up on the promise that one day it would go home.

THOSE WHO HEEDED Cyrus's decree and returned to the Land of Israel from Babylon found themselves in a region that was volatile—much as it remains today. Eventually, the small minority who did return managed to rebuild the Temple, though initially it was only a shadow of its former self. The Second Temple would stand for roughly six hundred years, but Jewish sovereignty would be intermittent.

After the rise and fall of the Persian Empire, the region was conquered by Alexander the Great. Greek rule was harsh at times, with religious freedom often viciously curtailed. Though there were many Jews who embraced the Hellenistic culture that surrounded them, there was a minority—in a pattern that would repeat in Jewish life in centuries to follow—that insisted that foreign cultural and religious influence had to be resisted. It was not enough, they believed, simply to live in their ancestral homeland. Living there would have meaning only if it were shaped by the ideals, beliefs, and commitments that had always been central to Jewish life.

In response to Greek suppression of Jewish religious liberty, Jewish resistance groups took up arms in what would become the most significant Jewish display of power since the Kingdom of David. In 164 BCE, a small band of Jews known as the Maccabees initiated a successful revolt against the Greeks. The Maccabees managed to create the first autonomous Jewish state in the Land of Israel in more than four hundred years, and Jews would forever celebrate that success through the holiday of Hanukkah.

The Jews were sovereign for about a century, however, after which they became a vassal state once more, this time to the Roman Empire. At first, life under Roman rule was fairly tolerable. Rome was far from Judea, and daily life for those Israelites living in the Land of Israel was not a crucial issue for the Roman leaders. Israelites were mostly left to their own devices, though like all subjugated peoples of that era, they were obliged to pay heavy taxes. With time, though, that changed. Roman rule grew increasingly oppressive—the Romans raised taxes and gradually erased Jewish religious autonomy. In 6 CE, Rome instituted direct rule of Judea, ending even the illusion of Jewish sovereignty.

Once again, the Jewish yearning for sovereignty led to rebellion. A small group, this time known as the Zealots, advocated military uprising against the Romans. At first, when rebellion actually broke out in 66 CE, the rebels forced the Romans to retreat. The Romans, however, were a massive power, and the rebelling Judeans were no match for them. By 70 CE, the Romans were ready to storm Jerusalem. The army besieged the city, allowing nothing to enter or exit. Food supplies ran out, and the population began to starve; soon thereafter, the Romans broke through Jerusalem's walls. They razed the city of Jerusalem and burned the Second Temple to the ground. The Romans massacred much of the Jewish population, and exiled many of the region's remaining Jews, inaugurating a two-thousand-year-long exile.

The Second Jewish Commonwealth had come to a brutal end.

Jerusalem was no longer. The drive not to succumb to Roman rule
was so impassioned, however, that a few pockets of resistance remained. The best known, the Zealots' outpost on Masada (a fortified mountain on the western edge of the Dead Sea), held out the
longest. But they, too, were doomed to defeat; Rome was simply
too massive, and the Zealots knew it. The Romans eventually surrounded them, but rather than let the Romans kill them—or worse,
sell them into slavery or prostitution—these last Jewish fighters decided to take their own lives. A few people killed almost all the
women, children, and most of the men, until one remaining Zealot
killed himself; of the almost one thousand Jews on Masada, only
two women and five children were found alive.[12]

The long war against Rome had exacted a horrific price. Jose-
phus, the historian who provides most of the information we have
about that period, notes that hundreds of thousands of Jews died in
the war, while many others were sold into slavery or forced to work
in Roman mines.

Astonishingly, even the devastating defeat at the hands of Rome
did not snuff out the Jewish longing to restore their sovereign rule
over their ancestral land. In 130 CE, some sixty years after the Second Temple was destroyed, the emperor Hadrian announced plans
to rebuild Jerusalem. Rather than restoring Jerusalem to its former
Jewish glory, however, he renamed it Aelia Capitolina and planned
to place a pagan altar there. He began referring to the region as
Syria Palestina, the origin of today's name, Palestine.

At that provocation, Simeon Bar Kokhba, with the support of
the aging sage Rabbi Akiva, plotted a revolt. Hundreds of thousands of fighters joined him. The revolt began in earnest in 132 CE,
and as had been the case in 66 CE, the Jews at first managed some
victories against the Roman forces. Bar Kokhba captured Jerusalem
and large swaths of additional territory. In each place that he liberated, he instituted autonomous Jewish rule. Modern archaeologists have found numerous coins with the Hebrew inscriptions "the
redemption of Israel," "the freedom of Israel," or "the freedom of

Jerusalem" from that period, products of Bar Kokhba's short-lived sovereignty.[13]

As it had in the past, however, the massive power of the Roman Empire vastly exceeded that of the rebels. Hadrian's military overpowered Bar Kokhba and his fighters, forcing them to retreat to a city south of Jerusalem named Betar. In 135 CE, the Romans put down the last remnants of the three-year-long rebellion. Ancient accounts claim that some 580,000 men were killed, while many more were sent to the slave market.

Judea had fallen for a third time. Once again, Jewish sovereignty ended. This time, there would be no quick recovery after seventy years, no rebellion sixty years after the loss. This time, it was really over.

FOR ALMOST TWO MILLENNIA—1,762 years, to be precise—the Jews would live without political autonomy. They would make their homes in lands ruled by others, hosted by people who would treat them better at times, worse at others. For the most part, there would be no serious attempt to restore Jewish sovereignty until 1897, when Theodor Herzl gathered his delegates in Basel at the First Zionist Congress. Herzl's message was a call to push back, to restore the glory of ancient Israel, to end the long, corrosive exile. No longer should Jews live at the whim of those who ruled the countries in which they found themselves. It was time, he insisted, for the Jews to take history into their own hands.

WHEN THEODOR HERZL STOOD at the podium at the First Zionist Congress in Basel in 1897, Jews had sustained their dream of returning to their ancestral land for almost two millennia. How had they done that? How had they been able to keep alive memories of a place they had never seen? How had they, to use George Eliot's language, managed to "give that early home a familiar unmistakable difference" even when they had never lived there or even visited, and probably never would?

What the Jews had done, to some degree in planning for the day in Basel that they dreamed might someday come, was to cyclically relive moments in history, even if they themselves had not experienced them. The genius of the Jewish tradition was that in their liturgy and holidays, the Jews invoked the past in a way that made it seem present and real. No matter what they did, said, or thought about, the Land of Israel remained their central focus. When they prayed, three times each day, they faced Jerusalem. For century upon century, they fasted on the ninth day of the Hebrew month of Av, the date on which tradition has it that both Temples were destroyed. When they sat in Spain or in Poland, reciting their Grace-after-Meals, they included a blessing that read, "Praised are You, Lord, who rebuilds Jerusalem in mercy." At the conclusion of the Passover Seder, Jews all around the world—in Africa and in Europe, in Yemen and in Iraq—sang "Next year in Jerusalem." At Jewish weddings, the groom traditionally breaks a glass, reminding the celebrants that even in their hour of joy, they ought to recall Jerusalem destroyed. There are dozens, if not hundreds, of other Jewish religious practices that kept the dream of Zion (Jerusalem) alive for generations of Jews who had never seen it and knew that they never would.

It was that strategy for preserving Jewish memory that explains how, when Bialik published "To the Bird" in 1892, it fell on such receptive ears. The words of the poem were new, but the dream to which it gave expression was not. Bialik was in some ways simply a continuation of what Jeremiah, Hananiah, and the Book of Psalms had all said—Jews might live in many different places, but only one place would ever truly be home.

The magic worked. As Europe turned on the Jews at the end of the nineteenth century, as nationalism swept across the continent and as many Jews sensed that Europe could not be their home for much longer, they instinctively knew that they had a home elsewhere. Religious and secular, intellectuals and not, eastern European and western, they had been raised in a tradition with so much reference to the dream of Zion that when Herzl wrote *The Jewish State*, it spoke of a dream that to the Jews sounded intimately familiar. Herzl's ideas spread so rapidly largely because they were not entirely new; he was bringing to life a dream that the Jews had harbored for many centuries.

We should therefore not be surprised by an observation by one of the delegates to the congress in Basel that "Everyone sat breathless, as if in the presence of a miracle. And in truth, was it not a miracle which we beheld? And then wild applause broke out; for fifteen minutes the delegates clapped, shouted and waved their handkerchiefs."[14] After all, to those Jews who had despaired of Europe, to those Jews for whom Zionism was the beginning of a renewed dream and a renewed hope, Herzl was Abraham, who first wandered "to the place that I will show you." He was Moses, leading his flock to the Promised Land. He was David, with the promise of renewed Jewish sovereignty. He was Bar Kokhba, insisting that the time had come to push back against the forces of history. Almost single-handedly, Herzl had brought an ancient dream to life, restored hope, and given Jews the inspiration to imagine for themselves a very different future.

After the First Zionist Congress, political Zionism was aloft, but it was, in many respects, nothing new. It was, quite simply, an ancient dream revived.

A CONVERSATION, NOT AN IDEOLOGY

Zionist Divisions at the Turn of the Century

*Kishinev exists wherever Jews undergo bodily or spiritual torture,
wherever their self-respect is injured and their property despoiled
because they are Jews. Let us save those who can still be saved!*
—Theodor Herzl at the Sixth Zionist Congress, 1903[1]

"We entered upon the dawn of the Twentieth Century in high hope for our country, our Empire and the world," Winston Churchill wistfully recalled in 1949. "The latter and larger part of the Nineteenth Century had been the period of liberal advance. In 1900 a sense of moving hopefully forward to brighter, broader and easier days was predominant."[2]

At the turn of the century, many Jews shared Churchill's optimism. The liberal advances of which Churchill spoke should have heralded a period of new opportunity for European Jews. And the First Zionist Congress in 1897, with its portending the Jews' joining the family of nations, made the future appear even brighter.

Therefore, when these optimistic expectations were dashed and when the twentieth century opened with a paroxysm of violence against Jews, many Jews were shaken to their core. In Russia, it began with the publication of *The Protocols of the Elders of Zion*, a forgery of "minutes" of a fictional meeting in which Jews were alleged to have plotted to take over the world by manipulating the press and world economies. The *Protocols* were translated into numerous languages and disseminated across the globe.

Shortly thereafter, Russia's hostility to Jews moved from words to violence. The attack that stunned them more than any other was the Kishinev pogrom of 1903. The horror began on Easter Sunday, April 19:

> Initially, young people began hounding Jews to leave Chuflinskii Square, their cause gradually taken up by adults in an increasing state of holiday drunkenness. Late that afternoon, some twenty-five bands, averaging thirty-fifty each, simultaneously fanned out across the Jewish quarter of Bessarabia's capital, teenage boys taking the lead in smashing the windows of houses and stores. Students and seminarists from the Royal School and the city's religious colleges, iron bars and axes in hand, followed the hooligans; aided by looters, they plundered and demolished property. The local police made no attempt to interfere, Chief of Secret Police Levendal even exhorting the gangs on. . . . Passing through the streets in his carriage, Orthodox bishop Iakov blessed the mostly Moldavian attackers.[3]

Once it became clear to the mob that the governor was not going to intervene, matters got even worse. The wanton cruelty was virtually beyond description. What followed was

> murder and massacre during the night. . . . 50,000 Jews (a third of the population) now fell prey to barbarism . . . a boy's tongue was cut out while the two year old was still alive. . . . Meyer Weissman, blinded in one eye from youth, begged for his life with the offer of sixty rubles; taking this money, the leader of the crowd destroying his small grocery store gouged out Weissman's other eye, saying "You will never again look upon a Christian child." Nails were driven through heads; bodies hacked in half; bellies split open and filled with feathers. Women and girls were raped, and some had their breasts cut off.[4]

As the horror was unfolding, the *St. Petersburgskiye Vedomosti* later reported, the upper class "walked calmly along and gazed at these horrible spectacles with the utmost indifference."[5] It was only when the minister of the interior sent a telegram to the governor telling him to put a stop to the massacre that the troops were deployed and, by the morning of April 21, martial law went into effect.

The toll was horrific. Thirty-four men (including two babies) and seven women were murdered during the pogrom; another eight Jews later died from their wounds. There was massive property damage. A journalist who arrived in the town soon after the pogrom noted that the local non-Jewish citizens displayed "neither regret nor remorse."[6]

SHORTLY AFTER THE POGROM, the Jewish Historical Commission in Odessa asked Chaim Nachman Bialik to go to Kishinev, to interview survivors and to tell the story. Bialik was a natural choice for the assignment. Ever since the publication of his poem "To the Bird" a decade earlier, his reputation had soared. By the time a collection of his poetry was published in 1901, he was widely considered one of the greatest—if not *the* greatest—Hebrew writers of his generation. Ze'ev Jabotinsky, another Zionist leader and himself a gifted writer, said Bialik was "the one poet in all of modern literature whose poetry directly molded the soul of a generation."[7]

What Bialik saw and heard when he arrived in Kishinev shocked him. His literary response, the epic poem "In the City of Slaughter," however, directed his fury not only at the marauding, raping, murdering mob, but also, surprisingly, at the Jews themselves. In the middle of the lengthy and complex poem, Bialik describes the basement of a house, where a gang of Cossacks rapes the Jewish women mercilessly, time and again. While the savage assault is unfolding, according to Bialik's rendition, the Jewish men hide behind casks, unable to stop the attackers, too frightened to even try. These "sons of the Maccabees," Bialik calls them with bitter irony, are the very symbols of what Bialik believes has gone wrong with European Jewry.

Then, Bialik turns his rage on the Jewish tradition itself. Bialik "describes" how after the attack, these men of priestly descent stepped over the broken bodies of their still-living wives and ran to the rabbi to ask, "Is my wife still permitted to me?"[8]

"*That* is what worries you?" Bialik virtually screams. The people you love are broken, wounded, raped, and lying on the ground, and all that concerns you is a question of Jewish law, the matter of whether your wives are still sexually permitted to you? What has happened to your humanity? What have you become?

It makes no difference, of course, whether the scene as Bialik describes it ever took place. He was, after all, a poet and not a historian. What matters was his horror, both at what Europe was capable of doing and—because of the passivity that Jewish tradition had fostered in them—at what the Jews could not do.

The exile of the Jew from his own land, Bialik claims, has more than robbed the Jew of his strength and his courage. It has eroded his capacity to feel. Exile has destroyed him. And the legal system of the Jewish tradition, which might once have created moments and spaces of purity and holiness in a spoiled world, now rots the Jew's soul by turning his attention away from what really matters. The Jewish tradition, Bialik essentially says, is a cancer that has destroyed the Jew's humanity.

For Bialik therefore, and for many of his contemporaries, the point of Zionism, of the return to the Jewish homeland, was not simply to create a refuge or to fix the "Jewish problem" in Europe. The reason that Jews needed to return to their land was that it was only there that the Jews could fashion a "new Jew." It was time, he insisted, to re-create the Maccabees of old. It was time for the Jewish nation to be reborn.

BIALIK WAS FAR FROM the only Jewish leader for whom the events in Kishinev were transformative. To Herzl, Kishinev was simply further evidence that the Jews desperately needed a home—wherever they could create it. Because he was making little progress with the Ottomans, Herzl, who had earlier entertained the possibility of Argentina as a location for his state, had begun to consider places other than Palestine.

At the Sixth Zionist Congress, which began on August 23, 1903, he invoked Kishinev, insisting that Kishinev was not an event or a place, but rather a condition. "Kishinev exists wherever Jews undergo bodily or spiritual torture, wherever their self-respect is injured and their property despoiled because they are Jews. Let us save those who can still be saved!" he insisted.[9] He wrote to his colleague Max Nordau that they should accept Great Britain's offer of territory in East Africa. That offer, he reminded Nordau, "is the only one. . . . We must, in a word, play the politics of the hour."[10]

Those "politics of the hour" were a proposal made by Joseph Chamberlain (the British colonial secretary), who—in response to Herzl's diplomatic pressure—had suggested that instead of insisting on returning to Palestine, the Jews should take a piece of territory in East Africa. Herzl presented the option, which became known as the Uganda Plan (even though the land in question was technically in modern-day Kenya, an area that not long before had been part of the Uganda protectorate[11]), at the Sixth Zionist Congress. The ensuing debate, predictably, was vociferous. Those who supported the plan argued that "Uganda" would not be the Jews' final destination; it would merely be a temporary stopover on the way to their permanent return to their ancestral homeland in Palestine. Surprisingly, some national-religious delegates, who as religious Jews might have been expected to insist on redeeming the Land of Israel, shared Herzl's sense of desperation and voted in favor of the plan.*

---

* Uganda was far from the only suggested alternative to Palestine. So desperate were Jews to find a place to which to go that they advocated, and pursued, several other possibilities. In the early 1800s Grand Island, New York, was suggested as a possibility. In the decades that followed, other suggestions included Uasin Gishu in East Africa (1903–1905), the

But resistance to the idea was fierce. How many people would uproot themselves to move to a place that they would then have to leave soon thereafter? Jews would either not move to "Uganda" at all, many feared, or, if they did, they would not move once again should Palestine become a possibility. The Uganda Plan could derail the hope of ever returning to Palestine. Zionism was not only about obtaining a home for the Jewish people—it was about reestablishing a home in their ancestral homeland. Even many secular Zionists (who did not share a *religious* attachment to the land) voted against the proposal, insisting that "giving up Zion for even an hour seemed like a severe and elemental ideological heresy."[12] Some Russian representatives, "among them those from Kishinev"[13] who should have felt more than anyone the urgency of finding a safe haven for the Jews, vigorously opposed the idea of a Jewish state in East Africa.

Herzl quickly realized that he had unwittingly unleashed a tempest he could not control. The Zionist congress—and the Zionist movement—were now deeply divided. There was nothing immediate that Herzl could do to undo the damage.

The Zionist community was now embroiled in deep and vituperative debate, and it would remain so—forever. The Uganda idea itself would fade and become irrelevant. But other issues would arise. Zionism, it was already becoming clear, would never be a simple political movement. Zionism was centered around the Jewish future and the subject of a Jewish national home—but precisely how those needs ought to be met would remain the subject of often messy and acrimonious disagreement. As much as it was a movement, Zionism was actually a complex and often feisty conversation.

Benguela Plateau in Angola (1907–1914), Madagascar (1933–1942), Port Davey, Tasmania (1940–1945), and Suriname (1938–1948). It was only Israel's creation in 1948 that put an end to these seemingly endless searches for a new Jewish home. (Adam Rovner, *In the Shadow of Zion: Promised Lands Before Israel* [New York: NYU Press, 2014].)

Because everyone involved understood that a messy show-down would serve no one, the congress sought to dodge the Uganda issue and voted merely to investigate the viability of the proposal. Yet even that left some of the delegates incensed, and after the vote, Yechiel Tschlenow—who had led the opposition to the proposal—stormed out of the hall with 128 other opposition delegates in tow.

Herzl left the conference dejected. In poor health and plagued by the dire situation of Russia's Jews, he had watched his prized congress come apart at the seams due to a divisive proposal that he himself had made. By the spring of 1904, he apparently realized the severity of his tactical error; at a meeting of the Zionist Executive, which would later be dubbed "the reconciliation conference," he said that "for us a solution can only be found in Palestine."[14]

As Herzl suspected would be the case, the Uganda Plan was ultimately rejected at the Seventh Zionist Congress in July 1905. But Herzl did not live long enough to attend that congress. Only forty-four years old, he died of heart failure on July 3, 1904.

Herzl had known since his youth that he had heart problems. Yet he had given the risk to his own life no consideration; he knowingly sacrificed himself in the pursuit of a dream that he believed could save his people. Jews recognized not only his sacrifice, but the enormous change in Jewish history for which he was largely responsible.

"Vienna," said one writer, "had never before seen such a funeral."[15] Stefan Zweig, a Jewish writer who attended Herzl's funeral, wrote:

> It was a strange day that day in July, unforgettable to everyone who witnessed it. Suddenly, from every station, from every train, day and night, from every region, from every port, they arrived and came in their thousands. Jews from western and eastern Europe, Russian and Turkish Jews, from every district and every remote hamlet, they flowed into the city, the shock

of the bad news still on their faces. And the truth that had been
obscured for so long by dissents and gossip was now revealed to
us in all its might—that this man who is now being laid to rest
was the leader of a great movement. Suddenly, Vienna is learning that it was no ordinary writer or poet who has died, but one
of those people who shape ideas, the like of whom appear so
rarely on the stages of history. A terrible pain has cut through
the hearts of an entire nation, and for the first time I have come
to realize how much courage and hope this singular man has
instilled in the world by means of his vision.[16]

It had been hundreds of years since the Jewish people had had
such a leader.

HERZL AND BIALIK WERE hardly the only Zionist leaders for
whom Kishinev was transformative. "The killing in Kishinev has
completely filled my heart and I cannot think of anything else,"
wrote Asher Zvi Ginzberg. He also agreed that the Jewish people
needed to become something other than what they were. "It is a
disgrace for five million human souls to unload themselves on others, to stretch their necks to the slaughter and cry for help, without
as much as attempting to defend their honor and lives."[17]

Born in 1856 in Ukraine (four years before Herzl's birth), Asher
Zvi Ginzberg took on the pen name Ahad Ha'am ("One of the
People"), by which he is universally known. Recognized early for
his sheer brilliance, Ahad Ha'am was born into a family deeply
entrenched in the Hasidic world, where they expected he would
remain. Like Bialik and others, however, Ahad Ha'am was drawn
to the larger intellectual world that Europe and the *haskalah* offered. A pattern was emerging. Many of the most prominent Zionist thinkers of those days had been born into Orthodox families but
to some degree or another left the world of Jewish tradition. Under
their leadership, Zionism would become a fusion of profound Jew-

ish knowledge and, at the same time, hostility to much of the tradition in which they had been raised.*

Unlike some of the others who left the traditional Jewish world, Ahad Ha'am retained a love for the spiritual world that had shaped him. Lore has it that his father warned him that he would no longer have access to his father's library if he continued to read heretical texts. Ahad Ha'am was so nervous about this that he even once burned a book to hide his forays into this foreign literary world[18]; he would simply not risk being banished from his father's library of Jewish classics.

In deference to his father, he even agreed to marry a wife from an appropriately religious background, and by the age of fourteen, was betrothed to a woman from a prestigious Hasidic family with whom he was not particularly taken.[19] Somewhat surprisingly, the union lasted.

After his father fell upon difficult times (another biographical detail common to many of the early Zionist leaders), Ahad Ha'am decided to move to Odessa, the hub of the intellectual Jewish renaissance to which he was so drawn. The sole Russian city in which Jews were permitted to live, Odessa was home to a thriving Jewish intellectual milieu; many of Zionism's greatest thinkers would emerge from there.

Ahad Ha'am threw himself into the hotbed of Jewish culture that was Odessa, but unlike some of the Zionist thinkers who did the same, it was not without inner conflict. He retained an instinctive commitment to the aesthetics of the Hasidic world. In an uncharacteristically revealing article, *"Ketavim Balim"* ("A Tattered Manuscript"), he wrote in 1888:

---

* The number of Zionist writers for whom this was their religious and intellectual trajectory is astounding. The list includes, among numerous others, Max Nordau, A. D. Gordon, Eliezer Ben-Yehuda, Micha Josef Berdyczewski, Ahad Ha'am, Chaim Weizmann, Yosef Brenner, and Berl Katznelson, all of whom figure later in the book.

During those long winter evenings, at times when I'm sitting in
the company of enlightened men and women, sitting at a table
with *tref* [nonkosher] food and cards, and my heart is glad and my
face bright, suddenly then—I don't know how this happens—
suddenly before me is a very old table with broken legs, full of
tattered [sacred] books, torn and dusky books of genuine value,
and I'm sitting alone in their midst, reading them by the light
of a dim candle, opening up one and closing another, not even
bothering to look at their tiny print . . . and the entire world is
like the Garden of Eden.[20]

That unabashed love for the world he had chosen to leave set
him apart from some of his other Zionist counterparts. What the
Jews needed, he insisted, was not sovereignty. Jews, he believed,
had an innate sort of spirituality, different from that of non-Jews.
Gentile nationalism, he argued, is rooted in power, while in Judaism, the spirit is meant to triumph over material power. "A political ideal which does not rest on the national culture," Ahad Ha'am
wrote at about the same time, "is apt to seduce us from our loyalty
to spiritual greatness, and to beget in us a tendency to find the path
of glory in the attainment of material power and political dominion, breaking the thread that unites us with the past."[21] Zionism,
he thought, should focus on creating a spiritual center in Palestine,
not a state.

Ahad Ha'am was particularly incensed by the fact that there was
nothing distinctly Jewish about Herzl's vision. "It would be better
if the Jewish people were to disappear from the face of history," he
wrote, "than to find itself trapped in the meaningless power mon-
gering of a small state populated by individuals of Jewish ancestry
but which would otherwise not be a Jewish state."[22]

Herzl may have been trying to save the Jewish people, Ahad
Ha'am believed, but he thought Herzl's plan terribly misguided:

Not only did he fail to take culture into account, but in his style
of politics he represented a sharp, sinister break with Jewish his-

tory: his cultivation of the masses (which Ahad Ha'am immediately denounced as demagoguery) coupled with his promise
of rapid redemption conjured terrifying comparison with messianic pretenders of the past. . . . He went so far as to charge Herzl
with heresy.[23]

Ahad Ha'am had an alternate proposal. Rather than working
to create a state, he thought Jews ought to establish a "colony" in
Palestine. Populated by the elites of the Jewish world, this spiritual
center would enrich the Jewish spirit everywhere.[24] "From Zion
shall go forth Torah," the biblical prophet Isaiah had proclaimed
optimistically thousands of years earlier.[25] Ahad Ha'am clearly
thought Zionism ought to fulfill the prophet's prediction.

To his mind, the Jewish future would rest not solely on Jewish
fortunes in Zion. Since Jewish sovereignty was not critical for him,
he was open to the idea of different kinds of Judaism flourishing
in multiple places. And, he was convinced, Jews could also flourish in America. "To *Eretz Israel* (the Land of Israel) or to America?"
he asked. "The true answer . . . is: to America *and to Eretz Israel*.
The economic side of the Jewish question needs to be answered in
America, while the idealistic side . . . it is only in *Eretz Israel*."[26]

After the publication of Herzl's *Altneuland* in 1902, the battle between Herzl and Ahad Ha'am (who was by then Herzl's most vociferous critic) grew even uglier. But just a year later, the pogrom in
Kishinev led even the apolitical Ahad Ha'am to back off—everyone
understood that the Jewish people needed to set aside differences
and to prepare a way to escape Europe. But he never dropped his
objection to Herzl's plan for a Jewish state. Statehood, he was convinced, would be an enormous mistake for the Jews.

Ahad Ha'am lost that battle with Herzl, of course, for Zionism
did go on to establish a state. Yet his ideas continued to resonate in
the Zionist world and continue to do so to this very day.

Among Ahad Ha'am's earliest devotees was a group of intellectuals in Palestine who established *Brit Shalom* (the Covenant
of Peace), an organization that sought to promote peace between

Jews and Arabs, primarily by advocating that the Jews give up
their quest for statehood. *Brit Shalom* members were convinced
that since a Jewish state would forever be in conflict with the region's Arabs, Jews would be better served by creating a binational
state of Jews and Arabs. There was no reason that Jews and Arabs
could not share the region, and even neighborhoods, living in
utter harmony.

The movement never had more than about a hundred members,
but its influence far outstripped its numbers. Prominent members
included Arthur Ruppin, an economist who held a senior position
in the Jewish Agency; the philosopher Martin Buber; and Gershom
Scholem, the world-renowned philosopher and historian. Albert
Einstein never joined the movement but was supportive; so, too,
was Judah Magnes, an American Reform rabbi and pacifist who
by virtue of his role in shaping the culture of Hebrew University
(he was the university's first chancellor and later its president), was
able to influence the thought of generations of Israeli students and
scholars. Subsequent generations of American Jewish leaders were
at the very least deeply influenced by Ahad Ha'am, and his followers, especially in Israel's early years, wondered aloud whether in
pursuing a state, Zionism did not make a critical strategic blunder,
unwittingly leading the Jews astray.

What both the statist and nonstatist visions had in common was
that for either to be realized, no small number of Jews would have
to pick themselves up and move to an Ottoman province. In that
regard, at least at this stage, the realization of either vision seemed
entirely unlikely.

OTHER IMAGES OF ZIONISM were also emerging during this time.
Max Nordau, a highly regarded public intellectual, had become
wrapped up in the Zionist cause at around the time of the Dreyfus
affair. Nordau had been born into an Orthodox family in Pest, was
a correspondent in Paris for the *Vossische Zeitung,* a liberal German
paper based in Berlin, and had left the Jewish world to become a

German intellectual. He even changed his name from Südfeld in an attempt to distance himself from Jewish heritage.

Nordau, in some sense, had foreseen Kishinev. As early as the Second Zionist Congress, he advocated the creation of the *Muskeljuden*, "muscle-Jews." The new Jewish state that the Zionists were anxious to create, he argued, needed to be populated by the new Jew—a strong, empowered figure for whom the yeshiva was a distant memory.

> For too long, all too long have we been engaged in the mortification of our own flesh. . . . Or rather, to put it more precisely— others did the killing of our flesh for us. Their extraordinary success is measured by hundreds of thousands of Jewish corpses in the ghettos, in the churchyards, along the highways of medieval Europe. . . . In the narrow Jewish street our poor limbs soon forgot their gay movements; in the dimness of sunless houses our eyes began to blink shyly; the fear of constant persecution turned our powerful voices into frightened whispers, which rose in a crescendo only when our martyrs on the stakes cried out in their dying prayers in the face of their executioners. . . . Let us take up our oldest traditions; let us once more become deep-chested, sturdy, sharp-eyed men.[27]

Nordau was hardly alone in feeling that Zionism needed to usher a new era of overt physicality into the consciousness of the Jewish people. The Kishinev pogroms shook no one in the Zionist establishment more than Vladimir Ze'ev Jabotinsky.[28] Born in Odessa in 1880, the secular, somewhat assimilated Jabotinsky (who later used the first name Ze'ev) spent his early years as a journalist and foreign correspondent in Europe and in the Russian Empire.

Jabotinsky was delivering a lecture to the Jewish literary society in Odessa on Pinsker's *Auto-Emancipation* when he received the news of the Kishinev pogrom. Though horrified by the news, he, too, was not entirely surprised. Even before the massacre, rumors had been circulating about an impending pogrom, and Jabotinsky

and a few others started gathering pistols and spoke of both the
legality and importance of self-defense.

Over the course of his career, Jabotinsky would increasingly lock
horns with the Zionist establishment, particularly as he became
convinced that the Zionists were too weak and passive in the face
of opposition—first from the Ottomans and then the British—to
ever accomplish their goals of creating a Jewish state. He hoped
to "revise" mainstream Zionism's accommodating and gradual approach to acquiring land and building on it; so he founded a splinter
movement, Revisionist Zionism.

In theory, Revisionist and mainstream Zionism were not all
that different. Both believed in the "establishment of Jewish settlements in Palestine, the right to a Jewish armed force, and free Jewish immigration to Palestine, all accomplished through diplomacy
with the British." Both of them also endorsed Jewish settlement
of the entire Land of Israel as outlined in the Bible, including both
sides of the Jordan River. Where they differed was in the degree to
which they might be willing to use force—if needed—to achieve
their goals.

Jabotinsky began by organizing Jewish self-defense units across
the Russian Empire, placing a heavy emphasis on the youth. Several years later, in 1923, Jabotinsky established a Revisionist youth
movement, Betar, named for the last standing fortress of the Bar
Kokhba rebellion against the Romans in 135 CE. Betar was designed to teach military tactics and to physically train the youth of
Europe. As Jabotinsky explained in his essay "The Idea of Betar,"
the aim of the movement was

> very simple though difficult: to create that type of Jew which
> the nation needs in order to better and quicker build a Jewish
> state. . . . The greatest difficulty is encountered because, as a
> nation, the Jews today are neither "normal" nor "healthy" and
> life in diaspora affects the intelligent upbringing of normal and
> healthy citizens.[29]

Betar spread throughout Europe, building chapters in Poland, Latvia, Lithuania, Austria, Czechoslovakia, Germany, and Palestine. In a decade, the movement would come to include seventy thousand members.

Unlike Ahad Ha'am and *Brit Shalom*, Jabotinsky was no pacifist. If the Jews wanted Palestine, he warned, they were going to have to go to battle. While other Zionist camps often felt that military prowess and the use of force were somehow at odds with Zionism's fundamental ethos, neither Jabotinsky nor the Revisionists who would follow him would apologize for being willing to fight when Jewish destiny demanded it.

Jewish destiny, they believed, would periodically require the use of force. Sadly, history would prove Jabotinsky and the Revisionists prescient.

If Nordau and Jabotinsky thought that physical power should be key to the essence of the new Jew, for others, the new Jew needed to focus on an entirely different form of physicality. In the first decade of the twentieth century, the Kishinev pogrom and the failure of the Russian Revolution forged a deeply ideological wave of immigrants, whose primary spokesperson was Aaron David Gordon (almost always referred to as A. D. Gordon).[30] A devotee of Ahad Ha'am's philosophy, Gordon would become the philosopher of Labor Zionism. He agreed that it was time for a new Jew. But for him, the new Jew would emerge not from discarding the past, not from a deep otherworldly spirituality, nor from Jews building their physiques. The new Jew would emerge from working the land.

Born in 1856 in Podolia, a small village in the Ukraine, near the modern-day border with Moldova, Gordon spent most of his life managing the estate of a wealthy relative. In 1904, at age forty-seven, Gordon, ignoring the advice of others, decided to head to Palestine. He left his wife and two children with whatever money he had, hoping that he would soon be able to bring them over. A white-collar worker his entire life and no longer young, physically weak but undeterred, Gordon was determined to be a laborer on the land. He succeeded. Whether at the wineries of Petach Tikvah, in the Galilee, or, finally at Degania (the first kibbutz* of the Labor Zionist movement), he worked the land until he was essentially spent. He became seriously ill in 1921, but disregarded his health and continued working until—like Herzl who had preceded him—he died.

Yet Gordon left a legacy that would inspire generations of Jews in the Yishuv† and later in Israel, particularly in the early kibbutz movement. His new Jew would be sustained by a "religion of labor":

> Labor is not only the force which binds man to the soil and by which possession of the soil is acquired; it is also the basic energy for the creation of a national culture. This is what we do not have—but we are not aware of missing it. We are a people without a country, without a living national language, without a living culture. . . . A vital culture, far from being detached from life, embraces it in all its aspects. . . . Farming, building, and road-making—any work, any craft, any productive activity—is part of culture and is indeed the foundation and the stuff of culture. [31]

Jews needed to return to nature and to working the land with their bare hands; for too long, Gordon felt, they had relied on their intellect for their livelihoods. This had distorted their national soul

---

* A kibbutz (plural—kibbutzim) is the name for a collective community originally based largely on socialist ideals and rooted in agricultural work. The kibbutz became an iconic Israeli institution in the state's first decades. Technically, Degania was the first *kevutza*, a community slightly smaller than a kibbutz, but today it is commonly called the first kibbutz.

† Yishuv means "area of settlement." It is also the term often used for the prestate Jewish community in Palestine. The "New Yishuv" refers to those Jews who began arriving with the immigrants described here; the "Old Yishuv" refers to those Jews who were already living in Palestine when the new immigrants began to arrive.

(an accusation with which Bialik and Ahad Ha'am would certainly have agreed). For Gordon, the remedy was to be found in the land; it was time for the Jews to return to a life of labor. "Labor has afflicted us," Gordon said, "and labor will heal us."[32]

It is impossible to exaggerate the degree to which Gordon's worldview would profoundly shape the first decades of renewed Jewish life in Palestine. The centrality of agriculture to the early kibbutz movement, the image of Jews resettling the land as farmers (though even at the peak, only a very small percentage of Jews worked in agriculture), was in a large measure the result of the power of Gordon's image. The pride that early prestate Zionists took in what might have seemed to some menial labor was also a reflection of Gordon's influence. The commitment to *avodah ivrit* ("Jewish labor"), which persists in some circles, is an evocation of A. D. Gordon's sense that genuine Jewish spirituality would come from calloused hands caked with the dirt of the Land of Israel.

BIALIK AND AHAD HA'AM never lost their love for traditional Jewish texts and the world that those texts evoked, and each wove their influence into his writing. Some Zionists, though, felt that Zionism was not only about transforming Judaism, but about moving beyond it altogether. Perhaps the best-known exponent of this position was Russian scholar Micha Josef Berdyczewski (pronounced Berdichevsky), who famously opined that Zionism needed to be a complete revolt against Judaism.[33] It was time for Jews to free themselves of the dogmas of Jewish tradition, history, and religion, and essentially to reinvent themselves. He said, "We can be the last Jews or the first Hebrews."[34]

It is therefore not at all surprising that if many of the Zionists rejected traditional Judaism, much of the traditional Jewish world also rejected Zionism. Though there were religious Jews among the Zionists, for many others, religious commitments were an explicit reason *not* to join the movement.

The reasons dated back millennia. A much-discussed passage in the Babylonian Talmud* refers to three oaths to which Israel and the nations of the world committed themselves. The nations of the world swore that they would not oppress the nation of Israel excessively, while Israel swore not to enter the Land of Israel by force and not to rebel against the nations of the world.[35]

Over the course of centuries, this brief text became the bedrock of those who argued that Jews should not return to their ancestral homeland until God returned them. It was clear to most that any return to the land was going to require at least some force, which they had sworn not to do. Ironically, religious anti-Zionists and largely secular pacifists like some members of *Brit Shalom* both opposed Zionism because it would inevitably involve using force.

Those oaths, though, were hardly the central issue. The real issue at the heart of religious anti-Zionism was deeper. Over the centuries of dispersion, Jews had come to see their world as composed of two spiritual states—exile and redemption.[36] Implicitly evoking Jeremiah's sense that the Jews would return to the land when their Creator decreed that it was time, Jews, particularly those in eastern Europe, felt they had a religious duty to remain in exile until God redeemed them. To them, Zionism—which sought to place history and the fate of the Jews in human hands—was a violation of the essence of Judaism. The fact that most of the movement's leadership was not only fiercely secular, but rabidly antireligious, just confirmed their sense. They railed against the Zionists and would have nothing to do with them.

Yet there were also religious Zionists. Not opposed to Zionism in principle, as were the ultra-Orthodox, they had no compunction about the Jews taking history back into their own hands.

---

* The Babylonian Talmud, composed approximately 200 CE to 500 CE by Jewish communities in Babylonian exile, is the most important Jewish postbiblical text. A massive work (the traditional version is printed in twenty volumes), it is still the primary religious text studied by traditional Jews around the world.

Still, they had a different vision for Jewish revival from the secular mainstream. There had been faint strains of a religious Zionist movement even in the late 1800s, but it was in 1902, when the Fifth Zionist Congress stated that Zionism would focus on Jewish culture, that Mizrachi, religious Zionism's first significant organization, was founded. Culture alone could never sustain Judaism, the religious Jews who founded it insisted. God and the observance of the commandments had always been the heart of Jewish life. Ever since the revelation of the Torah at Mount Sinai, fealty to Jewish law had been the key to Jewish survival. Nothing could ever change that. If Zionism was to have any merit, they said, religion needed to be at its core.

The Mizrachi met for its first world convention in what is today Bratislava in 1904, a year after Kishinev and the year of Herzl's death. Largely alone, they rejected both the anti-Zionism of the religious eastern Europeans as well as the antireligious sentiments of many in the Zionist world. They would remain relatively peripheral but dogged until 1967, when they would suddenly change Zionism and Israel forever.

ZIONISM HAD BECOME a series of unresolved debates. Some (Herzl) sought a state while others (Ahad Ha'am) insisted that statehood would lead to spiritual bankruptcy, so the Jews should seek only a spiritual center. Some (Bialik) thought religion was the cancer that had destroyed the Jew (though Bialik retained a love for Jewish religious texts), while others (religious Zionists) saw in religion the only hope for sustaining the Jewish people. Some ignored the Arab issue so consistently that they seemed to imagine a Palestine in which there were simply no Arabs. Still others (Herzl), not that different, hoped that the progress Jews would bring to the region would earn them the respect and admiration of their Arab neighbors. Others (Jabotinsky), however, thought those views foolish and said that if Jews were not willing to fight, they had no future in Zion. Some (Nordau) imagined a

Jew redeemed by a new physicality, while others (A. D. Gordon) insisted that the physicality had to be rooted in working the land. Zionism was a movement, but it was also a collection of competing dreams.

A Jewish state was still a long way off; decades would pass before the Jews would actually establish the state about which they were already disagreeing. When Zionists ultimately succeeded in creating a state, however, all these rival factions would have to live together in what would become a hastily declared and built country. As much as they disagreed with one another, they would have to live, love, go to battle, build a country—and die—together. Israel's fractious politics and turbulent political life are, in many respects, the result of these early, unresolved Zionist debates. When it eventually arose, the Jewish state would be one that Jews were constantly struggling to learn how to share. As the great Hebrew writer and early Zionist Yosef Brenner put it, Zionism was in some ways "forced to put forth branches before it [had] time to strike root."[37]

FROM A DREAM TO
GLIMMERS OF REALITY

The two things without which the Jews would not have become a
nation are the land and the language.

—Eliezer Ben-Yehuda[1]

A s Herzl was writing in German in the last decade of the nineteenth century, the best-known Jew in the English-speaking
world was Israel Zangwill. A novelist and a playwright (and deeply
involved in the women's rights movement), he, too, had left the
traditional household in which he had been raised and became a
Zionist.

Early in his career, Zangwill wrote a series of articles in which
he described Palestine as "a wilderness . . . a stony desolation . . .
a deserted home" and a land that had "gone to ruin."[2] The popular rendition of his view was that Palestine was a "land without a
people, waiting for a people without a land."[3]

That, of course, was not entirely accurate. Neither, though, was
it entirely wrong. While there *were* people in Palestine, they were
not organized in any way approximating what Europeans would
have expected. The Ottomans (Turkish Empire) had controlled Palestine since 1517, yet had done virtually nothing to develop it:

Loosely divided between the provinces of Beirut and Syria, the Palestine of the early 1800s was hardly less than an administrative shambles. Centuries of Turkish indifference and misgovernment had encouraged recurrent warfare between local pashas and had permitted Bedouin robber bands to terrorize the country's 400,000 inhabitants (by 1840). Trade was minimal.[4]

Yet, though poor, badly organized, and without any cohesive identity, there *were* people living there; the land was not empty. There were several hundred thousand people in Palestine, the majority of whom were Arabs.[5] For the most part, they led rural lives, dispersed over seven or eight hundred villages throughout the area. Most lived as tenant farmers in a somewhat feudal system with landowners, but some lived in towns like Gaza, Hebron, Haifa, and elsewhere. While Arab national identity during this period had not yet developed, its early stirrings could already be felt. As early as 1891, some of the wealthier Palestinian Arabs began to urge the Turkish authorities not to allow Jewish refugees to settle in Palestine; they understood, with great clarity, that the "'Arab' character" of the region was about to change.[6]

By the late 1870s, there were also about twenty-seven thousand Jews already living in Palestine, concentrated primarily in Jerusalem, where they constituted a majority. These Jews were almost exclusively poor, deeply religious, and committed to having as little to do as possible with people outside their community; they lived off the financial support of a *halukka* (distribution) system that collected money from Jews outside Palestine for scholars, widows and orphans, and other needy Jews. It was a simple way of life, virtually untouched by modernity, one to which the Jewish and Arab inhabitants had long been accustomed.

Ironically, it was European anti-Semitism that would change Palestine. As Jewish life in Europe became increasingly intolerable, a massive Jewish exodus from Europe began. So, too, did renewed Jewish immigration to Palestine.

In his undeniably utopian *Altneuland*, Herzl had described a future in which the Jews brought significant progress to Palestine. As a result, he believed, the Arabs would welcome them with open arms. Zangwill, as well, whether idealist or naive, imagined that the influx of Jews from Europe would be good for everyone. In an article from 1903, entitled "Zion, Whence Cometh My Help?," he said that the Jews would redeem the land and lead it to modernity. European Jews would find a home, at last, and local residents would benefit from an improved economy.

But European Jews were about to encounter a culture that they essentially did not understand:

> What was more than a little unreal, then, was the claim that the Sultan and his government ruled their domains in the sense in which Europeans understood government and administration. What was real in the Ottoman Empire tended to be local: a tribe, a clan, a sect, or a town was the true political unit to which loyalties adhered. This confused European observers, whose modern notions of citizenship and nationality were inapplicable to the crazy quilt of Ottoman politics.[7]

European notions of nations and citizenship, which Zionists from Europe would bring with them, were about to clash with the tribal, clannish, local system of the Palestinian Arabs. European Jews, in turn, would find themselves in tension with the insular Jews of Palestine, who remained opposed both to modernity as well as to the Jews from Europe who were importing it into the Middle East. To no small degree, those differing conceptions of nation and society, competing sensibilities regarding honor and memory, and many other missed cues would fuel the conflict between Jews and Arabs in the years to come.

THE FIRST WAVES OF Jewish immigration to the New Yishuv were for the most part not hardened ideologues. They were Jews who fled to Palestine in the late nineteenth and early twentieth centuries for the very same reasons that millions of other Jews had fled to North America. Largely Russian, these immigrants had set out looking to escape the dangers of a darkening Europe, seeking a place where they could lead simple lives in relative security.

Some, though, were passionate about creating a different Jewish future. They came to Palestine with a vision of a renewed Jewish society, many of them hoping that that new society would embody the socialist ideals then in vogue in Russia. (Karl Marx, the father of socialism, had died in 1883; the Bolshevik Revolution would follow in 1917.) That renewed Jewish life, they felt, could be realized only in their ancestral homeland, Palestine.

The first wave of Jewish immigration, known as the First Aliyah, began in 1882 and continued, with breaks, until 1903.* This was the period in which Diaspora organizations designed to foster the growth of Jewish life in Palestine (and later, in Israel) also began to develop. Two organizations critical to the First Aliyah got their start in 1882. The first was *Hovevei Zion* ("Lovers of Zion"), which Pinsker had helped create. The second, known as *Bilu*,[†] was composed of a tiny group of university students (called *Biluim*), who in spite of their small numbers—and relatively minimal accomplishments—became legendary for their passion and fervor and for the settlement they helped establish, Gedera.

The influx of European Zionists alarmed the Jews already living in Palestine, commonly known as the Old Yishuv. The Old Yishuv Jews were pious to the core and deeply loyal to their rabbinic authorities. To them, the new, ideologically ultrasecular Yishuv seemed alien, even blasphemous.

---

* Each wave of immigration was called an *aliyah*—*aliyot* in the plural—Hebrew for "those who went up." Classical Jewish sources always refer to going to the Land of Israel as "going up."

† Bilu is an acronym for the Hebrew phrase "House of Jacob, let us go up." The Hebrew words are *beit ya'akov lechu ve-nelcha* (Isaiah 2:5).

AT LEAST ONE CENTRAL figure in the Yishuv hoped that he might bridge the gap between the two communities. Born in 1865, Rabbi Abraham Isaac Kook moved to Palestine in 1904 (the year Herzl died), already a widely venerated scholar. Orthodox to his core, Rav Kook (Hebrew for Rabbi Kook, and the name by which he was universally known) was not about to sanction the antireligious, avowedly secular lifestyle and philosophy of the New Yishuv. But neither was he willing to write them off. While he certainly disagreed with Bialik and others who savagely attacked traditional Judaism and what it had done to the Jewish people, he was not beyond acknowledging that something had, indeed, gone wrong in Jewish life. He believed that "many young people disrespected authority because they had somehow risen above it, and the absence of an intellectual program to match their undoubted moral passion was the source of their confusion, bitterness and cynicism. Their rebellion was itself a sign of their 'thirst for thought, and reason, and with it for richer, more drenched feeling, fresh and alive.'"[8] Unlike most rabbinic authorities of the era, Rav Kook was unwilling to simplistically see the New Yishuv as apostates. The pioneers, he believed, "were filled with love, justice and power; the task of rabbis was to bring them to self-awareness. Rather than seeking to stifle these young people, spiritual leaders should be empowering them, precisely via the Torah that they earnestly—and even justifiably— despised."[9]

Rav Kook was thus a blend of passions in whom some sought a bridge between two seemingly utterly disconnected worlds. Exceedingly traditional in his appearance, Kook looked precisely like those Jews of the old guard who repudiated everything about Zionism. But unlike those rabbis, Kook was smitten with the ideological fervor of the pioneers and the New Yishuv. "Passing through the fields, he pointed and said, 'Look! A Jewish cow!' Once, on the way to Rishon Le-Zion, he told a traveling companion, 'I could kiss every stone in this land—and even the mules on the way.'"[10]

When he died in 1935, Rav Kook left a profound legacy of

ideas that some people hoped might form bridges between communities—with most of the bridging still undone. A generation later, his son, Zvi Yehudah Kook, would become one of Israel's most impassioned ideologues, and—some would say—a deeply divisive figure, as well.

THE REBIRTH OF HEBREW was yet another of Zionism's early revolutions. If Theodor Herzl was the father of political Zionism and Ahad Ha'am was the progenitor of the spiritual side of the Zionist movement, Eliezer Perlman—who later changed his name to Eliezer Ben-Yehuda (which means Eliezer the Son of Judah)—is the father of modern Hebrew. Zionism was a revolution in many respects. It restored the Jewish people's role as actors on the stage of history, it reestablished an ancient commonwealth, and, thanks to Ben-Yehuda, revived the language of the Bible, the language in which the Jewish people had first defined itself.

Ben-Yehuda had an upbringing similar to that of many of Zionism's leaders and the *haskalah*'s men and women of letters. Reared in an Orthodox home, he found himself more drawn toward the secular Zionist world. But instead of turning to poetry as did Bialik, Ben-Yehuda began to focus on how the ancient Hebrew language might support modern-day prose and everyday conversation. As a student at the Sorbonne, he witnessed the profound effect of the French language on French nationalism and decided that Jewish nationalism needed nothing less. He wrote to his future wife, Devorah, in 1880, "I have decided . . . that in order to have our own land and political life it is also necessary that we have a language to hold us together. That language is Hebrew, but not the Hebrew of the rabbis and scholars. We must have a Hebrew language in which we can conduct the business of life."[11]

Once Ben-Yehuda and his wife had settled in the Land of Israel in 1881, they spoke only Hebrew to each other and to their children. They would not permit their children to speak to anyone else in any language other than Hebrew. Since there were, essentially, no other Hebrew speakers, their children could speak only to their family. In his own way, Ben-Yehuda was no less the impassioned revolutionary than Herzl or anyone else in the Zionist leadership.

With time, Ben-Yehuda found partners in the battle. He and a small group of other Hebrew enthusiasts penned Hebrew literature at an extraordinary pace. Writers represented an unusually high proportion of the society; in that milieu, they were seen not only as artists, but as voices of the revolutionary national Jewish revival, as well.

That revolutionary zeal was reflected in Ben-Yehuda's inviting numerous women to publish in his various journals. Women, he argued, would be uniquely able to "insert emotion, tenderness, flexibility and subtlety into the dead, forgotten, old, dry and hardened Hebrew language."[12] The Yishuv was far from an egalitarian society, but just as the Second Zionist Congress had granted women the right to vote and to run for office, there were early feminist leanings in the Yishuv, as well.

Despite the revolutionary zeal of the Yishuv's intellectual elite, Hebrew was not a top priority for the average Jewish immigrant. (Even Herzl himself had doubted that Hebrew would be the language of the Jewish state.[13]) Given all the challenges they had to endure after moving to Palestine, the early pioneers were understandably not keen on speaking a language in which they could not fully express themselves. For many, the preferred language was Yiddish, the language of eastern European Jewish communities. Yiddish plays, regularly staged in Jaffa, drew large audiences who were anxious to be entertained in a language they could understand with ease. It was the classic revolutionary elite versus the rank and file. The Hebrew writers were determined to create high culture, but the immigrants were equally desperate to relax, to not work their minds as hard as they had to work their bodies.

Ben-Yehuda and his partners had other obstacles beyond a population that was not terribly enthusiastic about reviving a language. For religious Jews, the revival of Hebrew was no less problematic than Zionism itself. Hebrew was the sacred language of the Bible, the Mishnah (the first major work of rabbinic literature), and the liturgy, and they insisted that Jews must not sully it by using it for purely ordinary matters. They relentlessly attacked Ben-Yehuda's efforts to create a Hebrew lexicon. They stoned his office and reported him to the Ottomans, who jailed him briefly. Then the religious leadership excommunicated him. When Ben-Yehuda's first wife, Devorah, died of tuberculosis in 1891, they would not allow her to be buried in the Ashkenazi* cemetery. After Devorah's death, Ben-Yehuda married her younger sister, Hemda.

The religious community was not entirely wrong about Ben-Yehuda. He made no secret of the fact that, like Bialik and others, he saw Zionism as a rebellion against the very world of those other religious residents of Jerusalem. Following the Uganda controversy, Ben-Yehuda wrote:

> Another great and terrible argument of the "Zion Zionists," is that "they, the Ugandists" are turning their back on our entire history. How much cynicism in this argument?! Men who have turned their back on the past accusing others of doing the same thing! For let there be no illusions. The only ones who haven't turned their backs on the past are the "committee for the investigation of sins" [his religious opponents in Jerusalem]. All of us, all of us, have turned our backs on the past, that is our glory and splendor![14]

A loner in many ways, Ben-Yehuda aroused the scorn not only of the religious, but even of some of those who were deeply committed to the revival of Hebrew. Even "[t]he other leading cultural nationalists—Ahad Ha'am, Bialik—disdained him as a soulless linguistic mechanic, though none of them could compete with his ability to create, from scratch, Hebrew words."[15]

---

* "Ashkenazi" is the term for Jews of European descent, while "Sephardi," or "Mizrachi," refers to Jews from the Orient (primarily North Africa and the Middle East).

Yet slowly but surely, Ben-Yehuda earned himself a broad following in the Yishuv. The Orthodox establishment had first failed in their attempt to convince European Jews not to join the Zionist movement, and now they failed to derail the revival of Hebrew. Ben-Yehuda became recognized as a key player in the revitalization not only of the language, but of the entire people that spoke it. When he died in Jerusalem in December 1922, some thirty thousand people attended his funeral, and the Yishuv observed three official days of mourning.

IN PALESTINE, JUST AS had been the case in Europe, literature would be one of the settings in which Jews would set forth competing visions of what the Jew could, and should, be. Quickly, Hebrew literature became a vehicle for imagining a Jewish national home reconstituted, and at the same time, a medium for expressing the conflicts and divisions in Zionist life. Authors and poets would play a central role in shaping the movement, both in the Yishuv and after Israel's establishment.

The first book of modern Hebrew literature in the Yishuv was written by Ze'ev Yavetz, who moved to Palestine in 1887. Deeply unsettled by those immigrants who seemed insufficiently committed to re-creating the Jew, he used his sharp pen to attack those who he felt failed to appreciate that the decision to come to Palestine ought to flow from a passion for revolution. In one of his stories, he compares two types of Jews, which he frames as opposites: the Diaspora Jew, who is "the Tourist," and the Pioneer, who is "the Resident."[16] His preference was obvious. Overdressed and physically weak, solely concerned with his own comfort and appearance, the Diaspora Jew had "his beard shaved, his mustache made up. . . . [H]is bag was on his thigh and his cane and parasol were in his hand, curved and ruffled . . . but his appearance was very pale and his face deficient."[17]

In Yavetz's story, the Diaspora Jew refuses to join the pioneer men, women, and children sitting on the ground and taking pleasure in the view since it would mean getting his trousers wet. Unlike the "Tourist," the "Resident" is earthy and active; he is dressed simply in Arabic style clothing, holds a weapon for self-defense (instead of a parasol), and rides a white horse. He embodies health, confidence, and a passion for life. He is Bialik's new Jew who would not hide behind a cask during a pogrom, a new Jew who is determined to break with his victimlike past, the new Jew intent on taking control of his destiny. Now, thanks to Yavetz, that literary discussion of the new Jew had moved from Europe to Palestine, from exile to the budding Yishuv.

Yavetz was but one of a number of writers shaping the Yishuv. Another, who became a leading writer not only of the Yishuv but of the Western world, was Shmuel Yosef (Shai) Czaczkes, who became a frequent visitor to Rav Kook's home. Like many members of the New Yishuv, he was infuriated with the Judaism of the Diaspora; like many, though, he also harbored a lifelong love for its texts and was loath to leave that entire heritage behind. To Czaczkes, Rav Kook offered the possibility of that synthesis. Not long after meeting Kook, Czaczkes published his short story "Agunot," about women locked in broken marriages whose husbands could use Jewish law to hold them captive by refusing to grant them a religious divorce. He published the work under his recently adopted pseudonym, Shai Agnon.[18] In 1966, he would win Israel's first Nobel Prize.

IT WAS ONE THING for people like Yavetz to write about the "earthy" pioneers, utterly comfortable in the dirt of their new home, but entirely another matter to actually live that life. The young, somewhat hotheaded ideologues came to Palestine with an abundance of ideals, but they had virtually no agricultural experience. Their utopian socialist agricultural settlements failed almost immediately, and they found themselves forced to scavenge for financial assistance anywhere they could find it.

As would be the case even after the State of Israel's founding decades later, much of the assistance that the Yishuv needed came in the form of support from Diaspora Jews. Key among these philanthropists was Baron Edmond de Rothschild. Soon known as "The Benefactor," the baron poured part of his fortune into providing the settlements with everything from housing to equipment to livestock. By the turn of the century, his monetary assistance totaled $6 million, equivalent today to almost $150 million.

Sometimes also called the "godfather of the moshavot,"* Rothschild sent European agricultural experts to Palestine to advise the newly arrived immigrants, and he acquired extensive land holdings there. All told, he purchased about two hundred square miles of land, on which some forty villages were established. The communities he supported stretched from Metulla, situated at the very north, to Mazkeret Batya (Ekron) in the south, as well as other now significant towns such as Rishon Lezion, Rosh Pina, and Zichron Yaakov. He supported agricultural communities of all sorts (moshavim and kibbutzim) as well as towns. With his financial assistance, more than thirty such communities were founded between 1880 and 1895 alone. Given that there were roughly 160 villages in Palestine by 1937, Rothschild contributed to about a third of them. (See Map 2.)

The Jewish purchase of land, while entirely legal, aroused the concern of both the Ottomans and the local Arabs. Fully aware of the Jews' growing interest in establishing a foothold in Palestine, the empire began to push back. Even before the Biluim set out for Palestine, local Turkish officials announced that Palestine would be closed to the Jews of Odessa (a pronouncement very pointedly intended for the Biluim, as Odessa was where they were based). In 1856 the Ottomans had passed a law allowing foreigners to buy land in the empire, but by 1881, the Ottomans began banning land purchases by Jews and Christians and, in what was a very clear

---

* A moshav (moshavot or moshavim in plural) is the term for a cooperative rural Israeli town, usually in an agricultural area.

message, declared that year that Jews were still permitted to immigrate to the Ottoman Empire, with the exception of Palestine. The ban on the sale of lands in Palestine to Jews lasted for the duration of Ottoman rule.

The ban, though, did little to prevent Jewish acquisition of land in Palestine. "The central authorities were ambivalent and inconstant in their attitudes to land acquisition by foreigners, the formulation of the laws and regulations were unclear and open to different interpretations, and corruption and openness to bribery was widespread at all levels in the Ottoman bureaucracy." The legal path to Jewish acquisition of land in Palestine remained open,[19] and the Yishuv made the most of the opportunity. With the help of Old Yishuv Jews who spoke Arabic and were already familiar with Ottoman culture and government, the Zionists deftly navigated the back channels of the convoluted and corrupt Ottoman bureaucracy. Even Herzl, when he wished to meet the sultan, had to secure the meeting through bribery.

WHILE THESE NEW COMMUNITIES in the Yishuv could probably not have survived without Rothschild's beneficence, Rothschild and the pioneers were often at odds. The young, idealistic immigrants felt that making use of his abundant wealth was compromising the socialist utopia they had hoped to create. Rothschild, in turn, was dismayed by what struck him as an attitude of entitlement among the workers, and had his local administrators keep a watchful eye on them, which only reinforced youthful immigrants' sense that the capitalist hierarchy that they had sought to escape had followed them to their new home.

It was a pattern that would repeat decades later, in relations between Israel and its Diaspora supporters. Especially with regard to matters of Israeli foreign policy and religious pluralism in Israel, Diaspora Jews (and particularly American Jews) would act out of the best of intentions, while Israelis at times resented what they saw as the "rich Diaspora Jews meddling."

ALL TOLD, THE FIRST Aliyah brought twenty to thirty thousand Jews to Palestine. Yet some 60 to 90 percent of these early immigrants ended up leaving just a few years after they arrived.

Returning to their ancestral homeland was both an exhilarating and frustrating experience for these new, ideologically impassioned immigrants. They had come as idealistic visionaries, but found themselves dependent on the largesse of others. For many immigrants, the radical disparity between the idealized image of the sun-soaked, tranquil land that had animated them and the reality of the Jaffa port—filthy and fetid, clogged with people pushing, shoving, and spitting on the ground—was the first indication that life in their new home was going to be unlike anything they had anticipated. Many left. Those who stayed discovered a chasm between what they had dreamed of building and what they were actually able to accomplish. Some even felt undermined by developments in Europe, and in particular, the Uganda Plan of 1903. If the Zionist ideologues of Europe were giving up on Palestine, why should they toil endlessly for a land in which they were not wanted and about which the world Zionist movement seemed not to care?

Still, these early pioneers were successful far beyond what their self-criticism allowed them to appreciate. They could not know it with certainty then, but they had paved the road for future waves of immigration. They had laid the groundwork of communities that would become Israeli villages and cities. Most important, perhaps, they were the first to model what it would take to translate Herzl's vision into the beginning of a reality.

SHORTLY AFTER THE KISHINEV POGROM and then the rapid rise and fall of the Uganda Plan, the Second Aliyah (1904–1914) began. During this period, approximately forty thousand Jewish immigrants made their way to the Land of Israel, mostly from eastern Europe. This wave of immigration left an even more profound and lasting mark on the growing Jewish community in Palestine. It established the first kibbutz, Degania, just south of the Kinneret

(Hebrew for the Sea of Galilee)*; the first Jewish self-defense organization; and the suburb of Jaffa that would become Tel Aviv. This
was the wave of immigration that would become iconic, inspiring
generations of Israelis who followed; it would also produce leaders
for the Yishuv who would become some of the state's early pivotal
political and military figures.

Even for these pioneers, however, life was difficult and doubts
abounded. As was the case with the First Aliyah, the most poignant
expression of the hardships of this period appears in the literature
that the Second Aliyah produced.

One of the greatest Hebrew writers of the period was Yosef
Haim Brenner (1881–1921). Born to a poor traditional Jewish family
in a shtetl in Ukraine, he studied at the yeshiva in Pochep but, like
others in the Zionist world, became enamored of secular culture.
In his case, it was Russian culture—particularly writers like Dosto-
evsky and Tolstoy (whose work he later ended up translating into
Hebrew)—that cast the spell. War, though, interrupted Brenner's
intellectual pursuits. From 1901 to 1904, he served in the czar's
army; with the outbreak of the Russo-Japanese War, he escaped to
London and lived there until 1908. London, though, also felt like
exile, so in 1909, Brenner immigrated to Palestine, where he pio-
neered a new wave of modern Hebrew literature and became one
of the leading intellectuals of the Yishuv.

Brenner was passionate but complex. In a way that would somehow characterize the Zionist movement in decades to come, he

---

* Unlike many traditional rabbis, Rav Kook would occasionally go to entirely secular communities, sometimes to officiate at funerals of Jews
who had been killed by the local Arab population. At Merhavia, not far
from Haifa, Kook and others conducted a service in memory of two Jews,
one of them from Degania. The man from Degania, Moshe Barsky, had
been killed while going to get medicine for his friend, Shmuel Dayan.
To honor Barksy's memory, Shmuel named his firstborn son, one of the
first children to be born in Degania, Moshe Dayan. (Yehudah Mirsky,
Rav Kook: Mystic in a Time of Revolution [New Haven, CT: Yale University
Press, 2014], p. 84.)

was both deeply dedicated to the movement and, at the same time, an unremitting pessimist. Intensely committed to creating a new form of Hebrew culture in Palestine, he sometimes felt that his ideals notwithstanding, there was nothing utopian about what the Zionists were building. Exile, he said, had simply relocated to the Land of Israel.[20]

He was, in many ways, "the tortured secular saint of Hebrew letters."[21] A product of the religious world of Europe who was enamored of the Enlightenment, he was precisely the sort of person that Rav Kook hoped to attract to his new religious worldview.

But in what was a telling manifestation of the deep heartbreak at the core of many of the Yishuv's early writers and thinkers, Brenner did not fall under the rabbi's spell. His "pitiless, nearly ascetic lucidity about the depth of Jewry's predicaments and the spiritual crises of his time would not let him be drawn into the rabbi's mystic theodicy of his and his generation's rebellion and longing." About Kook, Brenner had this to say: "At times one senses in . . . certain lines of Rav Kook—that we are dealing here with people of soul, storming, seething—a puddle, but with a tempest roiling its waves."[22]

This, then, was the Zionist world of the time. Passionate souls desperate for a reborn Jewish people, torn between the world of tradition and a brave new—but uncharted—world. Ideologues determined to fashion a new society bumping up against the harsh realities of life in Palestine. Old Yishuv and New Yishuv. Searchers versus builders. It was a fascinating, tempestuous time, infectious with potential and rife with danger.

The state that Zionism would produce would reflect many of these tensions.

Brenner was at points rather pessimistic that the enterprise could even survive. In his short story "*Atzabim*" ("Nerves," 1911), his fear for the future of Zionism is clear. A nameless protagonist tells the nameless narrator the saga of his voyage to Palestine, struggling with the question of whether it was worthwhile. The protagonist leaves Ukraine for New York, where he works in a sweatshop sewing buttons, but eventually sails to Palestine in hope of finding a

better future. What he encounters, however, is a reality no less te-
dious than the one he had hoped to leave behind. The only difference is that now, instead of sewing buttons, he is picking oranges. If
Zion had once been a dream, it now seemed to him nothing more
than an irrational impulse—a fit of "Jewish nerves."

Brenner was not alone in being worried about the ways in which
the Zionist dream was unfolding. One Second Aliyah immigrant,
David Ben-Gurion (who would later become Israel's first prime
minister), felt that it was the people of the First Aliyah who had ca-
pitulated. "The pioneers of the First Aliyah became speculators and
shopkeepers trading in the hopes of their people and selling the aspirations of their youth for pennies. They introduced the idol of exile
into the temple of rebirth," he said, "and the creation of the homeland
was sullied by 'idolatry.'"[23] It was a harsh, and not entirely fair accusation, but it reflected the profound introspection and self-criticism
that would reflect both the Yishuv and the state that would follow.

Brenner, complex though he was, was perhaps *the* cultural icon
of the Second Aliyah. His work, still considered brilliant, surfaced
issues with which Israel continues to wrestle. He would have undoubtedly done even more than he managed in his brief life, but he
was murdered by an Arab mob in the 1921 Jaffa riots.

THE SECOND ALIYAH BEQUEATHED two enduring legacies that
influenced the Jewish state for decades to come: the revival and
ultimate embrace of a renewed Hebrew language, and perhaps Zionism's most iconic institution—the kibbutz.

Built largely on land the Jewish National Fund had purchased
from the Ottomans, the kibbutz movement was rooted in strong
socialist ideals, with an emphasis on collective responsibility
and A. D. Gordon's ideal of working the land. This collectivism,
informed by the immigrants' origins in Russia, eventually represented the single greatest contribution of these early aliyot to Israel's ethos. Equality was emphasized above all. Everything was
shared: food, profits, responsibility for protection of the land. Even

the nuclear family was secondary to the kibbutz collective; children were raised not by their parents, but communally; they slept not in their parents' homes, but in children's houses.

It was a passionate, ideologically rich life that embodied the social and economic vision that many of the pioneers had brought with them. At night, all members of the kibbutz would gather in the common dining hall to discuss both matters of business and kibbutz ideology. Most of the kibbutzim were also explicitly secular; the members believed that through their manual labor they were transforming themselves into the new Jew of which Bialik, Gordon, and so many others had written decades earlier.

Yet the ideological intensity of the kibbutz often came with its costs, especially when those ideologies began to splinter. When the early kibbutzim, for example, largely influenced by the Russian Revolution, could not agree on how to respond to Stalin and Communism's tarnished image, some split into two. When they did, it was not uncommon for couples to split permanently, one spouse living in each of the new communes, families torn asunder and children the unwitting victims of their parents' principled feuding.

The early kibbutz movement unearthed yet another struggle with which Israeli society would later have to wrestle—the tension between building the collective and the significance of the individual. That was true of many revolutionary movements, no less so for Zionism. In Israeli lore, the iconic case that illustrates this tension is that of Rachel Bluwstein Sela, known by her pen name, Rachel HaMishoreret, or Rachel the Poetess.

Rachel, as everyone called her, immigrated to Palestine as a young woman. In 1919, age twenty-nine, she moved to Degania. Shortly after her arrival, though, she fell ill with tuberculosis, which she may have contracted when she traveled for a period to Russia. Concerned for the health of the rest of the community, the kibbutz forced her to leave.

For the rest of her very short life, Rachel wandered, barely eking out a living; she died in a sanatorium in 1931. Yet her poetry, studied in Israeli schools to this day and considered a national treasure, continued to reflect both her nostalgia for the kibbutz and her pain at having been so summarily discarded by the community she had joined.[24] One of her most famous poems, "Perhaps," still sung in Israel almost a century later, evokes that wistfulness.

> *Perhaps it was never so.*
>
> *Perhaps*
> *I never woke early and went to the fields*
> *To labor in the sweat of my brow*
> *Nor in the long blazing days*
> *Of harvest*
> *On top of the wagon laden with sheaves,*
> *Made my voice ring with song*
> *Nor bathed myself clean in the calm*
> *Blue water*
> *Of my Kinneret. O, my Kinneret,*
> *Were you there or did I only dream?*[25]

Did those who gave everything for the cause not deserve more in return? Was the collective all that mattered? Did the new Jew not have some obligation to the individual, even if that meant some risk to the collective?

Though Rachel's poetry raised painful questions about the richness and dangers of ideological passion, the kibbutz movement of the 1930s flourished because the kibbutz embodied a distinct pioneering state-building spirit. So intertwined were the collectivist and national ideologies that "a young pioneer who left the kibbutz in 1934 was betraying his friends and his movement, [while in] 1937–9, he would feel that he was also betraying his country."[26]

The movement never attracted more than a small fraction of the Yishuv's population, however. At its peak in 1947, the kibbutzim accounted for only 7 percent of the Jews living in the Yishuv. Yet it had an enormous impact on what would become Israeli society.[27] The kibbutzim produced much of Israel's early leadership, and even for those who did not live there, it was a symbol of the country's pioneering ethos. By virtue of having been purposely established on the dangerous borders of Israel, the kibbutzim would also become critical to Israel's ongoing defense. That, in turn, created a culture of patriotic devotion in these communities.

In the 1960s, when only 4 percent of Israelis lived on kibbutzim, some 15 percent of members of the Knesset hailed from those settlements. In the Six-Day War, "kibbutz members were represented among the war casualties at a rate almost five times higher than their proportion of the population as a whole. Almost a fifth of fallen soldiers came from a kibbutz. Almost every third officer killed in the war was a kibbutz member."[28] If Israel had a "factory" for passionate dedication to the new state in its first decades, that factory was the kibbutz.

WHILE MANY IMMIGRANTS WERE caught up in the excitement of creating a Jewish model of an ideal socialist society, others longed for a place to live that was reminiscent of the urban landscape they left behind in Europe. A few integrated into existing Arab cities, but found those communities uncomfortably Middle Eastern, dramatically different from the European norms to which they were accustomed. Some sixty modest professionals decided to create the first "Jewish suburb" in Palestine just north of Jaffa. In contrast to what Jaffa, an ancient port city, had to offer, these people were committed to building "'something clean, beautiful and healthy.' It seemed wrong—'anti-Zionist'—to exchange the conditions of a European ghetto for a Middle Eastern one."[29]

In 1909, Tel Aviv was born. "Tel Aviv" was the title of the Hebrew translation of Herzl's utopian novel, *Altneuland*.* The new

---

* A *tel* is a hill created by the remains of homes and buildings of many generations of people who had lived and rebuilt communities on the same location. With time, the level of the hill rises, creating a mound that can be excavated layer by layer to discover the various stages of life there. *Tel* was a reference to the past. *Aviv* is the Hebrew word for "spring." Tel

suburb, which would become a world-class city in a matter of decades, was not intended to be a "farming village but . . . a city that emulated a variety of European models with which they were familiar. For some it was to be a Palestinian Odessa. For others it was to be Vienna on the Mediterranean."[30] Tel Aviv was envisioned as a place where highbrow Zionist culture could flourish; Bialik and many other leading writers of the period made their homes there. The commitment to Hebrew worked; "by 1930 there were more than 13,000 Hebrew-speaking children in municipal schools."[31]

That Tel Aviv ultimately became known as the "first Hebrew-speaking city" now sounds unremarkable. Yet the mere fact that any city, anywhere, could become a "Hebrew-speaking city" is itself another by-product of the sometimes radical Zionist revolution and was largely a product of the ideological fervor of the immigrants of the Second Aliyah. Ben-Yehuda's success was

> augmented by the iron willpower of the Zionist settlers themselves, and notably the immigrants of the Second Aliyah. Plainly it was an excruciating ordeal for Yiddish- and Russian-speaking Jews to employ Hebrew as their daily idiom at home and in the field, when every instinct cried out for relaxation. But they submitted to this discipline as tenaciously as they faced the other hardships of life in Palestine. Most of the Zionist farmers and workers by then had accepted fully Ben-Yehuda's contention: a nation was its language, no less than its sweat and blood.[32]

The Yishuv cultivated a growing literature, an intellectual class, a world of publishing and avid readers, unlike anything the region had seen. And Tel Aviv, with its educated, elite literary circles quickly turned into "'the second Leipzig,' a Hebrew publishing center in Europe."[33] No longer was Hebrew the project of a small group of ideologues animated by revolutionary zeal.

Aviv, therefore, captured the Old-New Land to which Herzl referred in *Altneuland*.

Menachem Ussishkin, one of the leaders of the Zionist movement and founder of the Hebrew Teachers' Federation in Palestine, remarked:

> Whether the children in the village school learn more or less of the rudiments of elementary grammar . . . more or less of history, more or less of science, does not matter. What they have to learn, though, is this: to be strong and healthy villagers, to be villagers who love their surroundings and physical work, and most of all to be villagers who love the Hebrew tongue and the Jewish nation with all their hearts and souls.[34]

The intellectual commitments of the Yishuv extended far beyond Hebrew and beyond the intellectual ferment of Tel Aviv. At the First Zionist Congress in 1897, Zvi Hermann Shapira had urged the creation of a university in Palestine, making education a central focus of the movement. By 1903, the Yishuv had founded the Teachers Association, a clear indication of the central role that education would play in the Yishuv and then in the Jewish state.

That Israel would, decades later, win numerous Nobel Prizes and become known as the "Start-Up Nation" was due in no small measure to the emphasis on education that had characterized Judaism for thousands of years and the Zionist revolution from its earliest days.

THE PASSIONATE IDEOLOGUES as well as the rank-and-file immigrants of the first two aliyot left an indelible stamp on the Yishuv. Though many left and for those who stayed life in Palestine was far from easy, those who remained built the first new Jewish settlements and established the kibbutz movement. They revived the Hebrew language, founded Tel Aviv, the first Hebrew-speaking city, and then both developed theater in their "new" language and produced numerous publications on a host of subjects.

These were the first steps of both Herzl's and Ahad Ha'am's

dreams coming to life. The road to independence would still be a long one, but the Jews had begun to build the infrastructure that would ultimately create the state Herzl so desperately sought. At the same time, reminiscent of Ahad Ha'am's belief that Palestine should become a cultural center for the Jews, for the first time in millennia, Jews were doing more than building infrastructure and laying the ground for political sovereignty. They could also see, hear, and feel what a Jewish society was about. It would have language, a literature, a distinct way of life.

For the first time since the Romans had exiled the Jews, Zionism was providing them a sense of what a renewed Jewish people might be.

THE BALFOUR DECLARATION

The Empire Endorses the State

His Majesty's Government view with favour the establishment in Palestine of a national home for the Jewish people.

—Balfour Declaration, 1917

Life in the Yishuv was improving, but in Europe, catastrophe loomed. The century would witness the worst bloodbath in human history. In the two world wars that would cast their pall upon the first half of the century, some eighty to one hundred million people—combatants and civilians—would die. Stalin would then murder some twenty million more.

Ze'ev Jabotinsky was one of those who had seen the devastation coming. Predicting a tragedy akin to the World War I before it began, he spoke of "a devastating war between two or more first-class powers, with all the grand insanity of modern techniques . . . with an incredible number of casualties and with such an expenditure of money—direct, indirect and incidental—that there would not be enough digits for accountability."[1]

Still others understood that whatever was to transpire, the horror about to unfold would not end quickly. British foreign secretary Sir Edward Grey remarked, "The lamps are going out all over Europe. We shall not see them lit again in our lifetime."[2]

FOR THE ZIONISTS, ONE critical question on the eve of World
War I was whether the Ottomans would lose control over the Middle East and whether, if they did, Britain would assume control of
the region. The movement quickly divided over how to handle the
uncertainty. Max Nordau insisted that the Zionists should curry
the Ottomans' favor to whatever extent possible. As if to prove him
wrong, though, Djemal Pasha, who had recently been appointed as
Ottoman commander of the Egyptian front, made his anti-Zionist
stance eminently clear just a few weeks after the Ottomans entered
the war. He disbanded a Turkish-loyalist Jewish defense organization, which had been founded by labor leaders Ben-Gurion and
Yitzhak Ben-Zvi; he closed down the Zionist newspaper *Ha'achdut;*
and he proclaimed every Zionist an enemy of Turkey and liable to
death.

Ben-Gurion had initially thought that the Zionists' hopes lay
with the Ottomans, but when the Turks began deporting Jews
from Tel Aviv, he realized he had been mistaken and switched his
allegiance to the British. Others, Jabotinsky chief among them, had
insisted from the outset that aligning the movement with the British was the best way to advance their cause. Convinced that continued Ottoman rule would make creating a Jewish state virtually
impossible,[3] Jabotinsky was both anxious to see the Ottoman Empire dismantled and certain that it would happen. He thought the
time had come to prevail upon British political leaders, who were
about to go to war against Germany and the Ottomans (among
others), and to impress upon them the justice of the Zionist cause.
"If we do not declare any orientation, if we play with both sides, we
shall lose everything. We must come out in favor of the Allies and
help them, with our Jewish soldiers, to conquer Eretz Israel."[4]

When Djemal ordered mass deportations of Jews from Palestine, some were sent to the Gabbari barracks in Egypt. Jabotinsky
was among those deported, and it was at Gabbari that he first met
Joseph Trumpeldor. Born in the Caucasus in 1880, Trumpeldor
had lost his left arm in 1904 while fighting for the Russians in the
Russo-Japanese War. Decorated five times for gallantry by the czar

himself, he eventually became the second Jew to become an officer in the Russian army. In 1912, he departed Russia to Palestine and worked the fields near the shores of the Sea of Galilee. In 1914, Djemal deported him along with thousands of others.

At the same time, Lieutenant Colonel John Henry Patterson, an Irish Protestant veteran of the Boer War in South Africa, arrived in Egypt just as the British were seeking an officer to command a Jewish military unit to help fight the Turks. Patterson, deeply knowledgeable of Jewish history and sympathetic to the Zionist cause, got the post. Ultimately, Jabotinsky and Trumpeldor worked with Patterson (who later described Trumpeldor as "the bravest man I ever knew") to form the Zion Mule Corps.

The Zion Mule Corps, the first organized group of Jews to fight under a Jewish flag since Bar Kokhba had led his revolt against the Romans some eighteen hundred years earlier, came to symbolize the renewal of an ancient Jewish pride. Several of its members later formed the core of what would become the Israel Defense Forces. Ironically as a result of Djemal's mass deportation, for the first time in two thousand years, the Jews had the beginnings of an army.

Trumpeldor died in 1920 while defending the settlement of Tel Hai, saying as he died, according to Zionist tradition, "It does not matter, it is good to die for our country." When Jabotinsky founded Betar three years later, he named it not only for the place in which the Simeon Bar Kokhba had made his last stand, but for Trumpeldor, as well.*

THOUGH THE ZIONISTS were not naive about the Ottomans' antipathy to the Zionist movement, many of them thought it unwise to take sides in the conflict between the Ottomans and the British. So the movement opened a liaison office in Copenhagen, which was in a neutral country. Others, though, were much more confi-

---

* Betar is also an acronym for **Brit Yosef Trumpeldor**, "The Covenant of Joseph Trumpeldor."

dent that the British would prove victorious and would acquire Palestine, and they thus worked feverishly to cultivate relationships with London.

No one was better suited to that task than Chaim Weizmann, who would later become Israel's first president. Born in 1874 in Motal, near Pinsk (in today's Belarus but then part of the Russian Empire), Weizmann was, like many other Zionist leaders of his era, the product of a traditional Russian Jewish family; he, too, was then drawn to the broader intellectual world Europe had to offer. Deeply intelligent, he was also an intellectual free spirit; one of his first teachers would later remark, "He was either going to be a genius or a convert."[5]

Weizmann studied chemistry, first in Germany and then at the University of Fribourg, Switzerland, where he earned a Ph.D. in organic chemistry in 1899. Weizmann had not attended the First Zionist Congress in Basel in 1897 (though he had intended to), but he was present at all subsequent gatherings and rapidly became a central figure in the movement. One of his chief early causes was advocating the creation of institutions of higher learning in Palestine. He was instrumental in the creation of Hebrew University in Jerusalem, and his efforts to create a university focused on science and technology ultimately resulted in the founding of the Technion—Israel's Institute of Technology—in 1912. He was also among the founders of the Weizmann Institute of Science, which became an internationally renowned research center, in 1934.

In 1904, Weizmann was appointed senior lecturer at Manchester University, where he was introduced two years later to Arthur Balfour, an up-and-coming Member of Parliament. Balfour, who had initially supported the idea of the Uganda Plan, was impressed with Weizmann. Gradually, Weizmann was able to draw Balfour closer to the Zionist cause.

In 1916, Weizmann became director of the British Admiralty laboratories and moved from Manchester to London to carry out his work. His research led to the development of acetone, a critical ingredient in the naval explosive cordite, which played a central role in the British war effort. Widely lauded for this discovery, Weizmann was able to capitalize on his newly minted status to gain access to influential British figures of which other Zionist leaders could only dream.

MEANWHILE, AS IT BECAME clear that the Ottoman Empire was crumbling, Britain and France began to consider how they would divide the Middle East between them, even though neither of those powers yet had any real claim to the land.

Toward the end of 1915, the two nations convened a series of meetings in which both could present their expectations. As its representative, Britain appointed Sir Mark Sykes, a Catholic who had studied the Middle East, traveled to Palestine during his honeymoon in 1903, and spent much of his career at the Foreign Ministry. The French appointed François Georges-Picot, also a career diplomat who was the first secretary of the French embassy in London at the time of the negotiations. Sykes had previously recommended that Palestine should come under Britain's control, though without stipulating what the boundaries of its territory should be. The agreement reached by Sykes and Picot, technically called the "Asia Minor Agreement" but commonly known as the Sykes-Picot Agreement, gave the French control over modern-day Syria and Lebanon. Britain, which needed unfettered access to the Suez Canal (see Map 8) because of the importance of India to the empire (Britain's need for the canal would later figure centrally in Israel's 1956 war, the Sinai Campaign), was to get control of the coastal strip from the Mediterranean Sea to the river Jordan, an area of land that comprises modern-day Jordan, southern Iraq, the ports of Haifa and Acre and the entire Negev. Western Palestine, south of the Sea of Galilee and north of Gaza, would be under international rule, according to the agreement.[6] The agreement also made provisions for the holy sites of Jerusalem and proposed placing them under international supervision and administration.

At no point did Sykes or Picot consider the interests of either the Zionists or Palestine's Arab population, and both Arabs and Jews were appalled by the agreement. The Arabs, who resented two foreign powers taking it upon themselves to divide the Middle East (before they had even won the war, no less), were livid. In earlier discussions between Sir Henry McMahon (the British high commissioner in Egypt) and Hussein bin Ali (the sharif of Mecca), McMahon had urged the Arabs to overthrow the Ottomans. They convinced Ali that it was in British interests not only to rid Palestine of the Turks but to work toward the establishment of an Arab state between Syria in the north and Yemen in the south. The Sykes-Picot Agreement seemed to them an outright violation of that British promise, as well. Relations between the British and the local Palestinian population were off to a most inauspicious start.

The Zionists were just as unhappy. Given French antipathy to Zionism, joint French-British control was likely to undermine their aims. Weizmann and other Zionists much preferred the idea of a British protectorate, believing that Britain "afforded her (white) colonial subjects more liberty than any other imperial power did," whereas France, they felt, "insisted upon making her colonial subjects into French citizens, erasing their national identities."[7] The Zionists, therefore, were determined to ensure that Palestine came under British control. They were going to be disappointed, however, when they eventually discovered that the British would be much less supportive of the Zionist cause than Weizmann and others had hoped.

AS ALL THIS WAS UNFOLDING, the Jews of Palestine witnessed the Ottoman massacre of its Armenian population. Beginning in 1915, forced labor of the able-bodied male population followed by the deportation of women and children on death marches into the Syrian desert led to the deaths of approximately one and a half million Armenians. The Yishuv was deeply worried; if the Ottomans could commit genocide against the Armenians, would they hesitate to do the same with Palestine's Jews?

A small group of Jews, working on their own initiative, decided to help rid Palestine of the Ottomans. Formed and then led by the Aaronsohn family, a small spy ring banded together. The primary operatives were Aaron Aaronsohn, an agronomist who had earned a degree of fame for his discovery of an ancient form of wheat in the Galilee; his sisters, Sarah and Rivka; and Avshalom Feinberg, Rivka's fiancé. The group called themselves Nili.*

When a plague of locusts struck the area, the Turks appointed Aaron Aaronsohn to head the effort to contain the outbreak. This immediately gave Aaronsohn virtually unfettered access to government offices and military installations throughout the area, where he gathered copious amounts of information that he then offered to the British. Initially dubious, the British ultimately decided that Aaronsohn could be useful. He stayed in Cairo, serving as a contact with the British, while his sister Sarah, brother Alexander, and Feinberg (along with some twenty to sixty others—estimates vary) carried out the day-to-day work of the spy ring.

Nili's principal activity was communicating information regarding Ottoman fortifications and troops, rail lines, and water sources to the British, all to assist them with their plans for a surprise attack. Nili transmitted the stolen information by means of a secret code and signal lights with a small British naval yacht that anchored off the coast of Atlit (just south of Haifa) every two weeks. When the ship stopped coming, they began to use homing pigeons instead.

The homing pigeons, however, led to the group's demise. In September 1917, the Turks intercepted one of the pigeons with a coded message attached to it, giving the Ottomans proof that a spy ring was at work. By the fall of 1917, most of Nili had been arrested. Several of them, subjected to relentless torture, gave up information about the others. Some were sentenced to death, and one was publicly hanged in Damascus.

When Sarah, then twenty-eight years old, was arrested in Zi-

---

* Nili is an acronym for the biblical phrase Netzach Yisrael Lo Yeshaker ("The Glory of Israel Does Not Deceive"), I Samuel 15:29.

chron Yaakov, she, too, was viciously tortured. Using a ruse, though, she received permission to return to her home, ostensibly to retrieve some fresh clothes to replace the blood-soaked clothing in which she had been tortured. Determined not to break, she shot herself in the mouth with a pistol she had hidden at home. She lingered several days before dying.

Nili's activities likely had no significant impact on the outcome of the war. Yet the story of Nili and of Sarah's self-sacrifice became Yishuv legend, in no small measure because it illustrated with utter clarity the sort of determination and courage that would be required to get foreign powers—first the Ottomans, and several decades later, the British—out of Palestine.

IN LONDON, CHAIM WEIZMANN was meanwhile working tirelessly to advance Zionism's cause. He held no official position in the movement, though, and many thought him a loose cannon. Yet disciplined or not, he had unparalleled access to the British corridors of power, access that he used to charm, cajole, and argue the cause of the Jews in Palestine.

The work was not easy. The largely Arabist Foreign Office believed that the Arabs had a stronger claim to Palestine, and as a practical matter, was loath to arouse the ire of Palestine's Arabs.[8] Opportunity struck, however, when David Lloyd George became prime minister in 1916. Lloyd George, who had served as the lawyer representing the Zionist movement's interests at the time that Herzl was negotiating the Uganda Plan, both acknowledged Zionism's ancient roots and had no doubt that the Jews would do more for the land than would its Arab inhabitants. "The Four Great Powers are committed to Zionism," he said. "And Zionism, be it right or wrong, good or bad, is rooted in age-long traditions, in present needs, and future hopes of far profounder import than the desires and prejudices of the 700,000 Arabs who now inhabit that ancient land. In my opinion that is right."[9]

Sensing a rare opportunity with Lloyd George's political rise, Weizmann charmed both Lloyd George and Balfour (who was then serving as the United Kingdom's foreign secretary). He also worked his relationship with Sykes, the influential British Foreign Office diplomat, referring to him as "one of our greatest finds."[10]

There was feverish action on both sides. While Weizmann pushed his agenda relentlessly, some Jewish MPs continued to rail against Zionist ambitions, fearing a rise in anti-Semitism in Britain and elsewhere, particularly if Arabs responded angrily. Sykes and others in the Foreign Office worked to convince other government officials that the Jews had a legitimate claim to Palestine.

Weizmann won. What was by far his life's greatest accomplishment—Lloyd George later wrote in his memoirs that the Balfour Declaration was given to Weizmann as "a reward for the important work he had done in producing acetone"[11]—came in the form of a letter that Balfour wrote to Lord Walter Rothschild* on November 2, 1917. It read:

> Dear Lord Rothschild,
>
> I have much pleasure in conveying to you, on behalf of His Majesty's Government, the following declaration of sympathy with Jewish Zionist aspirations which has been submitted to, and approved by, the Cabinet.
>
> "His Majesty's Government view with favour the establishment in Palestine of a national home for the Jewish people, and will use their best endeavours to facilitate the achievement of this object, it being clearly understood that nothing shall be done which may prejudice the civil and religious rights of existing non-Jewish communities in Palestine, or the rights and political status enjoyed by Jews in any other country."

---

* Walter Rothschild was a member of the British branch of the vast Rothschild family; he was not the same Rothschild who had supported the early aliyot to the Yishuv.

I should be grateful if you would bring this declaration to the
knowledge of the Zionist Federation.

Yours sincerely,

Arthur James Balfour[12]

Only twenty years had passed since Herzl had gathered his fledgling movement in Basel in 1897, and now, the most powerful empire on the planet had recognized the Zionist movement, had sided with it, and had promised to do what it could to advance its cause. Had he not died thirteen years earlier, Herzl would have been astounded.

CONSIDERING ITS HISTORIC IMPORTANCE, the Balfour Declaration of 1917 is an astonishingly ambiguous document. While it speaks of a "national home for the Jewish people," there is no mention of a Jewish state. There was no timetable as to when (or how) this "national home" would be created. There was no indication of how a "national home" for Jews could be created in Palestine without somehow impinging on "the civil and religious rights of existing non-Jewish communities in Palestine." Nor was there any indication of what the declaration meant by "Palestine," for it provided no maps or definitions of the territory. Finally, the document did not acknowledge the fact that at the time of the declaration, Palestine was still under control of the Ottomans. Though the British were confident that they soon would, they did not then even have Palestine to offer.

There were, however, at least implicit answers to some of these questions. Among British political leaders, there did seem to be a sense that the intent was to create a state in areas where Jews constituted a majority of the population.[13] The intended territory was apparently vast. Some twenty years later, the Palestine Royal Commission of 1937 stated that "the field in which the Jewish national home was to be established was understood at the time of the Balfour Declaration to be the whole of historic Palestine," meaning both sides of the Jordan River in what is today Israel and Jordan. (See Map 3.)

As for the fact that Britain did not yet control Palestine, they were certain that the Ottoman Empire was crumbling and that given the understandings outlined in Sykes-Picot, Palestine would soon be theirs. Indeed, within six weeks of the Balfour Declaration's publication, the Egyptian Expeditionary Force under the command of General Edmund Allenby drove the defending Ottomans out of Jerusalem. In a ceremony filled with British pomp, hundreds of onlookers and soldiers from armies that had fought for Jerusalem alongside the British lined the streets as Allenby entered Jerusalem's Old City through the Jaffa Gate on foot out of deference to the sanctity of the city.[14]

The British now had Palestine—and they had promised it to the Jews. They would retain control of the Jew's ancestral homeland for thirty-one years, until May 1948—when the State of Israel would be established.

ALL THE WHILE, the Yishuv continued to develop. The Eleventh Zionist Congress, held in Vienna in 1913, determined that a university should be established in Jerusalem and that its construction should begin within five years.[15] On July 24, 1918, less than a year after Balfour, thousands of people gathered for the ceremonial cornerstone laying for Hebrew University on Mount Scopus. The centrality of intellectual life to the Yishuv and to the state it would ultimately create was clear from the outset.

With the end of World War I in 1918, it was once again possible for people to move across the globe. That freedom of movement, combined with a new round of anti-Semitism in Europe and armed clashes in Russia in which some 100,000 to 200,000 Jews were killed, led to the next wave of immigration to Palestine. The Third Aliyah (1919–1923) brought 35,000 people to Palestine. Spurred by the changed international landscape that the war had wrought, the members of the Third Aliyah helped build the developing prestate institutions that would eventually make Jewish sovereignty possible. This first wave of Jewish immigration after the Balfour Declaration brought to Palestine the first immigrants to come with the sense that their cause was now internationally recognized.

The influx helped bring about technological advances in numerous areas; prime among them was water, a scarce commodity in that part of the world. In fact, when the British limited Jewish immigration during that period, they justified the move by claiming that the region's natural resources could not support the thousands of Jews who hoped to immigrate to Palestine.[16] That made water research an urgent matter. Leaders of the Yishuv understood that they not only needed to provide water to those who had already arrived, but needed to prove to the British and the world that the region could support significantly more immigration than the British claimed it could.

Given the nature of the land, that was going to be no small challenge. Most of the Zionist movement's land purchases in the period of 1880–1914 were centered in the coastal plain between Jaffa and Haifa in the west and the Jezreel and Jordan valleys in the east, and the lands they acquired were largely swamp-ridden, undeveloped, and void of inhabitants. Petach Tikvah, originally established by Jews from Jerusalem in 1878, failed in large measure because of malaria. When Russian immigrant-pioneers reestablished it several years later, they, too, had to leave due to outbursts of malaria. More than half of the inhabitants of Hadera died in the first two decades of its existence, also of malaria.[17] But undeterred, they pressed on. Pioneers returned to Petach Tikvah only two years later, drained the swamp, worked the soil, and transformed the area into a hub for citrus, known especially for its orange groves. David Ben-Gurion, too, contracted malaria while working in the orange groves in Petach Tikvah.

Kibbutzim shared in the effort of draining swamps and ridding the land of the disease. Baron de Rothschild was also instrumental in the process and brought in Egyptian workers whose assistance in draining the swamps and ridding the land of malaria was critical. Slowly and determinedly, the members of the kibbutzim made progress.

At the same time, the Zionist movement's leadership displayed vision to match the courage of those on the ground. They bought seemingly uninhabitable swampland, often at a steep price. When questioned about the wisdom of such a move, Menachem Ussishkin, who had been secretary of the First Zionist Congress and later headed the Jewish National Fund, insisted that virtually no price could be too high. "The cost of land in Palestine would increase from year to year; while what was not redeemed today could quite possibly never again be redeemed by us."[18]

Their progress was extraordinary. By 1938, when the U.S. Department of Agriculture sent Walter Clay Lowdermilk, a soil scientist, to do a survey of the soil of Europe, North Africa, and Palestine, the Yishuv had advanced water technology far beyond what it had been when the Jews arrived. Lowdermilk wrote that he was "astonished" by what the Jews had accomplished and described the agriculture land reclamation in which the Yishuv was engaged as "the most remarkable" such work he had seen during his extensive travels throughout the world.[19]*

The Yishuv also developed its political institutions during that same period. On April 19, 1920, it held elections for the *Asefat Ha-nivharim* ("Assembly of Representatives"), the parliamentary assembly of the Jewish community in British-controlled Palestine. There were 314 seats in the Assembly (the one and only time there were so many representatives). Continuing the voting tradition of the World Zionist Organization from Herzl's day, parties were allocated seats proportionally, based on the percentage of the vote that they received. A party that received 30 percent of the vote would be awarded 30 percent of the seats, and so forth.

No party won an outright majority in the 1920 elections. In fact,

---

* Lowdermilk later compiled his findings in a book, *Palestine, Land of Promise,* which became a bestseller. The book was found open on Franklin Delano Roosevelt's desk when the president died. It was likely the last book FDR ever read. (Seth M. Siegel, *Let There Be Water: Israel's Solution for a Water-Starved World* [New York: Thomas Dunne Books, 2015], p. 30.)

no party would ever win an outright majority in any subsequent vote, either in the Yishuv's Assembly of Representatives or in the Israeli parliament, which would replace it after independence. In the vote of 1920, the Labor movement, with only 70 seats, was the largest single faction. The newly elected Assembly became the parliament of the Yishuv's government-in-waiting.

HOW IS IT THAT the Yishuv developed a democratic tradition? Most of the immigrants to the Yishuv, after all, had come from nondemocratic countries. Russian and Polish Jews had not lived in democracies. The Jews who had lived under the Ottomans had not lived in a democracy. Nor was the Jewish tradition a distinctly democratic one. The biblical kings were not elected. The rabbis of the Talmud, while not the products of dynasties, were hardly elected through a democratic process. From where did this democratic impulse— both in the Yishuv and later in Israel—emerge?

The Jewish community's democratic impulse had developed after exile. Forced to wander from their ancestral homeland to places throughout Europe, they continually had to build communal structures from scratch. Beginning in 1580 and continuing until 1764, the Council of Four Lands (based in Lublin, Poland) served as the central locus of Jewish authority for Greater Poland, Little Poland, Ruthenia, and Volhynia. This elected council dealt with matters such as taxation, relations with the outside Gentile community, and more. The Council of Four Lands, as well as smaller and more local councils throughout European Jewish communities, were all democratically elected. That pattern was replicated by the Zionist congresses. By the early twentieth century, European Jews had been voting, legislating, and taxing themselves for some 350 years.[20]

That tradition withstood the distinctly nondemocratic environment of Palestine in the nineteenth and early twentieth centuries, and once the Jewish state was founded in 1948, it would succeed in transforming the massive waves of Jewish immigration from countries that had no democratic tradition, as well. Indeed, of the approximately one hundred countries that were created after World War II (mostly as a result of the collapse of empires), Israel would be one of the very few that began as a democracy and has continued to function as a democracy without interruption.

ON THE VERY SAME DAY in April 1920 that the first Assembly of Representatives was elected in Palestine, the fate of the Yishuv was also being discussed in Italy, in the town of San Remo. At a meeting known as the San Remo Conference, Britain, France, Italy, and Japan convened to discuss the division of the land that had been held by the Ottoman Empire. They did not draw up precise maps, but agreed on general principles. For the Yishuv, the most significant element of the San Remo Conference was that on April 25, the participants recognized the 1917 Balfour Declaration, incorporating it into its Resolutions and officially granting Britain the Mandate for Palestine.

That the Jews would have a national home in Palestine was now not only British policy—it was the express position of the victors of World War I.

Palestinian Arabs were infuriated, and, in a pattern that they would often repeat, they responded with violence. In 1920, rioting Arabs in Jerusalem killed six Jews and wounded others. In 1921, there were riots in Jaffa that soon spread; they left in their wake four dozen dead Jews, including Yosef Chaim Brenner.

Ironically, the riots also led to the early beginnings of Israel's eventual army. There had been Jewish defense organizations for some decades already. In 1907, Bar-Giora, a small clandestine guard group, one of the first of these organizations, was founded. Bar-Giora, and others like it, were small bands of Jews who offered their services as guards for a fee; Bar-Giora guarded Sejera (today called Ilaniya), the settlement where Ben-Gurion had worked the fields shortly after arriving in Palestine. Two years later, in 1909, Bar-Giora disbanded in order to develop a larger defense group,

Hashomer ("The Watchman"). Hashomer began to broaden its scope to provide security to Jews and their villages. It was the first attempt to provide organized defense for Jewish communities in Palestine.

Hashomer planned to replace Arab guards on Jewish farms and even had grandiose notions, which came to naught, of placing watchmen on farms in Ukrainian Cossack villages.[21] Now, in the wake of spreading Arab violence, and recognizing that the British were not going to offer sufficient protection to the Jews, the Yishuv's leaders decided in 1921 to create the Haganah ("The Defense") to protect Jewish farms and villages. It broadened its mandate to include preventing and rebuffing attacks. For the first several years of its existence, though, the Haganah was only loosely organized and not entirely effective.

Yet even as the Yishuv was learning to defend itself, it suffered a serious diplomatic blow. In 1921, just four years after the Balfour Declaration and one year after Balfour was included in the San Remo Resolutions, Winston Churchill, who had been appointed Secretary of State for the Colonies and who had until then been seen as a friend of the Zionists, decided to redraw the map of the Middle East without consulting his Zionist allies.[22] He carved away the portion of Palestine that was east of the Jordan River and created the country of Transjordan (later called Jordan).[23]

With the successes of Balfour and San Remo still fresh, those Zionists who believed that the map of the Mandate would be the map of their future state suddenly saw three-quarters of their future national home given away. The Jewish state was going to be significantly smaller than what they had imagined. Though they could of course not know it then, it would shrink even further in the decades to come.

AS CHURCHILL WAS DIVIDING UP the Mandate, Palestinian Arab anger over Jewish immigration and international support for a Jewish state erupted in renewed attacks on the Yishuv. The Zionist leadership now realized that they had not sufficiently factored Arab resistance into their planning. Ahad Ha'am noted this failing directly: "We are used to thinking of the Arabs as primitive men of the desert, as a donkey-like nation that neither sees nor understands what is going on around it. But that is a great error."[24]

Ahad Ha'am, who did not seek a state, might have had some reason to hold out some hope that Jews and Arabs might live peacefully together. To those deeply committed to Jewish statehood, however, the worsening relations with the Arabs were even more ominous. No one was more direct about this mounting tension than Ze'ev Jabotinsky, who in 1923 wrote two pamphlets, "The Iron Wall" and "Beyond the Iron Wall." It was a mistake to underestimate the Arabs, Jabotinsky insisted. They were as attached to Palestine as any other people was to the land on which it lived:

> Our Peace-mongers are trying to persuade us that the Arabs are either fools, whom we can deceive by masking our real aims, or that they are corrupt and can be bribed to abandon to us their claim to priority in Palestine, in return for cultural and economic advantages. I repudiate this conception of the Palestinian Arabs. Culturally they are five hundred years behind us, they have neither our endurance nor our determination; but they are just as good psychologists as we are, and their minds have been sharpened like ours by centuries of fine-spun logomachy. We may tell them whatever we like about the innocence of our aims, watering them down and sweetening them with honeyed words to make them palatable, but they know what we want, as well as we know what they do not want. They feel at least the same instinctive jealous love of Palestine, as the old Aztecs felt for ancient Mexico, and the Sioux for their rolling Prairies.[25]

That meant, he said, that the Arabs would never voluntarily come to agreement with the Zionists. If the Zionists wanted a foothold in Palestine, Arab violence would have to be met with an Iron Wall:

[t]his does not mean that there cannot be any agreement with
the Palestine Arabs. What is impossible is a voluntary agreement. As long as the Arabs feel that there is the least hope of
getting rid of us, they will refuse to give up this hope in return
for either kind words or for bread and butter, because they are
not a rabble, but a living people. And when a living people yields
in matters of such a vital character it is only when there is no
longer any hope of getting rid of us, because they can make no
breach in the iron wall. Not till then will they drop their extremist leaders, whose watchword is "Never!"[26]

In what would become the guiding spirit of Israel's political
Right in decades to come, Jabotinsky said, "[T]he only way to obtain such an agreement, is the iron wall, which is to say a strong
power in Palestine that is not amenable to any Arab pressure. In
other words, the only way to reach an agreement in the future is to
abandon all idea of seeking an agreement at present."[27]

Jabotinsky sadly proved prescient. A new wave of violence,
which would leave an ancient Jewish community utterly destroyed,
soon erupted.

Tensions surrounding the Temple Mount in Jerusalem had been
simmering for months. In September 1928, Jews erected a temporary divider in front of the Western Wall so that men and women
could pray there separately on Yom Kippur, in keeping with Jewish
tradition. In response, the grand mufti, Haj Amin al-Husseini, demanded restrictions on Jewish activity at the Western Wall, beginning a pattern of incitement that only further inflamed matters.[28]

Rumors that the Jews had designs on the al-Haram al-Sharif
("Noble Sanctuary," known to Jews as the Temple Mount) then
began to spread as did the circulation of falsified images of damage
at the site of the Dome of the Rock*; Muslim leaders claimed the

---

* Rumors of Jews taking over the Temple Mount or destroying the mosques
  on the site have been a consistent theme in the Arab-Jewish conflict and
  have proven incendiary since the first days of the violence between the

"damage" was done by Jews.[29] On Friday, August 23, 1929, Arab youths hurled rocks at yeshiva students in Hebron. Later that day, when a young man named Shmuel Rosenholtz went to the yeshiva alone, Arabs forced their way into the building and killed him. He would be the first of dozens to die in the unfolding riot.

The following morning, on the Jewish Sabbath, Arab mobs, wielding clubs, knives, and axes, began to surround the Jewish community of Hebron. Arab women and children threw stones at the Jews, while men ransacked Jewish homes and destroyed Jewish property. The rioters turned to one of the community's rabbis, in whose house many frightened Jews were hiding, and offered him a deal. They would spare the local Middle Eastern Jewish community if the rabbi turned over the Ashkenazi Jews. When he refused, the rioters killed him. The rioting that ensued soon spread beyond Hebron. By the end of the rampage, 133 Jews lay dead, 67 of them in Hebron alone.[30] Hundreds of Jews who survived the massacre were saved by their Arab neighbors, some of whom hid Jews in their own homes at great personal peril.[31] Nonetheless, the Hebron Jewish community, which had been established four centuries earlier by Jewish refugees from Spain and was one of the oldest Jewish communities in the world,[32] had been utterly destroyed.

Kishinev had come to Palestine.

In reaction to the Arab riots of 1929 and the wholesale massacre of the Hebron Jewish community, the Yishuv began to develop its paramilitary capabilities. The Haganah acquired foreign arms and

---

two communities. In 1929, these rumors led to the destruction of the centuries-old Jewish community of Hebron, which essentially ignited the Arab-Jewish conflict. In 2000, an announced and legal visit to the Temple Mount by then MK Ariel Sharon (he did not enter any of the mosques) enraged Muslims, which Yasser Arafat used as a pretext for unleashing the Second Intifada, which lasted from 2000 to 2004 and claimed thousands of victims. In 2015, (false) rumors that Israel planned to change the status quo of who could visit the Temple Mount and who could pray there led to incitement and then to yet another outbreak of Arabs stabbing and shooting Jews, and attacking them with vehicles.

manufactured its own. Eventually, it established twenty branches with twenty-five thousand men and women volunteers. Within a relatively short period, it transformed itself from an untrained military into a well-organized underground force. A Jewish army was beginning to develop.

AT THAT TIME, the Haganah subscribed to a policy called *havlagah*, or "restraint." Its fighters were instructed to do nothing but defend Jewish communities. They could prevent attacks to the best of their abilities, but they were not to initiate any actions before they learned that an attack was being planned.[33]

As Arab violence against Jews in Palestine increased, though, the *havlagah* policy became controversial. Zionists needed to meet violence with violence, Jabotinsky had written in "The Iron Wall," and the situation in the Yishuv seemed to prove him right. In 1931, a group of fighters deeply influenced by Jabotinsky broke away from the Haganah, creating their own fighting faction. They would no longer wait to be attacked, but rather, they would take the battle to the enemy. The group was first called Haganah Bet (Haganah "B"). It later changed its name to the Irgun Tzva'i Leumi (the "National Military Organization"), and was known as the Irgun.* Intially, most of its fighters were members of Jabotinsky's Revisionist movement or Betar; Jabotinsky, in fact, was the group's supreme commander, a figurehead position since the British had exiled him from Palestine. He retained that title until his death in 1940.

The Irgun had a very different orientation to the use of force than that of the Haganah. Unlike *"Hatikvah,"* the anthem of mainstream Zionism (of which the Haganah was part) that does not mention war or battle, Betar's anthem (a reflection of Jabotinsky's worldview and the position of his disciples who would follow him

---

* The Irgun was also known at the Etzel, which is an acronym for the Hebrew words Irgun Tzva'i Leumi.

in Yishuv and Israeli politics) was distinctly committed to saving the Jewish people through battle if necessary:

> *In the face of every obstacle*
> *In times of ascent, and of setbacks*
> *A fire may still be lit*
> *With the flame of revolt*
> *For silence is dirt*
> *Sacrifice blood and spirit*
> *For the hidden glory*
> *To die or to conquer the mountain*
> *Yodfat, Masada, Betar*

AS JEWS IN THE YISHUV were slowly learning to defend themselves, Jews in Europe were becoming ever more vulnerable. As horrific as World War I had been, an even more devastating war for the Jews was about to erupt. The violence that had erupted in Kishinev and Hebron would soon pale relative to what was about to transpire in Europe. The darkest, most horrific period that the Jewish people had ever experienced was about to unfold.

NOWHERE TO GO, EVEN IF THEY COULD LEAVE

We will fight with the British against Hitler as if there were no White Paper; we will fight the White Paper as if there were no war.

—David Ben-Gurion in 1939

In 1925, Adolf Hitler published *Mein Kampf.* The Jews intended to take over the world, he wrote, and when they did, they would destroy humanity. "If . . . the Jew is victorious over the other peoples of the world, his crown will be the funeral wreath of humanity and this planet will, as it did thousands of years ago, move through the ether devoid of men."

Zionism, Hitler declared, was part of the Jewish plot:

When the Zionists try to make the rest of the world believe that the new national consciousness of the Jews will be satisfied by the establishment of a Jewish State in Palestine, the Jews thereby adopt another means to dupe the simple-minded Gentile. They have not the slightest intention of building up a Jewish State in Palestine so as to live in it. What they really are aiming at is to establish a central organization for their international swindling and cheating.[1]

In January 1933, Hitler was appointed chancellor of Germany. In March, elections were held and the Nazis remained the largest party in the Reichtag. Given that Hitler had published *Mein Kampf* almost a decade earlier, Germans had every reason to understand exactly what they had elected. "The Jewish people will be the first victim of the strengthening of national hatreds, of suppression, of the denial of freedom, and of dictatorship," predicted David Ben-Gurion.[2]

David Gruen, who later changed his name to David Ben-Gurion, had been born in 1886 in the small town Plonsk (now in Poland but then part of the Russian Empire). Like many early Zionist leaders, he had been raised in a religious family committed to both secular studies and to Zionism. As a young child, he witnessed his father's hosting *Hovevei Zion* meetings in their home. Influenced by those meetings and later by Abraham Mapu's biblical and Zion-yearning novel, *The Love of Zion*, the young Gruen—who would come to see in the Bible a program for the moral basis of a Jewish state— became a committed Zionist.

When he was seventeen, Gruen learned of the Uganda Plan discussions at the Sixth Zionist Congress and was livid that the movement would even consider giving up on the notion of a Jewish state in the Jewish people's ancestral homeland. Concluding that creating a Jewish state in Palestine required action, not words, Gruen decided to move to Palestine.

Gruen eventually arrived at the Jaffa harbor—the same harbor that Herzl had described in *Altneuland*—on September 7, 1906, and shortly thereafter was working the orange groves in Petach Tikvah. A believer that physical labor was key to building the Jewish state (following in the tradition of A. D. Gordon), he migrated through the Galilee, working on a number of different farms. In 1910, he moved to Jerusalem in order to serve on the editorial board of Poalei Zion's official journal, *Achdut (Unity)*. When he published his first article there, he did so under his newly adopted and Hebraicized last name, Ben-Gurion.

With the Ottomans in control of Palestine, Ben-Gurion decided that if he was to have any role in leading the Yishuv, he needed a Turkish education. In 1911, he departed Palestine for Turkey to study law (though he did not complete the degree) and then continued on to America to spread the word of the pioneering movement and to attend Poalei Zion conferences. While living in New York, he met Paula Munweis and married her in 1917. They would have a son and two daughters.

After the Balfour Declaration, Ben-Gurion switched his allegiance from the Turks to the British. He joined the British Army's Jewish Legion and fought with the British against the Turks in the Palestine Campaign. Though he continued working with Poalei Zion, he also launched his own political party, *Achdut Ha'avoda* ("Unity of Labor"), composed mostly of the more left-leaning members of Poalei Zion after that party split. In 1921, Ben-Gurion became secretary of the Histadrut, the Yishuv's labor union. He led the Histadrut for thirteen years, firmly establishing his place as a member of the Yishuv's senior leadership. By the time Ben-Gurion predicted Europe's disaster in 1933, he was widely recognized as the authoritative voice of the Yishuv.

THE SENSE OF IMPENDING HORROR in Europe evoked conflicting emotions in the Yishuv. To some degree, what was unfolding confirmed the fears of those who had come to Palestine; it proved their foreboding sense of history accurate. While that undoubtedly provided a measure of validation to those in the Yishuv who had left Europe earlier, many Jews living in Palestine were committed to doing whatever possible to assist European Jewry.

Some of them hoped that applying economic pressure and boycotting Germany might lead Hitler's regime to relent and to pull back from its increasingly anti-Semitic, but not yet murderous, policies. Jabotinsky hoped that if a united Jewish front could inflict significant economic damage on Germany, that might both keep civil rights in Germany intact as well as promote Jewish emancipation.[3]

Much of the Yishuv was opposed to a boycott of Germany, however, and insisted that the most effective way to deal with Nazi Germany was through direct negotiations. There were several reasons for this position. The Yishuv feared that a boycott would infuriate Germany and only make matters worse for Jews there; it also hoped that negotiations with the Germans might encourage the immigration of Germany's Jews to the Yishuv.

The controversy surrounding the boycott led to one of the more bizarre incidents in the history of the Yishuv, one still shrouded in mystery. Chaim Arlosoroff, then the head of the Jewish Agency's political department and effectively its foreign minister, had moved with his family from Ukraine to Tel Aviv in 1924 to escape pogroms. On the way to Palestine, he spent time in Germany, where he earned a Ph.D. in economics.

While in Germany, he had an affair with a woman named Magda Ritschel, who would eventually marry Joseph Goebbels, the Nazis' notorious minister of propaganda. In June 1933, after having risen to the top of the Yishuv's leadership, Arlosoroff returned to Germany to negotiate with German officials, apparently using contacts through his former mistress to gain access to the people he needed to see.[4] His mission in Germany was to advance a plan called the *Ha'avarah* ("Transfer Agreement") that would allow German Jews to leave Germany without having to forfeit all their assets. Jews emigrating from Germany would deposit their money in a fund that was made available to Palestinian banks. Those banks would then purchase German goods that were shipped to Palestine. In Palestine, merchants would purchase the goods, and the money from the purchase would then be returned to the Jews who had emigrated from Germany.[5] Everyone seemed to benefit. Germany got rid of Jews it did not want, the Yishuv benefited from an influx of immigrants, the Jews who departed Germany could keep some of their assets, and Palestine was able to import German goods that it desperately needed. Some twenty thousand German Jews availed themselves of this plan, and $30 million moved from Germany to the Yishuv.

Yet as Germany tightened the noose around its Jews, the Transfer Agreement became increasingly controversial. Arlosoroff, many said, had made a pact with the devil. Ben-Gurion defended the plan as a means of sustaining the Yishuv while increasing immigration, but others believed that Germany had to be boycotted, and that the Transfer Agreement would undermine the boycott's impact. Jabotinsky railed against the Transfer Agreement; he thought it a foolhardy attempt to undermine Germany's economic isolation. The Revisionist newspaper *Hazit Ha'am* (*The People's Front*), ran a column on June 16, 1933, condemning Arlosoroff's agreement, warning that the Jewish people "will know how to respond to this odious act." The article personally identified Arlosoroff.[6]

Later that same night, Chaim Arlosoroff and his wife, Sima, went for a stroll on the Tel Aviv beach. Out of the dark, two men approached, one shining a flashlight in Arlosoroff's face while the other pulled a gun and fired. Arlosoroff was rushed to the hospital, but died a few hours later on the operating table.

Jabotinsky's Revisionist Party was immediately blamed for the murder. Two days later, Avraham Stavsky, a member of the Revisionist movement's organization Betar, was arrested, after Sima identified him as the man with the flashlight. Two other Revisionists were arrested, one as an accomplice and the other as the gunman. The Left blamed Jabotinsky both for having "primed" the gun as well as for masterminding the plan. Jabotinsky, in turn, invested tremendous effort and resources in defense of the three. Stavsky, who had initially been convicted and sentenced to death, was freed in July 1934 after his conviction was overturned by the British Court of Appeals in Palestine.

No one else was ever convicted of the crime, and Arlosoroff's assassination remains a mystery. His murder, though, would not be the last time Jews killed Jews over political disagreements in the Jewish state.

AS SOME MEMBERS OF the Yishuv had anticipated, the worsening conditions in Europe were actually a boon for immigration. Arab violence had subsided, and the Yishuv's infrastructure was developing. Slowly, life in Palestine was becoming less harsh. Because the United States had tightened its immigration restrictions (so, too, had the USSR, though Jews were hardly clamoring to go there), by the 1930s Palestine was becoming a central destination for Jewish immigration. The Jewish Agency, short of money and under pressure from the Mandatory government, limited the number of immigrants it allowed into Palestine. "Certificates" were required for immigration; competition for them sometimes became ugly, and there were accusations that the agency was admitting wealthier classes and those more likely to support Ben-Gurion's political views. Immigration was a fraught subject that could explode at a moment's notice; it would remain so throughout Israel's history.

While the Fourth Aliyah (1924–1929) had been composed primarily of middle-class, city-dwelling Polish immigrants, those arriving now in the Fifth Aliyah (1932–1936) were perceived to be well-educated, wealthy Germans desperate to escape an increasingly frightening anti-Semitic environment in Europe. In fact, though, most of the immigrants of the Fifth Aliyah were from central and eastern Europe, like the members of the aliyot before them. The number of immigrants was growing, as well. In 1934, as it became clearer that Hitler's vicious anti-Jewish policies would only intensify, the Yishuv witnessed the highest number of immigrants ever in a single year until that point; some forty-two thousand Jews made their way to the Land of Israel. The Yishuv was slowly moving toward the critical mass of Jews it would need for statehood.

WHEN CHAIM NACHMAN BIALIK had written "The City of Slaughter" after the Kishinev pogrom, neither he nor his readers could have imagined the darkness into which Europe would descend. Bialik had eventually left Russia for Germany in 1921 and then in 1924 moved to Palestine. Once in Palestine, Bialik devoted himself largely to public affairs and wrote much less than he had previously, but he remained the voice of an entire generation. In the summer of 1934, Bialik traveled to Vienna to undergo prostate surgery. He died on July 4, 1934, after the surgery failed.

The funeral of the Yishuv's poet laureate shut down the city of Tel Aviv. Giant posters announced the time of the funeral, and even in the scorching heat of a blazing Middle Eastern summer day, in a scene reminiscent of Eliezer Ben-Yehuda's mass funeral in 1922, many thousands of people took to the streets as part of the procession. Religious and secular, Ashkenazim and Mizrachim—they came not only from Tel Aviv but from all over Palestine. Blue-and-white flags, with black ribbons attached to them, adorned almost every building. Bialik's coffin was taken to the local cemetery, where he was buried with Ahad Ha'am to his right and Chaim Arlosoroff to his left. The political activist (Arlosoroff), the poet (Bialik), and the philosopher (Ahad Ha'am) lay side by side—a fitting image of Zionism's deep intellectual roots and many different voices, and also, of the ability of those many streams to come together at critical moments.

IN 1935, THE NAZIS passed the Nuremberg Laws, which stripped German Jews of their citizenship and outlawed both marriages as well as extramarital sexual relationships between Jews and Gentiles. Immigration to Palestine reached another all-time high of 61,000 Jews. In all, between 1933 and 1936, the Jewish population of Palestine grew in size from 234,967 to 384,078; Jews, who had been but a fifth of the population, now constituted almost a third.

A veritable explosion of cultural and intellectual development was changing the Yishuv, and very quickly, it reflected a blend of tradition and modernity, religious and secular Jews, Ashkenazim and Sephardim, socialists and the free-market city dwellers.

A Jewish folk culture began to emerge. In the late 1920s, for example, Tel Aviv hosted the Queen Esther Beauty Pageant, centered on the holiday of Purim.[7] Designed to build bridges, it purposely included contestants from both Ashkenazi and Mizrachi backgrounds. Much more than a mere beauty pageant, the competition was intended to help officials select an unofficial representative of the Yishuv. The pageant was shut down in 1929 due to pressure from the Yishuv's religious elements, but the European influences now shaping and changing the Yishuv were clear. Palestine had undergone a radical change; it was already entirely unlike the undeveloped land to which the First and Second Aliyot had immigrated.

In 1932, the Yishuv inaugurated the Maccabiah games, a nineday sporting event with competitions for Jewish men and women from all over the world in categories such as gymnastics, basketball, track and field, swimming, and tennis. There were ideological motives for the games, as well. Nordau's "muscular Jews" were on display, while Ahad Ha'am's vision of Palestine as a center for Jewish culture also got a boost. The Yishuv also hoped that bringing many Jews to Palestine for the competition would increase immigration.

Dance, both theatrical and folk, became a pillar of Yishuv life. Theatrical dancers competed in the National Dance Competition while folk dancers showcased their talent at the then iconic Dalia Festival, first staged a few years later, in 1944.[8] What began as a mere competition in the Yishuv ended up shaping much of Zionist culture for decades thereafter, as "Israeli folk dance" would remain a central feature of Zionist activity. "Already by the 1940s Israeli folk dances were exported and viewed as significant markers of the new Jew." Folk dance became "an important symbol of Israeli identity and one of the most significant and successful exports of Israeli culture around the world."[9]

Intellectual and economic life in the Yishuv also underwent a transformation. The influx of German immigrants led to a dramatic rise in the number of students at Hebrew University. Banking and finance also developed. Because German Jews and some middle-class Polish Jews had come to Palestine with substantial financial assets, Palestine soon had department stores and upscale cafés. Money from the Transfer Agreement (over which Arlosoroff had apparently been murdered) began to flow into the Yishuv. Jews purchased increasing amounts of land from local Arabs, many of whom were more than willing to exchange their property for cash.

YET WHAT LOOKED TO the Yishuv like great progress felt to the Arabs a profound dislocation. Many of the locals sensed that their way of life was being displaced by the rapidly increasing tide of Jewish immigration. Once again, Arab frustration exploded in violence.

On April 15, 1936, Arabs shot three Jewish drivers near Tulkarm (in what is today the West Bank, east of Netanya). One died on the spot. Another died five days later, while the third survived. Two days later, in response, a radical Jewish faction shot and killed two Arabs living in a shack in Petach Tikvah. That same day, during the funeral for one of the Jewish victims, anti-Arab and anti-British protests raged. An Arab was beaten, as was a police officer who came to his defense. Jews assaulted Arab shoeshine boys and peddlers. The Arabs then struck back. On April 19, unemployed peasants and migrant workers stormed through Jaffa, killing nine Jews and injuring sixty. Jaffa quickly descended into utter chaos, with Jews and Arabs searching for and fleeing from one another. Thousands of Jews fled to Tel Aviv.

The Arab revolt of 1936–1939 had begun.

Once again, the Arab community had decided to resist Jewish immigration and the Yishuv's development with violence. During the revolt, violence would flare regularly. Arabs burned farmland and orchards that Jews had cleared and planted. They destroyed Jewish stores and attacked houses. The Arab community staged strikes in the hopes of harming the Yishuv's economy, but the strikes had precisely the opposite effect—the Arabs unwittingly boosted Jewish business. Jewish shops and factories filled the vacuum, and the Yishuv's Jewish economy expanded.

Whatever economic progress it might have made, the Yishuv was deeply worried by the phenomenon of continued Arab violence. Jews who had believed that they could live in peace with

Arabs were now increasingly dubious. To make it clear that the Jewish population would not give up on its dream of statehood, even in the face of violence, the Yishuv established more villages.

With their attempts to demoralize the Jewish community failing, the Arab leadership used the revolt as an opportunity to press its demands with the British. They met in Jerusalem and demanded an absolute freeze on Jewish immigration. They also sought a prohibition on land sales and called for an Arab majority government. Even as they were making these demands, the violence continued.

At first, since the Arab revolt also targeted them, the British response to Arab violence was ruthless. They chased out the mufti and leveled portions of Jaffa. But then, they changed tactics. Desperate to avoid violence and hoping to keep the peace in an increasingly volatile region, they sought to appease the rioting Arabs. In mid-1936, they proposed limiting Jewish immigration to 4,500 in the following half of the year. In 1935, just a year earlier, 61,000 Jews had immigrated to Palestine. In proposing an annual limit of 9,000 Jewish immigrants, the British were effectively suggesting an *85 percent reduction* in Jewish immigration. Astonishingly, however, the Arabs rejected even that offer, insisting that there be no immigration at all.

The violence continued. The British, hoping that the violence would subside on its own and not wanting to risk Anglo-Arab relations, responded to the Arab violence with restraint. But their policy was an utter failure. After six months, two hundred Arabs, eighty Jews, and twenty-eight British were dead. Something clearly had to change.

As immediate measures, the British responded by sending more troops to Palestine and providing arms to some Jews in order to make it possible for them to protect themselves. They also established a nightly curfew and guard patrol. Yet they also understood that the situation required a long-term solution. To explore what that solution might be, the British established the Palestine Royal Commission (better known as the Peel Commission, since it was headed by Lord William Robert Wellesley Peel) to study the situation in Palestine and to make recommendations.

The Peel Commission arrived in November 1936 to survey the land and to hear extensive testimony from both Jewish and Arab representatives. On July 7, 1937, the commission released its 404-page extensive brief, which (unlike the Balfour Declaration) included maps of its plan. The Peel Commission's recommendation was that because Jews and the Arabs had fundamentally opposed interests, and since both claimed rights to the same land, they were unlikely to be able to share territory; the only possible solution was partition. (See Map 4.)

Peel was the first time that anyone had proposed a division of Palestine to accommodate the two peoples who claimed it. The coastal plain from Rosh Hanikrah to south of Be'er Tuvia, the Galilee, and the Jezreel and Jordan valleys would be assigned to the Jews. Aside from Jerusalem and Bethlehem, which would remain under the Mandate's control, everything else would be assigned to the Arab population. It also assumed that the Arab state within Palestine would be attached to Transjordan. Significantly, the commission called for a population transfer to separate the Jewish and Arab communities; in years to come, the subject of population transfers would remain a highly contentious issue in the region.

The area that Peel proposed assigning to a Jewish state was substantially smaller than what the Zionist movement had had reason to expect. While Balfour had not defined what was meant by "Palestine," the Peel Commission itself acknowledged that "the field in which the Jewish national home was to be established was understood at the time of the Balfour Declaration to be the whole of historic Palestine."[10] That area included today's Gaza, Israel, the West Bank, and all of what is now Jordan. Peel was proposing a Jewish state on a small fraction of that land; 20 percent was allocated to the Jews, while some 70 to 75 percent was allocated to the Arabs.[11]

Many Zionist leaders, including Jabotinsky and his followers, were outraged by Britain's reneging on the map they believed had been implied in the Balfour Declaration, and they were despondent at the notion of giving up even more land after Churchill's creation of Transjordan in 1921.

Once again, it was through poetry that Jewish dismay found expression. Uri Zvi Greenberg, one of the leading poets of the era, had been born to a Hasidic family in Austria-Hungary, but moved to Palestine in 1923 at the age of twenty-seven after he narrowly escaped being killed in a Polish pogrom. After the Hebron riots of 1929, his political position hardened. He eventually became a follower of Jabotinsky's Revisionist Zionist movement, so Greenberg was therefore naturally among those vociferously opposed to the Peel plan to divide the land.

In his "One Truth and Not Two," written in 1936 as the Peel Commission proposal was being developed, he played off the classic, ubiquitous phrase in rabbinic literature, "Our rabbis taught," and wrote:

> *Your rabbis taught, the Messiah will come in generations to come*
> *and Judea shall rise without fire or blood . . .*
> *And I say: if your generation lags*
> *and does not force the end with blows and bare hands . . .*
> *The Messiah will not come even in the distant generations.*
> *Judea shall not rise.*[12]

"Blood for blood," Greenberg warns later in the poem, is the rule for Jews no less than for Gentiles. Jews will have to wage battle for Judea to rise. It was an ideological position that some Israeli leaders would espouse, even decades later.

While many agreed with Jabotinsky, only a minority of Jews actively opposed the plan. Weizmann and Ben-Gurion worked feverishly to ensure that the Jewish community rallied behind the Peel recommendation. As Ben-Gurion put it, implicitly reminding the Zionist community that this was an extraordinary accomplishment given that a mere forty years had passed since the First Zionist Congress, "Herzl would have accepted as a godsend a charter for any part of Palestine, and put his stake in a Jewish state, without any commitment that this and only this will always be the Jewish state."[13] As Weizmann noted, the Peel Commission recommendation intended a Jewish state significantly smaller than they had hoped it would be. Still, it meant that Herzl's vision—at long last—would be realized. The Jews, Weizmann said pithily, "would be fools not to accept it, even if it were the size of a tablecloth."[14]

In August 1937, the Twentieth Zionist Congress in Zurich approved Peel's recommendations. Though they were hardly enthusiastic about all its details, they were going to get a state, which was more than they could have imagined just a few years earlier.

While the Jewish community accepted the Peel recommendations, the Arabs rejected them outright. King Abdullah of Transjordan apparently favored the plan, since it would reunite Arabs in Palestine with his kingdom and allocate to it more arable land. The rank and file Arab population was inexorably opposed, however, and Abdullah understood that he could not ignore them. Haj Amin al-Husseini, the mufti of Jerusalem (eventually a supporter of the Nazis), was also vociferously opposed and ensured that the Arab Higher Committee would reject it.

In what was already their standard pattern, Arabs responded to Peel with yet another round of violence, directing their venom not only at Jews but at the British as well. Among the dead was Lewis Andrews, the British official responsible for organizing the travel arrangements for Peel commissioners in Palestine. A known Zionist, Andrews was shot on September 26 on his way to church.

By mid-October 1937, the raging violence had surpassed that of a year earlier. Settlements, buses, Jewish civilians, and British patrols were all targets. The new airport at Lydda was burned, and oil lines were damaged. Much of the country's public transportation had to be discontinued, and due to mines and explosives planted at the sides of roads, the British prohibited travel at night. They also brought in more troops and instituted the death penalty for those involved in the violence, a punishment to which they would frequently resort in the years to come. All those steps, though, were only minimally effective.

Palestine was sinking into war.

MEANWHILE, MATTERS IN EUROPE were growing ever more ominous. In February 1938, Ben-Gurion said, "Germany is swallowing up Austria and tomorrow it will be Czechoslovakia's turn."[15] He was eerily prophetic. Nine months later, in November 1938, Europe's major powers agreed to Germany's annexation of portions of Czechoslovakia (which the Germans called Sudetenland). While Neville Chamberlain, Britain's prime minister, argued that his acquiescence to Germany's aggression was preserving the peace, Ben-Gurion understood that it was nothing more than appeasement that would encourage Hitler. He wrote to Eliyahu Golomb, then responsible for Jewish self-defense in Palestine, and said, "In my opinion, today is one of the blackest days Europe has ever known and who is to tell if, after the 'peaceful' Czechoslovakia 'settlement,' it won't be our turn soon."[16]

As Ben-Gurion predicted, the West was far more interested in appeasing the Arab leadership than it was in protecting Jews. In December, the Yishuv presented to the British a proposal to save the Jewish children from Germany and bring them to Palestine. At the same time, the mufti asked the Mandate to release any members from the Arab Higher Committee imprisoned in the Seychelles so that they might serve as representatives on the Palestine Arab delegation in London. No lives were at stake in the request that the Arabs made; nonetheless, the British responded in the affirmative to the Arabs' request and denied the Yishuv's plea to save the ten thousand Jewish children.[17]

On November 9 and 10, 1938, the Nazi propaganda, rhetoric, and discriminatory laws bore their inevitable fruit. After a mentally imbalanced Jew killed a German official in Paris, Germany and Austria erupted in hate-fueled violence against Jews. Jewish homes, synagogues, and businesses throughout Nazi Germany and Austria were destroyed. Two hundred sixty-seven synagogues were burned and seventy-five hundred Jewish-owned commercial stores were ruined. Firefighters were instructed to intervene only if the fire threatened non-Jewish-owned property. Nazi SS troops and Hitler Youth stormed into Jewish homes, attacking civilians. Many women were raped; others committed suicide rather than face the same fate. Twenty-six thousand Jews were sent to concentration camps, many dying almost immediately as a result of ruthless treatment. The attack, a return to the pogrom from decades earlier, is remembered as *Kristallnacht,* the "Night of Broken Glass." In many ways, it marked the beginning of the Holocaust.

A month later, in December, when leaders of the Yishuv met to discuss what had happened in November, they used the term *shoah* for the first time in that context.[18] It was a biblical term, taken from the Book of Zephaniah, in which the prophet predicts "a day of calamity and desolation, a day of darkness and gloominess, a day of dense clouds."[19] The fact that they had to resort to a little-used biblical term, rather than use a more common word, meant that the Yishuv's leaders, as had been the case with Jabotinsky and Herzl before them, foresaw a calamity with no historical precedent. Jewish history, they intuited, was about to change forever.

FIVE MONTHS LATER, in May 1939, the British issued a White Paper (a generic term for an official government policy document) that accepted most of the demands the Arabs had made in the wake of the 1936 riots. Europe was becoming a death trap for the millions of Jews who lived there, but the British decided nonetheless that Jewish immigration to Palestine would be restricted to seventy-five thousand people over a five-year period; any increase would require Arab consent. The White Paper also included a restriction on the sale of land to Jews in many areas and a ten-year plan in which Palestine would become an independent state with an Arab majority.

Astonishingly, the Arab Higher Committee rejected the White Paper, claiming that the length of the transitional period favored the Jews. To the Jewish community, of course, the limitations on immigration meant both that Jews who sought to flee Europe could not go to Palestine and that the growth in Jewish population that establishing a state would eventually require would be stymied. They held demonstrations in synagogues and public meetings throughout Palestine. In protest of the policy, a Jewish military group inspired by Ze'ev Jabotinsky—flaunting its disregard for the Haganah's continued cooperation with the British—bombed a few government buildings in Jerusalem and Tel Aviv. Subsequently, they attacked strategic elements of the British infrastructure, including electric facilities and radio and phone communication lines. They opposed the Haganah's restraint, and to make their case to the people, they also established an underground newspaper and radio system. Even the leadership of the Yishuv sensed that it needed to alter its strategy. It began to endorse illegal immigration and exerted more effort in helping Jews to enter Palestine.

The Yishuv was now losing any real hope that the British would fulfill the promise they had made in the Balfour Declaration. Twenty-two years earlier, Lord Balfour had called for "a national home for the Jewish people" in Palestine, but without immigration, no Jewish national home was going to be possible. And even with Hitler menacing Jews across Europe, Britain made it clear to the Nazis that the fate of the Jews was not its concern.

The Twenty-First Zionist Congress met in Geneva in August 1939. When Chaim Weizmann closed the Congress on August 24, there was a sense of impending tragedy. "It is with a heavy heart that I take my leave," he said. "If, as I hope, we are spared in life and our work continues, who knows—perhaps a new light will shine upon us from the thick, black gloom."[20] The audience wept.[21]

The First Zionist Congress in 1897 had closed with a sense of great promise; in 1939 there was dread. A week later, on September 1, 1939, Germany invaded Poland. Two days later Britain and France declared war on Germany. World War II had begun. Most of the European delegates to the Twenty-First Zionist Congress would be dead by the war's end.

With Britain now fighting the Nazis, the Yishuv found itself in an almost untenable position. The British were the enemies of the Yishuv because of their restrictions on immigration, but the British were also fighting the Nazis. With whom should the Yishuv side? In what became the de facto description of the Yishuv's position, Ben-Gurion said famously, "We will fight with the British against Hitler as if there were no White Paper; we will fight the White Paper as if there were no war."[22]

NOTHING BETTER CAPTURES the existential condition of the Jews across the globe during this period than the stories of three different refugee ships. One was the *St. Louis*. In May 1939, the *St. Louis* sailed from Hamburg to Cuba with 937 passengers. After Kristallnacht, the mostly German Jewish passengers understood that they needed to flee, so they had bought legal Cuban visas. When the vessel arrived at its destination, however, Cuban president Federico Laredo Brú refused to allow them to enter the country. The non-Jewish German captain of the ship, Gustav Schroder, committed himself to finding a home for each one of his passengers. Weeks of negotiations ensued, but when both America and Canada refused the immigrants a safe haven, Schroder had no choice but to return to Europe, where he negotiated with various European countries that agreed to take some of the passengers; 181 could go to Holland, 224 to France, 228 to Great Britain, and 214 to Belgium. For others, though, Schroder found no home. More than a month after they had set sail from Europe, the passengers disembarked back on European soil in mid-June. As the war progressed, many of them—though they had been just ninety miles from the shores of the United States—found themselves once again under Nazi rule. By the end of the war, 254 of the passengers, just over a quarter of them, had been killed in the Holocaust.[23]

The second ship in question arrived not in Cuba, but at the shores of Palestine. In November 1940, the SS *Atlantic* reached Haifa Bay from Romania, carrying 1,730 refugees from Germany.

The Mandate refused to let them enter Palestine and ordered them onto another ship, the *Patria*, which would take them to Mauritius, an island in the Indian Ocean. Members of the Jewish military resistance placed explosives on the *Patria* in order to delay its departure. But the plan backfired; as the first group of illegal immigrants was being escorted to the *Patria* the following morning, the explosives did significantly more damage than had been intended; the ship blew up and sank. More than 250 of the detainees drowned. The British sent the remaining immigrants who had arrived on the *Atlantic* to an internment camp in Atlit, not far from Haifa.

The third ship, the *Struma*, set sail from Romania on December 16, 1941, carrying 769 Jewish refugees to Palestine for what should have been a voyage of just a few days. Due to engine trouble, it anchored in the harbor of Istanbul. The Turkish government denied the passengers even temporary sanctuary, so the refugees lived on the boat for two months. The ship was equipped with only four sinks, one freshwater faucet, and eight toilet stalls that had no toilet paper. It had no life preservers.[24] The Jewish Agency intervened and pleaded with the British to let the Jewish passengers enter Palestine, even temporarily, just to relocate them later to Mauritius. The British refused, and on February 24, 1942, the Turks ordered the *Struma* to leave the harbor. They towed the boat into the Black Sea, abandoning it there with no functioning engine. A Soviet submarine, operating under then secret orders to sink all neutral and enemy shipping in the Black Sea (to prevent raw materials from making their way to Nazi Germany), torpedoed the boat.[25] The *Struma* sank almost immediately, drowning almost all the men, women, and children on board. There was but one survivor.

The *St. Louis*, the *Patria*, and the *Struma* brought home a single point with terrible clarity. For Jews who had no place to go, a Jewish state—Herzl's dream and Balfour's promise—was more critically necessary than it had ever been before. The creation of a Jewish state was now literally a matter of life and death.

Twenty-seven thousand Palestinian Jews enlisted in the British Army. At the same time, the Yishuv resisted the White Paper's immigration policy. To help those fleeing Europe enter Palestine, in late 1938, the Haganah established an organization, *Mossad le-Aliyah Bet* (Organization for Immigration B) to aid in this illegal immigration. The *Mossad le-Aliyah Bet* procured ships and crews, gathered the prospective immigrants, had them sail to Palestine, and arranged for them to be assisted and hidden once they had reached the state-in-waiting. In many ways successful, the project was still bittersweet; Benny Morris, one of Israel's foremost historians, points out, "During the period 1934–38 about forty thousand Jews had entered Palestine illegally, and another nine thousand by September 1939. But less than sixteen thousand made it during the following six years, when the need for sanctuary was at its most acute."[26]

Many of these illegal immigrants—*ma'apilim* as they were known in Hebrew[*]—succeeded in making their way into Palestine but were then caught by the British, who placed them in detainee camps. The largest such camp was in Atlit, where the Nili spy group had been active on behalf of the British.

Determined to stop Jewish immigration, the British also exerted diplomatic pressure on countries from which the illegal boats sailed and, as a punitive measure, drastically reduced the immigration quotas. Their excuse, which no one believed, was that Axis spies could have infiltrated Jewish refugees. For nineteen of the first thirty-nine months of the war, the British approved no Jewish immigration at all.

---

[*] The term *ma'apilim* is of biblical origin. In Numbers 15, Moses instructs the Israelites not to enter the land, "lest you be routed by your enemies . . . for the Amalekites and the Canaanites will be there to face you." (Num. 14:42–43) But the Israelites, desperate to reach their homeland, disobeyed. "Yet defiantly they marched toward the crest of the hill country." (Num. 14:44) *Ma'apilim* is taken from the Hebrew word *va-ya'apilu*, which means "defiantly they marched." The use of a biblical term for this defiant illegal immigration stressed that this was a return home, the continuation of an ancient and sacred story.

When these steps failed, the British resorted to force. Their coast guard attacked illegal ships and brought the refugees to internment camps. Initially situated in Mauritius and eventually in Cyprus, heartbreakingly close to Palestine (it was less than three hundred miles away), these internment camps were intentionally harsh. The initial hopes for the camps was that they "should be sufficiently punitive to continue to act as a deterrent to other Jews in Eastern Europe."[27] In a tragic historic coincidence, despite their obvious differences, both the Germans and the British were putting Jews into camps behind barbed wire.

WHILE THE YISHUV DID what it could to support the Allies' war effort, some Arabs pledged their allegiance to the Axis powers. They saw the British as accomplices to Zionism and attributed to the British responsibility for defeat of the Arab uprisings from 1936 to 1939. The Mufti of Jerusalem, Haj Amin al-Husseini, pushed out of Palestine by the British in 1936, fled to Berlin in 1941, where he helped develop Nazi propaganda in the Middle East. When Churchill announced in the House of Commons that Britain would be training a Jewish legion to fight on the front lines, the Mufti wrote a letter to the head of the SS, Heinrich Himmler, proposing an Islamic army in Germany.

In no way dissuaded by the Mufti's threat, the British helped train Jewish fighters, many of whom contributed to the British war effort. In 1943, a Jewish legion composed of men from the Yishuv formally joined the British Army. They fought in North Africa and Italy. In total, almost thirty thousand Jews from Palestine served in the British Army during the war. In the process, the British had also given training to many of the men who would form the backbone of the Haganah, and later, Israel's army.

This military cooperation notwithstanding, many British policies struck Jews as arbitrary and dismissive. One in particular was the rule forbidding Jews to sound the shofar (ram's horn) or to bring Torah scrolls to the Western Wall, which had been sacred to the Jews for two millennia.*

A few Jews resisted these policies as a matter of principle and pride. For example, on the holy day of Yom Kippur in 1930, Moshe Segal (one of the founders of the Irgun, the militant group inspired by Jabotinsky) defied British orders and sounded the shofar at the *Kotel*, as the fast ended at sundown as mandated by Jewish tradition. Though he was arrested and sent to jail, resistance continued; every Yom Kippur until 1947, young Jewish men somehow managed to smuggle a shofar into the area near the Western Wall and blow it—despite the warnings and patrols of British forces. Though some managed to escape, most of the shofar blowers were imprisoned. It was only after two decades passed—when Israel would capture the Old City of Jerusalem from Jordan in June 1967—that Jews would again sound the shofar at their holiest site without fear of harassment or imprisonment.

AFTER THE GERMAN INVASION of the Soviet Union in June 1941, the Nazis began their systematic liquidation of Europe's Jews. *Einsatzgruppen*, or special operating units, would round up Jewish communities and shoot them all—men, women, and children— destroying entire communities in only a few hours. Hundreds of thousands of Jews were murdered in just a few months.

That same year, the Haganah created a strike force called the Palmach.† Initially, the Palmach was designed to be an elite unit preparing for the possibility of a German invasion. It attracted the

---

* What is today known as the Western Wall is a remaining section of the retaining wall around the ancient Second Temple in Jerusalem that once stood on the site but was destroyed by the Romans. It has been venerated and visited by Jews as a place of prayer for two thousand years.
† Palmach is an acronym for the Hebrew words *Pelugot Machatz*, which mean "strike force."

best and brightest of the young men and women in the Yishuv, and between 1942 and 1943, the British helped train them. When it first started, the Palmach consisted of 100 men; by May 1948, when the State of Israel declared independence, the elite unit had grown to 2,100 well-trained fighters with another 1,000 who had completed their training and could be mobilized if need be.[28] They would become the core of the elite echelons of Israel's eventual army.

In January 1942, the Nazi senior officials met in Wannsee, Germany. The Wannsee Conference disseminated the new plan of action to Nazi leaders across Europe: Germany would round up Jews and send them to extermination camps in Poland to be gassed and incinerated. By the spring of 1942, one million Russian Jews and hundreds of thousands of Polish Jews had been murdered. Five million more would be killed over the next four years. By the time the war was over, one-third of the world's Jews would be dead; in Poland, the Jewish capital of the world and a place where Jews had lived in a thriving community for six hundred uninterrupted years, 90 percent of the Jews would be murdered. As far as Polish Jewry was concerned, Hitler won the war.

Hitler's forces extended their progress far beyond Europe. When Field Marshall Erwin Rommel's forces reached El Alamein deep in Egypt in 1942, the Yishuv was convinced that they might be next. In preparation for the dreaded Nazi invasion, the Yishuv's leadership drew up plans to take over British fortresses in Palestine (believing that the British would abandon the Mandate in the event of a Nazi invasion), prepared to blow up strategic bridges and even to make a last stand against the invading Nazis.

The Nazis' atrocities and the Yishuv's fears led to a shift in the Yishuv's attitudes to the fate of European Jewry. Years earlier, in December 1938 (a month after Kristallnacht), Ben-Gurion had said, "If I knew it was possible to save all the (Jewish) children of Germany by their transfer to England and only half of them by transferring them to the Land of Israel, I would choose the latter—because we are faced not only with the accounting of these children but also with the historical accounting of the Jewish People."[29] Zionism, it had then seemed, trumped any sense of urgency with regard to saving the Jews of Europe.

Now, though, as matters in Europe descended into a hell worse than anyone could have imagined, even Ben-Gurion—the hardened and single-minded Zionist—criticized the Yishuv's complacent attitude to the unfolding disaster and warned against "Yishuvism," a term he coined to define a state of mind that saw the Yishuv as responsible only for Jews in Palestine.[30] He understood that the Yishuv and Europe's Jews were too interdependent to allow for complacency. "The destruction of European Jewry," he said, "is the death-knell of Zionism."[31] But there was little the Yishuv could do.

On May 6, 1942, as the British War Cabinet agreed upon an official statement that "all practicable steps should be taken to discourage illegal immigration into Palestine," Zionist leaders met at an Extraordinary Zionist Conference at the Biltmore Hotel in New York to express international Jewry's resolve to create a Jewish state with or without British assistance. The participants agreed that Britain could not be trusted; the Jewish Agency, it decided, should replace the Mandate as the governing power in Palestine. It was now the official policy of the Zionist movement to bring an end to all restrictions on immigration and to establish a "Jewish Commonwealth" in Palestine.

The horrors unfolding in Europe had done what half a century of debate could not. For the first time, the Zionist movement had adopted an official policy that its goal was the creation of a Jewish state.[32]

THE YISHUV RESISTS THE BRITISH, THE ARABS BATTLE PARTITION

In a revolutionary war, both sides use force. . . . Fighters for free-dom must arm; otherwise they would be crushed overnight.

—Menachem Begin, *The Revolt*[1]

On November 22, 1942, for the first time since the outbreak of World War II, the Jewish Agency held a meeting devoted entirely to the fate of European Jewry. The following day, it published its first official acknowledgment that the Nazis were systematically murdering Jews in the hopes of exterminating the Jewish people.

Shortly thereafter, a group of young men in the Yishuv gathered to discuss what they might to do to save European Jewry. One of those in attendance was Yechiel Kadishai, a Jewish soldier from the Yishuv serving in the British Army, who had been given a furlough of several days from his base in Ismailia, Egypt.

In the middle of the meeting, Kadishai would later recall,[2] a man in his twenties, wearing shorts and glasses with small, round frames, entered the room and sat quietly at the side. In the middle of the discussion, the late arrival spoke up and said that there was only one thing that Jews in Palestine could do to save Polish Jewry. As long as Jews in Europe knew that they had nowhere to go, there was no impetus for them to flee Poland, the latecomer said. Furthermore, he pointed out, Hitler had not yet advanced to Hungarian or Romanian Jewry, and there was still time to save those Jews.

For anyone to be saved, though, the young man continued, the British would have to open Palestine to Jewish immigration. But the British would not open the shores of Palestine until the Jews used massive force, he said. If the Yishuv wanted to help Jews in Europe, it needed to attack the British in Palestine. Then he sat down.

The meeting ended inconclusively, but as they were departing, Kadishai, who had been struck by the newcomer's audacity, asked a friend who it was who had spoken up about the British. "He was the head of Betar in Poland," Kadishai's friend told him. "He was imprisoned by the Soviets, and just got here. The name is [Menachem] Begin."

The Jewish revolt against the British was about to start.

THE NAZI GENOCIDE of the Jews, somewhat surprisingly, was not much discussed in Palestine, a fact for which the leaders of the Yishuv would later be criticized. Occasionally, there were wistful conversations like that at which Yechiel Kadishai first heard Menachem Begin speak, but realistically, there was little that the Yishuv could do. One of those conversations hatched the idea of assisting the British in their war against the Nazis by parachuting Jews into Europe to gather intelligence and find survivors.

The most famous of those parachutists was Chanah Senesh. Senesh, who had been born in Hungary, moved to Palestine in 1939, upon graduating high school, and shortly thereafter joined the Haganah. In March 1944, she parachuted into Yugoslavia in the hopes of making her way into her native Hungary; the goal was to help Jews there who were about to be sent to the Auschwitz death camp. The Germans captured her on the Hungarian border, however, then jailed, tortured, and eventually executed her in Budapest in late 1944. Almost immediately, her story—like that of the Nili's Sarah Aaronsohn—became an iconic mainstay of Israeli lore and Zionist education. Her remains were brought to Israel in 1950; she is buried in Jerusalem, on Mount Herzl, not far from Herzl, Jabotinsky, and several of Israel's prime ministers.

In both Europe and Palestine, however, the Jews needed more than inspiring missions, no matter how courageous, to help them. In Europe, the Nazis were exterminating Jews by the millions. In Palestine, the Yishuv faced enemies in the form of both the Arabs and the British. Some senior British figures made no attempt to disguise their distaste for the Jews. In his letters to his lover, the commander of the British forces in Palestine, General Evelyn Barker, frequently expressed his hatred for the Jews. In one letter he wrote, "I loathe the lot. . . . Why should we be afraid of saying we hate them—it's time this damned race knew what we think of them— loathesome [sic] people."[3]

Among some members of the Yishuv, the feeling was mutual. Soon after Menachem Begin's arrival in Palestine, the Irgun asked him to become its head. He accepted, and almost immediately— though he knew that the leadership of the Yishuv was opposed—he decided to rid Palestine of what he thought was the Jews' greatest enemy after Hitler. Begin unleashed "The Revolt" against the British.

THE IRGUN, THOUGH FAR more willing to use violence and much more openly hostile toward the British, was hardly the Yishuv's most extreme underground group. That position was occupied by yet another group that split off from the Irgun in July 1940. It was led by Avraham Stern, a prolific writer who penned dozens of poems, which bespoke an erotic love for the Land of Israel. Stern had planned to do doctoral work in Italy, but convinced that others were not doing enough to liberate Palestine from the British, he put those aspirations aside to found his even more militant organization to help do so.

Several dozen Irgun members joined Stern and established their own underground militia. They took the name *Lochamei Cherut Yisrael* ("Fighters for the Freedom of Israel"), the acronym of which,

Lechi, is how the group is most commonly known. (The group's opponents derisively called it the "Stern Gang.") Unlike the Irgun, which was hesitant to wage an all-out war against the British as long as the British were at war with the Nazis, the Lechi saw the British as the greater enemy of the Yishuv. They unleashed more intensive guerrilla warfare against the British, usually conducting small-scale operations, most notably assassinating British military and government leaders.* Stern was killed in February 1942 in a shoot-out with British forces after a massive manhunt.

On November 6, 1944, just as Chanah Senesh was executed in Budapest, the Lechi incurred the wrath of the Yishuv.[4] Two of its members, Eliyahu Bet-Zuri and Eliyahu Hakim, assassinated Lord Moyne, the British minister of state in the Middle East, just outside his home in Cairo. They shot Lord Moyne's driver, as well. They were captured immediately after being surrounded by an angry crowd and were eventually convicted and hanged. During their trial, the "two Eliyahus" insisted that they killed Lord Moyne

---

* Just as the Jewish underground had its radical elements, such as the Lechi, which used force with much less discretion than did the Irgun, so, too, did the British sometimes resort to tactics no less horrific than those of the underground they were seeking to dismantle. In one notorious incident, Major Roy Farran, after having served in the British Army in Europe during World War II, was sent to Palestine, where he helped create a covert British team to extract intelligence information from Irgun and Lechi fighters. On May 6, 1947, Farran's team kidnapped Alexander Rubowitz, a sixteen-year-old who was distributing Irgun leaflets. Years later, it was determined that Rubowitz was tortured mercilessly but refused to divulge information. During the interrogation, Farran smashed in Rubowitz's head with a rock and the boy died. Despite extensive efforts, his body was never recovered. A year later, in revenge, the Lechi mailed a bomb to the Farran residence in England, but the package was opened not by Roy, but by his brother Rex, who was killed on the spot. Roy Farran eventually made his way to Canada, where he became a successful businessman and politician, serving as a member of the Legislative Assembly of Alberta Province from 1971 to 1979. (Bruce Hoffman, *Anonymous Soldiers: The Struggle for Israel: 1917–1947* [New York: Alfred A. Knopf, 2015], pp. 422 ff.)

because his opposition to Jewish immigration constituted a crime against the Jewish people. The British court, of course, was unmoved; the fact that the driver had been killed as well convinced many in the Yishuv that the Lechi acted more as a band of killers than a disciplined fighting force.

The Yishuv's leadership grew increasingly worried that the extremist Jewish paramilitary groups would bring down the wrath of the British on the entire Yishuv. With Ben-Gurion's approval, the Haganah decided to eliminate the other paramilitary groups. Between November 1944 and March 1945 (a period now known as the *Saison,* or the "hunting season"), special forces from the Palmach searched out members of the Irgun and Lechi, arrested them, and handed them over to the British, knowing full well that the British might hang them. Begin refused to temper his activity against the British, but also refused to fight the Haganah. He would simply not turn his hand against Jews. Ben-Gurion had no similar compunctions; Anita Shapira, one of Israel's leading historians (and an ideological disciple of Ben-Gurion) later noted that "the *Saison* was not Ben-Gurion's finest hour, [but] he never expressed remorse for it."[5]

MEANWHILE, IN EUROPE, the Allied war against the Nazis progressed. On May 8, 1945, the Germans surrendered unconditionally and World War II ended four months later on September 2. Some sixty million people died in the war (about 3 percent of the world's population in 1940), including the six million Jews (constituting one-third of the Jewish people) who had been murdered in the Holocaust. Ben-Gurion, years later, would reflect on the horrific toll of the Holocaust and note that "had partition been carried out [as it was proposed in the Peel Commission,] the history of our people would have been different and six million Jews in Europe would not have been killed—most of them would be in Israel."[6]

With the war's end, Britain was in desperate financial straits, Cold War fears were ubiquitous, and Arab oil was a critical factor. Still unwilling to incur Arab wrath, the British Labour government did not change the White Paper's policy and did nothing to create the Jewish state that the Zionists believed Balfour had promised.

The British were hardly the only ones exhibiting distaste for the Jews. It seemed that everywhere they turned, the Jews encountered hostility. The United Nations Relief and Rehabilitation Administration (UNRRA) housed the war's displaced persons in refugee camps, placing Jewish and German displaced persons together. When the Jews complained that they did not want to be with the people who until very recently had been their persecutors, the UNRRA authorities responded cynically that separating the Jews from the Germans would be tantamount to perpetuating the Germans' racist policies.

Nor were all leading American figures entirely sympathetic. In 1945, General George S. Patton wrote an entry in his journal in which he said, "[Others] believe that the Displaced Person is a human being, which he is not, and this applies particularly to the Jews who are lower than animals."[7] Patton recalled taking his commander, General Dwight D. Eisenhower, to see a temporary synagogue that had been constructed to allow the Jewish displaced persons to commemorate Yom Kippur. "We entered the synagogue, which was packed with the greatest stinking mass of humanity I have ever seen. Of course, I have seen them since the beginning and marveled that beings alleged to be made in the form of God can look the way they do or act the way they act."[8]

The displaced persons had survived the war, but they were desperate, and immigration became an ever more pressing issue. When UNRRA did a poll of the Jewish refugees, 96.8 percent said that they wanted to go to Palestine. The United States pressured Britain to back off the prohibition on land sales and to allow one hundred thousand Jews to enter Palestine. But the United States had also closed its borders to Jews during the war and had little moral authority to summon; the British refused.

So the Yishuv stepped up illegal immigration. Between 1945 and 1948, in what constituted a massive and often heroic effort to save the remnants of European Jewry, it assisted many thousands of Jews who—desperate to survive—sought to enter Palestine illegally. Sometimes at great personal peril, those living in the Yishuv would greet boats, large and small, coming to shore, help the survivors onto land, and seek to hide them before they could be caught.

Many, though, were caught. In a devastating twist of fate, survivors of the Holocaust who had finally made their way to Palestine often found themselves imprisoned once again, this time by the British. To delouse them, the British told them to undress and take a shower; revisiting that image was almost too much for many of them to bear.

ON JUNE 26, 1945, at a press conference in New York, Ben-Gurion declared that if the British insisted on maintaining the White Paper's policies with its restrictions on Jewish immigration, the Yishuv would have no choice but to respond with "constant and brutal force."[9] The Haganah, Irgun, and Lechi joined together to establish the *Tnu'at Hameri Haivri* (United Resistance Movement), which Ben-Gurion would lead. They agreed to join together to fight the British in a coordinated strategy, attacking "critical strategic points, destroying the infrastructure and symbols of power that legitimated the British mandate." The Haganah was given veto power over any operations that were decided upon.

The most successful attack by the United Resistance Movement was on June 16 and 17, 1946. Eleven coordinated attacks destroyed road and rail bridges and damaged the Haifa railway system, isolating Palestine from its neighboring countries and blocking Britain's ability to move goods and soldiers beyond its borders. The attacks cost the British Mandate over four million pounds sterling, an exorbitant sum at that time.

Twelve days later, the British retaliated. In Operation Agatha (which the Yishuv called Black Sabbath), the British placed Jerusalem, Tel Aviv, Ramat Gan, Haifa, and Netanya under lockdown. Some seventeen thousand British soldiers crisscrossed Palestine in search of militants, illegal weapons, and incriminating documents.

They arrested twenty-seven hundred Jews, many from the Zionist leadership. Ben-Gurion escaped arrest only because he was in Paris.

As the Jews were being rounded up in Palestine, they were also still being killed in Europe. Five days after Black Sabbath, on July 4, 1946, some 150 to 200 Jewish survivors from the war who were being housed in Kielce, Poland (some had come from Kielce and had gone back to their erstwhile home, while others were en route elsewhere), were attacked in what was the first major postwar pogrom. In the attack by the violent mob (in which the Polish army and police were involved from the outset), forty-two Jews were killed, while the rest were beaten or stoned. The war was over, but pogroms had returned to Europe. It was clear that even postwar, Poland would not be safe for Jews.

Kishinev had not been relegated to the past.

Word of the attack spread quickly. Within twenty-four hours of the attack, five thousand Jews in Poland left their houses, moving toward the Czechoslovakian border in hopes of reaching Palestine. The British, though, stopped them at the entrance to the occupied zone in Austria.

The mass of refugees from Europe was growing yet had nowhere to go. The leadership of the Yishuv was being jailed. And the British had seized many of the Jewish Agency's documents, some of which they could then use to prosecute leaders of the Yishuv. The volatility was undeniable; it was clear that the region was about to explode.

WORD REACHED THE YISHUV leadership that many of the documents that the British had seized during the Black Sabbath were being stored at the iconic King David Hotel building. The Yishuv was relatively certain that the British had sufficient documents in storage at the building to arrest, and possibly execute, a number of leaders of the Yishuv, including Golda Meir.[10] In retaliation for the British crackdown, and in order to destroy the incriminating evidence, the Irgun proposed staging an attack on the hotel, the southern wing of which had served as the British Mandate's military and administrative headquarters since 1938 (other rooms continued to be used as guest accommodations).

On July 1, 1946, Moshe Sneh, then head of the Haganah, sent Menachem Begin a secret note authorizing the bombing of the King David. The Irgun was to bomb the King David, while the Haganah and Lechi would attack other buildings. The Haganah and Lechi backed out of their roles, and two days before the scheduled attack, Weizmann told Sneh that he would resign from the World Zionist Organization, splitting the Yishuv, unless Sneh sought to stop the Irgun's plan. Sneh delayed the bombing a few times, but when the Irgun's leadership realized that the Haganah was getting cold feet, it decided to proceed on its own.

The King David received its milk in large tin canisters. On July 22, seven milk containers filled with TNT explosives were placed strategically in the building. Twenty minutes before the designated detonation time, an Irgun member called the King David and passed on a warning—in English and in Hebrew—of an impending attack in the building. The staff ignored the warning. The Irgun also placed calls to the French Consulate and the *Palestine Post*, warning them of the impending explosion. Those calls, too, went unheeded.

At 12:37 P.M., the explosives detonated, creating a blast equivalent in pressure to a direct hit by a 500-kilogram aerial bomb. Many occupants were killed immediately, with dozens more buried under the rubble. Ninety-one people died as a result of the attack. Twenty-eight were British, forty-two were Arabs, and seventeen were Jews, including one of the Irgun militants carrying out the operation. The dead also included two Armenians, one Russian, and one Greek.

Not surprisingly, the attack elicited reactions of outrage. American and British newspapers condemned the attack, predicting that it would set back the Zionist cause. The Jewish Agency also denounced the bombing, ignoring the critical fact that the Yishuv leadership had initially approved it. The Haganah, including Ben-Gurion, falsely denied any involvement in the plan. So intense was the backlash that from that point on, the United Resistance Movement was effectively dead. The Irgun and Lechi continued to work on their own, usually in defiance of the Haganah.

ON DECEMBER 9, 1946, some five months after the King David bombing, the Twenty-Second Zionist Congress met in Basel, in the same building in which Herzl had first convened the congress almost fifty years earlier. The aftershocks of the bombing defined the conversation; the central question at the congress was how to deal with the British—to use force or to wait for the British to change their position. It was a debate not unlike that between the biblical Jeremiah and Hananiah thousands of years earlier. Weizmann said terrorism was a "cancer in the body" and argued that creating a Jewish state by "un-Jewish methods" would defeat the entire purpose. Appropriately, he concluded his remarks by quoting Jeremiah: "Would that I had a tongue of flame, the strength of prophets to warn you against the paths of Babylon and Egypt. . . . 'In justice shall Zion be redeemed,' not by any other means."[11]

Weizmann's entreaty convinced Ben-Gurion that the congress no longer had the courage it would take to create a Jewish state. Ben-Gurion stormed out of the convention and returned to his room—the very same room in which Herzl had stayed. When other delegates appealed to him to stay, he relented. The vote to determine whether it was time for the Yishuv to begin to resist the British with greater violence was cast at dawn. By a slight majority of 171 to 154, Ben-Gurion won.

After thirty years of influence, Chaim Weizmann had lost not only his appeal for restraint but also the admiration of some erstwhile supporters. He had devoted his life to the cause and had paid a painful personal price in the war—his son, a fighter pilot for the British, had been shot down and killed. He would remain an important figure in Zionist and Israeli affairs, and would be instrumental in convincing President Harry Truman to recognize the State of

Israel, but he emerged from this loss with his standing in the movement significantly tarnished.

WORLD WAR II HAD EXACTED a terrible toll on Britain, and the empire needed to retrench. India would achieve independence in 1947, and in the Middle East, the cost of maintaining the Mandate had simply climbed too high. Some one hundred thousand British soldiers (one-tenth of the empire's entire army) were stationed in Palestine, one soldier for every eighteen inhabitants.[12]

In the meantime, the leadership of the Yishuv sought to establish as many facts on the ground as it could to expand whatever future borders the Jewish state would have. On October 6, 1946 (immediately upon the conclusion of the Yom Kippur fast), the Jewish Agency worked feverishly to establish—over the course *of a single night*—eleven new settlements in the northern Negev. They were built in an area that had not been included in the territory allocated to the Jewish state by the Peel Commission, and which, presumably, might not otherwise be included in future partition plans.

The Yishuv's intuition that it needed to move quickly proved prescient. Six months after the July 1946 bombing of the King David, the British announced on January 22, 1947, that they were washing their hands of Palestine and turning the fate of that territory—and of any future Jewish state—over to the United Nations.

ON MAY 15, 1947, the UN created the United Nations Special Committee on Palestine, better known by its acronym, UNSCOP. Composed of representatives of eleven countries, UNSCOP was charged with doing what the British had been unable to do—finding a solution to Palestine. The Arabs immediately announced that they would boycott all UNSCOP meetings and discussions. On June 2, UNSCOP committee members traveled to Palestine and remained there for three months of intensive study and investigation.

As there were still hundreds of thousands of Jewish survivors of the Holocaust desperate for a place to go, illegal immigration continued apace. While UNSCOP deliberated, another ship carrying homeless Jews once again captured headlines. This ship was the *Exodus*; again, the British were still unwilling to allow its passengers to disembark in Palestine.

The *Exodus*, formerly named SS *President Warfield*, sailed from Port-de-Bouc to Sète, where some 4,500 Jewish survivors of the war from Germany and Poland embarked. Filled far beyond capacity, it reached Palestine in July 1947. After a brief skirmish with the British Royal Navy killed three Holocaust survivors, the passengers were taken off the *Exodus*. The British transferred them to the *Empire Rival*, which would take them not to Cyprus, where many other Jewish refugees had been taken before, but back to Europe.

The survivors were devastated. Aubrey Eban (who later, as Abba Eban, became Israel's ambassador to both the United Nations and the United States) convinced members of the UNSCOP committee to come witness the transfer. When they arrived, Eban later wrote, they saw "British soldiers using rifle butts, hose pipes, and tear gas against the survivors of death camps. Men, women and children were forcibly taken off to prison ships, locked in cages below decks and sent out of Palestine waters."[13] When the UNSCOP members returned to Jerusalem, "they were pale with shock" at the British cruelty they had witnessed.[14]

UNSCOP heard from leaders of the Yishuv and even met secretly with members of the Haganah to determine whether the Jews could defend themselves against the Arabs once the British departed. On September 1, 1947, UNSCOP officially proposed a partition of Palestine into Jewish and Arab states; Jerusalem would remain a separate entity under international auspices. (See Map 5.) While the Zionists had moved one major step closer to statehood, that state was still going to be smaller than their original expectations. The Jewish state proposed by UNSCOP was at least larger than the area designated to them by Peel; Peel had proposed 20 percent of Palestine west of the Jordan for the Jews, and 80 percent for the Arabs. UNSCOP, on the other hand, proposed 55 percent for the Jews and 45 percent for the Arabs. Though much of the land assigned to the Jews was desert, UNSCOP's plan was still a major step forward for the Jews, and a significant setback for the Arabs.

For the Jews, however, the projected population balance of the two proposed states was cause for grave concern. The Jewish state proposed by UNSCOP would have 498,000 Jews and 407,000 Arabs.[15] The Arab state would be home to 725,000 Arabs and a mere 10,000 Jews.[16] Given the differential in Jewish and Arab birthrates and the ease with which additional Arabs could have been convinced to move to the area from surrounding countries, had the Arabs accepted UNSCOP's recommendations, all of Palestine might have been theirs in a generation. Just as had happened after Peel, though, the Jewish Agency accepted UNSCOP's recommendations, and the Arab Higher Committee rejected them outright.

In 1947, the United Nations was merely two years old and composed of fifty-six member countries. In the last week of November 1947, its General Assembly met in New York to debate Resolution 181, a slight modification of UNSCOP's proposal. Initially, the Americans offered only tepid support for the Zionists. The State Department, under George Marshall, had long assumed a staunchly anti-Jewish-independence stance; to make matters worse for the Yishuv, a day before the vote, a secret CIA report urged President Truman not to lend his support. The Jewish state would not be able to defend itself, the CIA had concluded, and the United States would be drawn into the conflict that was bound to ensue. "The Jews will be able to hold out no longer than two years," the CIA predicted.[17]

The president ignored the CIA and the State Department, and gave the partition plan not only America's vote, but pressured other countries to which the United States gave aid, as well.[18]

The Soviet Union had already made clear that it would back Jewish independence. Believing that the Jewish state might well become socialist (and undoubtedly delighting in the humiliation that the entire affair caused the British, a symbol of Western imperialism), the Russians threw their support behind Jewish independence. Andrei

Gromyko, the Soviet representative, said, "The Jewish people had been closely linked with Palestine for a considerable period in history. . . . As a result of the war, the Jews as a people have suffered more than any other people . . . the Jewish people were therefore striving to create a State of their own, and it would be unjust to deny them that right."[19]

Even with Soviet and American support, however, the Zionists feared that they were still a few votes short of the two-thirds majority they needed. The General Assembly vote was scheduled for Wednesday, November 26, but the Jewish Agency calculated that it needed more time to persuade several other countries, including Haiti, Liberia, and the Philippines to support them. Help came in the form of Rodriguez Fabraget, Uruguay's UN delegate, who launched a filibuster that ended up delaying the vote.[20] Because the vote would now have to wait until after the Thanksgiving holiday, the Zionist coalition had another day during which they could lobby a few countries whose votes were critical. Eban and others worked around the clock, calling people in the middle of the night, pleading the Jewish people's case and urging representatives to help establish the first Jewish commonwealth in two thousand years.[21]

When the General Assembly reconvened on November 29, Jews around the world, desperate for good news and a renewed lease on Jewish life after the horrors of the Holocaust, huddled around their radios. American Jews and Europeans, Australian Jews and Jews in the Yishuv, suddenly united by a sense that in the coming moments their people's history might be radically changed, held their breath and listened to the roll call. As expected by that point, the Soviet Union and the United States voted in favor. The British, responsible for Palestine, abstained. What was less expected was that seven of the seventeen countries who had indicated on November 25 that they planned to abstain now voted in favor.[22] The filibuster had worked. Resolution 181 for the Partition of Palestine passed by a vote of 33 in favor, 13 opposed, and 10 abstentions.

The Jews were going to have their state. Following the First Zionist Congress in 1897, Herzl had written in his diary, "At Basel I founded the Jewish state. If I said this out loud today, I would be answered by universal laughter. Perhaps in five years, and certainly in fifty, everyone will admit it."[23] Now it was 1947, exactly fifty years later, and Herzl's wild dream was about to come true.

Around the world, Jews hugged and wept. In Palestine, synagogues opened in the middle of the night for the reciting of prayers of thanksgiving; Jews by the thousands took to the streets and began to dance. According to one account, the following morning "great bonfires at Jewish collective farms in the north were still blazing. Many big cafes in Tel Aviv served free champagne. . . . Jews jeered some British troops who were patrolling Tel Aviv streets but others handed them wine."[24]

Amos Oz, who would become one of Israel's greatest novelists and was several times considered a contender for the Nobel Prize for Literature, later recalled that night in his autobiographical memoir, *A Tale of Love and Darkness*. He told how, merely eight years old, he rode on his father's shoulders in a surging crowd of celebrants in Jerusalem, and at three or four in the morning, still wearing his dirty clothes, crawled into bed. Moments later, Amos felt his father get into bed with him, not to scold him for still being in his clothes, but to tell him how when he (Amos's father) had been a boy, students at his Polish school had stolen his pants. When Amos's grandfather went to the school to complain, the boys—joined by the girls—attacked him, too, taking his pants as well. It was a story of utter humiliation.

Then, Oz relates, his father said to him early that morning of November 30, 1947, "Bullies may well bother you at school or in the street someday. . . . But from now on, from the moment we have our own state, you will never be bullied just because you are a Jew. . . . Not that. Never again. From tonight that's finished here. Forever."[25]

Finally, Oz writes, "I reached out sleepily to touch his face [and] instead of his glasses, my fingers met tears. Never in my life, before or after that night, even when my mother died, did I see my father cry."[26]

Not everyone in the Yishuv joined in the reverie. Menachem Begin did not dance, for he knew that war was looming. The Arabs had responded to immigration and to Peel with violence, and it was obvious to him that they would do the same now. The same was true of Begin's nemesis, David Ben-Gurion. "I could not dance," Ben-Gurion later recalled. "I knew that we faced war and that in it we would lose the best of our youth."[27]

Nothing expressed the Yishuv's overwhelming sense of anticipation better than the poem "The Silver Platter," by Natan Alterman. Alterman, who was born in Warsaw in 1910, moved to Palestine with his family in 1925. By 1941, he was recognized as one of the leading poetic voices of the Yishuv; he gradually assumed Bialik's unofficial position as the poet laureate of the Zionist movement. He wrote "The Silver Platter" on December 26, 1947, barely a month after the vote in the UN General Assembly and shortly after Chaim Weizmann had remarked, "A state is not given to a people on a silver platter."[28]

In "The Silver Platter," Alterman analogized the nation waiting for statehood to the biblical Israelites in the desert waiting for the revelation of the Torah at Mount Sinai. The Yishuv, Alterman said, was awaiting "the one miracle and only." As the nation waited, a boy and a girl, the only characters in the poem, walk slowly and silently toward the assembled throngs. The two are almost immobile and say nothing. Awestruck, the nation watches the young man and woman caked in dirt or blood, and then asks them who they are. "We," the boy and the girl reply, "are the silver platter on which the Jewish state has been given to you," whereupon they collapse. With that, the poem ends.

Though the bloodshed had already started, Alterman was reminding the nation that a still heavier price was about to be paid. Yet he was saying something even more important. The state-in-waiting was the new Sinai. The Jewish state about to declare independence would be the setting for the creation of a new Jew, the Jew that Bialik had virtually demanded in "The City of Slaughter" almost half a century earlier.

A "new religion"—a secular Judaism—would become the state's unofficial religion, intimated Alterman. To traditional Jews, when the nation assembles waiting for "the one miracle and only," that miracle is the revelation of the Torah at Mount Sinai. Not so for Alterman; for him, the "one and only" miracle is the creation of the state. In the biblical account, as the nation prepares to receive the Torah, Moses tells the men not to approach the women. In "The Silver Platter," however, the central characters—the boy and the girl—are inseparable, virtually indistinguishable. If the Torah demanded separation of the sexes at the foot of Mount Sinai,[29] Zionists rejected it without question. In the Torah, God commands the Israelites to wash their clothes as part of their preparation for revelation[30]; in Alterman's poem, the boy and the girl are caked with dirt, and they do not wash.

Saving the Jews, Alterman suggested, would require getting very dirty. No longer would purity and holiness guarantee the Jews' survival; now, staying alive would require young men and women who were willing to die.

THE YISHUV BEGAN a hurried preparation for the war. Ben-Gurion reached out to King Abdullah of Transjordan, with whom the Yishuv had long had a much better relationship than it did with other neighboring leaders, hoping (in vain) that Transjordan would remain neutral. The Haganah, technically still an illegal militia since the British had not yet left Palestine, created four brigades, established hideouts for arms, and recruited Jewish fighters who had battle experience from World War II. Even displaced persons in Cyprus—using wooden rifles local carpenters made them—received training from Haganah fighters.

There had been months of sporadic Arab terror, but now, with the UN vote, the violence that everyone knew was coming erupted in earnest. The war, which would last until early 1949, had two major phases. In the first phase, from the UN vote in November 1947 until Israel's declaring independence in May 1948, the

Haganah and other Jewish military groups fought marginally organized local Arab fighters and irregular Arab forces from other countries who attacked the Yishuv. In many ways, it resembled a civil war between Jews and Arabs more than a conflict between two standing armies. In the second phase of the war, which began in May 1948 and ended in early 1949, Israel—now a country with an official army—would find its forces pitted against the armies of five different countries—Lebanon, Syria, Iraq, Jordan, and Egypt.

The day after the UN vote, an Arab opened gunfire on a Jewish ambulance on its way to Hadassah Hospital. No one was injured, but the attack was an ominous indication of how vulnerable were the hospital's personnel. Later that day, Arabs, using machine guns and hand grenades, attacked a bus carrying passengers from Netanya to Jerusalem. Those people were not as lucky; five Jews died, including a young woman on the way to her wedding. The five and a half months that would make up the first half of the War of Independence were now under way.

Technically, as they had not yet departed Palestine, the British were responsible for maintaining order in the region. But they made little or no effort to prevent Arab violence. When Arabs attacked a group of Jews and a Haganah platoon went to defend them, the British blocked the Jewish fighters from crossing the street to break up the violence. Consistent with the long-standing but now irrelevant White Paper policy, the British also continued their efforts to block ships carrying "illegal" immigrants.

Jewish tactics remained similar to what they had been, as well. The Haganah, still committed to "restraint," limited itself to reprisals against individual Arabs who had participated in attacks. But the Irgun and Lechi increased their activity against the British and the Arabs, leading to an endless cycle of attacks. After a mere six weeks, 1,069 Arabs, 769 Jews, and 123 Britons had died.

Ben-Gurion insisted that his forces abandon no territory, even in the face of attack, and for the most part, the Yishuv held on. There were exceptions, however. The most significant (and now iconic) was the attack on four settlements known as the Etzion bloc, located in the Hebron Hills south of Jerusalem. In the first two weeks of 1948, the four settlements (Kfar Etzion, Massuot Yitzhak, Ein Tzurim, and Revadim) were besieged. Led by Abdel-Kader al-Husseini, the mufti's cousin, a thousand Arab villagers surrounded a few hundred Jewish men in the bloc (women and children had been previously evacuated). With the Jews poorly armed, hundreds of Arab women and children joined the siege with empty suitcases, ready to plunder the possessions they imagined would be left behind. On January 14, the Jewish defenders repelled an attack and succeeded in holding the Arab attackers at bay, killing 150 of the Arab villagers. But they had used a significant portion of their meager ammunition, and the siege continued.

Two days later, on January 16, 1948, a relief mission set out for the Etzion bloc. The column, consisting of thirty-five men, many of them the brightest of Hebrew University's students, departed from Hartuv (now an industrial zone near the city of Beit Shemesh). Because they departed later than planned, they lost the cover of darkness. They also had no radio or means of communication.

The convoy (known as the Lamed Heh, for two Hebrew letters that represent the number thirty-five) never reached Etzion. According to one account, the convoy encountered an Arab shepherd on its way. They knew they could either kill him, or risk his revealing their whereabouts. But he swore to them that he would say nothing, so they let him go. Another account, which emerged decades later, claimed that two Arab women from the village of Tzurif, on the western side of the hills of the Etzion bloc, were looking for firewood in the early morning. They happened upon two of the thirty-five Palmach fighters and ran back, screaming, toward their village. The soldiers chose not to kill them.[31]

Either way, with their cover blown, the thirty-five young men were ambushed before they could get the supplies to the Etzion bloc. They were killed and their bodies were mutilated, some beyond recognition.

Entirely cut off from the Yishuv and now facing the more powerful Arab Legion, there was no way the Etzion bloc could hold out.

It fell into Arab hands some months later, on May 13, 1948, one day before the State of Israel declared independence. Those who had not been killed defending the area had no choice but to surrender; many of those who surrendered were then murdered by the victorious Arabs.

The loss of the Etzion bloc was a painful blow to the Yishuv's morale. Just a day before independence, the future Jewish state was already losing ground and had lost some of its finest young men.

Even in wartime, poets had the ear of the Yishuv. Thanks in part to Haim Gouri, another leading poet of the Yishuv born in Tel Aviv in 1923, the death of the thirty-five men quickly became an iconic moment in the battle for the state and in the mythology of Israel thereafter. Entitled "Here Lie Our Bodies," the poem—dedicated to the fallen men—speaks in their voice. "Look, here our bodies lie in a long, long row. Our faces have changed. Death reflects from our eyes. We do not breathe."[32]

Gouri's poem was ultimately not about death, but about faith that the state would emerge, and the determination required to make that happen. "Will you bury us now?" the men figuratively ask. "For we shall rise, and we will emerge again as before . . . because everything inside us is still alive and streaming in the veins." As for the sacrifice that statehood would require, the men point to the way they died: "We did not betray. Look, our rifle is beside us and empty of ammunition. . . . [I]ts barrels are still hot and our blood is sprayed on the paths step by step."

Gouri's message resonated. With the death of the Lamed Heh and its impact on the Yishuv's morale, the Haganah altered its strategy. "Restraint" was now a thing of the past. Henceforth, villages from which attacks emanated would themselves be subject to reprisal. The war spread, and casualties—among both civilians and soldiers—rose dramatically. No one was immune, and virtually the entire population was affected. Shlomo Lavi, a childhood friend of Ben-Gurion's, a Zionist activist and later a member of Israel's Parliament, lost both his sons in the fighting—one in the Galilee and one in the Negev.[33] Such stories abounded.

All three underground militias were working feverishly, often without coordination. To amass ammunition without it being discovered by the British (or in the case of the Irgun and the Lechi, without it being discovered by the Haganah), each of the military groups created its own secret caches of guns, grenades, bullets, and the like, all in preparation for wars looming with either the British or Palestine's Arabs. These secret stashes, called "slicks" (possibly based on the Hebrew word meaning "to remove," though the etymology of the term remains unclear), were hidden in storehouses, some underground, even under reservoirs, throughout cities, moshavim, and kibbutzim.[34]

By 1948, there were more than fifteen hundred slicks in the Yishuv. There was, some experts say, scarcely a single kibbutz or moshav throughout the entire country that did not have a slick. One of the Haganah's largest slicks and main source of bullets was an underground bullet factory (today called the Ayalon factory), constructed in a kibbutz right outside Rehovot. Between 1945 and 1948, the factory—situated beneath a working laundry and bakery and operated by a group of young Palmach members—produced two million 9 mm bullets, making a significant contribution to the war effort.

Those who knew about each slick were sworn to secrecy. So hallowed was the aura of secrecy that, in many cases, these people died decades later without having ever mentioned the "slick"; the ammunition caches were discovered only when the area was dug up for new construction or some other purpose. Many will likely never be discovered.

WITH THE WAR TURNING into a slog, international opinion began to shift. There were calls to revisit the UN's partition vote, with the U.S. State Department pushing Truman hard to change the Americans' prior position. Ensuring the support of the president was now of prime importance. Truman, though, was unwilling to discuss Palestine. Indeed, in February 1948, when Weizmann traveled to the United States to muster support for partition, Truman refused to see him. So American Jewish leaders, desperate and having exhausted all their other options, turned to Truman's longtime Jewish friend Eddie Jacobson, with whom Truman had owned a haberdashery decades earlier. The two had remained friendly.

Frank Goldman, president of the national B'nai B'rith (then a leading American Jewish organization), called Jacobson and asked him to intervene. Jacobson wrote the president, but Truman would not budge. There was nothing new that Weizmann could tell him, he replied in a letter. Jacobson then traveled to Washington, where, on March 13, as Truman's long-standing friend, he gained entry to the White House via a side door. Waiting for the president outside the Oval Office, Jacobson was warned not to raise the subject of Palestine with the president.

Much to Truman's ire, however, that is precisely what Jacobson did. The president scolded him harshly, but Jacobson refused to back down. Pointing to a statue of Andrew Jackson that Truman had in his office, Jacobson said to his longtime friend, "Harry, all your life you have had a hero. . . . I too have a hero, a man I never met, but who is, I think, the greatest Jew who ever lived. . . . I am talking about Chaim Weizmann." Jacobson continued, "He is a very sick man, almost broken in health, but he traveled thousands of miles just to see you and plead the cause of my people. Now you refuse to see him just because you are insulted by some of our American Jewish leaders. . . . It doesn't sound like you, Harry, because I thought you could take this stuff they have been handing out."

Jacobson later reported that neither man said anything for what seemed "like centuries." Then, though, Truman turned to Jacobson and said, "You win, you baldheaded son-of-a-bitch. I will see him." It worked. Weizmann, whom Truman had met earlier and described as "a wonderful man, one of the wisest people I think I ever met," convinced Truman.

THE WINTER OF 1948 was a particularly harsh one. In Jerusalem, snow fell and blanketed the city. Beginning in February 1948, Arab forces blocked the roads to Jerusalem to prevent food and ammunition from reaching the Jewish population. Arab snipers picked off people waiting on line for food and water. Even the struggle for rudimentary supplies meant risking one's life.

Fighting in the north was also fierce. On January 10, the Arab Liberation Army, based in Syria, took nine hundred of its men to attack Kfar Szold, only two hundred yards from the Syrian border. In this instance, the defenders were well prepared and the Arab attackers retreated after suffering heavy casualties.

But the Yishuv was losing the battle for the roads, and as a result, the battle for Jerusalem. The Arabs were increasingly emboldened and the Jews dispirited, and perhaps most important, observers abroad started to believe that the Jews could not win a war against the Arab states if they couldn't even beat the local Palestinian Arabs or hold on to the territory assigned to it. The U.S. State Department began pushing its trusteeship plan, which effectively meant canceling the partition decision to create a Jewish state, and Truman was wavering as advisers told him the Jews might lose and be slaughtered.

The once-in-two-millennia chance to establish a Jewish state seemed to be slipping through the fingers of the Yishuv, and decisive action was needed.

In March 1948, Ben-Gurion instructed the Haganah to "gain control of the territory of the Hebrew state and defend its borders." So began Plan Dalet (Plan "D"). According to the plan, if Arab towns were strategically positioned, essential for communication, or could be used as enemy bases, the Haganah would aim to destroy the enemy's armed forces and drive the enemy civilian population to areas outside of the borders of the state. The assumption was that Arabs would be forced out of their villages only if they resisted; if they did not fight back, they could remain in their towns under Jewish sovereignty. Many Arabs fled, however, preferring to leave rather than live under Jewish rule. By May 14, 1948, the date the State of Israel declared independence, some three hundred thousand Arabs had already left Palestine. The problem of Palestinian refugees, today still far from being resolved, had begun.

A GROUP OF ISRAELI scholars known as the "new historians," often associated with Israel's political Left, argues that Ben-Gurion's motivation was at least as much about demography as it was about territory. He understood, they claim, that the demographic balance that the UN's partition plan would create was untenable for the Jewish state in the long run. If the new state were to be both Jewish and democratic, it would need a substantial Jewish majority. In their view, Plan Dalet and others like it were largely intended to get many of the Arabs to leave. Arab historians make the same claim, while mainstream Jewish historians see matters very differently and argue that the Arabs largely *fled*, both because their leadership had fled before them, and because of fear of the advancing Jewish forces. To this day, the decisions and actions that led to the Palestinian refugee problem remain one of the most hotly contested dimensions of the War of Independence.

Some Jewish leaders, including the mayor of Haifa, Abba Hushy, encouraged, even begged, the Arab residents to stay in the city where, for years, they had worked side by side with their Jewish counterparts. The Arab residents ignored Hushy's request and followed in the footsteps of the city's Arab leaders who had fled earlier (presumably to avoid the violence with the hopes of returning when it subsided).

The Yishuv was not oblivious to the human tragedy unfolding, and some of its leaders explicitly expressed their sympathy for what the Arabs were enduring. Golda Meir, who had replaced Moshe Shertok as the head of the political department of the Jewish Agency, said on May 6, after seeing Haifa empty following the flight of its Arab population, "I found children, women, the old, waiting for a way to leave. I entered the houses, there were houses where the coffee and pita were left on the table, and I could not avoid thinking that this, indeed, had been the picture in many Jewish towns [as Jews fled their homes in World War II]."[35] The Arabs had refused to accept the partition plan and had started the war, but there could be no denying that the resulting human suffering was immense.

IN ALL, THE WAR was not going well. Ben-Gurion, a master of timing and strategy, understood that he simply had to turn the war around or all would be lost.[36] Arabs had control of the roads; Jerusalem was cut off and was desperate for food and supplies. It seemed that the Jews might well lose the war.

To make matters worse, the Americans indicated that they were inclined to withdraw their support for partition and might favor putting Palestine under an international trusteeship. Ben-Gurion understood that time was against him and ordered the Haganah to undertake an attack of unprecedented scale. Operation Nachshon in April 1948, in which he dispatched fifteen hundred soldiers to break through to Jerusalem, tipped the scales of the war.

Thanks to arms shipments that finally arrived from Czechoslovakia (one of the few countries willing to violate the international arms embargo), Jewish forces were also able to conquer Tiberias, Safed, and Haifa's all-important port. Ben-Gurion had acted just in time, and the tide of the conflict began to shift.

BEYOND THE LEGITIMATE ACCUSATION that Jewish forces at times forced Arab populations to leave their homes, this portion of the war also prompted what the historian Benny Morris called the "atrocity factor"[37]—allegations that in the midst of the War of Independence, Jewish forces committed numerous atrocious and heinous acts, including rape and outright murder. Most of those accusations have been soundly debunked by contemporary scholars.

The key example, very controversial and still commonly cited by Israel's enemies, was the fierce battle for the Arab village of Deir Yassin. On March 22, 1948, Arab forces successfully cut off Jerusalem from any outside Jewish settlements. As the Haganah was assembling its platoon of fifteen hundred men for Operation Nachshon, three times larger than any force it had used before, the Irgun and Lechi, seeking to help relieve the siege of Jerusalem, decided to take the town of Deir Yassin, from which Arab forces were shooting onto the road into Jerusalem. Deir Yassin was one of the last villages on the western side of Jerusalem that the Arabs had not yet abandoned. Barely trained and ill equipped, the Irgun fighters were unlikely to stand their ground in a real battle, but no one expected significant resistance.

The operation began on April 9. A truck with a loudspeaker was sent to the village to instruct the villagers to leave or surrender. But the truck got stuck before it was close enough to be heard, the communication equipment between the Irgun and Lechi fighters failed, and the fighters encountered far more resistance than expected. In their panic, the ill-trained fighters tossed grenades into homes, with a horrendous death toll. Early accounts suggested that 250 people had been killed, and that the Jewish fighters raped villagers.

The Irgun admitted a high body count but insisted that the number of dead was closer to one hundred. It also absolutely denied the rape charges. The denials fell on deaf ears, however, largely because all parties had incentive to make the most of the charges. The Haganah used the incident to accuse the Irgun of being irresponsible and murderous. The Arabs used it to claim to the international community that the Jews were butchering them and in so doing helped cement the determination of surrounding Arab countries to enter the fray. And the Yishuv as a whole, including Ben-Gurion, benefited from the Arab panic and the increased Arab flight that ensued. Getting the Arabs out of the territory assigned to the Jews was precisely what Ben-Gurion wanted.

But had there been genocide or rape? Later scholars, both Israeli *and* Palestinian, agreed that there had been no rapes whatsoever, and that the death toll was almost precisely what the Irgun had claimed.[38] Both the Haganah and the Arabs had inflated the numbers. There was a heavy battle, to be sure, with heavy losses. Yet killing civilians had never been the intent.

But that was never how the Arabs described it. At the time, their assertions of a horrific massacre spread and prompted more Arabs to flee their homes in Palestine, ultimately making them refugees. To this day, they use Deir Yassin as part of their claim that Israel was "born in sin."

IN MARCH 1948, Abd Al-Qader Husseini, a leader of Arab forces in the Jerusalem area, threatened to attack and destroy Hadassah Hospital on Mount Scopus. Less than a month later, on the morning of April 13, hundreds of Arab militiamen ambushed a caravan of vehicles headed for the hospital. Though some of the smaller vehicles managed to escape and to return to Jerusalem, the two heavy armor-plated buses remained trapped. As Haganah defenders fought desperately for hours to hold the attackers at bay, Haganah headquarters pleaded with the British to intervene. Yet the British did not arrive for more than six hours, by which time it was too late.

Seventy-eight Jewish teachers, doctors and nurses (and, ironically, two members of the Irgun who had been wounded at Deir Yassin four days earlier) were massacred, many of them burned alive. Only thirty bodies remained; of the others, nothing remained but ash. The hospital, which had been treating Jews and Arabs alike since its opening years earlier, closed; it would not reopen on Mount Scopus until after the 1967 Six-Day War.

ON MAY 10, 1948, Golda—disguised as an Arab woman—went to see King Abdullah of Jordan. Meir knew that the Arab states were about to join the fray and that the war was heading into a new, more lethal phase. She pleaded with him not to attack the new Jewish state, insisting that Israel and Jordan could be allies. But Abdullah understood the larger political world in which he operated, and he told Golda that he might have no choice but to join the war against the Jewish state. He then asked Meir not to hurry in proclaiming a Jewish state. "We have been waiting for two thousand years," she said to the king. "Is that hurrying?"

Creating a state, Golda Meir understood, was about much more than sovereignty. It was key to ensuring the future of the Jewish people. After all the Jews had been through, there was no time to waste. And failure was simply not an option.

But the king remained noncommittal. As she departed his office, Meir turned to Abdullah and said, "If you can offer us nothing more than you have just done, then there will be a war and we will win it. But perhaps we can meet again—and after the war and after there is a Jewish state."[39]

INDEPENDENCE

The State Is Born

By virtue of our natural and historic right . . . we hereby declare the establishment of a Jewish State in the Land of Israel, to be known as the State of Israel.

—Israel's Declaration of Independence

Thirty years had passed since General Edmund Allenby had entered Jerusalem's Jaffa Gate in 1917, signaling the beginning of Britain's control over Palestine. Now, on May 14, 1948, the last Union Jack slid down the flagpole at Haifa's port, symbolically bringing the Mandate to an end. The empire was crumbling, and in Palestine, the British had been humiliated, forced out of Palestine by the fledgling Yishuv. Like the Greeks of old who had battled the Maccabees, they had underestimated the sheer grit of the Jews of Palestine.

The hopes that the Zionists had had for British rule when they anxiously awaited the fall of the Ottomans and the beginning of British dominion over Palestine had long been dashed. The British had gone from the Balfour Declaration's endorsement of Zionism to the barely veiled hostility of the 1939 White Paper to outright hostility. Evelyn Barker's last act as commander of the British forces in Palestine was to urinate on the ground.[1]

Yet despite all the enmity at the end, the British had left Palestine far more advanced than it had been when they had received the Mandate. They had built up the country's infrastructure and had allowed the Yishuv to create and cultivate the institutions that would form the backbone of a state. Despite their later limitations on immigration, under the British the Jewish population of the Yishuv had increased tenfold; it had soared from 56,000 to approximately 600,000—a number sufficient to make a small state viable.

The British were finally leaving. The dream that Theodor Herzl had shared with the world, that Lord Balfour had supported but that the British had later blocked, was at long last about to be realized.

BEN-GURION, WHOSE GENIUS INCLUDED an extraordinary sense of historical timing, understood that the opportunity then presented to the Yishuv might not come again, and he adamantly opposed any delay in declaring independence. That Harry Truman had promised his support was all the more reason to move forward.* Yet some members of the Yishuv's leadership disagreed. They worried that the Yishuv was not ready for the war that would follow, and they feared that the U.S. State Department and the Central Intelligence Agency's assessment that the Jewish state might not be able to withstand the inevitable Arab onslaught might be more correct than others in the Yishuv wished to admit. Independence, they insisted, should wait.

---

* Truman apparently remained very proud of his role in Israel's formation. Years later, when Truman's longtime friend Eddie Jacobson introduced the former president as "the man who helped create the state of Israel," Truman responded, "What do you mean 'helped to create'? I am Cyrus," an allusion to the last verses of the Bible (II Chronicles 36:22–23), in which Cyrus (King of Persia) instructs the Jews of his kingdom to return to Jerusalem and to build a temple there. (John B. Judis, "Seeds of Doubt: Harry Truman's Concerns about Israel and Palestine Were Prescient—and Forgotten," *New Republic* (January 16, 2014), http://www.newrepublic.com/article/116215/was-harry-truman-zionist.)

Ben-Gurion understood the enormity of the danger, admitting, "We . . . must be prepared for the heavy loss of territory and people, as well as public shock within the Yishuv as a whole."[2] Yet he insisted that for Jewish sovereignty, it might be "now or never." Mordecai Bentov, who had been part of the Jewish Agency's delegation to the United Nations, later wrote, "In the room sat ten Jews who had to make what was perhaps the most important decision in the history of the People of Israel for 2,000 years."[3] By a slim margin of 6–4, the People's Administration voted in Tel Aviv on May 12, 1948, to declare the first sovereign Jewish state since Judea had fallen two millennia earlier.

On Friday, May 14, 1948, as the British were departing, the People's Assembly gathered in the packed Tel Aviv Museum. Due to fears of an Arab bombing, word of the ceremony was disseminated as late as possible; formal invitations went out the day before. But word leaked, and outside the museum, a crowd of hundreds gathered, buzzing with anticipation.

The hall was not large enough to accommodate all the invitees; some were stranded outside while the Palestine Philharmonic Orchestra, invited to play the national anthem, had to be moved to the floor above the main hall. Everything had been prepared with great haste, but even in the heat of all the activity, the meaning of the day was lost on no one. "We moved about our duties . . . as if in a dream. . . . The days of the Messiah had arrived, the end of servitude under alien rulers," Ben-Gurion's assistant, Ze'ev Sharef, later recalled.[4]

Inside, the scene was consciously reminiscent of the First Zionist Congress in Basel fifty-one years earlier. And forty-two years after he had arrived in Palestine, David Ben-Gurion stood at the podium under an enormous portrait of the founder of modern Zionism, Theodor Herzl.

Promptly at four P.M., as photographers' bulbs continued to flash without interruption, all those in attendance stood and sang "Hatikva."[5]

Ben-Gurion, sixty-two, a five-foot, three-inch pragmatist with rock-hard convictions, who had devoted his life to amassing power, for himself and his people, with the aim of resurrecting Jewish self-determination in Palestine, a land he had reached (from Poland) in 1906 on the back of an Arab stevedore who carried him from skiff to shore—then read out the declaration, "Scroll of the Establishment of the State of Israel."

The Declaration of Independence opened with a series of preambles. In the Land of Israel, it declared, the Jewish people had been born. It was in the Land of Israel that the Jews had developed the civilization they had shared with the world. They had never ceased dreaming that they would return to their ancestoral homeland. Then, Ben-Gurion continued in a voice both tremulous and strident, "By virtue of our natural and historic right and on the strength of the resolution of the United Nations General Assembly, [we] hereby declare the establishment of a Jewish State in the Land of Israel, to be known as the State of Israel."[6]*

When Ben-Gurion had finished reading the declaration, Rabbi Yehuda Leib Fishman-Maimon, who headed the religious Zionist Mizrachi Party and had been flown in to the signing from Jerusalem, which was under siege, recited the *shehecheyanu* blessing, precisely as had Dr. Karl Lippe in Basel at the First Zionist Congress in 1897. "Blessed are You, Lord, our God, King of the universe, who has kept us alive, sustained us and enabled us to reach this moment."[7]

After those assembled sang *"Hatikva"* a second time, David Ben-Gurion declared, "The State of Israel is established! This meeting is adjourned." The proceedings had lasted a mere thirty-two minutes. A new era of Jewish history had dawned. Two millennia of exile had ended, and for the first time since the Romans, the Jews were sovereign in their ancestral homeland.

---

* The entire text of the Declaration of Independence is included in Appendix C at the end of this volume.

THE BRIEF MOMENT OF religiosity representd by the *shehecheyanu*
notwithstanding, the proceedings were distinctly secular. Ben-
Gurion, as had been the case with Herzl some fifty years earlier,
stood with his head uncovered. Half a century earlier, Herzl's contemporaries had pleaded for the creation of a new Jew. The day's
symbolism was clear; that Jew had, in fact, emerged and, now, was
establishing a sovereign Jewish state.

Israel's Declaration of Independence is not a theological document, but a historical one. Unlike the American Declaration of
Independence, which speaks both of "God" and of the "Creator,"
the Israeli declaration makes no mention of God. To pacify the religious elements who hoped for a more overtly religious text, the
declaration does say, "Placing our trust in the Rock of Israel, we
affix our signatures to this proclamation at this session of the Provisional Council of state," but that was an intentionally ambiguous
phrasing. To the religious, "Rock of Israel" was a traditional phrase
that always meant God.[8] (Rabbi Maimon made the reference explicit when above his signature he added three Hebrew letters, an
acronym meaning "by the grace of God."[9]) To the secularists, statehood had nothing to do with God; the Rock of Israel was therefore
Jewish history, Jewish grit, or the newfound ability of the Jews to
defend themselves.*

While the declaration omitted God, it was saturated with history. It spoke of the birth of the Jewish people in the Land of Israel,
the glories of the Jewish past in that land, and the Jews' horrific
suffering in the twentieth century. Reflecting Ben-Gurion's love of
the Bible and his belief that the "Book of Books" was a road map
for the Jews' young state, it promised that the new state would "be
based on freedom, justice and peace as envisaged by the prophets
of Israel."

---

* Not all of the declaration's signatories were able to sign it that Friday
  morning in Tel Aviv. The siege around Jerusalem continued, and roads
  across the country were dangerous. Many would sign only in the days to
  come when they could be brought to a safe place to do so.

Yet the declaration was no ethereal document. Zionism had been a movement born of a keen awareness of a rapidly changing world, and the declaration was deeply cognizant of the historical circumstances in which it was written. It referred explicitly to the war already under way. As if Ben-Gurion had a premonition that the world's sympathy for the Jewish people and its newborn state might be short-lived, it asserted that UN Resolution 181 was irrevocable. Declaring that "[t]he State of Israel will be open for Jewish immigration and for the Ingathering of the Exiles," it explicitly voided the policies of the White Paper. Even in the midst of war, it offered Israel's enemies peace. "We extend our hand to all neighboring states and their peoples in an offer of peace and good neighborliness," it said, "and appeal to them to establish bonds of cooperation and mutual help with the sovereign Jewish people settled in its own land."

The declaration is a complex and nuanced text. It stresses equality, promising that the state "will ensure complete equality of social and political rights to all its inhabitants irrespective of religion, race or sex." Addressing "the Arab inhabitants of the State of Israel," it invited them "to preserve peace and participate in the upbuilding of the State on the basis of full and equal citizenship." It stressed that the ethical foundations of the Jewish tradition would be key to the new Jewish state ("as envisaged by the prophets of Israel") and would serve as a refuge particularly for the Jewish people yet would "foster the development of the country for the benefit of all its inhabitants."

Ensuring that the state would be a distinctly Jewish state while also guaranteeing the rights of non-Jewish minorities would never be simple. Debates about how to strike this balance continue in Israel to this day.

The Declaration of Independence was signed by a broad coalition of Jews, ranging from Communists on the left to the ultra-Orthodox Agudath Yisrael on the religious right. Many of these groups had sparred over ideological issues ever since the First Zionist Congress in 1897, but now, in a stunning demonstration of Jewish unity at a critical moment in Jewish history, those differences were set aside. There would be future moments—both of great opportunity and of grave danger—when a politically divided Israel would recognize that the future of the Jewish people was at stake and would set aside even major disagreements.

Ever since the Second Zionist Congress in Basel in 1898, when they were accorded full membership rights in the Zionist political system (long before European governments did anything similar), women had played a significant role in both the Zionist movement and the Yishuv. Two women—Golda Meir (who would later become Israel's fourth prime minister) and Rachel Kagan-Cohen (a veteran women's and social welfare campaigner)—also signed the Declaration of Independence.

Not surprisingly, absent from the signing ceremony was Ben-Gurion's political foe Menachem Begin, who had led the Irgun. (Yitzhak Shamir, who had led the Lechi, would presumably not have been invited, either, but in any case he had been exiled by the British and was in detention.) Ben-Gurion detested Begin no less than he had Jabotinsky. The Declaration of Independence was a central part of Ben-Gurion's project of shaping Israel's foundational narrative, and if he could have his way, neither Begin nor the Irgun would figure prominently in the story that the state told about itself. Chaim Weizmann was abroad at the time, so could not sign, either; upon his return, Ben-Gurion, still vindictive even in that historic hour, refused to allow Weizmann to add his signature to the scroll.

The new country's name also had deep symbolic resonance.*

---

* Several days before the May 14 declaration, the leadership of the Yishuv met to discuss the name of the soon-to-be-established country. Some wanted to name it Judah, the name of the ancient Jewish kingdom. Since most of historic Judah was not included in the land to be given to the Jewish state in the partition plan, that name was rejected. Other names were also suggested, including "Zion" and "Tzabar" (Sabra)—but then someone suggested "Israel" and a vote was held. The name Israel won by 7–3. The first person to suggest that name for Israel was not Ben-Gurion,

Several possible names for the new country were proposed, but Israel was the name given to the biblical Jacob after he wrestled with an angel. "Your name shall no longer be Jacob, but Israel, for you have struggled with God and with men."[10] Little could anyone have known how apt that name would be.

THOUGH THE THRONGS OUTSIDE the Tel Aviv Museum were euphoric, the leadership once again found itself unable to celebrate. Ben-Gurion wrote in his diary, "In the country there is celebration and profound joy—and once again I am a mourner among the celebrants, as I was on November 29."[11] He told Shimon Peres (then a young leader of the state, and eventually its prime minister and, later, president), "Today everyone's happy. Tomorrow, blood will be spilled."[12]

THE SECOND PHASE of the war began the next day. It would last until January 1949, consisting of three major phases of fighting, punctuated by two internationally mandated cease-fires.

The first month would be the deadliest of the entire conflict. Israel would lose 876 soldiers and some 300 civilians. The Haganah (which would soon become the IDF, the Israel Defense Forces) found itself facing armies from five Arab states: Jordan, Egypt, Lebanon, Iraq (which did not even share a border with Israel), and Syria—augmented by troops from Sudan, Yemen, and Saudi Arabia. For Ben-Gurion, who consistently saw the new state in light of the Bible's narrative, the fact that Israel was arrayed against Egypt and Syria was enormously important. During the war, he wrote

---

but a Jewish Galician writer named Isaac Pernhoff, who in a short 1896 article responding to Herzl, predicted that when a state was established, it would be called the State of Israel. (Elon Gilad, "Why Is Israel Called Israel?" *Haaretz* [April 20, 2015], http://www.haaretz.com/israel-news/.premium-1.652699.)

in his diary: "Our planes need to bomb and destroy Amman [and] across the Jordan, and then Syria will fall. We will bomb Port Said, Alexandria and Cairo. Thus will we end the war and settle our ancestors' score with Egypt, Assyria and Aram."[13]

Those lofty aspirations notwithstanding, the first days did not go well. In the north, the Israelis confronted Iraqi and well-armed Syrian armies. Nor did matters appear much better in the south. Egyptian troops were quickly advancing in the Negev and were soon able to launch air attacks on Tel Aviv—where the Israeli General Staff was headquartered. As Yigal Yadin, the IDF's head of operations during the War of Independence and later its chief of staff, reflected:

> I was suddenly shocked . . . when I realized . . . the whole of the north might be lost. In the south, the Egyptian army was advancing on Tel Aviv. Jerusalem was cut off, and the Iraqis were putting pressure on the middle of the country. This was a moment that I suddenly felt that the dream of generations was about to disintegrate.[14]

Ben-Gurion, too, sensed that the next few days would determine the fate of the country: "This is a race [against] time," he said on May 19, just five days after independence. "If we hold out for two weeks—we will win."[15]

In spite of the protracted fighting on all sides, Ben-Gurion urged Yigal Yadin as early as May 19 to push on to Jerusalem, a task for which Yadin feared the Haganah was woefully underprepared. Not assigned to either the Jewish or Arab states in the United Nations partition plan, Jerusalem was supposed to be governed by an international protectorate, but it was commonly understood that that was not likely to happen. The UN had no power, the major international power brokers had no interest in enforcing the resolution, and both the Arabs and the Jews were uninterested in internationalizing the city. Had there been tremendous international pressure, the Jewish community might have agreed, but it was equally clear that the Arabs would reject the suggestion, just as they had rejected Peel and partition.

So a battle over the city ensued. The Arab Legion—intent on assisting Arabs in Jerusalem who were also running short on supplies—began its push toward Jerusalem. Ben-Gurion decided that the Israelis needed to push back.

The problem was how to get there. For the Israelis to have any chance of taking control of the road to Jerusalem, they needed to conquer Latrun, a hilltop outpost about fifteen miles outside the city (today an armored corps memorial just outside Jerusalem). Ben-Gurion ordered a new unit, the Haganah's Seventh Brigade, to carry out the task. But Yadin resisted, pointing out that many of the fighters who would be sent to the front lines for the battle for Latrun had pitifully little experience and only the most rudimentary weaponry—many of them were without even a canteen. Yadin pleaded with Ben-Gurion to appreciate the devastating irony of what Ben-Gurion was asking: many of these soldiers had been liberated from Nazi death camps, only to be placed in internment camps in Cyprus, to then finally arrive at the shores of Palestine, where they were given outdated weapons and sent to battle with no military training whatsoever. Ben-Gurion understood but was undeterred; the first battle for Latrun began on May 24.

As Yadin had predicted, the battle was a disaster, and the Israeli forces were repelled. Ariel Sharon, then a young platoon commander (later the hero of the Yom Kippur War and still later prime minister of Israel), was wounded. The Israelis launched a second assault on Latrun on June 1, but that also failed. Official counts put the number of killed Israeli troops at 139, though others suggest that the number was higher.

As Yadin had further predicted, Latrun would be remembered as "the place where the blood of Holocaust survivors . . . was spilt."[16] This was true not only of Latrun. Slightly more than a hundred thousand Jews enlisted in Israel's army during Israel's War of Independence. And, as one historian notes, "many of the newcomers who had come from Europe to die in the war for Israel were Shoah survivors."[17] Many died in battle almost immediately upon arrival and are buried in unidentified graves. They gave their lives defending a state in which no one even knew their names. It would not be the last time that Israeli society would grapple with its treatment of victims of the Holocaust, but their deaths were also testimony to the depth of their conviction that—given what they had seen in Europe—the creation of a Jewish state mattered more than anything, even more than their own survival.

The failed Latrun operation was followed by another devastating loss days later, when the Jewish Quarter of Jerusalem's Old City fell to the Arab Legion, the best-trained and equipped of the Arab forces, still fighting under British commanders. Yitzhak Rabin, future prime minister of the state, looked upon the Old City in horror as he saw the Jewish residents surrender to the Arab Legion, white flags waving, the profundity of the loss etched on their faces. Jews had been exiled from Jerusalem after their defeat at the hands of the Babylonian king Nebuchadnezzar in 586 BCE and again under the Romans in 70 CE. Now, once again, long lines of defeated Jews, their meager belongings slung over their shoulders, were exiled from the city and made their tearful way out of Jerusalem. The Jordanians, like the conquerors who had come before them, would show the city no mercy. They would turn synagogues into stables and use gravestones as latrines. Nineteen years would elapse until Jews would once again be able to touch the Western Wall and to pray at Judaism's most sacred site.

THE HAGANAH GAVE UP trying to capture Latrun and decided to seek an alternate route that became known as the Burma Road (so called because it provided Jerusalem's Jews with supplies, just as the Burma Road between Burma and China enabled supplies to be shuttled to the Chinese under Japanese siege during World War II). The desperate struggle to build the Burma Road on what had been an ancient path reflected the ingenuity that had characterized the underground in the days of the Yishuv and now reflected the character of the IDF. Necessity was the mother of invention, and the newly born state, knowing that Jewish blood would flow if it were defeated, was both ingenious and industrious at numerous points during the war. At the Burma Road, for instance:

> Using bulldozers, tractors, and manual labor, the engineers began the nearly impossible task of creating a passable road to the bluff at the head of the orchard and a road to the valley below. At night, against the background of Jordanian shelling, the scene was almost unreal: hundreds of porters silently carrying food and supplies down the hill to waiting trucks and jeeps and even mules. Even herds of cows were led along this route because we desperately needed to ship beef into the city.[18]

Using this alternate route, the Harel Brigade (under the command of Yitzhak Rabin, then twenty-six years old) succeeded in resupplying and defending the western parts of the city—but they were still unable to recapture the Old City.

The Burma Road was hardly the only example of this sort of creativity and ingenuity. Short of heavy weaponry during much of the war, the Yishuv also relied on the Davikda, a homemade three-inch mortar, which more often than not missed its target or failed to explode.[19] If the Davidka had any redeeming value, it was that when it did explode, no matter how inaccurate, the bomb caused a bright flash and an exceptionally loud noise, which then triggered mass panic among the local Arab populations.[20] The Davidka was most effective in the battles for Jerusalem and Safed, because the panic it triggered led the local population to leave or to surrender more quickly. In the battle for Safed, from May 6–9, the Davidka's loud sounds convinced the local Arabs that the Jews were using "atom bombs." "A Haganah scout plane, flying overhead, reported 'thousands of refugees streaming by foot toward Meirun.' . . . The Arab neighborhoods, literally overnight, turned into a 'ghost town.'"[21]

The air force employed similar creativity. In addition to genuine bombs loaded onto planes, the ground crews also began loading whatever empty soda bottles they could find—on base or from surrounding areas. They had heard that the falling empty bottles created a loud whistling noise that sounded to those on the ground like a bomb shrieking its way earthward and that the tactic was weakening the enemy's resolve.

THE FLEDGLING JEWISH STATE was still outgunned, however, and desperately struggled to hold on. Casualties were high. Israel was desperate for heavy weaponry that had been purchased but that had yet to arrive. And the Egyptians controlled the skies. Israel had barely finished declaring independence, and its fate hung in the balance.

The international community, concerned about the bloodshed, was eager to impose a break in the fighting. On May 22, the United Nations Security Council demanded an immediate cease-fire; the UN secretary-general appointed Count Folke Bernadotte, a Swedish diplomat, to negotiate the truce.

Bernadotte was an interesting choice, to say the least. During World War II, in his role as head of the Swedish Red Cross, he had saved many thousands of Jews from the death camps, but he had also met with senior Nazi leaders, notably Heinrich Himmler, seeking back channels to end the conflict. By the time he stepped into his role as negotiator at the peak of the war in Palestine, he was seen as "the gung-ho Swedish aristocrat, 'optimistic . . . and eager for action,' . . . the 'humanitarian' Don Quixote."[22] Charged with ending the war, Bernadotte took on a task that no one had thus far been able to accomplish. He was undaunted, however, and set out to secure a break in the fighting, and afterward, to seek a more permanent peace.

In part due to Bernadotte's political maneuvering and in part due to the exhaustion of all parties engaged in the fighting, the two sides eventually agreed to a truce. Originally scheduled to begin on June 1, the truce proved so complicated to implement that it officially took effect only ten days later, on June 11.

The terms of the respite dictated "a blanket embargo on arms and additional military personnel on Israel and the Arab states,"[23] but both sides violated these conditions. The Arab states fortified their combat units and intermittently fired across the Israeli lines. The Israelis used the lull in the fighting to import massive amounts of weapons, including some they had purchased from the United States as well as from other Western powers. The Yishuv also received a massive shipment of arms from Czechoslovakia, including "more than twenty-five thousand rifles, five thousand machine-guns, and more than fifty million bullets."[24] In what was surely an ironic twist, some of the Czech arms were standard German Mauser rifles and MG machine guns, and—having been produced for the Germans before May 1945—arrived with swastikas on them (as had the uniforms that the volunteer pilots had been given). Guns manufactured for the Germans during World War II were now in the hands of Jews desperately seeking to inaugurate a new chapter of Jewish history.[25]

It was not only weapons that arrived from abroad. At the start of the war, Israel had no military aircraft at all and very few pilots.[26] The American armed forces, on the other hand, had surplus planes by the hundreds after World War II, and Jewish veterans who had flown for the United States. Israel began a clandestine project of seeking out these pilots, many of whom were highly assimilated. Something about the Holocaust, however, awakened a sense of Jewish commitment in some of these men, and a few, in violation of American law, helped purchase American surplus planes and fly them to Europe and then to Israel. They were outfitted with used uniforms, which like some of the guns of those fighting on the ground had Nazi insignias—in this case, Luftwaffe patches—on them.

Germany had built factories for the manufacture of Messer-schmitt warplanes in Czechoslovakia, which continued to produce the planes even after World War II ended. The American pilots flew some of these Messerschmitts to Israel to join the battle.

Almost immediately upon landing in Israel, the Americans were told that Egyptian forces were a mere six miles from Tel Aviv, and that if they did not attack immediately, there would be ten thousand Egyptian troops in Tel Aviv the next morning.[27] So they took off, flying primitive, single-engine planes on their first bombing missions, and quickly changed the tide of battle. Later, air attacks on the advancing Iraqi forces convinced them to stay put and not to continue into Israel.[28]

In all, some 3,500 people from around the world volunteered to come to Israel and helped with the war effort. Many, interestingly, were not Jewish. Some 190 of the volunteers served in the air force.[29] Several of the pilots lost their lives in action. After the war, most of the Americans returned home. Others, though, decided that it was Israel that was home, stayed, and flew for El Al or worked in Israel's aircraft industry.

Benny Morris notes that in addition to its military significance, this wave of volunteers helped Israelis understand that though they were outnumbered, they were not alone.[30] It was a dramatic change in Jewish fate from the Holocaust and boosted the morale of the country significantly.

THE DESPERATE NEED FOR rearmament led to one of the most potentially catastrophic events of the war. On May 26, David Ben-Gurion had brought the Haganah out of "clandestine status" and declared in a simple one-page typewritten memo of twenty brief lines that it would now become the Israel Defense Forces, the official army of the new state of Israel. The memo also stipulated that no other armed groups would be permitted to operate. In what was an indication of both the degree to which the country was being stitched together day by day and the broad powers Ben-Gurion was taking for himself, the prime minister wrote, "Any action taken in accordance with this order shall be considered legal even if it contradicts another directive in an existing law."[31]

Ben-Gurion and Menachem Begin had reached an agreement that stipulated that Irgun members would enlist in the newly created IDF. Their arms and equipment, as well as installations for the manufacture of arms, would be turned over to the army. There would be no special Irgun units within army brigades, and separate purchasing activities would end. Ben-Gurion understood that if Israel were to be a legitimate state, it could not be home to competing militias.

Begin understood and agreed that the Irgun would cease operating as a distinct military unit within the State of Israel. Yet some of Begin's Irgun fighters remained in beleaguered Jerusalem, which was not then technically part of Israel and therefore not governed by Begin's agreement to fold his force into the IDF. With their ammunition running dangerously low, Begin was committed both to equipping his men, and more broadly, to doing whatever was possible to hold on to Jerusalem.

In the meantime, unbeknownst to Begin, the American arm of the Irgun—with which Begin had long been at odds—purchased an old ship and named it *Altalena* (the Italian word for "seesaw," which had been Jabotinsky's nom de plume as a journalist). The ship eventually docked in France; the French, hoping to curb British influence in the Middle East, donated munitions valued at 150 million francs (more than half a billion dollars in today's currency).[32] The arms loaded on the *Altalena* included 5,000 rifles, 250 Bren guns, 5 million bullets, 50 bazookas, and 10 light armored vehicles called Bren carriers. In addition to much-needed arms, some 940 immigrants, many of them survivors of the war, as well as some veteran members of the Irgun—including Yechiel Kadishai—also boarded the ship. Originally scheduled to reach Palestine by May 14, the ship departed late and sailed for Israel on June 11—the day the cease-fire banning the import of arms had gone into effect.

Begin was committed to upholding the truce and had not been informed of the ship's departure. By the time he learned that it had sailed, the ship was very close to Israel's territorial waters. He desperately tried to reach its captain, Eliyahu Lankin, to instruct him not to enter Israel's territorial waters. But the communication equipment malfunctioned, and when Begin realized that there was

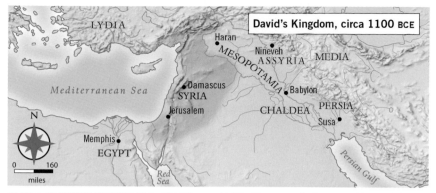

MAP 1. DAVID'S KINGDOM, CIRCA 1100 BCE: King David, the second king of the ancient Israelites, expanded what had begun as a small collection of tribes into a substantial
kingdom. For Zionists, creating a Jewish state in the Middle East would be the fulfillment of
the Jewish people's longstanding dream of returning to their ancestral homeland. Political
Zionism in the late nineteenth century transformed that dream into a political movement,
but the vision itself predated modern Zionism by thousands of years. See Chapter 2: Some
Spot of a Native Land.

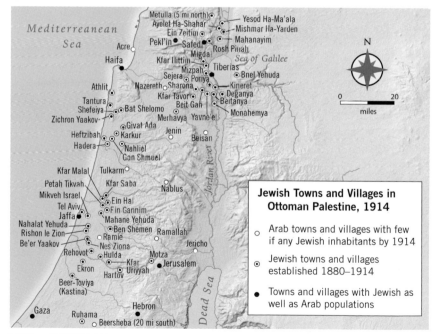

MAP 2. JEWISH TOWNS AND VILLAGES IN OTTOMAN PALESTINE, 1914: With
the launch of political Zionism at the end of the nineteenth century, Jewish immigration to
Palestine began in earnest. The Ottomans, who then controlled Palestine, sought to limit
Jewish immigration. Nonetheless, many Jewish settlements were established then and in
the century that followed. Some of them became the basis for the kibbutz (a symbol of Zionism's engagement with socialism), while others turned into modern, European-like cosmopolitan centers such as Tel Aviv. See Chapter 4: From a Dream to Glimmers of Reality.

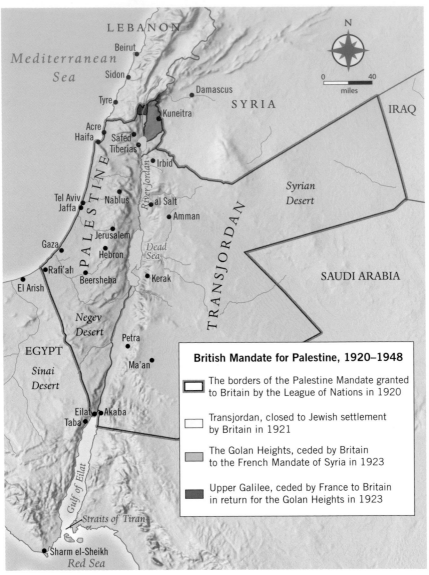

British Mandate for Palestine, 1920–1948

The borders of the Palestine Mandate granted to Britain by the League of Nations in 1920

Transjordan, closed to Jewish settlement by Britain in 1921

The Golan Heights, ceded by Britain to the French Mandate of Syria in 1923

Upper Galilee, ceded by France to Britain in return for the Golan Heights in 1923

MAP 3. BRITISH MANDATE FOR PALESTINE, 1920–1948: Following the defeat of the Ottomans in World War I, Palestine came under control of the British Empire in what is called the British Mandate for Palestine. The Balfour Declaration, issued in 1917, stated that the British looked with favor upon "the establishment in Palestine of a national home for the Jewish people," but it did not make explicit what the boundaries of that national home would be. The 1937 Palestine Royal Commission, however, intimated that it was meant to include the whole of historic Palestine, including both sides of the Jordan River. In 1948, the State of Israel was created on a small portion of Mandatory Palestine. See Chapter 5: The Balfour Declaration.

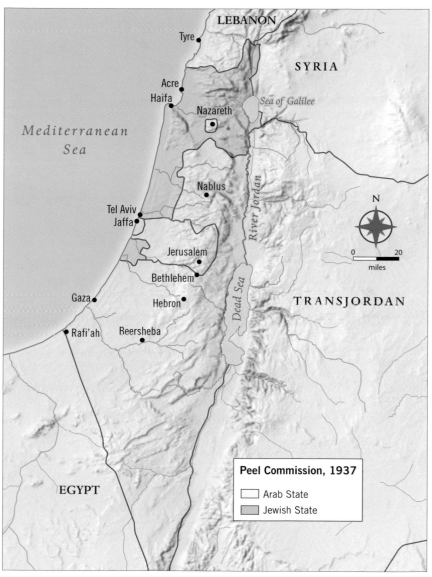

MAP 4. PEEL COMMISSION, 1937: The Peel Commission was a British delegation dispatched to Palestine in 1936 to find a solution to the widening conflict between the Jews and the Arabs. In 1937, when it issued its report, the commission became the first body to formally suggest dividing the land between Jews and Arabs (essentially the first version of a "two-state solution"). While the Yishuv, the Jewish community in Palestine, accepted the proposal, even if unhappily, the Arab leadership rejected it. See Chapter 6: Nowhere to Go, Even If They Could Leave.

MAP 5. UNITED NATIONS PARTITION PLAN, 1947: In 1947, the United Nations Special Committee on Palestine (UNSCOP) recommended the partition of Palestine into two states: one Jewish, one Arab. The United Nations General Assembly approved the plan, then called Resolution 181, on November 29, 1947. Though the land allocated to the Jewish state was but 12 percent of Mandatory Palestine, the Jewish community decided to accept the partition. The Arab leadership rejected it and launched what became Israel's War of Independence the next day. See Chapter 7: The Yishuv Resists the British, the Arabs Battle Partition.

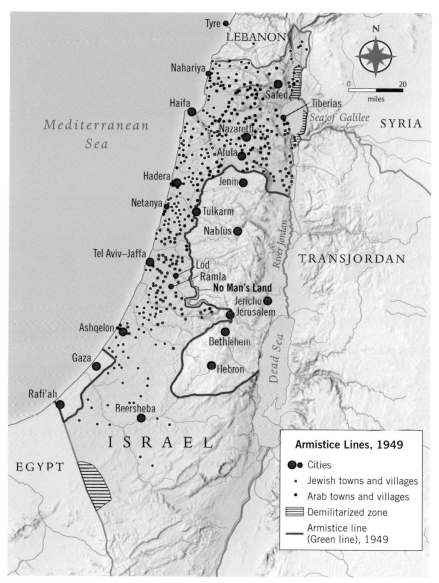

MAP 6. ARMISTICE LINES, 1949: During the War of Independence, Israel expanded its borders beyond what the United Nations had allocated to it in 1947. Though the Arab states at war with Israel refused to sign peace treaties with the Jewish state, the armistice agreements at the end of the war essentially became Israel's borders until the 1967 Six-Day War. See Chapter 8: Independence.

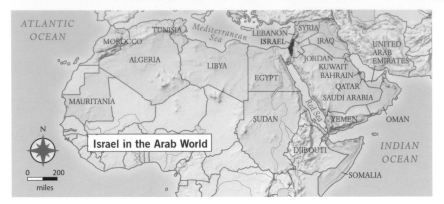

MAP 7. ISRAEL AND THE ARAB WORLD: After World War II, the Middle East was divided into the modern nation states that make up today's map. Until 1979, when Egypt became the first Arab nation to sign a peace treaty with Israel (Jordan later followed), the entire Arab Middle East was committed to Israel's destruction. Even the creation of a formidable military force has not entirely erased Israel's sense that it is a small island in a sea of hostile neighbors.

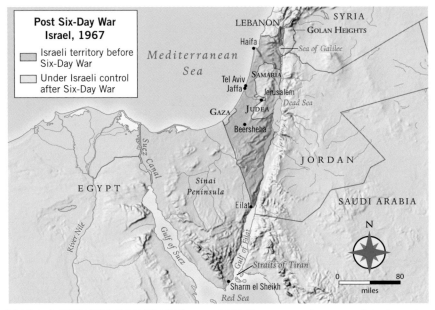

MAP 8. AFTER THE SIX-DAY WAR, 1967: With Egypt preparing to attack in June 1967 and its president, Gamal Abdel Nasser, threatening to destroy the Jewish state, Israel's air force launched a preemptive strike, essentially destroying the Egyptian air force before the war began. In six lightning days, Israel more than tripled its original size, gaining forty-two thousand square miles. It captured the Gaza Strip and Sinai Peninsula from Egypt, the West Bank of the Jordan River from Jordan, and the Golan Heights from Syria. Years later, Israel's pre-1967 borders would become the framework for peace negotiations and the proposed borders of an eventual Palestinian state. See Chapter 12: Six Days of War Change a Country Forever.

The Allon Plan

- ☐ Areas to be returned to Jordan
- ▨ Areas to be retained by Israel
- ○ Principal Arab towns in Jordan
- ○ Israeli settlements in 1970 to be annexed to Israel
- • Israeli settlements built in the two decades after the initial Allon Plan

Sea of Galilee

River Jordan

Jenin ○

Tulkarm ○

Kalkiya ○

Nablus ○

Mediterranean Sea

JORDAN

Ramallah ○

Jericho ○

Ma'ale Adurnmim ○

Jerusalem ●

ISRAEL

Bethlehem ○
Gush Etzion ○

Dead Sea

Hebron ○ Kiryat Arba ○

Gaza ○

GAZA

N

EGYPT

0 ——— 20
miles

MAP 9. ALLON PLAN, 1970: In 1970, Yigal Allon presented his proposal of what to do with the territories acquired by Israel during the Six-Day War. His plan suggested Israel create a bloc of settlements along the Jordan Valley to serve as an early-warning system for a potential attack from the east. The remainder of the West Bank would be returned to Palestinian or Jordanian rule. While the plan was never adopted as official Israeli policy, and was in fact rejected by Jordan, among others, many Israeli settlements were established in the areas suggested by Allon. The plan also became a harbinger of other proposed divisions of the West Bank that would follow decades later. See Chapter 13: The Burden of Occupation.

MAP 10. OSLO ACCORDS, 1993: The Oslo Accords were designed to be the first step in the creation of an eventual Palestinian state. The accords stipulated that the Palestinian Authority would gain control of the Palestinian territory in stages. Area A was transferred to the Palestinian Authority in the first stage of the enactment of the accords, Area B was under joint Israeli-Palestinian security control, and Area C was under the control of the Israelis. In the years following the accords, the agreement disintegrated following the assassination of Prime Minister Yitzchak Rabin and a surge in Palestinian violence. See Chapter 16: Taking a Page from the Zionists.

nothing he could do to turn the ship around, he informed Ben-Gurion.

Ben-Gurion understood that the ship's arrival would constitute a highly visible breach of the truce, but at the same time was loath to give up on such a desperately needed arms cache. The ship, which reached the Israeli shore on June 20, was ordered to sail to Kfar Vitkin (just north of Tel Aviv), where it was assumed UN observers might not see it. Yet there was no agreement between Ben-Gurion and Begin regarding what would happen with the arms. While Begin offered the vast majority to the IDF, he insisted on keeping 20 percent for his Irgun fighters, still struggling to hold out against the Jordanians in Jerusalem. Ben-Gurion dismissed the proposal out of hand. He feared that allocating any arms at all to the Irgun (even the Irgun in Jerusalem) would lend legitimacy to the idea of an army within an army.

News of the ship spread quickly, along with a rumor that Begin himself might appear on the beach at Kfar Vitkin. Irgun soldiers, anxious to meet the man who had been in hiding as they had been fighting under his command, deserted their units and made their way to Kfar Vitkin. This only confirmed Ben-Gurion's suspicion that Begin was up to something nefarious, so the next day, he called a meeting of the cabinet. Ben-Gurion told his ministers—falsely—that Begin had hidden the *Altalena* plan until the ship was already at sea. His long-standing mistrust of Begin now governed everything he said and did. He said to his cabinet:

> There are not going to be two States and there are not going to be two armies. And Mr. Begin will not do whatever he feels like. We must decide whether to hand over power to Begin or to tell him to cease his separatist activities. If he does not give in, we shall open fire.[33]

Yisrael Galili, the army's chief of staff, ordered IDF pilots—many of whom were those Americans and other volunteers who had been Allied pilots during World War II—to strafe the ship.

They refused. "We came here to fight for the Jews, not against the Jews," they said.[34]

By this time, Begin had boarded the ship and had instructed the Irgun men to use the cover of darkness to begin unloading the cargo. Begin received an ultimatum to hand over all the weapons to the IDF, but did not respond to it; he later claimed that the ultimatum was thoroughly unrealistic and gave him virtually no time to respond.

A firefight broke out between the Haganah forces and those loyal to the Irgun. The *Altalena* pulled away from shore and sailed south, toward Tel Aviv, and—in full view of hotel guests and beachgoers, reporters and UN observers—ran aground and could not move. Suddenly, Palmach fighters on the beach (the Palmach were the most hostile to the Irgun; among their commanders was Yitzhak Rabin) fired on the *Altalena*. Irgun fighters returned fire. Jews had begun to fire on Jews. Barely five weeks old, the Jewish state was on the verge of civil war.

More cannon fire stuck the ship, still heavily loaded with ammunition. Throughout, Begin instructed his men not to return fire. The ship was hit and the munitions on board began to explode. Begin, still on board, gave the order to abandon the ship; though he wanted to stay until the very end, his men forced him off the ship and got him to shore. As he was making his way to shore, bursts of gunfire were directed in his direction; many of those present were convinced that the Haganah men were trying to kill Begin. Shortly after Begin left the ship, the remainder of the ammunition caught fire, and the ship exploded. IDF soldiers, no doubt deeply ambivalent about what was unfolding so soon after Israel had declared independence, leaped into the water to save the *Altalena*'s passengers.

Meanwhile, on shore, the fighting continued. With Haganah and Irgun soldiers shooting at each other, the beginnings of a Jewish civil war moved from the waters of the Mediterranean to the streets of Tel Aviv. There were casualties on both sides. But Begin had insisted that his men not fire on Jews, and men on both sides understood that Israel could not afford a civil war. The firing ended.

All told, factoring in the firefight in Kfar Vitkin, the death toll included sixteen men from the Irgun and three from the IDF. One of those killed was Avraham Stavsky, who had been charged with the 1933 murder of Chaim Arlosoroff but was later exonerated. He had been one of the passengers on the *Altalena* and died just off the beach where Arlosoroff had been killed fifteen years earlier.

Begin took to the airwaves and delivered a radio address to his Irgun community that lasted over an hour. He reiterated his claim that the Irgun had done nothing wrong, yet even so, he reminded his men time and again, "Do not raise a hand against a brother, not even today." In what emerged as a refrain, he insisted that Jew not fight Jew, for "it is forbidden that a Hebrew weapon be used against Hebrew fighters." "There must not be a civil war with the enemy at our gates!" he virtually shouted in his radio address.

Ben-Gurion, incensed, refused to allow the dead Irgun men a burial in Tel Aviv.

Begin was vilified by some for having imported the arms. Yet others praised him for his pivotal role in bringing the fighting to an end (just as he had refused to attack the Haganah during the *Saison*). He would later claim that his greatest contribution to Israel was his having averted all-out civil war. Ben-Gurion also remained defiant in the aftermath, insisting that he had saved the country from a militia's uprising. The cannon that sank the *Altalena*, he insisted in a comment that was oft repeated, was so sacred that it deserved to "stand close to the Temple, if it is built."[35]

It was only in 1965 that David Ben-Gurion admitted, following a government inquiry into the *Altalena* affair, "Perhaps I was mistaken."[36]

More than anything else, what the *Altalena* came to represent in Israeli mythos was the understanding that for a state to be legitimate, all its military force had to be subject to the political echelon. In years to come, as Israelis watched Palestinian elected officials unable to rein in their multiple armed factions, they would say, "The Palestinians haven't yet had their *Altalena*."

THE NEXT PHASE of the war, which lasted only ten days, began
with the resumption of fighting on July 8, 1948 (the cease-fire had
been in effect for about a month). This phase of the conflict led to
one of the war's most controversial moments, including one battle
still much discussed.

This battle, the battle for Lydda, has become emblematic in the
"war of narratives" not only over Israel's War of Independence but
much of Israel's history. "Great wars in history eventually became
great wars about history," wrote Michael Oren, a leading historian
of Israel (and later Israel's ambassador to the United States),[37] and
no country in the world has evoked a "war about history" as vociferous as the one still waging about Israel.

Why is that? As Oren notes, "The unusual ferocity of the debate
over Arab-Israeli history is directly related to the singularly high
stakes involved. The adversaries are not merely vying for space on
university bookshelves, but grappling with issues that have a profound impact on the lives of millions of people: Israel's security,
the rights of Palestinian refugees, the future of Jerusalem."[38] Nor
is this exclusively a battle of Israelis versus Arabs; among Israelis
themselves, a group of scholars known as the "new historians"
have sought at numerous turns to upend Israel's mainstream narrative about the conflict. And they are unabashed about their aims.
As Israeli Ilan Pappe—a member of this group—put it, the goal is
to "reconsider the validity of the quest for a Jewish nation-state in
what used to be geographic Palestine."[39]

The war over history, then, is a war over Israel's legitimacy, and
therefore, over its future. It is thus not surprising that key moments
in the War of Independence, and particularly those that contributed to the flood of Palestinian Arabs leaving Israel (a politically
fraught issue to this very day), would become a key battleground
between these various schools of historians.

Lydda is a case in point. Jerusalem, under Jordanian attack,
was barely hanging on in the summer of 1948, and Ben-Gurion
was now determined to open another road to the city. To do so,

the military brass determined that it needed to capture Lydda, an Arab city of some twenty thousand inhabitants. Situated along the route from Tel Aviv to Jerusalem, Lydda's population had grown dramatically due to Arab flight from other towns during the fighting. The Transjordanian Arab Legion also had an infantry company of some 125 soldiers stationed there; both the soldiers and armed locals had long been preparing for battle against the IDF.

That battle came in the form of Operation Dani. On July 11, Israeli troops attacked the town but were unable to subdue it entirely. Later in the evening, an additional battalion moved into the city, taking over both the town's Great Mosque and the Church of St. George. The IDF ordered the population to report to the mosque and the church; soon, both structures were overflowing with people. According to most accounts, the Israeli troops later allowed the women and children to leave.

With about three hundred Israeli soldiers holding on to the city and fighters from the Arab Legion barricaded in the local police station to which they had retreated, a tense stalemate prevailed. The next day several more vehicles from the Arab Legion suddenly entered the city, spraying fire in all directions. Local fighters joined the renewed attack, firing at the Israelis from numerous buildings. Some of the sniping was coming from a smaller mosque in the city, from the top of which Arab snipers posed a deadly danger. The soldiers received an order to put an end to the Arab fire, and in the battle that ensued, Israeli forces fired an anti-tank grenade at the mosque. Though accounts differ, it is clear that there were many casualties.

Precisely how the fighting unfolded, how many Arabs died in the mosque and elsewhere, and how many of the dead were civilians remain the subjects of great debate. Some of the revisionist new historians have indicted the IDF's conduct at Lydda. One well-known Israeli author, summarizing their views, contended that "in thirty minutes, at high noon, more than two hundred civilians are killed.'[40] He continued accusatorially, suggesting that fault lay not only with the soldiers present but somehow with the larger movement of which they were a part, "Zionism instigated a human catastrophe in the Lydda Valley.'[41]

Many historians reject that revisionist conclusion categorically. In 2014, a highly regarded historian painstakingly reviewed archival evidence about the Lydda battle and demonstrated that the drive to upend Israel's narrative led revisionist historians to push too far and to skid off the evidentiary tracks. In Lydda, he demonstrates, the number of dead was far lower than the revisionist accounts suggest and those killed were almost exclusively combatants. While people on both sides died, no massacre of the sort the new historians described had taken place.[42]

Interestingly, even Benny Morris, at one point a member of the new historians school and very critical of the classic Israeli narrative, does use the word *massacre*. Nonetheless, he insists, whatever happened at Lydda has to be understood in the larger context of the war and the ways in which Israeli and Arab combatants conducted themselves:

> Lydda wasn't, however, representative of Zionist behavior. Before 1948, the Zionist enterprise expanded by buying, not conquering, Arab land, and it was the Arabs who periodically massacred Jews—as, for example, in Hebron and Safed in 1929. In the 1948 war, the first major atrocity was committed by Arabs: the slaughter of 39 Jewish co-workers in the Haifa Oil Refinery on December 30, 1947.
>
> True, the Jews went on to commit more than their fair share of atrocities; prolonged civil wars tend to brutalize combatants and trigger vengefulness. But this happened because they conquered 400 Arab towns and villages. The Palestinians failed to conquer even a single Jewish settlement—at least on their own. The one exception was Kfar Etzion, which was conquered on May 13, 1948 with the aid of the Jordanian Arab Legion, and there they committed a large-scale massacre.[43]

The War of Independence was a brutal war, a war of honor for the Arabs and a war of survival for the Jews. There were brutal acts on both sides; what Morris notes, though, is that on the Israeli side they were the exception. On the Arab side, he says, brutality was the rule.

When the battle in Lydda ended, the remaining Arab forces withdrew. The IDF and local Arab leadership reached an agreement that the population would leave the town and move to the east. Once again, fighting during the war had resulted in a long line of refugees leaving their homes. Shmarya Gutman, a Jewish archaeologist, witnessed the column of refugees and later recalled:

> A multitude of the inhabitants walked one after another. . . . Women walked burdened with packages and sacks on their heads. Mothers dragged children after them. Occasionally warning shots were heard. Occasionally, you encountered a piercing look from one of the youngsters in the column, and the look said, "We have not yet surrendered. We shall return to fight you."[44]

Everywhere one turned in the area, there were lines of devastated refugees. Jews were being pushed out of the Old City of Jerusalem. Arabs were fleeing Israel's north by the tens of thousands. Shortly thereafter, hundreds of thousands of Jews who lived in North African Arab countries would flee, some expelled and others pushed out by mistreatment or the threat of violence. Ultimately, seven hundred thousand Jews would have to leave Arab lands—and make their way to the newly founded state. For Jews and Arabs alike, it was a period of horrific dislocation. The anger and the bitterness these mass movements of people were engendering would poison the region for decades to come.

ON NOVEMBER 19, 1948, Natan Alterman published a poem in *Davar*, the Histadrut newspaper, which he titled *Al Zot* ("For This"). The poem does not mention a specific incident; it may have been a reference to Lydda (though several months had elapsed and it would have been strange for him to wait so long to respond to that battle), some other incident he did not identify, or a general sentiment about the ugliness of war. He wrote of a young man, "a lion cub flexing," on a jeep. He comes across an old man and woman, who out of fear, turn and face the wall along which they were walking. The boy smiles and says to himself, "I'll try out the gun." Then, says Alterman, "The old man just cradled his face in his hands, and his blood covered the wall." While we do not know which specific incident Alterman was reacting to, we do know how the country's leadership responded. Not only was Ben-Gurion not displeased with Alterman, he thanked him. Extraordinarily, even in the midst of the war, as soon as Ben-Gurion had read the poem, he wrote Alterman, saying:

> My dear Alterman,
>
> Congratulations—on the moral force and the expressive power of your most recent column in Davar. You have become the voice—a pure and loyal voice—for the human conscience. If that conscience is not active and does not beat in our hearts during these days—we will not be worthy of the achievements we have had thus far. . . . I am requesting your permission for the Ministry of Defense to reprint the column—no armed column in our army, even with all its weaponry, has [your poem's] power—in one hundred thousand copies and to distribute it to every soldier in Israel.
>
> With appreciation and with thanks,
> D. Ben-Gurion

Many people on both sides of the conflict suffered. What distinguished Israeli society then, though, and what would continue to characterize it in years to come was its almost compulsive tendency to self-critique. Still in its infancy, Israel was becoming a highly self-reflective society. Poets and politicians alike insisted that if Israel was to merit the independence it had recently achieved, it had to reflect the values of the tradition from which the dream of a Jewish state had emerged. That self-critical voice would become one of Israel's great strengths in the decades to follow.

BETTER EQUIPPED because of the weapons they had clandestinely imported during the first truce and single-minded in their determination to survive, Israeli forces gradually consolidated their gains throughout the country. The United Nations then pushed for a second truce, which would take effect beginning on July 19—bringing to an end ten days of intense fighting.

Just as with the first truce, both sides hemmed, hawed, and eventually agreed; and just as with the first truce, both sides used the quiet as an opportunity to rearm and to bolster troops and fortify their positions. Even while they feverishly prepared for the next round of fighting, Israelis sensed that the tide of the war had shifted, that the conflict might soon be over, and that they would win. Reveling in the respite, they even staged Jerusalem's first annual military parade on July 27, beginning a tradition that would continue for years.[45]

Meanwhile, the Arabs had begun to realize that the war to annihilate Israel had failed. They therefore set their sights on a new issue: the fate of the Arab refugees.

During the War of Independence, some seven hundred thousand Arabs fled their homes. Benny Morris has shown that the Arabs left for many different reasons. In Jaffa, Haifa, and other large cities and towns, urban society simply collapsed, particularly as the Arab leadership fled. In other cases, rumors of Jewish atrocities, the vast majority of them false, led Arabs to believe that fleeing was the only way to save their lives. In still other cases, Israel pushed Arabs out. Even Benny Morris understands that Ben-Gurion really had no choice. Ben-Gurion's responsibility was to create a viable Jewish state. And, says Morris, Ben-Gurion "understood the demographic issue and the need to establish a Jewish state without a large Arab minority."[46] Nothing else would have been viable.

By the war's end, these seven hundred thousand Palestinian refugees (almost precisely the number of Jews who would have to flee Muslim countries) had sought refuge in Lebanon, Syria, Jordan, and Gaza. The Arabs pressed Count Bernadotte, still working on behalf of the United Nations to keep the warring sides apart, to make the issue of Arab refugees central to any resolution of the conflict.

The Israelis insisted that they would not discuss the refugees as long as the Arabs continued fighting in an effort to destroy the Jewish state. So the Arabs shifted their approach, insisting that there would be no peace talks until the issue of the refugees was resolved. Resolving the refugee problem would not be a goal of the negotiations that would follow, but rather, had to be a precursor to any talks. Essentially, this meant that the refugee problem would forever remain unaddressed. From Israel's perspective, it seemed that rather than solving the problem of the refugees, Lebanon, Syria, and (to a lesser extent) Jordan chose to keep the refugees as an ace in their pocket. They would use this "asset" in future negotiations with the Zionist enemy—for even then, they were determined not to end the conflict until Israel no longer existed.

COUNT BERNADOTTE PRESSED ON, not only urging Israel to permit the refugees to return, but suggesting it relinquish the Negev, Jerusalem, the Haifa port (which would be internationalized), the international airport at Lydda (today, Ben-Gurion International Airport, Israel's largest), and more. Not only was Bernadotte ignoring the fact that Israel was now winning, but his proposal actually took away land that had been assigned to Israel by the UN partition plan. That stance, for many Israelis, impugned any pretense that Bernadotte was a fair arbiter. He was, many felt, undeniably an enemy who was now clearly siding with Israel's foes.

On September 17, 1948, four Lechi members, taking the matter into their own hands, donned IDF uniforms and assassinated Bernadotte, with the yet-unpublished draft of his plan in hand, in west Jerusalem. The international outcry was immediate, and Ben-Gurion was mortified. David Remez, minister of transportation and a signatory to the Declaration of Independence, said "Since the crucifixion of Jesus we have not had such an accusation directed at us."[47] Ben-Gurion was determined to snuff out any remaining embers of the Irgun and the Lechi, and he convinced the cabinet to give him broad powers to end acts of terrorism, including administrative detention without trial. The era of the Jewish underground, important as it had been in uprooting the British, was now over.

BEN-GURION UNDERSTOOD THAT TIME was not on his side. He had mobilized half of Israel's able-bodied male population and some of the women, and the conflict clearly could not go on endlessly. Yet there were still Syrian, Egyptian, and Jordanian forces in pockets of the land originally assigned to Israel under the partition plan, and Ben-Gurion wanted them out. So he pushed the IDF to establish control of those areas assigned to Israel, determined to bring the fighting to an end.

By the end of October, Syrian and Arab Liberation Army forces in the north were dislodged. By January 1949, the IDF had managed to push the Egyptians out of the portions of the Negev that had not been given to Israel in the partition plan—though Egypt held on to the Gaza Strip. (See Map 6.) The Jordanians, for their part, were also anxious for the war to be behind them. They and the Israelis had had an understanding to limit the scope of their fighting and to partition the land in such a way that the Jordanians would get the West Bank. No more battles were needed. The war was essentially over.

Some of Ben-Gurion's generals wanted to take the West Bank of the Jordan River, frustrated that Israel had forfeited an opportunity to establish a secure natural frontier, but Ben-Gurion demurred. He had several reasons. The last thing Israel needed, he believed, was to control an even greater number of Arab civilians. As it was, Ben-Gurion was worried about those Arabs who remained in Israel. They were Israeli, because they had stayed inside the state, but the only thing that distinguished them at that point from Israel's enemies on the other side of the line was that they had not fled, while their family members had. Ben-Gurion did not dare imagine that they yet had any loyalty to the new state.

Ben-Gurion was also concerned that the Americans would look askance on Israel taking more territory. No less important, Ben-Gurion chose not to conquer the West Bank because his mind had moved on to other challenges. He was, as Anita Shapira notes, "already immersed in the vital mission of bringing in masses of new immigrants and absorbing them."[48]

THE ARABS WERE RETICENT to sign armistice agreements, because, their denials notwithstanding, signing any agreement with Israel meant admitting that the battle to destroy the Jewish state had been lost. Eventually, though, Egypt signed on February 24, 1949; Lebanon, on March 23; and Jordan on April 3. Syria was the last to sign, on July 20, 1949.

Israel had secured the victory that the U.S. State Department had said it could not, but it nonetheless emerged from the war badly battered. Some six thousand Israelis had been killed—one-quarter of them civilians. This amounted to nearly 1 percent of the fledgling state's Jewish population. More than 500 women had been killed, 108 of them in military service.[49] Percentage-wise, the Palestinian Arabs lost roughly an equivalent number—about 1 percent of the civilian population.

The biggest losers in the conflict were Palestine's Arabs, who came to refer to this period as the Nakba, "the Catastrophe." Some seven hundred thousand Palestinian Arabs were displaced by the war and thousands more died. It was a terrible human toll.

That so many Palestinian Arabs had to leave their homes was undeniably heartbreaking. And Israel had, without doubt, played a role in their displacement. At the same time, however, what turned the heartbreak into genuine human tragedy was the decision of their new host countries to deliberately perpetuate their homelessness to foment international condemnation of Israel. Maintaining the refugee status of the Palestinians who had entered their countries gave the Lebanese, Syrians, Jordanians, and Egyptians a card they were intent on playing as the conflict unfolded.

Israel did precisely the opposite with Jews who were homeless. When hundreds of thousands of Jews evicted from Arab countries reached Israel's shores, the Jewish state granted them citizenship. One was a response of cynicism and manipulation, while the other was a commitment to peoplehood and a vision of a brighter future. Those differing responses made all the difference in what the future would hold for each population.

IN THE TWO YEARS that had passed since the UN vote on November 29, 1947, Israel had declared independence, had triumphed in a war that its Arab neighbors had initiated in order to destroy it and that many thought Israel could not survive, and had made tremendous progress on numerous fronts. Ben-Gurion, though, was anything but naive. He understood that the very existence of the Jewish state was anathema to Israel's Arab neighbors, and he assumed—correctly—that they would simply regroup in order to attack once again. Eventually, the war was bound to resume.

For now, though, the prime minister put war out of his mind and turned his attention elsewhere. It was time to build a nation.

FROM DREAMS OF A STATE TO THE REALITY OF STATEHOOD

Thus you shall say to the House of Jacob and declare to the children
  of Israel:
"You have seen what I did to the Egyptians,
how I bore you on eagles' wings and brought you to Me."

—Exodus 19:3–4

On January 25, 1949, an aura of sanctity pervaded the new state. Israel had been independent for some eight months, and on that day, with the war essentially over, it held its first national elections.

Given that it had been two thousand years since the Jews had been sovereign, the symbolic significance of these elections was lost on no one. Rabbi Moshe Yekutiel Alpert, an ultra-Orthodox rabbi, had served as the mukhtar (leader) of several Jewish communities in Jerusalem during the Mandate.

The time is 5:35 A.M. I woke up. Me, my wife and my brother R' Shimon Leib, and my brother in-law Rabbi Netanel Saldovin and my son, Dov. After drinking our morning coffee, we dressed in our Sabbath attire in honor of this great and sacred day, "because this is the day God has made to be happy and rejoice." (Psalms

118:24) Because after thousands of years or more of exile, that since the six days of creation, we have never been blessed with such a day, to be able to go and vote in a Jewish state. . . . "Blessed is the One who has kept us alive, sustained us, and brought us to this time."[1]

Alpert finished his coffee, and armed with his Israeli identity card, set out to the polls, which opened at six A.M. "The entire way I marched along as if it was [the holiday of] Simchat Torah,* as if I was carrying the Torah scroll in my arms and doing *hakafos,* simply because my Israeli identification card was in my hands. There were no limits to the happiness and joy I felt that very morning."

The first to arrive, Alpert waited just minutes before being handed a card, on which, along with his name, was stamped the number "1."

And then I experienced the holiest moment in my life, a moment that my father and grandfather were not privileged to experience. Only I, in my lifetime, was privileged to be at such a holy and pure moment. "Happy and blessed am I, happy and blessed is my portion!" I made the *shehecheyanu* blessing and I deposited the envelope in the ballot box.[2]

Only after he voted did Rabbi Alpert, who normally began his day with his morning prayers, return home to recite them.

Alpert was hardly alone in his enthusiasm. Tel Aviv was mobbed, but the crowds were patient. Police and ambulances who had been sent to one of the city's central traffic hubs reported that they had nothing to do.[3] In Netanya, as people waited in lines for the polls to open, they spontaneously began to sing *"Hatikvah,"* once the anthem of the Zionist movement and now the anthem of the Jewish state.

---

* Simchat Torah is one of the most joyous days of the Jewish calendar year, when Jews celebrate the gift of the Torah. In traditional communities, they dance in circles seven times—those dances are called *hakafot* or *hakafos.*

The 440,095 people who turned out to vote represented nearly 87 percent of those eligible. When the results were announced several days later, few were surprised that David Ben-Gurion's party, Mapai, had received 36 percent of the vote, giving them 46 out of the 120 seats of the Israeli Constituent Assembly, which a few weeks later became the Knesset, or parliament.*

The coalition in Israel's first Knesset was a broad-based one, including religious and secular, Jews and Arabs. It was composed of forty-six members of Mapai, two Arab members representing the Democratic List of Nazareth, sixteen members of the United Religious Front, five members of the Progressive Party, and four Sephardi List members. David Ben-Gurion—as head of the largest party—became prime minister and also assumed the role of minister of defense.† Ben-Gurion refused, in no uncertain terms, to include either the Communists or Menachem Begin's *Herut*

---

* Technically, these first elections were for a Constituent Assembly that would draft a constitution and then disband. But that Assembly decided to declare itself the legislature and put off the writing of a constitution.

The Knesset (its name taken from the Hebrew term for the Great Assembly, a Jewish legislative body in Talmudic times) was composed of 120 seats and used the same system of proportional representation that the Zionist congresses had employed. A political party that received a quarter of the vote, for example, would win 30 seats in the Knesset. Given the many competing parties, though, most typically received much smaller proportions of the vote, and prime ministers therefore had to cobble together coalitions of parties in order to control 61 seats, the minimum number for a majority of the 120. Because parties typically had dissimilar agendas, many coalitions were unhappy marriages from the outset. Small parties, by threatening to leave the coalition, could hamstring the prime minister, resulting in a tumultuous and unstable governmental system that has plagued Israel since its founding.

† Israeli prime ministers have the right to keep certain cabinet portfolios, which would normally be assigned to another minister, as their own realm of responsibility. Ben-Gurion was not the only prime minister to serve contemporaneously as minister of defense. Levi Eshkol and Yitzhak Rabin did the same. Other prime ministers retained other portfolios for themselves.

("Freedom") Party in the coalition; both, he felt, would under-mine the very values of the newly born state.

Israel's founders knew well that they owed everything to a man who had not lived to see the momentous accomplishment. So several months later, on August 17, 1949, Theodor Herzl's remains were moved to Israel, to what is now the national cemetery named Mount Herzl. Thousands of people followed a procession of sixty-four vehicles on the road from Tel Aviv to Jerusalem, which was lined with even more people. The procession's first stop was Mikveh Israel, where Herzl had first met with Kaiser Wilhelm in 1898. It then advanced to Rishon LeZion, where Herzl had spent his first night on the only visit he made to Palestine. Over the course of the journey to the capital, two hundred thousand—one-quarter of the country's inhabitants—came to pay their respects.[4] When the coffin finally lay in state in Jerusalem, some twenty thousand people lined up to walk past it. The entire cabinet and all members of the Knesset were present, as were some six thousand people who had been invited to attend. Herzl's casket was then covered with 380 small blue and white sacks filled with soil from settlements across the Land of Israel.[5] Herzl was then laid to rest on a hilltop in the capital of a newly founded state that was the product of his vision, for which he had given his life.

THE NEW NATION NEEDED a flag. Decades earlier, Herzl had written in *The Jewish State*, "I would suggest a white flag, with seven golden stars. The white field symbolizes our pure new life; the stars are the seven golden hours of our working-day."[6] On that score, Herzl did not get his way. In October 1948 the State of Israel adopted the flag that had represented the Zionist movement since the 1890s. A white background with a light-blue Jewish star in the center between two horizontal light-blue stripes, the flag was designed to evoke the image of the *tallit*, the Jewish prayer shawl. There were limits even to the hypersecularism of the new state.

The Knesset met for the first time on February 14, 1949. As the parliament did not yet have a permanent home, it met in the Jewish Agency building in downtown Jerusalem. Its first matter of business was appointing the country's president, Chaim Weizmann, who three decades earlier had been instrumental in convincing Lord Balfour to issue the Balfour Declaration. Though Israel's presidency is a largely honorific position, Weizmann's personal history brought gravitas to the office, and once elected, he rose to address the plenum.

Half a century earlier, in *The Jewish State,* Theodor Herzl had seen the renewal of a Jewish home as a model for people everywhere. "Whatever we attempt to accomplish there for our own welfare," he wrote then, "will have its powerful effect, promoting the happiness and wellbeing of all Mankind."[7] Now, at the dawning of the state that Herzl had envisioned, Weizmann said something very similar; what the Jews had just accomplished, he hoped, would inspire other oppressed peoples around the world.

Today we stand on the threshold of a new era. We leave the dawn light of provisional authority and enter the full sunshine of ordinary democratic rule. . . . Let us not be over-arrogant if we say that this is a great day in the history of the world. In this hour a message of hope and good cheer goes forth from this place in the Sacred City to all oppressed people and to all who are struggling for freedom and equality.[8]

Weizmann then turned his attention to the "tens of thousands of our brethren from countries near and far who are entering the gates of the country which stand wide open to receive them."[9] He continued, "It is our whole prayer that this gathering of exiles will increase and embrace an ever-larger multitude of our people who will strike roots here and work side by side with us in building the state and making our unproductive places fruitful again."[10]

A year later, on July 5, 1950, the Knesset enacted one of the most symbolic laws Israel would ever pass. It created the Law of Return, giving every Jew the right to immigrate to Israel. Another law then granted these immigrants full citizenship immediately upon arrival. "Home is the place where, when you have to go there, they have to take you in," Robert Frost wrote in his poem "The Death of the Hired Man,"[11] and for the Jewish people, the Jewish state was now that home. No longer would there be thousands of Jews in displaced persons camps in Europe with no one willing to take them in. Never again would ships loaded with Jews desperately seeking a place to live traverse the oceans. With the Law of Return, the era of the homeless, wandering Jew came to an end.

In the 1939 White Paper, the British had succumbed to Arab pressure and had essentially ended Jewish immigration; by outlawing the immigration that was necessary for the state to arise, the White Paper had for all intents and purposes revoked the Balfour Declaration. Now, by stating that there would be no limits on Jewish immigration to the State of Israel, the Law of Return was upending the British White Paper of 1939.

The Law of Return was also a symbolic overturning of the Nazis' Nuremberg Laws; the Nazis had defined as Jewish anyone with at least one Jewish grandparent, and the Law of Return used the same definition.* "If you were Jewish enough for the Nazis to seek to kill you," the Knesset essentially said, "you are Jewish enough to be taken in and protected by the State of Israel."

Jews began to migrate to the newly created state in unprecedented numbers. Between independence on May 15, 1948, and the end of 1951, no less than 686,739 Jews arrived in Israel. They hailed from seventy different countries and constituted, relative to the size of the population they were joining, the largest single migration of the twentieth century. It was, by any measure, one of the most extraordinary absorptions of immigrants in modern history:

---

* Traditional Jewish law defines as Jewish someone who is born of a Jewish mother or who converts to Judaism. The Law of Return thus opted for a definition of Jewishness derived not from Jewish tradition, but from Nuremberg.

100,000 new immigrants had arrived during the war, more than in any previous year. This was the first hint of what would happen later. In the first forty-two months of the state's existence, the average monthly number of new immigrants reached some 16,000. All in all 690,000 immigrants arrived in Israel, and within three years the Jewish population doubled. The vast scope of this immigration relative to the size of the host population [was] unheard of in any immigrant country.[12]

Israel would continue to be a country built by waves of immigration.* In 1948, merely 6 percent of the world's Jews lived in Israel; by 2015, that number had grown to some 46 percent, or almost half of the world's Jews.

Many of them came from Arab countries in North Africa. In 1948, when its Jewish population stood at approximately 75,000, Egypt began arresting Jews and confiscating their property. Cairo's Jewish Quarter was bombed. Jews left. In 1956, Egypt evicted another 25,000 of its Jews. Another wave of persecution in 1967 led to more emigration, and Egypt's Jewish population dropped to 2,500. By the 1970s, just a few hundred remained.

Libya was home to some 38,000 Jews in 1948. After pogroms by the Nazis, who had taken over Benghazi, and then by the local population after the Nazis left, 30,000 Jews fled, most of them in 1949. Even more decided to leave, worried about what lay ahead, after Libya became independent in 1951. In 1967, when Jews were subjected to pogroms again after the Six-Day War, virtually all the remaining Jews left.

Morocco had a Jewish population of 265,000 in 1948. With Israel's independence came riots and economic boycotts of Jews. By 1958, 65,000 Jews had left. In 1963, another 100,000 Jews were forced out

---

* By 2015, the Jewish population of Israel had increased more than tenfold since the country's creation in 1948. Estimates suggest that the population of the Jewish Diaspora dropped from 10.5 to 7.8 million over the same period.

of their homes. By 1968, only about 50,000 Jews remained. Similar stories unfolded in Algeria, Iraq, Syria, Tunisia, and Yemen. Some Jewish communities in Arab countries essentially ceased to exist; of the Jewish communities of Libya, Iraq, and Yemen, some 90 percent left within a decade of Israel's founding.[13] Between 1948 and 1951, a period of merely three years, over 37 percent of the Jews from Islamic countries immigrated to Israel.[14]

Even in non-Arab lands, similar patterns unfolded. Almost all the Jews of Bulgaria moved to Israel, and after the fall of Communism in 1991, nearly all the Jews of Albania did the same.

While arriving in Israel was no longer a problem for Jews, leaving their host countries was in some cases becoming increasingly problematic. The Iraqi government decided to let Jews leave, but only if they agreed to waive their citizenship. Most had estimated that between 10,000 and 40,000 Jews would leave. But they were shocked and embarrassed when more than 120,000—almost 90 percent of the entire Iraqi Jewish population—migrated. When the Iraqi government began to take note, they froze Jews' assets and began (in 1951) to prohibit Jewish families from taking their wealth with them. Almost overnight, they turned a previously affluent cohort of Iraqi society into a virtually penniless segment of Israel's new population.

To complete the immigration, which was becoming ever more dangerous for Iraq's Jews, Israel launched "Operation Ezra and Nehemiah"—named for the leaders of the Babylonian Jewish community who had led the return of Jews to Judea under Cyrus some twenty-five hundred years earlier. So eager was the Israeli government for Iraqi Jews to immigrate that the chief rabbinate—in violation of standard Jewish religious practice—allowed planes carrying the immigrants to fly on the Sabbath.

Ben-Gurion was keenly aware that the new country faced overwhelming financial challenges, but in a few areas, he was unwilling to let finances govern policy. One of those was immigration. Only massive immigration would give Israel the human capital it needed to survive, he knew, and he was committed to taking in Jews—

wherever they might be coming from—without regard for what financial burden even an enormous immigration might impose on Israel. When Levi Eshkol, then the treasurer of the Jewish Agency (later to become Israel's third prime minister) expressed concern about the massive Iraqi immigration, saying, "We don't even have tents. If they come, they'll have to live in the street,"[15] Ben-Gurion remained adamant. Israel would take in every Jew who wanted to immigrate to Israel.

That passionate commitment to immigration led to operations of epic proportions. One was "Operation Magic Carpet," in which the entire Yemenite Jewish community was flown to Israel between June 1949 and September 1950.* Yemenite Jews made their arduous way to prearranged collection points where DC-4 Skymaster planes, hired from Alaska Airways, flew them to Israel.[16] Israeli medical staff awaited them at the collection points to prepare the immigrants-to-be for their journey to Israel. In a massive airlift, Israel flew 45,640 people in transport planes from which the seats had been removed, enabling each plane to carry some 500 to 600 people on each flight. An additional 3,275 Jews were flown in from the seaport city, Aden, by the Red Sea. Golda Meir would later recall,

> Sometimes I used to go to Lydda and watch the planes from Aden touch down, marveling at the endurance and faith of their exhausted passengers. "Had you ever seen a plane before?" I asked one bearded old man. "No," he answered. "But weren't you very frightened of flying?" I persisted. "No," he said again, very firmly. "It is all written in the Bible, in Isaiah, 'They shall mount up with wings of eagles.'"† And standing there on the

---

* Egypt had closed the Suez Canal to all Israeli shipping, making passage by sea impossible.

† The official name for the operation was "On Eagles' Wings." "Magic Carpet" was a commonly used nickname. The phrase "on eagles' wings" actually comes from Exodus 19:4, not Isaiah: "You yourselves have seen what I did to Egypt, and how I carried you on eagles' wings and brought you to myself."

airfield, he recited the entire passage to me, his face lit with the
joy of a fulfilled prophecy—and of the journey's end.[17]

Many of the immigrants arrived needing urgent medical care;
three thousand children from Yemen arrived in grave condition.[18]
Hundreds lost their lives en route.

The Israel to which these immigrants came had virtually no
immigrant housing prepared for the hundreds of thousands of new
arrivals. It had almost no money with which to provide food, medical care, employment, and other basic needs to the immigrants.
It is impossible to understand the politics of the State of Israel in
the decades that followed—including the eventual demise of Ben-
Gurion's party's hegemony in the years to come—without appre-
ciating the resentment of the prime minister and his autocratic
nature that began to simmer in these early years.

At first, immigrants were housed in temporary camps, but conditions in them quickly became almost intolerable. The director of
one such camp near Haifa, heartbroken that Israel was unable to do
better, described the lives of these new immigrants:

> The immigrants were locked in, surrounded by barbed wire
> fences, and guarded by armed police. At different periods the
> crowding in the wood and stone huts left by the British Army
> reached brutal levels. Three times a day they stood in long lines
> for their food ration. The lines wound for kilometers around
> the medical and customs services. On more than one occasion,
> the immigrants had to wait for hours for their turn in the bath-
> houses, while the latrines overflowed. There was not always suf-
> ficient water in the camp, there were frequent power cuts, and at
> night, the camp was in total darkness.[19]

Desperate to improve the conditions, the government began
the construction of permanent housing in 1950. But Israel was a
state with enormous challenges on many fronts, and construction

lagged behind schedule. So Israel developed *ma'abarot* ("transit camps"), designed to alleviate the terrible conditions of the immigrant camps and to serve as temporary dwelling places until "real" housing was available.

Soon, though, conditions in the *ma'abarot* were just as bad as they had been in the immigrant camps, and for many immigrants, the *ma'abarot* became permanent housing. In the years to come, some of the *ma'abarot* morphed into small cities, and often, into Israel's poorest cities. As most of the residents of the *ma'abarot* were Mizrachi (Middle Eastern) Jews, these camps created a groundswell of resentment that would fester for decades. That resentment and the growing number of Mizrachim would eventually make them a powerful political force with which the Labor Party would have to reckon.

Even with limited resources, another issue to which Ben-Gurion was deeply committed was free childhood education. Long the foundation of Jewish community life, education had been a focus of the early Zionist congresses. The Yishuv had built dozens of educational institutions, and if the new state was to thrive, education was going to have to continue to play a major role. In 1949, the Knesset enacted the Compulsory Education Law, one of its first laws, which called for free education for all children between the ages of five and thirteen. The state adopted the three existing parallel systems for Jewish children—a general school system, a politically socialist school system (which was abandoned shortly later), and a religious Zionist school system. A school system for the ultra-Orthodox community was established and the state took responsibility for the already existing Arab education system.

Prior to 1948, schools for Arab children had been run through the British government for public schools and through a variety of religious institutions for private schools. Even as late as 1948, however, only 30 percent of Arab children were enrolled, most of them in elementary school; there were only ten Arab high schools. Israel changed that situation entirely when it applied the Free Compulsory Education Law to Arab children as well.[20]

DECADES EARLIER, THE OFTEN-PRESCIENT Herzl had written that "if the Jews should indeed return home, the next day they would discover that for many years they have not belonged together. They have been rooted for centuries in their homelands, nationalized, different from each other."[21] He was right. In ways that would color Israel's emerging society and its politics for decades, the massive and unprecedented flow of immigration created cultural clashes as well.

Some of these became evident even before the new immigrants landed on Israeli soil. On one transit ship, the *Pam Crescent,* the Hungarian girls frequently sunbathed in their bikinis to the shock and dismay of Moroccan men who came from communities where women were never so exposed.

Even those arriving from the Middle East—and grouped together under the terms "Mizrachim"—were actually very different from each other. As one historian notes:

From Iraq, the professional and educated elite departed. From Kurdistan, virtually all the immigrants were illiterate. In Egypt, Jews considered themselves to be part of the "European" community. They were both the mainstay of the business elite and the founders of the Communist party. In Yemen, they were artisans and peddlers who embraced Zion with a messianic expectation.[22]

Different though they were in many respects, these Jews often encountered a widespread condescending worldview on the part of the European immigrants who had been part of the previous major aliyot, who had developed the Yishuv and who were now running the country. The issue was not racism—it had nothing to do with skin color. It was a matter of cultural elitism, a genuine belief that European culture was the more developed of the cultures, and that it would be best for the newborn country if that elite culture would be the one that was taught to all.

It did not help, of course, that most of the Mizrachi immigrants had brought meager financial resources to the fledgling state. Some had long been poor in their countries of origin, while others had been stripped of their wealth by the countries that expelled them. Even when they did manage to arrive with some assets, the state often assumed that immigrants from North African countries or Iraq were destitute.

Ben-Gurion, the great advocate of Jewish immigration, was no exception to this elitist tendency, and wrote

> The dispersions that are being terminated [that is, entire communities, such as the Bulgarian and Iraqi Jews, that were liquidated through immigration to Israel] and which are gathering in Israel still do not constitute a people, but a motley crowd, human dust lacking language, education, roots, tradition or national dreams. . . . Turning this human dust into a civilized, independent nation with a vision . . . is no easy task, and its difficulties are no less than those of economic absorption.[23]

Determined to make the state as culturally advanced as it could possibly be, Ben-Gurion went so far as to suggest segregating schools and educating Mizrachi and Ashkenazi children separately, worrying that Israel would become "Levantine" and "descend" to be "like the Arabs."[24]

To avoid having Ashkenazi children "descend" to the level of Mizrachim, many new communities had an unwritten rule of segregation. New residents to these forming communities had to be approved, and not surprisingly, many of the new Mizrachi immigrants were denied a place. They were simply told that they were "not attuned to the community."[25]

This dimension of Israel's early years, aside from sowing the seeds of later political seismic shifts, was recognized by many even in the Ashkenazi world as far from Israel's finest moment. Leading Ashkenazim in the entertainment world understood that Israel, though admittedly beset by numerous financial and other challenges, was not living up to its vision of how it would treat incoming

Jews. Perhaps the best-known treatment of this issue in popular Israeli culture was the 1964 Israeli film *Sallah Shabati*, directed by the
satirist Efraim Kishon (himself an immigrant from Hungary and
a survivor of the Holocaust, including the Sobibor concentration
camp). The film, interestingly, was the first from Israel to garner
international recognition and was nominated for an Oscar for Best
Foreign Film.

Sallah Shabati is the name of the main character of the story
(though his name, ostensibly a Mizrachi name, was also a play on
the words for *selichah she-bati*, or "forgive me for coming"), who
upon arrival in Israel is tossed into a transit camp. Mired in challenging living conditions and subject to a dismissive European
culture he does not understand, Sallah Shabati struggles to make
sense of his new life in the Jewish state. The movie traces his often-
hilarious attempts to both earn a living and to restore the sense of
dignity he had had in his native country (presumably Yemen, as
Sallah Shabati is meant to sound like a Yemenite name).

It was precisely because *Sallah Shabati* struck such a powerful
nerve that it became such a success. Its skewering of the kibbutzim
for not being more open to immigrants aroused the resentment
of kibbutz members—but probably because they recognized themselves in its portrayal. *Sallah Shabati* was, even more important, a
reminder to Israelis that getting Jews to Israel was only the state's
first step in living up to its obligations to these people who now
made the Jewish state their home.

THE MASSIVE IMMIGRATION PRESENTED Ben-Gurion with the
challenge of forging a state out of such different masses of people.
He grew determined to impress on Jews of all backgrounds not
only the state's political authority, but its moral and cultural centrality as well. In his mind, it was imperative that everyone and
everything be subordinate to the newly formed state. "A state is
more than a formal entity, framework, regime, international status, sovereignty, or army," he said. "The state does not exist unless

it has been internalized inside people's hearts, souls, and consciousness. A state is mental awareness, a sense of responsibility . . . [that
connects] all the people, the citizens of the state."[26] He even created a term for what he was trying to create: *mamlachtiyut*. There is
no adequate English translation of the term, but "statism" or "state
consciousness" comes closest.

It was in the realm of *mamlachtiyut*—his absolute determination to build a national culture with the state at its core—that Ben-
Gurion's genius as well as his tendencies to the autocratic were
most on display. With astonishing determination and wisdom, Ben-
Gurion led the charge to build the state's institutions and culture.
The Histadrut, which he had helped lead decades earlier, became
a powerhouse, responsible for workers' rights, education, health
care, some banking, and more. To many workers, the Histadrut
was the way that Ben-Gurion's government cared for them. As one
laborer noted years later, "Just as the religious believe that God pro-
tects them, I knew that the Histadrut was taking care of me."[27]

At the same time, so determined was the new prime minister to
build the new state, so convinced was he that only he could do it,
that many other considerations became secondary. Israel's Declaration of Independence, for example, had stipulated that the Knesset
would ratify a constitution by October 1, 1948. But Ben-Gurion was
anxious to avoid the battles between the fledgling state's religious
and secular powers, a political and cultural conflict that might derail his efforts at state-building. Ben-Gurion also understood that
a constitution might well create a judiciary that could strike down
laws, would entrench the electoral system of proportional representation that made it impossible for a party to win a majority, and
could, in myriad ways, curtail the powers of the prime minister.*

---

* Years later, Menachem Begin, the head of the opposition, would assail
Ben-Gurion for not having ratified a constitution. Yet Begin had not
raised vigorous opposition to Ben-Gurion's delaying the constitution,
both because his own party was divided on matters of religion and state,
and because as a staunch believer in individual rights, he may have feared

For the long run, he favored a role for the prime minister that would be governed by standard democratic limits, but for the time being, he felt that he needed the broad powers that not defining his role allowed him.* So he delayed the adoption of a constitution—a document that to this day Israel has never ratified.

Worried that the Palmach, the Yishuv's most elite military unit, was too linked to the political Left and determined to create an apolitical military whose sole loyalty would be to the state, Ben-Gurion dismantled the Palmach in September 1948—to the great dismay of many, who felt he had undone one of the great institutions of the Yishuv.

For all intents and purposes, Ben-Gurion also banned television and he refused to allow the establishment of a government TV station. Even when Yigal Yadin, who had been a senior officer in the Haganah and was now the IDF's chief of staff, claimed that television could help immigrants as an educational and unifying medium, Ben-Gurion refused to back down. He claimed that television's lowbrow culture would be terrible for society as a whole.† The government also controlled the airwaves. The two bodies that governed radio broadcasting—the Broadcasting Authority and the army radio station—were both under the aegis of the government.

There was a vibrant press, but even there, Ben-Gurion exerted pressure. Ben-Gurion made clear to the press that if they cooperated with the government, they would get information that they could not find elsewhere, sometimes from the prime minister himself.[28] The press was often merciless in attacking Ben-Gurion; that tradition of skewering the political echelon persists to the present.

---

that a socialist Ben-Gurion government would ratify a constitution more sympathetic to the needs of the collective than to individuals' rights.

* Neither Ben-Gurion nor any prime minister who followed passed a constitution. Israel has a category of laws known as Basic Laws, which effectively function as a constitution, but a constitution as such—despite the pledge of the Declaration of Independence—has never been ratified.

† Television was introduced to Israel in the mid-1960s, under Moshe Sharett's tenure as prime minister.

Ben-Gurion, in turn, sought to use what power he had to try to shape how certain issues were reported.

No issue better illustrates the perception of Ben-Gurion's heavy-handed commitment to *mamlachtiyut* than the accusation— never proven but passionately believed by many in the Yemenite community—that the government took babies born to Yemenite mothers shortly after their arrival in Israel between 1949 and 1952, when they were living in *ma'abarot*, and gave them to Ashkenazi families.[29] Over time, the government established three commissions to investigate the charges and concluded that there were no cases where this had clearly happened. As late as 2001, a government commission looked into over 800 cases of missing infants and concluded that 750 of the children had died. The other 56 of them remain a mystery.[30] Many Israelis, including Yemenite families, remain convinced that their children were stolen and given to families of higher socioeconomic standing for the "children's benefit." Whatever the case, the mere accusation is a reflection of how life felt to those who became Israel's underclass in the country's trying early years.

Ben-Gurion's focus on *mamlachtiyut* clearly led to excesses, and Israeli society has been grappling with the implications of many of those policies ever since. Yet Ben-Gurion also faced enormous challenges. He had founded a state and now had to build a country out of new citizens who had long seen governments as entities that one evaded, deceived, and cheated. That was certainly true of the Middle Eastern Jews who came to Israel, and even those from Europe had come to Palestine and then to Israel with no love for the governments they were escaping. Life under the British during the Mandate had imbued the Jews of the Yishuv with much the same sentiment. Fashioning a coherent, stable, and unified society and democracy out of that variegated human raw material was not going to be easy, and Ben-Gurion understood that. There were excesses, but there was also vision and great genius. Given all the trials Israeli society was yet to face, it is quite possible that it was precisely Ben-Gurion's sometimes heavy-handed determination to create a society with a devotion to state and government at the center that enabled a fledgling Israel to survive.

ANOTHER POPULATION THAT PRESENTED Ben-Gurion with significant challenges was the religious community. In the early years of political Zionism, long before the state was established, Europe's ultra-Orthodox Jews had refused to participate in the movement to create it. Theologically, some of their leaders argued that Zionism was forcing God's hand; faithful Jews should wait for God to end the exile, rather than trying to end it (by returning to Palestine) on their own. Others saw in Zionism's overt secularism an outright abomination. These Jews, who call themselves Haredim,* also created a political party, which was vehemently opposed to anything that smacked of Zionism. They expelled dissidents, often dividing families in the process. Leaving for Palestine, its leaders said, was utterly forbidden and a violation of everything Judaism stood for.

It was Hitler who changed that. By the end of the Holocaust, many Haredi communities had been destroyed, some literally without a trace. Hundreds of thousands of Haredi Jews had been murdered, gassed, and burned. Though they found the Yishuv's hypersecularism misguided, even abhorrent, the Haredim could no longer deny that the Zionists had been right about Europe.

So their stance regarding Zionism began to soften, and they moved from a vehement *anti*-Zionism to an ambivalent *non*-Zionism. They continued to rail against Zionism's secularism, comparing Mapai to the Hellenized Jews of the Greek period. And Ben-Gurion, they were convinced, was intent on waging ideological war against them. If they did not push back, the state would educate their children in mainstream Zionism's nonreligious (actually antireligious) tradition and would pressure them to change their way of life.

---

* The word *Haredim* appears in Isaiah 66:5 and means "those who tremble before God."

Grudgingly, they entered Israeli politics. They signed the Declaration of Independence. Once the state was established, they would have preferred to stay apart from the state's institutions, but doing so would have precluded them from having a role in shaping Israel's policies and character. Gradually, they became increasingly involved in Israel's political process.

Ben-Gurion, for his part, did not have a long-term plan for how to handle the Haredim, for he was convinced that their ultra-Orthodox way of life was but a vestige of European Jewish life that would soon disappear. He did not need yet another battle on his hands, and so—not terribly concerned about their long-term role in Israeli politics—he agreed to maintain the status quo on matters of religion to which he had agreed in 1947. The Sabbath would be a public day of rest, government and army kitchens would be kosher, religious law would govern matters of personal status such as marriage, divorce, and conversion, and the religious communities would maintain their autonomy in matters of education.

Politics made for very strange bedfellows. Because Ben-Gurion was deeply suspicious of the political Left and the Communists—and refused to even consider including Menachem Begin's *Herut* Party in the coalition—he had little choice but to include the third-largest party, the United Religious Front, which was actually an amalgam of two religious Zionist parties and two religious non-Zionist parties. The Haredim used their leverage (by leaving the coalition, they could bring the government down and theoretically force new elections) to establish an independent school system (in which students were taught virtually no non-religious subjects) and to procure an exemption from military service for their sons so that the young men could continue studying in *yeshivot* and be spared exposure to the secular Jews they would undoubtedly encounter during military service.

Ben-Gurion was wrong about the Haredim disappearing. Their numbers ultimately grew dramatically, and they now constitute a massive economic and political force in Israel. They exert significant political pressure on governments both left and right, while still refusing (with rare exception) to have their members serve as ministers so as to prevent them from giving tacit approval to government decisions that go against Jewish law.

It was in the matter of exemptions from military service where the folly of Ben-Gurion's decision was most apparent. Whereas in Ben-Gurion's time, 400 exemptions from military service were given each year, by 2010, the number of Haredim excused from military service through the same arrangement would reach 62,500 annually—an increase of 15,000 percent, when Israel's population had grown only 1,200 percent in the same period.[31]

AFTER THE WAR OF INDEPENDENCE, the Arab population of Israel numbered 156,000, about 20 percent of the country's total population. Most lived in the Negev (those were largely the Bedouin) and in the Galilee, in an area known as the "Little Triangle" (which had been transferred to Israel by Jordan as part of the armistice agreement). Poorly organized as they had been under the Ottomans and the British, they had had no effective leadership. To make matters worse, whatever leadership they did have between the early 1920s to the late 1940s had fled abroad, leaving behind those who were, on balance, poorer, less educated, and less capable of playing leadership roles. That flight of Palestine's Arab leadership would shape the plight of Israel's Arabs for decades to come.

Israel's Arabs posed a significant challenge for Israel. The Declaration of Independence, of course, had promised "full and equal citizenship and due representation in all its provisional and permanent institutions," and there is little doubt that Ben-Gurion was committed to that ideal. At the same time, Israel's leaders recognized that it was only accidents of history—who had fled and who had not—that determined who was now a Palestinian refugee residing in Lebanon, Syria, and Jordan, and who was an Israeli citizen living inside the borders of the newborn state. For that reason, Israel's Arabs had never been drafted into the army. In 1954, the government decided to draft Arabs, and after the decision was reported in the press, some sixty thousand Arabs volunteered to join the IDF.[32] In the end, though, the country got cold feet. Would Israeli Arabs really go to war against armies on the other side of the line that included—quite literally—members of their own family? The government therefore never drafted Israeli Arabs in large numbers. With time, the reasons for why shifted. In the early years of the state, the Jewish majority was worried about their loyalty. Decades later, very few Arabs even wished to serve.

The worry about Israel's Arab population and its loyalty to the new state had much more far-reaching consequences than the military draft. Much of Israel's leadership was understandably worried that the Arabs inside Israel were no less hostile to the new state than were those who had fled it and who now lived in enemy countries. Could they be trusted? Were they already, or might they become, a fifth column and undermine Israel's security? Ben-Gurion was convinced to impose a military government on Israel's Arabs. It was an ironic decision, given that the military government Israel imposed was based on the British Mandate Defense Laws that had been used against the Yishuv. Under the military government, Israel's Arabs were tried by military courts and their freedom of movement was restricted (they had to obtain permission to leave their villages), opportunities for higher education were de facto severely limited, and employment in the center of the country was difficult to find. Even elementary education was affected; under the military administration, the security services determined who could teach in Arab schools, and not always on the basis of their pedagogical skills.[33] With the exception of the Communist Party, Arabs were for the most part not included in Jewish political parties.[34]

As Israel became more secure and less worried about an internal fifth column, many Israeli leaders—including Menachem Begin, whom Ben-Gurion was still portraying as a fascist—insisted that given Israel's commitment to democracy, the time had come to end the military administration that then governed Israel's Arabs. Years later, in 1966, under Levi Eshkol's much softer premiership, Israel abolished the system.*

The military administration over Israel's Arabs was a response to a very real challenge. Yet it had a long-term effect on Israel's Arabs and their attitude to the state, and would thus color Israel's politics and policies for decades.

SURPRISINGLY, AT LEAST TO Ben-Gurion, there was one major Jewish community virtually unaffected by the veritable miracle of the fulfillment of the ancient vision of the "ingathering of the exiles."† As hundreds of thousands of Jews were streaming to Israel from Europe and Arab countries from which they had been banished, fewer than two thousand came from the United States, which had a Jewish population of over five million.

Ben-Gurion, an ideologue to the very core, was disgusted. Years after Israel's creation, Ben-Gurion recalled with some bitterness, "For hundreds of years, a question-prayer hovered in the mouths of the Jewish people: would a country be found for this people? No one imagined the frightening question: would a people be found for the country when it would be created?"³⁵ Jews in dangerous

---

* Eshkol, an underrated prime minister, relaxed several of Ben-Gurion's stances, including Ben-Gurion's refusal to allow Jabotinsky, the father of Revisionist Zionist and the ideological forefather of Menachem Begin, to be buried in Israel. In 1964, both Jabotinsky and his wife, in accord with Jabotinsky's request in his will, were reinterred in Jerusalem in the national cemetery on Mount Herzl. (Shmuel Katz, *Lone Wolf: A Biography of Vladimir [Ze'ev] Jabotinsky* [Fort Lee, NJ: Barricade Books, 1995], p. 1790.)

† The "ingathering of the exiles," the notion that the Jewish people would one day be regathered to its ancestral homeland, was a central dimension of the narrative that the Jewish people had told about itself—and about its future—for millennia. The Bible promises the ingathering long before it tells of the people's exile: "The Lord your God will restore your fortunes and take you back in love. He will bring you together again from all the peoples where the Lord your God has scattered you." (Deut. 30:3–4)

places or in places where they could not stay came to Israel. Those who were comfortable did not come.

While Ben-Gurion compared American Jews to the Jews of Babylonia who preferred to stay in exile after King Cyrus had permitted them to leave, American Jews did not think of themselves as being in exile. Rather, they claimed that after two thousand years of not living in Zion, dispersion was now a normal dimension of Jewish life. Why did Ben-Gurion believe that they had some obligation to uproot themselves from a secure, increasingly prosperous existence and move to a country that was barely surviving?

In fact, precisely because they did not believe that they were in exile, despite the fervent support among many American Jews for the budding state, some leading American Jews had actually been opposed to the idea of the creation of a Jewish state. The American Council for Judaism, then a national American Jewish organization, existed primarily to argue against the creation of the state; it not only engaged in virulent anti-Zionist propaganda, but also helped Arab spokespeople prepare their speeches at the United Nations when the decision on partition was pending.

Most Jewish groups, though, did not go that far, even if they shared some ambivalence about what statehood would do to Judaism and to the position of American Jews. The American Jewish Committee (AJC), perhaps the most important and powerful American Jewish communal institution at the time, did not reject the idea of a Jewish state and would certainly not act against it— but neither was it willing to grant to Israel the role of the center of the Jewish world. Even Jacob Blaustein, president of the American Jewish Committee, told his membership that when the AJC agreed to support the 1947 partition plan, that was largely because a Jewish state would solve a demographic problem. "We had cooperated" in the approval of partition, he said, "in the conviction that [a Jewish state] was the only practicable solution for some hundreds of thousands of the surviving Jews of Europe."[36] Ben-Gurion saw Israel as a rebirth of Jewish peoplehood; many of American Judaism's leaders either opposed the idea of a Jewish state, or saw it as merely a solution to the challenge of resettling Europe's homeless Jews.

Indeed, no lesser a figure than Albert Einstein, as close as one could get to Jewish royalty in the United States, told celebrants at a Passover Seder before World War II, "My awareness of the essential nature of Judaism resists the idea of a Jewish state with borders, an army, and a measure of temporal power." History had changed the Jew, he felt. "I am afraid of the inner damage Judaism will sustain— especially from the development of a narrow nationalism within our ranks. We are no longer the Jews of the Maccabee period."[37] Even Israel's creation changed his view only marginally. "I have never considered the idea of a state a good one, for economic, political and military reasons," he told a friend. "But now, there is no going back, and one has to fight it out."[38] It was hardly an inspiring endorsement.

After the state was created, Blaustein made clear to Ben-Gurion that the leadership of the American Jewish community would not tolerate Israel overstepping its bounds. In a major position paper, he wrote:

> American Jews—young and old alike—Zionists and non-Zionists alike—are profoundly attached to this, their country. America welcomed our immigrant parents in their need. Under America's free institutions, they and their children have achieved that freedom and sense of security unknown for long centuries of travail. We have truly become Americans, just as have all other oppressed groups that have ever come to these shores.
>
> We repudiate vigorously the suggestion that American Jews are in exile. The future of American Jewry, of our children and our children's children, is entirely linked with the future of America. We have no alternative; and *we want no alternative*.[39]

Since America was not exile, Blaustein warned Israel, pleas to American Jews to immigrate to the Jewish state were both misplaced and bound to fail. As for Ben-Gurion's claim (and that of many of Israel's leaders) that Israel was now *the* center of the Jewish world or *the* spokesman for Jews everywhere, Blaustein was equally direct:

> [T]here can be no *single* spokesman for world Jewry no matter
> who that spokesman might try to be.[40]

Blaustein's statement was a direct attack on many of the assumptions of both the Zionist movement and many of Zionism's
leaders. Ever since the First Zionist Congress in 1897, Zionists had
seen themselves as the central address for the world's Jews. As the
Nazis had eradicated Polish Jewry, American Jews were now the
largest and most significant Jewish community in the world—and
they were warning Israel to back off that sentiment. As for immigration, Blaustein was equally clear: the Jews who would move to
Israel would be mostly those who had nowhere else to go. Most
American Jews were unlikely to budge.

In many respects, despite a shift in rhetoric, not much has
changed. American Jews have never moved to Israel in significant
numbers, and the disproportionate majority of those who did make
aliyah were from the Orthodox community, which comprised
about 10 percent of American Jews. Ninety percent of America's
Jewish community has never produced any statistically significant
immigration to Israel.

American Jewish attitudes to Israel did warm considerably in
the late 1960s (after the Six-Day War) and the early 1970s, and commitment to Israel became one of the pillars of American Jewish
identity. With time, however, Israel's role as a centerpiece of Jewish
identity in the United States began to wane. The rise of Palestinian
nationalism, the ongoing conflict with the Palestinians, and American Jewish concern over Israel's continued presence in the West
Bank would later erode some of that enthusiasm. The phenomenon
that so distressed Ben-Gurion in the state's early years would persist for generations to come.

HIS DISAPPOINTMENT IN AMERICAN Jews notwithstanding, Ben-

Gurion presided over a project of immigrant absorption of unprecedented proportions. Never in human history had such a small population absorbed so many immigrants so successfully. The *ma'abarot* were built, but eventually dismantled. With time, Mizrachim began to assert themselves and made their way into the center of Israeli culture and political power. Military administrative rule over Israeli Arabs was ended. And out of the motley mass of Jews from all across the globe, many indigent and illiterate, Ben-Gurion built a state and a society. Nothing was more astounding than the numbers of immigrants relative to the population—"unheard of in any immigrant country"—and the fact that a new democracy had been forged out of immigrants who came mostly from nondemocratic countries. Of the many states created after World War II, Israel is among the very few that has remained democratic to its core.[41]

Life in Israel would remain complicated and dangerous for many decades, but most Israelis continued to believe that, whatever the challenges, they were part of a project so surprisingly successful that it seemed—even to many secularists—almost cosmically extraordinary. Nor would they lose sight of the fact that their state might never have come into being were it not for the uniquely talented and visionary leader the country had in David Ben-Gurion, not only its first prime minister, but in more ways than could be counted, the man who against all odds had turned Herzl's dream into a state.

ISRAEL ENTERS THE INTERNATIONAL ARENA

We mustn't flinch from the hatred . . . of Arabs, who live around us and are waiting for the moment when their hands may claim our blood. We mustn't avert our eyes, lest our hands be weakened. That is the decree of our generation . . . to be willing and armed, strong and unyielding, lest the sword be knocked from our fists, and our lives severed.

—Moshe Dayan, eulogy for Roi Rotberg, 1956

In the days of the Mandate, there had been numerous attacks on Jews, but British officials had been able (when they wished) to identify the attackers and administer punishment. In the postarmistice Middle East, however, it was increasingly difficult for Israel to identify the culprits in these attacks, especially because they often traversed the border from Jordan or Egypt. While during the Mandate, the British had had a stake in maintaining law and order in the region, with the British gone, the governments of Arab countries bordering on Israel had no such interest. Indeed, for them, the less settled Israel's borders were, the better. When infiltrators would sneak into Israel to tend unmanned farmland (which they claimed was theirs), to loot border villages, or to carry out violent and often deadly attacks, they could then return across the border, where Arab officials were ambivalent at best about imposing any sort of punishment.

By 1953, the State of Israel was five years old. The War of Independence had ended more than four years earlier, but Israel's citizens now faced regular attacks by these Palestinian infiltrators crossing the Jordanian and Egyptian borders. The attacks were relentless. In the three years following independence, there were *thousands* of such infiltrations and attacks each year.[1]

On October 13, 1953, Susan Kanias, aged thirty-two, and her three young children were sound asleep in their home in the small town of Yehud, just north of Lod (formerly Lydda), near the narrowest section of Israel. A mere nine miles separated the Mediterranean Sea on the west and the armistice line on the east; located almost equidistant between the sea and the border, Yehud was less than five miles from the armistice line, and like many villages, eminently vulnerable. In the dark of night, Palestinian infiltrators crossed the border, made their way to her home, and lobbed a grenade into her apartment, killing Susan and two of her children, and wounding the third.

The murder of the Kanias family was hardly a lone instance. Between 1951 and 1956, several hundred Israelis were killed by *fedayeen* (Arabic for "self-sacrificers") infiltrators, and many more were wounded.[2] When the Kanias family was attacked, the IDF—which at first had been uncertain how to respond to these attacks—was prepared. The "activist" camp in Israel—reminiscent of Jabotinsky's argument in "The Iron Wall" in 1923 some thirty years earlier—had long felt that to induce the neighboring states to deal with the perpetrators seriously, Israel had to hit back and hit back hard. In early 1953, the IDF began to train a small elite force dedicated to the swift and ruthless punishment that these hard-liners deemed necessary to bring a modicum of quiet to Israel's borders. It formed Unit 101, composed largely of choice volunteers, some of whom had served in the Haganah's elite Palmach unit before independence. The unit was under the command of Ariel Sharon.

Training was intense, including "navigation exercises often taking them across the border; encounters with enemy patrols or village watchmen . . . forced marches . . . calisthenics, judo, and weapons and sabotage training."[3] Commanders apparently even provoked real firefights, which they considered the best practice for the missions that would follow.

The night after Susan Kanais and her children were murdered, Unit 101 got the green light to strike back. The soldiers made their way to the West Bank border village of Qibya, located just over the armistice line.

> The main body of IDF troops . . . prepared some 700 kilograms of explosives for detonation. Working with pocket flashlights and unhindered by Jordanian interference, the sappers proceeded to demolish 45 houses. The destruction took some three hours, lasting from 00:30 to 03:20. The troops failed to search the houses for inhabitants, some of whom hid in cellars and attics. It is possible that, at that stage, the troops believed that there was no one (alive) in the houses. Altogether, some 50–60 of the inhabitants died, both during the takeover of the village and in the demolitions. . . . Two to three days after the event, after sifting through the rubble, the Jordanians announced that 69 (or 70) persons had been killed, most of them women and children.[4]

The creation of Unit 101 illustrated a challenge that Israel would face for many decades. Surviving in the Middle East, surrounded by often violent neighbors who did not recognize its right to exist and swore that they would never do so, meant that Israel had to invest tremendous amounts of money and share of mind in maintaining a militarily superior force. That is precisely what it did with Unit 101. The rigor of this round-the-clock regimen created a fighting force of a capacity unprecedented in the IDF. Israel now had its first world-class Special Forces unit.

The reprisal raids were intentionally brutal; they were meant to convey a clear message that Israel would not tolerate attacks on its innocent citizens, and as such, these reprisal raids were taking place over the border and were killing some innocent Arabs.

It was too much for even some of the hardened soldiers who had volunteered. Some were traumatized by what had transpired in Qibya. Still others, including even those who had been members of the Palmach and had carried out countless attacks during the War of Independence, refused to participate in these new raids. One member of the unit later recalled the questions that haunted him about these operations: "Is this screaming, whimpering multitude the enemy? How did these *fellahin* ('farmers' or 'laborers') sin against us? War is indeed cruel. The depression is general. No one tells stories. All are silent and self-absorbed."[5]

Israel's need to wage what would become an often painful and nearly century-long war* evoked a tradition of profound soul-searching among Israelis about how they could best balance the need to fight for their survival and at the same time maintain the moral standards that they believed were critical to becoming the society they sought to be.

That reflection had begun as early as the War of Independence. Shortly after the war, the Israeli author S. Yizhar (a pen name; his real name was Yizhar Smilansky) published *Khirbet Khizeh,* a work of historical fiction that sought to capture the moral complexity of some actions Israeli forces had taken against an Arab village toward the end of the war. Everything moves slowly in *Khirbet Khizeh,* as if the narrator sees the world through fog, or as in a dream. Slowly, though, he comes to realize the human toll being exacted from the Arabs who were being forced from their homes: "Something struck me like lightning. All at once everything seemed to mean some-

---

* Many date the beginning of the conflict to 1929 with the outbreak of the Hebron riots and the destruction of the Jewish community there. Almost ninety years later, Israel was still locked in conflict with the Palestinians and other actors in the Muslim world, many of whom (Hamas and Hezbollah among the Palestinians, Iran among states) declared that they would never accept Israel's existence.

thing different, more precisely: exile. This was exile. This was what exile was like. This was what exile looked like."[6]

Yizhar was by no means questioning the legitimacy of Israel's establishment, or even Israelis' need to fight their War of Independence. Like many Israeli men and women of letters who would follow him, though, he asked Israelis to take note of the cost not only to themselves, but on the other side of the fight, as well. (Israelis knew well, of course, that had their enemies engaged in similar soul-searching, the region might well have looked very different over the years.)

Toward the end of the book, Moishe, one of the soldiers, tells the narrator: "Immigrants of ours will come to this Khirbet [Arabic for "destroyed village"] what's-its-name, you hear me, and they'll take this land and work it and it'll be beautiful here!" A. D. Gordon's dreamy vision of Jews working the land and the very project that was so central to Ben-Gurion's *mamlachtiyut* become the objects of the novel's narrator's derisive cynicism:

And hooray, we'd house and absorb—and how! We'd open a cooperative store, establish a school, maybe even a synagogue. There would be political parties here. They'd debate all sorts of things. They would plow fields, and sow, and reap and do great things. Long live Hebrew Khizeh! Who, then, would ever imagine that once there had been some Khirbet Khizeh that we emptied out and took for ourselves. We came, we shot, we burned; we blew up, expelled, drove out, and sent into exile.[7]

No less important than the potency of Yizhar's critique is the fact that Israelis did not shy away from the book or turn its author into a pariah. Instead, *Khirbet Khizeh* became an Israeli bestseller and by 1964 was included in the Israeli high school curriculum.[8] S. Yizhar was elected to the Knesset several times. Self-critique would remain one of the most defining characteristics of Israeli society.

Not everyone was equally conflicted by Unit 101 or the Qibya episode. Other soldiers acknowledged that the attacks were morally complex but insisted that they were necessary. Meir Har-Zion, an al-most mythical member of Unit 101 whom Moshe Dayan called "our greatest warrior since Bar Kokhba,"[9] insisted, "Our operations were not accompanied by hatred of the Arabs or any sort of hatred. In all that we were ordered to do we saw a necessity of safeguarding [Is-rael's] existence."[10] Hundreds of innocent Israelis had been murdered until the IDF came up with an effective countermeasure. For people like Har-Zion, Ariel Sharon and Unit 101 were the embodiment of that new Jew that Nordau and Bialik had insisted the Jews needed to create. "No more Kishinevs," people like Har-Zion essentially said. Having a Jewish state meant that Jews were no longer going to die simply because they were Jews.

THE RAID ON QIBYA also marked the beginning of the public—and controversial—career of Ariel Sharon, Israel's daring and brilliant military commander. Sharon would prove difficult to label. Born in 1928 to Vera and Samuil Scheinerman, two Russian immigrants, Sharon (he later Hebraicized his name) was raised on Kfar Malal, a moshav (cooperative agricultural community) just outside of Tel Aviv. His parents, committed Zionists, did things their own way. They raised crops—like peanuts and sweet potatoes—that their moshav thought would not survive. Arik (as he was commonly called) and his sister both attended high school, then considered a superfluous luxury for the people of this collectivist and land-focused community.

From an early age, Arik's parents also instilled in him the im-port of strength and military might. For his bar mitzvah, Samuil gave his son an ornate dagger, an unusual gift, to say the least, but one with an obvious message.[11] The new Jews who had been born and who had come of age in the Yishuv spoke Hebrew, were physi-cally strong, and were intent on taking their fates back into their own calloused hands. That was Arik's world.

The raid on Qibya was the embodiment of that worldview. Sha-ron created Unit 101, led the raid on Qibya, and never apologized for it. "The orders were clear. Qibya was to be a lesson," he wrote in his memoir many years later. "I was to inflict as many casualties as I could on the Arab home guard."[12] Sharon was a devout believer in the effectiveness—and legitimacy—of brute force when necessary.

Like the state to which he devoted his life, Sharon seemed to lack a coherent, consistent policy, and at times appeared internally contradictory. In his mind, however, his principles never varied: Israel's survival depended on being both powerful and smart. Survival would require very different policies in different periods. Sometimes it would demand taking the fight to the enemy, wherever it might be; at other times, it would mean retrenching and withdrawing from territory Israel once held. Sharon did both, and more. Decades later, a government commission would censure Sharon for allowing Lebanese Christians to slaughter Muslims in the Lebanon War of 1982. But years after he was censured, Sharon was elected prime minister, and in 2005, he single-handedly initiated and masterminded Israel's withdrawal from Gaza.

AFTER QIBYA, CONDEMNATIONS POURED in from across the globe, including from the American Jewish community.[13] But Ben-Gurion was unmoved. When the prime minister called Sharon in to discuss the details of the notorious night, Sharon recalled Ben-Gurion's reaction: "It doesn't make any real difference what will be said about Qibya around the world. The important thing is how it will be looked at here in this region. This is going to give us the possibility of living here."[14] The IDF's most prominent "activist," Moshe Dayan, drew an additional conclusion from the vociferousness of the world's reactions to Qibya, "What was allowed to Arabs—and to other peoples—would not be forgiven the Jews or Israel."[15]

Dayan was a passionate advocate of the reprisals. He was appointed chief of staff of the IDF just months later, in December 1953, in what was a clear indication of the direction in which Israeli policy was heading. Dayan, who as the second child born on Israel's first kibbutz was almost naturally emblematic of the new Jew, became a virtual icon when he lost an eye in 1941 while serving in a Palmach unit that was assisting a British invasion of French-controlled Syria. From then on, he wore his trademark eye patch.

Upon his appointment as the top general of Israel's young army, Dayan set out to reorganize the IDF's structure and rethink its strategies. Dayan ordered the most intelligent and best-educated men out of the headquarters and into fighting units. He required that officers stay in top physical condition and (in what is still a characteristic of the IDF) personally lead their men into battle. After the painful losses of the War of Independence and recognizing that the conflict with Israel's neighbors was not nearly over, Dayan was determined to make the cost of killing Israelis prohibitive. He was determined to transform the Israel Defense Forces into the most fearsome military in the Middle East.

AS THE ISRAELIS SHIFTED their strategy, though, so, too did their enemies. The Arab infiltrations morphed from attacks by individual infiltrators to incursions by armed and well-trained squads of fedayeen who were supported and equipped by their host governments, particularly the Egyptian military.

One of the kibbutzim that was the target of repeated such incursions was Nachal Oz, on the Gaza border. On April 29, 1956, twenty-one-year-old Roi Rotberg was patrolling the fields of Nachal Oz, where he lived, on horseback. Accustomed to seeing Gazans illegally picking the kibbutz's fields, when Rotberg saw a group of Arabs in the fields, he rode toward them to get them to leave. But it was a trap, and as Rotberg approached the "farmers," a group of fedayeen suddenly appeared, shot and killed Rotberg, then dragged his body into Gaza, where it was horrifically mutilated.

Coincidentally, Dayan had met Rotberg a few days earlier. He attended the funeral and delivered a brief eulogy (merely 238 words in total) that became Dayan's—and then, many Israelis'—classic statement about the inevitability of a long and costly conflict between Israel and its neighbors. Dayan reminded his listeners that there was nothing surprising about Arab resentment and violence. "Let us not hurl blame at the murderers," he said. "Why should we complain of their hatred for us? Eight years have they sat in the refugee camps of Gaza, and seen, with their own eyes, how we have made a homeland of the soil and the villages where they and their forebears once dwelt."[16]

Yet if mere Israeli survival was going to evoke Arab anger, Dayan then warned both his listeners and his entire newborn nation, Israelis had better be prepared to live by the sword. In language filled with biblical imagery, as if to remind his listeners that the battle to stay in the land was not new but was a story that had begun thousands of years earlier, Dayan continued, "We mustn't flinch from the hatred that accompanies and fills the lives of hundreds of thousands of Arabs, who live around us and are waiting for the moment when their hands may claim our blood. We mustn't avert our eyes, lest our hands be weakened. That is the decree of our generation. That is the choice of our lives—to be willing and armed, strong and unyielding, lest the sword be knocked from our fists, and our lives severed."[17]

It was a worldview that would guide not only Dayan, but the country he was helping to found, for decades to come.

AS ISRAEL WAS ADJUSTING to the inevitability of a long conflict, Egypt was undergoing a dramatic political transformation. In 1952, the Free Officers Movement, spearheaded by Colonel Gamal Abdel Nasser, staged a coup and ousted Egypt's then monarch, King Farouk. Determined to rid Egypt of the last vestiges of colonialism, which Nasser believed had strangled the Arab world and prevented it from achieving its real potential, the new Egyptian leader was determined to usher in a new era for the Arab world, with himself at the helm.

Israel played a unique role in Nasser's worldview and plan. In one sense, Nasser saw Israel and the Israelis as the region's latest manifestation of colonialism. At the same time, though, Israel served a positive purpose, for it was the enemy around whose destruction the entire Arab world could unite. "Arab unity," Nasser exhorted, was the "prerequisite to successful revenge."[18]

The Arab world had sought that revenge, the "second round" that would destroy the Jewish state, from the moment it lost the War of Independence. Azmi Nashashibi, a senior Jordanian official, declared as early as April 1949 that "the war in Palestine will be renewed, sooner or later." Arab leaders told Kenneth Bilby, an American journalist, that even if the struggle lasted for a hundred years, "the day of vengeance would come."[19] Nasser's call for Arab unity and vengeance against the Jews thus fell on receptive ears. By 1956, Ben-Gurion was warning the Israeli public that war was drawing ever nearer: in a speech in April of that year, he hinted that Israel was about to be tested even more fiercely than it had been in 1948.

One key element of Nasser's planned Arab renaissance was the construction of the Aswan High Dam on the Nile. To finance the extraordinarily ambitious project, which he hoped would restore Egypt's glory, Nasser borrowed enormous sums from the Americans and the British. Yet Nasser was also well aware of the Cold War tensions between the Americans and the Soviets, and he cunningly played them off each other. Even as he was receiving financial support from the West, Nasser appealed to the Soviets for increased funding for the dam, and—in what the West saw as a conscious act of belligerence—he chose to recognize Communist China.

Egypt also began acquiring copious quantities of armaments, building an arsenal of the sort that it had never previously possessed. In August 1955, the Egyptians signed an arms deal of unprecedented scope with Czechoslovakia, which was essentially doing the bidding of the USSR. (The sale of arms to Egypt was painfully ironic given that in the War of Independence, Israeli soldiers had used arms from Czechoslovakia.) By enabling the Egyptians to purchase $320 million of Czech arms, which included tanks, bombers, and fighter planes, the Soviets had created a new military Goliath in the Middle East and had altered the region's balance of power.

In retaliation for the arms deal and in response to recognition of China, the United States announced that it would no longer provide the Egyptians with support for the Aswan Dam, and the British soon followed suit. The Americans and British, though, had unwittingly played into Nasser's hands, precisely as he had hoped. On July 26, 1956, Nasser addressed an enormous crowd in Alexandria and told the Americans to "go choke on your fury."[20] Then he played his trump card and announced that Egypt was nationalizing the Suez Canal (see Map 8), the revenues from which he would use to finance the construction of the Aswan Dam. Instantaneously, Nasser was the hero of the Arab world.

British prime minister Anthony Eden was infuriated. British ships used the waterway (which had opened in 1869) daily. Having the canal under Nasser's control threatened critical interests of both France and England. British and French stockholders of the Suez Canal Company were also enraged at the "theft" of their asset. If Nasser had been hoping to dent the prestige of the colonialist power that had previously held Egypt, he had succeeded perfectly.

As summer progressed, Nasser's confrontational stance continued, and his ambitions moved from the diplomatic—seizing the Suez Canal—to the militaristic. Israelis listened, and with concern. Nasser's arms acquisitions meant that Egypt was now a formidable threat, and Israel's security was very much in danger. The French, too, were growing alarmed. A new independence movement was gaining steam in Algeria, and the French worried that the Egyptians were going to use their increasing momentum in the Arab world to support it. Advanced Czech weapons in the hands of the Algerian "separatists" could spell disaster for the French.

As British and French concern over Nasser's muscle flexing deepened, Israeli leaders were growing increasingly worried. Many doubted that Israel would be able to survive this new boost in Egyptian power. Nasser made no attempt to hide the reason for his acquiring the weaponry; the new Soviet weapons could quite possibly enable him to destroy the Jewish state.

With the Holocaust still fresh in Israelis' minds, Israel was not about to take Egypt's threats lightly. Tens of thousands of Israelis volunteered to dig trenches. People donated scarce money and treasured jewelry to a weapons fund.* Schoolchildren gave their lunch money to the cause.

Yet Israel's international standing had changed dramatically since 1948. Now, after less than a decade, the French and the British (who, not long before, had prohibited Jewish immigration and hanged members of the Jewish underground) saw in Israel a potential military partner. Israeli prime minister Moshe Sharett, who had become prime minister when Ben-Gurion stepped down (Ben-Gurion became prime minister once again a few years later), visited Paris on October 25, 1955, as part of a series of Israeli-French meetings designed to solidify relations between the two nations. "I've always been a friend of Israel," French prime minister Edgar Faure assured Sharett, "but now it is not a question of friendship. It is for reasons of political realism that France is called upon to help you."[21]

A year later, in October 1956, the three countries came to a secret agreement known as the Protocols of Sèvres. According to the agreement, Israel was to launch a massive attack against Nasser's forces and to try to reach the Suez Canal within a day. Then the French and British would call on both countries to cease hostilities and demand that Egypt open the canal to international shipping. Israel would be asked to withdraw its forces to a line several miles east of the canal, but the Protocols specifically stipulated that it was

---

* The notion of donating jewelry did not come out of nowhere. Here, too, the centrality of the biblical narrative reverberated for many Israelis. When the Israelis were building the Tabernacle and Moses asked them to donate what they could to the cause, the Bible recounts, "Men and women, all whose hearts moved them . . . came bringing brooches, earrings, rings and pendants—gold objects of all kinds." (Exodus 35:22)

understood that Israel would not be obligated to acquiesce—the demand would be for public appearance only.

Though Israel would be the country to put boots on the ground, it had much to gain from the agreement. France's partnership communicated a sense that the small state was no longer alone, not a mere pawn on the international chessboard. Israel was becoming a player. As part of the agreement, Israel would get air cover from the British and French in its campaign to eliminate Egypt as a threat, and the two European countries would provide international support as well. Furthermore, France provided Israel with arms, which began to arrive in early October.

Shimon Peres, then director-general of the Ministry of Defense, who had been instrumental in negotiating the deal, went to the Haifa port to witness the armaments' clandestine arrival. He took with him Natan Alterman, who had written "The Silver Platter" years earlier. So moved was Alterman by what he was witnessing that he wrote a poem, "It Will One Day Be Told"[22]: "I dreamed last night of steel, much steel, new steel," he wrote, and then described the stevedore, "the bearer of laden canisters, ringing on iron chains." This was no ordinary stevedore, though, Alterman wrote, for "with the first touch of the land he becomes the expression of the power of the Jews."

It was a dramatic transformation in Alterman's tone. No longer was he writing about the "state-in-waiting"; now Alterman was writing about "the power of the Jews."

Jewish power came not a moment too soon. Nasser began to send Egyptian troops into the Gaza Strip to support the fedayeen. Shimon Peres later recalled, "There was no doubt in Israel's mind . . . that Nasser was about to invade at any moment.'"[23]

ON OCTOBER 29, 1956, JUST as Israel was preparing to launch the war that would become known as the Sinai Campaign, tragedy struck the home front. Arab Israelis had then been living under military rule for eight years, and levels of distrust still ran high.

In preparation for the coming battle with Egypt, Israel issued a five P.M. curfew on all the Arab villages in the "Little Triangle" that abutted the Jordanian border, including a village by the name of Kafr Kassem.

News of the curfew was publicized just minutes shy of five o'clock, and most of the laborers did not receive the notice in time. Most workers who encountered army units after the curfew were allowed to pass without incident. But when one group of fifty laborers from Kafr Kassem, returning home after work beyond the five P.M. newly imposed curfew, encountered an IDF patrol, the Israeli soldiers shot and killed forty-seven people from the town—including many women and children. It was the largest massacre of Arabs since the founding of the state.

Though several officers were arrested and later convicted, all were released from jail shortly thereafter. Ben-Gurion called the incident a "dreadful atrocity,"[24] and in years to come, numerous Israeli officials expressed profound remorse for the massacre. In October 2006, Israel's minister of education, Yuli Tamir, instructed Israeli schools to commemorate the Kafr Kassem massacre and to reflect upon the need to disobey patently immoral orders. In December 2007, Israel's president, Shimon Peres, attended a reception in Kafr Kassem during the Muslim festival of Eid al-Adha, and asked for the community's forgiveness. "A terrible event happened here in the past, and we are deeply sorry for it," he said. In October 2014, Reuven Rivlin, Israel's tenth president, became the first to attend the annual memorial ceremony at Kafr Kassem.

Yet the incident had long-term legal implications for Israeli society. The trial was the first time that the Israeli judiciary discussed whether and when Israeli security personnel were obliged to disobey even a direct order that was manifestly illegal. Judge Benjamin Halevy (who heard the case as a sole judge) wrote that "the distinguishing mark of a manifestly illegal order is that above such an order should fly, like a black flag, a warning saying: 'Prohibited!'" In years to come, the phrase "a manifestly illegal order," a direct quote from Halevy's decision, would become ubiquitous in Israeli discussions of the morality of the conduct of war.

AT FIVE P.M. ON OCTOBER 29 (the very same hour as the curfew in Kfar Kassem), Israeli troops moved into the Sinai. Israel swiftly cut all communication between the Egyptian air force in the Sinai and the main bases of the Egyptian army. Soon thereafter, Israeli paratroopers, under the command of Ariel Sharon, made their way quietly toward the Mitla pass in Sinai, a crucial passageway on the road to the Suez Canal. By October 30, the paratroopers had made it across the expansive desert, had overtaken three Egyptian military bases with ease, and were within fifty kilometers of the canal.

On October 30, the British government issued the secretly planned public ultimatum to both Israel and Egypt, demanding that they withdraw their forces from the canal. The British were essentially ordering the Egyptians to relinquish their control of the canal that they had nationalized. As planned, the Israelis did not respond to the ultimatum. Egypt rejected it out of hand. The next day, British and French fighter planes bombed Egyptian airfields, but no British or French troops landed in the region for six days. Israel fought the Egyptians on its own.

Eventually, worried about the possibility of the contained conflict morphing into a major regional conflagration, the Americans demanded that the British, French, and Israelis remove their forces from the area. The Soviets made the same demand. The Russians had just crushed the Hungarian Revolution and had killed thousands of Hungarians in the process, so they had little moral authority to bring to the table. Still, the confluence of American and Soviet interests here meant that Israel, France, and Britain had to back down.

Israel, though, was not anxious to remove its forces from the Sinai, in large measure because it was loath to allow Gaza to become a launching pad for attacks once again. Ultimately, the

Americans recognized that Israel was insistent that it receive guarantees of safety before it pulled out. So the United States promised that if Israel agreed to a "complete and prompt withdrawal" from all the territory it had occupied in the brief war, the Americans would guarantee Israel's "right of passage" through the Straits of Tiran (narrow sea passages between the Sinai and Arabian peninsula). (See Map 8.) They would also guarantee Israel's "freedom to act to defend its rights" in the future.

It would not be long before the United States would have to make good on its promise.

On the British side, Prime Minister Eden systematically sought to destroy any trace of the agreement so that the United Kingdom could deny its role in the affair. It did him no good, though. Both Israel and France had archived copies, and Eden resigned under massive political pressure.

In all, the war lasted from October 29 through November 7. Israel lost 231 soldiers with another 900 soldiers wounded. Egyptian losses are estimated at between 1,500 and 3,000, with about 5,000 wounded.

For a short war, the Sinai Campaign had yielded profoundly important results. Israel had secured its right of passage in the Straits of Tiran and had won international guarantees from countries that not long before had doubted its ability to survive. For its citizens, it had established a sense of security and self-confidence after eight years of living under constant infiltration. As Michael Oren put it, the Sinai Campaign had been "Israel's second War of Independence."[25] The IDF, which astounded the world with its professionalism, had captured the Sinai Peninsula in a hundred hours, and as a result, Israel gained a decade of quiet. The Middle East had a new military power.

IN THE AFTERMATH of the war, it was increasingly obvious to David Ben-Gurion that Israel's relationship with the United States was becoming much more complex than many had anticipated or hoped. He had good reason for concern. When the United Nations had been discussing Israel's proposed borders prior to partition, the U.S. State Department encouraged the UN to redraw the borders and give more land to the Arabs. In 1953, John Foster Dulles, secretary of state at the time, suggested a "repatriation of specific numbers of Arab refugees to 'the area *presently controlled* by Israel.'" The words *presently controlled* suggested to some Israelis that Dulles did not believe Israel would long survive. After Egypt signed the arms deal with the Czechs, the United States refused to sell Israel weaponry to restore the balance of power (which is what sent Israel to the French looking for arms). Israel pleaded with the Americans, but to no avail. In fact, "President Eisenhower remarked to French Prime Minister Guy Mollet that there was no point in selling arms to Israel inasmuch as 1,700,000 Jews could not possibly defend themselves against 40 million Arabs."[26] (See Map 7.)

After the Sinai Campaign, the United States (along with the USSR) led the charge at the United Nations in denouncing Britain, France, and Israel for initiating the war. The American denunciation may have been a slap on the wrist, but Israel chose to make its case nonetheless and sent Foreign Minister Golda Meir to the United Nations. Meir, who was renowned for her wit, noted with bitter irony that a

> comfortable division has been made. The Arab states unilaterally enjoy the "rights of war" [while] Israel has the unilateral responsibility of keeping the peace. But belligerency is not a one way street. Is it then surprising if a people laboring under this monstrous distinction should finally become restive and at last seek a way of rescuing its life from the perils of the regulated war that is conducted against it from all sides?[27]

BY THE TIME BEN-GURION sent Golda Meir to the United Nations to defend Israel, she had already more than made her mark on the

Jewish state. Born Golda Mabovitch (later Meyerson, her husband's last name) in 1898 in Kiev, she soon thereafter moved with her staunchly Zionist family to Pinsk. When Meir's sister (who, upon hearing of Herzl's death, wore black for two full years) invited like-minded peers to Zionist meetings at her house, Golda would perch herself atop the family's coal stove to catch as many snippets of the conversations as she could. The family moved to Milwaukee, Wisconsin, in 1906, when she was eight years old.

It was at a parlor meeting there, discussing the kibbutz movement and the philosophy of A. D. Gordon, that Meir met her future husband, Morris, with whom she would have a tumultuous and largely loveless marriage. Soon thereafter, they decided to move to Palestine:

> I think it was while we were marching through town [in a parade] that I realized I can no longer postpone a final decision about Palestine. . . . Palestine, I felt, not parades in Milwaukee, was the only real, meaningful answer to Petlyura's murderous mobs. The Jews must have a land of their own again—and I must help build it, not by making speeches or raising funds, but by living and working there.[28]

She and Morris departed the United States in 1922. By 1956, she had climbed the ladder of Mapai party leadership, and David Ben-Gurion appointed her foreign minister. One of her first steps was to Hebrarcize her name, like many Zionist leaders who had come before her; she changed it from Meyerson to Meir.

Shortly after the Sinai Campaign, she pulled out *Altneuland* and read to the staff of the Foreign Ministry a passage from Herzl's classic novel:

> There is still one question arising out of the disaster of the nations which remains unsolved to this day, and whose profound tragedy only a Jew can comprehend. This is the African question. Just call to mind all those terrible episodes of the slave trade, of

human beings who merely because they were black, were stolen like cattle, taken prisoner, captured and sold. Their children
grew up in strange lands, the objects of contempt and hostility
because their complexions were different. I am not ashamed to
say, though I may expose myself to ridicule in saying so, that
once I have witnessed the redemption of the Jews, my own people, I wish also to assist in the redemption of the Africans.[29]

When she finished reading from *Altneuland*, Meir told the members of her staff that it was their task to ensure the fulfillment of
Herzl's vision in this vein. With the beginning of the massive wave
of African independence, Meir insisted that African nations and
Israel had many shared experiences and struggles: "Like us, their
freedom was won only after years of struggle. Like us, they had to
fight for their statehood. And like us, nobody handed them their
sovereignty on a silver platter."[30]

Meir hoped that Israel would be able to provide technology,
farming expertise, and most important, a model of a repressed
people that had achieved a long-awaited national revival, to African
countries that had histories very similar to Israel's. She hoped that
the Jewish story of rebirth and recovered sovereignty would speak
not only to Jews, but to nations worldwide.

For a short while, Israel did manage to foster positive relationships with several African countries and used its expertise in agriculture, hydration, and other technologies to help them advance
their own productivities. In the long term, Golda's was a naive
hope. The newly founded African countries would soon compose
a bloc that would become one of Israel's largest foes in the United
Nations. Israel's overtures had made no difference.

INTERNALLY, ISRAEL WAS LAYING the foundations of a world-class
military. As Dayan had noted in his eulogy for Roi Rotberg, the
conflict was not going to end anytime soon, and Israelis began to
develop the kinds of deterrent military capabilities they would need

both to survive and to provide safety for Israel's citizens. But Israel had also established a culture of self-reflection, of judicial oversight over military conduct, and had articulated clear moral limits on military orders.

On the global front, the Jewish state had become a player in international intrigue and even war. It had demonstrated a commitment to helping other countries that could benefit from its expertise.

A fledging state now felt less tenuous, and Israelis could begin to think not only about survival, but also about the future. What they were about to discover, however, was that building that future would first require them to confront head-on one of the most painful periods in the Jewish people's long history.

ISRAEL CONFRONTS THE HOLOCAUST

This is a chronicle of the planet of Auschwitz. . . . [The] inhabitants of this planet had no names, they had no parents nor did they have children. . . . [T]hey were not born there and they did not give birth; . . . [T]hey did not live—nor did they die—according to the laws of this world.

—Yechiel De-Nur, Testimony at Eichmann Trial[1]

At four o'clock in the afternoon on May 23, 1960, the plenum of the Knesset was packed to capacity. Prime Minister Ben-Gurion apparently had unprecedented news to relay to the nation. As those assembled waited to hear what the prime minister had to say, the feeling in the chamber was electric.

Ben-Gurion approached the podium and began:

I have to inform the Knesset that a short time ago one of the great Nazi war criminals, Adolf Eichmann, the man responsible together with the Nazi leaders for what they called the Final Solution, which is the annihilation of six million European Jews, was discovered by the Israel security services. Adolf Eichmann is already under arrest in Israel and will be placed on trial shortly under the terms of the Law for the Trial of Nazis and Their Collaborators.[2]

With that, Ben-Gurion walked away from the podium and departed the chamber.

The hall was silent. Each person in the room struggled with the enormity of the announcement and its implications. Would the State of Israel finally exact even a modicum of justice from one of the architects of the annihilation of European Jewry? Would some measure of retribution finally be found for the millions murdered and tortured, gassed and burned or buried alive, and the million children whose lives had been cut off by the Nazi genocidal machine? Would there be an accounting for those delegates of the Zionist congresses who had perished, for the sisters and brothers, parents and spouses of many of those who sat in the room and of the hundreds of thousands of others who made up Israeli society?

Adolf Eichmann had been a Nazi SS-*Obersturmbannführer* (lieutenant colonel) and one of the architects of the Holocaust, a central figure at the Wannsee Conference that decided on the Final Solution, and, at the time of his capture, the highest-ranking Nazi official still alive. He had spent most of his time after the war living under a pseudonym in Argentina. And now, the Mossad (one of Israel's security agencies) had located him, captured him, and secreted him out of Argentina and into Israel.

It was almost too much to imagine. Then, as if continuing the ten-minute ovation that Theodor Herzl had received in Basel sixty-three years earlier, those in the plenum shook the hall with spontaneous and thunderous applause.

PREDICTABLY, MUCH OF THE WORLD did not applaud. Condemnations poured in from around the globe. Argentinean officials, who unabashedly gave Nazis refuge, claimed that Israel's action was "typical of the methods used by a regime completely and universally condemned."[3] The United Nations Security Council passed Resolution 138, stating that Israel had violated Argentina's sovereignty and warned that future similar actions could undermine international peace. The United States, China, France, and Britain all joined in condemning Israel.

Argentinean civilians, following the lead of their government's reaction, responded with violent anti-Semitic attacks on the Argentine Jewish community. Both the *Washington Post* and the *New York Post* published condemnations, while the *Christian Science Monitor* said that Israel's decision to "adjudicate crimes against Jews committed outside of Israel was identical to the Nazis' claim on 'the loyalty of persons of German birth or descent' wherever they lived."[4] *Time* magazine, inexplicably, called Ben-Gurion's actions a form of "inverse racism."[5]

Israel proceeded, undeterred, animated by a sense of justice. David Ben-Gurion also had an educational agenda. Israel's young people had been raised in a society that had thus far avoided confronting the Holocaust. It was time for a public reckoning, the prime minister believed. "Israeli youth should learn the truth of what had happened to the Jews of Europe between 1933 and 1945."[6]

So in a bold move in which Israel claimed jurisdiction for a crime that had taken place on a different continent, before the state had been established, by a murderer nabbed from yet a third country, Israel placed Adolf Eichmann—symbol of the Nazi regime—on trial. This time the guards were Jews, not Nazis. Now it was not Jews who stood trapped behind barbed wire, but the accused Nazi who sat behind a protective glass cage in a court of Jewish judges, in Jerusalem, the capital of the Jewish state.

EICHMANN'S TRIAL WOULD BE the first time that Israeli society would publicly engage with the horrific details of the atrocity and with the nightmares that many Israelis—survivors of the inferno of Europe—carried with them every day. But the Nazi genocide had already colored Israeli policy on more than one occasion. In 1951, almost ten years before Ben-Gurion made his announcement to the stunned Knesset plenum, the governments of Israel and the German Federal Republic (West Germany) had begun negotiations over an agreement in which Germany would pay Israel monetary reparations for what it had done to the Jewish people during the Holocaust. Konrad Adenauer, the postwar German chancellor, said on September 27, 1951, that Germany was "ready, jointly with the representatives of Jewry and the State of Israel, which has received so many homeless refugees, to bring about a solution of the problem of material restitution."[7]

The announcement that Israel would even speak to a German government brought Menachem Begin out of a self-imposed political retirement. Begin had left the public stage, at least temporarily. Yet when Ben-Gurion announced that he would bring a motion to the Knesset on the subject of the reparations, Begin's longtime associates called him into action, convinced that Begin (who was still a member of the Knesset) was the only one who could give voice to the sentiment that making any deal with the Germans was unthinkable. Reparations, they also understood, would afford Begin an opportunity to reenter the political fray not as the object of Ben-Gurion's dismissive disregard, but as the Jewish voice accusing Ben-Gurion of abandoning the obligations of Jewish history and Jewish honor.

Begin, whose father, mother, and brother had been murdered by the Nazis, launched a merciless attack on Ben-Gurion and on the mere idea that Israel would accept monetary compensation from the Germans. The Germans, he raged, were not people with whom Jews with even a modicum of pride would ever consider negotiating.[8]

In the course of the debates that followed, Begin said, "They [the government] are on the verge of signing an accord with Germany and of saying that Germany is a nation, and not what it is: a pack of wolves whose fangs devoured and consumed our people."[9]

Arguably the finest orator in the country at that time, Begin aroused the passions of much of Israeli society. *Ma'ariv,* one of the country's leading newspapers, published a cartoon depicting a German holding a blood-soaked bag of money, extending his arm to give it to an Israeli. A December 1951 headline in *Herut (Freedom,* the newspaper of Begin's political party) asked, "How much will we get for a burnt child?"

Ever the pragmatist, Ben-Gurion countered that an economically flourishing Jewish state would arouse international admiration; Jews could safeguard their honor in more than one way. Ben-Gurion knew that the Israeli economy was on the verge of collapse. The government had instituted food rationing, Israel possessed virtually none of the heavy machinery necessary for getting the country on its feet, and the Jewish state desperately needed housing for the hundreds of thousands of destitute Jewish immigrants who had made their way to its shores. If German money could further Israel's becoming a stable country, that, too, would be a form of exacting justice.

The national dispute, which elicited unprecedented acrimony, reached its climax on January 7, 1952, the date set for the Knesset's vote. On a cold, wintry day, a huge crowd from all over Israel gathered in Jerusalem's downtown Zion Square to protest the debate in the Knesset, then unfolding only a few hundred yards away. Begin, who refused to enter the Knesset until the vote itself, addressed the crowd in a tone he had never previously assumed. He referred to Ben-Gurion as "that maniac who is now Prime Minister," the "now" pregnant with numerous possible implications.

Then Begin threatened the government. "There will not be negotiations with Germany, for this we are all willing to give our lives. It is better to die than transgress this. There is no sacrifice that we won't make to suppress this initiative." Referring to the fact that he had commanded his men to hold their fire on the day of the *Altalena,* he now changed his tune. "This will be a war of life and death," he told his supporters. "Today I shall give the order: 'Blood!'"[10]

Suddenly, the man who had helped avert civil war in the *Altalena* incident seemed to threaten civil war.

Ben-Gurion was neither convinced by Begin's rhetoric nor worried by his threats. To him, Begin was nothing more than a demagogue, a Polish Jew ill-suited to the Knesset's podium in a country of new post-European Israelis. The two men, beyond even their deep personal enmity, simply saw the Jewish world through profoundly different lenses. Begin insisted that a Jewish state that abandoned Jewish memory and a sense of the sanctity of the Jewish past would have no soul and no reason for being. For Ben-Gurion, the Jewish state was about looking forward, acknowledging the horrors of the European past but moving beyond it. For Prime Minister Ben-Gurion, who had left Europe long before the Holocaust, the Diaspora Jew for whom Begin still mourned was the pitiful, weak Jew of Chaim Nachman Bialik's painful epic poem "The City of Slaughter." Israel, he thought, had created something better.

The debate inside the Knesset was vicious. And outside the Knesset's acrimonious session, violence erupted. Some of Begin's supporters had followed him up Ben-Yehudah Street* from Zion Square to the Knesset and, in rage, threw rocks at the windows. Suddenly, the sound of shattering glass interrupted the Knesset's debate. Tear gas that the police had used to disperse the crowd outside wafted into the Knesset, and the proceedings were temporarily suspended. Eventually, though, the debate continued, and as expected, the Knesset voted 60–51 on January 9 to proceed with the negotiations with Germany. Begin conceded defeat, but for his inflammatory rhetoric, both outside the building and in the plenum, he was banned from the Knesset for three months.

As Ben-Gurion had hoped, the reparations, combined with other foreign aid sources, got Israel on its feet. The money was used to improve housing, create an Israeli shipping fleet and national airline, build roads and telecommunication systems, and establish electricity networks. Reparations also helped finance Israel's National Water Carrier project, critical to bringing water to arid parts of the country, making them habitable—no small challenge in the

---

* One representation of the deep historical awareness that pervades Israel is in its naming of streets. Many streets are named for Jewish scholars, writers, and heroes of the past—biblical, rabbinic, and modern, famous dates in Jewish history and the like. Many Israeli cities have a Ben-Yehudah Street, named for the father of Modern Hebrew.

parched Middle East. Per capita (and adjusted for inflation), the tiny state spent on the National Water Carrier roughly six times the amount that the United States had expended to build the Panama Canal, and "far more than other iconic U.S. public works like the Hoover Dam or the Golden Gate Bridge."[11] At the height of the project, one of every fourteen able-bodied people in the country was working on the carrier, whether digging, pipefitting, welding, or performing some other task.[12] It cost about 5 percent of Israel's GDP, an extraordinary amount for any country—all the more so in an economically fragile one like Israel. Without the reparations, the project would likely not have been possible then.

By the mid-1950s, Israel had the world's fastest-growing economy, ahead even of Germany and Japan.[13] There were also unanticipated consequences to the reparations, as well, far beyond the financial. For years, both Holocaust survivors and Israeli society had avoided speaking about what had happened in Europe in the 1940s. For the survivors, the memories were simply too painful. For Israeli society, the subject evoked both images of the Yishuv's inability to help, and the image of a European Jew-as-victim that Israel sought to transcend.

Now, in the aftermath of the reparations, the Israeli refusal to engage the subject of the Holocaust had its first crack. And the man now associated with the role of safeguarding Israel's Jewish conscience was David Ben-Gurion's political adversary, Menachem Begin. The reparations debate had afforded Begin the opportunity to represent Israel's Jewish soul, the sanctity of Jewish memory, no matter how painful.

It was not only the seeds of Ben-Gurion's Mapai Party's fall that had been planted. This was also a turning point for the kibbutzim. Until that point in Israeli history, many of the kibbutzim outlawed private property with no exceptions. Members shared everything, including clothing and other gifts that kibbutz members might receive from friends or family. Children were raised not by their parents, but in communal children's residences, where they slept from infancy.

With the reparations, though, a crack in that policy also appeared. Survivors suddenly resisted the notion that the money they would receive for their own indescribable suffering should be shared with those who had not been through the Holocaust. Some kinds of property, they insisted, were simply not meant for everyone. On some kibbutzim, the debate that the issue evoked was no less vociferous or acrimonious than the heated debate in the Knesset.

Several kibbutzim settled on a compromise position; members could keep some of the reparations that they received, but the rest would be deposited in the collective coffers. The kibbutz as an institution would survive for decades, but the absolute egalitarianism of the kibbutz was over. Decades later, when kibbutzim would privatize and abolish public property, some would ironically see the roots of the change in the influence that German reparations money had on Israel's signature socialist institution.[14]

IF REPARATIONS PRECIPITATED ISRAEL'S first serious reckoning with the Holocaust, matters only intensified several years later with the riveting trial of Rudolf Kasztner. In June 1955, Malkiel Gruenwald, an eccentric Holocaust survivor, published a pamphlet in which he accused Kasztner, who had been head of the Zionist Rescue Committee in Hungary during the war, of having made a pact with the Germans in 1944. The deal, which became known as "blood for goods," involved Kasztner's transferring trucks to the Germans in exchange for a trainload of Jews who would not be sent to Auschwitz. The deal led to the release of some seventeen hundred Jews, among them Kasztner's own family and other wealthy Jews who had paid a premium price to get spots on the train. There were also orphans, Hasidim, and select others included in the deal, which was entirely public. And because in addition to saving those lives, Kasztner had also arranged for a significant number of Jews to be sent to labor camps rather than to Auschwitz, many Hungarian Jews thought him a hero of that horribly dark period.

Others, though, held a much less charitable view. They argued that Kasztner had saved his own family, had lived very well under the

Nazis, and perhaps most egregiously, had failed to tell the Jews whom he could not save what awaited them. Kasztner, they said, was no hero, but rather, was complicit in the deaths of many thousands of Jews.

After the war, Kasztner moved to Israel, began to work with Ben-Gurion's Mapai Party, and lived his life mostly out of the limelight. When Gruenwald made his accusation that Kasztner was the "vicarious murderer" of five hundred thousand Hungarian Jews, fifty-eight of whom were members of Gruenwald's own family, Kasztner was serving in a senior position of the Israeli Ministry of Industry and Trade. To protect its reputation, the government decided to prosecute Gruenwald for slander.

Though elderly and without resources, Gruenwald refused to go down without a fight. He hired a lawyer named Shmuel Tamir, who had been a member of Begin's Irgun. In a stunning display of ingenious courtroom strategy, Tamir, a talented advocate and skillful rhetorician, managed to turn the trial on its head. Tamir argued that Gruenwald was right, and that Kasztner had been a collaborator. In essence, Kasztner—and by association, the government that had taken up his cause—now had to defend itself against Gruenwald's accusations.

The court eventually exonerated Gruenwald and declared that Kasztner had "sold his soul to the devil." Publicly humiliated, Kasztner became a virtual recluse. The Supreme Court eventually reversed that decision, but too late for Kasztner. On March 4, 1957, Kasztner was assassinated by Ze'ev Eckstein outside his home in Tel Aviv.[15]* Eerily similar to the Arlosoroff murder in 1933 in apparent response

---

* Eckstein had been an agent for the Shin Bet, which assigned him to keep an eye on the radical Right (but not to do more than that). As he did so, however, the ideology of the Right eventually won him over and he went rogue. He served seven years in prison for the murder, and later, almost six decades after the murder, published his autobiographical *Quilt Blanket*, in which he said, "I wouldn't do it today. I wouldn't shoot. There's no doubt about it." (Elad Zeret, "Kastner's Killer: I Would Never Have Shot Him Today," *Ynetnews.com* [October 29, 2014], http://www.ynetnews.com/articles/0,7340,L-4585767,00.html.)

to the Transfer Agreement, Kasztner's murder was the second time a high-profile Jew was assassinated for his role in negotiating with the Germans. This time, though, the killing took place in postindependence Israel. It was the first time a Jew had assassinated a Jew for political reasons in the Jewish state. Tragically, it would not be the last.

Just as the reparations agreement had unexpected consequences, so, too, did the Kasztner trial. In condemning Kasztner, the judge—however unintentionally—essentially reinforced a perception that those Jews who had survived the Holocaust must have done something distasteful. Otherwise, many implicitly wondered, why had *they* survived when so many millions of others had perished?

Ironically, the public attention to the Holocaust actually made some survivors less inclined to talk about their experiences. Their burden became one they would bear alone and that, too, reinforced the sense that they were somehow "different." Ariel Sharon, commander of Unit 101 and eventually prime minister, would recall that on the kibbutz in which he grew up, survivors seemed to live in a world of their own:

> The survivors had their own codes, and [one] could never be sure what they were really saying. They were either not speaking to each other because of some obscure insult or else ready to die for each other. A kibbutz was supposed to be a place of trust; who could build a commune with such people?[16]

FAR FROM THE PUBLIC EYE, the Holocaust was having yet another major influence on Israel's development. By 1955, David Ben-Gurion had come to a far-reaching decision. The Arab-Israeli conflict, he understood, was not going to be resolved at any time in the near future. Given the vagaries of world history, he did not wish to be exclusively dependent on the West. He decided that Israel needed to become a nuclear power.

At that time, only the United States, Britain, and the USSR had nuclear weapons. Israel did not even manufacture transistor radios.

The mere notion that a small country with no technological expertise and that was home to fewer than two million citizens would
go nuclear seemed fanciful to some of Ben-Gurion's advisers and a
bad idea to others. But for the prime minister, the conflict with the
Arabs coupled with the sense of vulnerability that the Holocaust
created was a deciding factor. Israel was meant to end Jewish vulnerability, whatever that would take.

When she later reflected on the importance of Israel's nuclear
capacity, Golda Meir harked not back to the Holocaust but to the
pogroms of her childhood. She called Israel's nuclear capacity *va-
renye;* that was the name eastern European Jews used for the fruit
preserves they kept secreted away so that should a pogrom erupt,
they would have that to eat until the threat passed.

Ben-Gurion sent Shimon Peres to Paris in 1956 to try to convince
the French (who were developing their own nuclear program at
that time) to help Israel develop its nuclear capacity. Mired in anti-
Arab sentiment (which came to the fore most obviously in the 1956
Suez Campaign) and a sense of obligation to the Jews in light of the
pro-Nazi Vichy French government's treatment of the Jews, France
agreed.* Its desire to extend its reach in light of its misfortunes in

---

* An interesting side story to Israel's acquisition of a nuclear weapon involved American Jews, as well. Most notable among them was Zalman
Shapiro, a chemist, inventor, and deeply committed Zionist. When a
1965 inventory of the Nuclear Materials and Equipment Corporation
(NUMEC) found some 200 to 600 pounds of uranium missing, Shapiro,
who had founded NUMEC, was accused of espionage and of having di-
verted nuclear materials to Israel. Seymour Hersh, the author of *The Samson Option: Israel's Nuclear Arsenal and America's Foreign Policy,* argues that
Shapiro did nothing wrong and quotes one of the chief investigators as
saying, "I know of nothing at all to indicate that Shapiro was guilty." Shapiro was never indicted, but rumors of illegal American Jewish involvement in Israel's nuclear program dogged him for the rest of his life. To
many American Zionists, for his role in abetting Israel's security, Shapiro
was an uncelebrated hero. (Seymour Hersh, *The Samson Option: Israel's
Nuclear Arsenal and America's Foreign Policy* [New York: Random House,
1991], pp. 243, 250, 252, 255.)

Algeria and the dimming light of colonialism undoubtedly made the idea of cooperating with Israel even more appealing. France made a commitment to provide engineers and technicians, a facility for separating plutonium, and missile capabilities. Israel would become one of only a handful of countries to have nuclear capacity. In the shadow of the Holocaust, Israel's insightful journalist and commentator Avi Shavit notes, it was not lost on the very few who knew about the plan that for the first time in history, the Jews could have the ability to annihilate other peoples.[17]

By 1960, the United States knew that France was helping Israel build a nuclear reactor. When he became president in early 1961, Kennedy, committed to nuclear nonproliferation, was deeply concerned; accordingly, Israel and the United States signed an agreement that stipulated that beginning in 1962, U.S. officials could visit Dimona, where the reactor was situated, once a year. For some time, the Americans could uncover no evidence of a nuclear program. As the Americans became more suspicious, Israel went to ever greater lengths to hide what was really taking place at Dimona. The Israelis built simulated control rooms; they covered entrances to the underground portions of the facility and even spread pigeon droppings around some buildings to make it appear that they were not in use.

Though Israel passed these inspections, it was clear that the ruse would not work forever. In 1969, Golda Meir, by then prime minister, reached an agreement with Richard Nixon—who had just been elected president—that Israel would pursue its program, but would not reveal that it had the weapon. Israel could have the security that it needed to ensure that Holocaust-like genocidal campaigns against the Jews were a relic of the past, without goading the Arab world into seeking a weapon of its own.

IT WAS AGAINST THIS complex background—German reparations, the Kasztner trial, and (though known only to a small elite) Israel's pursuit of a protective nuclear weapon—that Eichmann's capture hit Israelis like a thunderbolt. Israelis applauded, foreign countries condemned, and even American Jews were very conflicted. Indeed, with Eichmann's capture, the fragile agreement between Ben-Gurion and Jacob Blaustein reached ten years earlier came close to unraveling. Not wishing Israel to establish itself as the central address for world Jewry, the American Jewish Committee believed that the Eichmann trial should not be held in Israel; some of its members even met with Golda Meir to emphasize their displeasure at the prospect. Infuriating the Israeli officials, AJC leaders charged that trying Eichmann in Jerusalem would undermine the fact that he had committed "unspeakable crimes against humanity, not only against Jews."[18]

Ben-Gurion, incensed by these sentiments, unleashed his criticism in a number of public ways. As to the charge levied against the Israelis by the American Jewish Committee, Ben-Gurion took to the *New York Times* the following December to say:

> Now I see it argued, by Jews among others, that Israel is legally entitled to try Eichmann but ethically should not do so because Eichmann's crime, in its enormity, was against humanity and the conscience of humanity rather than against Jews as such. Only a Jew with an inferiority complex could say that; only one who does not realize that a Jew is a human being.[19]

The reference to "a crime against humanity"—as opposed to a crime against the Jewish people—was a thinly veiled attack on the AJC's greater comfort in speaking about crimes against humanity than crimes against the Jewish people.*

---

* Ben-Gurion's comments were part of an ongoing tendency of Israeli leaders to criticize American Jews for any one of a number of faults, in this case, their having a greater comfort with American universalism than with Jewish particularism. Others, however, pointed to different failings in American Jews. Upon completing his term as Israel's ambassador to the United States, Michael Oren wrote of American Jews—in his memoir entitled *Ally: My Journey Across the American-Israeli Divide*—"I wanted

Ben-Gurion's anger was directed not only at the AJC, but at American Jews at large, whom he now accused of downplaying Jewish suffering in the Holocaust. The "Judaism of Jews of the United States is losing all meaning and only a blind man can fail to see the day of its extinction," he said. Those Jews who did not live in Israel faced "the kiss of death and the slow . . . decline into the abyss of assimilation."[20] Rhetoric such as this constituted a flagrant violation of the spirit of the Blaustein agreement just ten years earlier. Ben-Gurion had to know that these comments would send Blaustein into a rage. He apparently did not care.

It took extended effort to get Blaustein back from the brink, and some of the damage was irreparable. Just as reparations had hastened the unraveling of the kibbutz's foundational ethos, it was ironically the capture of a Nazi that drove a further wedge into the relationship between the Jews of Israel and those of the United States.

THE EICHMANN TRIAL BEGAN in Jerusalem on April 11, 1961.

The prosecution began by evoking centuries of Jewish history. It accused Eichmann of standing in a long line of enemies of the Jewish people, including Pharaoh and Haman.* The prosecution was intent on making the trial about not only what had happened to the specific survivors who would testify, but what the Nazis had done to the Jewish people as a whole. While some witnesses called to the stand had actually crossed paths with Eichmann during the war,

---

to accuse them [American Jews] of that most narcissistic of sins: ingratitude." (Michael Oren, *Ally: My Journey Across the American-Israeli Divide* [New York: Random House, 2015], p. 267.)

* The two are, in the biblical narrative, classic villains who sought to eradicate the Jewish people. Pharaoh commanded that all male Israelite babies be cast into the Nile (Exodus 1:22). Haman is the villain of the biblical Book of Esther, who told the King, "There is a certain people . . . whose laws are different from those of any other people. . . . If it please Your Majesty, let an edict be drawn for their destruction" (Esther 3:8–9).

the trial also heard from survivors who had not encountered Eich-mann but could speak of the horrors of the war, of the indescribable suffering and the devastation wrought by the Nazis' assault on Europe's Jewry. Some observers objected to this decision, but Gideon Hausner, the chief prosecutor, insisted that their ultimate responsibility was to give the Holocaust "its place in history."[21]

Israel's youth received the education Ben-Gurion believed they needed. The trial spared no details. Witnesses described watching women, men, and children murdered in cold blood. One witness described how her child was shot as she held him in her arms. Another described a horrific scene in which thousands of French children, separated from their parents and without any adult supervision, were herded into dank, squalid rooms: "It was not uncommon for them to awake during the night screaming for their parents. Some were too young to know their own names."[22] The children were deported—"struggling and screaming"[23]—to Auschwitz, where they were murdered and incinerated.

Another witness attempted to read the last letter her husband would ever write to her and the last words he would impart to his children: "My dear wife and children . . . We are setting out upon a very long journey. . . . I shall somehow bear my fate whatever it may be. I do not want to make you sad but I would want very much to live yet in your midst. May God grant us that we may be allowed to achieve that."[24] The woman to whom the letter had been addressed became so overwrought that she could not read it; she passed it on to one of the lawyers to read on her behalf, but he, too, found reading the letter almost unbearable.

A prisoner at Birkenau described being separated from his wife and daughter, who were "sent to the 'left'—that is, the gas chambers. He recalled that, despite the crush of people, he could identify them because of his little girl's red coat. 'The red spot was a sign that my wife was near there. The red spot was getting smaller and smaller. . . .' He never saw them again."[25]

Perhaps the most memorable testimony was given by Yehiel De-Nur, who had been a prisoner in Auschwitz. De-Nur had already

written under the pen name Ka-Tsetnik 135633,* but when he testi-
fied at the trial, his true identity became known to many Israelis
for the first time. De-Nur began his testimony with a spell-binding
description of the world of Auschwitz, a world, he said, which was
for all intents and purposes a different planet. He called Auschwitz
the "planet of ashes."

Quickly, though, De-Nur's testimony became quirky and then
incoherent, and then he fainted.[26] The image of De-Nur slumped
on the witness stand with police officers trying to revive him gave
Israelis a sense of the horror of which many were hearing for the
first time.

Just as world Jewry had huddled around radios in November 1947 to follow the vote on partition at the UN's General Assembly, Israelis were now glued to their radios, transfixed by the
stories and horrors. Implicitly, the testimony of the witnesses gave
the thousands of Israeli survivors "permission" to begin speaking
about their experiences. That had not always been the case. Given
the Israeli focus on the "new Jew" who could defend himself, these
survivors with tattooed numbers on their arms, who seemed psy-
chically and physically broken, had represented precisely the Jews
that Israelis wanted to forget and to transcend. They often unfavor-
ably compared Holocaust victims to the new, powerful Jews of the
Yishuv who dislodged the British and fought off the Arabs with
strength and military might. Tellingly, "[t]hose killed in the Holocaust were said to have 'perished,' while Jews who died fighting in
Palestine had 'fallen.'"[27]

Tommy Lapid, a survivor of the Budapest ghetto and ultimately
a well-known Israeli journalist and successful politician (and father

---

* Both De-Nur's name and his pen name were symbolically laden. He had
been born Yehiel Feiner in Europe, but changed his name (as did many
European immigrants to Israel) to De-Nur, which in Aramaic means "out
of the fire." His pen name, Ka-Tsetnik 135633, is a shortening of the *Konzen-
trationslager,* which means someone in a concentration camp. 135633 was
De-Nur's prisoner number.

of Yair Lapid, also a much admired journalist and founder of the political party *Yesh Atid*), recalled years later how veteran members of the Yishuv essentially accused the survivors for what they had endured. "'Why didn't you fight back?' they would ask. 'Why did you go like sheep to the slaughter?' They were First-Class Jews who took up arms and fought, while we were Second-Class Yids whom the Germans could annihilate without encountering resistance."[28] Perhaps worse still, those who had been born in the Yishuv and come of age there made light of the horrific uses that Nazis had for the bodies of the murdered Jews. They knew, for example, that the Nazis had used the bodies of Jews to make soap. Lapid recalled:

> At the time, there was a cook . . . who was a survivor of Auschwitz with a number tattooed in blue on his arm. The long-time staffers called him Soap, a twisted play on the famed Nazi plan to use Jewish body fat to make soap. "Hey, Soap," they would say. "What's for lunch today?" to which Soap would chuckle uncomfortably and fill their plates.[29]

Now, with the trial, matters began to change. The prosecution made no attempt to dodge the question of why survivors had not resisted. One poignant moment silenced those questions. A witness by the name of Beisky was describing, in traumatic detail, how fifteen thousand prisoners watched while a young boy was hoisted up on a chair to be hanged. The rope on the noose broke, agonizing the poor boy, who began to cry out for mercy. The SS soldiers then reissued the order for the hanging. In a seemingly merciless move, one of the lawyers in the case asked the witness describing this horrific scene why the thousands of prisoners who watched this unfold did not react. The witness said the following:

> I cannot describe this . . . terror inspiring fear. . . . Nearby us there was a Polish camp. There were 1,000 Poles. . . . One hundred meters beyond the camp they had a place to go to—their

homes. I don't recall one instance of escape on the part of the
Poles. But where could any of the Jews go? We were wearing
clothes which . . . were dyed yellow with yellow stripes. [In] the
hair at the centre of [our] head . . . they made a kind of swath
in a stripe 4 centimeters in width. And at that moment, let us
suppose that the 15,000 people within the camp even succeeded
without armed strength . . . to go beyond the boundaries of the
camp—where would they go? What could they do?[30]

IN 1943, YEARS BEFORE the establishment of the state, as news of
Nazi atrocities had begun to spread in the Yishuv, the Ukrainian-
born Hebrew writer Haim Hazaz published "The Sermon." The
short story's main character is Yudke (a diminutive of Yehudah,
Hebrew for Judah), a kibbutz member usually reticent to speak.
One evening, though, Yudke erupts with a speech that became an
Israeli classic.

> I want to state that I am opposed to Jewish history. . . . [W]e
> didn't make our own history, the goyim made it for us. . . . What
> is there in it? Oppression, defamation, persecution, martyrdom.
> I would simply forbid teaching our children Jewish history. Why
> the devil teach them about their ancestors' shame? I would just
> say to them: "Boys, from the day we were exiled from our land
> we've been a people without a history. Class dismissed. Go out
> and play soccer."[31]

Finally, even if belatedly, the Eichmann trial forced Israeli society to see that Yudke was wrong. No Jewish person present could
have meaning unanchored from a Jewish past. The new Israeli had
wanted to start the Jewish narrative over, but the trial had made
it clear to Israeli society—Jewish life could not be lived without a
profound attachment to Jewish history, no matter how painful that
might sometimes be.

THE COURT SENTENCED EICHMANN to death. (Coincidentally, one of the three judges was Benjamin Halevy, who had presided over the Kafr Kassem trial.) He was hanged on May 31, 1962, two years after his capture. In order that his grave not become a shrine, he was cremated and his ashes were dumped into the sea outside Israel's territorial waters. No mere murderer, Eichmann was an almost mythical enemy of the Jewish people. His execution has been the only instance of capital punishment by a civil court in the history of the Jewish state.*

The Holocaust had long been a troubling dimension of Jewish history for the Yishuv and the early state. In large measure, that was because the new Jew of the Yishuv was seeking to create an image of Jews very different from the helpless, tortured victims in Europe. Now that new Jew had come to be. It was time to add nuance to the story that Israelis told about themselves and their people.

It was a painful process for the young state, but if anything, it made even clearer to a generation that had known little of the Holocaust how critical it was that the Jews have a state they could call their own.

---

* On June 30, 1948, some six weeks after Israel declared independence and in the midst of the War of Independence, an IDF officer named Meir Tabiansky was falsely accused of espionage and sentenced to death in a drumhead court martial. He was executed by firing squad, but was later exonerated. (Shabtai Teveth, *Ben Gurion's Spy: The Story of the Political Scandal That Shaped Modern Israel* [New York: Columbia University Press, 1996], pp. 31–54.)

SIX DAYS OF WAR CHANGE
A COUNTRY FOREVER

*All that I love was cast at my feet. . . . The old Land of Israel, the
homeland of my youth, the other half of my cleft country.*

— Israeli poet Haim Gouri, after the Six-Day War

By 1967, the Jewish state had survived an onslaught of unre-
lenting attacks, had absorbed over a million immigrants,[1] had
emerged as a player on the international stage, and was quickly cultivating national, political, and cultural traditions. Many challenges
undoubtedly lay ahead, but nineteen years after its founding, Israel
had fared far better than anyone might have dared imagine when
the United Nations had voted in November 1947 to create a Jewish
state.

Yet Jerusalem was still divided. In the War of Independence, the
fledgling Israel Defense Forces had been unable to hold on to the
eastern portion of Jerusalem and the Old City, which was now in
Jordanian hands. For nearly two decades, a wall of cinder block and
barbed wire ran through the heart of the country's capital. Even
if the Israeli government was prepared to live with that, for many
Jews, most particularly (but certainly not exclusively) in the religious community, it was a wound that refused to heal.

As Independence Day 1967 approached, Jerusalem mayor Teddy

Kollek commissioned songs about Jerusalem that could be broadcast on national radio as part of the second annual Israeli Song Festival. Until then, few Israeli poets or composers had written songs
about Jerusalem. The handful that had been written since the turn
of the century made no mention of the facts that the city was divided or that Jews could not approach the Western Wall or even
enter the Old City.

So Kollek asked five people, including songwriter Naomi
Shemer, to compose songs about Jerusalem. Intimidated by the
challenge of writing a popular song about such a fraught subject, all of them declined. Eventually, though, Shemer relented
and wrote a song. She called it "Jerusalem of Gold."

"In the slumber of tree and stone, hostage to her dream," the
first verse declared, "is the city that sits alone, while in her heart
there lies a wall."[2] Then came the now well-known refrain:

> *Jerusalem of gold, and of bronze and of light*
> *Behold for all your songs, I am the violin.*[3]

The song, originally sung by a young, unknown soprano
named Shuli Natan, became an instantaneous hit, heard on the
radio seemingly incessantly. "Israelis had suppressed their longing
for the missing parts of Jerusalem," wrote one of Israel's keenest
observers, "but now they were singing along with Shuli Natan,
mourning their divided capital."[4] Now Jerusalem, like Israel itself,
had an (unofficial) anthem.

IN THE RELIGIOUS COMMUNITY, the despair over Jerusalem's division was particularly poignant. The Western Wall—the only remnant of the ancient Temple in Jerusalem—was off-limits to Jews.
For two thousand years, Jews had prayed there, albeit in small
numbers. Now, because Israel had lost the Old City of Jerusalem
in the War of Independence, and because Hebron and other traditionally sacred Jewish sites were also in enemy hands, the Jewish

state ironically had sovereignty over no traditionally Jewish sacred places.

Just a day before Naomi Shemer's song hit the airwaves, Rabbi Zvi Yehuda Kook (son of the mystic bridge builder Rabbi Abraham Isaac Kook) spoke to his disciples about his own experience of the day of the UN vote nineteen years earlier. Like David Ben-Gurion and Menachem Begin, he, too, had been unable to celebrate, but for a different reason:

> The whole nation flowed into the streets to celebrate its feelings of joy. . . . [But] I couldn't go out and join in the rejoicing. I sat alone, and burdened. In those first hours I couldn't make my peace with what had happened, with the terrible news that the word of God in the book of the Prophets had not been fulfilled: "They divided my land!" . . . Where is our Hebron? Have we forgotten it? And where is our Shechem [Nablus]—have we forgotten it? And where is our Jericho—have we forgotten it? And where is the other bank of the Jordan River? Where is every clod of earth? Every piece of God's land? Do we have the right to cede even a centimeter of it? God forbid! . . . In that state, my whole body was stunned, wounded and severed into pieces. I couldn't celebrate. "They divided my land!" They divided the land of God! . . . I couldn't go outside to dance and rejoice. That is how the situation was nineteen years ago.[5]

According to those who were present, the reaction was "[t]otal silence. The students had never heard such grief, such outrage, from their rabbi."[6] What, they wondered, was he trying to tell them?

FOR SOME TIME, the region had been growing increasingly tense. Syria had declared its intention to divert water away from Israel's National Water Carrier, by up to 35 percent. Israel had responded that it would consider such a diversion an act of war, but the Syrians continued. Border clashes ensued, with Syria firing on Israeli villages while Israel attacked heavy earth-moving equipment the Syrians were using for the project.

In the spring of 1967, outside parties consciously added fuel to the fire. The Soviets informed Egyptian and Syrian representatives that Israel had brought twelve brigades to the north in preparation for attack. Prime Minister Eshkol denied the claims, and on April 26, he even invited the Soviet ambassador, Dmitri Chucakhin, to go to the north with him and to see for himself. (Chucakhin declined.) Though the United States also insisted that the Soviet reports were utterly false, the Syrians chose to believe the Soviets. By informing Syria and Egypt that Israel was planning a war, the Soviets were, in essence, sparking one.

A few weeks later, on May 15, Israel staged its annual Independence Day Parade. Typically held in a different location each year, in 1967 the parade was scheduled to take place in Jerusalem.[*] As always, the parade was largely military in nature, designed to highlight the army's strength by displaying massive amounts of armor. That year, though, in keeping with Israel's 1949 armistice agreement with the Jordanians that Israel would limit the number of tanks it brought to Jerusalem, the parade included much less armor than usual. To the Egyptians and Syrians, on high alert because of the Soviets' warning, the small number of tanks in the parade seemed to confirm that the tanks were elsewhere, preparing for war.

As the parade proceeded, an Israeli official passed a note from IDF intelligence to Yitzhak Rabin—now the IDF's chief of staff— who in turn passed it on to Prime Minister Eshkol.[†] Egyptian ar-

---

[*] The last annual parade took place a year later, in 1968. Israel discontinued the parades due to their high costs. One final parade was held in 1973, in honor of Israel's twenty-fifth anniversary.

[†] According to the historian Michael Oren, Rabin and Eshkol actually received a note the night before the parade telling them of the Egyptian troops entering the Sinai. They continued to receive notes throughout the next day at the parade, updating them on the situation. (Michael Oren, *Six Days of War: June 1967 and the Making of the Modern Middle East* [Oxford: Oxford University Press, 2002], pp. 61–63.)

mored vehicles, it said, had entered the Sinai Peninsula. Eshkol and Rabin chose to act with restraint, but as the day went on, the notes became more frequent and urgent. What was supposed to be a day of celebration was quickly turning into something much more ominous.

The Israeli leadership was not certain how to respond. On the one hand, they knew that Nasser was an aficionado of such military displays and still hoped that he was not intent on war; on the other, they knew that Egypt and Syria had signed a mutual defense treaty several months earlier. But Israel's hope that the crisis might be resolved diplomatically or with a minor military action eroded when Cairo Radio announced, "Our forces are in a complete state of readiness for war."[7] On May 15, a day that Arab nations marked with mourning for their defeat in the 1948 war (and the day of the parade), Nasser declared, "Brothers, it is our duty to prepare for the final battle in Palestine."[8] The long-anticipated "next round" in the Arab campaign to destroy Israel seemed increasingly likely.

THE NEXT THREE WEEKS—known in Israel as the *hamtanah* ("the waiting period")—were one of the most stressful periods in Israel's history. The Egyptians poured five divisions of troops and equipment into the Sinai, each one composed of 15,000 men, 100 tanks, 150 armored personnel carriers, and a supply of Soviet artillery.

Did Nasser truly intend to go to war, or was this all a matter of posturing, of restoring Arab pride, that ultimately got out of hand? Scholars remain divided on that subject. Whatever his true intentions, Nasser's actions created the sense among Israelis that his goal was war. On May 16, he raised the stakes by taking the impending conflict into the international arena. Since 1957 (after the 1956 Sinai Campaign), the UN Emergency Force had stationed several thousand troops in dozens of observation posts along the international border of Gaza and Sharm al-Sheikh (the name of the area at the very southern tip of the Sinai Peninsula). The troops were to stop infiltrations into Israel and to make sure that Egypt did not close the Straits of Tiran. (See Map 8.) Now, though, Egyptian troops were streaming into the Sinai.

In what was a clear act of belligerency, Nasser instructed U Thant to remove the UN troops from the region. Israel assumed that the secretary-general would put up at least some pro forma resistance. But U Thant complied immediately, without so much as informing the General Assembly. By May 19, there was no UN presence in the area. The United Nations, it was painfully clear, was not going to offer Israel protection against an onslaught.

The political and military brass agreed that Israel would consider Egyptian steps to close the Straits of Tiran (which connected the southern Israeli port of Eilat with the Red Sea and was Israel's critical commercial link to the east)⁹ a casus belli (an act that justifies war). Two days later, Egypt did just that. In the space of eight days, Egypt had successfully erased every diplomatic gain Israel had made in the 1956 Sinai Campaign.

THE DIPLOMATIC FRONT NOW became the most critical. The man at the center of Israel's international efforts was Abba Eban. Born in Cape Town in 1915, Eban moved with his family to London when he was an infant. He later studied classics and Oriental languages at Cambridge, at which time he became very involved with the Federation of Zionist Youth and edited its journal. At the start of World War II, Eban began his career by working with Chaim Weizmann at the World Zionist Organization. He then served as a British Army intelligence officer, in both Egypt and Palestine.

By 1947, Eban was appointed liaison to the United Nations Special Committee on Palestine (UNSCOP), at which point he Hebraicized his first name to Abba. He later served both as Israel's ambassador to the United States and, simultaneously, its ambassador to the United Nations. He returned to Israel in 1959 and was elected to the Knesset. In 1966, he began what would be an eight-year stint as foreign minister.

In Eban, Israel had a uniquely brilliant, articulate, and eminently qualified representative. (Years later, President Lyndon Johnson told Eban, "I think you are the most eloquent speaker in the world today.") Eban rushed to France, which only eleven years earlier had been Israel's chief ally in the Sinai Campaign and was still its main supplier of armaments. But Eban departed for France worried that those sands were shifting. Hervé Alphand, secretary-general of the French Foreign Ministry, had stated not long before that "there was no contradiction between France's recognition of 'Israel's existence' and France's friendship with the Arab states."[10] It was not lost on the Israelis that Alphand had spoken merely of "Israel's existence" but of actual "friendship" with Arab states.

Eban's meeting with French president Charles De Gaulle confirmed his fears. De Gaulle insisted that the situation had to be resolved by France, Britain, the United States, and the Soviet Union. But that was a patently cynical demand that no one could satisfy; the USSR was fanning the flames of the conflict and was not going to facilitate a diplomatic solution. De Gaulle also warned that Israel must not be the one to "shoot first." When Eban pointed out that the closing of the Straits of Tiran constituted a casus belli, De Gaulle rejected the notion out of hand. That Egypt was crippling Israel's economy could not have mattered less to the French leader. When Eban pointed out to De Gaulle that in 1956 France had promised that it would recognize Israel's right to fight if Egypt imposed a blockade, which is precisely what had happened, De Gaulle responded nonchalantly that 1967 was not 1956.

Disappointed by France, Eban proceeded to London and met with the Labour prime minister, Harold Wilson. There he found some support. Wilson told him that the cabinet had met and "that the policy of blockade must not be allowed to triumph."[11]

In return for Israel's leaving the Sinai in 1957, the United States had promised to recognize Israel's right to self-defense should Egypt ever close the Straits of Tiran again. But Eban's meeting with President Lyndon Johnson, his next stop after London, was disappointing. Johnson agreed that Egypt's closing the Straits was "illegal" and told Eban that the United States was formulating a "Red

Sea Regatta" plan, to use an international convoy of ships from forty maritime powers, affirming free passage through the Straits of Tiran to guarantee international maritime rights.

Eban left the meeting uneasy. Israel was facing an existential threat, while Johnson—clearly preoccupied with the American war in Vietnam—was unlikely to be able to act on the Regatta plan. Like De Gaulle, Johnson also warned Israel not to be the first to attack. "Israel will not be alone unless it decides to go alone," said the American president.

It was a far cry from the commitments the United States had made in 1957. The United States, like France, was reneging on its 1956 promise.

AS EBAN TRAVERSED THE world with only marginal success, matters in Israel became increasingly tense. The primary question facing the country's leadership was whether to wait before shooting, as America had demanded, or to gain the upper hand by attacking first. Prime Minister Levi Eshkol insisted that Israel had to wait: "It is not politically, diplomatically and perhaps even morally logical to start a war," he said. "Now we have to restrain ourselves and to maintain our forces for a week or two or even longer. . . . [M]aturity demands that we stand up to this test."[12]

On May 27, the cabinet voted to wait before acting. The next day, May 28, Eshkol took to the airwaves, seeking to calm an already rattled public. Israel, he said, still hoped to settle the crisis diplomatically, with the assistance of the United States.

His speech, though, was a disaster. As Yehuda Avner, the prime minister's English speechwriter, would later recall:

> There then came the sound of more paper being rustled, accompanied this time by repeated grunts of "Err, err," as if Eshkol had lost his place, or was struggling to decipher scribbled alterations about "responsible decision-making" and "unity of purpose." . . . [H]e stumbled along, speaking in fits and starts, stuttering "Err,

err" over and over again. . . . His audience was a frightened nation, and the more he stumbled over his reading, the more indecisive and panic-stricken he sounded, even when he rounded off with an assurance that Israel would know how to defend itself if attacked.[13]

Eshkol's radio disaster became known as the "Stammering Speech." "Suddenly, the country seemed powerless and leaderless," Avner later recalled. "Israel's enemies rejoiced while Israeli soldiers in the trenches smashed their transistors and broke down in tears."[14] "It's amazing how a people who suffered a Holocaust is willing to believe and endanger itself once again," wrote a leading columnist for the *Ha'aretz* newspaper.[15]

In fairness to Eshkol, he had originally planned to record the speech at his home, but he was late reviewing it and by the time he finished making changes to the text, the pages were filled with cross outs, comments, and arrows. The studio then informed him that it was too late to prerecord the speech, and the prime minister was forced to read the speech live, from pages that were heavily and almost illegibly marked up.

But the damage had been done, and public confidence in Eshkol had evaporated. Calls for his removal followed, along with suggestions that Ben-Gurion reassume the role of prime minister. Another *Ha'aretz* columnist wrote the following day:

> If we could truly believe that Eshkol was really capable of navigating the ship of state in these crucial days, we would willingly follow him. But we have no such belief after his radio address last night. The proposal that Ben-Gurion be entrusted with the premiership and Moshe Dayan with the Ministry of Defense, while Eshkol takes charge of domestic affairs, seems to us a wise one.[16]

The military brass was deeply frustrated by the prime minister's decision to wait. Ariel Sharon, by then a general, an infantry brigade commander, and still a rising star in the IDF, thought Israel's delay was a major strategic blunder:

Today we have removed with our own hand our most powerful weapon—the enemy's fear of us. We have the power to destroy the Egyptian army, but if we give in on the free passage issue, we have opened the door to Israel's destruction. We will have to pay a far higher price in the future for something that we in any case had to do now. . . . The people of Israel are ready to wage a just war, to fight, and to pay the price. The question isn't free passage but the existence of the people of Israel.[17]

On May 29, Jordan's King Hussein flew to Cairo to meet with Nasser. Nasser brought to the meeting the defense pact he had signed with Syria a year earlier, and Hussein said, "Give me another copy; let us replace the word Syria by the word Jordan and the matter will be arranged."[18]

Israel had invested a great deal in building a relationship with Jordan. In the War of Independence, the relationship had held fairly firm despite fighting in and around Jerusalem. Palestinian incursions notwithstanding, there had been relative peace on the Israel-Jordan border for nineteen years. But now, under unbearable pressure, the king felt he had no choice but to go to war. The Jordanians also signed a mutual defense pact with Syria, and Israel was now facing the possibility of war on three different fronts: Syria, Jordan, and Egypt. A day later, Iraqi troops reached Egypt, just as they had in 1948, eager to join the fight.

In the meantime, the United States did little. There were no ships in the area that could support an effort to break the blockade, and Israel had no time to spare. American and British requests for other countries to join them went mostly ignored. Johnson announced that he could see no way out of the crisis, while the White House—focusing on its endless problems in Vietnam and wary of expending precious political capital on yet another military venture—simply ignored Israel's pleas for missiles, tanks, and jets.

The news from France was even worse. De Gaulle had earlier told Eban that France would impose an arms boycott on whichever country fired first. But De Gaulle changed his mind and banned all weapons sales to Israel even before the outbreak of any hostilities. France apparently did not believe that Israel could defeat the Arabs and therefore saw this as an opportunity to revive its long-term relations with the Muslim world.

So great was the stress that even Rabin, the IDF's chief of staff, began to falter. He barely ate, was smoking some seventy cigarettes a day, and drank copious amounts of coffee—and then suffered a nervous breakdown. Knowing that its lead soldier had collapsed on the eve of a war would have sent an already frightened country into uncontrolled panic, so his ailment was called "nicotine poisoning."[19] Rabin's doctor was only slightly more honest and called it "acute anxiety." As Yossi Klein Halevi, a profound observer of Israeli society, noted, "Israel was facing not just a war but a war of survival, the end of the Jewish dream of sovereignty, and the responsibility had overwhelmed Rabin."[20]

Rabin rested for a day, was medicated, and returned to active duty.

ISRAEL'S PRIME ALLY at the moment of crisis was world Jewry. European and American Jews, listening to the rhetoric coming from Arab capitals, understood that this was no game. Knowing that they had underreacted during the Holocaust, American Jews were not prepared to make the same mistake again. They contributed money, organized rallies, and applied political pressure in Washington.

A rally in New York in support of Israel attracted 150,000 people, the largest rally American Jews had ever staged. (AIPAC—the American Israel Public Affairs Committee, which would eventually become American Judaism's central voice on Capitol Hill in support of the U.S.-Israel relationship—existed during this period, but would achieve genuine influence only a decade later.)[21] Within six months, the United Jewish Appeal's "emergency campaign" raised $307 million. American Jews were deeply moved—a new relationship between American Jews and Israel was dawning, just

as Jews everywhere wondered whether the Jewish state would survive an inevitable onslaught. Across America, individual Jews dug
deep, just as Israelis had, to do what they could to ensure the state's
survival. One couple in Beachwood, Ohio, for example, who had
been painstakingly saving money for years toward a renovation of
their home, pledged all the money they had saved to Israel.[22]

But the Arab world had also awakened. On May 26, Nasser announced, "Our basic objective will be to destroy Israel."[23] Ahmed
Shukeiri, who had been the Saudi ambassador to the United Nations from 1957 to 1962 and who would eventually become the Palestine Liberation Organization's chairman, declared, "In the event
of a conflagration, no Jews whatsoever will survive."[24] Protests
were held in Cairo, Baghdad, and Damascus, and throngs of people
gathered in the streets, chanting, "Death to the Jews!" and "Throw
the Jews into the sea!"[25]

Herzl and Bialik's Europe had come to the Middle East. Just
twenty-two years after the ovens of Auschwitz had burned thousands of Jews daily and five years after Israelis had been riveted
and horrified by the Eichmann trial, the Arab world consciously
evoked Holocaust imagery. One cartoon in an Egyptian newspaper
depicted a hand stabbing the heart of a Star of David; it was signed,
"Nile Oils and Soaps Company," a clear reference to the Nazi practice of making soap out of the bodies of dead Jews.

Israel prepared for the worst. Rabbis across the country cor-
doned off areas to be used as mass graves. The Ramat Gan stadium
was consecrated as ground for the burial of up to forty thousand
people. Hotels were cleared of guests so the facilities could be used
as massive emergency first-aid stations. Schools were converted
into bomb shelters, there were daily air raid drills, and in an ironic
twist on the Kindertransport of 1938–1940 in which Jewish children
were shuttled out of harm's way (mostly to England), plans were
prepared to send Israeli children to Europe. Israeli intelligence reported to Eshkol that poison gas equipment had been detected in
the Sinai but that Israel had no stockpiles of gas masks. Eshkol mut-
tered in Yiddish, the language of his youth from Europe, "Blood

is going to spill like water." There was even black humor; Israelis joked that there was a sign at the country's only international airport that read, THE LAST ONE TO LEAVE, PLEASE TURN OUT THE LIGHTS.[26]

BY JUNE 1, IT WAS clear that Johnson's Regatta plan—the international effort to open the waterways—had aroused no international interest and was not going to happen. Asked if the United States would seek to restrain Israel from firing first, U.S. secretary of state Dean Rusk replied, "I don't think it is our business to restrain anybody."[27] Israel had the first indication that it might be allowed to attack.[28]

Domestically, Eshkol understood the country's mood and decided that, more than anything, the government needed to make a show of unity. He established Israel's first "unity government," bringing leaders of the opposition into the cabinet. Among those opposition leaders was Menachem Begin, who under Ben-Gurion had been banished to the political desert. Eshkol's unity government moved Begin closer to the center of Israeli politics.

In response to widespread demand, Moshe Dayan, who was a member of Ben-Gurion's Rafi Party and not Eshkol's Labor Party, was appointed defense minister. Israel's nervous public, which had never seen a unity government before, greeted Dayan's appointment with cheers.

Then, in a move that astounded his colleagues, Begin actually suggested that Ben-Gurion be brought back to serve as prime minister during the crisis. Ben-Gurion declined, but the gesture softened his attitude to Begin and a tentative relationship began to develop. "If I knew Begin like I know him now," he would later say, "the face of history would have been different."[29]

At the unity government's first meeting on Thursday, June 1, 1967, the decision was made that the political echelon would meet with the general staff and defense committee the next morning, in the "Pit," an underground operations center at the IDF headquarters in Tel Aviv. At that meeting, on Friday, the government made the decision to go to war. On Saturday, June 3, the generals (Sharon, Rabin, Yeshayahu Gavish, and others) presented their war plans, and Dayan said that the cabinet would meet the next day to authorize the army to act.

On Sunday, in a seven-hour meeting, Dayan presented his military proposal to the cabinet. The situation was dire: the Egyptians had at least 100,000 troops and 900 tanks in the Sinai. To the north, Syria had readied 75,000 men and 400 tanks, while the Jordanians had amassed 32,000 men and almost 300 tanks. In total, Israel faced a potential force of 207,000 soldiers and 1,600 tanks. With full mobilization, Israel could muster 264,000 soldiers but had only 800 tanks. When it came to planes, the situation was even worse. The Arabs had 700 combat aircraft, while Israel had only 300.

But Dayan insisted that Israel could win if its forces struck soon. He asked the cabinet to approve a first strike, with the further request that he and Rabin alone would determine the timing. The cabinet voted 12–5 to authorize a preemptive attack on Egypt. The timing of the attack was left to Dayan and Rabin.

ON THE MORNING OF June 5, the Fifty-Fifth Paratrooper Brigade was stationed at the Tel Nof air force base, not far from Rehovot, a small Israeli city along the Mediterranean Sea situated about twelve miles south of Tel Aviv. At 7:10 A.M., the Israeli soldiers were astonished to see dozens of planes taking off, flying extremely low and heading south. Thanks to their location, they were some of the very few soldiers who saw the planes taking off and then returning for the next ninety minutes.

By seven thirty A.M., two hundred Israeli jet-fighters were flying toward Egypt, ready to attack. Israel knew that at that hour Egypt's pilots would be eating breakfast, and that their planes would be entirely unattended. The attacking force represented a huge portion of Israel's air force; only twelve planes stayed behind to defend the entire country, a terribly risky move. The attacking planes flew dangerously low, often at an altitude of only fifteen meters, to evade Egypt's radar. One paratrooper later recalled that the planes were flying so low that it felt that if he reached his arm up, he could have touched one of them.

The pilots observed strict radio silence. All had been told that under no circumstances were they to radio for help, no matter how dire their position. If they were desperate, they were to crash their planes into the sea.

Jordanian radar detected the Israeli jets, but they were unable to warn the Egyptians, who had changed their frequency codes without informing the Jordanians. It was a costly mistake. In just three hours, in successive waves of attacks (Israeli aircraft returned to base, were refueled and rearmed, then set out for Egypt again), Israel destroyed hundreds of Egyptian aircraft. A third of Egypt's pilots were killed, thirteen bases were no longer functional, and twenty-three radar stations and antiaircraft sites were knocked out of service. For all intents and purposes, Egypt no longer had an air force.

The Israelis lost seventeen planes and five pilots. One of its planes suffered damage and strayed over Dimona, the site of Israel's nuclear reactor. Because the pilot was unable to communicate over the radio, Israeli hawk missiles shot the Israeli jet out of the air.

At 10:35 A.M., about three hours after the first Israeli planes had taken off, Yitzhak Rabin received a simple report: "The Egyptian air force has ceased to exist."[30] Israel would suffer many losses in the days that would follow, but the IDF's leadership understood what had just happened—Israel had essentially won the war before it had even begun.

THE ISRAELIS APPROACHED JORDAN'S King Hussein, pleading with him not to enter the conflict. Though Jordan had begun firing on Israel, the Israelis said that if the Jordanians held their fire, Israel would continue to accept the terms of the armistice the two countries had signed in 1949. But King Hussein—who may well have believed Nasser's protestations that Egypt was faring well in the

conflict and had to worry about fury among his own population
if he did not join the battle—responded by instructing his troops
to cross the armistice line and by putting his air force on alert to
prepare for action.

At 11:50 A.M., Jordanian, Syrian, and Iraqi planes attacked Israel,
but over the next two hours, the IAF shot down or repelled all the
enemy aircraft and destroyed Jordanian and Syrian air force bases.
On June 5 alone, Israel destroyed four hundred Arab planes. Its air
dominance was now established.

On the ground, Israeli troops cut off the Gaza Strip from the rest
of Egypt. The next day, Israeli soldiers captured Sharm el-Sheikh
without firing a single shot and reopened the Straits of Tiran.

AS HE WAS ON HIS WAY to his swearing-in ceremony on June 5,
Menachem Begin heard the sounds of Jordanian shelling. Yet Begin
sensed not danger, but opportunity. As the cabinet gathered in a
dusty subterranean storeroom filled with used furniture and clean-
ing materials (the cabinet had been instructed to meet there since
shells had fallen on the Knesset lawn, shattering some windows),
Begin suggested that Israel make the most of Hussein's decision to
enter the conflict. Israel, he said, should reclaim the Old City of Jerusalem. When Eshkol expressed concern about the costs that such
a battle would exact, Begin—as he often did—described the conflict in the context of Jewish history. "Gentlemen," he exhorted in
his characteristically impassioned tones, "the Jordanian army is all
but smashed, and our own army is at the city's gates. Our soldiers
are almost in sight of the Western Wall. How can we tell them not
to reach it? We have in our hands a gift of history. Future generations will never forgive us if we do not seize it."[31]

Within a few hours, the IDF command issued the order that two
battalions "break through the barrier separating East and West Jerusalem, navigating through the minefields and trenches and reach
Mount Scopus." The soldiers were told to prepare to take the Old
City and to "erase the shame of 1948."[32] The next day, June 6, para-

troopers entered Jerusalem by bus. Though they could hear shelling on the far side of the city, West Jerusalem—which had been in Israeli hands since 1948 and was now Israel's capital—was silent. Moved but also discomfited by the stillness, the soldiers broke the silence by singing Naomi Shemer's lyrics that had become so familiar to the country in just three weeks. "Jerusalem of gold, and of bronze and of light," they sang. "Behold for all your songs, I am the violin." Little did those "violins" know that they were about to take part in the fiercest battles of the war.

The attack did not begin auspiciously. Based on faulty intelligence, Israel sent ground troops to a Jordanian stronghold now called Ammunition Hill, just outside the Old City, believing that the Israeli force would be three times as large as the defending Jordanian force. But the Jordanians had stationed many more troops there than Israel had expected. The battle began on June 6 at two thirty A.M. and ended at six thirty A.M. As Michael Oren describes the outcome, "The point Israeli squads were all but annihilated. One of their three Shermans was knocked out; the other two could not depress their guns low enough to fire at the submerged Jordanian positions. Unable to call for artillery support without endangering themselves, with their packs too wide to maneuver through the enemy trenches, the paratroopers were compelled to advance without cover over open ground."[33] It was one of the bloodiest battles in the history of the Israeli-Arab conflict. Israel lost thirty-five soldiers in the four-hour battle; seventy-one Jordanian soldiers died.

Still, by four thirty the next morning, after the night of heavy fighting, Israeli soldiers had crossed into the no-man's-land area close to the Old City, and a few hours later, Israel had control of all the Arab areas outside the ancient walls. The soldiers hunkered down, waiting to hear what the cabinet would decide and what orders would come their way. At nine fifteen A.M. Motta Gur, then the commander of the Fifty-Fifth Paratrooper Brigade (and later the IDF's chief of staff) was told—"Go into the Old City immediately and capture it."

Motta sat on the ground and gazed at the walled city. It was a bright, cool morning, and the sun was on his back. The gold and silver domes of the Temple Mount glowed before him. He closed his eyes, as if in prayer. He was about to enter the Jewish pantheon, along with King David, who'd conquered Jerusalem and turned it into his capital; Judah the Maccabee, who'd purified the Temple after its desecration by the Hellenists; Bar Kochba, who'd thrown himself against Rome and lost the Jews' last desperate battle for Jerusalem. Then came the centuries of enforced separation, landscape transformed into memory. And now landscape was re-emerging from dream, shimmering back into tangible reach.[34]

Gur commanded his paratroopers to make their way to the Lion's Gate. An hour later, they had burst through the gates of the Old City and had reached the Temple Mount. Motta Gur took the radio and relayed a report that has now become an iconic Israeli phrase: "The Temple Mount is in our hands."

Only three weeks earlier, Rabbi Zvi Yehuda Kook had stunned his students with his agonized cry, "Where is my Jerusalem?" Now, along with the paratroopers who had just captured the city, he descended from the Temple Mount to the Western Wall. Rabbi Shlomo Goren, chief rabbi of the IDF (and later, chief rabbi of Israel) was also there. Shofar and Torah in hand, he was hoisted onto someone's shoulders. Too moved by the emotion, though, he was unable to sound the traditional ram's horn. Another soldier, who played the trumpet, told Goren to hand him the shofar, and he blew it. The last time that the shofar had been sounded at the Western Wall, it had been by young men of the Irgun who had defied British orders and who had to flee immediately. No longer. For the first time in thousands of years, the Temple Mount and the Western Wall were in sovereign Jewish hands.

BY JUNE 7, JUST TWO DAYS after the war had begun, the Egyptian and Jordanian forces were all but defeated. Nasser ordered a general retreat. Still, though, he refused to sign a cease-fire, because he wanted a clause similar to that of 1956 that would require Israel to leave the Sinai. But De Gaulle had been right: 1967 was not 1956; Israel was not going to agree. Only when he saw that he had no hope of regaining any of the territory he had lost did Nasser accept a cease-fire at midnight on June 8.

AS THE WAR IN the south and in the center of the country had unfolded, the IDF's leadership had struggled with what to do in the north. Dayan and Eshkol were against taking the Golan Heights from the Syrians. Syrian troops, they both insisted, had thus far made no effort to cross the northern border, and both feared that extending the war to the north would provide the Soviets with an excuse to intervene.

But others disagreed. On June 8, David Elazar (commander of Israel's northern front) went to Eshkol to try to convince him to take the Golan. For years, he reminded the prime minister, citizens of Israel's north had lived under regular Syrian shelling and with the constant fear of Syrian infiltration. Syria would start to shell, Israelis would descend to bomb shelters and come out a short while later to find their homes, public buildings, or their fields ablaze. They lived in terror for themselves and their children, and with daily uncertainty about their future. This was Israel's chance to erase these dangers once and for all and to provide the north with a modicum of normalcy.

An emergency Ministerial Committee on Defense convened to hear Elazar's petition as well as Rabin's plan for taking the mountainous region. Even after the presentations, though, Dayan remained unmoved. He was still worried that taking the fighting to the north would provide the Russians with an excuse to enter the battle. Earlier that day, in a case of mistaken identity, Israel had accidentally strafed and bombed an American ship, the USS *Liberty*, just off the coast of Egypt, killing 34 U.S. crewmen, wounding 171, and causing extensive damage to the U.S. Navy's ship. It was a catastrophic moment in U.S.-Israel relations, and the prospect of having the Russians enter the battle just as the Americans were enraged with Israel seemed reckless.

After the meeting, Rabin called Elazar to tell him of the committee's decision. Elazar was disappointed and felt that the government had once again abdicated its responsibility to citizens living on the border. "After all the trouble they've caused, after the shelling and the harassments, are those arrogant bastards going to be left on the top of the hills riding on our backs?" he would later mutter. "If the State of Israel is incapable of defending us, we're entitled to know! We should be told outright that we are not part of the State, not entitled to the protection of the army. We should be told to leave our homes and flee from this nightmare!"[35]

At two A.M., the exhausted military command dispersed and went to bed. But at six, Dayan awakened with a sudden change of heart. He called the central command, which informed him that although Israel had not attacked in the north, Syrian units on the Golan Heights were crumbling and fleeing. At a quarter to seven, Dayan phoned Elazar directly and ordered him to begin the attack on the Golan Heights immediately.[36] When Rabin awoke to the news, he called Elazar and warned him that the central command's assessment was entirely wrong. "The Syrian army is nowhere near collapse. You must assume that it will fight obstinately and with all its strength!"[37]

Rabin was right. The fighting was vicious, and Israeli losses were intense; 115 soldiers were killed in that battle alone, and 306 were wounded. But Syrian losses were greater, and by the night of June 9, the Israelis had the upper hand and Syrian defenses were collapsing.*

---

* While Israeli losses were very high, they would have been even worse were it not for the work of Eli Cohen, one of Israel's most famous spies and now an Israeli legend. Cohen was born in Alexandria, Egypt, in 1924 and enlisted in the Egyptian army in 1947. Following Israel's establishment, Cohen was harassed by the Muslim Brotherhood at the university where

Soon thereafter, the IDF was on its way to capturing Kuneitra, a Syrian town just forty miles west of the Syrian capital, Damascus. When Israel occupied Kuneitra, Syria agreed to a cease-fire. At six thirty P.M. on June 10, the Six-Day War was essentially over.

THE WAR HAD BEEN exceedingly brief—it had lasted a mere 132 hours. And Israel's victory had been decisive. The Egyptians lost between 10,000 and 15,000 men, 5,000 more were missing, and thousands were injured. Jordan lost 700 soldiers, with an additional 6,000 missing or wounded. On the northern front, 450 Syrians died and almost 2,000 were missing or injured. Only 15 percent of Egypt's military hardware remained intact. Israel lost 679 soldiers (some Israeli sources later adjusted that number to about 800) and 2,567 were wounded.*

In terms of territory, the war changed Israel dramatically. Israel had gained forty-two thousand square miles in the war, more than tripling its original size.[38] (See Map 8.) It captured the Gaza Strip, the Sinai Peninsula, the West Bank of the Jordan River (including East Jerusalem), and the Golan Heights. Israel felt like a different country. Haim Gouri, who had become accustomed to Jews not having access to those lands, said after the Six-Day War, "It seemed

---

he was studying; his family, like many other Jewish families, moved to Israel. Cohen, who spoke fluent Arabic, became an Israeli spy and gathered critical intelligence in Syria between 1961 and 1965 after he became chief adviser to the Syrian minister of defense. He was discovered, sentenced to death, and hanged in a Damascus public square in May 1965. Information that he supplied to Israel about Syrian defenses contributed to Israel's lightning capture of the Golan Heights during the Six-Day War.

* Just as had been the case in 1948, Diaspora Jews again paid the price for Israel's victory. Angry mobs attacked Jews and burned synagogues in Egypt, Yemen, Lebanon, Tunisia, and Morocco. In Tripoli (Libya), a pogrom left 18 Jews dead and 25 injured. In Egypt, 800 of the country's 4,000 Jews were arrested. Some 7,000 Jews were expelled from Arab countries, many with nothing but the clothes they were wearing and a small bag of possessions. (Michael Oren, Six Days of War, p. 307.)

to me I'd died and was waking up, resurrected." The once-divided country had finally been reunited. "All that I love was cast at my feet, stunningly ownerless, landscapes revealed as in a dream," Gouri said. "The old Land of Israel, the homeland of my youth, the other half of my cleft country."[39]

DURING THE WAR OF INDEPENDENCE, some seven hundred thousand Arabs had left Israel and made their way to neighboring countries (which would, for the most part, turn them into permanent refugees by refusing to make them citizens). The Six-Day War radically altered their lives once again. They now found themselves living not under Jordanian rule, but Israeli control. There were, in 1967, some 1.25 million Palestinians in the West Bank and Gaza, and their fate would become an issue of international concern.

It is therefore not surprising that as was the case in the 1948 war, revisionist historians (the school of "new historians") would once again seek to fashion a narrative about the Six-Day War that was different from the mainstream Israeli narrative. Some asserted that the war was a result of enduring belligerence of Palmach members who had been frustrated by Ben-Gurion's decision in 1948 not to take the West Bank. Haim Hanegbi, a Jewish Israeli political columnist, for example, wrote, "It must be remembered that in 1967 the army was still commanded by former members of the Palmach who were burning to exploit the Six Day War to complete what was denied them in 1948: To take over the Palestinians' remaining territories and, through the power of conquest, realize the true Greater Israel."[40] Others argued that the war was the product of economic failure, with the government seeking to avert attention from high levels of unemployment. "The process of escalation that started in 1964 was 'not necessary' in the sense that it did not stem from the exigencies of the Arab-Israeli conflict. The force of Israel's reactions in those years expressed . . . a certain strategy . . . compensating for the state's retreat from its social principles."[41]

Over the years, it has become clear that these allegations have argumentative power but not historical merit. Indeed, once thirty years had passed since the war and Israel's State Archive declassified documents from that period (Arab archives remain closed, indefinitely), it was possible to review the diplomatic history and to prove, as Michael Oren did in his magisterial *Six Days of War*, that "Israel was *desperate* to avoid war and, up to the eve of the battle, pursued every avenue in an effort to avert it."[42]

WITH THE GUNS SILENCED and the danger averted, Israel was in the throes of virtually unbridled euphoria. The Jewish state had more than survived. Betrayed by the French, put off by the Americans, and rattled by the Russians, Israelis had been left entirely on their own. And they had won, decisively. The ragtag band of fighters that had pushed the British out of Palestine had now been transformed into a highly professional army. Israel was the region's most powerful country, by a wide margin. And the Jews were out of danger. Gone were the days when one could threaten the Jewish people with impunity. Gone were the days when Jews would cower in fear as their enemies amassed arms. Gone were the days when Jews had to wonder about whether another Holocaust was just around the corner. Those early Zionist thinkers had dreamed of a world in which the Jews, sovereign on the land of their ancestral home, would finally be safe. That day had finally come.

Israelis were not the only ones in the thralls of the euphoria. Soviet Jews, witness to a different image of the Jew than that on which they had been raised, suddenly felt a new pride in being Jewish.[43] Their demands to leave the USSR for Israel would become only more vociferous in the years to come. American Jews were also jubilant. In the year after the war, sixteen thousand American Jews moved to Israel, which was more than the total number of American Jews who had made that move since Israel's creation.[44]

As the paratroopers in Jerusalem were celebrating the capture of the Old City, Naomi Shemer was in the Sinai, preparing to sing to a group of soldiers. But then she heard a radio broadcast of soldiers singing her song, "Jerusalem of Gold," in which she'd written of Jerusalem as a "city that sits alone, while in her heart there lies a wall," and she realized that six days of war had made her song outdated. So using a soldier's back as a desk, she quickly scribbled an additional verse:

> We've returned to the water holes, to the market and the square
> A shofar calls out on the Temple Mount, in the Old City
> And in the caves in the rock, thousands of suns shine
> We will once more return to the Dead Sea, [this time] by the Jericho road.[45]*

A long-cultivated Zionist dream had come true. It was a dream of safety, of confidence, of pride, of international admiration.

It would not last long.

---

* Israelis had had access to the Dead Sea prior to the war, but only by driving south toward Beersheba and through Arad, a several-hour journey from Jerusalem through a barren desert. Now, with access to the Jericho road due east from Jerusalem, the Dead Sea was barely more than half an hour away.

THE BURDEN OF OCCUPATION

Jerusalem is mine, yet a stranger to me . . .
People live there, strangers . . .
they are living where they have always lived and I am the stranger.
—Amos Oz, shortly after the Six-Day War

We have returned to the well / the market and the square . . . [and to] the Temple Mount in the Old City," Naomi Shemer had written. And return they did. The wall in the heart of the city was gone, while the Wall at the base of the Temple Mount was theirs once again. For the first time since the Romans had destroyed the Temple almost two thousand years earlier, Jews traveled en masse to the Western Wall.

They went to touch the stones, to explore the markets, to see with their own eyes the place for which Jews had yearned for millennia, and which for the last nineteen years had been entirely out of reach. "There were women wheeling baby carriages and grandmothers in kerchiefs and kibbutzniks in floppy hats and Orthodox men in prayer shawls and Hasidic fur hats and black fedoras and berets and knitted kippot. . . . Strangers smiled at each other: We are the ones who made it to the end of the story."[1]

Yet it was not "the end of the story." Beyond the celebration, there was also eeriness, a sense that the conquest was more complicated than the euphoria suggested. Yes, the still young state had overcome seemingly insurmountable odds in a war that many thought would spell the end of the country; yes, the nation of Israel had returned to the lands of the Bible, to the places Jews had read about in their most sacred texts for centuries.

Yet those markets about which Naomi Shemer had sung had not been uninhabited. Amos Oz—whose father had promised him on that fateful night in November 1947 that Jewish history had changed forever—now sensed that the tides of history might be shifting once again. He traveled to Jerusalem straight from his military service in the Sinai, wandered the streets, and thought to himself:

> Jerusalem is mine, yet a stranger to me. . . . [T]he city is inhabited. People live there, strangers: I do not understand their language, they are living where they have always lived and I am the stranger. . . . Their eyes hate me. They wish me dead. Accursed stranger. . . . [I am] stalking its streets clutching a submachine gun, like a figure from one of my childhood nightmares: an alien man in an alien city.[2]

"Even unavoidable occupation is corrupting occupation," he wrote soon after the war in a column for *Davar*, then the Labor Party newspaper. It was a position he would espouse, along with other Israeli novelists like David Grossman, for decades.[*]

---

[*] While many high-profile Israelis, along with rank and file, came to oppose the occupation, not all Israelis agreed that Israel's presence in the West Bank constituted an "occupation," in legal terms. A 2012 report headed by former Israeli Supreme Court Justice Edmund Levy argued that because there was never a sovereign entity in the West Bank, and especially viewed in light of Jordan's renouncement of claims to the territory, Israel had a legal basis as the rightful sovereign of these lands. (Amb. Alan Baker, "The Legal Basis of Israel's Rights in the Disputed Territories," http://jcpa.org/ten-basic-points-summarizing-israels-rights-in-judea-and-samaria/.)

BLACK-AND-WHITE PHOTOGRAPHS OF THE Western Wall taken prior to the war depict a tight, narrow alley running along the wall, far too small to accommodate even several hundred people, much less the thousands of celebrating citizens that the government anticipated would make their way to Judaism's holiest place. Just beyond that narrow alley was a squalid encampment called the Mughrabi Quarter. Displaced by the fighting in 1948, some 135 Arab families had sought refuge there and had lived there ever since. On the evening of June 10, with the military's approval, the families in the Mughrabi Quarter were instructed to leave the area so it could be cleared out to create a wide plaza to accommodate large crowds in front of the Western Wall. Soon thereafter, army bulldozers rolled into the square to level the homes and to enable mass access to the wall. The commander of the Mughrabi Quarter operation would later recall, "The order to evacuate the neighborhood was one of the hardest in my life. . . . When you order 'Fire!' [in battle], you're an automaton. Here you had to give an order knowing you are likely to hurt innocent people."[3]

Some scholars see the Mughrabi Quarter* incident as a reflection of a wider phenomenon of quickly cobbled together policies and hastily made decisions, some of which would come to shape Israel for decades to come. The removal of Mughrabi on June 10 unfolded without a national conversation about what to do with the towns and neighborhoods that Israel had just captured. As Israelis would soon learn, decisions they made about the territories captured—and the people who lived there—would create challenges to the

---

* The Mughrabi Quarter, too, had long been a bone of contention between Jews and Arabs. As early as 1929, with tensions between Jews and Arabs simmering over Jews' access to the Western Wall, Haj Amin al-Husseini called for restricting Jewish access to the site. In response, Rabbi Avraham Yitzhak HaKohen Kook, the Ashkenazi chief rabbi of the Yishuv, called for evacuating the Mughrabi Quarter. Now, his suggestion—which had never been acted on—came to fruition. (Hillel Cohen, *Year Zero of the Arab-Israeli Conflict, 1929* [Waltham, MA: Brandeis University Press, 2015], p. xvii.)

Jewish state that were no less existential than the threats that the
Six-Day War had sought to end.

ISRAELIS EVERYWHERE HAD PASSIONATE reactions to what was
unfolding. To religious Israelis, the mere fact that the Jewish state
had averted disaster—and in such a dramatic and decisive fashion—
was a sign of nothing less than God's hand active in human history. Some believed that the war was the herald of the age of the
Messiah. It seemed to them that God had heard Rabbi Zvi Yehuda
Kook's pained cry. Those religious passions were about to fuel a
movement that would soon change Israel forever.

For secular Israelis, as well, floodgates of emotion suddenly
opened. And once again, it was Israel's leading poets who gave expression to the sentiments of a nation. Natan Alterman had long
marked major Israeli moments with poems that became iconic. He
had become the voice of the nation.

Between 1967 and his death in 1970, however, Alterman became
a more divisive figure as he took up his pen on behalf of Israel's
hawkish postwar contingent. This movement insisted that in capturing the West Bank, Israel had rightfully regained sovereignty
over the biblical Land of Israel. "Israel must give up nothing, particularly not 'the cradle of this nation,'" he said. "The meaning of
this victory is that it erased the difference between the State of Israel and the Land of Israel. . . . The state and the land are henceforth
one essence."[4]

It was lost on few that Alterman was a secular Jew.[5] Though the
commitment to keeping the territory that Israel acquired in the Six-
Day War would later be associated with the religious community,
acquiring land and building on it had been the essence of secular
Zionist activity since its beginnings at the end of the nineteenth
century. During the earlier aliyot, young socialist Jews had come
from Russia, and often with the help of Diaspora-based benefac-
tors, purchased land from Arabs who wished to sell. When Arabs
had attacked the Yishuv in 1947 in a war that would last until 1949,

Israel had captured more land. Building on that land in the 1950s, too, in the years after the War of Independence, seemed the natural next step of Zionism.

There was another reason that secular Zionists embraced the new land with such zeal. For some time, classic Labor Zionism had grown tired. In the six years before the Six-Day War, a mere ten new moshavim or kibbutzim were established. Collective agricultural settlement had been largely the project of European socialist Jews, and since the vast majority of those Jews had met their ends in Hitler's gas chambers, there were far fewer potential immigrants. Secular Zionism was ready for an infusion of passion.

The diminished ideological passion of secular Zionism created a vacuum that afforded religious Jews an opportunity to become Zionism's new leaders, the pioneers of Israel's third decade. If previous Jewish religious leaders had *assailed* Zionism because it was overly secular and had sought to create a new Jew, after the war, some religious leaders actually chose to *lead* a reenergized Zionism. This newfound passion was exemplified by no one better than Rabbi Zvi Yehuda Kook. Before the war, Rabbi Kook had lamented the fractured state of the Land of Israel; now, after the war, he suddenly sounded like a modern-day biblical prophet, recounting the glory of the Zionist movement:

> The rabbi spoke from a lectern draped with an Israeli flag. In covering a lectern that held holy books with the flag of secular Israel, Rabbi Zvi Yehudah was saying: This flag is no less holy than the velvet cloth covering the Torah ark behind me. . . . Voice strong, tone defiant, the rabbi warned the world not to interfere with God's plan and try to wrench the liberated lands from Israel's control. Not even the democratically elected government of Israel, he continued, had the right to withdraw from the territories.[6]

Rabbi Kook's confidence that he had the right to warn the government about what it did and did not have the right to do was an ominous warning of things to come. Most Israelis missed the signs completely.

Not all religious Jews saw matters that way, however. A notable exception was one of Israel's most important public intellectuals, an Orthodox Jew, Professor Yeshayahu Leibowitz. For Leibowitz, the principal religious obligation that flowed from the victory in June 1967 was for Israel to save its soul. To do that, he insisted, Israel needed to withdraw from the territories it had captured, so Israelis would not be imposing their rule on a foreign population.

Three years after the war, he wrote a letter to an Israeli twelfth-grade student, summarizing what he had been saying from the moment that the shooting had stopped in 1967:

> I am in favor of an immediate exit from the territories that are inhabited by one and a quarter million Arabs, for reasons that have nothing to do with peace. I have always spoken about *exiting* the territories and not *returning* them, for I have no idea to whom we would "return" them. To Hussein? To Fatah? To Nasser? To the local residents? It is not our business, nor is it our obligation or our right, to be concerned with what the Arabs will do with the territories once we get out of there. We need to entrench ourselves in our Jewish state and to defend it. If we do not get out of there with honor—i.e., by our own free will, as a result of an understanding of the genuine needs of the Jewish people and our state—the Americans and the Russians will force on us a humiliating withdrawal.
>
> Understand this—the problem of the "territories" does not interest me in the least. Rather [what interests me is] the problem of the 1,250,000 Arabs who live there, and not out of concern for the Arabs but out of concern for the Jewish people and our state. Including these Arabs (in addition to the 300,000 who already live in the state) in the area under our control will mean the elimination of the State of Israel as a Jewish state, the destruction of the Jewish people in its entirety, and the ruin of the social edifice we have built in the state.[7]

MOST RELIGIOUS JEWS DISAGREED with the iconoclast Leibowitz. Among them was Hanan Porat, one of the paratroopers who liberated the Old City and the Temple Mount. As he approached the Western Wall and saw the weathered, sacred stones, he whispered, "We are writing the next chapter of the Bible."[8]

Zionism had long been a revolution of the young. Chaim Nachman Bialik wrote his 1892 poem "To the Bird" when he was nineteen years old. Yitzhak Rabin was a mere twenty-six years old when, as commander of the Harel Brigade, he was instrumental in the battle for Jerusalem. Now, armed with nothing more than passion and drive, the twenty-four-year-old Hanan Porat and his generation had launched a movement that would change Israel forever.

Born in 1943 and raised on Kfar Etzion, a newly established religious kibbutz in the Judean Hills outside of Jerusalem, Porat knew exile firsthand. During the War of Independence, Kfar Etzion had been one of the kibbutzim overrun by Arabs just a day before independence, on May 13, 1948; all the men were gathered together and shot or were killed by grenades. He and his friends had survived because the women and children of Kfar Etzion evacuated the kibbutz and took refuge in Jerusalem, while the men had stayed behind to try to defend their homes.

When the kibbutzim in the area fell, the dead included the fathers of Porat's closest friends (with whom he had been raised on the kibbutz). When Porat said he was going to redeem the "land of his fathers," he meant it quite literally.

Others did, too. In the weeks after the Six-Day War, Yoel Bin-Nun, an enormously popular Bible teacher, took his students to the places of which they had been reading for years:

> Pocket-size Bible in hand, wearing sunglasses and the kibbutzniks' brimless hat, Yoel led his students through the biblical landscape. They searched for springs, ruins, the topography of biblical accounts that would reveal the sites of ancient battlegrounds. They traced the route where Abraham walked from Hebron to Jerusalem, and the route of the Palmach fighters of

1948 who tried to break the siege on Kfar Etzion—a seamless history as though uninterrupted by twenty centuries of exile.⁹

Bin-Nun could now make the Bible come alive in a way that had not been possible until his students could walk the hills of which it spoke. In Bin-Nun's teaching, Porat had a newfound outlet for his religious passion—his drive to resettle the land on which his friends' fathers had been killed, land that would already have been part of Israel had the kibbutz not fallen.

On September 25, 1967, just over three months after the end of the war, Hanan Porat managed to arrange a meeting with the prime minister, hoping to secure the government's permission to resettle Kfar Etzion. He recounted the interaction numerous times, for it illustrated the complete misunderstanding the political leadership had of this newfound religious fervor:

> "What do you want, kinderlach?" Eshkol asked, using the Yiddish endearment for children. "To go up," said Hanan. "Nu, kinderlach, if you want to go up, then go." "Listen," Hanan pressed, "in ten days it will be Rosh Hashanah," the Jewish new year. "We very much want to pray in the place where our parents prayed." "Nu, kinderlach," said the prime minister, "if you want to pray, then pray."¹⁰

It is not clear from this recounting of the conversation whether the prime minister was being dismissive, encouraging, or merely skeptical. "Eshkol's comments were retold . . . as everything from warm approval to an absolute no, overcome only by the activists' defiance."¹¹ What is fairly clear, however, is that whatever Eshkol thought of Porat, he vastly underestimated Porat's determination.

The return to Gush Etzion was far more than a general drive to settle the land, or to change Israel's physical and political landscape. Porat and his friends were going home. They were returning to the land where most of them had been born, the land that their mothers and fathers had cultivated and on which they had built their homes and their community. It was the place their fathers had died trying to defend, where their parents had been massacred. If Zionism writ large was about the Jewish people returning to their ancestral homeland, Porat and his partners wanted to return to their own families' homes. "For we shall rise, and we will emerge again as before," Haim Gouri had written when Kfar Etzion and the surrounding Jewish villages fell in May 1948. The sons and daughters of the men who had died there were determined nineteen years later to fulfill the promise that Gouri had made to the nation.

Eshkol's noncommittal endorsement was all that Porat needed. Within two days, Hanan Porat and his friends (known as "the children of Kfar Etzion") had begun to resettle Kfar Etzion. In beat-up trucks and buses, they traveled back to the land on which the kibbutz had stood.

When they arrived, they unloaded mattresses and threw them on the floors of the makeshift aluminum structures that they would now call home. They then hung a picture of Rabbi Zvi Yehuda Kook in the men's dormitory and settled in to sleep for their first night in the first resettlement in the West Bank.

Kfar Etzion, which was widely seen as having fallen in the defense of Jerusalem, occupied a unique place in Israeli collective memory. Its resettlement inspired Israelis of all walks of life. In Tel Aviv, a "dentist about to retire offered to sell his office equipment and donate the proceeds to Kfar Etzion,"[12] and the Tel Aviv University rector remarked that "The pioneers of Kfar Etzion are showing the way."[13] A student offered to forgo his higher education if that would enable him to join the kibbutz; a couple put in a request to honeymoon on the kibbutz.

The settler movement picked up steam and never looked back.

By the end of 1973, just six years later, Israelis had established seventeen settlements in the West Bank (most of them in the Jordan Valley), and by May 1977, there were thirty-six. By 1973, seven settlements had been established in the Gaza Strip and in the northwestern corner of the Sinai Peninsula (the Rafa approaches), and

by 1977, there were sixteen. In Sinai proper, by 1973, there were
three settlements; by 1977, seven.[14]

In 1974, those Israelis intent on settling the land captured in 1967
formed their first significant political entity, which would become a
cornerstone of the religious Zionist movement. Called Gush Emunim ("Bloc of the Faithful"), it was not only the embodiment of
Rabbi Zvi Yehuda Kook's ideology, but was also in many ways a
reinvigoration of an early Zionist ethos. Years later, Ariel Sharon
would recall that when someone asked him, "Who are these Gush
Emunim people?" he had responded, "They are much like we were
in the 1940s, only more serious."[15] Gush Emunim would leave an
indelible mark on Israeli society: by 2012, approximately 341,000
Israelis were living in settlements.

Whereas some Israelis were intent on Israel's retaining the West
Bank for religious and ideological reasons, others were motivated
not by theology but by security. In 1970, Yigal Allon, a founder of
the Palmach then serving as deputy prime minister and minister of
immigrant absorption, proposed returning some of the territories
Israel had captured in 1967 and retaining others. His suggestion,
now known as the Allon Plan (see Map 9), called for Israel to retain control of the Jordan Valley, East Jerusalem, and the Etzion
bloc as well as Kiryat Arba, a new Jewish neighborhood on the
outskirts of Hebron. In these areas, Israel would build civilian settlements, which in addition to providing housing, would serve as
early-warning systems to detect attacks from the east. The blocs that
Israel would not control would be released to Jordan (in one version
of the plan) and would be connected by highways. Allon proposed
returning most of the Sinai to Egypt, but retaining a substantial portion of the Golan. Though the plan was controversial in Israel (and
although extensively discussed was never formally voted on by the
Israeli government), that ended up being moot, for King Hussein of
Jordan rejected it out of hand.

A few decades later, it would be clear to most Israelis that some
division of the West Bank was inevitable (because of international

pressure, among other reasons). But by that time, matters had become infinitely more complex than they had been when Allon proposed his plan. By 2015, hundreds of thousands of Israeli Jews were living in the West Bank. Both Israelis and Palestinians had become more entrenched in their (mutually exclusive) demands in negotiations, and the conflict had in many ways morphed from a political one to a religious one in which religious ideologues on both sides claimed that God had assigned the land to them. Allon's plan came too early, but had it been adopted, the history of the Middle East might have unfolded very differently.

WHAT TO DO WITH the captured territories now became the most contentious issue in Zionism. In the movement's early years, Herzl had sought a state, while Ahad Ha'am insisted that statehood would be a mistake and that the Jews should build a cultural center—but nothing more—in Palestine. Later there had been the battle between Ben-Gurion and Jabotinsky, between the mainstream Zionists and the Revisionists, about how much to resist the Ottomans and the British to push them out of Palestine. Years later, Ben-Gurion and Menachem Begin locked horns over German reparations—and more deeply about the role that Jewish memory ought to play in determining Israel's policies and political agenda. Now, it was Right versus Left, settlers versus those who thought Israel should relinquish the land it had captured. As with the prior ideological debates, this was no pro-Zionist/anti-Zionist split. It was a deep divide between two camps who loved the Jewish state and who were committed to its flourishing—but who disagreed about what course of action would best protect its soul.

Where Gush Emunim saw virgin territory, biblical lands calling young Jews back to the birthplace of their people, other Israelis saw people, approximately 1.25 million Arabs who now found themselves under Israeli rule. Where Allon saw the possibility for enhanced security, Leibowitz saw a cancer that would consume Israel's character. Suddenly, the issue of Israel's borders was no longer simply a question of security and diplomacy; it was a religious matter, and thus infinitely more complex. Israeli society was becoming divided in a way it had never been before; to this day, that chasm has never been bridged.

LIKE HANAN PORAT, Meir Ariel—a shy, curly-haired, artistic paratrooper—was also at the battle for the Old City of Jerusalem. Yet while Porat had stood in wonder when he reached the Western Wall, Meir's experience was distinctly different. "At '[a]ny moment,' he thought, 'it's going to hit me: here I am, a fulfillment of two thousand years of longing.' But it did not happen. Meir Ariel felt no exultation, no sense that the next chapter of the Bible was now being written. 'What's wrong with me?' he wondered. 'What kind of Jew am I?'"[16] Musical by instinct, he took out his pen and wrote a different version of Naomi Shemer's song.[17]

While Shemer had begun her song with "The mountain air is clear as wine, / And the scent of pines is carried on the breeze of twilight," Ariel opened his version, which he entitled "Jerusalem of Iron," with the Hebrew word *be'machshakayich*, "in your darkness."[18] "In your darkness, Jerusalem . . . ," he wrote, "we came to expand your borders and to evict the enemy."

Where Naomi Shemer saw the Jewish people reunited with the ancestral lands on which it had been born, Meir Ariel could not see beyond the suffering the war had caused. He ended his song by using the phrase "Jerusalem of gold" but with a very different sentiment. Jerusalem was not only the city of gold, but "of lead and of dreams" as well. And Ariel ended with a prayer:

> Forever amidst your walls
> May peace dwell.

After the war, Ariel made a low-budget recording of his version of the song, which somehow made its way to Israeli radio, where— suddenly—it was played over and over. The popularity of the painful, quasi-satirical rebuke of Naomi Shemer was no accident. Israel was facing a gathering storm. What should it do with those lands it had captured? Leibowitz and Porat had diametrically opposed views. Shemer and Ariel offered radically different answers. Ariel would go on to become, in the words of Yossi Klein Halevi, the Bob Dylan of Israel. He became the voice of his generation's sense of disillusionment. It would take another decade for this disillusionment to produce the Peace Now movement; but here, as was often the case in Israeli society, musicians and poets were augurs of movements still to come.

EVEN SOME OF THE IDF BRASS understood that there was an underbelly to the great victory. Yitzhak Rabin later said: "We could have extended the area under our control. There was no Egyptian force capable of halting the IDF had we intended to occupy Cairo. The same held for Amman, and on June 11 it would not have required much effort to take Damascus. But we had not gone to war to acquire territories, and those we already occupied presented enough of a burden."[19]

Burden was the instructive word. Many Israelis intuited that occupying the lands that Israel had just captured and ruling over 1.25 million Arabs was going to be complicated. David Ben-Gurion, who in 1948 had refused his generals' pleas that Israel take the West Bank, spoke up from his retirement. Israel should keep Jerusalem and the Golan, he said, but get rid of everything else. On that matter, he agreed with Yeshayahu Leibowitz: what was at stake was Israel's soul.

In a dramatic departure from what previously had been considered the appropriate, stiff-upper-lip behavior expected from Israel's warriors, veterans of the conflict also began to share their misgivings about what they had seen. In a set of interviews with kibbutz members who had fought in the war, published in a book called *Soldiers' Talk,* Israelis heard sentiments they had not heard expressed before. Soldiers spoke about the pain of killing another person, of their anger at having to fight, of the shame they felt when children who were the age of their own children raised their hands in surrender.

The publishers of the interviews expected at best a modicum of interest in their book. To their amazement, it sold a hundred thousand copies—an astronomically high number in a market of Israel's size. The book sold so well for the same reason that Meir Ariel's song "Jerusalem of Iron" became so popular. Some Israelis had a sixth sense that they were approaching a reckoning—with a people whose national movement was just beginning and that the Israelis themselves had helped ignite.

WHILE THE SIX-DAY WAR divided Israelis, it united the vanquished Arab Palestinian community. Israel's victory had dealt a fatal blow to Nasser's pan-Arabist movement. It was now clear how little Nasser or any of the other Arab leaders had done for the Palestinians (those who had fled the war in 1948 and their descendants) about whom they ostensibly cared so deeply. Nasser had been utterly humiliated, but so too had the Palestinians, even though they were mostly pawns in a much larger battle. Many of the seven hundred thousand Palestinians who had been dispossessed during the fighting in 1948 and had relocated to the West Bank and Gaza now found themselves living under the very people they held responsible for uprooting their families.

The change was dislocating for Palestinians in numerous ways. The erasure of the 1949 armistice line as a meaningful border represented an opportunity to visit the cities and the homes from which they had fled in 1948, nineteen years earlier. But that brought with it complicated emotions. As one historian of the period notes:

> [I]n the streets of Qatamon and Baqa—West Jerusalem neighborhoods whose mansions had been abandoned by wealthy Arabs in 1948 and subdivided among Jewish immigrants—packed cars with Jordanian plates rolled slowly by, as families from East Jerusalem and beyond looked at houses left behind. . . . American

consul-general Evan Wilson [wrote in a cable:] "Arab owner of grand piano, which has been in living room of our New City residence for 19 years since he entrusted it for safe-keeping to my predecessor . . . in 1948 when leaving in a hurry, has come to claim it back."[20]

Some Palestinians, however, suspected that Israelis had more nefarious motives. Ghassan Kanafani, a leading Palestinian author of the period (and a leader of the Popular Front for the Liberation of Palestine, a violent terrorist organization), described in "Returning to Haifa" (one of his many published short stories) how Palestinians returned to Haifa from the West Bank to see the places that had been home until 1948. The main male character says to his wife as they drive through Israel:

> They opened up the border as soon as they completed the occupation, suddenly and immediately. That has never happened in any war in history. You know the terrible thing that happened in April 1948, so now, why this? Just for our sakes alone? No! This is part of the war. They're saying to us, "Help yourselves, look and see how much better we are than you, how much more developed. You should accept being our servants. You should admire us."[21]

There were other dividends. Some West Bank Palestinians found employment in Israel, and their standard of living rose. With time, under Israel's rule, educational opportunities expanded. Yet the most salient factor for Palestinians was that they were now living not under Jordanian Muslims, but Israeli Jews. They were now occupied, and it would be only a matter of time until ending that occupation became their primary national objective.

IN THE LATE 1950S, Yasser Arafat had founded Fatah, the Palestinian National Liberation Movement.

Arafat was born in Cairo in August 1929. His father had come from Gaza City, while his mother had grown up in Jerusalem. When his mother died, his father sent him to live in Jerusalem's Old City with his mother's family. He eventually moved back to Cairo, where he studied civil engineering (though he took time off from school to fight alongside the Muslim Brotherhood in the 1948 war). After the Sinai Campaign, when all the fedayeen were expelled, Arafat moved to Kuwait where he lived among many Palestinian refugees, and in 1959, he founded Fatah.

In 1968, Fatah became part of the PLO (Palestine Liberation Organization, which had been founded in 1964—before Israel had even occupied the West Bank) and fairly quickly became its dominant element. Arafat's rise to power affected not only Israel, for the PLO essentially invented international terrorism and thus left the entire world vulnerable.

While in Israel there were voices who advocated relinquishing lands so that the two people might live side by side, the PLO was hardly open to compromise. Its attitude to Zionism was explicit in its charter:

Zionism is a colonialist movement in its inception, aggressive and expansionist in its goals, racist and segregationist in its configurations and fascist in its means and aims. Israel in its capacity as the spearhead of this destructive movement and the pillar for colonialism is a permanent source of tension and turmoil in the Middle East in particular and to the international community in general.[22]

Now, in 1967, with the Palestinians (and the PLO, which had been associated with the Arab League and Egypt) humiliated, the Arafat-led Fatah was suddenly more appealing to millions of Palestinians than it ever had been. Fatah took over the PLO, and Arafat—now an international figure—became its chairman. Yasser Arafat was for all intents and purposes the political leader of the Palestinians.

The Palestinians were making political moves and, as had been the case with the Zionists, were also finding a literary voice. They did so most notably in the poetry of Mahmoud Darwish, a Palestinian born in the western Galilee whose family fled their village of al-Birwa during the War of Independence. Drawing upon both centuries of Arab verse and the homelessness that he and his fellow Palestinians felt, Darwish penned "Identity Card" in 1964 (the year of the PLO's founding).[23] "Write down! / I am an Arab," he announced to his reader, and then turned to the accusation at the heart of the Palestinian narrative: "You have stolen the orchards of my ancestors, / And the land which I cultivated." Wherefrom their desperation? "And you left nothing for us, / Except for these rocks." Then came the threat.

> If I become hungry
> The usurper's flesh will be my food.
> Beware.
> Beware.
> Of my hunger.
> And my anger!

Darwish, like other Palestinian writers and poets, was the voice of a people seeking independence and freedom. The anger of which he warned was undeniably real, and would soon become one of the most significant threats to Israel's continued flourishing.

ON SEPTEMBER 1, 1967, THE Arab League, which had gathered in Khartoum (the capital of Sudan) three months after the end of the Six-Day War, issued a statement that insisted, in part:

> The Arab Heads of State have agreed to unite their political efforts at the international and diplomatic level to eliminate the effects of the aggression and to ensure the withdrawal of the aggressive Israeli forces from the Arab lands which have been

occupied since the aggression of June 5. This will be done within the framework of the main principles by which the Arab States abide, namely, no peace with Israel, no recognition of Israel, no negotiations with it, and insistence on the rights of the Palestinian people in their own country.[24]

"No peace, no recognition, and no negotiations" became a mantra of the Arab world.

Israel had achieved a stunning military victory in six days of June 1967. But that victory had not ended the Jewish state's conflict with the Arab states that surrounded it. Now, it was clear, the triumph had also awakened a new conflict—with the Palestinians. Both sides reacted to the extraordinary change with ideological passion. On the Israeli side, Gush Emunim emerged, giving new ideological passion to the settlement movement. For the Palestinians, Israel's victory added energy and fuel to their own nationalism—and to their desire to eradicate the Jewish state.

Ironically, as a result of its victory in 1967, the Jewish state now had a new and increasingly potent enemy that was going to dramatically alter Israel's future.

YOM KIPPUR WAR

The "Conception" Crashes

You promised . . . peace . . . [and] you promised to keep your promises.

—From the Israeli song "Winter '73"

In the spring of 1973, when Yitzhak Rabin returned to Israel after a five-year stint in Washington as Israel's ambassador to the United States, he sensed that he had come back to a country transformed. "The Israel I came home to had a self-confident, almost smug aura to it," he said, "as befits a country far removed from the possibility of war."[1]

If the weeks prior to the Six-Day War had been a time of unprecedented self-doubt and pervasive despair, the years following the war heralded a period of great confidence. Israel, it seemed, had moved beyond the threat of destruction; the Diaspora-like nervousness of Israel's earlier generations now appeared a vestige of the Jewish past.

Later, Israelis would refer to the new national mind-set—a worldview that was especially deeply rooted in the military's top brass and Israel's intelligence community—as the *conceptzia*, the "conception." Rank-and-file Israelis as well as their leaders had complete faith in the IDF's military superiority. Certain that it would take years for Egypt to recover the military might that the Jewish state had summarily destroyed in six lightning days, they assumed that Syria also knew better than to attack Israel's northern border. Thanks to the IDF, they asserted, Israel was now invulnerable.

Israeli life had changed in numerous ways. If in the early years of the state military leaders spoke of their accomplishments with a sense of humility—the pervasive culture insisted that they were merely "doing their duty to serve the nation"—Israel now venerated IDF generals and treated them as heroes. Some of those generals then parlayed their newfound popularity to move into politics, eroding what had been Ben-Gurion's policy of insisting upon a clear divide between the military and the political sphere. David Ben-Gurion, Moshe Sharett, and Levi Eshkol, the three men who had served as prime minister from 1948 through the Six-Day War, had virtually no military experience to speak of. In the years to follow, however, many of Israel's prime ministers would be former generals or highly decorated soldiers.

The near asceticism of Zionist leaders like Ben-Gurion, A. D. Gordon, or Golda Meir also disappeared. Israel's early leaders had eschewed physical comforts, and even when they reached the peak of the political ladder, they lived in small, plain apartments with astonishingly few comforts. That, too, was gone. Israeli leaders began to permit themselves to live well—very well, indeed.

Yitzhak Rabin was right. Israel had changed.

With this new mind-set, Israel staged the largest military parade in its history on Independence Day in the spring of 1973. It would also be the last.

DESPITE ISRAELIS' BRAVADO and sense of invincibility, though, Israel was still not at peace. Along the Sinai in particular, Israeli and Egyptian forces remained "eyeball to eyeball"[2]—both sides clearly visible to the other, with nothing but the narrow canal between them. Israel began construction of defensive positions along the canal named the Bar-Lev Line (for General Chaim Bar-Lev, the IDF's chief of staff). Though no one thought it would successfully block a full-scale Egyptian invasion, its proponents believed it would be an effective early-warning system should Egypt ever attack, and if necessary, would hold off the Egyptians long enough for additional forces to arrive.

From the outset, though, Israeli military officials disagreed about the likely efficacy of the Bar-Lev Line. Ariel Sharon, then head of Southern Command, believed that the Bar-Lev Line was dangerous because it invited an unjustified sense of security. "I knew with absolute certainty that I was right and they [generals and former chiefs of staff] were wrong," he later said with his characteristic self-assuredness. "[T]he Bar-Lev Line was bound to bring us disaster. But it was no pleasure when four years later it did exactly that."[3] But most of the brass were not terribly worried, and the construction continued. For some, the Bar-Lev Line became *the* symbol of Israel's impregnability on the southern border.

While Israel was building defensive fortifications, Egyptian president Nasser assumed a more aggressive posture. Determined to force Israel to leave the Sinai Peninsula that it had captured in the Six-Day War, Nasser unleashed limited artillery barrages and small incursions into the Sinai. When they proved ineffective, Egypt began another offensive on March 8, 1969, which became known as the War of Attrition.

The War of Attrition, often omitted from the lists of Israel's armed conflicts, lasted from March 1969 until August 1970. When a cease-fire eventually went into effect, the border had not moved an inch, but the toll for both sides had been significant. Though scholars disagree about the precise numbers, one Israeli military historian suggests that 921 Israelis died; 694 of them were soldiers and the rest civilians. Israel lost about two dozen aircraft in the dozens of battles that constituted the war, in addition to a navy destroyer.

As had been the case in all the previous wars, though, Arab casualties were much higher. Benny Morris believes that Egyptian losses approximated ten thousand soldiers and civilians killed; at certain points during the war, the Egyptians were losing some three hundred soldiers a day.[4] The Egyptians lost about a hundred aircraft and several naval vessels. In a loss that was surely symbolic as well as tangible for Egypt, the Egyptian chief of staff lay among the dead.

IN APRIL 1970, EGYPTIAN PRESIDENT Nasser invited Nachum Goldmann, president of the World Zionist Congress (the body responsible for the Zionist Congresses since Herzl had convened the first congress in Basel in 1897), to travel to Cairo to discuss a possible resolution to the conflict. Prime Minister Golda Meir, believing it was a trap, pressured Goldmann not to go.[5] Some Israelis began to wonder aloud if Israel was really doing enough to exit the cycle of violence. In a step that then struck many as an unpardonable violation of Israel's collectivist ethos, fifty-eight high school students sent a letter to Meir on April 28, 1970. They wrote, "We and many others are therefore wondering how we can fight in a permanent, futureless war, while our government's policy is such that it misses chances for peace."[6] Public unrest regarding Golda Meir had begun.

It was a simple letter—still known as the "Twelfth-Graders' Letter"—but it shook the nation. The letter was one of the first indications of cracks in the facade of Israel's collective ethos (one dimension of Ben-Gurion's larger *mamlachtiyut* project). No less important, Israel had the beginnings of a peace movement; a tradition of Israeli civilians questioning the sincerity and motives of their government's foreign policy had been born.

Several months later, Egypt's president died of a heart attack. Gamal Abdel Nasser succumbed knowing his life's central cause had failed. He had not delivered on his promise to push Israel into the sea and his grand vision, the pan-Arab movement, was losing steam. His death was in many ways the final nail in the coffin of the Egyptian-led pan-Arab movement.

IF PAN-ARABISM WAS DYING, however, Palestinian nationalism was awakening. Ever since Israel's independence and the Palestinian

Nakba ("Catastrophe") that had unfolded during the War of Independence, Arab countries had continuously said that the Palestinian cause would be one of the central foci of the pan-Arab movement. Yet nothing had materialized. Arab states' devotion to the Palestinian cause, Palestinian activists began to realize, was nothing but rhetoric. The Palestinians came to realize that if they were to make any progress, and particularly if they were to reverse the territorial losses of the 1967 war, they would have to do it themselves.

The man who took up the cause most effectively was Yasser Arafat. He managed to get Palestinian national aspirations onto the world's agenda, but to do so, he fashioned a tradition of Palestinian violence worldwide. Ultimately, Arafat unleashed a campaign of terror not only against Israeli civilians, but against targets in Europe and beyond as well.

The campaign of terror began in earnest in the mid-1960s. In early 1965, Fatah gunmen began crossing the Israeli border to execute more deadly raids. In May 1965, as their attacks intensified, they fired at a farm truck, a chemical tanker, and residents of a kibbutz, injuring several. Between June 1967 and March 1971, attacks continued relentlessly, with numerous Israeli dead and wounded.

From the outset, Arafat was explicit in his assertion that even Israel's returning to the pre-June 1967 borders would not be sufficient. The Palestinians had a much more ambitious—and deadly—goal in mind. "We are not concerned with what took place in June 1967 or with eliminating the consequences of the June war," Arafat said in August 1970. "The Palestinian revolution's basic concern is the uprooting of the Zionist entity from our land and liberating it."

Palestinian terror took the revolution overseas as well, hijacking numerous planes. On February 21, 1970, forty-seven passengers and crew members were killed in Zurich when a Swissair plane was sabotaged; seventeen of the victims were Israeli. That same day, seven elderly Jews were killed in a Palestinian attack on a home for the aged in Munich.

Though Arafat quickly became an internationally reviled figure, his campaign succeeded. Palestinian nationalism was an international concern, and eventually, it would put Israel on the diplomatic defensive.

IRONICALLY, IT WAS THE Arab world that first struck back at Arafat. By 1970, the Kingdom of Jordan, to which many of the hundreds of thousands of Palestinians fled during the War of Independence and later during the Six-Day War, was becoming an important base of operations for Arafat's radical and deadly Palestine Liberation Organization. Soon though, the PLO overreached and set its sights on Jordan's Hashemite monarchy. King Hussein survived two assassination attempts by PLO militants in merely three months. Further PLO attacks on Jordanian soil, designed to overthrow the Hashemite dynasty, included the hijacking of three airliners to Jordan and their subsequent televised destruction.

With his monarchy at stake, King Hussein responded with a brutal crackdown now known as "Black September." What he unleashed was actually a civil war, fought between PLO terrorist organizations and the Jordanian armed forces, which began in September 1970 and lasted for ten months, until July 1971. The war left some two thousand PLO fighters dead; thousands of Palestinian noncombatants also lost their lives. Jordan was in such turmoil that Syria saw an opportunity to invade Jordan—claiming that its goal was to prevent the annihilation of the Palestinians. Only when Israel concentrated tanks on the Golan Heights, within striking distance of Damascus, did the Syrians stand down.

Though Hussein managed to save his kingdom, he unwittingly brought about the destruction of another Middle Eastern country. The PLO leadership and thousands of its fighters, expelled from Jordan, fled to southern Lebanon. By 1975, civil unrest had broken out in Lebanon—which had long had a precarious and tense agreement between Muslims and Christians—and all-out civil war would follow. The "Paris of the Middle East" would eventually lie in rubble, and largely because of Arafat, Lebanon's days as a functioning country were numbered.

WITH THE COLD WAR raging, the United States and the USSR both saw the Middle East, and Egypt in particular, as a critical place to establish their influence. The Soviet Union took Egypt and Anwar Sadat— who had twice served as Egyptian vice president under Nasser and succeeded him as president when Nasser died—under its wing. But Sadat resented what he saw as Soviet meddling in internal Egyptian affairs and ordered Soviet advisers out of Egypt.

Israel and the United States were convinced that Sadat had made a significant strategic blunder by giving up such an important ally, but the Egyptian leader was much cleverer than they believed. Sadat knew that the Soviets were worried that Egypt would launch another war against Israel. If Egypt lost again, it would cast the Soviets, who were assisting Egypt, in a bad light. The Soviets, however annoyed they might have been with Sadat, could not afford to let him lose.

The Soviets "punished" Egypt by strengthening the Syrians. They provided them with hundreds of tanks, planes, and SAMs (surface-to-air missiles). Almost overnight, Syria became the most heavily armed Arab nation, per capita, in the world. Given that the Syrian Baath regime remained committed to the "liquidation of all traces of Zionist aggression,"[7] this was an ominous development for Israel. The Soviets also knew that they could not abandon Egypt. Despite their frustration with Sadat, they provided him with jet fighters, tanks, anti-tank missiles, SAMs, and Scuds that could threaten Israel's major cities.

Sadat got precisely what he wanted. Suddenly, the Middle Eastern balance of power was not nearly as disproportionate as many Israelis wished to believe. With most Israelis unaware of how quickly the region was shifting, the *conceptzia* was becoming a profound liability.

SADAT WAS DETERMINED TO restore Egypt's pride. By March 1973, Sadat and Syrian president Hafez al-Assad reached a general agreement to launch a joint offensive against Israel. They left many of the details unplanned, largely because the two nations had different objectives in mind. Syria still hoped to destroy Israel, but Sadat was willing to settle for a restoration of Egyptian dignity by undoing some of the humiliation of the 1967 defeat. If his forces could establish a beachhead on the east bank of the Suez Canal and overrun the Israeli defenses and the symbolic Bar-Lev Line, the campaign would be a success. To ensure that Israel's air power would have limited impact, the plan was to stay within the twelve-kilometer range of safety afforded by the SAMs that the Soviets had provided him.

Even while he was planning for war, Sadat may have been pursuing an alternate, parallel track, as well. In early 1971, Sadat made overtures to Israel suggesting that Israel and Egypt could come to an interim agreement if Israel withdrew to a distance of forty kilometers from the Suez Canal. Golda Meir, utterly confident in Israel's security and dubious that Sadat had any serious intent of making peace, rejected the suggestion out of hand.[8]

In late 1972 and unbeknownst to most Israelis, Sadat appointed Hafez Ismail, a longtime diplomat, to the position of national security adviser. He instructed Ismail to conduct secret negotiations with U.S. President Richard Nixon's National Security Advisor, Henry Kissinger. The purpose was to make clear that Egypt would be willing to end its conflict and establish normal relations with Israel if Israel were willing to withdraw from the territories it had captured from Egypt in 1967.

Kissinger and Ismail met twice in 1973,[9] but this Egyptian proposal, too, went nowhere. Why that is the case remains unclear. According to some scholars, Ismail was "forthcoming . . . in seeking a settlement with Israel, one in which territory would be returned and normalized relations established."[10] Or had Sadat decided to go to war to restore Egyptian pride no matter what, making Ismail's efforts a diversionary tactic only?[11] Whatever the reason, the proposal never received serious attention.

Some on the Israeli side floated proposals as well. Israeli defense minister Moshe Dayan was willing to explore an economic arrangement with the Egyptians. He was confident that if Israel withdrew from the banks of the Suez and the Egyptians began to allow Israel to use the canal for shipping, the two countries might be able to avoid war.[12] Neither the Israeli government nor the Egyptians were very interested in Dayan's proposal, however, and eventually, it, too, was shelved. No one seemed terribly worried about avoiding a war they were confident the Egyptians knew better than to start.

IN THE SPRING AND summer of 1973, Egyptian forces began military exercises along Israel's southern border. The Israeli high command—in the grips of the *conceptzia*—assumed that these were routine exercises. Yet they were nothing of the sort. Preparing to cross the Suez Canal, the Egyptians were trying to desensitize the IDF to Egyptian activity across the border. As time went on, Israeli intelligence gathered additional evidence that the Egyptians were planning an attack, but the high command misread all the information. So pervasive was the *conceptzia*—Israel's sense of invulnerability and the IDF's disparaging attitude to the Egyptian armed forces—that those in charge of the IDF either dismissed the mere notion that Egypt would attack or assumed that Israel's superior intelligence could give them ample warning so they could repel anything thrown at them.

In May, after Egypt put its military on high alert, David "Dado" Elazar, the IDF chief of staff, ordered a partial mobilization of the IDF, but at a huge financial cost. When the Egyptians called off their alert, many on Israel's side believed that Dado had overreacted—Israeli generals would be hesitant to mobilize too early the next time around.

Toward the end of September, King Hussein made a secret visit to Jerusalem, where he met with Prime Minister Meir. He told her that Egypt and Syria were planning to attack Israel.[13] The meeting left Golda shaking, but her senior command reassured her. Again, Israel did nothing.

At the beginning of October, the Israeli intelligence community received further information from a senior Mossad agent, Ashraf

Marwan, who was both Egyptian president Nasser's son-in-law and an Israeli spy. Marwan warned the Israelis that Egypt was planning an attack, which it would disguise as a military drill. This information never made its way to the prime minister's office.[14]

In Israel's Southern Command, Lieutenant Benjamin Siman Tov submitted a document on October 1 to his officer, Lieutenant Colonel David Gedaliah, stating that the Egyptian deployment on the western side of the canal was indicative not of military exercises, but of preparation for war. Two days later he submitted a second report insisting that there was a high likelihood that the Egyptians were preparing for a major conflict. Gedaliah did not distribute these reports, nor did he include them in the Southern Command intelligence report to General Headquarters. Siman Tov's reports received no attention whatsoever.

On October 4 and 5, Soviet advisers departed Egypt and Syria, along with their families. This, too, Israeli HQ ignored. On those same days, aerial photographs of Egypt and Syria indicated an unprecedentedly high number of tanks, infantry units, and SAMs. Still, Israel did not react. At twelve thirty A.M. on October 5, the Mossad headquarters in Tel Aviv received a cable that was marked as urgent. The cable, from Marwan again, stated that war was imminent. He insisted that he speak to the Mossad head, General Zvi Zamir, and when he was put through, he told Zamir that an attack would begin the following day, October 6, which was Yom Kippur, the holiest day of the Jewish year. Marwan stated incorrectly, however, that the attack would take place at sunset.

On Friday, the eve of Yom Kippur, the Israeli cabinet met in emergency session. General Eli Zeira, the head of military intelligence, informed the government that he had incontrovertible evidence that an Egyptian attack would follow the next day at six P.M. Chief of Staff General Elazar immediately requested permission for a preemptive air strike, in what would have been similar to how Israel had handled the crisis of June 1967. Golda Meir refused. Yitzhak Rabin, then serving as Israel's ambassador to the United States, had agreed to Henry Kissinger's demands—which were coupled to American threats—that Israel not strike first. Unwilling to risk losing American sympathy and assistance, Meir and Dayan refused the request; not wishing to appear as the aggressors, they also denied the brass's request for a full IDF mobilization and decided instead on a very limited one. They did agree that should war break out the next day, Golda Meir would have full authority to mobilize the reserves on her own.

YOM KIPPUR IS TYPICALLY an eerily silent day in Israel. By law, all businesses are closed, and scarcely a vehicle moves on the streets. Children sometimes ride their bicycles on the abandoned lanes of Israel's major highways. Though a religious holiday, it is observed in some way by the vast majority of secular Jews, as well. Most Israeli Jews, even those who are not ordinarily religious, fast for twenty-five hours. Many who usually do not attend synagogue go for at least part of the day. It is a day of stillness, of utter quiet and of deep, intensely private contemplation.

At two P.M. on Yom Kippur in 1973, the silence that had enveloped the entire country was suddenly shattered by air raid sirens. They were the first such sirens Jerusalemites had heard since the Six-Day War. Israelis who turned on their radios at first heard nothing—even most of the radio stations went off the air for Yom Kippur. Those who kept their radios on, however, soon heard precisely what they did not want to hear. "The sirens are not a false alarm. When the siren sounds again, everyone must go to their shelters." For lack of other prepared programming, the radio stations cut to Beethoven's *Moonlight Sonata*, known for its evocative funereal tone.

Just over an hour later, at three thirty P.M., another announcement followed. "Egypt and Syria have attacked. Partial mobilization has been ordered." More air sirens followed, throughout the country—the calm of Yom Kippur was now but a faint memory—and hundreds, then thousands, and finally tens of thousands of people ran, panicked, to bomb shelters. By four P.M., the streets were increasingly filled with vehicles bearing signs that they were being used to transport soldiers to the front, and radio announcements instructed all nonessential traffic to stay off the roads. Gas stations would be opening, public transportation—shut down for the holiday—was going to resume while all nonemergency patients in hospitals would be discharged and sent home to make way for wounded soldiers. That final announcement was the first indication to the public that whatever was happening, it was serious.

In some families, fathers, brothers, and sons were called up, all making their way to their units. Shortly thereafter, a radio announcer confirmed people's worst fears: "The Egyptians have crossed the Suez Canal and are on the east bank." By five P.M., the public was informed that "Syrian planes are in action in the Upper Galilee. A fierce air battle is in progress." Citizens were instructed to stick tape over their windows, mirrors, and pictures to prevent glass shards from flying through their homes.

Moments later, Israelis heard from the prime minister. She reported that even as her cabinet was discussing a possible invasion, Egypt and Syria had opened fire on land and in the air. That was a dramatic understatement. What the prime minister chose not to tell the public was that in the first fifteen minutes of the war, 240 Egyptian fighter jets had crossed the canal, giving support to 2,000 Egyptian soldiers who fired 10,000 shells at Israeli positions in the very first minute of the attack. The barrage of shelling lasted fifty-three minutes.[15] The Israelis, on the east side of the canal, had only 436 soldiers, many of them recent immigrants with no battle experience. The prime minister also failed to note that 1,400 Syrian tanks were making their way down the Golan Heights toward Israel's Galilee, and that facing the main Syrian force of 600 tanks, Israel had only 57 tanks. Syria was on the verge of slicing into Israel's heartland.

Later in the evening, Moshe Dayan revealed the extent to which the *conceptzia,* even in the midst of battle, still prevailed. Israeli casualties, he predicted, would be in the "tens"—the losses would not reach hundreds, he said. As for the Golan, he said, "I don't think it was a bad day for us." By eight P.M., however, the radio reported that all women and children had been evacuated from the Golan, precisely as had been the case in Gush Etzion before it fell to the Jordanians in May 1948.

By midnight, Israel had mobilized 200,000 reservists, many of whom had been sent directly into battle. When they reached their posts, many found broken and unusable equipment and poorly maintained tanks. In the words of Ariel Sharon's biographer, "This was not an army primed and poised for war, but rather one that had grown lax and decadent, basking in its overconfidence."[16] Those poorly equipped reservists found themselves facing 300,000 Syrian troops and 850,000 Egyptian soldiers. Once again, as it had done in 1948 and 1967, Iraq joined the fray and sent 14,000 soldiers to the battle. Lebanon fired daily. The IDF was outnumbered six to one.

The Jewish state was twenty-five years old in 1973, and for the third time in its brief history was facing a war for its very survival. For what seemed like an eternity, during the first portion of the war when Israel was on the defensive, the outcome was by no means a foregone conclusion.

THE FIRST FIVE DAYS of what would be a sixteen-day war were the worst for Israel; half of Israel's total losses occurred in those opening days. With the exception of a few counterattacks, the IDF focused mostly on holding the enemy at bay. Israel's soldiers were bewildered. Ariel Sharon noted after he visited a base on October 7, "Suddenly something was happening to them that had never happened before. These were soldiers who had been brought up on victories. . . . It was a generation that had never lost. Now they were in a state of shock. . . . How was it that [the Egyptians] were moving forward and we were defeated?"[17]

The situation was critical. In the first two days of fighting alone, Israel lost 10 percent of its aircraft. An IDF armored division on the front line lost more than half its tanks. The Bar-Lev Line—the much vaunted symbol of Israel's impermeability—disintegrated.

By October 8, Israel had lost 180 of the 290 tanks it had deployed in the Sinai Desert. Dayan, who by then understood the absurdity of his earlier cavalier overconfidence, gave a press conference shortly thereafter, shocking his listeners with his tone of despair. Golda Meir intervened to prevent him from giving a televised interview when she was told that he was going to discuss the possible "destruction of the Third Temple."[18]

Golda Meir appealed to President Nixon for assistance, going so far as to hint that Israel was on the brink of destruction; though every hour was critical for Israel, Nixon took his time.* Speaking on television, the prime minister appealed to Jordan not to make the same costly mistake it had made in 1967. Given the level of cooperation between Israel and Jordan, she had reason to believe that Jordan would not take a very active role, if any, in the war. With regard to American aid, however, all she could do was wait and see.

On the fifth day of the war, October 10, the prime minister addressed the Israeli public on television. She condemned the USSR for heavy losses that the Egyptians and Syrians were inflicting on Israel. "Everything that is in the hands of the Syrian and Egyptian soldier, all this comes from the Soviet Union."[19]

Nixon, too, understood that Israel was in some ways an actor in a larger drama—a proxy war between the two superpowers—in which others had significant influence. The president instructed his national security adviser that Israel was to get the military hard-

---

* Years later, it became clear Nixon had more than a mild distaste for Jews. Henry Kissinger, his right-hand man, was reputed to have a complex relationship with his Jewishness. Ambassador Yehuda Avner later wrote that for Kissinger, being Jewish was a "source of neurosis." In the Nixon tapes released in 2010, Kissinger can be heard telling the president, "If they put Jews into gas chambers in the Soviet Union, it is not an American concern." (Yehuda Avner, *The Prime Ministers: An Intimate Narrative of Israeli Leadership* [Jerusalem: Toby Press, 2010], p. 269; Gil Troy, "Happy Birthday, Mr. Kissinger," May 23, 2013, *Tablet*, http://www.tabletmag.com/jewish-news-and-politics/132819/happy-birthday-mr-kissinger#xCoSwz6BrWoHxhzI.99.)

ware it had requested—with the sole exception of laser-guided bombs—as long as Israel did the transporting of the equipment on El Al planes.[20] According to some reports, Nixon was motivated not only by increasing American concern regarding Israel's survival, but also by reports that Israel—worried about its own survival— had taken off the covers of its nuclear arsenal.[21]

AFTER AN ISRAELI ATTACK in the Sinai on October 8 failed miserably, the IDF General Staff understood that to avert disaster, Israel needed to change the course of the war—immediately. So the IDF's leadership decided to give priority to the northern border, where the Syrians had made significant headway, and to instruct the south to remain in a defensive position for the time being. It worked. Within two days, by October 10, Israeli forces had pushed the Syrians back to the border from which Syrian president Hafez al-Assad had attacked four days earlier. By October 11, the outskirts of Damascus were within range of Israeli artillery. Shortly thereafter, IAF planes bombed the Syrian Defense Ministry building in Damascus.[22] Much more optimistic than he had been just days earlier, Dayan now issued a threat: "The Syrians must learn that the road from Damascus to Israel is also the road from Israel to Damascus."[23]

Suddenly, with Syria rather than Israel on the defensive, superpower concerns began to dominate. With the Soviet Union alarmed at Israel's proximity to Damascus, Anatoly Dobrynin, the Soviet ambassador to the United States, intimated to Kissinger on October 11 that Soviet airborne forces were on alert and Soviet warships were heading to Syrian coastal towns, all to defend Damascus. Two days later, on October 13, Richard Nixon ordered American planes to assist in the military airlift to Israel.

Now Israel had to address the threat from the south. On October 14, the Egyptians made a serious tactical mistake. They pushed beyond their SAM umbrella in order to launch a new attack, exposing themselves to the Israeli Air Force. In the battle that ensued,

Egypt lost 250 tanks while Israel lost only 20. The tide in the south had begun to shift.

Israel exploited the momentum. On October 15, under the command of General Ariel Sharon, Israeli forces began a strike that would enable them to cross the Suez Canal. In what was a very bloody battle (Israel lost three hundred soldiers in that battle alone—almost half of what it had lost in the entire Six-Day War), the first Israeli troops made it to the other side of the canal. Within a week, the IDF had crossed the canal en masse and had captured its western bank. On October 19, the Soviet Union and the United States began to pressure Egypt and Israel, respectively, to call for a cease-fire. Fighting continued, however, in both the north and the south.

On October 22, the United Nations Security Council met and then passed Resolution 338, calling for a cessation of fighting at 6:52 P.M. that day. Just two minutes before the deadline, Israeli radio announced that Israel would accept the terms of the cease-fire.

Still, the battles persisted. But at two A.M. on October 24, after the IDF had encircled the Egyptian Third Army and could have wiped it out, Egypt and Syria agreed to the cease-fire. When it went into effect at one P.M., the war was essentially over.

BY THE END OF THE WAR, the IDF had performed admirably. In dogfights, the IAF shot down 277 Arab planes, losing only 6 of its own (a 46:1 ratio). Altogether, the Arab armies lost 432 planes to Israel's 102. The cost in men had been very high. Arab casualties numbered 8,258 dead and 19,540 wounded, though some Israeli estimates of Arab casualties claim that the real losses were twice that—15,000 dead (among them 11,000 Egyptians) and 35,000 wounded (25,000 of them Egyptian).[24]

Israel lost 2,656 soldiers, with another 7,250 wounded. It was a figure dramatically lower than the Arab losses, but it was more than three times what Israel had lost in 1967—when it had tripled its size in a lightning war of six days. In this war, which had dragged on for much longer, Israel ended up essentially where it had started. There had clearly been egregious blunders in the days leading up to the war, and the country was reeling from the astounding number of casualties. Many Israeli assumptions about land, peace, and war were shattered. Though Israelis had cause to have confidence, once again, in the soldiers at the front, they had less confidence in their leadership; and their hope for any possibility of peace in the region had eroded. Gone, for many, was the hope that there would ever be a "last war." As Yigal Yadin noted after the conflict, "This [was] the first war in which fathers and sons have been in action together. We never thought that would happen. We—the fathers—fought in order that our sons would not have to go to war."[25]

Damaged, too, was Israelis' confidence in their allies. Particularly among Israel's political Right, there were many who would never forgive Kissinger for having delayed arms shipments when they had been so desperately needed. France's support of the Arab state by supplying military equipment surprised few, but Israelis were stunned that Britain—which, like much of post-oil-boycott Europe, was abandoning Israel and moving toward the Arabs—had imposed an embargo on military aid to the region. When Britain finally broke its own embargo, it was by training Egyptian helicopter pilots. When Israel complained, Britain told Israel that they were better off having those pilots training in England than at the front in the Middle East. Third World countries, including those in whom Israel had invested significant money and expertise, cut off ties with the Jewish state.

Oil, too, had entered the picture once again. On October 17, in the midst of the war, Arab countries imposed an oil embargo as punishment of the United States and other countries that had supported Israel. The embargo threw the American and other Western economies into chaos, placing Israel squarely in the crosshairs of international intrigue once again. OPEC (Organization of Petroleum Exporting Countries, dominated by Saudi Arabia) emerged and would color U.S. foreign policy for decades.

THE *CONCEPTZIA* HAD BEEN replaced by a deep sense of gloom, a loss of faith in the country's leaders, and a realization that the IDF was not invincible. A country that had grown accustomed to being the victor slowly and painfully came to terms with the magnitude of its losses. The media showed footage of Israeli POWs, a phenomenon to which Israelis were unaccustomed and that they found horrifying. There were pictures of burned-out Israeli tanks and dead IDF soldiers. One kibbutz, Beit Hashita, lost eleven of its sons. The film of a caravan of eleven army jeeps, each carrying a coffin draped in an Israeli flag, was more than many viewers could bear.

It was also more than many of the kibbutz members could bear. The absolute rejection of religion and the utter commitment to secularism of the founding generation began to give way. It was too early to tell then, but Israel was going to move away from its early image of the new Jew—secular, confident, dismissive of religion—and would begin to search for meaning in places that previous generations would have dismissed out of hand.

Naomi Shemer, who had written "Jerusalem of Gold" in 1967, proved almost prophetic once again. Shortly before the 1973 war, she wrote a Hebrew version of the Beatles song "Let It Be." After the war, she changed the lyrics and the melody, though the refrain still subtly evokes the Beatles' melody. Her song, which took the country by storm and is still widely sung, captured the sadness of an entire nation.[26] "There is still a white sail on the horizon," she wrote, but "beneath a heavy black cloud." And in an obvious invoking of the Beatles, yet with a distinct 1973 Israeli resonance, she wrote:

> All that we long for, let it be.
> Please, let it be, let it be
> All that we long for, let it be.

Even with the passage of time, the country's sadness did not abate. On Israel Independence Day in 1995, Israelis heard the first performance of a song that would soon become an Israeli classic. Titled "Winter '73," it begins: "We are the children of winter of '73." Their parents, the children sang, "First dreamt us at dawn, when the battles ceased." Creating them, these children understood, was an act of desperation, of their parents' passionately clinging to the very possibility of hope: "And when you conceived us with love in winter of '73, / You wanted to fill your bodies with all that the war had taken away."[27]

Yet their parents had made promises, too. "You promised to do everything for us, to turn our enemy into a loved one." Even a whole generation later, though, that had not happened. Hence the refrain that had Israel in its grip, and which still evokes goose bumps among a population that continues to sing the song:

> *You promised peace;*
> *You promised spring at home and blossoms;*
> *You promised to keep your promises;*
> *You promised a dove.*

When that song appeared in 1995, more than two decades after the Yom Kippur War, no dove had come. Israel was a country with a still-broken heart, a country still at war. Even the religious holiday of atonement, Yom Kippur, would never be the same in the Jewish state. A religious holiday of deep personal introspection had been transformed into—and remains to this very day—an annual remembrance of incompetence, grief, loss, and the shattering of Israeli illusions.

In many ways, the Yom Kippur War irrevocably shattered part of Israel's soul.

THE WAR HAD PROFOUND political ramifications, as well. As early as November 13, 1973, Menachem Begin attacked both Golda Meir and the government in the Knesset for what he said was their incompetent handling of the war. Begin had been relegated to the opposition for decades, but now Israelis were listening. Even more damaging to the Labor Party's hegemony, however, was the Agranat Commission, established to investigate what had happened in the period leading up to the war. The commission was appointed on November 21, 1973, and published its findings on April 1, 1974. It held the army brass accountable for numerous failures, but for the most part, sidestepped placing blame on the government. Three senior army officials—David Elazar (chief of staff), General Eli Zeira (head of the intelligence branch), and Shmuel Gonen (chief of the Southern Command)—were stripped of their positions. Gonen left Israel immediately thereafter, living out the rest of his life in Africa. He died of a heart attack at the age of sixty-one. David Elazar also died of a heart attack, in April 1976, less than three years after the war. He was fifty-one years old.

Though the Agranat Commission was less critical of Golda Meir and Moshe Dayan, that in some ways actually made matters worse for the political echelon. They seemed to be getting a "pass"; the public grew angry and disgusted and began to clamor for politicians' resignations.

Peaceful mass protests began. The best known was Motti Ashkenazi's lone demonstration across from the prime minister's residence in Jerusalem, where he held a sign that read: "Grandma [the nickname given to Prime Minister Golda Meir], your defense minister is a failure and 3,000 of your grandchildren are dead."[28] Prior to the war, speaking that way to an elected official would have been unthinkable; this time, it galvanized a nation. The Labor Party won the postponed elections in December 1973, but Golda Meir resigned in April 1974 and was succeeded by Yitzhak Rabin. Rabin had a smaller majority than Meir had had in her first term, and with the country still seething, he was in many ways presiding over a party whose hegemony was about to end.

Rabin's rise to the office of prime minister marked the beginning of a new era. He was the first prime minister born in the twentieth century and the first native-born. He was the first who had received his entire education in Israel and was the first to emerge from the ranks of the army. Israelis felt ready for a new sort of leader.[29]

American Jews sensed the change, and some, who had found a self-confident, pugnacious Israel difficult to deal with post-1967, were actually relieved that some of the wind had been taken out of Israel's sails. "It will be a pleasure," several American Jewish leaders occasionally remarked, "to deal with a lesser Israel."[30] In the ongoing tension between the views of Jacob Blaustein and David Ben-Gurion, those of Blaustein were once again on the ascendancy.

IN DECEMBER 1973, to add even more pain to a country still in agony, just months after the war, David Ben-Gurion died. He had been ailing for some time, but given the trauma that Israel had just endured, the death of the country's founder and father figure was another painful blow.

He had autocratic tendencies and probably stayed in politics just a bit too long. But born in Europe, he came to Palestine early, out of pure ideology, and picked oranges, built labor unions, and rose to the top of Yishuv politics. Then, David Ben-Gurion nimbly guided the Yishuv through the turbulent years of British rule, building prestate institutions and then a state itself. He had an impeccable sense of timing, knew when to wait and when to move, and declared the state even before it was ready, because he knew that another opportunity might never arise.

Not a military man, he guided the fledgling state through the War of Independence with courage and strategic brilliance. If Herzl had given life to political Zionism, David Ben-Gurion had given life to the State of Israel. He was, Yitzhak Navon (Israel's fifth president) firmly believed, "the greatest Jew who had lived since the destruction of the Second Temple" two thousands years earlier.[31] And now he was gone.

Israelis, already shattered and heartbroken after the war, watched David Ben-Gurion's funeral on television, one Israeli author noted, "as if they were watching their own."[32]

THE WAR HAD BEGUN with disaster and it shattered the *conceptzia*. Yet there were also remarkable dimensions to Israel's conduct during the Yom Kippur War. Syrian tanks had been poised to slice through the north of Israel, but the public, while worried, did not flee. The military had made terrible mistakes before the war and in its early days, but under unimaginable pressure, it regrouped, retooled its strategy, and ultimately demonstrated once again Israel's military supremacy. Israel's soldiers had died by the hundreds and then by the thousands, to some extent because of mistakes made by higher-ups, but Israeli soldiers stayed at the front. They did not flee, they did not surrender. Though they had not heard Dayan's comment to the prime minister that the Third Temple—the renewed Jewish commonwealth—was at stake, they intuited that they had come close to losing everything. Israel was not going to fall on their watch.

As it always had, Israel's democracy worked away, with civilians holding accountable both military brass and the country's public leadership.

Israel's military position at the end of the war was overwhelming. It had the Egyptian Third Army encircled and could have destroyed it. In the north, Israeli armor was poised to reach Damascus. Especially given the element of surprise and Israel's initial losses, it was a stunning military accomplishment. The Yom Kippur War, in fact, was the last time that Israel would face an enemy's standing army.[33] Despite the failures leading up to the war and in its first days, the IDF had convinced its neighboring Arab states that attacking Israel head-on was a self-destructive, losing proposition.

Still, Israel had not "won," not in the way to which it had become accustomed. Years later, Shlomo Gazit (head of military intelligence from 1974 to 1979) admitted in a televised interview that the Yom Kippur War had had no victor.[34] That military deadlock, he believed, made both sides more open to the possibility of a peace treaty than they had ever been before.

THE ARAB BATTLE TO destroy Israel was far from over. Having lost on the battlefield, Israel's enemies took their campaign elsewhere. For years, the Palestinians had also been engaged in a diplomatic assault on Israel. Now, European countries, intimidated by the Arab oil embargo, kowtowed to Arab and Palestinian pressure, enabling that diplomatic assault to become more effective. In November 1974, Yasser Arafat was invited to speak at the United Nations. In what became known as the "Olive Branch and Gun" speech, he spoke not about peace with Israel, but about the "Jewish invasion of Palestine." Threatening violence as much as he alluded to peace, he said, to great applause, "Today I come bearing an olive branch in one hand, and the freedom fighter's gun in the other. Do not let the olive branch fall from my hand. I repeat, do not let the olive branch fall from my hand."

Responding to the applause, Arafat clasped his hands above his head, and a holster on his belt came into view. The holster, which Arafat had brought with obvious symbolic intent into the plenum of the General Assembly, was a thinly veiled threat of continuing violence, but it had no impact on the applause. Arafat had declared war on Israel's existence, and the UN responded with adulation and a standing ovation. Merely a year later, the General Assembly granted the PLO observer status at the United Nations.

The UN's assault on Israel continued. In November 1975, the General Assembly approved—by a vote of 72 to 35 (with 32 abstentions)—Resolution 3379, which stated that "Zionism is a form of racism and racial discrimination." The United States voted against the resolution. Daniel Patrick Moynihan, U.S. ambassador to the United Nations, denounced what he understood was really happening: "The United Nations is about to make anti-Semitism international law." Moynihan thundered his now famous declaration, "The [United States] . . . does not acknowledge, it will not abide by it, it will never acquiesce in this infamous act. . . . A great evil has been loosed upon the world."[35]

Even Moynihan had no idea how far and how fast international delegitimization of the Jewish state would soon spread. Though wars against standing armies were now behind it, Israel was in some ways less secure. In many ways, the Jewish state was about to become an international pariah—and would find itself far more vulnerable than it had ever been before.

REVOLUTION WITHIN THE REVOLUTION

The Rise and Revenge of Israel's Political Right

We will be nobody's cowering Jew. . . . Those days are over. . . . Without readiness for self-sacrifice, there will be another Ausch-witz. And if we have to pay a price for the sake of our self-defense, then we will have to pay it.

—Prime Minister Menachem Begin[1]

In the 1970s, the Israeli music scene—like much of political, cultural, and public life in Israel—was dominated by Ashkenazim, white Jews of European extraction, as it had been ever since long before the beginning of the modern aliyot and independence. Naomi Shemer's parents had immigrated from Vilna. Arik Einstein, the uncontested king of Israeli rock in the 1960s, was born in the Yishuv in 1939, also to parents from Europe. When the first Eurovision competition was staged in 1973, Israel was represented by one of the country's most popular singers—Ilanit. Her parents had immigrated to Palestine from Poland. In 1974, the band representing Israel at Eurovision and that sang *"Natati Lah Chayai"* ("I Gave Her My Life")—an Israeli hit to this very day—was the enormously popular *Kaveret* (Beehive), a playful comedic group of five white (Ashkenazi) men.

Israeli radio stations mostly ignored music written and performed by Mizrachim, and record companies had little interest in them. To the music establishment, the Middle Eastern timbre of Mizrachi music sounded strange, foreign, almost Arab. Nothing about the way these Mizrachim looked, sounded, or expressed their Jewishness was what Bialik, Alterman, and others had imagined when they thought of the new Jew who would emerge in the Jewish state. The music scene was but one representation of a much wider phenomenon—Mizrachim were relegated to the periphery of Israeli society in almost every way.

It was the invention of the soon-to-be-ubiquitous audiocassette that helped bring about a dramatic change. In the early 1970s, Mizrachi musicians, ignored by recording studios, began to disseminate their music on cassettes, first in Tel Aviv and later in other areas, as well. This North African, Middle Eastern, somewhat renegade music was soon called *muzikat ha-kasetot*—"the cassette music."* Soon, it began to change the Israeli music scene. Mizrachi music burrowed its way into Israeli life. Musicians like Zohar Argov (whose parents had come not from Europe, but from Yemen) got their first breaks with the cassette music revolution[2] and eventually became national stars.

THE MIZRACHI "REVOLUTION," JUST beginning in the 1970s, would affect much more than the music industry. Israeli political life, too, was about to undergo a seismic shift. The Mizrachim had long lived under the thumb of Arab majorities. They came to Israel when their host countries pressured or forced them to leave. Often expelled without most of their assets, many of them quickly became a subset of Israeli society largely locked in poverty. Yet the Israel to which they came was itself confronting withering eco-

---

* At approximately the same time and in essentially the same region, Ayatollah Ruhollah Khomeini was using audiocassettes to distribute his subversive anti-Western (and anti-Shah) sermons, preparing the way for what would be the 1979 Iranian Revolution.

nomic pressures, and it had meager resources to expend as these Mizrachim made Israel their new country.

The Jewish state took them all in, made them all citizens, gave them an education and basic housing. But the government had placed them in far-flung *ma'abarot*. The government's decision to place these immigrants far from the center of the country was in some ways motivated by national considerations. Years earlier, placing the kibbutzim—with their deeply entrenched tradition of military training—near Israel's borders had contributed to the country's defense. Similarly, situating the *ma'abarot* far from the center of the country was a conscious decision to populate the state's periphery lest Israel's possession of those areas ever be contested in the future.

Yet for the Mizrachim, understandably, the decision to place the *ma'abarot* so far from the country's center created a sense that they had literally been relegated to the periphery of Israeli society, and that unless they took action, nothing would change. Much of the immigrant generation remained docile in the face of government decisions, but for their children, a sense of injustice became a central pillar of their identity. They began to organize in the early 1970s. One group, the Black Panthers (named for the American group with the same name), arranged a meeting with Prime Minister Golda Meir in 1971 in which they expressed their frustration. After the meeting, all Meir had to say about them was "they're not nice."[3] The leadership of Mapai was utterly out of touch; the country was ripe for revolution. The Agranat Commission and Golda Meir's subsequent resignation only reinforced that sense.

Yitzhak Rabin, who succeeded Meir, did not last long either. In 1977, the Israeli press revealed that Rabin's wife, Leah, maintained a small overseas bank account (left over from their years when he had served as Israel's ambassador to the United States), a practice then prohibited by Israeli law. An angry, exasperated, and depressed Israeli public had had enough of Labor leaders who seemed incompetent, corrupt, or out of touch when the rest of the country was struggling financially and Rabin, like Meir before him, resigned.

Israel was ready for change.

RELEGATED TO THE POLITICAL opposition since Israel's first elections in 1949 (except for the brief period of the unity government beginning with the Six-Day War), Menachem Begin had by 1977 spent twenty-nine years failing to make much political headway. A disciple of Ze'ev Jabotinsky, Begin had mostly established his reputation—for better and for worse—in the latter part of the pre-state era and during the first decade of independence.

After he was appointed to lead the Irgun, he had declared the revolt against the British. He had masterminded the attack on the King David Hotel building, which proved critical to the British decision to leave Palestine. Begin also had played a critical role in ensuring that the fighting after the *Altalena* did not become a full-fledged civil war. Though he lost his political battle against taking German reparations, the fight earned him the reputation among many Israelis as the watchman for the Jewishness of Israel's soul.

David Ben-Gurion, on the other hand, had continually cast Begin as a fascist, a label that stuck even with American Jews. In advance of Begin's trip to the United States in 1948, leading American Jewish figures—Albert Einstein and Hannah Arendt among them—wrote a letter to the *New York Times* in which they also called him a fascist, noting that Begin "preached an admixture of ultranationalism, religious mysticism, and racial superiority."[4]

By 1977, Begin had not shaken the accusation entirely, but many Israelis had come to intuit that he was much more complex than his enemies suggested. It was Begin who had been one of the most impassioned voices pushing for the end of military rule over Israeli Arabs,[5] and after a 1965 Knesset reinvestigation of the *Altalena* affair in which some people alleged Ben-Gurion had tried to have Begin killed,[6] it was Begin who emerged largely vindicated.

Throughout his years as head of the opposition, Begin had cultivated a relationship with Mizrachi Jews. He reminded them, time and again, that when he ran the Irgun, his fighters came from Tunisia, Yemen, Syria, Argentina, South Africa, Iraq, Persia, and other non-European Jewish communities:

> [I]n all the divisions of the Irgun we had members who came from all Jewish communities and of all classes. . . . We were the melting-pot of the Jewish nation in miniature. We never asked about origins: we demanded only loyalty and ability. Our comrades from the eastern communities felt happy and at home in the Irgun. Nobody ever displayed stupid airs of superiority toward them and they were thus helped to free themselves of any unjustified sense of inferiority they may have harbored.[7]

In the Irgun, unlike the Knesset, he noted, Mizrachi men attained the highest positions of power.

One might have expected that the Mizrachim would see Begin, a suit-wearing, "proper," and gentlemanly Polish Jew, as highly European—and therefore part of the same problem that Labor represented. Ironically, Begin's Polish background served him well with Israel's North African immigrants. In the early 1950s, as he visited the ma'abarot (and called the Mizrachim living there "my brothers and sisters"), residents of the transit camps took note of his formal attire, the dark suits that seemed so out of place among the Yishuv leaders. They saw his dress as a form of respect for them; to the Mizrachim, the T-shirts and shorts that Ben-Gurion favored when he visited them seemed dismissive, not respectful. Begin capitalized on their simmering anger. As early as 1959, he told a largely Mizrachi audience that Ben-Gurion had turned Israel into a divided country of "Ashkenazim and non-Ashkenazim."[8]

THE COMBINATION OF THE Yom Kippur War, Meir's resignation after the Agranat Commission, Rabin's resignation under a cloud of financial scandal, and the abiding frustrations of the

Mizrachi population was Begin's perfect storm. On Election Day in May 1977, exit polls (the first in Israel's history) stunned the nation. Begin's Likud won 43 seats, while voters gave the Alignment (Ben-Gurion's reconfigured Mapai Party) only 32 seats (a decrease of more than a third of its previous number). Menachem Begin became the only leader in history to have lost eight consecutive elections only to win the ninth.[9]

The victory was dubbed the *"Mahapach"* or "Reversal," by Israeli newscaster Chaim Yavin. (That word was related to *mahapeicha*, the Hebrew word for "revolution.") Many Israelis, especially Mizrachi voters, took to the streets, chanting with jubilation, "Begin! Begin!" Israel had a new crowned prince. It was not only Begin's day; the Mizrachim felt that it was theirs, too. Finally, they felt, they had played a central role in charting the nation's course.

The Ashkenazi elite was in shock. Those Israelis who had grown up under Ben-Gurion and had revered him could not imagine a country led by any other party. As one keen observer noted, "they could not comprehend how one could hate the party that had built the state and absorbed millions of Mizrachim, and they were stunned by its defeat."[10]

On Election Day, as the results came in, reporters shoved microphones at Begin waiting to hear what he would say. Though not punctiliously observant, Begin always carried a *kippah* with him, and now, he donned it and recited the *shehecheyanu*, the traditional blessing to mark an achievement and good fortune. Israelis had never witnessed such an act by a high-ranking politician. Ben-Gurion had not even donned a *kippah* during the Declaration of the State in 1948. When another reporter, in the midst of an exuberant crowd, asked him what style prime minister he would be, Begin paused for a moment at the odd question, and then responded, "In the style of a good Jew."[11]

Israelis are still divided about what Begin meant when he said that, but Israel was already rethinking what it meant to be a "good Jew." That year, a wildly popular comedian, actor, and director of the Israeli stage, Uri Zohar, put on a *kippah* for the first time on the television game show he hosted.[12] That was but one instance of a wider phenomenon; religion was reentering Israeli life, in both politics and culture.

IN AN IMPRESSIVE DEMONSTRATION of Israelis' deep commitment to their democracy, the transition from Mapai to Likud, after almost three decades of Mapai rule, was entirely uncontested. Begin assumed leadership of the government.

The first major development during his administration focused not on the Mizrachim, but on peace. For years, Henry Kissinger had been engaging in shuttle diplomacy between Israel and Egypt and had succeeded in getting both sides to agree to two disengagement agreements, disentangling their forces after the Yom Kippur War. But those ended a previous conflict—they did little to avert the likelihood of a future one.

Just months after Begin's election, however, after a series of secret back-channel communications (some of them through Romania's president Nicolae Ceaușescu), Egyptian president Anwar Sadat departed from his prepared remarks to the Egyptian Parliament on November 9, 1977. Israel "will be stunned to hear me tell you," he announced, "that I am ready to go to the ends of the earth, and even to their home, to the Knesset itself, to argue with them, in order to prevent one Egyptian soldier from being wounded."[13]

In an almost immediate response to Sadat's gambit, Begin issued his own radio broadcast—aimed directly at the Egyptians—in which he invited Sadat to Jerusalem. Eight days later, to many Israelis' disbelief, Sadat's plane landed in Tel Aviv. Begin met Sadat at the bottom of the steps leading from the plane, and the two men embraced on the red carpet laid out for Sadat and his procession. Israeli and Egyptian flags fluttered in the breeze. In the minutes that followed, Sadat met a veritable "who's who" of Israeli leadership. The man who had waged war on Israel was now standing on Israeli soil, meeting the country's leaders and being shown a warm welcome. He was introduced to Moshe Dayan and Yitzhak Rabin, who had led Israel's stunning victory in 1967, and to Golda Meir, who had defeated him in 1973.

Rabin later recalled being immediately impressed with Sadat: "Here he was meeting all his former arch-enemies, one after another, in the space of seconds, and he nonetheless found a way to start off his visit by saying exactly the right thing to each and every one of them."[14] He also made a deep impression on the citizens of Israel, who watched on television with rapt attention. "The citizens of Israel were ecstatic. If Sadat wanted to persuade them of his peaceful intentions, he had won them over in a single dramatic gesture."[15]

The following day, Sadat became the first Arab leader to address the Knesset. He laid out five conditions for peace: Israel's complete return to the 1967 borders, independence for the Palestinians, the right for all to live in peace and security, a commitment not to resort to arms in the future, and the end of belligerency in the Middle East.

Sadat's demands were steep, and the negotiations were painstaking, acrimonious, and slow going. The United States, under President Jimmy Carter, joined the negotiations as intermediaries. Begin and Sadat developed a mutual respect (though their relationship, too, had ups as well as many downs), but relations between Begin and Carter were toxic. Carter invited Begin and Sadat to Camp David, where he thought the bucolic setting might help move matters forward. Even there, though, negotiations almost collapsed. Begin and Sadat locked horns and hardly saw each other. Carter called Begin a "psycho,"[16] while Begin thought Carter was purposely and callously ignoring the enormity of the concessions the president was asking the prime minister to make. Begin was inclined to depart.

Eventually, the sides were able to narrow their differences. Begin sacrificed the Sinai but kept the West Bank. He resisted Sadat's demands that land from the West Bank be given to the Palestinians, stating that he did not intend to sign an agreement with one enemy while creating a state for another. The Egyptian president got the

Sinai back by being the first Arab head of state to make peace with Israel and by selling out the Palestinians.

On September 28, 1978, at roughly three A.M., after hours of acrimonious debate, the Knesset voted 84 in favor, 19 opposed, and 17 abstentions; the Camp David peace agreement was approved. Begin had the beginning of his peace with Egypt. The man the British had once called terrorist number one had made peace with Israel's most powerful enemy. For the sake of peace, Israel was agreeing to withdraw from land it had captured in a war it had not started and in which it had lost thousands of its sons. To those who recalled that Meir's left-leaning government had refused to take Sadat up on his ostensible offers to negotiate, it was a stunning move.

It would also not be the last time Israel made the choice to cede land in the hopes of peace.

Israelis took note of the fact that it was a right-wing prime minister—in fact, the country's first right-wing prime minister—who had agreed to withdraw from territory. Part of the reason was parliamentary politics. If the Left sought to withdraw, the Right would try to block the move. But when the Right advocated giving up territory, the Left (which always claimed to be *more* inclined to compromise for peace) would obviously have to support the move. The Right, it ironically seemed, might be the key to peace in the future, as well. A significant part of the formula in this case, though, was Begin himself. Much more decisive than many of his predecessors, when he saw opportunities, he rarely hesitated to act.

Shortly thereafter, the Nobel Committee decided to award the Peace Prize to both Begin and Sadat. Sadat's willingness to make peace with Israel, however, had made him the most reviled leader in the Arab world. (The Arab League ostracized and expelled Egypt, closing its headquarters in Cairo. Egyptian students studying abroad were expelled from other Arab states.) Fearful for his life (and perhaps not wishing to be seen with Begin at this stage, with negotiations still unfolding), Sadat chose not to attend the Nobel ceremony on December 10, 1978, and sent his son-in-law instead.

In Israel, too, old party animosities endured. Golda Meir, embittered and an heir to Ben-Gurion's instinctive resentment of Begin, remarked—with her characteristic wit still intact—that Begin deserved not a Nobel, but an Oscar.[17] She died while he was in Oslo receiving the prize.

Sadat's precautions and his decision not to attend the Nobel ceremony did not save him, however. Attitudes toward the Egyptian president only worsened when Israel passed the 1980 Jerusalem Law, which stated that all of Jerusalem was Israel's capital, and was interpreted as Israel's annexation of East Jerusalem. On October 6, 1981, in a moment eerily evocative of the 1951 murder of Jordan's King Abdullah I after rumors spread that he was considering peace talks with Israel, Anwar Sadat was assassinated by soldiers in his own army (who were affiliated with the Egyptian Islamic Jihad) while attending the annual parade in Cairo commemorating the Egyptian crossing of the Suez during the October War (the Egyptians' term for the Yom Kippur War).[18]

THERE WAS ACRIMONY and resentment inside Israel, too. As early as the signing of the Camp David Accords in 1978, Jewish residents of the Sinai protested the Knesset's decision to withdraw. The largest standoff took place at Yamit, a smallish secular town near the border with Gaza, where the withdrawal began in earnest in April 1982—shortly after Sadat's assassination. Though many left peacefully in exchange for compensation, some of the residents refused to abandon their homes.[19] They clung to rooftops, and IDF soldiers had to use powerful water hoses to dislodge them. One extreme group locked itself in a bunker in Yamit and said they would blow themselves up if the army sought to dislodge them. Begin refused to back down. Ultimately, Israeli authorities destroyed the settlement entirely. They dismantled its greenhouses and uprooted orchards. What had been transformed into fertile land almost immediately became, once again, desert.

Though there were no significant injuries in the withdrawal, the sight of Israeli citizens scuffling with Israeli soldiers cast a pall over the country. Israelis would witness similar scenes of anguish almost a quarter of a century later when Israel left Gaza in 2005. Yet both of the withdrawals were actually remarkable displays of Israeli democracy at work, as well as restraint by the settlers and by the military. There were no serious injuries in either, despite great sadness and gloomy predictions of violence.

At the same time, Israelis intuited that were Israel ever to leave the West Bank, scenes infinitely more violent were likely to unfold.

THOUGH THE LIKUD WAS not a religious political party, most of its leadership and many of its voters felt a natural kinship to Gush Emunim, the religious-nationalist movement that had spearheaded settlement growth. These settlers were passionate and unabashed Zionists in an era in which many Israelis had started to grow cynical about the ideological fervor of previous generations. The Gush Emunim pioneers saw themselves as doing what the early pioneers had done—continuing to build on land that was the Jewish ancestral homeland that Israel had now captured in a defensive war it had not sought.

Begin's identification with the settler movement had begun years earlier. In 1974, Gush Emunim members had sought permission to build one of the first settlements, Elon Moreh. As was the case in the beginnings of many settlements (including that in Hebron), when permission was refused, settlers went anyway. Eventually, after numerous requests, the (left-wing government) acquiesced and approved what the settlers had already started.

The issue of settlements in the newly occupied territory was perhaps the most divisive political question of the time, and largely in hopes of dodging it, Labor governments waffled. That indecisiveness allowed the settlers to create their facts on the ground. Begin, in contrast, was committed to continuing that policy, as a matter of principle and not only political expediency. In May 1977, two days after the elections, Begin and Ariel Sharon visited the temporary

Elon Moreh site. "Soon," Begin said, "there will be many more Elon Morehs."[20]

When reporters following the prime minister-elect asked whether Begin's firm commitment to the settlements implied a future annexation of the West Bank, they got a tongue-lashing in return:

> We don't use the word "annexation." You annex *foreign* land, not your own country. Besides, what was this term "West Bank"? From now on, the world must get used to the area's real—biblical—name, "Judea and Samaria." . . . [I]s it so difficult for you to use these words?[21]

A different Israeli ethos had come to power. During the course of Begin's tenure as prime minister, the number of settlements doubled. Given that this number would later increase under right-wing Israeli governments and that the Right was always much more unabashed about defending the legitimacy of the settlement movement, the international community would later speak of settlements as the creation of the Israeli political Right, but that was incorrect. When Begin took office, there were already seventy-five settlements—and they had been created under the governments of Golda Meir and Yitzhak Rabin. Settling land—whether purchased or captured in conflicts that Israel did not seek—was not a policy of the political Right or Left. It was a central pillar of Zionism's ethos from the very outset.

That was how the Jews had built their state. Many Israelis saw no reason to give up on the very ideology that had made their country possible in the first place. What was different about the Right was that it made that claim entirely unapologetically.

WHILE ISRAEL HAD PEACE (even if a "cool" peace) with Egypt, new threats continued to emerge. Iraq's Saddam Hussein was threatening to "drown" the Jewish state "with rivers of blood."[22]

Toward that end, Iraq—with the active assistance of the French—was building a nuclear reactor. The French, who had once helped Israel build its own reactor in Dimona, had now decided to assist a country committed to destroying the Jewish state. Upon his election, Begin began to insist that under no circumstances could Hussein, who was intent on destroying the Jewish state, be allowed to acquire a nuclear weapon.

In August 1978, Begin convened the first of dozens of secret cabinet meetings to determine the appropriate course of action. Any military action was fraught with danger. On the diplomatic front, Israelis knew that the United States, interested in protecting its broader interests in the Arab Middle East, might well condemn and isolate Israel following an attack, especially since the U.S. State Department continued to claim as late as 1980 that there was "no hard evidence that Iraq has decided to acquire nuclear explosives."[23] Militarily, the mission to destroy Iraq's reactor would be no less treacherous. The pilots would be flying twelve hundred miles across enemy territory, dangerously low and close to the ground to avoid radar (in fact, several pilots were killed in training for the mission).

Yet for Begin, there was no question that the mission was critical. The Jewish people had not reestablished its national home after two thousand years only to live once again under the threat of extinction.

On June 7, 1981, eight Israeli fighter jets streaked east toward Iraq. Arriving undetected, they dropped their bombs; the Iraqi reactor at Osirak was completely destroyed, and all the planes returned safely to Israel. While the attack was a glorious moment for Israel's military, international reaction was immediate and unremittingly critical. The French were incensed as expected, but the Israeli government encountered a blanket of criticism even in the United States. Two days after the strike, the New York Times published an editorial lambasting the strike as "an act of inexcusable and short-sighted aggression."[24] With a hint at Begin's past, the paper declared that the prime minister "embraces the code of his weakest enemies, the code of terror. He justifies aggression by his profound sense of victimhood."[25] Joseph Kraft of the *Los Angeles Times* likened the attacks to Arafat's terrorism, insisting that "Americans need not be afraid to point out that the Palestinian leader, Yasser Arafat, looks no more prone to terrorist tactics than does Menachem Begin."[26]

The United States initially condemned Israel's actions, even supporting the unanimous UN Security Council Resolution 487, which depicted the attack as a "clear violation of the Charter of the United Nations and the norms of international conduct."[27] A decade later, in 1991, while at war with Iraq in Operation Desert Storm, the United States essentially recanted. U.S. secretary of defense Dick Cheney gave the Israelis a satellite photograph of the Osirak reactor remnants, on which he wrote:

> *For General David Ivri, with thanks and appreciation for the outstanding job he did on the Iraqi Nuclear Program in 1981, which made our job much easier in Desert Storm!*
> Dick Cheney, U.S. Sec. Def.[28]

The peace treaty with Egypt also survived the attack on Iraq. No Arab armies responded. The reactor was gone, the peace treaty survived, and everyone understood that even U.S. president Ronald Reagan was not as incensed as he had pretended. The attack was an unmitigated success.

Israel now had a policy known as the "Begin Doctrine," which would endure long after Begin himself was gone from the political arena. It held that Israel would not countenance any of its mortal enemies seeking to develop or acquire a weapon of mass destruction.[29]

THOUGH ISRAEL HAD PROVEN that it could make peace with nations willing to accept its existence and take on those who planned its destruction, the Jewish state's new challenge was not standing

AUSTRALIAN **JNF** CAMPAIGN 1947

The plough breaks through

RESTRICTIONS

BUILDING AND AGRICULTURE

Working the land and building the Yishuv were central to the ethos of early Zionism.

Top: Men working a field in 1932. *Daniel Kaplan, Israel Government Press Office*

Middle left: Building Tel Aviv Gymnasium (high school). *Central Zionist Archives*

Middle right: The plow breaks through. *Central Zionist Archives*

Bottom right: Men constructing a "tower and stockade" *(homa u-migdal)* settlement. *Central Zionist Archives*

HEBREW WRITERS

Renewing the Hebrew language was a central project of early Zionism, and Hebrew writers were widely revered as the voices of a reemerging nation.

Top: Learn Hebrew! *Central Zionist Archives*

Middle left: The purple 50 nis bill featured Shai Agnon, Israel's first Nobel Laureate. © 2014 *The Bank of Israel*

Bottom left: Agnon was later replaced on the 50 nis bill, but by another writer, the poet Saul Tchernichovsky. © 2014 *The Bank of Israel*

Middle right: Eliezer Ben-Yehuda surrounded by books. *Central Zionist Archives*

Bottom right: Hayim Nachman Bialik at his desk. *Central Zionist Archives*

ILLEGAL IMMIGRATION

Illegal immigration—in defiance of British restrictions—was critical in the early years, both to save Jews fleeing Europe as well as to amass a population sufficient for creating a viable state.

Top: British soldiers carefully watch a ship approaching with illegal immigrants. *Central Zionist Archives*

Middle left: Pulling an immigrant boat into shore. *Central Zionist Archives*

Middle right: Immigrants arrive on boat. *Central Zionist Archives*

Bottom: This Zionist poster shows a "new" muscular Jew helping European Jewish survivors reach shore. *Central Zionist Archives*

IMAGES OF THE NEW JEW

Early Zionism was focused on the creation of a "new Jew" who, unlike the Jews of Europe, could shape his or her own future. These early Zionist posters illustrate the focus on the new, muscular Jew, and weave together images of Jews who both work the land and defend it.

Top left: Join the Army! *Central Zionist Archives*

Middle left: Rifle and Hammer. *Central Zionist Archives*

Bottom left: Redemption of Nation and Humankind. *Central Zionist Archives*

Bottom right: Shoulder to Shoulder Gun and Shovel. *Central Zionist Archives*

DECLARING INDEPENDENCE

Israel's independence was seen as one of the most transformative moments in all of Jewish history.

Top left: David Ben-Gurion just moments before declaring the new state on May 14, 1948. *Frank Shershel, Israel Government Press Office*

Top right: A tally sheet the Zionist delegation used at the UN during the vote on Partition (later signed by many dignitaries). *Israel State Archive*

Middle left: Crowds celebrate and dance in Palestine after the vote. *Central Zionist Archives*

Bottom left: A telegram from Chaim Weizmann to President Harry Truman pleading for his help in ensuring that the motion for Partition would pass. *Courtesy of Yad Chaim Weizmann, The Weizmann Archives, Rehovot, Israel*

WESTERN UNION

TO PRESIDENT TRUMAN   NOVEMBER 25, 1947 19

Street and No. WHITE HOUSE

Place WASHINGTON D C

DEAR MR PRESIDENT AT THIS CRUCIAL HOUR WHEN DIFFICULT PALESTINE

PROBLEM IS ON THE VERGE OF A SOLUTION WHICH WOULD OWE SO MUCH TO

YOUR PERSONAL INITIATIVE I ADDRESS MYSELF TO YOU AGAIN STOP I AM

AWARE OF HOW MUCH ABSTAINING DELEGATIONS WOULD BE SWAYED BY YOUR

COUNSEL AND THE INFLUENCE OF YOUR GOVERNMENT I REFER TO CHINA

HONDURAS COLOMBIA MEXICO LIBERIA ETHIOPIA GREECE STOP I BEG AND

PRAY FOR YOUR INTERVENTION AT THIS DECISIVE HOUR TO BRING ABOUT

A SETTLEMENT WHICH WILL GO DOWN IN HISTORY PLEASE FORGIVE MY

TROUBLING YOU AGAIN   CHAIM WEIZMANN

PEOPLE WHO MADE
IT HAPPEN

Among the shapers of Israel's story
were fascinating and passionate men
and women, religious and secular
Jews, scientists and generals, writers
and politicians. They developed the
ideas behind Zionism, advocated
for the movement in international
circles, built Israel's democracy and
infrastructure, led its military and
turned from enemies of Israel to
peacemakers. These are but a few
of the most central figures.

OPPOSITE PAGE
Top left: Theodor Herzl visits Palestine.
The tuxedos illustrate the chasm
between Herzl's imagination the
realities of Palestine. *Israel Government
Press Office*

Top right: Rabbi Abraham Isaac Kook
meets with nonreligious Jews. *Central
Zionist Archives*

Middle right: Golda Meir addresses
members of the Histadrut labor union.
*Zoltan Kluger, Israel Government Press
Office*

Bottom: Dr. Chaim Weizmann and Lord
Arthur Balfour. *Central Zionist Archives*

THIS PAGE, FROM TOP TO BOTTOM
Menachem Begin beside a photo of his
political nemesis, David Ben-Gurion.
Joseph Roth, Israel Government Press Office

Yitzhak Rabin and his peace partner,
King Hussein of Jordan. *Ya'acov Sa'ar,
Israel Government Press Office*

Yitzhak Rabin, Hosni Mubarak, King
Hussein, and Bill Clinton putting on
their ties as Yasser Arafat watches.
*White House Photographer Israel
Government Press Office*

Ariel Sharon, though long a warrior
and politician, always saw himself as
a farmer. © *2016 Gideon Markowicz/
Flash90*

IMMIGRATION AND ETHNICITIES

Israel was built in large measure by successive waves of immigrants, bringing to the Jewish State Jews from all over the world.

Top left: A Russian immigrant arrives in Israel, still adorned with the medals of his former country. *Zion Ozeri.*

Top right: Operation Magic Carpet brings Yemenite Jews to Israel. © 2016 courtesy of the JDC

Middle right: Ethiopian Aliyah. © 2016 FLASH90

Bottom right: Survivors of Buchenwald concentration camp arrive in Israel. *Yad Vashem*

armies, but terrorism—most notably the Palestine Liberation Organization (PLO).

Since September 1970, when Jordan's King Hussein expelled Yasser Arafat and the PLO from his kingdom, the PLO had begun using Lebanon (on Israel's northern border) as a new base of activities against Israel. (See Map 8.) Lebanon, once a thriving Middle Eastern country, was now in the grips of an increasingly bitter civil war between numerous factions, which included the entrenched Maronite Christians and the country's Muslim populations, Syrians, and Druze. Lebanon was a country with deeply embedded rivalries; the country's disintegration and chaos made it a perfect launching pad for terrorist activity into Israel.

Terrorism, of course, was nothing new to Israel. Initially, the PLO opted for high-visibility attacks, many of which became iconic moments in Israeli history. Most infamous, perhaps, was the attack on the Munich Olympics in September 1972. Terrorists from the Black September Organization stormed the Israeli accommodation block in the Olympic Village and took Israeli athletes hostage. A German Special Forces team failed in its attempt to rescue the hostages, and by the end of the shooting, eleven Israelis were dead.[*] It was lost on very few Israelis that thirty years after the Holocaust, it

---

[*] Some forty years later, in late 2015, the *New York Times* and other news sources reported on information obtained decades earlier that revealed that the athletes, before they were killed in the firefight, had been beaten up and tortured. One hostage was shot and bled to death in front of his colleagues, who were bound and unable to help him. At least one other was castrated, quite possibly while he was still alive. In the 1903 Kishinev pogrom, marauding Russians had not only killed Jews, but had cut breasts off live women. The sport of not only killing, but of mutilating, Jews continued three-quarters of a century later. ("Horrifying Details of Murder of Athletes in Munich Revealed: 'They Were Tortured in Front of Their Friends,'" http://www.ynet.co.il/articles/0,7340,L-4733681,00.html [Hebrew]; see also Sam Borden, "Long-Hidden Details Reveal Cruelty of 1972 Munich Attackers," *New York Times* [December 2, 2015], http://www.nytimes.com/2015/12/02/sports/long-hidden-details-reveal-cruelty-of-1972-munich-attackers.html.)

was Germany—of all places—where Jewish blood was being spilled as the entire world watched the unfolding horror on television.

Four years later, in the summer of 1976, Palestinian and German terrorists hijacked an Air France plane and took it to Entebbe, Uganda, where they held more than a hundred hostages, most of them Jews and, of those, many Israeli. In a daring mission that became the stuff of Israeli legend, an Israeli Special Forces team flew to Entebbe on July 4 and rescued all the hostages (save for three who were killed in the fighting). The team's commander, Yonatan Netanyahu (brother of Benjamin Netanyahu, who would later become prime minister), was the only Israeli commando killed in the attack, and almost instantly—given the audaciousness of the successful rescue and his own bravery—was transformed into an Israeli hero.

THERE WAS UNREST ON the home front, too. Over the years, Israeli Arabs had begun to organize and to demand better social and economic conditions. In March 1976, the Israeli government announced plans to appropriate a large swath of land, some of it Arab owned, and to assign it to several Jewish cities, including Carmiel (an Israeli town approximately midway between Haifa and the Sea of Galilee). To Israeli Arabs, the continuous erosion of their control over lands that had long been theirs was symbolic of their general second-class status. On March 30, hundreds of thousands of Israeli Arabs began to protest. The land appropriation was the immediate trigger, but the huge turnout suggested that the protests were also about long-term simmering resentment. The protests grew violent; Arabs burned tires in the streets, blocked roads, and threw rocks (and some say, Molotov cocktails) at security forces. In the mayhem that followed, accounts of which remained highly contested, six Israeli Arabs—who were not armed—were killed by Israeli forces. In the minds of many of Israel's Arabs, it was a replay of the 1956 Kafr Kassem massacre and it became a turning point in Israeli Arabs' sense of self. Israeli Jews protested against the government regularly, the Arabs noticed. But Jews did not end up shot by soldiers and police. Land Day 1976, as it became known, was transformed into a defining and painful milestone in the Israeli Arab narrative.

While Israeli Arabs had protested mostly unarmed, Palestinian extremists outside of Israel turned ever more violent. Arafat changed tactics, and using southern Lebanon as his base, began firing rockets at Israeli civilians, hoping to make Israeli life unbearable. Cross-border assaults and rocket fire into northern Israel grew increasingly common; for Israel's citizens, bomb shelters were becoming a regular part of life, and a sense of siege descended on the northern portion of the country. By 1982, over fifteen thousand Palestinian guerrillas were operating in southern Lebanon, from Beirut down to the area increasingly called "Fatah-land."[30]

On March 11, 1978, early in Begin's tenure as prime minister, an eleven-man terror cell infiltrated Israel from the sea, hijacked a bus traveling Israel's coastal road en route to Tel Aviv, and killed thirty-eight Israelis and injured seventy-one. It was, *Time* magazine noted, "the worst terrorist attack in Israel's history.[31] An Israeli response, Operation Litani, forced a hasty PLO retreat to Beirut, but the PLO remained ensconced in Lebanon. It was an early indication that Israel would not easily win its war against terror by military means.

The threat against the north continued, as did shelling. Israelis in the north had to flee to bomb shelters as rockets from Lebanon struck their towns and cities. Israeli children were spending many nights belowground, terrified. Then—just as the coastal road attack had unleashed Israel's first foray into Lebanon—an attack in London by a Palestinian splinter terror group precipitated the second.

On June 3, 1982, Palestinian terrorists shot Israel's ambassador to England, Shlomo Argov, in London.* The attack on Argov was

---

* Though shot in the head, Argov did not die. He remained in a coma for three months, and after he regained consciousness, was returned to Israel, where he remained as a permanent patient in a rehabilitation hospital, blinded for life. He died in 2003, at the age of seventy-three, having been hospitalized for twenty-one years.

the final straw, but tensions had been rising. For Begin, a disciple of Jabotinsky who had inherited a passionate commitment to *hadar* (the notion that the core of Jewish life should be dignity), the image of Israeli children cowering in fear night after night was an outrage he would not abide. It was an image of what Jewish life in Europe had been like, and the opposite of the purpose of Jewish sovereignty. Evoking a bewilderment that had echoes of Bialik's "The City of Slaughter," Begin asked why the Jews should accept being attacked without being willing to defend themselves:

> We will be nobody's cowering Jew. We won't wait for the Americans or the United Nations to save us. Those days are over. We have to defend ourselves. Without readiness for self-sacrifice, there will be another Auschwitz. And if we have to pay a price for the sake of our self-defense, then we will have to pay it. Yes, war means bloodshed, bereavement, orphans—and that is a terrible thing to contemplate. But when an imperative arises to protect our people from being bled, as they are being bled now in Galilee, how can any one of us doubt what we have to do?[32]

Begin's plan was risky. The Israelis hoped that if the Christians could take control of Lebanon, rocket fire into Israel would cease. Furthermore, Begin hoped that in return for supporting Bashir Gemayel, the head of Lebanon's Christian Phalangist Party (the Phalangists were a Lebanese Christian paramilitary organization founded in 1936), in his ongoing battle against Lebanon's Muslims, Israel might be rewarded with a peace treaty. The entire plan, however, depended on Gemayel's success—over which Israel had virtually no control.

Operation Peace for the Galilee was launched on June 6, 1982. Despite some initial successes at ridding southern Lebanon of PLO fighters, Israel's plans quickly unraveled. Ariel Sharon took Israeli troops far beyond the forty-kilometer line to which the cabinet had agreed and that Begin had committed to Reagan he would observe. Not long thereafter, the IDF had Beirut under siege; Israel, it was clear, had invaded another country. Israeli casualties were also heavy—more than two hundred soldiers had been killed and a thousand more had been wounded. For the first time, many Israelis felt that they were fighting a war that Israel had chosen to start, not one that had been forced on them.

Lebanon was becoming Israel's Vietnam.

Israel's international image also suffered. Despite his own losses, Arafat refused to leave Beirut. He appeared on Western television regularly, showing pictures of maimed Palestinian children and still-smoldering Palestinian homes. As a result of Israel's attack on Beirut, to many millions of international viewers, Arafat was suddenly a hero, the redeemer of the Palestinian people.

Militarily, though, Arafat and the PLO were no match for Israel's massive firepower. Israel bombed Palestinian refugee camps in southwest Beirut, home to significant PLO positions, relentlessly—and successfully. By August 12, 1982, Arafat conceded. Forced out of Jordan in 1971, the PLO now had to leave Lebanon, too. Between August 21 and 30, some nine thousand PLO fighters (and another six thousand Syrian troops) were escorted out of the city. Arafat, in the company of some of his fighters, set sail for Tunisia.

From its outset, though, nothing about the Lebanese operation had gone as expected, and its end was no exception. On September 14, 1982, less than a month after Arafat's departure from Beirut, the Christian Phalangist headquarters in Beirut was bombed by a Syrian operative. Twenty-seven people were killed, among them Bashir Gemayel. Israel had lost its "Great Lebanese Hope" for peace, and the Christians had lost a leader many revered. The Israeli government's entire strategy was disintegrating.

Matters quickly grew infinitely worse. The bedlam following Gemayel's murder, Ariel Sharon believed, afforded Israel an opportunity to capture the overcrowded Palestinian refugee camps on the southwest edge of the city, which he said were serving as home to those PLO fighters who had not departed Lebanon.

Sharon told the cabinet that he planned to secure the Sabra refugee camp. He did not mention a second camp, Shatila, and emphasized that the Christian Phalangists "would be left to operate 'with their own methods.'"[33] Israelis, he promised, would not be doing the fighting.

On the evening of September 16, IDF divisions secured the perimeters of both the Sabra and Shatila camps. Under IDF watch, the Christian Phalangist forces, seeking revenge for the murder of Gemayel, entered the camps and encountered fierce resistance from Muslim PLO fighters. The Christians quickly overwhelmed them, and—enraged by the murder of Gemayel and fueled by long-standing hatred for their Muslim rivals—then began to open fire on civilians. For three days, the Christian Phalangists indiscriminately massacred Palestinian Muslims. By the time it was over, "groups of young men in their twenties and thirties had been lined up against walls, tied by their hands and feet, and then mowed down gangland-style with fusillades of machine-gun fire."[34] An estimated seven hundred to eight hundred men, women, and children had been killed.

On September 26, 1982, hundreds of thousands protested in Tel Aviv against the government, demanding a judicial inquiry into the massacre, and calling for the resignations of both "Sharon the Murderer" and "Begin the Murderer." It was a profound national crisis; Begin established the Kahan Commission to determine whether Israel was responsible for the massacre.

In the United States, the massacre had a profound impact on the attitudes of young Jews to Israel. Gone was the wall-to-wall support for Israel that had emerged after 1967. As one leading American Jewish social activist put it, "It was a shameful moment. . . . I think also we lost a lot of young people. . . . You can't behave that way as a nation and expect to spark in young, idealistic Jews a passion for Israel unless you're dealing with fanatics."[35] That tear in the fabric of relations between Israel and young American Jews would become even more pronounced in years to come.

After four months of deliberations, the commission announced its findings. It determined that while no Israelis were directly responsible for the massacre at Sabra and Shatila, Ariel Sharon, above all others, bore "personal responsibility" for the affair:

> It is impossible to justify the Defense Minister's disregard of the danger of a massacre. . . . His involvement in the war was deep, and the connection with the Phalangists was under his constant care. If in fact the Defense Minister, when he decided that the Phalangists would enter the camps without the IDF's taking part in the operation, did not think that the decision could bring about the very disaster that in fact occurred, the only possible explanation for this is that he disregarded any apprehensions about what was to be expected.[36]

The cabinet accepted the recommendations of the Kahan Commission. Embittered, Sharon agreed to step down as defense minister, but he remained in the government as a "minister without portfolio," not responsible for any particular ministry. Humiliated and widely detested, it would have been difficult to imagine then that just two decades later, that same pugnacious Ariel Sharon would become prime minister and would be the architect of one of Israel's most significant territorial withdrawals.

ISRAEL MAINTAINED a military presence in Lebanon, along the border, until Prime Minister Ehud Barak pulled Israel's troops out in 2000. At the time of the pullout, many Israelis felt that Israel had little to show for almost two decades in Lebanon, other than many hundreds of casualties. The drawn-out foray into Lebanon left much of the country permanently embittered, and—because of Sabra and Shatila—plagued by guilt. The country's mood was captured beautifully by Matti Friedman, an Israeli who served in Lebanon at the very end of Israel's presence there and who then went on to become an internationally recognized journalist and author:

The Israel that arrived in Lebanon in 1982 was still imagina-
tive and light on its feet, however unwise its ideas and however
wretched their execution. . . . [W]e thought we could make
things happen. The invasion [of Lebanon] was supposed to effect a dramatic change in our surroundings. . . . Underlying [ev-
erything] was the same sentiment—our fate was malleable, and
it was ours to shape. But most of us came to understand . . . that
we were wrong. . . . The Middle East doesn't bend to our dictates
or our hopes. It won't change for us.[37]

Israel's film industry also captured the competing feelings of the
country. *Two Fingers from Sidon* (1986) traced the daily life of Israeli
soldiers in Lebanon shortly before Israel's withdrawal, pointing to
the dangers there and the ethnic and moral complexities of the IDF
being in Lebanon. *Beaufort,* a 2007 film named for an Israeli outpost on a Lebanese mountain of the same name, was more critical,
portraying a group of soldiers stationed there toward the end of
Israel's years in Lebanon. The movie captured their fears at being
there and the moral conundrums they faced on the eve of Israel's
withdrawal, while conveying a deep sense of the endlessness and
utter futility of war.

But nothing captured the sensibilities of Israel's ongoing reckoning with the legacy of Lebanon better than *Waltz with Bashir,* an
Israeli film produced in 2008. The film tells the story of Ari Folman,
who in 1982 was a nineteen-year-old infantry soldier. In 2006, a
friend from the period of his army service recounts his nightmares
from the war, but Folman surprisingly remembers nothing. After
meeting with others who served, Folman eventually recalls that he
was among the soldiers who had fired flares into the sky to illumi-
nate the refugee camp for the Lebanese Christian Phalange militia
perpetrating the massacre inside,[38] and he confronts his sense that
he had blocked the memories because he felt that he was no less
guilty of the massacre than those who had actually committed it
firsthand.

Here was a continuation of the self-examination and self-criticism that had characterized Israeli society since its inception. Just as *Khirbet Khizeh* had become a bestseller when it questioned the behavior of some Israeli troops during the War of Independence and was then made part of the country's high school curriculum, *Waltz with Bashir* was viewed by thousands of Israelis. In a society long wrestling with its role in the war and in Sabra and Shatila, it was the subject of seemingly endless debate and analysis, part of an Israeli discourse about whether—in a conflict they could not end—Israelis were nonetheless losing their way.

The film was banned in Lebanon.[39]

MONTHS AFTER THE KAHAN Commission report, Menachem Begin—in poor health, depressed by the war, and profoundly alone in the wake of his wife's death—resigned and retreated to his home. For the next decade, until his death in 1992, he did not exit his apartment except for memorial ceremonies for his wife and medical appointments. Yitzhak Shamir, who had headed the Lechi during the British Mandate, succeeded the former head of the Irgun as prime minister.

While Begin had transformed Israel's political map, he had also brought new religious sensibilities to the fore of Israeli discourse. By no means scrupulously observant, he nonetheless unabashedly loved and honored Jewish tradition. As Minister Dan Meridor put it, "He spoke Jewish."[40] In the decades to come, Israeli society would begin to "speak Jewish" again, in ways that even Begin himself could not have imagined.

Yet Menachem Begin's legacy was also colored deeply by Lebanon. Begin had good reasons for invading, but the war had turned into a quagmire. Eventually, Lebanon would essentially cease to exist as a functioning state. The power vacuum that resulted from the violence there—violence in which Israel was deeply involved—would turn the erstwhile country into a base for Hezbollah, which would become an even more fearsome terrorist threat to Israel. Could that have been prevented? It is obviously hard to know. Did

Begin make critical decisions, or did Ariel Sharon mislead him? That, too, is still hotly debated even among people who were in Begin's government at the time.

THE BEGIN YEARS HAD not been easy ones for Israel, but they had been important. Israel had made peace with its once most potent enemy, Egypt. It had made clear that it would not tolerate weapons of mass destruction in the hands of its sworn enemies. It had shown that it would go to war—even a war that many Israelis eventually opposed—to protect the rights of its citizens and children to live normal lives and not to sleep in bomb shelters.

On the social front, the Likud had ushered in an era of freer capitalism, but that, too, had gone awry. Annual inflation reached 450 percent.[41] The Mizrachim were among the hardest hit by the economic downturn.[42] Yet by acknowledging the injustices of the past and the mistreatment of some of Israel's immigrants, Israelis had in some ways emerged more unified.

Perhaps most significant, the hegemony of a single party that had ruled Israel for decades had been broken. The Right, long relegated to the political desert, had ended Labor's grip on the nation's politics and policies. Israelis now had options as they charted their nation's future. More often than not, what would determine how they voted was how supported or isolated they felt. As the international community abandoned Israel in the decades to come, Israelis would seek security in toughness. Israelis who felt safe could attend to social issues and take greater risks for peace; when they felt threatened, they instinctively elected those they thought could protect them. That simple fact would change the destiny of the Middle East in the years to come.

TAKING A PAGE FROM THE ZIONISTS

The Rise of Palestinian Nationalism

We will continue the peace process as if there is no terror. And we will fight the terror as if there is no peace process.

—Prime Minister Yitzhak Rabin

When Begin's election ended decades of Labor's hegemony, it brought into the prime minister's office a man whose devotion to Jewish tradition differed radically from all those who had preceded him. Yet the reentrance of religion into the public sphere was most markedly represented by the sudden rise to political stardom of a precocious politician by the name of Aryeh Deri.

Deri's family were immigrants from Morocco who came to Israel when Arab states turned on their Jewish populations after Israel's 1967 victory in the Six-Day War—just as they had after the War of Independence. The Deri family arrived in Israel both poor and deeply committed to its traditional way of life. Animated by a belief that mainstream Israel was not giving immigrants like his family a fair chance, the singularly talented Deri entered political life. His rise was meteoric. By 1985, at the age of twenty-six, Deri was a close adviser to the minister of the interior, and by twenty-nine, he himself had taken over the position. Deri was, in the words of a leading Israeli journalist, "the most electrifying, promising figure of a new Israel."[1] Deri was eventually toppled by a series of scandals in the

1990s, but by the time he disappeared (temporarily) from public life, he had indelibly changed Israeli politics.

In 1984, as Deri was rising to political prominence, Rabbi Ovadia Yosef had just retired from the position as Sephardic chief rabbi of Israel.* Rabbi Yosef was both a legal genius who had produced an extraordinary corpus of rulings on a wide array of Jewish legal topics and also a populist with a knack for vitriol directed at non-Orthodox Jews, Arabs, or anyone else of whom he disapproved at any given moment. Leveraging his great popularity among the Mizrachim (and with the guidance of another leading rabbi, Rabbi Elazar Shach), Rav Ovadia, as his flock referred to him, formed a political party called Shas.† The party's name was the product of two Hebrew letters that are the acronym of *Shomrei Sefarad* ("The Sephardi Guards"), meaning the Sephardic guardians of the Torah. But the name was a double entendre, since the Hebrew could also be understood as "Guardians of the Sephardim."

That, in fact, is precisely how the Mizrachi community saw Shas. Religiously, Shas had an unabashedly Orthodox, highly traditional agenda, but Shas also took care of Mizrachi social and educational needs. Even Mizrachim who were not particularly religious were attracted to the party. Instead of supporting the largely secular Likud, Mizrachim now had their own—explicitly religious and politically successful—party to represent their interests.

---

* Though Jews are divided by ethnicity into three major categories—Ashkenazi, Sephardi, and Mizrachi, *religious* traditions are most generally divided into Ashkenazi and Sephardi. Each of these two groups has its own chief rabbi. Demographically, "Sephardi" and "Mizrachi," though technically distinct, can generally be used interchangeably.

† Rabbi Ovadia retained his enormous popularity and political weight through the end of his life. When he died in 2013, it was estimated that some eight hundred thousand people (in a country with a population of but eight million people, some six million of them Jews) "attended" his funeral. With a crowd that size, of course, the vast majority could get nowhere near the cemetery. But streets, and even highways, were packed with throngs walking in the direction of his burial, thus symbolically participating in his funeral.

Eventually, thanks to the charismatic and politically astute Aryeh Deri as its public face, Shas experienced a rapid rise in popularity and power. In 1984, the year it was founded, Shas received a mere 4 seats in the Knesset. By 1999, though, the same year that Deri was convicted of corruption (for which he ultimately went to prison), Shas received 13 percent of the vote, and 17 seats in the Knesset.

The rise of Shas heralded a new vision of what Zionism was and could be. Deri described his radical departure from the old Zionist ideal with no attempt at concealing his bitterness:

> Now secular Israelis are afraid that Shas will change the secular character of the state. They call themselves Zionists, but they are not really Zionists. Their movement is a movement of heresy. They see our fathers and mothers as primitives. They wanted to convert them. They sent them to remote towns and villages where life was hard. They gave their children a good-for-nothing education. Until we came and began taking care of all these people who were suffering in all these remote places. That's why they are afraid of us. That's why they persecute us. And this persecution is both ethnic and religious. But the more they humiliate us, the more we will grow. We shall change the character of the State of Israel.[2]

It was a promise that Shas kept.

AS RELIGION BEGAN TO OCCUPY a more prominent place in the Israeli public square, a similar phenomenon was transpiring elsewhere in the Middle East, particularly in the countries that bordered Israel.

In the mid-1980s, the Arab world was still reeling from the death of the secular pan-Arab dream. The community organizers who were most successful at cultivating a following during this period were those who urged their listeners to put their faith in a new vision for the restoration of the Arab world's former glory: an Islamic revolution. With many of the repressive secular regimes that had ruled the Arab countries in the previous decades now weakened (the most prominent case being Sadat's regime in Egypt), the setting was ripe for an alternative source of hope. In many of the Arab countries surrounding Israel, due in part to the regional influence of the successful Iranian revolution that brought the regime of the ayatollahs to power in 1979, it was Islamism that filled the vacuum.*

During the 1970s and 1980s, the Muslim Brotherhood became the most prominent of the Islamist organizations. In many places in the Arab world, it began developing effective systems for providing critical social services—services that the secular governments had failed to provide.[3] Its social service organizations, though, brought with them a distinct, highly traditionalist religious message, which spread rapidly. Soon, the impact could be seen plainly on the Arab street. There were more women donning a hijab (a traditional Muslim headdress), more bearded men (also a sign of greater religious devotion). Twenty years after the Six-Day War, a new devotion to Islam could be seen in the religious institutions being created everywhere Israelis looked.

Stalled economic opportunity helped shift the dynamics of Muslim religiosity in the West Bank and in Gaza, as well. In many ways, Israeli rule had improved Palestinians' economic lot. In the years after the Six-Day War, between 1967 and the 1980s, annual per capita income in the Gaza Strip increased from $80 to $1,700. In the West Bank, the GDP tripled in the same period. The number of cars in the territories increased tenfold. In 1967, only 18 percent of households in Gaza had electricity. But in 1981, when Gazan com-

---

* There were two seismic events in the Middle East in 1979: the signing of the Egyptian-Israeli Peace Accords and the Iranian revolution. In the decades to follow, the question was which movement—toward realism in foreign policy or toward religious purism and the intermixing of religion and politics—would have greater influence on the region.

munities were connected to the Israeli electric grid, that number rose to 89 percent.

But Israeli rule had not erased crushing poverty among parts of the populations of Gaza; Gaza was still densely populated and over-crowded. Untreated sewage ran in the streets, and many homes did not have running water. Then, economic growth stalled in the mid-1980s. The frustration with the economic downturn was par-ticularly acute in the Palestinian refugee camps, where masses of people lived in squalor.

The well-mobilized Islamist movements, with their promises for brighter futures, resonated with the Palestinian refugees who had again and again been sorely disappointed by movements—such as Pan-Arabism—that had claimed that they would bring about change but had done nothing. The Muslim Brotherhood found it-self with more influence, more power—and increasing numbers of religiously devout followers.

Israel's open policies, ironically, contributed to the spread of Muslim fundamentalism in both Gaza and the West Bank. Prior to the Six-Day War, there had been no universities in the territo-ries. Hoping to foster the growth of more moderate movements, Israel encouraged higher education in the land it now controlled, and seven universities were established in the West Bank and Gaza. But to a large extent, the plan backfired. Many of the more radical Islamist movements grew exponentially in the university setting. When they did, Israel assumed—incorrectly as it turned out—that they were primarily religious movements and not political. That, however, was a major miscalculation and it would later cost Israel dearly.

In 1988, another Muslim organization, Hamas, was founded. For Hamas's followers, a central religious obligation was the libera-tion of all of historic Palestine from "Zionist occupation," claiming that the land "from the river to the sea" was a Muslim *waqf,* or "en-dowment." They vowed to wage holy war, or jihad, against Israel.

Hamas adopted a founding charter blatantly anti-Semitic in tone and content, perpetuating tropes found in Nazi propaganda against Jews, including the *Protocols of the Elders of Zion*. The language and its tenor were familiar to those who knew the history of the twentieth century:

> Today it is Palestine and tomorrow it may be another country or other countries. For Zionist scheming has no end, and after Palestine they will covet expansion from the Nile to the Euphrates. Only when they have completed digesting the area on which they will have laid their hand, they will look forward to more expansion, etc. Their scheme has been laid out in the *Protocols of the Elders of Zion,* and their present [conduct] is the best proof of what is said there.[4]

Hamas insisted that the Jews "founded the United Nations and the Security Council in order to rule over all the world."[5] Hamas placed responsibility for almost all international wars—including the revolutions in France and Russia, and World Wars I and II—at the feet of the Jews. Most important was the organization's attitude toward Israel. The introduction to Hamas's charter promised that "Israel will rise and will remain erect until Islam eliminates it as it had eliminated its predecessors."

Nasser was dead. Israel's military superiority had effectively neutralized any Syrian threat. Pan-Arabism was a thing of the past. Yet once again, Israel found itself arrayed against another enemy sworn to its destruction.

ON DECEMBER 9, 1987, an Israeli truck driver accidentally ran over four Arab workers in the Gaza Strip. The long-simmering Arab street in both the West Bank and Gaza exploded with fury and into violence. Hundreds, then thousands, of young people began seeking confrontations with Israeli soldiers, throwing rocks and Molotov cocktails at both soldiers and civilians. General strikes followed, enforced against reluctant store owners by gangs of thugs. With this new and unexpected resistance movement, dubbed the *intifada* (Arabic for "shaking off," as in the way a dog shakes water off its fur, a metaphor for how the Palestinians were going to shake Israel off their backs), Israel now faced a new military frontier.

There had been warning signs for quite some time. Beginning in the mid-1980s, Israel had begun to face a round of mass Palestinian violence unlike the targeted PLO attacks Israelis were used to. At first, there had been periodic flare-ups of rock throwing, stabbings, and burning tires. None of this particularly worried the Israeli security establishment, however. Now, after the reaction to the December 1987 accident, the leaders understood that they had a major problem, one unlike anything else they had ever had to face, and that they were not sure how to counter. Sari Nusseibeh, a Palestinian professor of philosophy and a public intellectual, likened the uprising to a volcano. "No one starts a volcano," he said. The conditions for the explosion simply build up, and when it erupts, it does so with fury.[6]

Never before had Israeli soldiers been on a battlefront in which they were facing teenagers with stones. This was not an enemy that elite IDF units could identify and then eliminate. Now, Israel's young men and women found themselves arrayed against frustrated, angry civilian populations, which while not carrying arms for the most part, used rocks and Molotov cocktails. Israel's technological edge was mostly useless in this new battle. Suddenly, the IDF was fighting in densely populated civilian areas, using rubber bullets, tear gas, clubs, and on occasion, more lethal weaponry. Rabin, some IDF officers said, had ordered the army to "break their arms and legs."[7] But that did not work, either; the resentment and despair ran too deep.

The intifada, during which Israelis came face-to-face with Palestinian rage over decades of being occupied since Israel had won the Six-Day War, exacted a heavy price from both sides. Schools in the territories, which served as centers of the uprising, were frequently closed. One Hebrew University professor of criminology reported that "In the academic year 1987–1988, pupils in the West Bank lost some 175 out of 201 school days because of forced closures."[8] The school closures and many other disruptions to daily Palestinian life—including curfews, roadblocks, and searches—further infuriated the Palestinians and fanned the flames of violence.

CHANGE IN JORDAN ALSO complicated the region. Jordan had lost the West Bank to Israel after Hussein's decision to join Egypt and Syria in the Six-Day War, but the kingdom had never renounced its claim to that territory. Palestinians from the West Bank continued to serve in the Jordanian Parliament and thousands of Jordanian civil service employees worked in the West Bank and were paid in part through Amman.

Hussein's kingdom, however, was governed by a Hashemite minority in which the Palestinian majority were decidedly second-class citizens, constituting a "disaffected majority."[9] The last thing the king needed was a spillover of the violence and instability from the West Bank across the Jordan River and into the center of Jordan; in light of the intifada, Jordan renounced its claim to the West Bank in July 1988.[10]

As long as they assumed that Jordan would one day take the West Bank back, Palestinians hedged their bets and hesitated to give their open support to the PLO, which was still an archenemy of Jordan. With Jordan out of the picture, however, the PLO was now viewed by local residents as the uncontestably rightful representative of the Palestinians in the West Bank. Israel's political predicament—in large measure because of an occupation it had never planned to begin and now could not end without a responsible party to assume control of the occupied territories—was becoming ever more complex.

The intifada (later called the First Intifada) was challenging Israeli society in ways it had never been challenged before. Eighteen- and nineteen-year-old conscripts had grown up hearing stories of the IDF's heroic exploits, of defending Israel against deadly and decidedly evil enemies. Their own service, though, was proving very different; they were busy with what felt like the dirty work of policing a civilian enemy population. One Israeli journalist coined a term for this disillusionment: *yorim v'bochim,* or "shooting and crying."[11] One reserve officer observed with sadness, "Eighteen year olds ask me if it is frightening to serve in the territories. I tell them the greatest fear is of myself—what I would become, what I could be drawn into. It's a jungle with its own laws."[12]

The intifada worked. Israelis were now worrying not only about the impact of the occupation on the Palestinians living under Israeli rule, but also about what being occupiers was doing to them, their children, and their humanity. Many were coming to agree with the Israeli Orthodox philosopher Yeshayahu Leibowitz, who had warned as early as 1967 that "Israel had to 'liberate itself from this curse of dominating another people,'" if it did not wish to "bring about a catastrophe for the Jewish people as a whole."[13]

The intifada also dealt a devastating blow to the Israeli political Right. As Yossi Klein Halevi noted, many Israelis, faced with this outburst of Palestinian rage, began to understand that the mere notion that peace could be had while Israel held on to Gaza and the West Bank and the millions of Palestinians who lived there was the stuff of sheer fantasy. As the West Bank continued to burn, the notion of an "enlightened" occupation that had pervaded Israeli discourse in the years after the Six-Day War—but that had its earliest roots in Herzl's *Altneuland* with its image of Arabs welcoming Jews because of the progress they would bring with them—went up in flames as well. The writing was on the wall—Palestinians had shown Israelis that Palestinian nationalism was not a force that Israel could ignore. It might take years or decades, but for increasing numbers of Israelis, there was now little doubt that Israel would have to leave most of the West Bank, sooner or later.

EUROPE, TOO, WAS EXPERIENCING seismic shifts. In late 1989, the Berlin Wall came down. By 1991, the Soviet Union had dissolved, and the United States stood alone as the world's uncontested super-power. Ever since Israel's founding, Israel and its Arab neighbor-enemies had been caught in a larger battle between the world's two superpowers. American-Russian relations impacted the wars of 1956, 1967, and 1973, and much in between. The United States had voted at the United Nations in favor of the creation of a Jewish state, though there had been difficult periods in relations between the two countries. By the time the Soviet Union fell, the United States was seen as Israel's protector while the Soviet Union had stood be-hind the Arab states. Now, the Arabs were going to have to find a new source of backing; in the years to come, European countries would play a much more central role in the conflict.

The fall of the Soviet Union changed Israel internally, as well. The Jewish state was about to embrace the largest infusion of im-migrants since its founding. The exodus of Soviet Jews had not come about overnight and had been, in fact, one of the key projects to which American Jewry had long devoted itself. Ever since Stalin had come to power, Soviet Jews had been living under a repressive, authoritarian regime that sought to snuff out Jewish learning, Zi-onist activity, and Jewish identity writ large. Stalin and the Soviet leaders who followed him here were successful in dramatically de-creasing the levels of Jewish knowledge among Soviet Jews over a period of some seventy years, but they failed to stem the desire of many to join their fellow Jews in Israel. That desire took on new en-ergy in 1967, when Soviet Jews saw in Israel a new model of what it meant to be Jewish, a model in which Jews were no longer victims and of which they therefore wanted to be a part.

Because the gates of the USSR were closed, freeing Soviet Jews became a central project of American Jews and the Israeli govern-ment. Organizations such as the Student Struggle for Soviet Jewry and political efforts like the Jackson-Vanik Amendment to the U.S. Trade Act of 1974 (designed to punish Communist-bloc countries that prohibited emigration) all played a role. So, too, did protests and demonstrations, and no small number of intrepid American Jews who applied for and received visas to visit Russia and used their visits there to take books, music, and other educational and religious items to bolster the spirits and deepen the education of the repressed community.

Slowly, the gates opened. In 1970, 992 immigrants to Israel came from the Soviet Union. By 1980, that number was 7,570. In 1990, it was 185,227. By the time the mass immigration had subsided, shortly after 2000, some one million Soviet Jews had made their way to the Jewish state, changing its character dramatically.

Like many who had come before them, Soviet immigrants often arrived with little money and needed significant support upon arrival. Many who had been highly trained in the Soviet Union had to settle for menial jobs in the competitive Israeli job market. The massive number of Soviet immigrants enabled them to publish their own newspapers and magazines, and often to live in largely Russian neighborhoods. Not infrequently, all this aroused resentment in some Israelis, who viewed it as a disinclination to acculturate.

But this population was very different from the earlier Mizrachi immigrants. While it took time for them to be integrated into Israel society, this was a Western aliyah in many ways, comprised in part of highly educated university graduates. The new immigrants included engineers and physicians and others specializing in the arts and particularly in music. Soviet Jews joined Israel's scientific and artistic communities, both supplying talent and creating a demand for educational and cultural services.

The man who became the public face of Soviet immigrants was the now iconic former Soviet Jewish "refusenik" Natan Sharansky. After having applied for permission to emigrate to Israel, Sharansky was imprisoned for nine years on trumped-up charges of having spied for the American Defense Intelligence Agency. After U.S. president Reagan finally placed great pressure on Soviet president Mikhail Gorbachev, Sharansky was released from prison. He immigrated to Israel, where he became an internationally acclaimed human rights activist and a Jewish symbol of courage. In 1996, he founded a political party named *Yisrael Ba-Aliyah* (a name that can mean both "Israel Making Aliyah" or "Israel on the Rise") that catered primarily to the needs of Russians, leading him to a prominent place in the Knesset. With time, as Russian immigrants felt less of a need for their own party, Sharansky left formal politics, but he retained his standing as one of Israel's leading statesmen and is among the Jewish people's greatest living heroes.

JEWS IN THE SOVIET UNION were not the only ones who would find refuge and forge new lives in the Jewish state. As civil war raged in Ethiopia, with famine contributing to its dire state of affairs, world Jewry became particularly concerned for the fate of the Jewish community there. Taking a page from Operation Magic Carpet some thirty-five years earlier, in which the IDF had airlifted the Yemenite Jews to safety in Israel, the Israeli government decided once again that Jews in danger—anywhere in the world—were its responsibility.

As early as 1984, Israel had sent both activists and Mossad agents to the Sudan to facilitate the covert immigration of thousands of Ethiopian Jews to Israel. But many more still remained. By 1991, conditions in Ethiopia were deteriorating, and dangers to the local Jews increased dramatically.

In May 1991, in a daring mission known as Operation Solomon, Israeli pilots landed lumbering converted C-130 jets on narrow airstrips in Ethiopia in the midst of the civil war. Planes were stripped of their seats to allow for the maximum number of passengers, and in some cases, more than eleven hundred people were jammed onto a single plane. Many of the desperately poor immigrants boarded their flight with nothing but the clothes on their backs and some basic cooking utensils. Many were so frail that 140 of them were met by ambulances upon landing in Israel and received medical care on the tarmac. Several women gave birth on the plane. In total, the nonstop flights of thirty-five Israeli Air Force C-130s and El Al Boeing 747s transported 14,325 Ethiopian Jews to Israel in a mere thirty-six hours.

Whatever the historical origins of the Ethiopian Jewish community (a highly contested issue itself), those Ethiopians being rescued had virtually nothing in common with the mostly Ashkenazi pilots who were risking their lives to save them. For thousands of years, Ethiopian Jews had been completely cut off from Jewish life in Babylonia, Palestine, Europe, and North Africa; they had preserved an ancient Jewish way of life that was now very different from what Israelis saw as "authentic" Judaism. Any Jewish development or tradition that was less than two thousand years old was largely foreign to these new immigrants. They knew nothing of the Talmud, which was written after they were exiled. Purim and Hanukkah had entered the Jewish calendar after the Ethiopians were cut off from the rest of the Jewish people. They knew nothing of the Holocaust or of any dimension of the rest of the Jewish experience over the past two millennia. They spoke Amharic, not Hebrew. For all intents and purposes, they knew virtually nothing about the modern State of Israel when they arrived. Modernity, too, was new to them. Their utter unfamiliarity with electricity, running water, or modern technology (some tried to light fires in the planes ferrying them to Israel because they were cold) just added to the challenge.

This was an immigration project unlike anything Israel had ever attempted before. Sadly, many Ethiopians became an Israeli underclass. There were, unfortunately, some cases of overt racism, and it would take decades for their children and grandchildren to begin to make their way up Israel's social, economic, educational, and military ladders. At the same time, Israel saved thousands of lives in bringing the Ethiopian Jewish community to Israel, and in so doing, with Caucasian pilots landing their planes to load up with thousands of black immigrants, illustrated that the Jewish state's commitment to saving the Jewish people transcended race and color.

There were, without question, instances of discrimination, and occasional outrageous examples of racism. For the most part, though, the barrier that Ethiopians faced had to do with the very

different culture from which they hailed, the vast difference between their Judaism and the religious culture of the country to
which they arrived—and the challenges that face immigrants all
over the world. As different as the Ethiopian Jews looked, sounded,
and behaved from the other Jews who already inhabited Israel, and
despite the significant absorption challenges that the Ethiopian
community represented, Israelis were convinced that bringing
them had absolutely been the right thing to do. They were part of
the Jewish people, and saving that people was Israel's raison d'être.

IRONICALLY AND SADLY, one thing that the Ethiopian and Russian
waves of immigration shared was uncertainty on the part of the
rabbinate as to whether or not they were actually Jewish. In the
case of the Russians, it was clear that many of those who were immigrating to Israel were not Jewish according to *halakhah* (Jewish
law). The Jewish community in the USSR had intermarried extensively; according to some estimates, only 25 percent of those who
came to Israel under the Law of Return (which defined Jewishness
the way that the Nazis had—having one Jewish grandparent—and
not as classic Jewish law did) were technically Jewish. Time and
again, the rabbinate was criticized (by many people, including
Orthodox rabbis), though not for determining that these new immigrants were not Jewish, but for putting up roadblocks as these
people sought to convert.[14]

Matters were even worse for the Ethiopians. It was the Sephardic chief rabbi who first ruled that these Ethiopians (whom he
referred to as *Falashas*, another commonly used name for that community) were Jews. In a historic 1973 ruling (issued long before the
masses of Ethiopian immigrants arrived), Rabbi Ovadia Yosef said:

> I have therefore come to the conclusion that the Falashas are de-
> scendants of the Tribes of Israel, who went southward to Ethio-
> pia, and there is no doubt that the above sages established that
> they [the Falashas] are of the Tribe of Dan . . . and [have] reached

the conclusion on the basis of the most reliable witnesses and evidence . . . and have decided in my humble opinion, the Falashas are Jews.[15]

Rabbi Shlomo Goren (a deeply learned scholar who had often issued cutting-edge pathbreaking rulings), the Ashkenazi chief rabbi, was far less courageous on this issue. It was not until 1981 that any piece of his own writing even *suggested* that he approved the immigrants' status as Jews.[16]

IN AUGUST 1990, Iraq's Saddam Hussein invaded Kuwait. The United States, along with a coalition of other primarily Western nations, went to war against Hussein. As retaliation for the American-led counterattack, Hussein fired missiles at Israel in January 1991. Israeli leadership had never been willing to sit passively while Israeli civilians were attacked, but this time, Israel had no choice but to stand down; U.S. president George H. W. Bush was adamant that he would not abide Israel's involvement in the battle (the United States, for example, refused to give the Israeli Air Force the codes it would need to ensure that coalition forces did not shoot down IAF planes). Prime Minister Yitzhak Shamir, who as head of the Lechi in the prestate era had never shied away from the use of force to protect Jews, understood that this time he had no options.

Israelis huddled in bomb shelters with stockpiles of food and gas masks (there were fears that Hussein would use the chemical weapons he had deployed during the invasion of Iran). They waited out the war in sealed rooms, gas masks and even gas-proof cribs for infants at the ready. They were both fearful of Hussein and—while grateful that their government was adopting a pragmatic approach to the Americans, who were also providing them with Patriot missiles for defense—dumbfounded that almost a century after Kishinev, Jews were hiding again, their men in shelters unable to protect their wives and children.

In one of his best-known poems, "On the Slaughter" (not to be confused with the "City of Slaughter," discussed earier), Hayim Nachman Bialik railed against God in fury after the massacre of Jews. "If there is justice—let it appear!" Bialik cried in one of the poem's most famous lines; the role of the Jew as victim-in-waiting simply had to end. Now, just about a century later, an Israeli political commentator responded to the IDF's being ordered to do nothing while missiles rained on Tel Aviv and wrote: "And if there is an IDF—let it appear immediately." The allusion was lost on very few.

AS EARLY AS THE YOM KIPPUR WAR, Shlomo Gazit (head of Israeli military intelligence in the late 1970s) said Israel and Egypt had battled to a stalemate; there were, he said, no winners in that war. In the battle with the Palestinians, too, the conflict continued to grind on with no decisive victory or accomplishment for either side. It was becoming increasingly obvious to many Israelis that the sides were going to have to talk.

Just as it had been a right-wing, Likud administration that had made peace with Egypt, it was a Likud administration that agreed to the first indirect talks with the Palestinians. In October 1991, with Yitzhak Shamir still prime minister, Israeli officials sat with Syrian, Lebanese, and Jordanian delegations in Spain, in what would become known as the Madrid Conference. Israel still refused to engage in direct negotiations with the Palestine Liberation Organization, which Israeli law defined as a terrorist organization. In a compromise, therefore, Israelis did allow Palestinian representatives from the West Bank and Jordan who were not formal PLO officials to join the Jordanian delegation. For the first time, Israelis and Palestinians sat across from one another at the negotiating table.

The goal of the Madrid Conference was not to produce a deal, but to launch bilateral negotiations. At that, it succeeded—the sides were finally talking. With peace with the Palestinians now clearly on the Israeli public agenda, in 1992, Israelis elected the man they believed could make that peace happen—Yitzhak Rabin. The man

involved in some of the most decisive battles in the War of Independence and the lightning victory of 1967, Rabin was someone who
Israelis were confident understood their security needs. Though he
had resigned under a cloud, Israelis now wanted him back; a deal
he would make would be a deal they could live with.

In a speech upon his swearing in, Rabin insisted that the Jewish
condition *had* changed, and that Israelis could now take risks for
peace:

> No longer are we necessarily "a people that dwells alone," and
> no longer is it true that "the whole world is against us." We must
> overcome the sense of isolation that has held us in its thrall for
> almost half a century. . . . We believe wholeheartedly that peace
> is possible, that it is imperative, and that it will ensue. "I shall be-
> lieve in the future," wrote the poet Shaul Tchernikovsky. "Even
> if it is far off, the day will come when peace and blessings are
> borne from nation to nation"—and I want to believe that the day
> is not far off.[17]

Early in 1993, Israel repealed the law forbidding Israelis from
negotiating with the PLO. The next day, secret back-channel negotiations began in Oslo, Norway, between Israeli and Palestinian
representatives. In time, the parties agreed upon the basic framework of Oslo I, itself the first set of agreements in what would become known as the Oslo Accords.

The accords, which outlined an arrangement that was intended
to last for up to five years while a permanent settlement between
the Israelis and Palestinians was negotiated, provided for the creation of a Palestinian Authority, which would administer the territory under Palestinian control. Israeli forces, in turn, would pull
back from portions of Gaza and the West Bank.

Shimon Peres signed the accord, in secret, when he visited
Oslo in August 1993. As part of a "mutual recognition" agreement,
the PLO recognized the State of Israel and pledged to abandon
violence against the Jewish state. Israel, in turn, recognized the

PLO as the representative of the Palestinian people and permitted Yasser Arafat—along with tens of thousands of his fighters from abroad—to return to the West Bank and Gaza.

Another agreement, Oslo II, followed in September 1995, dividing the West Bank into Areas A, B, and C (see Map 10), which would be controlled by the Palestinians, a joint Israeli-Palestinian authority, and the Israelis, respectively. Neither Oslo I nor Oslo II guaranteed the Palestinians that they would have a state, but the framework was intended to lead to that, eventually. In September 1993, Arafat, Rabin, and U.S. president Bill Clinton gathered on the Great Lawn of the White House and, with a handshake between Rabin and Arafat, seemed to usher in a new era for the Middle East.

FOR HARD-LINE MUSLIMS, the accords were heresy. Israel had no right to exist on Arab land, they insisted, and they would never accept a deal. As a result, rather than heralding a period of peace, the signing of the Oslo Accords began a period of renewed and intensified Palestinian violence against Israelis. Now, the violence was far more deadly than it had been during the intifada. Hamas and other extremist Islamist groups in Gaza and the West Bank were carrying out suicide bombings, aimed mostly at Israeli civilians in Tel Aviv as well as cities within the Green Line (the 1949 armistice line), including Jerusalem, seeking massive casualties wherever possible in the hopes that they could derail the accords. More Israelis died in these attacks between 1994 and 1996 than had ever been killed by terror in such a short span of time in Israel's history.[18] Arafat only rarely publicly denounced the culpable parties. Occasionally, he had them arrested, only to release them when the world's attention had shifted. To many Israelis, it was the ultimate unmasking of the Arafat at the UN General Assembly in 1974, who while extending an "olive branch" was wearing a holster. It was time for Arafat, many Israelis said, to tell his own people, in Arabic, that the violence had to cease. But Arafat would not do it.

THEN, AN INSTANCE OF Jewish terrorism made the region even more explosive. On February 25, 1994, Baruch Goldstein, a religious American immigrant to Israel, entered the Cave of the Patriarchs,* heavily armed, and opened fire on Muslims in the middle of prayer. He murdered twenty-nine Palestinian worshippers before he himself was killed by the enraged crowd.

Once again, Hebron had proved incendiary. In 1929, Hebron had been the site of the riots during which Arabs not only murdered Jews who lived there and destroyed the Jewish community there, but in effect inaugurated the Arab-Jewish armed conflict in the Middle East. After the 1967 Six-Day War, it was to Hebron that a group of young people moved to establish one of the first Jewish communities over the Green Line. Now, with the region at the height of tension and the future of the Oslo Accords very much in doubt, Hebron was once more the site of a massacre, this time at the Cave of the Patriarchs. Now, though, it was a Jew who had committed the atrocity and Muslims at prayer who were the victims.

Israelis were horrified by Goldstein's attack, and Jewish religious leaders across the spectrum decried his actions. But the damage had been done. Arab terror continued and grew even more violent, and the region was unraveling. According to some sources, even Rabin was privately beginning to give up on Oslo due to the terror it had unleashed. Former defense minister Moshe "Bogie" Ya'alon wrote years later, in 2008, that Rabin had told him that the prime minister "was going to 'set things straight' with the Oslo process, because Arafat could no longer be trusted."[19] And in an interview with one of Israel's leading newspapers, Dalia Rabin, the prime minister's daughter, said in 2010, "many people who were close to Father told me that on the eve of the murder he considered stopping the Oslo process because of the terror that was running

---

* The Cave of the Patriarchs is sacred to both Jews and Muslims. Jewish tradition asserts that it is the burial site of Abraham and Sarah. Like the Jews, Muslims also worship there, in a mosque that was built on the site in the sixth century CE.

rampant in the streets, and because he felt that Yasser Arafat was not delivering on his promises."[20]

Whatever his personal and private misgivings, Rabin remained publicly undeterred. Echoing Ben-Gurion's determination that the Yishuv would fight the White Paper as if there were no war and would fight the war as if there were no White Paper, he declared, "We will continue the peace process as if there is no terror. And we will fight the terror as if there is no peace process."[21] Despite its exasperation with Arafat's duplicitousness, Israel continued to carry out its obligations under the Oslo Accords. In May 1994, the IDF departed Jericho and almost all of the Gaza Strip, a mere nine days after the details of this agreement were finalized. Later, the IDF began withdrawing from large cities and territories in the West Bank and Gaza.

PEACE PROGRESSED ON ANOTHER FRONT, as well. In 1994, Jordan and Israel began serious negotiations designed to end the state of war between the two countries. King Hussein had officially renounced any claim to the West Bank (which he did not want because its large Palestinian population would make his Hashemite ruling minority an even smaller minority), so there were no insurmountable issues still dividing the two countries. When Shimon Peres, who was then serving as minister of foreign affairs, flew to Jordan that year to meet with King Hussein, he remarked that "the flight took only fifteen minutes . . . but it crossed a gulf of forty-six years of hatred and war."[22]

Israel and Jordan signed a peace agreement in October 1994. The two nations had agreed upon the border between them, had settled water rights, and now had full mutual recognition. Israel was officially at peace with two of its neighbors. For King Hussein, who as a young man had witnessed his grandfather, King Abdullah I, murdered by Palestinians in July 1951 for contemplating peace with the Israelis—the accomplishment had not

only political and economic significance, but deep personal resonance as well.

INCREASING NUMBERS OF ISRAELIS, horrified that a "deal" with
Arafat had unleashed terror rather than bringing peace, were beginning to believe that Israel had made a profound and existentially
dangerous mistake. For some, the issue was explicitly theological;
God had given the Land of Israel to the Jewish people, they believed, and any agreement to cede even a portion of it was heretical.
Israel's Jewish political and religious Far Right grew particularly
vicious. At its rallies, there appeared signs with photos of Rabin
made to look like Hitler—archenemy of the Jewish people. A few
extremist rabbis referred to Rabin as a *rodef* (a person seeking the
death of another), and a *boged* (traitor), categories that in Jewish law
merit death. On one occasion, Benjamin "Bibi" Netanyahu, who
would eventually become prime minister, was filmed speaking at a
downtown Jerusalem rally above a sign (of which he may well have
been unaware) that read DEATH TO RABIN.

Many Israelis worried that the unrestrained incitement would
result in disaster. Sixty-two years after his own father had been
gunned down on the Tel Aviv beach, Chaim Arlosoroff's son
pleaded with the nation in a column he wrote for one of Israel's
major newspapers. He believed it was incitement that had led to his
father's assassination, and that he was witnessing a chilling repeat
of the same phenomenon. "The leaders of the right must cease to
incite," he wrote, "and must explain to their followers what can
happen if incitement continues, otherwise all the blame will fall on
them, as it did with the murder of Arlosoroff."[23]

Despite his apparent private misgivings, Rabin continued to
shore up support for the Oslo Accords. To demonstrate to Israel
and to the world that the Jewish state remained behind the agreements it had signed with Arafat, he and Shimon Peres called for
a massive pro-peace rally in Tel Aviv on November 4, 1995. En

masse, Israelis answered the call. Estimates put the size of the crowd that gathered at 150,000, perhaps more.[24] Speaking to the thousands of exultant Israelis who still believed that peace was possible, Rabin said:

> I was a military man for twenty-seven years. I fought as long as there was no chance for peace. I believe that there is now a chance for peace, a great chance. We must take advantage of it for the sake of those standing here, and for those who are not here—and they are many. I have always believed that the majority of the people want peace and are ready to take risks for peace. In coming here today, you demonstrate, together with many others who did not come, that the people truly desire peace and oppose violence.
>
> Violence erodes the basis of Israeli democracy. It must be condemned and isolated. This is not the way of the State of Israel. In a democracy there can be differences, but the final decision will be taken in democratic elections, as the 1992 elections which gave us the mandate to do what we are doing, continue on this course.[25]

When he concluded his speech, Rabin joined the rally in singing "Shir La-Shalom," "A Song to Peace," which had become the anthem of the pro-peace camp. The Tel Aviv square reverberated with the sounds of the refrain:

> Don't [just] say the day will come,
> Bring that day about
> For it is no dream
> And in all the city's squares
> Cry out for peace![26]

As Rabin made his way to the car that awaited him, Yigal Amir, a twenty-five-year-old religious law student at Bar Ilan University, managed to work his way through Rabin's security detail and fired three bullets into the prime minister. Rabin was rushed to the hospital, and as news of the shooting spread, an anxious nation held its breath.

Not long thereafter, Rabin's close associate Etan Haber exited Ichilov Hospital, where Rabin had been in surgery, and to a shocked, horrified, and frightened crowd read a brief announcement that many Israelis still know by heart:

> The government of Israel announces in dismay, in great sadness, and in deep sorrow, the death of prime minister and minister of defense Yitzhak Rabin, who was murdered by an assassin tonight in Tel Aviv. May his memory be blessed.

A young state—that had never known peace and had experienced more than its share of tragedy—suddenly faced a horror unlike anything it had ever imagined. Deep shame hung in the air like a dark cloud that refused to dissipate. Thousands, spontaneously this time, returned to the square where the rally had been held and sang the same song they had sung earlier that night, in a country that was then very different. Thousands wept in the streets. Desperate to express what words could not convey, throngs of young Israelis lit hundreds of thousands of candles on the sidewalks of the entire country. Bewildered, they were slowly becoming aware of the magnitude of the tragedy of which they were all a part, of the dream that had died, of a country that might never be the same. They held one another and simply wept.

They sat, sang, and cried, staring at the flickering flames they had lit, seeking in the embrace of their friends some reassurance that somehow, sometime, their badly wounded nation would recover. They prayed for some glimmer of hope that all was not lost. And at the same time, they mourned for what they feared they might be losing—for the tiny country that had surpassed everyone's expectations, for the vision that had become a state, for the new lease on Jewish life that their grandparents, against all odds, had built out of nothing.

THE PEACE PROCESS STALLS

I am a failure, and you have made me one.

—Bill Clinton to Yasser Arafat

One million people passed by Rabin's coffin before his burial. "I never thought," said King Hussein of Jordan as he addressed dignitaries representing eighty different countries at Yitzhak Rabin's funeral, "that the moment would come like this, when I would grieve the loss of a brother, a colleague, and a friend." Rabin had been, Hussein said, "a man, a soldier who met us on the opposite side of a divide, whom we respected as he respected us. A man I came to know because I realized, as he did, that we have to cross over the divide, establish a dialogue, get to know each other and strive to leave for those who follow us a legacy that is worthy of them."[1]

Departing the podium, the king was visibly shaken. Given his grandfather's murder years earlier, the moment must have seemed agonizingly cyclical. Would the region forever languish in the grip of those who were determined to prevent peace at all costs?

Egyptian president Hosni Mubarak came to Israel for the funeral. So, too, did the clearly heartbroken U.S. president Bill Clinton. Clinton, who had ordered that flags in the United States be flown at half-mast,[2] concluded his eulogy by turning to Rabin's casket and whispering words that were then forever engraved on Israelis' memory. "*Shalom, chaver,*" he said, "Good-bye, friend," as he gently bowed before the body of the slain warrior-cum-peacemaker.

Shimon Peres, who had long had a bitter rivalry with Rabin over leadership of the Labor party, became acting prime minister upon Rabin's death. The next day at the prime minister's office, he declined to sit in Rabin's chair; he understood that Israel confronted a gaping chasm that no one could fill. Peres, who had been a young man serving among Ben-Gurion's entourage of founding fathers, knew that there was a country to run and a society to heal. Whether the latter could be accomplished was anyone's guess.

SHIMON PERES HAD SEEN IT ALL. Born Szymon Perski in 1923, in Wiszniew, Poland (now Vishnyeva, Belarus), Peres moved to Palestine in 1934 with his family and was drafted into the Haganah in 1947 to oversee personnel and arms purchases, roles in which he continued during the early stages of the War of Independence. Peres subsequently served in a number of significant roles beyond his being a member of the Knesset, including minister of foreign affairs, minister of defense, minister of finance, and prime minister from 1984 to 1986. Now, committed to Rabin's vision of peace, he pushed on with Oslo. In November and December 1995, Israel redeployed out of all the major cities of the West Bank (except Hebron) and allowed the Palestinian Authority to hold elections. Arafat was elected chairman and his Fatah Party won a majority of the council seats. Palestinian statehood seemed to be moving forward.

But Palestinian attacks did not stop. In fact, the rate of attacks and the casualty count were higher than ever before.[3] The pretense that Oslo was anything but an abject failure was becoming increasingly difficult to sustain. "Instead of thanks," said Peres, "we got bombs."[4] He moved Israel's elections up by six months, confident that Israelis, repulsed by the Right's assassination of Rabin, would elect him to lead the country. Indeed, polls showed him with a significant lead over his rival, Benjamin Netanyahu of the Likud Party. Palestinian terrorists changed that, however, with two attacks in Jerusalem, one in Tel Aviv, and another in Ashkelon, killing almost sixty Israelis in the heart of Israel's cities within nine days. Israelis were outraged and frightened, and Peres was voted out of office a mere seven months after he had assumed Rabin's place.

With security always their most pressing concern, Israeli voters often move to the political right after increases in terrorism; 1996 was no exception, and they elected Benjamin Netanyahu over Peres. Netanyahu did follow through on Israel's commitment (as stipulated in the 1995 Israeli-Palestinian Peace Agreement, also known as Oslo II) to redeploy from Hebron, then the last West Bank city under Israeli control. Under American pressure, Netanyahu also later signed the 1998 Wye River Memorandum, designed to resume implementation of the stalled Oslo II agreements.

From the outset, though, Netanyahu had thought Oslo a misstep for Israel, and during the three years of his administration, did whatever he could to reverse the dangers that he believed Oslo had wrought. But in the elections that followed, Israelis, seeking a more centrist figure, swung back to the left and elected Ehud Barak.

One of the most highly decorated soldiers in Israel's history, Barak had campaigned on a platform built on three fundamental promises. He pledged to get Israeli troops out of southern Lebanon, from which Israel had never figured out how to extract itself. He committed himself to making peace with Syria. And finally, despite increasing doubts about Oslo, Barak said he would make peace with the Palestinians.

Some of Israel's leaders felt that it would be wisest to combine two of these objectives—if Israel and Syria could sign a peace accord, then Israel could leave Lebanon through coordination with Syria. But that was not to be. Syria, in fact, was pleased that Israeli forces were still deployed in Lebanon, since that enabled it to attack Israeli troops through its proxy, Hezbollah.[5] The Syrian foreign minister stated that an act of Israeli withdrawal without Syrian consent would be considered an "act of war," which one leading

Israeli journalist remarked was "a mental contortion memorable even by local standards."[6]

If Barak was to get Israel out of Lebanon, he was going to have to execute a unilateral withdrawal, which he did on May 24, 2000; the troops then serving in Lebanon had been born around the time Israel had first invaded in 1982.

It would not be the last time that Israel would take unilateral action to withdraw from territory in the face of Arab violence. The coming years would demonstrate, however, that each time Israel withdrew from territory, it played into the hands of the Arab extremists. By 2000, Hezbollah had already shown that it could unleash lethal violence against one of the world's most professional armies—between 1985 (after the intense period of the Lebanon war) and 1997, more than 200 Israeli soldiers were killed and over 750 were wounded. With Israel's retreat, Hezbollah was able to solidify its position in southern Lebanon. During the last night of Israeli presence on the border, Hezbollah's deputy secretary-general described the night as "a light at the end of the Palestinian tunnel, a hope that liberation might be achieved by treading the path of resistance and martyrdom." "What happened in Lebanon," he promised, "can be repeated in Palestine."[7]

HAVING FULFILLED HIS PROMISE of getting Israeli troops out of Lebanon, Barak turned his attention to the Palestinians. In the summer of 2000, just months after May's pullout from Lebanon, Ehud Barak, Yasser Arafat, and Bill Clinton convened at Camp David— the same rural retreat where, twenty-two years earlier, Begin and Sadat had met with Carter to hammer out *their* deal.

For years, the thorniest issues that the Israelis and Palestinians had to resolve in order to reach a deal—the Palestinian demand that Palestinian refugees be allowed to return to their homes in Israel, the status of Jerusalem, and the final borders of a Palestinian state—had been tabled. Now, Barak was determined to reach a comprehensive agreement. He offered Arafat 92 percent of the

West Bank and sections of Jerusalem for the Palestinian state. To the surprise of the Israeli team, Arafat and his negotiating team refused to even consider the offer. First, Oslo had led to increased terror. Now, Arafat was turning down an offer—without even making a counteroffer—that the Israelis had thought he would consider either generous or at least a legitimate starting point from which to negotiate. Bill Clinton, too, was confused by the Palestinians' intransigence.

The Camp David negotiations collapsed and the participants disbanded. Barak returned to Israel politically wounded, having angered the Right for offering far more than they thought he should have, while disappointing the Left by returning empty-handed. Arafat, meanwhile, returned home a national hero. He had stood up to the Zionists, determined to show that the Palestinians would not be satisfied with anything less than receiving their full demands on Jerusalem, borders, and the right of return. His will had not been broken, he wanted his people to see, and he had remained faithful to their national aspirations.

Dennis Ross, the American diplomat and author who was involved in Middle East negotiations for decades and served as Bill Clinton's Middle East envoy, later wrote, "Both Barak and Clinton were prepared to do what was necessary to reach agreement. Both were up to the challenge. Neither shied away from the risks inherent in confronting history and mythology. Can one say the same about Arafat? Unfortunately, not."[8]

Israeli analysts and historians, even those long associated with the Left, understood Arafat's calculus.[9] As long as negotiations dragged on, the international community would fete him as a reformed fighter now dedicated to peace. Were he to sign an agreement, however, the international community would expect him to govern and would hold him accountable for what unfolded in his newly founded state. With time, fewer and fewer people were inclined to believe that Arafat had any intention whatsoever of making the transition.

Tensions in the region rose. Six months after the withdrawal from Lebanon, and just over two months after the Camp David summit, opposition leader Ariel Sharon decided to visit the Temple Mount. While perfectly within his legal rights as an Israeli, his visit struck some as a provocation. Others asserted that Sharon was seeking to make clear to Palestinians that Israel remained sovereign over East Jerusalem and the Old City; perhaps, still others thought, Sharon knew that Arafat would respond to a gesture like that with violence and he wanted Israelis to see that before the government made any more concessions.

Whatever his motivation, Sharon had "apparently been told that Shlomo Ben-Ami, the Minister of Internal Security, was told by Israeli intelligence that there was no concerted risk of violence. This was implicitly confirmed by Jibril Rajoub, the Palestinian head of Preventive Security on the West Bank, who told Ben-Ami that Sharon could visit the Haram, but not enter the mosque on security grounds."[10]

Sharon did not enter the mosque, but on September 28, 2000, accompanied by hundreds of Israeli policemen, he went up to the Temple Mount. The following day, twenty thousand Palestinian rioters stormed the Temple Mount; Israeli forces responded with small firearms, which only increased and intensified the rioting. In that day's clashes, seven Palestinian rioters were killed, and three hundred Palestinians and seventy Israeli police were wounded. Leaders of the Palestinian Authority used vicious anti-Israel rhetoric on television, and on the radio they called for jihad (a Muslim term for religious war against nonbelievers).

Within days, Arafat and his security forces fanned the flames of conflict, which caused clashes to spread throughout the country. Many members of Israel's security establishment believed that he had been planning the uprising for quite some time, and that Sharon's visit simply afforded him the excuse to launch it.

Several of the many incidents became symbolic of the beginning of a four-year battle that would become known as the Second Intifada. A French TV crew captured on film a horrific scene that purported to show twelve-year-old Mohammad al-Dura being killed in Gaza as his father desperately tried to shield him. Despite Israeli insistence (later shown to be correct) that IDF troops had not killed the boy, the incident ignited the Palestinian street. Less than two weeks after the September 30 al-Dura incident, two Israeli re-servist soldiers, called up for duty to serve as drivers, took a wrong turn on their way to the location at which they were to serve. Sur-rounded by a crowd in the Palestinian city of Ramallah, they were lynched and murdered. The image of one of the terrorists standing at a window and raising his blood-soaked hands before a cheering crowd made its way around the world; the images repulsed Israelis who felt, once again, that the Palestinians were far more interested in killing Jews than they were in creating a state of their own.*

This intifada, though much less of a mass revolt than the first, proved far more lethal due to the Palestinian Authority's security forces' use of weapons and suicide bombers.[11] The conflict then spread to Israel's Arabs as well, particularly in the heavily Arab-populated Galilee. Some Arab Israelis attacked Jewish property, vehicles, settlements, and institutions. Israeli Jews began rioting against mosques, Arab-owned businesses, and Arab residents in mixed cities.[12] In what became known as the October 2000 Events or the October Ignition, Israeli police and the Arab rioters clashed after a demonstration escalated into violence. Arabs threw rocks and firebombs, launched ball bearings in slingshots, and, in a few cases, fired live rounds. In response, the police fired live ammuni-tion, and in the course of a few days in October, thirteen Israeli Arabs were shot and killed by Israeli security forces.[13] The Or Com-mission, which would later investigate the incidents, found that the police were unprepared for the violence and in some cases had overreacted.

October 2000 was unlike Kafr Kassem in 1956, since in the later case, Arabs had without question resorted to violence. But in the

---

* The name of the lynching terrorist was Aziz Salha. He was later arrested by Israeli authorities and sentenced to life imprisonment for the murders, but in 2011, he was released as part of the Gilad Shalit prisoner exchange.

minds of Israeli Arabs, the incidents were related. Like the 1956 Kafr Kassem massacre and the events of Land Day in 1976, the October 2000 killings reinforced their sense that they were perpetually second-class citizens whose lives were valued differently from those of Jews. Even when Haredim burned tires on roads in protest and used low-level violence, the security forces never opened fire on them.

In light of both Sharon's visit and the deaths of Arabs on October 1, Arab violence became more intense. Molotov cocktails were thrown, buses were set on fire. Arab arsonists set forests afire. That was an intentionally symbolically laden attack; forestation had been a significant and emblematic Zionist project since the early aliyot, and in the past century, the Jewish National Fund had planted 250 million trees.[14] The trees not only contributed to land reclamation, but exemplified Zionism's drive to renew the Land of Israel. That progress was precisely what the arsonists were trying to destroy.

As the violence continued, President Clinton attempted one last-ditch effort to resuscitate the peace process. In late December 2000, Clinton presented his proposal, "The Clinton Parameters," which proposed that the new Palestinian state would include 94 to 96 percent of the West Bank (though the parameters did not mention Gaza, Clinton clarified in January 2001 that the Palestinian state would include the Gaza Strip). Israel would be allowed to annex the settlements that were situated in substantial blocks of Jewish population, thus incorporating some 80 percent of the settler population. Clinton proposed dividing East Jerusalem into Palestinian areas, inhabited overwhelmingly by Arabs, and Israeli areas in which Jews lived. To assuage Israeli concerns about security, Clinton proposed temporary international and Israeli presence in the Jordan Valley and for the longer term, three Israeli-controlled "early warning stations." Palestinian refugees would return only to Palestine, and not to Israel proper.

Technically, both the Israelis and Palestinians accepted the parameters, but as Clinton later noted in his autobiography, *My Life,*

"Arafat had said he accepted the parameters with reservations. The problem was that his reservations, unlike Israel's, were outside the parameters, at least on refugees and the Western Wall, but I treated the acceptance as if it were real, based on his pledge to make peace before I left office."[15]

Shortly before Clinton left office, Arafat called Clinton to thank him and told the president that he was a great man. President Clinton replied, "Mr. Chairman, I am not a great man. I am a failure, and you have made me one."[16] On the last day of his presidency, Clinton warned George Bush and Colin Powell not to trust a word Arafat would say to them. Believing Arafat, he told them, "was the biggest mistake I made in my presidency."[17] Clinton, who had orchestrated the famous handshake between Arafat and Rabin, left the White House without having succeeded in settling the Israeli-Palestinian conflict.

With the peace process sputtering and attacks on Israelis continuing unabated, the mood in Israel was grim. Israelis had had enough of Prime Minister Ehud Barak. Camp David had collapsed, yet Barak had continued to offer massive concessions to Arafat even as Arafat refused to budge. Having lost his support in the Knesset, Barak called for elections to be held in February 2001. Israeli Arabs boycotted the elections as a reaction to the events of October 2000, which further weakened the Left. Barak lost, and Ariel Sharon, heading the right-wing Likud party, was elected to replace him. Once again, Palestinian violence had returned the Israeli political right to power. Unlike Barak, Sharon was unwilling to participate in what he considered the charade of negotiations with the Palestinians. Arafat, he believed, had never intended to make a deal; it was time for Israel to be clear about that.

The peace process was dead. That realization was, for many Israelis, no less agonizing than the loss of the *conceptzia* after the 1973 Yom Kippur War. Ever since Israel's Declaration of Independence had extended "our hand to all neighboring states and their peoples in an offer of peace and good neighborliness," most Israelis had been raised on the belief that someday, somehow, the two warring sides would set their swords aside and usher in a new era for the Middle East. It had happened with Egypt, and then Jordan, too, had made peace with Israel. But the Palestinians, it still seemed, would settle for nothing less than Israel's disappearance. A heartbroken and exhausted Left, which had long been pushing for compromise as the only way to peace, felt both naive and deeply betrayed. They found themselves quoting Abner, the leader of King Saul's army: "Must the sword consume forever?"[18] With grave disappointment and profound worry, they found that they could not answer no.

IN 2001, more than a hundred Israelis died at the hands of suicide bombers. Dozens more died in attacks of other sorts. As the Palestinians grew increasingly brazen, they attacked more heavily trafficked locations seeking ever higher body counts. In the summer of 2001, a suicide bomber attacked a disco on the Tel Aviv beach, which left twenty-one Israelis dead, most of them teenage girls from Russian families who had immigrated to Israel. Over a hundred were injured. Barely two months later, a suicide bomber attacked a pizzeria in downtown Jerusalem, at one of the city's busiest intersections. One hundred and thirty people were injured in the blast, and fifteen were killed. Half of the dead were children.

Most of the perpetrators of the violence were coming from the West Bank. To make matters even worse, as Israelis saw it, Palestinian police and *tanzim* forces (from Fatah) were involved in many shooting incidents; Fatah operatives began carrying out suicide bombings, which they had not done previously. All this turned the Israeli public against Arafat, Fatah, and the Palestinian Authority and led most people to believe that Israel had no partner for peace.

On the first night of Passover in 2002, some 250 guests had gathered for the traditional Seder at the Park Hotel in the seaside city of Netanya. A Palestinian terrorist disguised as a woman managed to get past hotel security and detonated a large explosive in the crowd, many of whom were elderly and some of whom were Holocaust survivors. The blast killed 28 civilians and injured about 140 people. Twenty of the wounded were severely injured, and two later died of their wounds. Several married couples were killed, as was a ninety-year-old. A father was killed with his daughter.

In the aftermath of this attack, Ariel Sharon decided to respond, and shortly thereafter, Israel launched Operation Defensive Shield. The largest Israeli military operation in the West Bank since the Six-Day War, it was designed to uproot the terror infrastructures in the major Palestinian cities there. In essence, Israel took back the cities that it had transferred to the Palestinians in 1995 as part of the Oslo Accords.

Israel did not stop there. Committed to stopping the terror and the attacks on its citizens, the government decided in September 2002 to build a separation barrier cutting off Arab areas in the territories from Israel. The wall, which took more than five years to construct, covered 480 miles (though it was never completed). When the northern section of the wall was completed, it managed to stop all terrorist attacks from that section of the West Bank. Despite its undeniable effectiveness, the wall evoked widespread international condemnation for the inconveniences it imposed on innocent Palestinians, but Israel's leadership was not moved. Construction of the wall continued, and by December 2004, the number of suicide attacks had decreased by 84 percent.

Between September 2000 and September 2004, over a thousand Israelis had been killed and more than two thousand injured. Over twenty-seven hundred Palestinians had been killed. Beyond the toll of dead and injured lay another casualty—the Israeli peace camp. For decades, the Israeli Left had been predicated on a principle of "land for peace"—if Israel would only surrender most of the land that it captured in 1967, the Left insisted, the Palestinians would make peace. But Barak's offer to Arafat and the ensuing intifada had proven that thesis dangerously naive. Even if Barak's offer had not been sufficient, many Israelis believed, Arafat surely had a starting point from which to negotiate. But he never did that. Instead, Arafat unleashed round after round of violence proving to Israelis that he was a terrorist who would never make the transition to statesman. In the process, he eviscerated the Israeli political Left.

Israelis' position was perhaps best captured by Benny Morris, who had in years past been a symbol of the political Left. He called Arafat an "inveterate liar" and concluded, with sadness, that a peaceful coexistence between Israel and the Palestinians might well be impossible. Reflecting on the public bewilderment at his shifted position, he said:

> The rumor that I have undergone a brain transplant is (as far as I can remember) unfounded—or at least premature. But my thinking about the current Middle East crisis and its protagonists has in fact radically changed during the past two years. I imagine that I feel a bit like one of those western fellow travelers rudely awakened by the trundle of Russian tanks crashing through Budapest in 1956.[19]

Morris's grave disappointment was shared by many others, including U.S. president George W. Bush, who later remarked, "Arafat had lied to me. I never trusted him again. In fact, I never spoke to him again. By the spring of 2002, I had concluded that peace would not be possible with Arafat in power."[20]

In his 1923 paper "The Iron Wall," Ze'ev Jabotinsky had argued that the Arabs would never end the conflict until they understood that the Israelis would not budge—it sadly seemed that he had been right. Yossi Klein Halevi later commented that the years of 2000 to 2004 turned Israelis into centrists. They agreed with the Left that creating a Palestinian state was critical for Israel, so that Israel would not continue to rule over millions of Palestinians. Yet they also agreed with the Right that creating a Palestinian state would put Israel in grave danger.[21] They were stuck.

ON NOVEMBER 11, 2004, Yasser Arafat died at the age of seventy-five after a very brief illness. He was succeeded by Mahmoud Abbas (also known as Abu Mazen), whom he had appointed in March 2003 to the then newly created position of prime minister. Abbas had resigned out of frustration when Arafat prevented him from governing in any meaningful way, but he now assumed Arafat's former position.

Abbas, born in Safed in 1935, had fled during the 1948 war. He was later educated in Cairo and then in Moscow, where he wrote a doctoral dissertation entitled "The Other Side: The Secret Relationship Between Nazism and Zionism," in which he argued that Zionists had dramatically exaggerated the number of deaths of Jews at the hands of the Nazis. The notion that six million Jews had been killed, he insisted, was a "fantastic lie."[22] Abbas, one of the founding members of Fatah in 1959, had also been one of the Palestinian negotiators of the 1993 Oslo Accords.[23]

Though the Right harped on the issue of Abbas's dissertation, other Israelis actually saw his election as cause for hope. Might having a Palestinian leader who had advocated negotiation over violence open a new chapter in the region?

MATTERS WERE SHIFTING ON the Israeli side as well. In December 2003 at a conference in Herzliya, Prime Minister Ariel Sharon declared his intent to unilaterally withdraw the IDF from Gaza and to remove all the Jewish settlements from the area. On April 14, 2004, Sharon wrote a letter to President George Bush. "Having reached the conclusion that, for the time being, there exists no Palestinian partner with whom to advance peacefully toward a settlement," he said, "and since the current impasse is unhelpful to the achievement of our shared goals, I have decided to initiate a process of gradual disengagement with the hope of reducing friction between Israelis and Palestinians."[24]

For thirty-four years, there had been Jewish settlements in Gaza. In 2004, eighty-eight hundred Jews lived there, surrounded by over a million Palestinians. The territory in which they lived took up a fifth of the Gaza Strip. But defending those few thousand Israeli Jews was becoming very costly for Israel, requiring tens of thousands of soldiers over the years; despite the force Israel arrayed,

124 Israelis had been killed in Gaza in the preceding five years. Sharon decided that since there could be no negotiated withdrawal from Gaza, Israel would withdraw unilaterally.

That it was Ariel Sharon, widely perceived as the quintessential hawk, who decided that Israel should leave Gaza, surprised many. In his own party, the right-leaning Likud, the decision aroused dismay. Benjamin Netanyahu (then finance minister), in particular, publicly argued with Sharon, insisting that getting out of Gaza would constitute a grave danger for Israel. Hamas bolstered Netanyahu's argument when it began launching rockets from Gaza into Israel; in 2004 alone, Hamas fired 882 mortar shells and 276 Kassam rockets at Israel from Gaza.

Just as Rabin had been undeterred by the rise of violence after Oslo, Sharon insisted on plowing ahead even in the face of the rocket fire. To demonstrate the depth of his opposition to the strategy, Netanyahu resigned from his position as finance minister on August 7. The settlers in Gaza considered Sharon's decision an outright betrayal. Sharon had run for office with a commitment not to execute a unilateral withdrawal from Gaza and now he was doing just that. "Jews do not expel Jews" became the slogan of their movement; they wrote petitions, staged demonstrations, and held protests and hunger strikes. To mollify them, the government promised financial compensation for each family. To pressure them, the government also warned that those who resisted removal would be sent to prison.

In preparation for the removal of the settlers from Gaza and for the bulldozing of their homes and communities, the fourteen thousand police officers and IDF soldiers who were to be involved underwent special training in how to respond to any provocations. For the most part, the actual evacuation in August 2005 went smoothly. In some instances, settlers did pelt soldiers with stones and bottles filled with paint, but no one resorted to firearms. Elsewhere, settlers barricaded themselves in their homes to prevent soldiers from removing them.

Some of the settlers refused to believe that the Jewish state, which since the early aliyot at the close of the nineteenth century had been committed to acquiring land and building on it, would force some of the country's most passionate Zionists out of their homes. In the synagogue of Neve Dekalim, one of the Gaza settlements, a twenty-one-year-old Israeli told a reporter, "This building is the symbol of our life. I don't believe the army will come in here to take us out." She was wrong.

There were no serious injuries, and no deaths. Soldiers went door-to-door to inform the residents it was time to go. It was a hot summer day in Gaza; where necessary, soldiers distributed water to those they were evacuating. Embracing the civilians they were evicting, some soldiers wept; others sat down to join the evacuees in prayer.

The disengagement from Gaza evoked yet another incident from the past, as well. Mcnachem Begin had long said that the moment in his career of which he was most proud was when he was able to avert civil war on the day of the *Altalena* battle in June 1948. In Gaza, Israeli society demonstrated great maturity once again. The armed forces had been meticulously prepared for the operation, and the Jews who were removed from their homes also comported themselves with extraordinary dignity and restraint.

Ariel Sharon had run for office promising not to evacuate Gaza, and then never called for a plebiscite on the disengagement; the entire process struck many Israelis as fundamentally undemocratic. But no one resisted with any significant violence, and the rule of law held fast. It was a heartbreaking day for many Israelis, but a proud one, too, for what was still a young democracy.

WITH THE GAZA EVACUATION complete, getting Israel disentangled from Palestinians on the West Bank was next on Sharon's docket. To smooth his political path, he left the Likud and in November 2005 formed his own party, *Kadima Yisrael* ("Forward, Israel!"), recruiting centrists from both Labor and Likud. But four months after the Gaza disengagement, Sharon suffered a massive

stroke and fell into a coma. Seemingly indestructible, the "Bull
dozer," as Sharon had been called, had been felled.*

Sharon's successor, Ehud Olmert, the former mayor of Jerusalem, declared his intention to hand over the majority of Palestinian
territories in the West Bank to the Palestinian Authority. Unlike
some of his predecessors, Olmert was asserting that a Palestinian
state could be established *before* many of the thorniest issues in the
negotiations would be hammered out. "[I]f the Palestinians abandon the path of terror and stop their war against the citizens of
Israel," he said, "they can receive national independence and a Palestinian State, with temporary borders, even before all the complicated issues connected to a final agreement are resolved. All these
issues will be resolved later, during negotiations between the two
countries."[25]

On the very day that Olmert made that announcement, the
Palestinian Authority held elections. Hamas, a terror organization
long sworn to Israel's destruction, won the popular vote by a thin
margin,[26] but due to the Palestinian electoral system and to massive disunity within Fatah, they captured a large majority of the
seats in parliament. A thin popular victory turned into a landslide.

Upon their election, Hamas officials declared once again that
they would neither recognize Israel nor negotiate with it. Just as
Israel was offering to make a Palestinian state possible, Palestinians elected a government that would only end the conflict when
the Jewish state was destroyed. Any remaining glimmer of hope
for the peace process ended. When Ehud Olmert resigned as prime
minister in March 2009 after allegations of corruption, his initiative, too, died.†

---

*   Sharon lingered for almost nine years, but never regained consciousness.
    He died on January 11, 2014.

†   In February 2016, after a lengthy legal process, Olmert became Israel's
    first former prime minister to go to jail. He joined Moshe Katsav, who
    had resigned as president in July 2007 after he was accused of raping
    members of his staff. Katsav was also convicted and entered prison in
    December 2011. Katsav shared a cell with Shlomo Benizri, former minis-

IN WHAT WAS NOW a long-standing pattern, peace negotiations essentially ended; the violent conflict did not. And once again, the Israel Defense Forces was going to have to reimagine itself. That had happened in the First Intifada, when instead of facing standing Arab armies, the IDF found itself arrayed against a civilian population, armed more with stones than with firearms. It had changed again when the IDF had to learn how to fight the terror organizations behind the Second Intifada. Now, the IDF was battling terrorist organizations once again, but those terror groups now behaved much more like standing armies than anything Israel had faced in decades.

To the north, there was Hezbollah, and to the southwest, Israel faced Hamas. Both were unabashedly committed to Israel's destruction and to terrorizing Israel's population; both launched intermittent rocket attacks on Israeli population centers close to the border. Periodically, these attacks and Israeli retaliations escalated and became serious military engagements.

On June 25, 2006, using tunnels it had dug under the Israel-Gaza border, Hamas kidnapped Corporal Gilad Shalit, who was on active duty in a tank on the Israeli side of the border.* Israelis were stunned by Hamas's daring and military abilities. On July 12, 2006, Hezbollah fired anti-tank missiles on two Israeli military vehicles that were patrolling the Israeli side of the border fence, leaving three soldiers

---

ter of labor and social welfare, who had been convicted of fraud. Several dozen former ministers, members of the Knesset, and other public officials have been convicted of fraud or other crimes—a serious blow to the social ethos that Ben-Gurion had outlined when he proclaimed Israel's independence and read aloud the Declaration of Independence. While Israel could take some comfort in the fact that the judiciary was at least successful in prosecuting even the country's highest officials, increasing corruption was a trend that Israeli society proved unable to reverse.

* Shalit was held for five years and was released on October 18, 2011, when Israel traded approximately a thousand Palestinian prisoners, including many terrorists convicted of violent attacks against Israelis, for his freedom.

dead. Worse, though, from the Israelis' standpoint, was that two additional soldiers were kidnapped. Another group of soldiers sought to rescue them, and in the attempt, five more were killed.

Hezbollah demanded that Israel release prisoners in exchange for the soldiers (who, though unbeknownst to Israel, were already dead). Israel refused. Instead, the IDF sought to weaken Hezbollah, attacking both Hezbollah military targets as well as Lebanese civilian infrastructure, including Beirut's Rafic Hariri International Airport. But Hezbollah fought back for several intense weeks during what became known as the Second Lebanon War and held a seemingly much more powerful IDF at bay. It was an example of the relatively new phenomenon of asymmetrical war, in which public opinion regarding civilian deaths effectively restricts a stronger democratic power. More than 1,000 Lebanese and 165 Israelis were killed, and Israel caused extensive damage to Lebanon. For approximately a month, the two sides bludgeoned each other. With improved use of ground troops, Israel finally began to get the upper hand, but the United States pressured Israel into accepting a UN-imposed cease-fire.

DESPITE HAMAS HAVING WON the parliamentary elections, Fatah did not relinquish its power. In June 2007, Hamas militants staged a violent coup and took control of the Gaza Strip from Fatah, blowing up Fatah headquarters in the city of Khan Yunis and throwing Fatah personnel off buildings. Abbas had been dealt a humiliating blow.

Then, every year or two, Hamas began to fire hundreds and even thousands of rockets at Israeli cities over a period of weeks or months, disrupting what had seemed a semblance of normalcy and quiet. Invariably, since Israelis expected their government to protect them, these Hamas barrages invited an Israeli response, and within days, the two sides were engaged in full-scale warfare. Israel's air force punished Hamas from the skies, and in two of the conflicts,

Israel decided to enter with ground forces. Vicious battles ensued as Hamas tried to hinder the IDF's progress and sought to exact as high a price as possible in Israeli casualties. Hundreds of Palestinian terrorists, Israeli soldiers, and civilians would die in each round—many more of the casualties Palestinian than Israeli—but without substantial gains for either side. Time after time, the sides accepted a cease-fire, awaiting the next round.

It was lost on very few Israelis that what all these brief wars had in common was that they were all "wars that Israel was unable to win" in any decisive manner. In all of them, Israel and whoever it was fighting—Hezbollah (in Lebanon) or Hamas (in Gaza), depending on the conflict—bloodied each other but achieved no substantive strategic gain. Hezbollah and Hamas failed to get Israel to capitulate, withdraw, or change any major policy, while Israel was unable to destroy those terror networks or assure itself that they would not attack again. In fact, Israelis began to realize, they had not really won a war since 1973. True, the IDF had performed admirably in 2002's Operation Defensive Shield, which was in effect a short war, but Israel had had no decisive wins of the 1967 sort in decades and found itself arrayed against an enemy much more tenacious and brutal than many had previously imagined.

In the conflicts, as casualties mounted, Israelis took note of an additional change in their society. If in the 1960s it had been the kibbutzim that had produced officers—and suffered casualties—at rates disproportionate to their percentage of the population, it was now the national religious community that had taken on that role. By 2010, though the national religious community represented no more than 10 percent of Israel's population, they made up some 25 to 30 percent of soldiers in combat units. Similarly, there had been a dramatic increase in the percentage of graduates of the officers' training course who were from the religious community; that rate had risen from a mere 2.5 percent in 1990 to 26 percent in 2008.[27] Israel's military leadership—but also its patriotic passion—was now coming from a very different segment of society.

IF IN THE CONFLICT with the Palestinians Israel was stuck, in other realms it was flourishing. In the 1950s, Israel had been out of money and had no resources for housing or food for the hundreds of thousands of immigrants coming to its shores from North Africa and elsewhere. By the end of the twentieth century and the beginning of the twenty-first, Israel had become a technological powerhouse.

In the sixty years since its founding, Israel's economy had grown fiftyfold.[28] By 2008, Israel had an annual 3.1 percent growth rate in GDP, one of the highest in the world at that time.[29] It had the highest concentration of engineers and research and development spending in the world, as well as the highest concentration of start-ups.[30] In that same year, Israel had the second-highest number of companies listed on NASDAQ (the United States was first), with more companies on the list than the entire European continent combined.[31] Per capita venture capital investments in Israel were "2.5 times greater than in the US, thirty times greater than in Europe, 80 times greater than in China, and 350 times greater than in India."[32]

Several factors had contributed to this enormous success. One was the many thousands of educated Russians who had made their way to Israel, creating a cadre of very ambitious people anxious to overcome the deficits that immigration had wrought. "Immigrants," a leading Israeli policy expert noted, "are not averse to starting over. They are, by definition, risk-takers. Any nation of immigrants is a nation of entrepreneurs."[33] Israel was now reaping the benefits of having been committed, from the outset, to offering a home to Jews no matter where they came from. The integration of Russian immigrants into Israeli education, the army, society, and the economy enriched the still young state in numerous ways.

Other factors also contributed to Israel's becoming a "start-up nation." When in the mid-1980s, the joint U.S.-Israel program to design the Lavi fighter plane was shut down in response to mounting pressure from the U.S. Congress,[34] some fifteen hundred highly trained Israeli engineers suddenly found themselves unemployed. Many of those engineers were those who then created the start-ups that made Israel a leader in technology, brought tremendous wealth to part of Israeli society, and gave Israel once unimaginable positive visibility among investors and inventors across the globe.[35]

IN THE INTERNATIONAL COMMUNITY, however, Israel was perceived not as a start-up nation, but increasingly as a pariah state. Having made no significant headway through the use of terror, the Palestinians turned to another tactic—the international delegitimization of Israel. That was in many ways a natural outgrowth of the United Nations' 1975 claim that Zionism was racism. Now, other groups would pick up that baton and insist that Zionism itself was born in sin and that Israel, therefore, simply had no right to be.

The UN and its affiliates were ground zero for this battle. Ever since the 1970s, the UN had been a transparently anti-Israel forum. Ben-Gurion had called it the "theater of the absurd."[36] Abba Eban, Israel's eloquent—and often pithy—ambassador to the UN and later to the United States, once said of the UN, "If Algeria introduced a resolution declaring that the earth was flat and that Israel had flattened it, it would pass by a vote of 164 to 13 with 26 abstentions."[37]

By 2000, even the UN's pretenses were largely gone. Though the UN had ostensibly revoked the "Zionism is racism" resolution in December 1991, the culture there did not change. In 2001 and 2009, UN-sponsored conferences against racism in Durban, South Africa, decreed once again that Zionism was colonialism, that Israel was an apartheid state, and that Israel had been born in sin and established through "ethnic cleansing."[38] Copies of the Protocols of the Elders of Zion and Adolf Hitler's Mein Kampf were distributed at the conferences.[39]

Between 2003 and 2012, the UN issued 314 resolutions concerning Israel, nearly 40 percent of all resolutions passed in that time. That constituted six times more resolutions than those addressing any other country; the "runner-up" was Sudan.[40] At the end of 2013, Israeli deputy foreign minister Ze'ev Elkin pointed out that of the 103 resolutions about individual countries from the UN Human

Rights Council (UNHRC), 43 of them (42 percent) had condemned
Israel.[41] During the UNHRC's 2013 March session alone, six resolutions were adopted criticizing Israel, while only four addressed all
the remaining countries of the world combined.[42] Israel was the
subject of more emergency sessions in the UNHRC than any other
country.[43] At the same time, the UNHRC failed to pass a single resolution condemning two hundred thousand deaths in Darfur or
human rights violations by China, Cuba, Pakistan, Saudi Arabia,
Sudan, or Zimbabwe.[44]

There were some observers who understood the dynamic and
sought to right the scales. After the UN issued a scathing critique
of Israel's conduct in the 2014 war with Hamas and held Israel responsible for civilian deaths, Richard Kemp, a retired British Army
colonel and former commander of British forces in Afghanistan,
struck back. In an op-ed in the *New York Times,* he reminded his
readers who was responsible for the perpetuation of the conflict.
Though the UN had blamed "Israel's 'protracted occupation of the
West Bank and the Gaza Strip,' as well as the blockade of Gaza,"[45] it
knew that that was not the case. Israel had withdrawn from Gaza
a decade earlier, Kemp reminded his readers, but Hamas used the
disengagement as an opportunity to escalate the conflict. "The
conflict last summer, which began with a dramatic escalation in
rocket attacks targeting Israeli civilians," wrote Kemp, "was a continuation of Hamas's war of aggression."

As for the accusation that Israel had violated international humanitarian law, Kemp compared the IDF to other armies and said:

The [United Nations] commission could have listened to Gen.
Martin E. Dempsey, chairman of the United States Joint Chiefs
of Staff, who said last November that the I.D.F. had taken extraordinary measures to try to limit civilian casualties. Or to
a group of 11 senior military officers from seven nations, including the United States, Germany, Spain and Australia, who
also investigated the Gaza conflict recently. I was a member of
that group, and our report, made available to Judge Davis, said:

"None of us is aware of any army that takes such extensive mea-sures as did the I.D.F. last summer to protect the lives of the civilian population."[46]

The United Nations was even indicted by Samantha Power, then U.S. ambassador to the UN. Not usually regarded as a par-ticularly warm advocate of Israel, even Power acknowledged that something sinister was at play:

> [W]e have seen member states seek to use the UN Security Council, the General Assembly, and even the most arcane UN committees in ways that cross the line from legitimate criticisms of Israel's policies to attempts to delegitimize the state of Israel itself. The only country in the world with a standing agenda item at the Human Rights Council is not North Korea, a totali-tarian state that is currently holding an estimated 100,000 people in gulags; not Syria, which has gassed its people—lots of them. It is Israel. Bias has extended well beyond Israel as a country [but also to] Israel as an idea.[47]

Zionism had always been an idea as much as it was a country. Now Power had articulated precisely what had happened to the standing of that idea. In 1917, with the Balfour Declaration, Britain endorsed the idea of a Jewish state. In November 1947, at the UN vote on partition, the international community did the same. Less than seventy years later, though, most of the international com-munity had changed its mind. What had become objectionable was not the behavior of the Jewish state, but the notion that the Jews ought to have a country of their own.

The fact that the pretense was gone, however, did not mean that the bias would stop. It was clear that if the UN had to vote again on the creation of a Jewish state, unlike the outcome in Novem-ber 1947, this time the motion would have virtually no chance of passing.

Nor was the UN the only locus of the battle. Many ostensibly impartial human rights organizations focused their attention disproportionately on Israel, subjecting it to a transparent double standard. Human Rights Watch was a classic case in point. Robert Bernstein, who founded the organization in 1978 to advocate for victims of human rights violations, wrote an op-ed in the *New York Times* in 2009 denouncing the very organization he had created:

> Human Rights Watch has lost critical perspective on a conflict in which Israel has been repeatedly attacked by Hamas and Hezbollah, organizations that go after Israeli citizens and use their own people as human shields. . . . Leaders of Human Rights Watch know that Hamas and Hezbollah chose to wage war from densely populated areas, deliberately transforming neighborhoods into battlefields. They know that more and better arms are flowing into both Gaza and Lebanon and are poised to strike again. And they know that this militancy continues to deprive Palestinians of any chance for the peaceful and productive life they deserve. Yet Israel, the repeated victim of aggression, faces the brunt of Human Rights Watch's criticism.[48]

That sort of double standard was not uncommon. In the form of numerous organizations and with the complicity of much of the press and European governments, the delegitimization movement—a relentless criticism of the Jewish state that "exhibits blatant double standards, singles out Israel, denies its right to exist as the embodiment of the self-determination right of the Jewish people, or demonizes the state"—continued to gain momentum.[49]

In many cases, the organizations purporting to be devoted to ending the occupation barely sought to camouflage their opposition to the very idea of a Jewish state. The Boycott, Divestment and Sanctions Movement (BDS) was founded in 2005, just as Israel was pulling out of the Gaza Strip. It called for ostracizing the Jewish state until it not only ended the occupation of Palestinian land since 1967, but also gave equal rights to Arab-Palestinian citizens and granted the right of return to Palestinians who had fled the fighting in 1948 as well as to their descendants, who then numbered in the millions. There was no way that Israel could absorb all those Palestinians (thus ending a Jewish demographic majority) and still remain both Jewish and democratic. That, of course, was precisely the point. BDS was aimed at destroying Israel.

It was an exceedingly clever tactic. By using the language of human rights, which spoke powerfully to the sensibilities of American Jews, the BDS campaign and other organizations succeeded in convincing many young American Jews to wonder whether the Jewish state was not in some significant way a betrayal of the values that had long made Judaism a positive force in the world.

More sophisticated observers understood what was at play. At the first UN conference on anti-Semitism in New York in June 2004 (before BDS had even become a strategy), one noted human rights activist and scholar described the state of affairs. "[T]he evil of anti-Semitism today moves through the UN host like an opportunistic pathogen," she said. "First, discrimination of Israel followed by its demonization; the deification of the enemies of the Jewish state, the denial of Jewish victimhood; the denunciation of the Israeli who fights back; and finally, the refusal to identify the assailants."[50] In Europe, overt anti-Semitism increased, as did violence against Jews. European Jews understood that they had seen this "play" before, and in 2015, western European immigration to Israel hit an all-time high.[51] Once again, many Jews felt they had to flee.

OF MORE IMMEDIATE CONCERN to Israel's government was the spread of nuclear technology, and particularly the nuclear aspirations of governments committed to Israel's destruction. The Begin doctrine was tested in 2007 when Israel acquired incontrovertible evidence that Syria was building a nuclear reactor near the Euphrates River. After bringing President George W. Bush into the picture, Israeli prime minister Ehud Olmert ordered a covert military

strike on the facility. It was completely destroyed in a strike by Israeli aircraft, without a shot being fired by Syria.[52]

Israel faced a more formidable challenge to the Begin Doctrine
in Iran. In April 2006, Iran announced that it had managed to successfully enrich uranium for the first time, a critical step in the development of nuclear weaponry. Iran's intentions were clear. That
same year, Iranian president Mahmoud Ahmadinejad declared
without hesitation his desire to see "the Zionist regime wiped off
the map."[53] That policy persisted. In 2012, the Iranian chief of staff,
Hassan Firouzabadi, announced, "The Iranian nation is [commit-
ted to] the full annihilation of Israel."[54] Iran, though, is farther away
from Israel than Iraq. And hoping to forestall an Israeli attack, Iran
buried its nuclear program deep beneath the ground, out of the
reach of Israeli bombers and weaponry.

Prime Minister Benjamin Netanyahu invoked the Begin Doctrine, as well, and insisted that if the international community did
not prevent Iran from going nuclear, Israel would somehow do it
alone. But U.S. president Barack Obama and his administration
were not inclined to use force or even to give Israel the green light
(or weaponry) to stop Iran's march toward a weapon and to end
Iran's threat to annihilate the six million Jews living in Israel.* In
March 2015, world powers (the United States, the United Kingdom,
France, Russia, China, Germany, and the European Union) met
with representatives of Iran in Lausanne, Switzerland, to negotiate a framework deal to stall Iran's nuclear development in return
for an easing of some of the crippling economic sanctions that had
been enforced on the regime for decades. The deal, entitled the
Joint Comprehensive Plan of Action, was signed on July 14, 2015.

The agreement did not require Iran to dismantle its vast nu-

---

* The number six million raised horrifying assocations for Jewish Israelis.
  It was the number of Jews who had perished in a previous genocide, and
  who now found themselves in the crosshairs of a country sworn to their
  destruction.

clear infrastructure, and the restrictions that it imposed would expire after ten years. Lawmakers opposing the deal noted that at its foundation was trust of Iran, which, they said, was foolhardy. Henry Kissinger, a Republican who had proven over the years that he was hardly in Israel's pocket, coauthored an opinion piece with former secretary of state George Shultz, arguing that the West had made a terrible strategic mistake and had abdicated its moral responsibility:

> The threat of war now constrains the West more than Iran. While Iran treated the mere fact of its willingness to negotiate as a concession, the West has felt compelled to break every deadlock with a new proposal. In the process, the Iranian program has reached a point officially described as being within two to three months of building a nuclear weapon. . . . History will not do our work for us; it helps only those who seek to help themselves.[55]

Israelis of many walks of life saw the development as ominous. The United States, ostensibly Israel's most significant ally, had not only parted ways with Israel on a major policy, but incomprehensibly to Israelis, seemed to be lifting obstacles that might prevent a country determined to destroy the Jewish state from acquiring a nuclear weapon. This spelled, some thought, a dramatic shift in U.S.-Israel relations and left Israelis feeling alone and vulnerable in a way that they had not been in many decades. "Most disturbing for me personally," wrote Michael Oren, who had served as Israel's ambassador to Washington as the Obama administration was both negotiating with Iran and keeping Israel in the dark, "was the realization that our closest ally had entreated with our deadliest enemy on an existential issue without so much as informing us."[56]

In many ways, even Israelis who did not believe that Iran *would* attack Israel understood that an Iran that *could* attack Israel was a game changer. No one captured the sentiment of Israel's population better than Yossi Klein Halevi. What Israel would eventually decide to do, he said, would determine whether the creation of the state had ultimately made any difference at all.

"A Jewish state that allows itself to be threatened with nuclear weapons," said Klein Halevi, "will forfeit its right to speak in the name of Jewish history."[57]

A JEWISH RENAISSANCE IN
THE JEWISH STATE

This scent still tugs at my heart . . . opens doors . . . to that ancient
song we have passed down for generations.

—Israeli musician Rami Kleinstein, "Small Gifts"[1]

In early 2013, shortly after Israel held elections to the nineteenth Knesset, those newly elected to the Parliament—in keeping with long-standing tradition—took to the podium to deliver their inaugural addresses to the assembly. In that election, a new party had done surprisingly well. Named *Yesh Atid* ("There Is a Future"), it was led by a handsome, intelligent, widely admired television journalist and author, Yair Lapid. Lapid, whose Holocaust-survivor father had also been a member of the Knesset and a fierce opponent of religion in the Jewish state, had assembled an eclectic list of candidates, many of whom had never previously served as elected officials: men and women, Haredim, national-religious and secular, gay and straight, Ashkenazi, Mizrachi, and Ethiopian, immigrants and native-born Israelis.*[2] Part of the point of his list was that the

---

* Lapid's list also included the first American to be elected to the Knesset in thirty years. An interesting and surprising dimension of Israeli politics has been that while Russian (Natan Sharansky and Avigdor Lieberman,

silos dividing Israeli society needed to come down. Among the
MKs in his new party was Ruth Calderon.

When it came her turn to speak, Calderon walked to the podium with a volume of the Talmud in hand. "Mr. Chairman, honorable Knesset," she began, "the book I am holding changed my
life, and to a large extent it is the reason that I have reached this
day with the opportunity to speak to the Knesset of Israel as a new
member."[3]

Then Calderon continued by reminding the assembly of the history they all shared to some degree or another:

> I did not inherit a set of Talmud from my grandfather. I was
> born and raised in a quaint neighborhood in Tel Aviv. My fa-
> ther, Moshe Calderon, was born in Bulgaria and immigrated to
> this land as a young man. After the difficult war years, he began
> studying agriculture at the Hebrew University in Jerusalem, and
> was immediately conscripted to defend Gush Etzion during the
> War of Independence. . . . My German-born mother, who had
> the combined misfortune (at that time) of being Jewish, left-
> handed, and red-haired, made *aliyah* as a teenager, and met my
> father courtesy of the British siege of Jerusalem.

Yet her story was not the classic Zionist narrative that it sounded
like at first blush. In fact, she went to great lengths to explain, her
generation marked the beginning of the end of that narrative.

> I grew up in a very Jewish, very Zionist, secular-traditional-
> religious home that combined Ashkenaz and Sepharad, [Revi-

---

for example) and North African immigrants to Israel (Aryeh Deri and his
colleagues) have become very politically active, the thousands of American Jewish immigrants—despite the impression created by the iconic
Golda Meir—have chosen to remain largely on the political sidelines.
(http://www.jpost.com/Israel-News/Politics-And-Diplomacy/Dov-Lip
man-to-head-WZO-department-437000.)

sionist] Betar and [Socialist] Hashomer Hatzair, in the Israeli mainstream of the 60s and 70s. I was educated like everyone else my age—public education in the spirit of "from the Tanach to the Palmach."* I was not acquainted with the Mishna, the Talmud, Kabbala or Hasidism. By the time I was a teenager, I already sensed that something was missing. Something about the new, liberated Israeli identity of . . . Naomi Shemer's poems, was good and beautiful, but lacking. I missed depth; I lacked words for my vocabulary; a past, epics, heroes, places, drama, stories—were missing.

The new Hebrew [i.e., new Jew], created by educators from the country's founding generation, realized his dream and became a courageous, practical, and suntanned soldier. But for me, this contained—I contained—a void. I did not know how to fill that void, but when I first encountered the Talmud [with] its language, its humor, its profound thinking, its modes of discussion, and the practicality, humanity, and maturity that emerge from its lines, I sensed that I had found the love of my life.

Calderon's opening was far more than a mere autobiographical curiosity. The Zionist revolution, she was saying, had been successful, but also too successful. Zionism had created a new Jew, but that new Jew was rudderless, an "orphan in history."[4] Zionism had "cured" the Jew; but it had also *overcured* the Jew. Desperate to create a new Jew, to fashion a Jew who would not cower behind casks when Cossacks attacked Kishinev, Zionism had so eradicated connection with the Jewish tradition that a generation or two later, young Israelis were so divorced from their own tradition that Hillel Halkin, a well-known Israeli author and translator, called them

---

* "Tanach" is a Hebrew acronym for words that mean "the Bible." "Tanach to Palmach" is an Israeli phrase that, because of its rhyme, is a popular way of referring to the early Zionists' determination to ignore all Jewish tradition that developed between the period of the Bible and the return to Jewish sovereignty, represented by the rise of the Yishuv (and the Haganah's elite strike force, the Palmach).

"Hebrew-speaking goyim." Now they were hungry for meaning, yearning for roots, seeking to reconnect with what Zionism had taken from them.

Nor was she alone, Calderon insisted. There were so many young Israelis seeking the very reconnection she yearned for that multiple institutions were founded to address their needs. She and several others founded a "Home for Hebrew Culture" in Tel Aviv, and in Jerusalem, they created one of the first Israeli settings in which men and women, religious and secular, studied classic Jewish religious texts together.

Secular Israelis were studying these great works, seeking a rapprochement with the very tradition from which Ben-Gurion, Alterman, and Bialik (all of whom knew classical Jewish texts and cited them often, ironically) had felt Israelis needed to distance themselves. And religious people were now studying with secular people, suddenly aware that rather than simple "apostates," these secular Jews had interpretations of texts to offer from which the religious young people could learn a great deal, but which they were not going to hear in classic religious settings.

Though this new trend did not, of course, touch all of Israeli society, increasing numbers of Israelis were no longer certain that the Jewish state could be what Natan Alterman had intimated it would be in his poem "The Silver Platter"—a replacement for Sinai, the mountain that represented thousands of years of Jewish tradition. In fact, they sensed, without Sinai at the core, without a unique and particular Jewish message rooted in classic Jewish writings, Jewish statehood and sovereignty would be rendered meaningless.

THE ORIGINAL ZIONIST REVOLUTION was fading. Many early Zionist thinkers had seen Zionism as a therapeutic project. Zionism would heal the Jew. It would save the Jew from religion, from the dusty tomes of the yeshiva bookshelves. There had been an era in which having absolutely no religious faith was a badge of Zionist honor. Tommy Lapid—Yair Lapid's father—recounted an instance in which he and an ultra-Orthodox Jew appeared on the same television show. Lapid mentioned that he did not believe in God and then relayed what happened: "'If you don't believe in God,' some angry ultra-Orthodox politico shouted at me during one of the *Popolitika* television programs, 'then who defined you as a Jew?' 'Hitler,' I shouted back at him. For once there was silence in the studio."[5]

Lapid may have put it more starkly than others, but a rejection of classic Jewish religion was key to much of early Zionism. That was the power of Calderon's coming to the podium of the Knesset with a volume of the Talmud and teaching a passage to the assembly. She, the product of those new Jews that Zionism had sought to create, wanted some of the old Jew back.

THE IDEOLOGY OF CLASSIC ZIONISM was beginning to crack. Cracks could be seen far beyond the relatively small—even if widening—circles of Israel's young intellectual elites. The rock music scene was another lens into the phenomenon. Arik Einstein (1939–2013), the wildly popular "father of Israeli rock," grew up in Tel Aviv with all its attendant hypersecularism (and the lifestyle belonging to a rock musician). Einstein's closest friend was Uri Zohar, a comedian and film director, who in the 1970s began to turn to religion. In 1977, Zohar—long a symbol of the best of secular Israeli entertainment—left the entertainment world, became a rabbi, and joined the ultra-Orthodox community.

In the meantime, Einstein divorced his wife, Alona. Alona was from pure Zionist aristocratic stock. The daughter of one of the Israeli Air Force's first pilots, in itself sufficient to make her part of the secular aristocracy, she was also the granddaughter of Manya and Israel Schochet. Manya had been a revolutionary in czarist Russia, and both she and her husband made their way to Palestine during the Second Aliyah. Theirs was the classic, canonical Zionist narrative.

After she and Einstein divorced, Alona found her way to religion, as well, and she, too, became ultra-Orthodox. Ultimately, Arik and

Alona's two ultra-Orthodox daughters married Uri Zohar's two eldest sons, also ultra-Orthodox. In many ways, the story was a mere curiosity; but the image of Arik Einstein, the hypersecular king of Israeli rock, surrounded by ultra-Orthodox family members who had come from the secular aristocracy was a powerful symbol of the shifts taking place in parts of Israeli life.

Arik Einstein's family was not alone. Reengagement with religion became a defining characteristic of many Israeli musicians. Etti (Esther) Ankri achieved instant stardom with her first album, *I Can See It in Your Eyes* (1990), which reached double platinum in Israel. The very symbol of musical success, she was eventually named Israeli Female Singer of the Year. In 2001, she, too, began a slow return to religious observance, and when she released an album in 2009, it was a musical rendering of the poetry of the medieval Jewish poet and philosopher Rabbi Yehudah Halevi.

The Banai family, the first "Israeli musical family," illustrated the pattern best. The first generation of Banai performers, Yossi and Gavri Banai, were staunch secularists. In the next generation, first cousins Ehud and Yuval Banai were in bands that brought East-West fusion into Israeli culture, a reflection of the spiritual search that often took Israelis abroad. Still later, in the 1990s, Ehud and Evyatar (also first cousins) became religious and were soon bringing overt Jewish themes into their music. It was one family, with several stages of spiritual searching that represented Israeli life at large.

One could see the shift online and in bookstores, as well. YNet, Israel's most popular news website (hosted by the secular daily *Yediot Achronot*), almost always posted some overtly Jewish religious content on its rapidly changing pages. In 2005, when Israeli professor Malka Shaked published *I'll Play You Forever: The Bible in Modern Hebrew Poetry,* her anthology of modern Israeli poetry that was in clear dialogue with the Bible weighed in at well over a thousand pages.[6] The poetry had been written over decades, but now there was a popular market for volumes that would trace Israelis' ongoing dialogue with the Bible and attest to its being so ubiquitous in Israeli cultural life.

Micah Goodman, a popular teacher on the Israeli scene and one of its young public intellectuals, wrote his first three books on Maimonides's *Guide to the Perplexed*, Rabbi Yehudah Halevi's medieval classic, *The Kuzari*, and the biblical book of Deuteronomy—hardly subjects one would expect to attract mass attention. Yet all three of Goodman's books hit the Israeli bestseller list. Israelis were buying, reading, and thinking about books on subjects their grandparents had tried to evict from the Israeli conversation.

In the Israeli movie industry, major films began to examine, often with a sympathetic even if critical eye, the world of Jewish tradition that most of secular Israel had long ignored or viewed with derision. In 1999, *Kadosh* (Hebrew for "sacred") cast a critical but not entirely unsympathetic eye on the secular world's narrow and dismissive view of ultra-Orthodox life. *Fill the Void*, released in 2012, focused on a modern ultra-Orthodox twist of the biblical tradition of levirate marriage; the film tells the story of a young woman pressured into marrying her sister's husband after her sister dies in childbirth.* *Get* (Hebrew for "writ of divorce"), a 2014 film, explored the power that Jewish men could exert over their wives in government-sanctioned rabbinic courts. Perhaps the best known of the rapidly expanding genre was *Footnote,* a 2011 film that focused on the troubled relationship between a father and a son, both of whom are Israeli professors of Talmud. The father, interested in highly technical academic aspects of the Talmudic text, is appalled by his son's search for contemporary meaning in the text— and the throngs of students who are attracted to his son's new (and in the father's mind, insufficiently academically serious) approach. The battle between the generations, a realistic assessment of what

---

* In its original biblical formulation, levirate marriage required that the brother of a childless, deceased man marry his brother's widow, and the widow is obliged to marry her deceased husband's brother, in order to carry on the family tree of the deceased brother; the firstborn child of the new couple was treated as that of the deceased brother. Cf. Deuteronomy 25:5–6.

was transpiring in Israeli academe, was a clear reference to Ruth Calderon's generation yearning for exposure to the Talmud not as a scientific discipline, but as part of a journey of searching for life's meaning in the company of Jewish texts.

The shift was apparent even among Israel's most important establishment intellectuals. In 2003, Professor Ruth Gavison (a leading Israeli jurisprudential philosopher and later a nominee for the Israeli Supreme Court) and Rabbi Yaakov Medan (one of the leaders of the prestigious Har Etzion Yeshiva) published the Gavison-Medan Covenant, a proposed "agreement" between secular and religious Israelis about how to make Israel's public space palpably Jewish while respecting individual rights. The covenant covers many areas of daily life in Israel, including Jewish identity, marriage, the Sabbath, Kashrut, the Western Wall, and the IDF. Some of its groundbreaking progress included agreements that civil registration of marriages would be necessary for all those wishing to marry, while a religious service, if any, would be optional. The Sabbath would be deemed a day of rest for the State of Israel but restaurants, entertainment centers, and a limited number of grocery stores, gas stations, and pharmacies would not be forbidden from operating, and there would be modified forms of public transportation on the Sabbath, as well.

It was telling that Gavison, a nonobservant woman long associated with the Israeli Left (she had been at the helm of the Association for Civil Rights in Israel, in addition to her many academic endeavors) was the one insisting that the state could not survive without a substantive core of Jewish content. Her participation reflected two moves—secular and religious Israelis reaching across the divide, seeking common ground, and Israelis seeking to root their country in a discourse of Jewish meaning. If Israel were not democratic, she believed, it would have no *justification* for being. If it were not palpably Jewish, it would have no *reason* to be. The challenge of Israel's governmental policies, she insisted, "is not just to ensure the existence of the state, but also to ensure that it will include an effective legacy of Jewish identities . . . as a precondition for interest in Jewish history or Jewish sources. Only such a legacy will enable the continued willingness of most of the public that lives in the state to continue to support a state that is both Jewish and democratic."[7]

There was more. Across Israel, one could see indications that young religious Jews were anxious to meet their secular counterparts, and that secular Israelis, in addition to meeting their religious peers, were thirsty for serious exposure to the texts that the "Tanach to Palmach censorship" had long hidden from them. One-year post-high-school, pre-military-service programs for students cropped up all over the country, many of them designed specifically for a mixed population of secular and religious people. Thousands of students attended—applications far outstripped capacity.

Israel remained a complex and heterogeneous society, of course. Approximately a million immigrants from the former USSR had come to Israel very skeptical about religion, and as a whole they remained so—though many of their children who were not Jewish according to Jewish law (because their mothers were not Jewish) availed themselves of opportunities that the army afforded them to undergo conversion.

Israelis of Russian background typically share the right-leaning political dispositions of the Mizrachim—but not their instinctive allegiance to religious tradition. Tel Aviv remains a highly secular city, so different from much of Israel that it is sometimes called "the State of Tel Aviv." There is no one Israel, but many Israels—and religion plays a different role in each of them. Across the country, though, one could sense at least a new openness to the tradition that the Zionist founding fathers had jettisoned, a new spiritual searching that earlier generations had dismissed.

Scarcely more than half a century into its history, the very religious tradition that the founding fathers of the state had sought to banish was making its way back to the center of Israeli life. The State of Israel—and especially its foundational ideology—was going through a seismic shift. What had happened?

ONE MAJOR DEVELOPMENT WAS the rise of the Mizrachim to a place of social and cultural prominence in Israeli life. Mizrachi religiosity had always manifested itself differently than the philosophically more rigid Ashkenazi variety, and now secular Israelis were being exposed to its worldview. Mizrachi Jews *admired* rabbis more than their Ashkenazi counterparts did, but *obeyed* them less. As one leading Israeli philosopher put it, for Mizrachim, a Jew's relationship to Jewish tradition was less one of *obedience* (the central trope of classic Ashkenazi religiosity) and more a matter of *loyalty*.[8] One could be a deeply believing and loyal Jew, Mizrachim essentially asserted, without being committed to the observance of all the rigors of Jewish law. The Mizrachim made it possible for Ashkenazim to draw closer to Jewish tradition—with attendant sentiments of respect and loyalty—without the fear of becoming "religious," a label that was still anathema to many Israelis who had been raised in the secular world.

In some ways, Israelis were also growing tired of the burden of history, of having to constantly see their own lives as part of a grand historic pageant. Many decades had passed since Haim Hazaz had written his 1943 short story "The Sermon," in which he declared that he was opposed to Jewish history. But Israel had never given up on history or memory. Archaeology had become a national obsession, and some archaeologists, like Yigael Yadin, became virtual folk heroes. Israel also treated memory as virtually sacred, as seen even in street names. There are virtually no Broadways or Ninety-Sixth Streets in Israel: every street is named for a person of biblical, Talmudic, or historical importance; a biblical place or flower—but then, only a flower that is found in the Land of Israel; Zionist organizations; important dates in Jewish and Israeli history; and the like.

But the drive to play a pivotal role in a historic drama of epic proportions, which had so moved and animated the early generations, was wearing thin for Israelis two or three generations later. Yehuda Amichai, who in many ways replaced Natan Alterman as Israel's national poet (Alterman, who died in 1970, filled the role when Chaim Nachman Bialik died in 1934), often expressed the yearning to be relieved of the burden of history and narrative. His poem "Tourist" is one of his most famous. The narrator, a man carrying heavy baskets at his side, comes across a group of tourists with their guide. The guide points to the man with the baskets and says, "Just right of his head there's an arch from the Roman period. Just right of his head."⁹

But is the man, the person, the living human being less important than the ancient stones? Says the narrator (and thus, Amichai, too), "Redemption will come only if their guide tells them, 'You see that arch from the Roman period? It's not important: but next to it, left and down a bit, there sits a man who's bought fruit and vegetables for his family.'"

Israelis were seeking a new kind of redemption, one that would come not from courage on the battlefield or profound ideological intensity, but from a life of simple humanity. Many of them were seeking it in the texts and traditions that had shaped their people for thousands of years.

The renewed search for meaning also stemmed from Israelis' realization that peace was not going to come any time soon. After the devastation of the Yom Kippur War and the collapse of the *conceptzia*, Yehoram Gaon—one of Israel's most popular singers— came out with a song the refrain of which was "I promise you, my little girl, that this will be the last war." By the end of 2000, after a new Intifada had erupted, few Israelis believed that there would be a "last war." The conflict would go on, if not forever then for a very long time. The idyllic images of Theodor Herzl's *Altneuland,* where Jews and Arabs lived peacefully beside each other in a Jewish state thriving and welcomed by all, seemed terribly naive. If the pursuit of a lasting peace could no longer be many Israelis' source of inspiration and meaning, they would have to turn elsewhere.

EVEN AS SOME ISRAELIS were growing more interested in their religious roots, much of Israeli society was at the very same time worried about other religious phenomena in the Jewish state. The chief rabbinate, an institution that the Ottomans and British had established and shaped, was becoming ever more reviled. As the Haredim had become increasingly central to Israeli politics, they were able to ensure that the chief rabbis were either ultra-Orthodox or close to it. By the twenty-first century, Israel had not only chief rabbis who were occasionally indicted for misuse of funds, but were also not Zionists. Frightened by modernity and opposed to change, they dismissed and ridiculed all non-Orthodox forms of Judaism, alienating large swaths of Diaspora Jews, the vast majority of whom were not Orthodox. One Orthodox rabbi writing in 2016 and bemoaning what had happened to the rabbinate cited a recent poll in which 71 percent of Israelis said they were dissatisfied with the rabbinate and 65 percent favored abolishing the institution altogether.[10]

The Haredi world, varied though it is, on the whole had a strategy for Jewish survival that was fundamentally at odds with almost all branches of Zionism. If Zionism was predicated on erasing the passivity of the Diaspora Jew and taking the reins of history into Jewish hands, the Haredi world believed that it was in the Diaspora that Jewish life had reached its purest state. If Zionists wanted to create new Jews, Haredim sought to retain what they saw as the luster of the "old" (and therefore, "authentic") Jew and restore the primacy of Jewish *religious* life, even if that meant forcing it on non-believing Israelis. If Zionism believed that a powerful Jew could engage the non-Jewish world as an equal, the Haredi world eyed the Gentile world with suspicion and fear. They wanted to be left alone. The less contact with the Jewish state—and the world it was engaging—the better.

By 1963, when Ben-Gurion realized that he had been wrong to release Haredi students from army service, he wrote Eshkol, who was then prime minister: "I released yeshiva students from army service. I did so when their number was small, but now they are increasing. When they run amok, they represent a danger to the honor of the state."[11]

Much more than the state's honor was at stake, however, and Ben-Gurion had failed to recognize the full gravity of the mistake he had made. By 2014, Haredim constituted approximately 15 percent of Israel's Jewish population, and the percentage was growing; the average fertility rate for Haredi women was 6.2 children, while for the non-Haredi Jewish population it was 2.4.[12] Because the vast majority of Haredi boys cease their secular education at the age of fourteen, they are much less prepared for the job market and remain increasingly dependent on the government. In 2010, the universally liked and admired Bank of Israel governor, Stanley Fischer, warned that without a significant change in policy, Israel's prosperity in light of the Haredi numbers was simply "not sustainable."[13]

Interestingly, though, even as Israelis were deeply worried about the implications of the Haredim for democracy (many Haredim would prefer a theocracy or life under a non-Jewish government), secular civil rights, and economics, they were, at the same time, also fascinated by the devotion that way of life elicited in its followers. That, too, was reflected in popular Israeli culture, in a well-known television series discussed obsessively on social media after each episode. Named *Shtisel,* its plot follows a Haredi family of the same name. After decades of secular Jews showing either disinterest or disdain when it came to Haredim, *Shtisel* was a loving, understanding portrayal of a way of life Israelis still feared but also found fascinating. It was, as one of its coauthors readily noted, "the first time that a television show shows Haredim who love their way of life, their kids and their grandkids."[14] Tel Avivians who watched the show began speaking to each other with a smattering of Yiddish terms they learned from its characters.

The tensions with the Haredi world were not over, but the barriers were cracking. Israelis were searching, and were finding meaning in places that not long before would have seemed unthinkable.

WHATEVER CHALLENGES THE HAREDI world might have represented to Israel's democracy or economic sustainability, religion in the Jewish state also had other, more radical splinter groups. In the decades following Oslo, a small group of nationalist extremists began to establish outposts in the West Bank (or Judea and Samaria, the biblical name by which many Israelis refer to it). The "hilltop youth," as they are called, grew out of the Gush Emunim worldview but came to see even the hard-core Gush Emunim settlers as too passive and overly respectful of the state and its government. Their goal was not only to ensure Jewish sovereignty over the "whole land of Israel" but also to form a monarchy that would establish Jewish law as the law of the land. For them, Zionism was too new to afford them a sense of being part of a grand Jewish narrative. "I don't see myself as a continuation of Zionism," one told an interviewer. He was in search of "something deeper with more roots."[15] Even the sometimes militaristic rhetoric of people like Ze'ev Jabotinsky was insufficient for these young people. They were looking for a different, more violent sort of inspiration. They were the extreme manifestation of precisely what Yeshayahu Leibowitz had warned would happen if Israel did not exit the West Bank.

Their inspiration came in the form of Rabbi Yitzchak Ginsburgh, the author of a book named *Barukh Ha-Gever* (*Blessed Is the Man*). The book justified the actions of Baruch Goldstein, who killed 29 Palestinians and injured 125 in Hebron in 1994. *Barukh Ha-Gever* was actually a play on words, for it could mean either "Blessed Is the Man" or "Baruch Is the Man," and it became a manifesto for the violence-inclined post-Zionist hilltop youth.

Two of Ginsburgh's admirers then published a book in 2009 called *Torat Ha-Melekh* (*The Law of the King*). Among its most notorious (and repulsive) conclusions, *Torat Ha-Melekh* justifies the killing of Palestinian children because "it is clear that they will grow to harm us"[16] and asserts that the Bible's injunction "Thou shall not kill" applied only to the killing of Jews. Appalled by its tone and content, several Jewish groups filed a petition with Israel's High Court of Justice, asking that the book be banned and that its authors be charged with incitement.[17] But Israel has a long tradition of protecting freedom of expression and freedom of religion, and the High Court argued that the book, even if inflammatory, was not a call to action and therefore could not be banned. Successive governments were no less successful at containing this small but ugly phenomenon than they were at limiting the power of the Haredi community. In ways that no preeminent Zionist thinker had foreseen, the Jewish return to physical power had spawned an ugly, racist, and dangerous offshoot; and no matter how small it was, Israel would have to confront it.

DESPITE THESE WORRISOME DEVELOPMENTS, Judaism in the Jewish state was mostly a story of deep decency, vitality, and renewal. One hundred and twenty years after the First Zionist Congress, almost seventy years after the State of Israel had been created, Ahad Ha'am's dream had in many ways come true. Israel was once again bursting with Jewish energy, with Jewish creativity, with Jewish searching. In 1897, Ahad Ha'am could never even have dreamed of a state that would be home to eight million people, three-quarters of them Jews. Who, in Zionism's early days, could have imagined that there would be a sovereign secular state that would still be home to the thousands of *yeshivot* of which Rav Kook had dreamed, in which bookstores boasted hundreds of linear yards of shelves holding books written in a largely abandoned language that Eliezer Ben-Yehuda had revived?

Herzl's Jews had sought a state. Ahad Ha'am had proposed a vision of Israel as a great spiritual center. In ways that neither could have anticipated, though, the two dreams grew intertwined. Israel could never have become the Jewish spiritual center it was becoming were it not for the fact that it was also a nation-state. Ahad Ha'am's dream could come to fruition because Herzl, too, had won the day.

Yet Herzl's vision of a sovereign state had meaning, increasing numbers of Israelis believed, only if those new Jews rooted themselves and their humanity in the tradition they had inherited. Herzl without Ahad Ha'am was merely political sovereignty—and that, Israelis began to sense, was simply not enough.

Theodor Herzl. Ahad Ha'am. Two radically different personalities. Two opposing visions for the Jewish future. But a century after Balfour, it was dawning on Israelis that what made their country so extraordinary was the fact that they no longer believed they had to choose between the two. Both models had come to be, and in the process, the two together had created a new Jew far richer and more nuanced than either could have achieved alone.

Conclusion

————

A CENTURY AFTER BALFOUR—
"A NATIONAL HOME FOR
THE JEWISH PEOPLE"

But we are still here . . . clinging to this shore and living on this shore. Come what may.

—Ari Shavit, *My Promised Land*[1]

A century has passed since the 1917 Balfour Declaration's assertion that "His Majesty's government views with favour the establishment in Palestine of a national home for the Jewish people." A national home for the Jewish people has, indeed, been established in the Land of Israel, and it is now home to more Jews than any other place in the world.

The path to statehood was complex, and statehood itself has been far from easy. Ever since 1929, when Arab rioters destroyed the centuries-old Jewish community of Hebron in a matter of days, the region has been hostage to a grinding conflict that still has no end in sight. Thousands of people, on both sides, have died. In the decades that followed, one-third of the Jewish people was murdered by the Nazis and their enablers. In Poland, the seat of the greatest Jewish community in the world at that time, 90 percent of the Jews were killed. During the Holocaust, millions of Jews lost their homes in Europe; in Arab countries in North Africa, Iraq, Iran, and

.emen; and elsewhere. Hundreds of thousands of Palestinians also lost their ancestral homes in conflicts in 1948 and 1967.

There have been countless moments of grave uncertainty. When David Ben-Gurion and Menachem Begin both declined to join the revelry in the street on November 29, 1947, after the United Nations approved partition, they understood that the outcome of the war already under way was by no means certain. One percent of the Jewish citizens of the new state—a huge blow for any society—would die in the conflict.* In the early 1950s, Israel was short on food and faced severe shortages in housing as hundreds of thousands of immigrants arrived at its shores; the country's collapse was by no means unlikely. When Israel dug thousands of graves in 1967 in preparation for the massacre that Nasser promised the Arab world, it was far from evident that the Jewish state would survive. In 1973, in a grievous failure of Israeli military intelligence, a massive Egyptian force crossed the Suez Canal and Syrian tanks threatened to slice through the Galilee. When Saddam Hussein began construction of a nuclear facility, it was far from clear that Israel could destroy it. There have been wars and intifadas, economic boycotts and terrorism, massive immigrations to absorb and huge social inequalities with which to wrestle. Time and again, it was unclear whether the newly founded Jewish state could survive.

But Israel has more than survived—it has flourished. What began as a small collection of vulnerable settlements desperately in need of financial support from philanthropists from abroad has transformed itself into a modern state now home to some eight million people, six million of them Jews. On its sixty-eighth Independence Day, Israel's population was ten times what it had been in 1948.[2] That fact itself bespoke the extraordinary accomplishment that was Israel. Something grand and ancient had been reborn. Barbara Tuchman, the Pulitzer Prize–winning author and historian, once observed that of all the peoples of the world from three thou-

---

* In the United States today, the same percentage would mean the deaths of some 3.2 million Americans.

sand years ago, it is only the Jews who live in the same place, speak the same language, and practice the same religion.[3] The story of the return of the Jewish people to its ancestral homeland became, in short, one of the great dramas in the history of humankind.

What fueled that grit and determination? Why did the Jews succeed when so many others did not? There were many causes, but key among them was the fact that, as Golda Meir put it, "the Jews have a secret weapon: we have nowhere else to go."[4]

Part antiquity and part modernity, rooted in history but determined to forge a new path, the story of the State of Israel is, in many ways, nothing less than the story of the rebirth of the Jewish people. Charles Krauthammer, the noted columnist, captured the accomplishment perfectly. "Plant a Jewish people in a country that comes to a standstill on Yom Kippur; speaks the language of the Bible; moves to the rhythms of the Hebrew (lunar) calendar; builds cities with the stones of its ancestors; produces Hebrew poetry and literature, Jewish scholarship and learning unmatched anywhere in the world—and you have continuity."[5]

THE ZIONIST MOVEMENT HAD made the Jewish people a variety of promises. Some had come to fruition, others had not.

In *The Jewish State*, Theodor Herzl asserted that if the Jews had a state of their own, anti-Semitism in Europe would wither. That prediction has proven sadly naive; European anti-Semitism is growing at an alarming rate, French Jews are fleeing Europe, and all across the continent Jews are watching anti-Semitic parties on both the radical left and the fascist right with increased wariness.

In ways that Herzl would not have anticipated, however, the Jewish state has had a profound effect on the *Jews* of the Diaspora. Though Judaism is about much more than Israel, it is Israel that galvanizes Diaspora Jews more than any other issue. It is only Israel that gets Jews across the globe to join rallies and marches in huge numbers. Most other dimensions of Jewish life have been relegated to the realm of the private, and between denominations, differences in practice are so wide that varying Jewish communities often have little common ground. Where they do come together, and where Judaism leaves the private sphere and enters the public square, is when Diaspora Jews think about—and argue about—what is happening in the Jewish state. In ways that Jacob Blaustein could not have anticipated, American Jews agree with him that they are not in exile, yet Israel somehow captures their attention and concern in ways that no other Jewish issue does. So Herzl was not entirely wrong; the Jewish state *has,* indeed, transformed Jewish life in the Diaspora.

In *Altneuland,* Herzl shared a utopian vision of a reborn Jewish people in its ancestral homeland, entirely at peace with the surrounding populations. Parts of that vision have, indeed, come to fruition. Despite much work that remains, Israeli Arabs have made professional, academic, social, and economic progress in Israel. They are surgeons and engineers, lawyers and members of the Supreme Court. Bedouin women study medicine at Israeli universities.

As complex as the standing of Israeli Arabs is, the Jewish state's relations with Arabs outside Israel are infinitely more fraught. The conflict with its neighbors grinds on endlessly, with no end and no solution in sight. The international community has tired of the conflict, and inside the Jewish state, many Israelis feel stuck. They believe that the occupation is proving Yeshayahu Leibowitz correct. They fear that occupying another people has forced Israelis to be something they did not want to be, and yet for many, it is not clear at present what the alternative is. Polls show that most Israelis would like to end the occupation; polls also show that given the facts on the ground, most Israelis are not willing to take the security risks that relinquishing that land in the present circumstances would likely mean. The occupation in all its manifestations remains one of the most pained dimensions of contemporary Israeli life.

Yet many other facets of the Zionist dream have more than exceeded the Jewish people's wildest hopes. Eliezer Ben-Yehuda imagined a world in which the Jewish people spoke Hebrew again. But did he dare dream of millions of people speaking the language, of Hebrew writers being recognized as among the world's greatest novelists and poets? Could he have envisioned Israeli bookstores with thousands of volumes written in a language that a century and a half ago hardly anyone in the world spoke?

It is no accident that Israel's Declaration of Independence mentions the revival of Hebrew. For the renewal of that ancient language has become a metaphor for the renewal of the richness of Jewish life and the Jewish people that has unfolded in the Jewish state in a way that cannot be replicated anywhere else in the world.

A. D. Gordon urged the Jews to return to working their land, to revive their people by dirtying themselves with the earth of their ancestral home. They did. Even in the high-tech nation that Israel has become, Israelis are still farmers. Israel leads the world in water technology. Hiking the land, from north to south, is still an Israeli passion, for the young as well as for their parents and even grandparents. National parks are filled to capacity on holidays and vacations. Israelis have planted 250 million trees in the past hundred years, and Israel is one of only two countries in the world that ended the twentieth century with more trees than it had had a century earlier.[6] Israelis do not all have their hands in the earth the way that Gordon might have hoped, but they have, indeed, fallen in love with a land that not long ago was off-limits to most of the Jewish people.

Bialik, Nordau, and Jabotinsky all urged the Jewish people to be victims no longer, and Israel has realized that vision, too. Israel still fights terror and worries about the specter of an Iranian nuclear weapon, but for three-quarters of a century, Jews have defended themselves and, in ways that no one could have imagined, have become one of the world's leading fighting forces. Today's Israeli is radically different from the European Jews who were the objects of Bialik's accusation in "The City of Slaughter."

The use of military force is never morally uncomplicated, particularly when arrayed largely against a terrorist infrastructure purposely situated in the midst of a civilian population. Israel has not avoided those moral complexities, and it has at times stumbled—even very badly. But Colonel Kemp had pointed to a critical truth—the IDF, he said, goes to greater lengths than any other army in the world to avert civilian casualties.[7] Of that, too, the vast majority of Israelis, though deeply concerned about the conflict, are very proud.

Ahad Ha'am's dream of a spiritual renewal in the Land of Israel has come about as well. Israelis are engaging with Jewish tradition and their people's classic texts in ways that would have shocked David Ben-Gurion. Israel is a country where authors and poets are household names, where many of the leading social activists are the leading novelists, where poets and writers appear on the country's currency, where, when Israelis want someone to speak truth to power, they often turn to a writer.

Herzl promised the readers of *Altneuland* not only a Jewish safe haven, but a Jewish state that would be a source of progress and continuous growth. That dream, too, has been fulfilled. A tiny country the size of New Jersey with a population roughly equivalent to that of Los Angeles is a world leader in medical technology. In a 2015 ranking of the world's top universities, Hebrew University was ranked at number 67, the Technion (Israel's equivalent of MIT) at 77, the Weizmann Institute between 101 and 150, and Tel Aviv University between 151 and 200.[8*] The Jewish tradition's focus on learning, reflected in the suggestion at the First Zionist Con-

---

* In contrast, it is worth noting, there was not a single university from a Muslim country that ranked in the top 250, despite the oil-rich Arab nations that have no limit at all on the resources they could spend on creating such institutions. In the rankings mentioned in the text, King Fahd University of Petroleum and Minerals in Saudi Arabia was ranked highest among them at 266, and it was followed by the National University of Sciences and Technology in Pakistan, at 350.

gress that the Yishuv create a university even before statehood, has yielded extraordinary results, including numerous Nobel Prizes in science, economics, and literature.

Herzl's vision also spoke of a state that would share the wealth of its progress and technology with other peoples across the world, and Israel has done that, too. Menachem Begin's first act as prime minister in 1977 was to instruct an Israeli vessel to save dozens of Vietnamese boat people floating hopelessly and without drinking water on the open seas, after ships from other countries had ignored them. Israel brought them to its shores and made them all citizens. Later, U.S. president Jimmy Carter, hardly a friend of Israel, commended Begin for that decision. "It was an act of compassion, an act of sensitivity," Carter said, "and a recognition of him and his government about the importance of a home for people who were destitute and who would like to express their own individuality and freedom in a common way, again typifying the historic struggle of the people of Israel."⁹

Begin's decision had been rooted in Jewish history, precisely as Herzl had predicted. "We have never forgotten the lot of our people, persecuted, humiliated, ultimately physically destroyed," Begin responded to Carter. "Therefore, it was natural that my first act as Prime Minister was to give those people a haven in the Land of Israel."¹⁰ Over the years, Israel has led critical humanitarian missions to respond to many natural disasters, often setting up the first and largest emergency hospitals.

Herzl's Zionist congresses were democratic, and Israel has continued that tradition. Some one hundred countries have been created since World War II (mostly as a result of the collapse of empires), and Israel is one of the very few that began as a democracy and have continued to function as a democracy without interruption.

Although there is much work to do on gender equality in Israel, too, it is also worth noting that Israel is the only country in the democratic world in which women are drafted into the army and

have been since the state's creation. It was also one of the first democracies to elect a woman as prime minister and one of the first
to have a woman as head of its Supreme Court.

ISRAELIS HAVE MUCH TO be worried about and know that many
dimensions of their country need improving. But most still believe,
unabashedly, that their country is a story of extraordinary accomplishment. Nor are they the only ones who see matters that way.
Fouad Ajami, a Lebanese-born Shiite Muslim, was born in 1945 and
grew up in southern Lebanon, just over the border with Israel. In
1991, he recalled that

> at night, a searchlight from the Jewish village of Metullah could
> be seen from the high ridge on which my [own] village lay. The
> searchlight was a subject of childhood fascination. The search-
> light was from the land of the Jews, my grandfather said. . . . In
> the open, barren country, by the border, that land of the Jews
> could be seen and the chatter of its people heard across the
> barbed wire.[11]

Ajami chose to do more than to hear the chatter, and years later,
spent time in the Jewish state. Summarizing what he had encountered, he wrote:

> On a barren, small piece of land, the Zionists built a durable
> state. It was military but not militaristic. It took in waves of refu-
> gees and refashioned them into citizens. It had room for faith but
> remained a secular enterprise. Under conditions of a long siege,
> it maintained a deep and abiding democratic ethos. The Arabs
> could have learned from this experiment, but they drew back in
> horror.[12]

It would be difficult to summarize the accomplishments of the
Jewish state more succinctly.

WHAT LAY AHEAD? Israelis knew that they could not know. Zionists have known from the outset that they dare not even ask.

Natan Alterman wrote a poem in 1947, "Summer Quarrel," in which he depicted Israelis of varying sorts as different women. Who would Israelis be? What would they be like? What would their future hold?

> *How will be the cities between Sidon and Philistia?*
> *Will storms bring them thunders and rain? Shush your dispute!*
> *Tomorrow's Shulamit is dressing in her room.*
> *Do not dare peep through that keyhole!*[13]

Living in Israel meant knowing that there was no keyhole through which to glimpse the future. Yet while Israelis understood that they could not know what the future held, there were hints based on what they had already experienced. A century after Balfour, Zionism is a story of extraordinary accomplishments. Even when it seemed imposible, the Yishuv and then the state had always beaten the odds.

Most Israelis were convinced that they and their still young country would manage to overcome whatever challenges might come their way. They had no choice.

Ensuring that Israel would thrive was their most fundamental and profound responsibility. Just as failure had not been an option in 1948, it was not an option now. Too much was at stake, for Israel was much more than a state. Zionism had begun as the national liberation movement of the Jewish people, and Israel was the embodiment of a rich conversation still unfolding, of a grand idea that had become reality. What was at stake was much more than the virtually miraculous country that they, their parents, and their grandparents had created and cultivated. What was truly at stake, they knew, was the very future of the people that the Jewish state had been created to save.

ACKNOWLEDGMENTS

I have benefited from the support, assistance, and encouragement of many people while writing this book, and it is a pleasure to have an opportunity to thank them.

Shalem College, Israel's first liberal arts college, is a fascinating and inspiring place to work. Many of Shalem College's faculty and staff have made my work on this book possible. To Daniel Polisar, Seth Goldstein, and Ido Hevroni, my gratitude for their understanding of the time that this book took even as we were building a college together.

I cannot conceive of a colleague more supportive of another's work than Dan has consistently been of mine. Dan read this manuscript, with a fine-tooth comb and in its entirety, several times as it evolved, made invaluable suggestions about tone and scope, and saved me from numerous gaffes. The time he invested in this project, and his encouragement of it from the outset, have been far beyond what I had any right to expect. Dan's unique combination of prodigious knowledge, extraordinary competence, and utter selflessness is but one of the many reasons that so many of us at Shalem hold him in such high regard.

To Yudi Levi, David Messer, and Yair Shamir, chairs of our boards during the period that I wrote this book, and to the members of Shalem College's board of directors, my thanks for their consistent support, understanding, and encouragement.

Without the financial support of several generous friends, this book could not have come to be. Terry Kassel and Paul Singer, of the Paul E. Singer Foundation, championed the project before anyone else, and their generosity single-handedly made its launch possible. Jonathon and Joanna Jacobson of the Jacobson Family Foundation also contributed very generous financial support. Rabbi Robert Hirt and Virginia Bayer have supported previous books of mine and generously continued to underwrite my work with this one, as well. To all, my thanks for their friendship and profound generosity. For several years, I have had the honor of being the Koret Fellow at Shalem College. I am deeply grateful to the Koret Foundation for its support and to Anita Friedman and Jeffrey Farber for their friendship.

Many friends, colleagues, academics, and family members shared expertise, assisted with bibliographic searches, or provided materials I would otherwise not have come across. Warm thanks to Rina Bardin, Menachem Ben Sasson, Marc Brettler, Sergio Dellapergola, Elana Gordis, Barry Levenfeld, Samantha Margolis, David Matlow, Matthew Miller, Benny Morris, Fania Oz-Salzberger, Leah Sarna, Anita Shapira, Ariel Sheetrit, Yossi Siegel, Ken Stein, Nava Winkler, and Jacob Wright. David Brummer joined our team for several months and I am grateful for his contributions to the research. To Ari Hoffman, who spent a summer reading the manuscript even while working on his Ph.D. in literature at Harvard, my thanks for his insight and suggestions. To Yaacov Lozowick, the chief archivist at the Israel State Archives, and Guy Jamo of the Central Zionist Archive, many thanks for all their assistance. To Zion Ozeri, a longtime cherished friend and one of the world's leading photographers of the Jewish people, my thanks for permission to use his photograph of a Russian immigrant to Israel.

Several of Israel's thought leaders consented to be interviewed for the book, and their insights substantially enriched the final product. For their time and wisdom, my thanks to Ruth Calderon, Micha Goodman, Donniel Hartman, Avi Katzman, Yossi Klein Halevi, and Saul Singer.

Several friends and colleagues offered to read the manuscript in a late but not final stage and made substantive suggestions that dramatically improved the final product. At different stages, Martin Kramer and Seth Goldstein both read the manuscript and marked it up carefully, making many valuable suggestions. Several other friends and colleagues did the same. For this, my thanks go to Daniel Bonner, Yonatan Gordis, Yossi Klein Halevi, Jon Jacobson, Terry Kassel, Seth Klarman, Jay Lefkowitz, Jeffrey Swartz, Judy Swartz, Ilan Troen, and Lisa Wallack. Carolyn Hessel, a legend in the world of Jewish books, has been a mentor, friend, and muse for years; she, too, read early drafts of this book more than once, and for her many suggestions and ongoing encouragement, I am deeply grateful.

Several of these readers were in wide disagreement about the tone of this book. While some thought that I had set the vector more or less correctly, others felt that the book was far too critical of Israel in places while still others, who read identical versions, felt that I'd given Israel "a pass" in areas where much sterner critique was in order. That is the nature of a book like this—the discourse about Israel is too laden for any one approach or tone to satisfy everyone. In the end, the book reflects my own sentiments about Israel and my own read of this inspiring yet complicated country.

This book's tone has been enhanced and made more nuanced by the comments of all the readers—my friends—mentioned here, and I am grateful for their time, wisdom, and honesty. It goes without saying that responsibility for the tone and content of this book, as well as for any errors, is mine alone.

I HAVE BEEN WORKING with Richard Pine, my literary agent, for more than twenty years, and remain deeply grateful not only for his professionalism and friendship, but for the sage advice he has shared over these past two decades as well. To the entire team at Ecco/HarperCollins, many thanks for their excellence. To Emma Janaskie, my editor, and Miriam Parker, associate publisher, my thanks for all they did to improve drafts of this manuscript, photos, and maps. The maps in this book are as useful and attractive as they are thanks to the talents of Joe LeMonnier. To Suet Chong, senior design manager, my thanks for the design of this volume, and the layout of its maps and photos. And to Laurie McGee, much appreciation for her meticulous work in copyediting the manuscript.

MANY YEARS AGO, ELISHEVA and I were fortunate enough to meet David and Ellen Chaikof on a mountaintop in Colorado. Cherished friends ever since then, practically family now, they have during more than one summer afforded us a respite from the pressures of Israeli life. Parts of this book had their beginnings at a lakeside paradise in which they made us feel utterly at home. David's mother, Bayla Chaikof, is a revered educator in Toronto and a woman whose love for Israel and wistful recollections of an Israeli era long since gone have animated many an energetic summertime conversation. I've included Bayla in the dedication for this book as a small and inadequate token of our thanks to the entire Chaikof clan for their abiding friendship.

Not a day goes by when we do not feel deep appreciation to Pinchas and Sandy Lozowick for making it all possible when we first got to Jerusalem almost twenty years ago. Time has done nothing to erode our gratitude.

TRANSLATIONS FROM THE HEBREW Bible are based on the *Tanakh: The Holy Scriptures, The New JPS Translation According to the Traditional Hebrew Text,* though often with emendations on my part.

FROM THE VERY OUTSET of this project, I had the great fortune of working with two outstanding research assistants, Rachel Greenspan and Allie Mayer Feuerstein. During the second year of our work on the book, Rachel served as lead researcher. When Rachel moved on to a position at Jerusalem's City Hall, Allie stepped to the plate and carried an enormous load on her own, working intensively for months to complete the process of getting this book done. They are both extremely bright, hard workers, devoted colleagues, and excellent writers.

Rachel and Allie helped conceive the book's structure, did research, outlined, edited and reedited, attended to logistics such as bibliographies, notes, and permissions for photographs, and much, much more. While the three of us have much in common—we were all raised and educated on the East Coast of the United States and then made aliyah, for example—we are also of different generations and occupy different spots on the political and religious spectra, which by nature shaped our respective views of the events and epochs described in this book. For almost two years, we disagreed and cajoled, made our cases, and honed one another's views. This book has Rachel's and Allie's intellectual and moral fingerprints on every page, and I am grateful not only for their manifold contributions to the book, but for their collegiality and for the sheer pleasure of having worked with them both.

THE PERIOD IN WHICH this book was written was one of both great sadness and unmitigated joy for our family. Shortly after work on the book began, my father took ill and some months later, passed away. Elisheva and our children could not have been more supportive during a year that had more than its share of agonizing moments, and I am grateful to all of them for their unfailing love and devotion, both to my father and to me. For many years, by virtue of her decision that we should live in Israel, Elisheva has shown our children—Talia and Avishay, Avi and Micha—what it means to live a life shaped by principle and conviction; they are, I think, finally old enough to fully appreciate how extraordinary is the woman they are blessed to have as their mother. More recently, as she has taken the lead in caring for my mother, Elisheva has modeled for all of us once again what selflessness means.

Elisheva's voluminous knowledge of Israel and its history enriched this volume in ways too numerous to count. She is also an extraordinarily talented editor, and her keen eye for detail and style caught many a gaffe before it was too late. Even after many others had gone through the manuscript, she made numerous wise suggestions and improved countless passages in this book. For all that, and for infinitely more, I am deeply in her debt. No words could begin to suffice in thanking her or expressing our collective love for all she is and does.

JUST ONE WEEK BEFORE we lost him, my father had the privilege of meeting his first great-grandchild, to whom this volume is dedicated. Working on this book as Ella was born and began to discover the world around her, I was often reminded that she is, in our line of the family tree, the first child to be born in the Land of Israel in many centuries. That has been a humbling yet profoundly satisfying awareness. Though she is still just a very young child, she has brought into our lives more unbounded joy than any of us could have imagined.

I wish her, our first "daughter of Zion," to paraphrase the verse that appears in the dedication at the opening of this book, a life of great joy and grand dreams, of deep satisfaction and of devotion to her people.

Jerusalem
May 2016
5 Iyar 5776, the sixty-eighth anniversary of Israel's Independence

GLOSSARY OF PEOPLE MENTIONED

Aaronsohn Family (Aaron & Sarah)—Siblings Aaron and Sarah formed a spy ring, called Nili, during World War I to provide intelligence to the British. The Ottomans eventually discovered the ring and then jailed, tortured, and killed many of the group's members. Aaron and Sarah became Zionist heroes and icons.

Abbas, Mahmoud "Abu Mazen"—Appointed by Yasser Arafat as the Palestinian Authority's first prime minister, Abbas was a negotiator of the Oslo Accords. He took over as president of the Palestinian Authority after Arafat's death.

Ahad Ha'am (Asher Zvi Ginzberg)—A leading Zionist thinker opposed to Herzl's idea of a state, Ahad Ha'am favored establishing a Jewish spiritual center in Palestine.

al-Assad, Hafez—Syrian president from 1971 to 2000. In tandem with Anwar Sadat, Assad launched the Yom Kippur War attack on Israel in 1973, and as late as 1996, refused to make peace with Israel.

al-Hussein, Abdullah I (bin)—King of Transjordan (renamed Jordan in 1949) from 1946 to 1951, King Abdullah had warmer relations with the Yishuv and Israeli leaders than any other Arab leader. He was assassinated in 1951 after rumors spread that he was considering peace talks with Israel.

al-Husseini, Haj Amin—Grand mufti of Jerusalem between 1921 and 1937, al-Husseini, leader of the Arab Higher Committee, did all in his power to block Jewish immigration and settlement in Palestine. During World War II he assisted with the development of Nazi propaganda in the Muslim world.

Allon, Yigal—A founder of the Palmach, Israeli politician, and IDF general. Allon devised a plan to annex some of the land captured in 1967 and to return the rest to the Jordanians. The plan was never acted on.

Arafat, Yasser—Founder of Fatah in the late 1950s, and later chairman of the PLO, Arafat was recognized as the political leader of the Palestinians. Mastermind of a campaign of terror not only in Israel, but in the world at large, he also signed the Oslo Accords but ultimately refused to make peace with Israel.

Ariel, Meir—A soldier in the unit that helped capture the Old City of Jerusalem in 1967, Ariel became a leading Israeli musician and the voice of a generation unsettled by Israel's occupation of the West Bank. His alternative to Naomi Shemer's "Jerusalem of Gold," called "Jerusalem of Iron," helped launch his career.

Arlosoroff, Chaim—Head of the Jewish Agency's political department, Arlosoroff developed the *Ha'avara*, or Transfer Agreement, that enabled German Jews to move their money to Palestine, while creating a market for German goods. Many people in the Yishuv were furious that Arlosoroff negotiated with the Nazis. He was assassinated in 1933.

Balfour, Arthur—As the United Kingdom's foreign secretary, Balfour wrote a letter to Lord Rothschild declaring, "His Majesty's Government views with favour the establishment in Palestine of a national home for the Jewish people." It was the first step in the international community's endorsement of the idea of a Jewish state.

Bar Kokhba (Simeon Bar Kokhba)—Sixty-two years after the Romans had destroyed the Second Temple, Bar Kokhba staged a revolt against the occupying empire in 132 CE. Eventually, Rome's massive army in 135 CE overran Bar Kokhba's forces, but Bar Kokhba remained a symbol of rebelliousness against foreign occupying powers.

Barak, Ehud—Former IDF general who served as prime minister from 1999 to 2001. He withdrew Israeli troops from Lebanon in 2000 and participated in peace negotiations with Clinton and Arafat at Camp David.

Begin, Menachem—Leader of the Irgun during the revolt against the British and then leader of the political opposition from 1948 to 1977.

Begin was then elected prime minister. He made peace with Egypt, bombed the Osirak nuclear plant in Iraq, and invaded Lebanon.

Ben-Gurion, David (David Gruen)—After immigrating to Palestine in 1906, Ben-Gurion quickly rose to power and ultimately became the leader of the Yishuv. He declared Israel's independence and led the country as its first prime minister.

Ben-Yehuda, Eliezer (Eliezer Perlman)—The father of the modern Hebrew language, Ben-Yehuda believed that Jewish renewal in the Land of Israel also required a renewal of Hebrew as a spoken language.

Berdyczewski, Micha Josef—A Jewish Russian scholar who believed that Zionism was a revolt against Judaism itself. He famously said, "We can be the last Jews or the first Hebrews."

Bernadotte, Count Folke—A Swedish diplomat, Bernadotte was appointed by the UN secretary-general to negotiate cease-fires during the War of Independence. Bernadotte was assassinated by the Jewish underground.

Bialik, Chaim Nachman—The world's leading Jewish poet during his lifetime, he gave expression to the yearnings of an entire generation and became a key voice in the Zionist movement. His funeral in Tel Aviv in 1934 was attended by thousands.

Blaustein, Jacob—President of the American Jewish Committee, Blaustein reflected American Jews' ambivalent attitude toward Israel. His belief that Jews in America were no longer living in exile and that Israel dare not declare itself the center of Jewish life led to fierce conflict with Ben-Gurion.

Bluwstein Sela, Rachel (Rachel the Poetess)—After moving to Palestine, Bluwstein joined the kibbutz Degania. She soon thereafter fell ill with tuberculosis and was banned from the kibbutz. Her poetry is still studied and sung a century later.

Brenner, Yosef Chaim—One of the greatest Hebrew writers of the Second Aliyah, Brenner wrote about the many struggles of early Yishuv life. He was killed in Arab riots in Jaffa.

Cyrus, King of Persia—When the Persian Empire overtook the Babylonians in 539 BCE, King Cyrus allowed the Jews, who were then in exile, to return to their home and rebuild their temple in Jerusalem.

Darwish, Mahmoud—Palestinian poet who wrote about the homelessness of the Palestinian people and expressed their longing for their homes in Palestine.

Dayan, Moshe—A member of the Haganah, Dayan became the IDF's chief of staff in 1953. He oversaw the IDF's battle in the 1967 Six-Day War and was defense minister during the Yom Kippur War.

Deri, Aryeh—One of Israel's first successful Mizrachi politicians. As a leader of the Shas Party, Deri rose to national political prominence before being felled by corruption scandals.

Eban, Abba—An Israeli diplomat and politician, Eban served in many positions, including as Israel's ambassador to the United States and to the UN. Eban, serving as Israel's foreign minister during 1967, worked tirelessly to garner international support for Israel in the face of the looming war.

Eichmann, Adolf—A Nazi leader who was a key player in the Wannsee Conference and one of the architects of the Final Solution, Eichmann was captured by Israel's Mossad in 1960 in Argentina. He was later convicted and is, to date, the only person in Israel ever to have received the death penalty.

Elazar, David (Dado)—A top military general, Elazar was instrumental in capturing the Golan Heights during the Six-Day War. As the IDF's chief of staff during the Yom Kippur War, he was found responsible for multiple failures by the Agranat Commission and was stripped of his position.

Eshkol, Levi—Israel's third prime minister, Eshkol served from 1963 until his death in 1969. When many lost confidence in him during the weeks leading up to the Six-Day War, he became the first prime minister to forge a national unity government.

Gemayel, Bashir—Head of Lebanon's Christian Phalangist Party. Menachem Begin hoped that with Israel's help, Gemayel and his forces would control Lebanon, ending the PLO's dominance in the south. When Gemayel was killed, Begin's plan came to naught.

Goldstein, Baruch—An American religious immigrant to Israel, Goldstein killed twenty-nine Palestinians praying by the Cave of Patriarchs in February 1994. Reviled by most of Israel and the Jewish world, to a small radical fringe he became a hero.

Gordon, Aaron David (A. D. Gordon)—An influential shaper of Labor Zionism, Gordon believed the redemption of the Jews would come from working the land. Gordon's philosophy played a significant role in shaping the image of the new Jew working the land in Palestine and in the kibbutz movement.

Goren, Rabbi Shlomo—As chief rabbi of the IDF during the Six-Day War, Goren came to the Temple Mount after its capture with a shofar and Torah scroll in hand. Later, as Israel's chief rabbi, and despite his legal genius and history of courageous rulings, Goren was slow to recognize Ethiopian immigrants as Jews.

Gouri, Haim—An Israeli writer, Gouri captured many of Israel's pivotal moments through poetry, including poems on the Lamed Heh and the Six-Day War.

Greenberg, Uri Zvi—One of the leading poets of the Yishuv, Greenberg was a follower of Jabotinsky's Revisionist movement.

Hananiah—A little-known biblical prophet, Hananiah prophesied that redemption would come much more quickly than Jeremiah believed. His views were adopted by those who denied that Jews had to acquiesce to exile. (See *Jeremiah*)

Herzl, Theodor—The father of political Zionism, Herzl became a household name with the publication of his book *The Jewish State*. A year later, Herzl assembled Jews from all over the world at his Zionist congress, which launched the Zionist movement.

Hess, Moses—An early Zionist thinker and writer, Hess proposed the idea of a Jewish state in 1862 in his book *Rome and Jerusalem*. His book, while very similar in content to Herzl's *The Jewish State*, was largely ignored.

Hussein, ibn Tala—King of Jordan from 1952 until his death in 1999, Hussein waged war against Israel in 1967 but in 1973 warned Israel of an impending attack and did the best he could to stay out of that war.

In 1994 Jordan and Israel signed a peace treaty and King Hussein later gave a moving eulogy at Yitzhak Rabin's funeral.

Jabotinsky, Ze'ev (Vladimir)—The creator of Revisionist Zionism, Jabotinsky believed that establishing and maintaining a Jewish state in Palestine would require a willingness to use force. The forebear of the political Right in Israel, Jabotinsky was also Menachem Begin's prime inspiration.

Jeremiah—A leading biblical prophet during the Babylonian exile, Jeremiah prophesied that the exile would last for seventy years, following which the Jews would return home. He urged them to settle in their foreign lands and establish lives for themselves there. (See *Hananiah*)

Kadishai, Yechiel—An Irgun fighter, Kadishai became Menachem Begin's close friend and political confidant. He was a passenger on the *Altalena* but escaped the episode unharmed.

Kasztner, Rudolf—As head of the Zionist Rescue Committee in Hungary during the Holocaust, Kasztner made a deal with the Germans in 1944 to exchange trucks for Jews. After Malkiel Gruenwald called Kasztner a "vicarious murderer," Kasztner sued Gruenwald for slander but was publicly humiliated when Gruenwald was exonerated. Kasztner was later assassinated.

Kissinger, Henry—An American diplomat, Kissinger served as national security adviser from 1969 to 1975 and as secretary of state between 1973 and 1977. He played key roles in advising the White House during times of war, and, later, seeking to negotiate a Middle East peace.

Kook, Rabbi Abraham Isaac—A scholar and mystic, Rabbi Kook was one of the few religious Zionist leaders who embraced secular pioneers in Palestine. He later became the chief rabbi of the Yishuv.

Kook, Rabbi Zvi Yehudah—The son of Rabbi Abraham Isaac Kook, he was at the forefront as religious Zionists moved from the sidelines toward the center of Israeli society and politics. His ideology was a cornerstone of the Gush Emunim settlement movement.

Lapid, Tommy—An Israeli journalist and politician and a Holocaust survivor, Lapid served in the Knesset from 1999 to 2006. A well-known author and television personality, Lapid was a fierce political opponent of the ultra-Orthodox parties.

Lapid, Yair—Son of Tommy Lapid, Yair is also a journalist and politician and founder of the centrist Yesh Atid political party.

Leibowitz, Yeshayahu—An Israeli Orthodox public intellectual, Leibowitz was a strong advocate for returning the territories captured in the Six-Day War and predicted that ruling over another people would destroy Israel.

Lloyd George, David—Prime minister of Great Britain from 1916 to 1922 and sympathetic to the Zionist cause, Lloyd George supported the Balfour Declaration in 1917.

Mapu, Avraham—An early Zionist thinker, Mapu wrote the first Hebrew novel in 1853. Called *The Love of Zion*, the novel set in ancient biblical Israel sold very well and inspired many, including David Ben-Gurion.

Meir, Golda (Golda Meyerson)—Head of the political departments of both the Histadrut and the Jewish Agency, Meir served in the Knesset as minister of labor and foreign minister. She was elected as Israel's first female prime minister in 1969 and held that position until 1974.

Nasser, Gamal Abdel—Egypt's president from 1956 until his death in 1970, Nasser led Pan-Arabism and sought to unite the Arab people around destroying Israel. He nationalized the Suez Canal, which led to the 1956 Sinai Campaign, and later triggered the Six-Day War.

Nebuchadnezzar—King during Babylonia's rule over Judea, Nebuchadnezzar destroyed the First Temple in 586 BCE and exiled the Israelites.

Netanyahu, Benjamin—Leader of the Likud Party, Netanyahu served as prime minister between 1996 and 1999 and was elected again in 2009. He is considered by many the political disciple of Jabotinsky and Begin.

Nordau, Max—An early Zionist thinker, Nordau was a leader of political Zionism and an ally of Theodor Herzl. He championed a vision of a new Jew with a focus on physical strength.

Olmert, Ehud—An Israeli politician, Olmert replaced Ariel Sharon and served as prime minister from 2006 to 2009. He planned to continue

Sharon's disengagement policies but was felled by scandal. He became Israel's first former prime minister to be sent to jail.

Oz, Amos—One of Israel's leading novelists, Oz became a powerful voice for the Israeli Left.

Peres, Shimon—An Israeli politician and diplomat, Peres has held multiple government positions, including two stints as the country's prime minister, and was Israel's president between 2007 and 2014. Peres played a central role in developing Israel's nuclear capabilities and in negotiating the Oslo Accords.

Pinsker, Leon—An early Zionist thinker, Pinsker wrote *Auto-Emancipation* in 1882 encouraging Jews to strive for independence and national rebirth. Pinsker established *Hovevei Zion,* one of the first European organizations created to foster Jewish immigration to Palestine, in 1882.

Porat, Hanan—A paratrooper during the Six-Day War, Porat was one of the soldiers who captured the Old City of Jerusalem. The religious Porat and some of his friends built the first settlement rebuilt after the recapture of Gush Etzion in 1967.

Rabin, Yitzhak—An Israeli general and politician, Rabin fought in the Palmach and IDF, eventually becoming the army's chief of staff during the Six-Day War. Prime minister between 1974 and 1977 and again in 1992, Rabin made peace with Jordan and signed the Oslo Accords. He was assassinated in November 1995.

Rothschild, Baron Edmond—Called "The Well-Known Benefactor," Baron Rothschild almost single-handedly supported the Yishuv during its early years. While he poured millions of dollars into settling Palestine, many new immigrants resented what they saw as his interference in their pioneering work.

Rotberg, Roi—One of many Israelis killed by Arab infiltrators, called *fedayeen* (Arabic for "self-sacrificers"), Rotberg became known as a result of Moshe Dayan's eulogy at his funeral. Dayan spoke about the inevitability of a long and costly conflict between Israel and its neighbors.

Sadat, Anwar—Succeeding Nasser as president after his death, Sadat served as Egypt's president from 1970 until his assassination in 1981.

He waged war against Israel in 1973, but signed a peace agreement with Begin in 1978.

Senesh, Chanah—After volunteering as a paratrooper for the British army during World War II and parachuting into Yugoslavia, Senesh was captured by the Germans and was jailed, tortured, and eventually executed. She became a national Israeli hero.

Shamir, Yitzhak—A former leader of the Lechi, Shamir became an Israeli politician and served as prime minister twice, from 1983 to 1984 and 1986 to 1992, representing the Likud Party.

Sharansky, Natan—Imprisoned by the Soviet Union on false charges of being a spy, Sharansky became an international Jewish hero and human rights activist. Released after nine years, he immigrated to Israel, where he became involved in politics as the voice of the country's growing Russian population.

Sharett, Moshe—Sharett was Israel's second prime minister, from 1954 to 1955.

Sharon, Ariel—An Israeli general and politician, Sharon played an instrumental role in almost all of Israel's wars. After retiring from his military career, he joined the Likud Party and served as prime minister from 2001 to 2006. As prime minister, he created the Kadima Party and led the disengagement from Gaza.

Shemer, Naomi—An Israeli musician and songwriter, Shemer was a national star. Two of her most famous songs are "Jerusalem of Gold," written two weeks before the Six-Day War, and "Let It Be," written after the Yom Kippur War.

Stavsky, Avraham—A member of Betar, Stavsky was originally convicted but then acquitted of the murder of Haim Arlosoroff, the creator of the Transfer Agreement. He was killed in the *Altalena* battle.

Stern, Avraham—A former member of the Irgun, Stern, in 1940, broke away, creating his own underground fighting force called the Lechi. The British killed him in 1942 after a relentless manhunt.

Trumpeldor, Joseph—A war hero and Zionist activist, Trumpeldor helped create the Zionist Mule Corps, the first organized fighting force in the Yishuv. He was killed defending the settlement of Tel Hai in 1920.

Weizmann, Chaim—Weizmann was the president of the World Zionist Organization and Israel's first president. He was instrumental in securing the Balfour Declaration and in the establishment of Hebrew University. He also founded the Weizmann Institute of Science.

Yadin, Yigael—An Israeli archeologist, general, and politician, Yadin was head of operations for the Haganah during the War of Independence and served as the IDF's second chief of staff.

Yavetz, Ze'ev—After immigrating to Palestine in 1887, Yavetz was the first to publish a modern Hebrew novel there. After a falling-out with Baron de Rothschild, Yavetz left Palestine.

Yizhar, S. (Yizhar Smilansky)—An Israeli author, Yizhar published a novel, *Khirbet Khizeh,* that sought to capture the human suffering Israeli forces had caused the Palestinians during the 1948 war. His book became part of the curriculum in Israeli schools, and Yizhar was elected a member of the Knesset for several terms.

Yosef, Rabbi Ovadia—A legal genius and popular rabbi to Israel's Mizrachim, Rabbi Ovadia, upon completing his tenure as the Sephardic chief rabbi of Israel, formed the Shas Party, the first political party representing Mizrachim.

Zangwill, Israel—A novelist and playwright, Zangwill was a Zionist thinker who described Palestine as a "land without a people, waiting for a people without a land." Zangwill, like Herzl, believed that a mass migration of Jews from Europe to Palestine would serve both Jews and Palestine.

GLOSSARY OF NON-ENGLISH TERMS

aliyah—From the Hebrew verb "to go up," aliyah is used to refer to people moving to Israel. It is also used to describe a wave of immigration to Palestine or Israel, as in the First Aliyah or the Russian Aliyah.

Ashkenazi—The name for the Jews from most of Europe (Ashkenazim in the plural). The Ashkenazim built communities throughout central and eastern Europe, developing their own set of religious and cultural traditions and even creating their own language, Yiddish.

Biluim—Bilu is an acronym for the Hebrew phrase "House of Jacob, let us go up." Biluim, the plural of Bilu, refers to a group of Russian students who immigrated to Palestine during the First Aliyah.

Brit Shalom—Hebrew for "The Covenant of Peace," *Brit Shalom* was a group of intellectuals in Palestine founded in 1925 to promote peace between Jews and Arabs. They believed peace would come if the Jews abandoned their quest for national sovereignty.

conceptzia—A Hebrew word based on the English "conception," *conceptzia* was created to refer to Israel's cockiness and sense of invincibility in the years between the 1967 Six-Day War and the 1973 Yom Kippur War.

Eretz Israel—Hebrew for "The Land of Israel."

Fedayeen—Arabic for "self-sacrificers," *fedayeen* is a term commonly used to refer to guerrilla fighters who attacked Israelis mostly in the 1950s. Self-described freedom fighters, they crossed the Jordanian and Egyptian borders to attack Israeli villages and towns.

Fellahin—Arabic for "farmers" or "laborers."

Gush Emunim—Hebrew for "The Bloc of the Faithful," Gush Emunim was a political movement created in 1974 centered around building settlements in the post-1967 territories.

ha'avarah—Hebrew for "transfer," *ha'avarah* refers to the Transfer Agreement negotiated between Chaim Arlosoroff and the Nazis that allowed Jews leaving Germany to retain their assets through a complex arrangement with the German government.

Haganah—Hebrew for "The Defense," the Haganah was created in 1921 by Yishuv leaders to protect Jewish farms and villages by preventing and repelling Arab attacks. With time, it would develop into the Israel Defense Forces.

Halakhah—A term for "Jewish law."

Hamtanah—Hebrew for "the waiting period," it refers to the three weeks prior to the June 1967 Six-Day War, during which Israel and its leadership knew that another war with its Arab neighbors was imminent. The country prepared for the worst, converting hotels into hospitals and parks into mass graves.

Hanukkah—The Jewish holiday that commemorates the Maccabees' successful revolt against Greek rule in 164 BCE. The holiday lasts for eight days and is celebrated most notably by lighting a menorah.

Haredim—Hebrew for "tremblers," Haredim is the name commonly used for ultra-Orthodox Jews. Haredim have typically been opposed to or ambivalent toward the Jewish state and are now a major political and economic force in Israel.

Hashomer—Hebrew for "The Watchman," Hashomer was the Yishuv's first organized defense group created to protect Jews and their villages.

Hasid—From the Hebrew for Hesed, "loving-kindness," a Hasid is a member of an ultra-Orthodox sect of Judaism that was founded in the eighteenth century in eastern Europe.

Haskalah—The Jewish Enlightenment, the Haskalah, was active from the late eighteenth century to the late nineteenth century in western Europe. Designed to apply Enlightenment values and ideas to Judaism and to integrate the Jews into secular society, the movement had a profound influence on many early Zionist thinkers.

Hatikvah—Hebrew for "The Hope," "Hatikvah" is the name of Israel's national anthem. It was written in 1878.

Herut—Hebrew for "Freedom," Herut was the name of Menachem Begin's political party. Established in 1948, the party eventually merged with others and became the Likud Party.

Histadrut—The Yishuv's primary workers' union. It later became a powerful political force in Israel.

Hovevei Zion—Hebrew for "Lovers of Zion," Hovevei Zion was one of the first organizations in Europe that fostered Jewish immigration to Palestine. It brought idealistic eastern European Jews to Palestine during the First Aliyah.

intifada—Arabic for "shaking off," intifada refers to periods of attacks on Israel, primarily by Palestinians from the territories Israel occupied in 1967. The First Intifada took place from 1987 to 1991, while the Second Intifada lasted from 2000 to 2004.

Irgun—Irgun Tsva'i Leumi, the National Military Organization, was an underground fighting group commonly called the Irgun. It was also known by its Hebrew acronym, Etzel. Founded in 1931, the Irgun was led by Haganah fighters who were deeply influenced by Jabotinsky's ideology and were frustrated by the Haganah's policy of restraint. The Irgun functioned as a separate fighting force until the creation of the IDF during the War of Independence.

kibbutz—A kibbutz (plural—kibbutzim) is the name for a collective community originally based largely on socialist ideals and rooted in agricultural work. The kibbutz became an iconic Israeli institution in the state's first decades. While the kibbutz flourished, it never accounted for more than 7 percent of the population.

kippah—Hebrew for "skullcap," traditionally worn by Jewish men.

Knesset—The Israeli parliament, the Knesset, is composed of 120 seats and uses the same system of proportional representation that the Zionist congresses had employed. The first Knesset was elected in 1949.

Kotel—Hebrew for "wall," it is a reference to the Western Wall or Wailing Wall, the only remnant of the Second Temple. It has become a sacred site to Jews as well as a battleground for competing religious ideologies.

Kristallnacht—A German word that approximates "The Night of Broken Glass," Kristallnacht was a pogrom against Jews in Germany and Austria on November 9 to 10, 1938. Jewish businesses and synagogues were burned and destroyed and many Jews were killed or injured.

Lechi—An acronym of Lochamei Cherut Yisrael ("Warriors for the Freedom of Israel"), Lechi was an underground militia founded in 1940 by Avraham Stern. Originally a member of the Irgun, Stern broke off and founded his own fighting group.

Likud—Hebrew for "the Consolidation," Likud is a political party founded by Menachem Begin and leaders of several other right-wing parties in 1973. In 1977, Likud became Israel's ruling party for the first time under Begin.

ma'abarot—Transit camps, *ma'abarot* were temporary housing provided for the new immigrants who flooded the country after the Independence War. They were created to alleviate the terrible conditions in the immigrant camps until the state could provide "real" housing, but soon, the conditions in the *ma'abarot* were just as bad.

ma'apilim—*Ma'apilim* was the Hebrew name given to illegal immigrants who came to the Yishuv when immigration was severely limited during the British Mandate. Some of the *ma'apilim* were successful while others were caught by the British and put in detainee camps.

mamlachtiyut—Translated most closely as "statism" or "state consciousness," *mamlachtiyut* was the term for David Ben-Gurion's campaign to have the state be central to Israeli culture and policy.

Mapai—The acronym for the Hebrew of "Workers' Party of the Land of Israel," Mapai was Israel's secular Left party until it merged with another small left-leaning party and became the Israeli Labor Party in 1968. Mapai and then Labor were the ruling political parties from 1948 until 1977.

Mizrachi—Term for Jews who resided in the Orient (plural—Mizrachim), mostly in North Africa and the Middle East, after the Romans expelled the Jews from Judea. Over the centuries, they developed unique religious and cultural traditions.

moshav—Hebrew for "village" or "settlement," a moshav (plural—moshavim) is a cooperative rural Israeli town in an agricultural area. Many moshavim were established during the early aliyot.

Mossad—Literally, "the Institute," the Mossad is Israel's national intelligence agency.

Nakba—Arabic for "the Catastrophe," Nakba was the name given to the 1948 War of Independence by Palestine's Arabs.

Palmach—Acronym for Hebrew words that mean "strike force," the Palmach was created in 1941 as an elite unit within the Haganah. Trained by British forces, the Palmach was originally created to prepare for the possibility of a German invasion in Palestine. It consisted of many of the Yishuv's best fighters.

Poalei Zion—Poalei Zion, or "Workers of Zion," was a movement of Marxist-Zionist workers established throughout eastern Europe at the turn of the twentieth century.

Saison—French for "season," the *Saison*, also called the Hunting Season, refers to a period between November 1944 and March 1945 in which elite forces from the Haganah searched out Irgun and Lechi members and handed them over to the British.

Sephardi—Hebrew for "Spaniard," Sephardi (plural—Sephardim) refer to Jews who settled in Iberia and the Spanish Diaspora after the Roman exile. There, they established their own communities, developing their own set of religious and cultural traditions.

Shas—From an acronym for a Hebrew verse that translates to "the Sephardi Guards," Shas is the name of a political party founded in 1984. Its leader, Rav Ovadia Yosef, was a former Sephardi chief rabbi of Israel who created Shas to represent Israel's Mizrachi population.

Shehecheyanu—Hebrew for "who has given us life," *shehecheyanu* is a Jewish blessing commonly said at life-transforming moments. The blessing recognizes the grandness of the moment and gives thanks to God for having kept us alive to reach that point.

Shoah—A biblical term from the Book of Zephaniah that means "calamity," *shoah* is the Hebrew word used for the Holocaust.

shofar—A ram's horn, a shofar is an ancient instrument sounded in synagogue on Rosh Hashanah (the Jewish New Year) and at the conclusion of Yom Kippur (the Day of Atonement).

Sinai (Mount)—Mount Sinai is the place at which the Bible says the Torah was revealed by God to the Jewish people.

shtetl—A Yiddish term for a small village or town with a large Jewish population, found primarily in eastern and central Europe prior to World War II.

Talmud—The central text of Rabbinic Judaism. Composed approximately 200 CE to 500 CE by Jewish communities in Babylonian exile, the Talmud is the most important Jewish postbiblical text and is still the primary religious text studied by traditional Jews around the world.

Torah—The traditional Jewish term for the Five Books of Moses, from Genesis through Deuteronomy. The Torah tells the story of the birth of the Jewish people and their journey from Egyptian slavery toward the Promised Land.

yeshiva—The central institution of learning for religious Jewish men, in which the mainstay of the curriculum is the Babylonian Talmud.

Yiddish—Yiddish, mainly a fusion of German, Hebrew, and Aramaic, is a language created by Ashkenazi Jews. Many Jews who immigrated to Palestine, including Zionism's and Israel's greatest leaders, spoke Yiddish as their native tongue.

Yishuv—Hebrew for "area of settlement," Yishuv is commonly used for the prestate Jewish community in Palestine. The Yishuv, with its own government and army, eventually became the State of Israel.

Yom Kippur—The Day of Atonement is the holiest day of the year in the Jewish calendar. Focused on repentance and self-examination, the holiday is usually observed by a twenty-five-hour fast and a day of worship in synagogue.

Appendix C

_____

ISRAEL'S DECLARATION OF INDEPENDENCE

Issued at Tel Aviv on May 14, 1948 (5th of Iyar, 5708)

The Land of Israel* was the birthplace of the Jewish people. Here their spiritual, religious, and political identity was shaped. Here they first attained to statehood, created cultural values of national and universal significance, and gave to the world the eternal Book of Books.

After being forcibly exiled from their land, the people kept faith with it in all of the lands of their Dispersion and never ceased to pray and hope for their return to it and there to renew their political freedom.

Impelled by this historic and traditional attachment, Jews strove in every successive generation to reestablish themselves in their ancient homeland. In recent decades they returned in their masses. Pioneers, ma'apilim and defenders, they made deserts bloom, revived the Hebrew language, built villages and towns, and created a thriving community shaping its own economy and culture, seeking peace while defending itself, bringing the blessings of progress to all the country's inhabitants, and aspiring toward independent nationhood.

In the year 5657 (1897), at the summons of the spiritual father of the Jewish state, Theodor Herzl, the First Zionist Congress convened

_____

* This translation is reproduced from the State of Israel website, with minor modifications throughout. Almost all translations retain the name "Eretz Israel," which in this appendix is rendered as the "Land of Israel," to indicate that the declaration's intent is not the land of the State of Israel, but to the land that composed the ancestral home of the Jewish people. I have nonetheless changed that translation for the reader's ease.

and proclaimed the right of the Jewish people to national rebirth in its own country.

This right was recognized in the Balfour Declaration of November 2, 1917, and reaffirmed in the Mandate of the League of Nations, which, in particular, gave international sanction to the historic connection between the Jewish people and the Land of Israel and to the right of the Jewish people to rebuild its National Home.

The catastrophe that recently befell the Jewish people—the massacre of millions of Jews in Europe—was another clear demonstration of the urgency of solving the problem of its homelessness by reestablishing in the Land of Israel the Jewish state, which would open the gates of the homeland wide to every Jew and confer upon the Jewish people the status of a fully privileged member of the comity of nations.

Survivors of the Nazi Holocaust in Europe, as well as Jews from other parts of the world, continued to migrate to the Land of Israel, undaunted by difficulties, restrictions, and dangers, and never ceased to assert their right to a life of dignity, freedom, and honest toil in their national homeland.

In the Second World War, the Jewish community of this country contributed its full share to the struggle of the freedom- and peace-loving nations against the forces of Nazi wickedness and, by the blood of its soldiers and its war effort, gained the right to be reckoned among the peoples who founded the United Nations.

On November 29, 1947, the United Nations General Assembly passed a resolution calling for the establishment of a Jewish state in the Land of Israel; the General Assembly required the inhabitants of the Land of Israel to take such steps as were necessary on their part for the implementation of that resolution. This recognition by the United Nations of the right of the Jewish people to establish their state is irrevocable.

This right is the natural right of the Jewish people to be masters of their own fate, like all other nations, in their own sovereign state.

ACCORDINGLY WE, MEMBERS OF THE PEOPLE'S COUNCIL, REPRESENTATIVES OF THE JEWISH COMMUNITY OF THE LAND OF ISRAEL AND OF THE ZIONIST MOVEMENT, ARE HERE ASSEMBLED ON THE DAY OF THE TERMINATION OF THE BRITISH MANDATE OVER THE LAND OF ISRAEL AND, BY VIRTUE OF OUR NATURAL AND HISTORIC RIGHT AND ON

THE STRENGTH OF THE RESOLUTION OF THE UNITED NA-
TIONS GENERAL ASSEMBLY, HEREBY DECLARE THE ESTAB-
LISHMENT OF A JEWISH STATE IN THE LAND OF ISRAEL, TO
BE KNOWN AS THE STATE OF ISRAEL.

WE DECLARE that, with effect from the moment of the termination of the Mandate being tonight, the eve of Sabbath, the 6th Iyar,
5708 (15th May, 1948), until the establishment of the elected, regular
authorities of the state in accordance with the Constitution, which
shall be adopted by the Elected Constituent Assembly not later than
the 1st October 1948, the People's Council shall act as a Provisional
Council of State, and its executive organ, the People's Administration,
shall be the Provisional Government of the Jewish state, to be called
"Israel."

THE STATE OF ISRAEL will be open for Jewish immigration
and for the Ingathering of the Exiles; it will foster the development
of the country for the benefit of all its inhabitants; it will be based on
freedom, justice, and peace as envisaged by the prophets of Israel; it
will ensure complete equality of social and political rights to all its
inhabitants irrespective of religion, race, or sex; it will guarantee freedom of religion, conscience, language, education, and culture; it will
safeguard the Holy Places of all religions; and it will be faithful to the
principles of the Charter of the United Nations.

THE STATE OF ISRAEL is prepared to cooperate with the agencies and representatives of the United Nations in implementing the
resolution of the General Assembly of the 29th November, 1947, and
will take steps to bring about the economic union of the whole of the
Land of Israel.

WE APPEAL to the United Nations to assist the Jewish people in
the building-up of its State and to receive the State of Israel into the
comity of nations.

WE APPEAL—in the very midst of the onslaught launched against
us now for months—to the Arab inhabitants of the State of Israel to
preserve peace and participate in the upbuilding of the state on the
basis of full and equal citizenship and due representation in all its provisional and permanent institutions.

WE EXTEND our hand to all neighboring states and their peoples in an offer of peace and good neighborliness, and appeal to them
to establish bonds of cooperation and mutual help with the sovereign

Jewish people settled in its own land. The State of Israel is prepared to do its share in a common effort for the advancement of the entire Middle East.

WE APPEAL to the Jewish people throughout the Diaspora to rally round the Jews of the Land of Israel, in the tasks of immigration and upbuilding and to stand by them in the great struggle for the realization of the age-old dream—the redemption of Israel.

PLACING OUR TRUST IN THE "ROCK OF ISRAEL," WE AFFIX OUR SIGNATURES TO THIS PROCLAMATION AT THIS SESSION OF THE PROVISIONAL COUNCIL OF STATE, ON THE SOIL OF THE HOMELAND, IN THE CITY OF TEL-AVIV, ON THIS SABBATH EVE, THE 5TH DAY OF IYAR, 5708 (14TH MAY, 1948).

David Ben-Gurion	Rachel Cohen	Aharon Zisling
Daniel Auster	Rabbi Kalman	Moshe Kolodny
Mordekhai Bentov	Kahana	Eliezer Kaplan
Yitzhak Ben Zvi	Saadia Kobashi	Abraham Katznelson
Eliyahu Berligne	Rabbi Yitzhak Meir	Felix Rosenblueth
Fritz Bernstein	Levin	David Remez
Rabbi Wolf Gold	Meir David	Berl Repetur
Meir Grabovsky	Loewenstein	Mordekhai Shattner
Yitzhak Gruenbaum	Zvi Luria	Ben Zion Sternberg
Dr. Abraham	Golda Myerson	Bekhor Shitreet
Granovsky	Nachum Nir	Moshe Shapira
Eliyahu Dobkin	Zvi Segal	Moshe Shertok
Meir Wilner-Kovner	Rabbi Yehuda Leib	
Zerach Wahrhaftig	Hacohen Fishman	
Herzl Vardi	David Zvi Pinkas	

ISRAELI PRIME MINISTERS AND THE AMERICAN AND ISRAELI PRESIDENTS WITH WHOM THEY WORKED

	ISRAELI PRIME MINISTER	U.S. PRESIDENT	ISRAELI PRESIDENT Largely Honorific
1948			
1949	**David Ben-Gurion** May 14, 1948– January 26, 1954	**Harry S. Truman** April 12, 1945– January 20, 1953	**Chaim Weizmann** February 17, 1949– November 9, 1952
1950			
1951			
1952			
1953		**Dwight D. Eisenhower** January 20, 1953– January 20, 1961	**Yitzhak Ben-Zvi** December 16, 1952– April 23, 1963
1954	**Moshe Sharett** January 26, 1954– November 3, 1955		
1955			
1956	**David Ben-Gurion** November 3, 1955– June 26, 1963		
1957			
1958			
1959			
1960			
1961		**John F. Kennedy** January 20, 1961– November 22, 1963	
1962			
1963			
1964	**Levi Eshkol** June 26, 1963– February 26, 1969	**Lyndon B. Johnson** November 22, 1963– January 20, 1969	**Zalman Shazar** May 21, 1963– May 24, 1973
1965			
1966			
1967			
1968			

	ISRAELI PRIME MINISTER	U.S. PRESIDENT	ISRAELI PRESIDENT Largely Honorific
1969	*Note: Yigal Allon was interim PM from February 26 until March 7*	Richard Nixon January 20, 1969– August 9, 1974	Zalman Shazar May 21, 1963– May 24, 1973
1970			
1971			
1972	**Golda Meir** March 17, 1969– June 3, 1974		
1973			
1974			
1975	**Yitzhak Rabin** June 3, 1974– June 20, 1977	Gerald Ford August 9, 1974– January 20, 1977	Ephraim Katzir May 24, 1973– May 29, 1978
1976			
1977			
1978	**Menachem Begin** June 20, 1977– October 10, 1983	Jimmy Carter January 20, 1977– January 20, 1981	Yitzhak Navon May 29, 1978– May 5, 1983
1979			
1980			
1981		Ronald Reagan January 20, 1981– January 20, 1989	
1982			
1983			
1984	**Yitzhak Shamir** October 10, 1983– September 13, 1984		Chaim Herzog May 5, 1983– May 13, 1993
1985	**Shimon Peres** September 13, 1984– October 20, 1986		
1986			
1987	**Yitzhak Shamir** October 20, 1986– July 13, 1992		
1988			
1989		George H. W. Bush January 20, 1989– January 20, 1993	
1990			
1991			
1992			
1993	**Yitzhak Rabin** July 13, 1992– November 4, 1995	Bill Clinton January 20, 1993– January 20, 2001	Ezer Weizman May 13, 1993– July 13, 2000
1994			
1995			

	ISRAELI PRIME MINISTER	U.S. PRESIDENT	ISRAELI PRESIDENT Largely Honorific
1996	*Note: Peres was interim PM from November 4 until November 22* **Shimon Peres** November 22, 1995– June 18, 1996	**Bill Clinton** January 20, 1993– January 20, 2001	**Ezer Weizman** May 13, 1993– July 13, 2000
1997	**Benjamin Netanyahu** June 18, 1996– July 6, 1999		
1998			
1999			
2000	**Ehud Barak** July 6, 1999– March 7, 2001		
2001		**George W. Bush** January 20, 2001– January 20, 2009	
2002	**Ariel Sharon** March 7, 2001– April 14, 2006 *Note: From January 4, 2006, Sharon was in a coma; Olmert was acting PM*		**Moshe Katsav** August 1, 2001– July 1, 2007
2003			
2004			
2005			
2006			
2007	**Ehud Olmert** April 14, 2006– March 31, 2009		
2008			**Shimon Peres** July 15, 2007– July 24, 2014
2009		**Barack Obama** January 20, 2009– Incumbent	
2010	**Benjamin Netanyahu** March 31, 2009– Incumbent		
2011			
2012			
2013			
2014			
2015			**Reuven Rivlin** July 24, 2014– Incumbent
2016			

ISRAELI POLITICAL PARTIES AND THEIR CHANGING BALANCE OF POWER

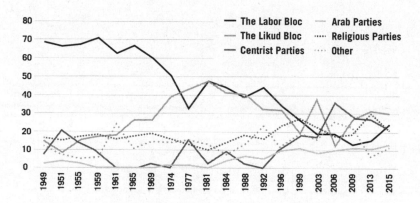

Israeli political parties are created, disappear, and merge with great frequency, so it can be difficult to monitor the relative fates of the major left- and right-wing blocs. Today's two major groups, commonly called Labor and Likud, are the products of the mergers of the following parties, many of which are mentioned throughout this book.

THE RIGHT

- Herut: 1948–1965 (Menachem Begin's party)
- Gahal: 1965–1973 (formed by a merger of Herut and the Liberal Party)
- Likud: 1973–Present (formed by a merger of Gahal, the Free Centre, the National List, and the Movement for Greater Israel)

THE LEFT

- Mapai: 1948–1968 (David Ben-Gurion's party)
- Labor Alignment: 1965–1968 (formed by a merger of Mapai and Ahdut HaAvoda); Ben-Gurion broke off from Mapai and created the Rafi Party
- Israeli Labor Party: 1968–2014 (a merger of Labor Alignment and Rafi)
- One Israel: 1991–2001 (a merger of the Israeli Labor Party, Gesher, and Meimad, the latter a liberal, socially conscious religious party)
- Zionist Union: 2014–Present (a merger of the Israeli Labor Party and Hatnuah, a new party that had been formed by Tzipi Livni)

FOR FURTHER READING

A book of this nature, by definition, covers Israel's history from a bird's-eye view. Every event, issue, and personality discussed in these pages has been the subject of much investigation and writing. There are many wonderful books that, by focusing on a much more narrow subject, can examine the issues we've discussed here in much greater detail.

For a list of suggested books and online resources for further reading, please see my website: http://danielgordis.org/books/israel-concise -history-nation-reborn/.

INTRODUCTION

1 Ben-Gurion made this comment in the course of a CBS television interview with Edward R. Murrow on February 3, 1956, https://www.youtube.com/watch?v=4Oo75OQmHAw [Last viewed on March 15, 2016].

2 Mark Twain, "Concerning the Jews," *Harper's Magazine*, March 1898.

CHAPTER 1: POETRY AND POLITICS

1 Lawrence Epstein, *The Dream of Zion: The Story of the First Zionist Congress* (Lanham, MD: Rowman and Littlefield, 2016), p. 16.

2 Robert M. Seltzer, *Jewish People, Jewish Thought: The Jewish Experience in History* (New York: Macmillan Publishing, 1980), p. 632.

3 Yaacov Shavit and Jehuda Reinharz, *Glorious, Accursed Europe* (Waltham, MA: Brandeis University Press, 2010), p. 88.

4 Walter Laqueur, *A History of Zionism* (New York: Schocken Books, 1976), p. 60.

5 David Patterson, "Introduction," in Abraham Mapu, trans. Joseph Marymount, *The Love of Zion & Other Writings* (Israel: Toby Press, 2006), p. xvi.

6 Alex Bein, trans. Maurice Samuel, *Theodor Herzl: A Biography* (Philadelphia: Jewish Publication Society of America, 1940), p. 232.

7 Shlomo Avineri, trans. Haim Watzman, *Herzl: Theodor Herzl and the Foundation of the Jewish State* (London: Weidenfeld & Nicolson, 2008), p. 33.

8 Amos Elon, *The Pity of It All: A Portrait of the German-Jewish Epoch 1743–1933* (New York: Picador, 2002), p. 213.

9 Bein, trans. Samuel, *Theodor Herzl*, p. 37.

10 Avineri, trans. Watzman, *Herzl*, p. 85 (quoting Herzl's diary).

11 Bein, trans. Samuel, *Theodor Herzl*, p. 19.

12 Yoram Hazony, *The Jewish State: The Struggle for Israel's Soul* (New York: Basic Books, 2000), pp. 84–85.

13 Conversation between the author and David Matlow, of Toronto, Canada. See also Raphael Patai, *The Jews of Hungary: History, Culture, Psychology* (Detroit: Wayne State University Press, 1996), p. 347.

14 Avineri, trans. Watzman, *Herzl*, pp. 61–62.

15 Ibid., p. 78.

16 Ibid., p. 69.

17 Theodor Herzl, *The Jewish State* (New York: Dover Publications, 1989), p. 47.

18 Ibid., pp. 92–93.

19 Ibid., p. 76.

20 Ibid.

21 Hazony, *The Jewish State*, pp. 99–100.

22 Avineri, trans. Watzman, *Herzl*, p. 116.

23 Patterson, "Introduction," in Mapu, trans. Marymount, *The Love of Zion*, p. xiv.

24 It was long asserted that Hess's wife, Sibylle Pesch, had been a prostitute and that Hess married her as a kind of atonement for the way in which men had long taken advantage of impoverished women, but the claim about Pesch's background is now a matter of some scholarly disagreement.

25 Moses Hess, *The Revival of Israel: Rome and Jerusalem, the Last Nationalist Question* (Lincoln: University of Nebraska Press, 1995), p. x.

26 Many mistakenly assume that Hess was referencing the Roman Republic in his title; in fact, he asserted that modern Italian nationalism should be interpreted by a Jewish national movement in Palestine. See Epstein, *The Dream of Zion*, p. 6.

27 Eric Cohen, "The Spirit of Jewish Conservatism," *Mosaic* (April 6, 2015), http://mosaicmagazine.com/essay/2015/04/the-spirit-of-jewish-conservatism/ [Last viewed April 6, 2015].

28 Laqueur, *A History of Zionism*, p. 54.

29 Ibid., p. 53.

30 Arthur Hertzberg, ed., *The Zionist Idea* (Philadelphia: Jewish Publication Society, 1997), p. 32.

31 Ibid., p. 188.

32 Ibid., p. 195.

33 Bein, trans. Samuel, *Theodor Herzl,* p. 226.

34 Ibid., p. 230.

35 Ze'ev Tzahor, "Chaim Arlosoroff and His Attitude toward the Rise of Nazism," *Jewish Social Studies,* Vol. 46, No. 3/4 (Summer–Autumn 1984), p. 322.

36 Epstein, *The Dream of Zion,* p. 86.

37 Avineri, trans. Watzman, *Herzl,* p. 141.

38 Ibid., p. 1.

39 Epstein, *The Dream of Zion,* p. 83.

40 Theodor Herzl, *Old New Land* (Princeton, NJ: Markus Wiener Publishers, 1997), p. 248.

41 Ibid., p. 174.

42 Avineri, trans. Watzman, *Herzl,* p. 167.

CHAPTER 2: SOME SPOT OF A NATIVE LAND

1 George Eliot, *Daniel Deronda,* introduction by Edmund White, notes by Dr. Hugh Osborne (New York: Modern Library, 2002), page 15. *Daniel Deronda* was initially published by William Blackwood and Sons in eight parts, from February to September 1876. It was subsequently republished in December 1878 with revisions primarily in those sections dealing with Jewish life and customs.

2 Genesis 12:1.

3 Genesis 12:7.

4 Exodus 1:9–10. The phrase lends itself to different interpretations. The JPS translation renders the phrase as "rise from the ground," based apparently on Ehrlich's *Mikrah Kifshuto.* The Babylonian Talmud (Sotah 11a) suggests that Pharaoh means "gain ascendancy over the country," but that meaning obscures the plain sense of the verse, which coheres with the dispersion that is central to the early chapters of Genesis. The simplest translation works best.

5 Deuteronomy 7:1.

6 Alex Bein, trans. Maurice Samuel, *Theodor Herzl: A Biography* (Philadelphia: Jewish Publication Society of America, 1940), p. 232.

7 Jeremiah 29:5–6.

8 Psalms 137:1.

9   Psalms 126:1–6.

10 II Chronicles 36:23.

11 J. Maxwell Miller and John H. Hayes, *A History of Ancient Israel and Judah* (Louisville, KY: Westminster John Knox Press, 2006), p. 509.

12 Jerome Murphy-O'Connor and Barry Cunliffe, *The Holy Land: An Oxford Archaeological Guide,* 5th ed. (New York: Oxford University Press, 2008), pp. 378–381.

13 Hayim Ben-Sasson, ed., *A History of the Jewish People* (Cambridge, MA: Harvard University Press, 1976), p. 332.

14 Bein, trans. Samuel, *Theodor Herzl,* p. 232.

CHAPTER 3: A CONVERSATION, NOT AN IDEOLOGY

1   Monty Noam Penkower, "The Kishinev Pogrom of 1903," *Modern Judaism,* Vol. 24, No. 3 (2004), p. 199. Unless otherwise noted, Penkower's work on Kishinev is the source for the history recounted in this chapter.

2   Winston Churchill, "MIT Mid-Century Convocation, March 31, 1949," *MIT Institute Archives,* https://libraries.mit.edu/archives/exhibits/midcentury/mid-cent-churchill.html [Last viewed December 7, 2015].

3   Penkower, "The Kishinev Pogrom of 1903," p. 187.

4   Ibid.

5   Ibid., p. 188.

6   Ibid.

7   Ibid., p. 211.

8   David G. Roskies, ed., *The Literature of Destruction: Jewish Responses to Catastrophe* (Philadelphia: Jewish Publication Society, 1988), p. 162.

9   Penkower, "The Kishinev Pogrom of 1903," p. 199.

10 Ibid.

11 Lawrence Epstein, *The Dream of Zion: The Story of the First Zionist Congress* (Lanham, MD: Rowman and Littlefield, 2016), p. 97.

12 Shlomo Avineri, trans. Haim Watzman, *Herzl: Theodor Herzl and the Foundation of the Jewish State* (London: Weidenfeld & Nicolson, 2008), p. 241.

13 Penkower, "The Kishinev Pogrom of 1903," p. 199.

14 Avineri, trans. Watzman, *Herzl,* p. 245.

15 Ibid., p. 259.

16 Ella Florsheim, "Giving Herzl His Due," *Azure,* No. 21 (Summer 5765/2005), p. 21, http://azure.org.il/include/print.php?id=182 [Last viewed May 1, 2016].

17 Penkower, "The Kishinev Pogrom of 1903," p. 194.

18 Steven J. Zipperstein, *Elusive Prophet: Ahad Ha'am and the Origins of Zionism* (Berkeley: University of California Press, 1993), p. 11.

19 Ibid., p. 14.

20 Ibid., pp. 18–19.

21 Ahad Ha'am, "The Jewish State and the Jewish Problem," in Arthur Hertzberg, *The Zionist Idea* (Philadelphia: Jewish Publication Society, 1997), p. 268.

22 Yoram Hazony, *The Jewish State: The Struggle for Israel's Soul* (New York: Basic Books, 2000), p. 127.

23 Zipperstein, *Elusive Prophet,* p. 129.

24 Arthur Hertzberg, ed., *The Zionist Idea* (Philadelphia: Jewish Publication Society, 1997), pp. 54–55.

25 Isaiah 2:3.

26 Alan Dowty, "Much Ado About Little: Ahad Ha'Am's 'Truth from Eretz Yisrael,' Zionism, and the Arabs," *Israel Studies,* Vol. 5, No. 2 (Fall 2000), p. 161 (quoting Ahad Ha'am). Italics added.

27 Max Nordau, "Jewry of Muscle," in Paul Mendes-Flohr and Yehuda Reinharz, *The Jew in the Modern World: A Documentary History,* 2nd ed. (Oxford: Oxford University Press, 1995), pp. 547–548.

28 Penkower, "The Kishinev Pogrom of 1903," p. 209.

29 Ze'ev (Vladimir) Jabotinsky, "The Basis of the Betarian Viewpoint Consists of One Idea: The Jewish State: The Ideology of Betar," *World Zionist Organization,* http://www.wzo.org.il/index.php?dir=site&page=articles&op=item&cs=3360&langpage=eng&category=3122&mode=print [Last viewed December 7, 2015].

30 Raymond P. Scheindlin, *A Short History of the Jewish People: From Legendary Times to Modern Statehood* (Oxford and New York: Oxford University Press, 2000), p. 224.

31 A. D. Gordon, "Logic for the Future (1910)," in Hertzberg, *The Zionist Idea,* p. 373.

32 Yehudah Mirsky, *Rav Kook: Mystic in a Time of Revolution* (New Haven: Yale University Press, 2014), p. 65.

33 Hertzberg, *The Zionist Idea*, pp. 291–292.

34 Micah Joseph Berdyczewski, "Wrecking and Building," in Hertzberg, *The Zionist Idea*, p. 293.

35 Babylonian Talmud, Ketubbot 111a.

36 Alan Nadler, "Piety and Politics: The Case of the Satmar Rebbe," *Judaism*, Vol. 31 (Spring 1982), p. 40.

37 Alan Lelchuk and Gershon Shaked, *8 Great Hebrew Short Novels* (New Milford, CT: Toby Press, 2012), Kindle Edition, Location 1029.

CHAPTER 4: FROM A DREAM TO GLIMMERS OF REALITY

1   The phrase is oft quoted. An example in a speech by Prime Minister Ariel Sharon can be found at http://www.pmo.gov.il/English/MediaCenter/Speeches/Pages/speech040105.aspx.

2   Hani A. Faris, "Israel Zangwill's Challenge to Zionism," *Journal of Palestine Studies*, Vol. 4, No. 3 (Spring 1975), p. 81.

3   Ibid.

4   Howard M. Sachar, *A History of Israel: From the Rise of Zionism to Our Time* (New York: Alfred A. Knopf, 1979), p. 23.

5   Anita Shapira, trans. Anthony Berris, *Israel: A History* (Waltham, MA: Brandeis University Press, 2012), p. 28.

6   Benny Morris, *1948: The First Arab-Israeli War* (New Haven and London: Yale University Press, 2008), p. 6.

7   David Fromkin, *A Peace to End All Peace: The Fall of the Ottoman Empire and the Creation of the Modern Middle East* (New York: Henry Holt, 2009), p. 36.

8   Yehudah Mirsky, *Rav Kook: Mystic in a Time of Revolution* (New Haven: Yale University Press, 2014), p. 59.

9   Ibid., pp. 59–60.

10 Ibid., p. 50.

11 Sachar, *A History of Israel*, p. 82.

12 Yaffah Berlovitz, *Inventing a Land, Inventing a People* (Tel Aviv: Hotza'at HaKibbutz HaMeuchad, 1996), p. 55 [In Hebrew].

13 Theodor Herzl, trans. I. M. Lask, *The Jewish State* (Tel Aviv: M. Newman Publishing House, 1954), p. 134.

14 Mirsky, *Rav Kook*, p. 54.

15 Ibid., pp. 53–54.

16 Berlovitz, *Inventing a Land*, pp. 18–19.

17 Ibid., p. 20.

18 Mirsky, *Rav Kook*, p. 66.

19 Ruth Kark, "Changing Patterns of Landownership in Nineteenth-Century Palestine: The European influence," *Journal of Historical Geography*, Vol. 10, No. 4 (1984), pp. 357–384.

20 Nurit Govrin, *Roots and Tops: The Imprint of the First Aliyah in Hebrew Literature* (Tel Aviv: Papyrus and Tel Aviv University, 1981), p. 43 [In Hebrew].

21 Mirsky, *Rav Kook*, p. 68.

22 Ibid., pp. 68–69.

23 Shapira, trans. Berris, *Israel: A History*, p. 46.

24 Tali Asher, "The Growing Silence of the Poetess Rachel," in Ruth Kark, Margarit Shilo, and Galit Hasan-Rokem, eds., *Jewish Women in Pre-State Israel: Life History, Politics, and Culture* (Waltham, MA: Brandeis University Press, 2008), p. 245.

25 Rachel Bluwstein, "Perhaps," *Palestine-Israel Journal*, Vol. 3, Nos. 3 and 4 (1996), http://www.pij.org/details.php?id=536 [Last viewed December 7, 2015].

26 S. Ilan Troen, *Imagining Zion: Dreams, Designs, and Realities in a Century of Jewish Settlement* (New Haven and London: Yale University Press, 2003), Kindle Edition, Locations 1358–1361.

27 Ibid., Locations 1368–1369.

28 Tom Segev, *1967: Israel, the War, and the Year That Transformed the Middle East* (New York: Henry Holt, 2007), p. 442.

29 Troen, *Imagining Zion*, Location 1541.

30 Ibid., Location 1566.

31 Ibid., Location 1609.

32 Sachar, *A History of Israel*, p. 83.

33 Troen, *Imagining Zion*, Location 1609.

34 Martin Gilbert, *Israel: A History* (New York: Harper Perennial, 1998), p. 24.

CHAPTER 5: THE BALFOUR DECLARATION

1 Shmuel Katz, *Lone Wolf: A Biography of Vladimir (Ze'ev) Jabotinsky* (Fort Lee, NJ: Barricade Books, 1995), p. 136.

2 Edward Grey, Viscount of Fallodon, *Twenty-Five Years 1892–1916* (New York: Frederick A. Stokes Company, 1925), p. 20.

3 While Herzl was still alive he had approached the ruling Turks with his proposals for Jewish settlement in Palestine, which they had flatly refused—fearing "introducing an additional non-Muslim element into the Middle East that would provide further grounds for European intervention." Anita Shapira, trans. Anthony Berris, *Israel: A History* (Waltham, MA: Brandeis University Press, 2012), p. 22.

4 Katz, *Lone Wolf,* p. 177.

5 Cited in a display in Chaim Weizmann's home in Rehovot, now a museum.

6 Shapira, trans. Berris, *Israel: A History,* p. 71.

7 Jonathan Schneer, *The Balfour Declaration: The Origins of the Arab-Israeli Conflict* (New York: Random House Trade Paperbacks, 2012), p. 197.

8 John Bew, "The Tragic Cycle: Western Powers and the Middle East," *New Statesman* (August 21, 2014), http://www.new statesman.com/world-affairs/2014/08/tragic-cycle-western-powers-and-middle-east [Last viewed December 7, 2015].

9 Shapira, trans. Berris, *Israel: A History,* p. 73.

10 Cecil Bloom, "Sir Mark Sykes: British Diplomat and a Convert to Zionism," *Jewish Historical Studies,* Vol. 43 (2011), p. 142.

11 Walter Laqueur, *A History of Zionism* (New York: Schocken Books, 1976), p. 186. While this is a widely held view, not everyone agrees that acetone had anything to do with the Balfour Declaration, and some scholars consider the linkage mere urban legend.

12 Arthur James Balfour, "Balfour Declaration" (1917), *The Avalon Project,* http://avalon.law.yale.edu/20th_century/balfour.asp [Last viewed December 7, 2015].

13 Shapira, trans. Berris, *Israel: A History,* p. 73.

14 Eitan Bar Yosef, "The Last Crusade? British Propaganda and the Palestine Campaign, 1917–18," *Journal of Contemporary History,* Vol. 36, No. 1 (January 2001), p. 100.

15 The Mount Scopus site was acquired in 1914—but World War I ensured that building was delayed until 1918.

16 Seth M. Siegel, *Let There Be Water: Israel's Solution for a Water-Starved World* (New York: Thomas Dunne Books, 2015), p. 22.

17 Martin Gilbert, *Israel: A History* (New York: Harper Perennial, 1998), p. 9.

18 Ibid., pp. 45–46.

19 Siegel, *Let There Be Water,* p. 28.

20 Shlomo Avineri, lecture at the Shazar Center in Jerusalem on December 30, 2014.

21 Anita Shapira, trans. Anthony Berris, *Ben-Gurion: Father of Modern Israel* (New Haven and London: Yale University Press, 2014), p. 28.

22 Michael Makovsky, *Churchill's Promised Land: Zionism and Statecraft* (New Haven: Yale University Press, 2007), Kindle Edition, Location 1463.

23 Martin Gilbert, *Churchill and the Jews: A Lifelong Friendship* (New York: Henry Holt, 2007), p. 50.

24 Tom Segev, trans. Haim Watzman, *One Palestine, Complete: Jews and Arabs Under the British Mandate* (New York: Little, Brown, 2000), p. 104.

25 Howard M. Sachar, *A History of Israel: From the Rise of Zionism to Our Time* (New York: Alfred A. Knopf, 1979), p. 186.

26 Ze'ev Jabotinsky, "The Iron Wall," Jewish Virtual Library, http://www.jewishvirtuallibrary.org/jsource/Zionism/ironwall.html [Last viewed December 7, 2015].

27 Ibid.

28 Hillel Cohen, *Year Zero of the Arab-Israeli Conflict, 1929* (Waltham, MA: Brandeis University Press, 2015), p. xvii.

29 Jeffrey Goldberg, "The Paranoid, Supremacist, Roots of the Stabbing Intifada," *Atlantic* (October 16, 2015), http://www.theatlantic.com/international/archive/2015/10/the-roots-of-the-palestinian-uprising-against-israel/410944/ [Last viewed December 7, 2015].

30 Schneer, *The Balfour Declaration,* p. 375.

31 Benny Morris, *Righteous Victims: A History of the Zionist-Arab Conflict, 1881–2001* (New York: Vintage Books, 2001), Kindle Edition, Location 2481.

32 Yoram Hazony, *The Jewish State: The Struggle for Israel's Soul* (New York: Basic Books, 2000), p. 210.

33 Daniel Gordis, *Menachem Begin: The Battle for Israel's Soul* (New York: Knopf Doubleday, 2014), p. 36.

CHAPTER 6: NOWHERE TO GO, EVEN IF THEY COULD LEAVE

1 Adolf Hitler, *Mein Kampf* (Boring, OR: CPA Book Publisher, 2000), p. 184.

2 Tuvia Friling, trans. Ora Cummings, *Arrows in the Dark: David Ben-Gurion, the Yishuv Leadership, and Rescue Attempts during the Holocaust*, Volume I (Madison: University of Wisconsin Press, 2005), p. 16.

3 Hava Eshkoli-Wagman, "Yishuv Zionism: Its Attitude to Nazism and the Third Reich Reconsidered," *Modern Judaism*, Vol. 19, No. 1 (February 1999), p. 26.

4 Colin Shindler, "Zionist History's Murder Mystery," *Jewish Chronicle Online* (June 16, 2013), http://www.thejc.com/comment-and-debate/comment/108596/zionist-historys-murder-mystery [Last viewed December 7, 2015].

5 Tom Segev, trans. Haim Watzman, *The Seventh Million: The Israelis and the Holocaust* (New York: Henry Holt, 1991), p. 21.

6 Ibid., p. 25.

7 Nina S. Spiegel, *Embodying Hebrew Culture* (Detroit: Wayne State University Press, 2013), p. 22.

8 Ibid., p. 135.

9 Ibid., p. 7.

10 Abba Hillel Silver, Moshe Shertok, and Chaim Weizmann, "Before the United Nations: October 1947," p. 7. Copy on file with the author.

11 Benny Morris, *One State, Two States: Resolving the Israel/Palestine Conflict* (New York: Vintage Books, 2001), Kindle Edition, Location 523.

12 Translation of Uri Zvi Greenberg, "One Truth and Not Two," is from Neta Stahl, "Jesus and the Pharisees Through the Eyes of Two Hebrew Writers: A Contrarian Perspective," *Hebrew Studies*, Vol. 56, No. 1 (December 11, 2015).

13 Yoram Hazony, *The Jewish State: The Struggle for Israel's Soul* (New York: Basic Books, 2000), p. 231.

14 Ibid., p. 232.

15 Friling, trans. Cummings, *Arrows in the Dark,* p. 19.

16 Ibid.

17 Howard M. Sachar, *A History of Israel: From the Rise of Zionism to Our Time* (New York: Alfred A. Knopf, 1979), p. 219.

18　Dina Porat, *The Blue and the Yellow Stars of David: The Zionist Leadership in Palestine and the Holocaust, 1939–1945* (Cambridge, MA, and London: Harvard University Press, 1990), p. 2.

19　Zephaniah 1:15.

20　Sachar, *A History of Israel,* p. 226.

21　Jack L. Schwartzwald, *Nine Lives of Israel: A Nation's History Through the Lives of Its Foremost Leaders* (Jefferson, NC: McFarland, 2012), p. 33.

22　Martin Gilbert, *Israel: A History* (New York: Harper Perennial, 1998), p. 101.

23　Mike Lanchin, "SS *St Louis*: The Ship of Jewish Refugees Nobody Wanted," *BBC World Service* (May 13, 2014), http://www.bbc.com/news/magazine-27373131 [Last viewed December 7, 2015].

24　Alan Guggenheim and Adam Guggenheim, "Doomed from the Start," *Naval History,* Vol. 18, No. 1 (February 2004), pp. 46–51.

25　Douglas Frantz and Catherine Collins, *Death on the Black Sea: The Untold Story of the* Struma *and World War II's Holocaust at Sea* (London: HarperCollins, 2003), p. 254.

26　Benny Morris, *Righteous Victims: A History of the Zionist-Arab Conflict, 1881–2001* (New York: Vintage Books, 2001), Kindle Edition, Locations 4035–4037.

27　Geneviève Pitot, trans. Donna Edouard, *The Story of the Jewish Detainees in Mauritius 1940–1945* (Lanham, MD: Rowman and Littlefield, 1998), p. 129.

28　Gilbert, *Israel: A History,* p. 151. Morris, *Righteous Victims,* p. 22, suggests numbers slightly lower.

29　Segev, trans. Watzman, *The Seventh Million,* p. 22.

30　Friling, trans. Cummings, *Arrows in the Dark,* p. 47.

31　Morris, *Righteous Victims,* pp. 162–163.

32　Gilbert, *Israel: A History,* p. 112.

CHAPTER 7: THE YISHUV RESISTS THE BRITISH, THE ARABS BATTLE PARTITION

1　Menachem Begin, trans. Samuel Katz, *The Revolt* (1951; reprint Bnei Brak, Israel: Steimatzky, 2007), pp. 59–60.

2　Interview with the author, April 18, 2013.

3　Bruce Hoffman, *Anonymous Soldiers: The Struggle for Israel: 1917–1947* (New York: Alfred A. Knopf, 2015), p. 333.

4   Accounts differ. Martin Gilbert (*Israel: A History* [New York: Harper Perennial, 1998], pp. 118–119) claims that Moyne was killed on the sixth and Senesh on the fourth, but other accounts suggest that she died a day before Moyne was assassinated. There was, of course, no cause and effect.

5   Anita Shapira, trans. Anthony Berris, *Ben-Gurion: Father of Modern Israel* (New Haven and London: Yale University Press, 2014), p. 138.

6   Lawrence Epstein, *The Dream of Zion: The Story of the First Zionist Congress* (Lanham, MD: Rowman and Littlefield, 2016), p. 120.

7   Eric Lichtblau, "Surviving the Nazis, Only to Be Jailed by America," *New York Times* (February 7, 2015), http://www.nytimes.com/2015/02/08/sunday-review/surviving-the-nazis-only-to-be-jailed-by-america.html [Last viewed December 7, 2015].

8   Ibid.

9   Gilbert, *Israel: A History*, p. 121.

10 Yehuda Avner, interview with the author on October 24, 2012.

11 Gilbert, *Israel: A History*, pp. 138–139.

12 Hoffman, *Anonymous Soldiers*, p. 379.

13 Gilbert, *Israel: A History*, p. 145.

14 Ibid.

15 These numbers vary slightly among scholars—Colin Shindler, *A History of Modern Israel*, 2nd ed. (New York: Cambridge University Press, 2013), puts the figures at 538,000 Jews, and 397,000 Arabs (p. 45).

16 Gilbert, *Israel: A History*, p. 149.

17 "CIA Report on the Consequences of the Partition of Palestine," p. 18. Copy on file with the author.

18 David McCullough, *Truman* (New York: Simon & Schuster, 1993), Kindle Edition, Locations 11804–11836.

19 Gilbert, *Israel: A History*, p. 150.

20 iCenter, "The Story of a Vote, Nov. 29, 1947," *iCenter* (November 4, 2012), http://www.theicenter.org/voice/story-vote-nov-29-1947.

21 Accounts of the chronology differ. In his autobiography, Abba Eban writes that the vote was postponed on Tuesday, November 26, and again on Wednesday, November 27, because of an appeal and a filibuster. It finally took place on Friday, November 29, after a third

hiatus for Thanksgiving on that Thursday. Asaf Siniver's biography of Eban says that the vote was postponed on Wednesday, but was ultimately held on Saturday. Anita Shapira writes the vote took place on Friday, while Benny Morris states that the date was Saturday.

22 Asaf Siniver, *Abba Eban: A Biography* (New York and London: Overlook Duckworth, 2015), p. 91.

23 Shlomo Avineri, trans. Haim Watzman, *Herzl: Theodor Herzl and the Foundation of the Jewish State* (London: Weidenfeld and Nicolson, 2008), p. 141 (quoting Herzl's diary).

24 A.A.P., "U.N.O. Passes Palestine Partition Plan," *Morning Herald* (December 1, 1947), http://trove.nla.gov.au/ndp/del/article/134238148 [Last viewed December 7, 2015].

25 Amos Oz, trans. Nicholas de Lange, *A Tale of Love and Darkness* (Orlando: Harcourt, 2004), p. 359.

26 Ibid.

27 Michael Bar-Zohar, trans. Peretz Kidron, *Ben-Gurion: A Biography, The New Millennium Edition* (Israel: Weidenfeld and Nicolson, 2013), Kindle Edition, Location 3028.

28 Daniel Gordis, *Saving Israel: How the Jewish People Can Win a War That May Never End* (Hoboken, NJ: Wiley, 2009), p. 170. *Ha'aretz* attributed this language to Weizmann on December 15, 1947, just two weeks after the United Nations voted to partition Palestine.

29 Exodus 19:15.

30 Exodus 19:10.

31 Nadav Shragai, "The Legend of Ambushed Palmach Squad '35,'" *Ha'aretz* (April 27, 2009), http://www.haaretz.com/the-legend-of-ambushed-palmach-squad-35-1.274876 [Last viewed December 7, 2015]. The original account was based on a eulogy Ben-Gurion delivered to his Mapai Party only a few days after the attack. Ben-Gurion apparently received his information from an Arab who supposedly was at the scene but did not take part in the massacre. The latter version surfaced sixty-one years later, when the story was told by Yochanan Ben-Ya'akov, born in Kfar Etzion and orphaned by the war.

32 Tamar S. Drukker, "'I Am a Civil War': The Poetry of Haim Gouri," in Hugh Kennedy, ed., *Warfare and Poetry in the Middle East* (London: I. B. Tauris, 2013), pp. 242–243.

33 Mati Alon, *Holocaust and Redemption* (Victoria, BC: Trafford Publishing, 2013), p. 168.

34 Yossi Melman, "Jews, Just Like Arabs, Hid Weapons in Immoral Places," *Ha'aretz* (January 27, 2011).

35 Shapira, trans. Berris, *Israel: A History*, p. 161.

36 Ibid., pp. 157–158.

37 Benny Morris, *Righteous Victims: A History of the Zionist-Arab Conflict, 1881–2001* (New York: Vintage Books, 2001), Kindle Edition, Location 6208.

38 Benny Morris, an internationally recognized and respected Israeli "new historian," who wrote numerous accounts of Israeli military excesses, believes that the accusations of rape were simply false. Most contemporary historians estimate the number killed at 100 to 120. Even Arab historians have changed their narrative; in 1987, two Palestinian scholars associated with Birzeit University near the West Bank city of Ramallah released a report after multiple interviews with witnesses. They put the number of dead at 107, and made no mention of rape in their report. Their conclusions were not unlike Begin's. Cf. Benny Morris, "The Historiography of Deir Yassin," *Journal of Israeli History: Politics, Society, Culture,* Vol. 24, No. 1 (August 2006), p. 87. See also my more detailed summary of the battle and the ways in which it was used by various parties in *Menachem Begin: The Battle for Israel's Soul* (New York: Knopf Doubleday, 2014), Chapter 6, "Deadly Road to Jerusalem."

39 Gilbert, *Israel: A History*, pp. 179–180.

CHAPTER 8: INDEPENDENCE

1 Bruce Hoffman, *Anonymous Soldiers: The Struggle for Israel: 1917–1947* (New York: Alfred A. Knopf, 2015) Kindle Edition, Location 8282.

2 Ariel Feldestein, "One Meeting—Many Descriptions: The Resolution on the Establishment of the State of Israel," *Israel Studies Forum,* Vol. 23, No. 2 (Winter 2008), p. 104.

3 Ibid.

4 Benny Morris, *1948: The First Arab-Israeli War* (New Haven and London: Yale University Press, 2008), p. 177.

5 Ibid., p. 178.

6 "Israel's Declaration of Independence 1948," *Avalon Project,* http:// avalon.law.yale.edu/20th_century/israel.asp [Last viewed December 7, 2015].

7 Anita Shapira, trans. Anthony Berris, *Israel: A History* (Waltham, MA: Brandeis University Press, 2012), p. 180.

8 II Samuel 23:3.

9 Yehudah Mirsky, "What Is a Nation-State For?"*Marginalia* (March 11, 2015), http://marginalia.lareviewofbooks.org/nation-state-yehudah -mirsky/ [Last viewed December 7, 2015].

10 Genesis 32:28.

11 Shapira, trans. Berris, *Israel: A History,* p. 164.

12 Amira Lam, "Peres Recalls Declaration of Independence: We Didn't Have Time to Celebrate," Ynetnews.com (December 21, 2014), http://www.ynetnews.com/articles/0,7340,L-4606090,00 .html.

13 *Tekumah (Rebirth: The First Fifty Years),* an Israeli television series, first broadcast 1998, Channel 1, Episode 3 at 29:25.

14 Martin Gilbert, *Israel: A History* (New York: Harper Perennial, 1998), p. 192.

15 Morris, *1948,* p. 237.

16 Shapira, trans. Berris, *Israel: A History,* p. 165.

17 Colin Shindler, *A History of Modern Israel,* 2nd ed. (New York: Cambridge University Press, 2013), p. 55.

18 Gilbert, *Israel: A History,* pp. 207–208.

19 Morris, *1948,* p. 142.

20 Ibid., p. 159.

21 Ibid.

22 Ibid., p. 365.

23 Ibid., p. 266.

24 Ibid., p. 268.

25 The curiosity of the swastikas on the Czech arms is mentioned at the Ayalon museum exhibit, and was corroborated as likely in an e-mail from Professor Benny Morris to the author. "The arms arriving from Czecho were standard German Mauser rifles and MG machineguns—so presumably many had Swastikas, having been produced, for the Germans, before May 1945 (as the Messerschmitts produced by the Czechs also, originally, did)." E-mail, dated May 1, 2016, on file with the author.

26 See, for example, Eliezer Cohen, trans. Yonatan Gordis, *Israel's Best Defense: The First Full Story of the Israeli Air Force* (New York: Orion Books, 1993), pp. 7–60. See also *Above and Beyond* (Playmount Productions and Katahdin Productions, produced by Nancy Spielberg, 2015) at 15:20.

27 *Above and Beyond* at 38:20.

28 *Above and Beyond* at 43:00.

29 *Above and Beyond* at 50:40.

30 *Above and Beyond* at 51:30.

31 Translation by the author. Photograph of the memorandum on file with the author.

32 Jerold S. Auerbach, *Brothers at War: Israel and the Tragedy of the Altalena* (New Orleans: Quid Pro Books, 2011), p. 50.

33 Yehuda Lapidot, trans. Chaya Galai, "The *Altalena* Affair," *Etzel*, http://www.etzel.org.il/english/ac20.htm [Last viewed December 7, 2015].

34 Zvi Harry Hurwitz, *Begin: His Life, Words, and Deeds* (Jerusalem: Gefen Publishing, 2004), p. 27.

35 Avi Shilon, trans. Danielle Zilberberg and Yoram Sharett, *Menachem Begin: A Life* (New Haven and London: Yale University Press, 2007), p. 130.

36 Auerbach, *Brothers at War,* p. 109.

37 Michael Oren, "Did Israel Want the Six Day War?," *Azure* (Spring 5759/1999), p. 47.

38 Ibid.

39 Ilan Pappe, "A Post-Zionist Critique of Israel and the Palestinians, Part II: The Media," in *Journal of Palestine Studies* (Spring 1997), pp. 37–43, cited in Oren, "Did Israel Want the Six Day War?," p. 48.

40 Ari Shavit, *My Promised Land: The Triumph and Tragedy of Israel* (New York: Spiegel & Grau, 2013), p. 108.

41 Ibid., p. 132.

42 See Martin Kramer, "What Happened at Lydda," *Mosaic* (July 1, 2014), http://mosaicmagazine.com/essay/2014/07/what-happened-at-lydda/.

43 Benny Morris, "Zionism's 'Black Boxes,'" *Mosaic* (July 13, 2014), http://mosaicmagazine.com/response/2014/07/zionisms-black-boxes/ [Last viewed December 7, 2015].

44 Gilbert, *Israel: A History*, p. 218.

45 Nadav Man, "1st IDF Parade from Behind the Lens," Ynet news.com (December 13, 2008), http://www.ynetnews.com/articles/0,7340,L-3637748,00.html [Last viewed December 7, 2015].

46 Ari Shavit, "Survival of the Fittest? An Interview with Benny Morris," *Ha'aretz* (January 8, 2004), http://www.haaretz.com/survival-of-the-fittest-1.61345 [Last viewed December 7, 2015].

47 Shilon, trans. Zilberberg and Sharett, *Menachem Begin: A Life*, p. 137.

48 Shapira, trans. Berris, *Israel: A History*, p. 172.

49 Morris, *1948*, p. 406.

CHAPTER 9: FROM DREAMS OF A STATE TO THE REALITY OF STATEHOOD

1 Pinhas Alpert and Dotan Goren, eds., *Diary of a Muchtar in Jerusalem: The History of the Beit Yisrael Neighborhood and its Surroundings in the Writings of Rabbi Moshe Yekutiel Alpert (1938–1952)* (Ramat Gan, Israel: Bar Ilan University Press, 2013), pp. 173–174 [In Hebrew]. English translation from Vered Kellner, "Longings and Disappointments: A Voter in Exile in New York," *Ha'aretz* (January 18, 2013), http://www.haaretz.com/opinion/longings-and-disappointments-a-voter-in-exile-in-new-york.premium-1.494743 [Last viewed August 5, 2016].

2 Vered Kellner, "Longings and Disappointments: A Voter in Exile in New York," *Ha'aretz* (January 18, 2013), online at http://www.haaretz.com/opinion/longings-and-disappointments-a-voter-in-exile-in-new-york.premium-1.494743 [Last viewed August 5, 2016]

3 Jewish Telegraphic Agency, "Israel to Vote Today in First National Elections; Campaign Reaches High Peak" (January 25, 1949), http://www.jta.org/1949/01/25/archive/israel-to-vote-today-in-first-national-elections-campaign-reaches-high-peak [Last viewed December 7, 2015].

4 *Tekumah (Rebirth: The First Fifty Years),* an Israeli television series, first broadcast 1998, Channel 1, Episode 21 at 00:35.

5 "Moving Ceremony Marks Reburial of Herzl's Remains; Israeli Cabinet in Full Attendance," *Jewish Telegraphic Agency,* http://www.jta.org/1949/08/18/archive/moving-ceremony-marks-reburial-of-herzls-remains-israeli-cabinet-in-full-attendance.

6   Theodor Herzl, trans. I. M. Lask, *The Jewish State* (Tel Aviv: M. Newman Publishing House, 1954), p. 137.

7   Ibid., p. 151.

8   JTA, "Of Weizmann's Address Opening Session of Israeli Constituent Assembly" (February 15, 1949), http://www.jta .org/1949/02/15/archive/of-chaim-weizmanns-address-opening -session-of-israeli-constituent-assembly [Last viewed December 7, 2015].

9   Ibid.

10   Ibid.

11   Robert Frost, "The Death of the Hired Man" (North of Boston, 1915), *Bartleby.com*, http://www.bartleby.com/118/3.html [Last viewed December 7, 2015].

12   Anita Shapira, trans. Anthony Berris, *Israel: A History* (Waltham, MA: Brandeis University Press, 2012), p. 208.

13   "Displacement of Jews from Arab Countries 1948–2012," *Justice for Jews from Arab Countries*, http://www.justiceforjews.com/main_ facts.html [Last viewed December 7, 2015].

14   Colin Shindler, *A History of Modern Israel*, 2nd ed. (New York: Cambridge University Press, 2013), p. 64.

15   Shapira, trans. Berris, *Israel: A History*, Kindle Edition, Locations 5437–5443.

16   Shindler, *A History of Modern Israel*, p. 93.

17   Golda Meir, *My Life* (New York: Dell Publishing, 1975), pp. 250– 251.

18   Esther Meir-Glitzenstein, "Operation Magic Carpet: Constructing the Myth of the Magical Immigration of Yemenite Jews to Israel," *Israel Studies*, Vol. 16, No. 3 (Fall 2011), p. 150.

19   Shapira, trans. Berris, *Israel: A History*, Kindle Edition, Location 5453.

20   Israel Ministry of Foreign Affairs, "Fifty Years of Education in the State of Israel," http://www.mfa.gov.il/mfa/aboutisrael/is raelat50/pages/fifty%20years%20of%20education%20in%20 the%20state%20of%20israel.aspx.

21   Herzl, trans. Lask, *The Jewish State*, p. 16.

22   Shindler, *A History of Modern Israel*, p. 94.

23   Shapira, trans. Berris, *Israel: A History*, p. 231.

24 Seth J. Frantzman, "David Ben-Gurion, Israel's Segregationist Founder," *Forward* (May 18, 2015), http://forward.com/opinion /israel/308306/ben-gurion-israels-segregationist-founder/ [Last viewed December 8, 2015].

25 Ibid.

26 Nir Kedar, "Ben-Gurion's Mamlakhtiyut: Etymological and Theoretical Roots," *Israel Studies*, Vol. 7, No. 3 (Fall 2002), p. 129.

27 *Tekumah*, Episode 17 at 12:00.

28 Shapira, trans. Berris, *Israel: A History*, p. 199.

29 Tamara Traubman, "A Mystery That Defies Solution," *Ha'aretz* (November 5, 2001), http://www.haaretz.com/print-edition/ news/a-mystery-that-defies-solution-1.73913 [Last viewed December 8, 2015].

30 Moshe Reinfeld, "State Commission: Missing Yemenite Babies Not Kidnapped," *Ha'aretz* (November 4, 2001), http://www.haaretz .com/news/state-commission-missing-yemenite-babies-not-kid napped-1.73778 [Last viewed December 8, 2015].

31 "15,000% Growth in Army Exemptions for Yeshiva Students since 1948," Hiddush website, http://hiddush.org/article-2338–0–15000 _Growth_in_army_exemptions_for_yeshiva_students_since _1948.aspx [Last viewed December 9, 2015].

32 *Tekumah*, Episode 11 at 31:45.

33 *Tekumah*, Episode 11 at 20:15.

34 Shapira, trans. Berris, *Israel: A History*, p. 197.

35 David Ben-Gurion, *Like Stars and Dust: Essays from Israel's Government Year Book* (Ramat Gan, Israel: Masada Press, 1976), p. 147. The translation from the Hebrew by the author. This passage also appears in my *Saving Israel: How the Jewish People Can Win a War That May Never End* (Hoboken, NJ: Wiley, 2009), p. 154.

36 Jacob Blaustein, "The Voice of Reason: Address by Jacob Blaustein, President, The American Jewish Committee, at the Meeting of Its Executive Committee, April 29, 1950," *American Jewish Committee Archives*, http://www.ajcarchives.org/AJC_DATA/ Files/507.PDF), p. 11. [Last viewed December 8, 2015]. Italics in original, p. 9.

37 Walter Isaacson, *Einstein: His Life and Universe* (New York: Simon & Schuster Paperbacks, 2007), p. 520.

38 Ibid.

39 Blaustein, "The Voice of Reason," p. 11. Italics original.

40 Ibid., p. 10. Italics original.

41 Shapira, trans. Berris, *Israel: A History*, p. 179.

CHAPTER 10: ISRAEL ENTERS THE INTERNATIONAL ARENA

1   Anita Shapira, trans. Anthony Berris, *Israel: A History* (Waltham, MA: Brandeis University Press, 2012), p. 274.

2   The number of Israelis killed is highly contested. Martin Gilbert claims that 967 Israelis were killed in these attacks (Martin Gilbert, *The Routledge Atlas of the Arab-Israeli Conflict* [New York: Routledge, 2005], p. 58). But Benny Morris calls that number "sheer nonsense." (See Benny Morris, *Israel's Border Wars, 1949–1956: Arab Infiltration, Israeli Retaliation, and the Countdown to the Suez War* [Oxford: Oxford University Press: 1993], p. 101.) Conservative estimates are several hundred.

3   Morris, *Israel's Border Wars, 1949–1956*, Kindle Edition, Locations 3037–3049.

4   Ibid., Locations 3123–3128.

5   Martin Gilbert, *Israel: A History* (New York: Harper Perennial, 1998), pp. 289–290.

6   S. Yizhar, trans. Nicolas de Lange and Yaacob Dweck, *Khirbet Khizeh: A Novel* (New York: Farrar, Straus and Giroux, 2014), p. 100.

7   Ibid., pp. 103–104.

8   Noah Efron, "The Price of Return," *Ha'aretz* (November 23, 2008), http://www.haaretz.com/news/the-price-of-return-1.258035 [Last viewed December 8, 2015].

9   Robert Slater, *Warrior Statesman: The Life of Moshe Dayan* (New York: St. Martin's Press, 1991), p. 149.

10 Morris, *Israel's Border Wars, 1949–1956*, Locations 3037–3049.

11 David Landau, *Arik: The Life of Ariel Sharon* (New York: Alfred A. Knopf, 2013), p. 7.

12 Gilbert, *Israel: A History*, p. 292.

13 Zvi Ganin, *An Uneasy Relationship: American Jewish Leadership and Israel, 1948–1957* (Syracuse, NY: Syracuse University Press, 2005), pp. 190–191.

14 Landau, *Arik*, pp. 26–27.

15 Morris, *Israel's Border Wars, 1949–1956*, Locations 3293–3299.

16 Translation from Mitch Ginsburg, "When Moshe Dayan Delivered the Defining Speech of Zionism," *Times of Israel* (April 26, 2016), http://www.timesofisrael.com/when-moshe-dayan-delivered -the-defining-speech-of-zionism/ [Last viewed on May 8, 2016]. See also Aluf Benn, "Doomed to Fight" (May 9, 2011), *Ha'aretz*, http://www.haaretz.com/weekend/week-s-end/doomed-to-fight -1.360698 [Last viewed December 8, 2015].

17 Ginsburg, "When Moshe Dayan Delivered the Defining Speech of Zionism." See also Chemi Shalev, "Moshe Dayan's Enduring Gaza Eulogy: This Is the Fate of Our Generation," *Ha'aretz* (July 20, 2014), http://www.haaretz.com/blogs/west-of-eden/ .premium-1.606258 [Last viewed December 8, 2015].

18 Morris, *Israel's Border Wars, 1949–1956*, Locations 208–213.

19 Ibid.

20 Howard M. Sachar, *A History of Israel: From the Rise of Zionism to Our Time* (New York: Alfred A. Knopf, 1979), p. 486.

21 Ibid., p. 487.

22 Gilbert, *Israel: A History*, p. 315.

23 Ibid., p. 317.

24 Morris, *Israel's Border Wars, 1949–1956*, Location 7962.

25 Michael B. Oren, "The Second War of Independence," *Azure*, No. 27 (Winter 5767/2007).

26 Sachar, *A History of Israel*, p. 483.

27 Gilbert, *Israel: A History*, pp. 326–327.

28 Golda Meir, *My Life* (New York: Dell Publishing, 1975), p. 59

29 Yehuda Avner, *The Prime Ministers: An Intimate Narrative of Israeli Leadership* (Jerusalem: Toby Press, 2010), Kindle Edition, Locations 1822–1829.

30 Ibid.

CHAPTER 11: ISRAEL CONFRONTS THE HOLOCAUST

1 David Mikics, "Holocaust Pulp Fiction," *Tablet Magazine* (April 19, 2012), http://www.tabletmag.com/jewish-arts-and -culture/books/97160/ka-tzetnik.

2 Deborah E. Lipstadt, *The Eichmann Trial* (New York: Knopf Doubleday, 2011), p. 3.

3 Ibid., pp. 21–22.

4 Ibid., pp. 24–25.

5 Ibid., p. 29.

6 Martin Gilbert, *Israel: A History* (New York: Harper Perennial, 1998), p. 337.

7 George Lavy, *Germany and Israel: Moral Debt and National Interest* (London: Frank Cass, 1996), p. 7.

8 Menachem Begin, *White Nights: The Story of a Prisoner in Russia* (New York: HarperCollins, 1979), p. 265.

9 Daniel Gordis, *Menachem Begin: The Battle for Israel's Soul* (New York: Knopf Doubleday, 2014), p. 104.

10 Gilbert, *Israel: A History*, p. 280.

11 Seth M. Siegel, *Let There Be Water: Israel's Solution for a Water-Starved World* (New York: Thomas Dunne Books, 2015), p. 40.

12 Seth M. Siegel, "50 Years Later, National Water Carrier Still an Inspiration," Ynetnews.com (September 6, 2014), http://www.ynetnews.com/articles/0,7340,L-4528200,00.html [Last viewed on May 10, 2016].

13 *Tekumah (Rebirth: The First Fifty Years),* an Israeli television series, first broadcast 1998, Channel 1, Episode 17 at 20:15.

14 Assaf Inbari, *HaBaita* (Tel Aviv: Yediyot Sefarim, 2009), pp. 169–170, 178 [Translations by Daniel Gordis].

15 Elad Zeret, "Kastner's Killer: I Would Never Have Shot Him Today," Ynetnews.com (October 29, 2014), http://www.ynetnews.com/articles/0,7340,L-4585767,00.html [Last viewed December 8, 2015].

16 Yossi Klein Halevi, *Like Dreamers: The Story of the Israeli Paratroopers Who Reunited Jerusalem and Divided a Nation* (New York: HarperCollins, 2013), p. 42.

17 Ari Shavit, *My Promised Land: The Triumph and Tragedy of Israel* (New York: Spiegel & Grau, 2013), pp. 179–180.

18 Lipstadt, *The Eichmann Trial*, p. 34.

19 David Ben-Gurion, "The Eichmann Case as Seen by Ben-Gurion," *New York Times* (December 18, 1960), http://timesmachine.nytimes.com/timesmachine/1960/12/18/99904385.html?pageNumber=182 [Last viewed December 8, 2015].

20 Lipstadt, *The Eichmann Trial*, p. 36.

21 Ibid., p. 53.

22 Ibid., p. 78.

23 Ibid.

24 Ibid., pp. 97–98.

25 Ibid.

26 "Planet Auschwitz" (filmed testimony of Yehiel De-Nur at Eichmann trial), https://www.youtube.com/watch?v=o0T9tZiKYl4.

27 Oz Almog, *The Sabra* (Berkeley: University of California Press, 2000), p. 84.

28 Yair Lapid, trans. Evan Fallenberg, *Memories After My Death: The Joseph (Tommy) Lapid Story* (London: Elliott & Thompson Limited, 2011), pp. 131–132.

29 Ibid.

30 Lipstadt, *The Eichmann Trial,* pp. 80–81.

31 Haim Hazaz, *The Sermon and Other Stories* (Jerusalem: Toby Press, 2005), p. 237.

CHAPTER 12: SIX DAYS OF WAR CHANGE A COUNTRY FOREVER

1 Jewish Agency, "The Massive Immigration," http://www.jewish agency.org/he/historical-aliyah/content/22097 [Last viewed December 10, 2015] [In Hebrew].

2 Many translations of the song have been published. This one is mine.

3 On her deathbed in 2004, Shemer admitted that the melody she wrote was largely based on a Basque lullaby. Tom Segev, "In Letter, Naomi Shemer Admitted Lifting 'Jerusalem of Gold' Tune," *Ha'aretz* (May 5, 2005), http://www.haaretz.com/news/in-letter -naomi-shemer-admitted-lifting-jerusalem-of-gold-tune-1.157851 [Last viewed December 8, 2015].

4 Yossi Klein Halevi, *Like Dreamers: The Story of the Israeli Paratroopers Who Reunited Jerusalem and Divided a Nation* (New York: HarperCollins, 2013), p. 58.

5 Ibid., p. 31.

6 Ibid., p. 34.

7 Michael B. Oren, *Six Days of War: June 1967 and the Making of the Modern Middle East* (Oxford: Oxford University Press, 2002), p. 63.

8 Ibid.

9 Ibid., p. 368.

10 Abba Eban, *Abba Eban: An Autobiography* (Lexington, MA: Plunkett Lake Press, 2015), Kindle Edition, Location 7223.

11 Ibid., Location 7352.

12 Oren, *Six Days of War*, p. 133.

13 Yehuda Avner, *The Prime Ministers: An Intimate Narrative of Israeli Leadership* (Jerusalem: Toby Press, 2010), p. 148.

14 Ibid.

15 Oren, *Six Days of War*, p. 132.

16 Avner, *The Prime Ministers*, p. 148.

17 Oren, *Six Days of War*, p. 134.

18 Martin Gilbert, *Israel: A History* (New York: Harper Perennial, 1998), p. 377.

19 Avraham Avi-hai, "The POSTman Knocks Twice: Yitzhak Rabin, Man of Contradictions," *Jerusalem Post* (September 11, 2014), http:// www.jpost.com/Opinion/The-POSTman-Knocks-Twice-Yitzhak -Rabin-man-of-contradictions-375134 [Last viewed March 23, 2016].

20 Halevi, *Like Dreamers*, p. 57.

21 Samuel G. Freedman, *Jew vs. Jew: The Struggle for the Soul of American Jewry* (New York: Simon & Schuster, 2001), p. 164. Michael Oren, *Power, Faith, and Fantasy: America in the Middle East, 1776 to the Present* (New York: W. W. Norton, 2007), p. 536.

22 Ibid., p. 319.

23 Gilbert, *Israel: A History*, p. 373.

24 Anita Shapira, trans. Anthony Berris, *Israel: A History* (Waltham, MA: Brandeis University Press, 2012), p. 298.

25 Avner, *The Prime Ministers*, p. 135.

26 Tom Segev, trans. Jessica Cohen, *1967: Israel, the War, and the Year That Transformed the Middle East* (New York: Henry Holt, 2005), p. 15. I have altered Segev's translation of the Hebrew slightly.

27 Gilbert, *Israel: A History*, p. 378.

28 Accounts of what happened, and when, differ slightly. Compare Shapira, Oren, and Gilbert to see the differences. The following account is based on Michael Oren's chronology.

29 Daniel Gordis, *Menachem Begin: The Battle for Israel's Soul* (New York: Knopf Doubleday, 2014), p. 126.

30 Oren, *Six Days of War*, p. 176.

31 Avner, *The Prime Ministers*, pp. 156–158.

32 Halevi, *Like Dreamers*, p. 69.

33 Oren, *Six Days of War*, p. 222.

34 Ibid., p. 88.

35 Gilbert, *Israel: A History*, p. 391.

36 Ibid., p. 392.

37 Ibid.

38 Oren, *Six Days of War*, p. 307.

39 Gershom Gorenberg, *The Accidental Empire: Israel and the Birth of the Settlements, 1967–1977* (New York: Henry Holt, 2006), p. 2.

40 Michael Oren, "Did Israel Want the Six Day War?," *Azure* (Spring 5759/1999), p. 49.

41 Ibid., p. 50.

42 Ibid., p. 51.

43 *Tekumah (Rebirth: The First Fifty Years)*, an Israeli television series, first broadcast 1998, Channel 1, Episode 19 at 20:35.

44 *Tekumah*, Episode 20 at 25:45.

45 Halevi, *Like Dreamers*, p. 98.

CHAPTER 13: THE BURDEN OF OCCUPATION

1 Yossi Klein Halevi, *Like Dreamers: The Story of the Israeli Paratroopers Who Reunited Jerusalem and Divided a Nation* (New York: Harper-Collins, 2013), p. 111.

2 Gershom Gorenberg, *The Accidental Empire: Israel and the Birth of the Settlements, 1967–1977* (New York: Henry Holt, 2006), p. 86.

3 Ibid., p. 43.

4 Ibid., p. 85.

5 Tsur Ehrlich, "Nathan the Wise," *Azure*, No. 28 (Spring 5767/2007), http://azure.org.il/include/print.php?id=445 [Last viewed December 8, 2015].

6 Halevi, *Like Dreamers*, p. 119.

7 Translation of Leibowitz's letter, which is reproduced on numerous websites, by the author.

8 Halevi, *Like Dreamers*, p. 94.

9 Ibid., p. 152.

10 Ibid., pp. 140–142.

11 Gorenberg, *The Accidental Empire*, p. 113.

12   Halevi, *Like Dreamers,* pp. 145–146.

13   Ibid.

14   Benny Morris, *Righteous Victims: A History of the Zionist-Arab Conflict, 1881–2001* (New York: Vintage Books, 2001), p. 335.

15   *Tekumah (Rebirth: The First Fifty Years),* an Israeli television series, first broadcast 1998, Channel 1, Episode 14 at 4:50.

16   Halevi, *Like Dreamers,* pp. 96–97.

17   Ibid.,p. 101.

18   Translation by the author.

19   Martin Gilbert, *Israel: A History* (New York: Harper Perennial, 1998), p. 393.

20   Gorenberg, *The Accidental Empire,* pp. 61–62.

21   Ghassan Kanafani, *Palestine's Children: Returning to Haifa and Other Stories* (Boulder, CO: Lynne Rienner, 2000), p. 151.

22   The Hamas charter is found in many places online. Translations vary slightly. This translation is from the Jewish Virtual Library.

23   Mahmoud Darwish, "Identity Card," http://www.barghouti.com/poets/darwish/bitaqa.asp.

24   "The Khartoum Resolutions," Ministry of Foreign Affairs of Israel (September 1, 1967), http://www.mfa.gov.il/mfa/foreignpolicy/peace/guide/pages/the%20khartoum%20resolutions.aspx [Last viewed December 8, 2015].

CHAPTER 14: YOM KIPPUR WAR

1   Martin Gilbert, *Israel: A History* (New York: HarperPerennial, 1998), p. 423.

2   Howard M. Sachar, *A History of Israel: From the Rise of Zionism to Our Time* (New York: Alfred A. Knopf, 1979), p. 744.

3   David Landau, *Arik: The Life of Ariel Sharon* (New York: Alfred A. Knopf, 2013), p. 75.

4   Zeev Schiff, *A History of the Israeli Army: 1874 to the Present* (London: Macmillan, 1985), p. 246.

5   *Tekumah (Rebirth: The First Fifty Years),* an Israeli television series, first broadcast 1998, Channel 1, Episode 9 at 36:20.

6   Anita Shapira, trans. Anthony Berris, *Israel: A History* (Waltham, MA: Brandeis University Press, 2012), Kindle Edition, Locations 7794–7795.

7   Sachar, *A History of Israel,* p. 748.

8   *Tekumah,* Episode 9 at 43:18.

9   William B. Quandt, *Peace Process: American Diplomacy and the Arab-Israeli Conflict Since 1967* (Washington, DC: Brookings Institution, 2005), p. 101.

10 "Kissinger and Ismail Conduct Secret Meetings," Center for Israel Education, http://israeled.org/kissinger-ismail-conduct-secret-meetings/ [Last viewed December 8, 2015].

11 Quandt, *Peace Process,* p. 455.

12 Mordechai Bar-On, *Moshe Dayan: Israel's Controversial Hero* (New Haven and London: Yale University Press, 2012), p. 156.

13 *Tekumah,* Episode 10 at 8:07.

14 Mitch Ginsburg, "Mossad's Tip-Off Ahead of Yom Kippur War Did Not Reach Prime Minister, Newly Released Papers Show," *Times of Israel* (September 20, 2012), http://www.timesofisrael.com/newly-released-papers-detail-depth-of-mishandling-of-yom-kippur-war-warnings/ [Last viewed December 8, 2015].

15 Gilbert, *Israel: A History,* p. 432.

16 Landau, *Arik,* p. 98.

17 Benny Morris, *Righteous Victims: A History of the Zionist-Arab Conflict, 1881–2001* (New York: Vintage Books, 2001), p. 416.

18 Shapira, trans. Berris, *Israel: A History,* p. 330.

19 Gilbert, *Israel: A History,* p. 440.

20 Herbert Druks, *The Uncertain Alliance: The U.S. and Israel from Kennedy to the Peace Process* (Westport, CT: Greenwood Press, 2001), p. 113.

21 Amir Oren, "CIA Report on Yom Kippur War: Israel Had Nuclear Arsenal," *Ha'aretz* (February 13, 2013), http://www.haaretz.com/news/diplomacy-defense/cia-report-on-yom-kippur-war-israel-had-nuclear-arsenal.premium-1.501101 [Last viewed December 8, 2015].

22 *Tekumah,* Episode 10 at 32:00.

23 Gilbert, *Israel: A History,* p. 442.

24 Abraham Rabinovich, *The Yom Kippur War: The Epic Encounter That Transformed the Middle East* (New York: Schocken Books, 2004), p. 497.

25 Gilbert, *Israel: A History,* p. 460.

26 Motti Regev and Edwin Seroussi, *Popular Music and National Culture in Israel* (Berkeley: University of California Press, 2004), p. 67.

27   Translation from the Hebrew by the author.

28   Rabinovich, *The Yom Kippur War*, p. 499.

29   Robert Slater, *Rabin: 20 Years After* (Israel: KIP-Kotarim International Publishing, 2015).

30   *Tekumah*, Episode 20 at 37:55.

31   *Tekumah*, Episode 7 at 45:30.

32   Assaf Inbari, *HaBaita* (Tel Aviv: Yediyot Sefarim, 2009), p. 242 [Translations by Daniel Gordis].

33   There was a brief exception in 1982, when Israeli troops faced the Syrian army, but that never led to genuine war with Syria.

34   *Tekumah*, Episode 13 at 11:40.

35   Gil Troy, *Moynihan's Moment: America's Fight Against Zionism as Racism* (Oxford: Oxford University Press, 2013), p. 18.

CHAPTER 15: REVOLUTION WITHIN THE REVOLUTION

1   Yehuda Avner, *The Prime Ministers: An Intimate Narrative of Israeli Leadership* (Jerusalem: Toby Press, 2010), p. 606.

2   Ben Shalev, "Zohar Argov's Flower That Launched a Million Cassettes," *Ha'aretz* (May 4, 2012), http://www.haaretz.com/weekend/week-s-end/zohar-argov-s-flower-that-launched-a-million-cassettes-1.428235 [Last viewed December 8, 2015].

3   Nir Hasson, "Jerusalem Neighborhood to Name Streets in Honor of Mizrahi Black Panthers," *Ha'aretz* (June 14, 2011), http://www.haaretz.com/jerusalem-neighborhood-to-name-streets-in-honor-of-mizrahi-black-panthers-1.369313 [Last viewed March 23, 2016].

4   Albert Einstein, "New Palestine Poetry: Visit of Menachem Begin and Aims of Political Movement Discussed," *New York Times* (December 4, 1948), https://archive.org/details/AlbertEinsteinLetterToTheNewYorkTimes.December41948.

5   In the fifth Knesset, Begin advocated for the gradual lifting of military law over areas with large Arab populations. It was, in his mind, an extension of the law that breaches individual liberties and freedoms and was a mark of Israel's character. "One of the founding principles of a free country," he posited, "is that military commanders should monitor soldiers and civilians [should monitor] civilians." Avi Shilon, trans. Danielle Zilberberg and Yoram

Sharett, *Menachem Begin: A Life* (New Haven and London: Yale University Press, 2007), p. 191.

6 Daniel Gordis, *Menachem Begin: The Battle for Israel's Soul* (New York: Knopf Doubleday, 2014), p. 88.

7 Menachem Begin, trans. Shmuel Katz, ed. Ivan M. Greenberg, *The Revolt: Story of the Irgun* (Bnei-Brak, Israel: Steimatzky Group, 1952), p. 78.

8 Ned Temko, *To Win or to Die: A Personal Portrait of Menachem Begin* (New York: William Morrow, 1987), p. 146.

9 Anita Shapira, trans. Anthony Berris, *Israel: A History* (Waltham, MA: Brandeis University Press, 2012), p. 357.

10 Assaf Inbari, *HaBaita* (Tel Aviv: Yediyot Sefarim, 2009), p. 248 [Translations by Daniel Gordis].

11 Israeli Broadcasting Authority (IBA), May 30, 1977. The Hebrew can be translated, equally correctly, either as "in the style of a good Jew," or "in a good Jewish style."

12 Benjamin Beit Halachmi, *Despair and Deliverance: Private Salvation in Contemporary Israel* (Albany: State University of New York Press, 1992), p. 55.

13 Gordis, *Menachem Begin*, p. 159.

14 Martin Gilbert, *Israel: A History* (New York: Harper Perennial, 1998), p. 489.

15 Shapira, trans. Berris, *Israel: A History*, p. 367.

16 Gordis, *Menachem Begin*, p. 171.

17 Ofer Grosbard, *Menachem Begin: The Absent Leader* (Haifa: Strategic Research and Policy Center, National Defense College, IDF, 2007), p. 271.

18 Mohamed Fadel Fahmy, "30 Years Later, Questions Remain Over Sadat Killing, Peace with Israel," CNN (October 7, 2011), http://edition.cnn.com/2011/10/06/world/meast/egypt-sadat-assassination/ [Last viewed December 8, 2015].

19 Ironically, most of these resisters were not residents of the town.

20 Gershom Gorenberg, *The Accidental Empire: Israel and the Birth of the Settlements, 1967–1977* (New York: Henry Holt, 2006), p. 361.

21 Temko, *To Win or to Die*, p. 198.

22 Hal Brands and David Palkki, "Saddam, Israel, and the Bomb: Nuclear Alarmism Justified?" *International Security*, Vol. 36, No. 1 (Summer 2011), p. 133.

23 Ibid., p. 146.

24 "Israel's Illusion," *New York Times* (June 9, 1981), http://www.ny times.com/1981/06/09/opinion/israel-s-illusion.html [Last viewed December 8, 2015].

25 Gordis, *Menachem Begin*, p. 192.

26 Joseph Kraft, "For Begin, the End? He Should Be Voted Out for Raid That Further Isolates Israel," *Los Angeles Times* (June 11, 1981).

27 "United Nations Security Council Resolution 487 (1981)," United Nations, http://www.un.org/documents/ga/res/36/a36r027.htm [Last viewed December 8, 2015].

28 Moshe Fuksman-Sha'al, ed., trans. Ruchie Avital, "Dick Cheney Letter to Menachem Begin," *Israel's Strike Against the Iraqi Nuclear Reactor 7 June 1981* (Jerusalem: Menachem Begin Heritage Center, 2003), p. 77.

29 Dan Raviv and Yossi Melman, *Spies Against Armageddon: The Mossad and the Intelligence Community* (Israel: Yediot Ahronoth Books, 2012), p. 334.

30 Gadi Bloom and Nir Hefez, *Ariel Sharon: A Life* (New York: Random House, 2006), p. 213.

31 "Middle East: A Sabbath of Terror," *Time* (March 20, 1978), http://www.time.com/time/magazine/article/0,9171,919454,00.html.

32 Avner, *The Prime Ministers*, p. 606.

33 Temko, *To Win or to Die*, pp. 283–284.

34 Thomas L. Friedman, *From Beirut to Jerusalem* (New York: Farrar, Straus and Giroux, 1989), p. 162.

35 *Tekumah (Rebirth: The First Fifty Years)*, an Israeli television series, first broadcast 1998, Channel 1, Episode 20 at 45:50. The speaker was Letty Cottin Pogrebin, editor of *Ms.* Magazine.

36 Gadi Bloom and Nir Hefez, *Ariel Sharon: A Life* (New York: Random House, 2006), pp. 246–247.

37 Matti Friedman, *Pumpkin Flowers: A Soldier's Story* (Chapel Hill, NC: Algonquin, 2016), p. 188.

38 The assertion that Israel fired flares is made by, among others, Thomas Friedman, *From Beirut to Jerusalem*, p. 161.

39 Nirit Anderman, "Israeli Film on Lebanon War 'Waltz with Bashir' Shown in Beirut," *Ha'aretz* (January 21, 2009), http://www.haaretz.com/news/israeli-film-on-lebanon-war-waltz-with-bashir-shown-in-beirut-1.268524 [Last viewed December 8, 2015].

40 Dan Meridor, interview with the author, January 2, 2013.

41 Michael B. Oren, *Ally: My Journey Across the American-Israeli Divide* (New York: Random House, 2015), p. 27.

42 Shilon, trans. Zilberberg and Sharett, *Menachem Begin: A Life*, pp. 374–375.

CHAPTER 16: TAKING A PAGE FROM THE ZIONISTS

1 Ari Shavit, *My Promised Land: The Triumph and Tragedy of Israel* (New York: Spiegel & Grau, 2013), p. 276.

2 Ibid., p. 278.

3 Nathan Brown, Amr Hamzawy, and Marina Ottaway, "Islamist Movements and the Democratic Process in the Arab World: Exploring the Gray Zones," *Carnegie Papers*, No. 67 (March 2006), http://carnegieendowment.org/files/CP67.Brown.FINAL.pdf [Last viewed December 9, 2015].

4 The Hamas Charter is widely available online. See, for example, http://www.acpr.org.il/resources/hamascharter.html.

5 Benny Morris, *Righteous Victims: A History of the Zionist-Arab Conflict, 1881–2001* (New York: Vintage Books, 2001), Kindle Edition, Locations 13929–13937.

6 *Tekumah (Rebirth: The First Fifty Years)*, an Israeli television series, first broadcast 1998, Channel 1, Episode 18 at 3:50.

7 *Tekumah*, Episode 18 at 16:25.

8 Martin Gilbert, *Israel: A History* (New York: Harper Perennial, 1998), pp. 533–534.

9 Morris, *Righteous Victims*, Location 6313.

10 Ibid., Locations 14578–14596. See also http://www.nytimes.com/1988/08/01/world/hussein-surrenders-claims-west-bank-plo-us-peace-plan-jeopardy-internal-tensions.html.

11 Morris, *Righteous Victims*, Locations 14501–14503.

12 Gilbert, *Israel: A History*, pp. 538–539.

13 Joel Greenberg, "Yeshayahu Leibowitz, 91, Iconoclastic Israeli Thinker," *New York Times* (August 19, 1994), http://www.nytimes.com/1994/08/19/obituaries/yeshayahu-leibowitz-91-iconoclastic-israeli-thinker.html [Last viewed December 9, 2015].

14 David Ellenson and Daniel Gordis, ed. Aron Rodrigue and Steven J. Zipperstein, *Pledges of Jewish Allegiance: Conversion, Law, and*

Policymaking in Nineteenth- and Twentieth-Century Orthodox Responsa (Stanford, CA: Stanford University Press, 2012), pp. 151–158.

15 Howard M. Lenhoff and Jerry L. Weaver, *Black Jews, Jews, and Other Heroes: How Grassroots Activism Led to the Rescue of the Ethiopian Jews* (Jerusalem: Gefen Publishing House, 2007), pp. 42–43.

16 Daniel Gordis, *Menachem Begin: The Battle for Israel's Soul* (New York: Knopf Doubleday, 2014), pp. 144–145.

17 Gilbert, *Israel: A History*, p. 552.

18 Jeff Jacoby, "Would Rabin Have Pulled the Plug on a 'Peace Process' That Failed?" *Boston Globe* (October 22, 2015), http://www .bostonglobe.com/opinion/2015/10/22/would-rabin-have-pulled -plug-peace-process-that-failed/fgHF1Y8bkh7leSbtgHfleL/story .html [Last viewed December 9, 2015].

19 Moshe Ya'alon, *The Longer Shorter Way* (Tel Aviv: Yedioth Ahronoth Books and Chemed Books, 2007). p. 82 [In Hebrew]. Also discussed in English in David M. Weinberg, "Yitzhak Rabin Was 'Close to Stopping the Oslo Process,'" *Jerusalem Post* (October 17, 2013), http:// www.jpost.com/Opinion/Columnists/Yitzhak-Rabin-was-close-to -stopping-the-Oslo-process-329064.

20 Weinberg, "Yitzhak Rabin Was 'Close to Stopping the Oslo Process.'"

21 Gilbert, *Israel: A History*, pp. 569–570.

22 Ibid., p. 572.

23 Ibid., p. 584.

24 *Tekumah*, Episode 22 at 00:20.

25 Ibid., p. 587.

26 Ibid.

CHAPTER 17: THE PEACE PROCESS STALLS

1 King Hussein's eulogy at Rabin's funeral, November 6, 1995. Transcript available at http://www.mfa.gov.il/mfa/mfa-archive/1995/ pages/rabin%20funeral-%20eulogy%20by%20king%20hussein.aspx.

2 "Clinton to Lead U.S. Delegation," CNN (November 5, 1995), http://edition.cnn.com/WORLD/9511/rabin/clinton/index.html [Last viewed December 9, 2015].

3 Jeff Jacoby, "Would Rabin Have Pulled the Plug on a 'Peace Process' That Failed?" *Boston Globe* (October 22, 2015), http://

www.bostonglobe.com/opinion/2015/10/22/would-rabin-have
-pulled-plug-peace-process-that-failed/fgHF1Y8bkh7leSbtgHfleL/
story.html [Last viewed December 9, 2015].

4 Martin Gilbert, *Israel: A History* (New York: Harper Perennial, 1998), p. 593.

5 Matti Friedman, *Pumpkin Flowers* (Chapel Hill: Algonquin Books, 2016), p. 155.

6 Ibid.

7 Ibid., p. 181.

8 "Dennis Ross and Gidi Grinstein, Reply by Hussein Agha and Robert Malley," *New York Review of Books* (September 20, 2001), http://www.nybooks.com/articles/archives/2001/sep/20/camp-david-an-exchange/ [Last viewed December 9, 2015].

9 Not surprisingly, not everyone agrees as to the reason for the collapse of talks. Even among Israelis, there are some scholars who hold Barak accountable and do not accept the Ross-Barak narrative.

10 Colin Shindler, *A History of Modern Israel*, 2nd ed. (New York: Cambridge University Press, 2013), p. 283.

11 Benny Morris, *Righteous Victims: A History of the Zionist-Arab Conflict, 1881–2001* (New York: Vintage Books, 2001), Kindle Edition, Locations 15878–15883.

12 Dan Rabinowitz, "October 2000, Revisited," *Ha'aretz* (October 19, 2004), http://www.haaretz.com/print-edition/opinion/october-2000-revisited-1.137855 [Last viewed December 9, 2015].

13 Jack Khoury, "Israeli Arabs Mark Fifteenth Anniversary of October 2000 Riots," *Ha'aretz* (January 10, 2015), http://www.haaretz.com/israel-news/.premium-1.678344 [Last viewed December 9, 2015].

14 Jewish National Fund, Tree Planting Center, http://www.jnf.org/support/tree-planting-center/.

15 Bill Clinton, *My Life* (New York: Vintage Press, 2005), p. 946.

16 Ibid., pp. 296–297.

17 Dennis Ross, *Doomed to Succeed: The U.S.-Israel Relationships from Truman to Obama* (New York: Farrar, Straus and Giroux, 2015), p. 297.

18 II Samuel 2:26.

19 Benny Morris, "Peace? No Chance," *Guardian* (February 21, 2002),

http://www.theguardian.com/world/2002/feb/21/israel2   [Last viewed January 10, 2016].

20   Ross, *Doomed to Succeed*, p. 312.

21   Interview between Rachel Greenspan and Yossi Klein Halevi, December 15, 2015.

22   Benny Morris, "Exposing Abbas," *National Interest* (May 19, 2011), http://nationalinterest.org/commentary/exposing-abbas-5335 [Last viewed December 9, 2015].

23   Gilbert, *Israel: A History*, p. 627.

24   "Exchange of Letters Between PM Sharon and President Bush," Ministry of Foreign Affairs of Israel website (April 14, 2004), http://www.mfa.gov.il/mfa/foreignpolicy/peace/mfadocu ments/pages/exchange%20of%20letters%20sharon-bush%2014 -apr-2004.aspx [Last viewed December 9, 2015].

25   Gilbert, *Israel: A History*, p. 637.

26   Ibid., p. 638.

27   Yagil Levy, *The Hierarchy of Military Death*, Open University of Israel (Lisbon, April 14–19, 2009), https://ecpr.eu/Filestore/ PaperProposal/2cfd87af-cab2-4374-b84d-eb03fbbc3cd1.pdf. 11.

28   Dan Senor and Saul Singer, *Start-Up Nation: The Story of Israel's Economic Miracle* (New York: Twelve, 2012), p. 15.

29   The World Bank, "GDP Growth (annual %)," http://data.world bank.org/indicator/NY.GDP.MKTP.KD.ZG?page=1.

30   Senor and Singer, *Start-Up Nation*, p. 11.

31   Ibid., pp. 11, 13.

32   Ibid., pp. 11–12.

33   Ibid., p. 129.

34   Ibid., p. 181.

35   Ibid., p. 182.

36   Manfred Gerstenfeld, *The War of a Million Cuts: The Struggle Against the Delegitimization of Israel and the Jews, and the Growth of New Anti-Semitism* (Jerusalem: JCPA, 2015), p. 250.

37   Daniel Freedman, "The World's Deadly Obsession with Israel," *Forbes* (June 24, 2010), http://www.forbes.com/2010/06/23/israel -hamas-middle-east-opinions-columnists-daniel-freedman.html.

38   Gerstenfeld, *The War of a Million Cuts*, pp. 13–14.

39   Joshua Muravchik, "Muslims and Terror: The Real Story," *Commentary* (February 1, 2015), https://www.commentarymagazine

.com/articles/muslims-and-terror-the-real-story-1/ [Last viewed December 9, 2015].

40 "Human Rights Actions," *Human Rights Voices,* http://www .humanrightsvoices.org/EYEontheUN/priorities/actions/ body/?ua=1&ya=1&sa=1&tp=1 [Last viewed January 10, 2016].

41 Michal Navoth, "Israel's Relationship with the UN Human Rights Council: Is There Hope for Change?" *Institute for Contemporary Affairs,* No. 601 (May–June 2014), http://jcpa.org/article/israels-relationship-un-human-rights-council/ [Last viewed January 10, 2016].

42 Irwin Cotler, "Israel and the United Nations," *Jerusalem Post* (August 15, 2013), http://www.jpost.com/Opinion/Op-Ed-Contributors/Israel-and-the-United-Nations-323252 [Last viewed January 10, 2016].

43 Gerstenfeld, *The War of a Million Cuts,* p. 254.

44 Ibid.

45 Richard Kemp, "The U.N.'s Gaza Report Is Flawed and Dangerous," http://www.nytimes.com/2015/06/26/opinion/the-uns-gaza -report-is-flawed-and-dangerous.html.

46 Ibid.

47 Samantha Power, *Remarks at the Israel Middle East Model United Nations Conference on "Building a More Model UN,"* transcript (February 15, 2016), http://usun.state.gov/remarks/7138 [Last viewed March 23, 2016].

48 Robert L. Bernstein, "Rights Watchdog, Lost in the Mideast," *New York Times* (October 19, 2009), http://www.nytimes .com/2009/10/20/opinion/20bernstein.html [Last viewed December 9, 2015].

49 The Forward and Nathan Guttman, "Want to Delegitimize Israel? Be Careful Who You Mess With," *Ha'aretz* (April 13, 2010), http:// www.haaretz.com/news/want-to-delegitimize-israel-be-careful -who-you-mess-with-1.284184 [Last viewed December 9, 2015].

50 Gerstenfeld, *The War of a Million Cuts,* p. 252.

51 Aron Heller, "Western Europe Jewish Migration to Israel Hits All-Time High," Associated Press (January 14, 2016), http://bigstory.ap .org/article/164bbc1445aa42fc883ee85e4439523a/western-europe-jewish-migration-israel-hits-all-time-high [Last viewed March 23, 2016].

52 David Makovsky, "The Silent Strike: How Israel Bombed a Syrian Nuclear Installation and Kept It Secret," *New Yorker* (September 17, 2012),

http://www.newyorker.com/magazine/2012/09/17/the-silent-strike [Last viewed January 10, 2016].

53 Gilbert, *Israel: A History*, p. 635.

54 "PM Says Iran's Chief of Staff Vowed Sunday to Eliminate Israel," *Times of Israel* (May 21, 2012), http://www.timesofisrael.com/pm-says-irans-chief-of-staff-vowed-sunday-to-eliminate-israel/ [Last viewed December 9, 2015].

55 Henry Kissinger and George P. Shultz, "The Iran Deal and Its Consequences," *Wall Street Journal* (April 7, 2015), http://www.wsj.com/articles/the-iran-deal-and-its-consequences-1428447582 [Last viewed December 9, 2015].

56 Michael B. Oren, *Ally: My Journey Across the American-Israeli Divide* (New York: Random House, 2015), p. 360.

57 Ibid., p. 183.

CHAPTER 18: A JEWISH RENAISSANCE IN THE JEWISH STATE

1 Rami Kleinstein, "Small Gifts," on the album of the same name. First verse. Translation is mine.

2 "Israel Election Updates Yesh Atid to Announce Openly Gay Candidate," *Ha'aretz* (January 26, 2015), http://www.haaretz.com/israel-news/elections/1.639040 [Last viewed December 9, 2015].

3 This translation of Calderon's speech is taken from Ruth Calderon, "The Heritage of All Israel," *Jewish Week* (February 14, 2013), http://www.thejewishweek.com/editorial-opinion/opinion/heritage-all-israel#tz8I4YxxRBluZ53i.99 [Last viewed December 9, 2015].

4 The phrase is Paul Cowan's. Paul Cowan, *An Orphan in History: One Man's Triumphant Search for His Jewish Roots* (Woodstock, VT: Jewish Lights Publishing, 2002).

5 Yair Lapid, trans. Evan Fallenberg, *Memories After My Death: The Joseph (Tommy) Lapid Story* (London: Elliott & Thompson Limited, 2011), page 23.

6 Malka Shaked, *I'll Play You Forever: The Bible in Modern Hebrew Poetry* (Tel Aviv: Yediot Achronot, 2005).

7 Ruth Gavison, "No 'Israeliness' Instead of 'Jewishness,'" *Liberal Magazine*, Vol. 15 (January 2015), http://theliberal.co.il/ruth

-gavison-israeliness-instead-jewishness/ [Last viewed December 9, 2015].

8   Meir Buzaglo, *Safa La-Ne'emanim* [Hebrew]. *A Language for the Faithful: Reflection on Tradition* (Tel Aviv and Jerusalem: Keter Publishing and Mandel Foundation, 2009).

9   Robert Alter, ed., *The Poetry of Yehuda Amichai* (New York: Farrar, Straus and Giroux, 2015), p. 299.

10 Elli Fischer, "Why I Defy the Israeli Chief Rabbinate," *Jewish Review of Books* (Winter 2016), https://jewishreviewofbooks.com/articles/1917/why-i-defy-the-israeli-chief-rabbinate/.

11 Akiva Eldar, "Border Control Getting in a State Over the UN Vote," *Ha'aretz* (September 13, 2011), http://www.haaretz.com/print-edition/features/border-control-getting-in-a-state-over-the-un-vote-1.384135 [Last viewed March 23, 2016].

12 "Israel's Haredi Population: Progress and Challenges," Myers-JDC-Brookdale (October 2015), http://brookdale.jdc.org.il/_Uploads/dbsAttachedFiles/Israels-Haredi-Population-2015–10-FINAL.pdf [Last viewed December 9, 2015].

13 Gwen Ackerman and Alisa Odenheimer, "Israel Prosperity Seen Unsustainable as Haredim Refuse to Work," *Bloomberg Business* (August 2, 2010), http://www.bloomberg.com/news/articles/2010–08–01/israel-prosperity-seen-unsustainable-as-haredim-refusal-to-work-takes-toll [Last viewed December 9, 2015].

14 Jessica Steinberg, "TV show 'Shtisel' Subtly Changes Ultra-Orthodox Perceptions," *Times of Israel* (January 13, 2016), http://www.timesofisrael.com/tv-show-shtisel-subtly-changes-ultra-orthodox-perceptions/ [Last viewed March 23, 2016].

15 Noah Feldman, "Violence in the Name of the Messiah," *Bloomberg View* (November 1, 2015), http://www.bloombergview.com/articles/2015–11–01/violence-in-the-name-of-the-messiah [Last viewed December 9, 2015].

16 The Forward and Daniel Estrin, "The King's Torah: A Rabbinic Text or a Call to Terror?" *Ha'aretz* (January 22, 2010,), http://www.haaretz.com/jewish/2.209/the-king-s-torah-a-rabbinic-text-or-a-call-to-terror-1.261930 [Last viewed December 9, 2015].

17 Jeremy Sharon, "'Torat Hamelech' Authors Will Not Be Indicted," *Jerusalem Post* (May 28, 2012), http://www.jpost.com/National

-News/A-G-Torat-Hamelech-authors-will-not-be-indicted   [Last viewed December 9, 2015].

CONCLUSION

1 Ari Shavit, *My Promised Land: The Triumph and Tragedy of Israel* (New York: Spiegel & Grau, 2013), p. 419.

2 "Israel Turns 68 with 8.5 Million People, 10 Times More Than in 1948," *Times of Israel* (May 9, 2016), http://www.timesofisrael .com/israel-turns-68-with-8-5-million-people-10-times-more-than -in-1948/.

3 Barbara Tuchman, "Israel: Land of Unlimited Impossibilities," in *Practicing History* (New York: Ballantine Books, 1981), p. 134.

4 Vice President Joe Biden, "Remarks by Vice President Biden: The Enduring Partnership Between the United States and Israel" (March 11, 2010), White House, Office of the Vice President, https://www.whitehouse.gov/the-press-office/remarks-vice -president-biden-enduring-partnership-between-united-states-and -israel [Last viewed December 7, 2015].

5 Charles Krauthammer, "At Last, Zion," *Jewish Ideas Daily* (September 21, 2012), http://www.jewishideasdaily.com/5057/fea tures/at-last-zion/ [Last viewed March 23, 2016].

6 Jewish National Fund, "Forestry & Green Innovations," http:// www.jnf.org/work-we-do/our-projects/forestry-ecology/   [Last viewed March 23, 2016].

7 Richard Kemp, "The U.N.'s Gaza Report Is Flawed and Dangerous," *New York Times* (June 25 2010), http://www.nytimes .com/2015/06/26/opinion/the-uns-gaza-report-is-flawed-and -dangerous.html; Samantha Power, *Remarks at the Israel Middle East Model United Nations Conference on "Building a More Model UN,"* transcript (February 15, 2016), http://usun.state.gov/remarks/7138 [Last viewed March 23, 2016].

8 Academic Ranking of World Universities 2015, http://www.shanghai ranking.com/ARWU2015.html [Last viewed August 10, 2016].

9 "Speech by Jimmy Carter on White House Lawn, Washington, D.C., July 19, 1977." Cited in Daniel Gordis, *Menachem Begin: The Battle for Israel's Soul* (New York: Knopf Doubleday, 2014), p. 143.

10 "Speech by Menachem Begin on White House Lawn, Washington,

D.C., July 19, 1977." Cited in Daniel Gordis, *Menachem Begin: The Battle for Israel's Soul* (New York: Knopf Doubleday, 2014), p. 143.

11   Martin Kramer, "Fouad Ajami Goes to Israel," *Mosaic* (January 8, 2015), http://mosaicmagazine.com/observation/2015/01/fouad -ajami-goes-to-israel/ [Last viewed March 23, 2016].

12   Fouad Ajami, "A Reality Check as Israel Turns 60," *U.S. News & World Report* (May 7, 2008), http://www.usnews.com/opinion/fa jami/articles/2008/05/07/a-reality-check-as-israel-turns-60   [Last viewed March 23, 2016].

13   Tsur Ehrlich, "Nathan the Wise," *Azure,* No. 28 (Spring 5767/2007), p. 77, http://azure.org.il/include/print.php?id=445 [Last viewed May 1, 2016].

WORKS CITED

———

A.A.P. "U.N.O. Passes Palestine Partition Plan." *Morning Herald* (December 1, 1947), http://trove.nla.gov.au/ndp/del/article/134238148 [Last viewed December 7, 2015].

"About the Organization." HaShomer HaHadash website, http://www.shomer-israel.org/index.php?option=com_content&view=article&id=100&Itemid=62 [Translation by Daniel Gordis] [Last viewed December 9, 2015].

Above and Beyond. Playmount Productions and Katahdin Productions, produced by Nancy Spielberg, 2015.

Ackerman, Gwen, and Alisa Odenheimer. "Israel Prosperity Seen Unsustainable as Haredim Refuse to Work." *Bloomberg Business* (August 2, 2010), http://www.bloomberg.com/news/articles/2010–08–01/israel-prosperity-seen-unsustainable-as-haredim-refusal-to-work-takes-toll [Last viewed December 9, 2015].

Ahad Ha'am. "The Jewish State and the Jewish Problem." In *The Zionist Idea,* ed. Arthur Hertzberg. Philadelphia: Jewish Publication Society, 1997.

Ajami, Fouad. "A Reality Check as Israel Turns 60." *U.S. News & World Report* (May 7, 2008), http://www.usnews.com/opinion/fajami/articles/2008/05/07/a-reality-check-as-israel-turns-60 [Last viewed March 23, 2016].

Almog, Oz. *The Sabra.* Berkeley: University of California Press, 2000.

Alon, Mati. *Holocaust and Redemption.* Victoria, BC: Trafford Publishing, 2013.

Alpert, Pinhas, and Goren Dotan, eds. *Diary of a Muchtar in Jerusalem: The History of the Beit Yisrael Neighborhood and its Surroundings in the Writings of Rabbi Moshe Yekutiel Alpert (1938–1952).* (Ramat Gan, Israel: Bar Ilan University Press, 2013) [In Hebrew].

Alter, Robert, ed. *The Poetry of Yehuda Amichai*. New York: Farrar, Straus and Giroux, 2015.

Anderman, Nirit. "Israeli Film on Lebanon War 'Waltz with Bashir' Shown in Beirut." *Ha'aretz* (January 21, 2009), http://www.haaretz.com/news/israeli-film-on-lebanon-war-waltz-with-bashir-shown-in-beirut-1.268524 [Last viewed December 8, 2015].

Asher, Tali. "The Growing Silence of the Poetess Rachel." In *Jewish Women in Pre-State Israel: Life History, Politics, and Culture*, ed. Ruth Kark, Margarit Shilo, and Galit Hasan-Rokem. Waltham, MA: Brandeis University Press, 2008.

Auerbach, Jerold S. *Brothers at War: Israel and the Tragedy of the* Altalena. New Orleans: Quid Pro Books, 2011.

Avi-hai, Avraham. "The POSTman Knocks Twice: Yitzhak Rabin, Man of Contradictions." *Jerusalem Post* (September 11, 2014), http://www.jpost.com/Opinion/The-POSTman-Knocks-Twice-Yitzhak-Rabin-man-of-contradictions-375134 [Last viewed March 23, 2016].

Avineri, Shlomo, trans. Haim Watzman. *Herzl: Theodor Herzl and the Foundation of the Jewish State*. London: Weidenfeld & Nicolson, 2008.

Avner, Yehuda. *The Prime Ministers: An Intimate Narrative of Israeli Leadership*. Jerusalem: Toby Press, 2010.

Baker, Amb. Alan. "The Legal Basis of Israel's Rights in the Disputed Territories." Jerusalem Center for Public Affairs (January 8, 2013), http://jcpa.org/ten-basic-points-summarizing-israels-rights-in-judea-and-samaria/ [Last viewed May 1, 2016].

Balfour, Arthur James. "Balfour Declaration." *Avalon Project* (1917), http://avalon.law.yale.edu/20th_century/balfour.asp [Last viewed May 1, 2016].

Bar-On, Mordechai. *Moshe Dayan: Israel's Controversial Hero*. New Haven and London: Yale University Press, 2012.

Bar-Zohar, Michael, trans. Peretz Kidron. *Ben-Gurion: A Biography, The New Millennium Edition*. Israel: Weidenfeld Nicolson, 2013.

Begin, Menachem. *White Nights: The Story of a Prisoner in Russia*. New York: HarperCollins, 1979.

———, trans. Samuel Katz, ed. Ivan M. Greenberg. *The Revolt: Story of the Irgun*. Bnei-Brak, Israel: Steimatzky Group, 1952.

Bein, Alex, trans. Maurice Samuel. *Theodor Herzl: A Biography*. Philadelphia: Jewish Publication Society of America, 1940.

Ben-Gurion, David. "The Eichmann Case as Seen by Ben-Gurion." *New York Times* (December 18, 1960), http://timesmachine.nytimes

.com/timesmachine/1960/12/18/99904385.html?pageNumber=182 [Last viewed December 8, 2015].

————. *Like Stars and Dust: Essays from Israel's Government Year Book.* Ramat Gan, Israel: Masada Press, 1976.

Benn, Aluf. "Doomed to Fight." *Ha'aretz* (May 9, 2011), http://www .haaretz.com/weekend/week-s-end/doomed-to-fight-1.360698 [Last viewed December 8, 2015].

Ben Hurin, Yitzhak. "Horrifying Details of Murder of Athletes in Munich Revealed: 'They Were Tortured in Front of Their Friends." *Ynet.co.il* (December 1, 2015), http://www.ynet.co.il/ articles/0,7340,L-4733681,00.html [Last viewed May 1, 2016].

Ben-Sasson, Hayim, ed. *A History of the Jewish People.* Cambridge: Harvard University Press, 1976.

Berdyczewski, Micah Joseph. "Wrecking and Building." In *The Zionist Idea,* ed. Arthur Hertzberg. Philadelphia: Jewish Publication Society, 1997.

Berlovitz, Yaffah. *Inventing a Land, Inventing a People.* Tel Aviv: Hotza'at HaKibbutz HaMeuchad, 1996.

Bernstein, Robert L. "Rights Watchdog, Lost in the Mideast." *New York Times* (October 19, 2009), http://www.nytimes.com/2009/10/20/ opinion/20bernstein.html [Last viewed December 9, 2015].

Bew, John. "The Tragic Cycle: Western Powers and the Middle East." *New Statesman* (August 21, 2014), http://www.newstatesman.com/ world-affairs/2014/08/tragic-cycle-western-powers-and-middle -east [Last viewed May 1 , 2016].

Biden, Joe. "Remarks by Vice President Biden: The Enduring Partnership Between the United States and Israel." White House, Office of the Vice President (March 11, 2010), https://www.white house.gov/the-press-office/remarks-vice-president-biden-enduring -partnership-between-united-states-and-israel [Last viewed December 7, 2015].

Billings, Lee. "'Beyond: Our Future in Space,' by Chris Impey." *New York Times* (April 30, 2015), http://www.nytimes.com/2015/05/03/ books/review/beyond-our-future-in-space-by-chris-impey.html [Last viewed December 7, 2015].

Bishop, Patrick. *The Reckoning: Death and Intrigue in the Promised Land, A True Detective Story.* New York: HarperCollins, 2014.

Blaustein, Jacob. "The Voice of Reason: Address by Jacob Blaustein,

President, The American Jewish Committee, at the Meeting of Its Executive Committee, April 29, 1950," *American Jewish Committee Archives*, http://www.ajcarchives.org/AJC_DATA/Files/507.PDF [Last viewed December 8, 2015].

Bloom, Cecil. "Sir Mark Sykes: British Diplomat and a Convert to Zionism." *Jewish Historical Studies*, Vol. 43 (2011).

Bloom, Gadi, and Nir Hefez. *Ariel Sharon: A Life.* New York: Random House, 2006.

Bluwstein, Rachel. "Perhaps." *Palestine-Israel Journal*, Vol. 3, Nos. 3 and 4 (1996), http://www.pij.org/details.php?id=536 [Last viewed December 7, 2015].

Borden, Sam. "Long-Hidden Details Reveal Cruelty of 1972 Munich Attackers." *New York Times* (December 1, 2015), http://www.nytimes.com/2015/12/02/sports/long-hidden-details-reveal-cruelty-of-1972-munich-attackers.html.

Brands, Hal, and David Palkki. "Saddam, Israel, and the Bomb: Nuclear Alarmism Justified?" *International Security*, Vol. 36, No. 1 (Summer 2011).

Brown, Nathan, Amr Hamzawy, and Marina Ottaway. "Islamist Movements and the Democratic Process in the Arab World: Exploring the Gray Zones." *Carnegie Papers*, No. 67 (March 2006), http://carnegieendowment.org/files/CP67.Brown.FINAL.pdf [Last viewed December 9, 2015].

Buzaglo, Meir. *Safa La-Ne'emanim* [Hebrew]. *A Language for the Faithful: Reflection on Tradition.* Tel Aviv and Jerusalem: Keter Publishing and Mandel Foundation, 2009.

Calderon, Ruth. "The Heritage of All Israel." *Jewish Week* (February 14, 2013), http://www.thejewishweek.com/editorial-opinion/opinion/heritage-all-israel#tz8I4YxxRBluZ53i.99 [Last viewed December 9, 2015].

Churchill, Winston. "MIT Mid-Century Convocation, March 31, 1949." *MIT Institute Archives*, https://libraries.mit.edu/archives/exhibits/midcentury/mid-cent-churchill.html [Last viewed December 7, 2015].

"CIA Report on the Consequences of the Partition of Palestine." Copy on file with the author.

"Clinton to Lead U.S. Delegation." CNN (November 5, 1995), http://edition.cnn.com/WORLD/9511/rabin/clinton/index.html [Last viewed December 9, 2015].

Clinton, Bill. *My Life*. New York: Vintage Press, 2005.

Cohel, Eric. "The Spirit of Jewish Conservatism." *Mosaic*, http://mosaic magazine.com/essay/2015/04/the-spirit-of-jewish-conservatism/.

Cohen, Eliezer, trans. Yonatan Gordis. *Israel's Best Defense: The First Full Story of the Israeli Air Force*. New York: Orion Books, 1993.

Cohen, Hillel, trans. Haim Watzman. *Year Zero of the Arab-Israeli Conflict: 1929*. Waltham, MA: Brandeis University Press, 2015.

Cotler, Irwin. "Israel and the United Nations." *Jerusalem Post* (August 15, 2013), http://www.jpost.com/Opinion/Op-Ed -Contributors/Israel-and-the-United-Nations-323252 [Last viewed January 10, 2016].

Cowan, Paul. *An Orphan in History: One Man's Triumphant Search for His Jewish Roots*. Woodstock, VT: Jewish Lights Publishing, 2002.

Cunliffe, Barry, and Jerome Murphy-O'Connor. *The Holy Land: An Oxford Archaeological Guide from Earliest Times to 1700*. Oxford: Oxford University Press, 2008.

Darwish, Mahmoud. "Identity Card," 1964. http://www.barghouti .com/poets/darwish/bitaqa.asp [Last viewed May 1, 2016].

David, Assaf, and Asaf Siniver, eds. "Jordan's War That Never Was." In *The Yom Kippur War: Politics, Legacy, Diplomacy*. Oxford: Oxford University Press, 2013.

"Dennis Ross and Gidi Grinstein, Reply by Hussein Agha and Robert Malley." *New York Review of Books* (September 20, 2001), http:// www.nybooks.com/articles/archives/2001/sep/20/camp-david -an-exchange/ [Last viewed December 9, 2015].

Dermer, Ron. "Israeli Ambassador: The Four Major Problems with the Iran Deal." *Washington Post* (July 14, 2015), https://www .washingtonpost.com/opinions/a-bad-deal-today-a-worse-deal -tomorrow/2015/07/14/5d34ba00–2a39–11e5-a250–42bd812efc 09_story.html [Last viewed December 9, 2015].

"Displacement of Jews from Arab Countries 1948–2012." *Justice for Jews from Arab Countries*, http://www.justiceforjews.com/main_facts .html [Last viewed December 7, 2015].

Dowty, Alan. "Much Ado About Little: Ahad Ha'Am's 'Truth from Eretz Yisrael,' Zionism, and the Arabs." *Israel Studies*, Vol. 5, No. 2. Bloomington: Indiana University Press, 2000.

Drukker, Tamar S. "'I Am a Civil War': The Poetry of Haim Gouri."

In *Warfare and Poetry in the Middle East,* ed. Hugh Kennedy. London: I. B. Tauris, 2013.

Druks, Herbert. *The Uncertain Alliance: The U.S. and Israel from Kennedy to the Peace Process.* Westport, CT: Greenwood Press, 2001.

Dunstan, Simon. *The Yom Kippur War: The Arab-Israeli War of 1973.* Oxford: Osprey Publishing, 2007.

Eban, Abba. *Abba Eban: An Autobiography.* Lexington, MA: Plunkett Lake Press, 2015.

Efron, Noah. "The Price of Return." *Ha'aretz* (November 23, 2008), http://www.haaretz.com/news/the-price-of-return-1.258035 [Last viewed December 8, 2015].

Eglash, Ruth. "Ten Years On, Pain of Dolphinarium Bombing Still Strong." *Jerusalem Post* (May 29, 2011), http://www.jpost.com/National-News/Ten-years-on-pain-of-Dolphinarium-bombing-still -strong [Last viewed December 9, 2015].

Ehrlich, Tsur. "Nathan the Wise." *Azure,* No. 28 (Spring 5767/2007), http://azure.org.il/include/print.php?id=445.

Eldar, Akiva. "Border Control Getting in a State Over the UN Vote." *Ha'aretz* (September 13, 2011), http://www.haaretz.com/print -edition/features/border-control-getting-in-a-state-over-the-un -vote-1.384135 [Last viewed March 23, 2016].

Eliot, George. *Daniel Deronda.* Introduction by Edmund White, Notes by Dr. Hugh Osborne. New York: Modern Library, 2002.

Ellenson, David, and Daniel Gordis. *Pledges of Jewish Allegiance: Conversion, Law, and Policymaking in Nineteenth- and Twentieth-Century Orthodox Responsa.* Stanford Studies in Jewish History and Culture, edited by Aron Rodrigue and Steven J. Zipperstein. Stanford, CA: Stanford University Press, 2012.

Elon, Amos. *The Pity of It All: A Portrait of the German-Jewish Epoch 1743–1933.* New York: Picador, 2002.

Epstein, Lawrence. *The Dream of Zion: The Story of the First Zionist Congress.* Lanham, MD: Rowman and Littlefield, 2016.

Eshkoli-Wagman, Hava. "Yishuv Zionism: Its Attitude to Nazism and the Third Reich Reconsidered." *Modern Judaism,* Vol. 19, No. 1 (February 1999).

"Exchange of Letters between PM Sharon and President Bush." Ministry of Foreign Affairs of Israel website (April 14, 2004), http://www.mfa.gov.il/mfa/foreignpolicy/peace/mfadocuments/pages/

exchange%20of%20letters%20sharon-bush%2014-apr-2004.aspx [Last viewed December 9, 2015].

Fahmy, Mohamed Fadel. "30 Years Later, Questions Remain Over Sadat Killing, Peace with Israel." CNN (October 7, 2011), http://edition.cnn.com/2011/10/06/world/meast/egypt-sadat-assassination/ [Last viewed December 8, 2015].

Fallows, James. "Who Shot Muhammed Al-Dura." *Atlantic* (June 2003), http://www.theatlantic.com/magazine/archive/2003/06/who-shot-mohammed-al-dura/302735/ [Last viewed January 10, 2016].

Faris, Hani A. "Israel Zangwill's Challenge to Zionism." *Journal of Palestine Studies,* Vol. 4, No. 3 (1975).

Feldestein, Ariel. "One Meeting—Many Descriptions: The Resolution on the Establishment of the State of Israel." *Israel Studies Forum,* Vol. 23, No. 2 (Winter 2008), p. 104.

Feldman, Noah "Violence in the Name of the Messiah." *Bloomberg View* (November 1, 2015), http://www.bloombergview.com/articles/2015–11–01/violence-in-the-name-of-the-messiah [Last viewed December 9, 2015].

"15,000% Growth in Army Exemptions for Yeshiva Students Since 1948." Hiddush (February 8, 2012), http://hiddush.org/article-2338 –0–15000_Growth_in_army_exemptions_for_yeshiva_students _since_1948.aspx [Last viewed December 9, 2015].

Fischer, Elli. "Why I Defy the Israeli Chief Rabbinate." *Jewish Review of Books* (Winter 2016), https://jewishreviewofbooks.com/articles/1917/why-i-defy-the-israeli-chief-rabbinate/.

Florsheim, Ella. "Giving Herzl His Due." *Azure,* No. 21 (Summer 5765/2005).

"Forestry & Green Innovations." Jewish National Fund, http://www.jnf.org/work-we-do/our-projects/forestry-ecology/ [Last viewed March 23, 2016].

The Forward and Daniel Estrin. "The King's Torah: A Rabbinic Text or a Call to Terror?" *Ha'aretz* (January 22, 2010), http://www.haaretz.com/jewish/2.209/the-king-s-torah-a-rabbinic-text-or-a-call-to-terror-1.261930 [Last viewed December 9, 2015].

The Forward and Nathan Guttman. "Want to Delegitimize Israel? Be Careful Who You Mess With." *Ha'aretz* (April 13, 2010), http://www.haaretz.com/news/want-to-delegitimize-israel-be-careful-who-you-mess-with-1.284184 [Last viewed December 9, 2015].

Frantz, Douglas, and Catherine Collins. *Death on the Black Sea: The Untold Story of the Struma and World War II's Holocaust at Sea*. London: HarperCollins, 2003.

Frantzman, Seth J. "David Ben-Gurion, Israel's Segregationist Founder." *Forward* (May 18, 2015), http://forward.com/opinion/israel/308306/ben-gurion-israels-segregationist-founder/ [Last viewed December 8, 2015].

Freedman, Daniel. "The World's Deadly Obsession with Israel." *Forbes* (June 24, 2010), http://www.forbes.com/2010/06/23/israel-hamas-middle-east-opinions-columnists-daniel-freedman.html.

Freedman, Samuel G. *Jew vs. Jew: The Struggle for the Soul of American Jewry*. New York: Simon & Schuster, 2001.

Friedman, Matti. "Mizrahi Nation." *Mosaic* (June 1, 2014), http://mosaicmagazine.com/essay/2014/06/mizrahi-nation/ [Last viewed December 9, 2015].

———. *Pumpkin Flowers*. Chapel Hill, NC: Algonquin Books, 2016.

Friedman, Thomas L. *From Beirut to Jerusalem*. New York: Farrar, Straus and Giroux, 1989.

Friling, Tuvia, trans. Ora Cummings. *Arrows in the Dark: David Ben-Gurion, the Yishuv Leadership, and Rescue Attempts During the Holocaust*, Volume 1. Madison: University of Wisconsin Press, 2005.

Fromkin, David. *A Peace to End All Peace: The Fall of the Ottoman Empire and the Creation of the Modern Middle East*. New York: Henry Holt, 2009.

Frost, Robert. "The Death of the Hired Man." (North of Boston, 1915), *Bartleby.com*, http://www.bartleby.com/118/3.html [Last viewed December 7, 2015].

Fuksman-Sha'al, Moshe, ed., trans. Ruchie Avital. "Dick Cheney Letter to Menachem Begin." *Israel's Strike Against the Iraqi Nuclear Reactor 7 June 1981*. Jerusalem: Menachem Begin Heritage Center, 2003.

Ganin, Zvi. *An Uneasy Relationship: American Jewish Leadership and Israel, 1948–1957*. Syracuse, NY: Syracuse University Press, 2005.

Gavison, Ruth. "No 'Israeliness' instead of 'Jewishness.'" *Liberal Magazine*, Vol. 15 (January 2015), http://theliberal.co.il/ruth-gavison-israeliness-instead-jewishness/ [Last viewed December 9, 2015].

"GDP Growth (annual %)." World Bank, http://data.worldbank.org/indicator/NY.GDP.MKTP.KD.ZG?page=1.

Gerstenfeld, Manfred. *The War of a Million Cuts: The Struggle Against the Delegitimization of Israel and the Jews, and the Growth of New Anti-Semitism.* Jerusalem: JCPA, 2015.

Gilad, Elon. "Why Is Israel Called Israel?" *Haaretz* (April 20, 2015), http://www.haaretz.com/israel-news/.premium-1.652699.

Gilbert, Martin. *Churchill and the Jews: A Lifelong Friendship.* New York: Henry Holt, 2007.

———. *Israel: A History.* New York: HarperPerennial, 1998.

———. *The Routledge Atlas of the Arab-Israeli Conflict.* New York: Routledge, 2005.

Ginor, Zvia Ben-Yoseph. "'Meteor-Yid': Abba Kovner's Poetic Confrontation with Jewish History." *Judaism,* Vol. 48, No. 1 (Winter 1999).

Ginsburg, Mitch. "Mossad's Tip-Off Ahead of Yom Kippur War Did Not Reach Prime Minister, Newly Released Papers Show." *Times of Israel* (September 20, 2012), http://www.timesofisrael.com/newly-released-papers-detail-depth-of-mishandling-of-yom-kippur-war-warnings/ [Last viewed December 8, 2015].

———. "When Moshe Dayan Delivered the Defining Speech of Zionism," *Times of Israel* (April 26, 2016), http://www.timesofisrael.com/when-moshe-dayan-delivered-the-defining-speech-of-zionism/.

Goldberg, Jeffrey. "The Paranoid, Supremacist, Roots of the Stabbing Intifada." *Atlantic* (October 16, 2015), http://www.theatlantic.com/international/archive/2015/10/the-roots-of-the-palestinian-uprising-against-israel/410944/.

Gorali, Moshe. "How God and Democracy Were Left Out." *Ha'aretz* (May 5, 2003), http://www.haaretz.com/print-edition/features/how-god-and-democracy-were-left-out-1.11023 [Last viewed December 9, 2015].

Gordis, Daniel. *Menachem Begin: The Battle for Israel's Soul.* New York: Knopf Doubleday, 2014.

———. *Saving Israel: How the Jewish People Can Win a War That May Never End.* Hoboken, NJ: Wiley, 2010.

Gordon, A. D. "Logic for the Future (1910)." In *The Zionist Idea,* ed. Arthur Hertzberg. Philadelphia: Jewish Publication Society, 1997.

Govrin, Nurit. *Roots and Tops: The Imprint of the First Aliyah in Hebrew Literature.* Tel Aviv: Papyrus and Tel Aviv University, 1981. [In Hebrew].

Grayzel, Solomon. *A History of the Jews.* Philadelphia: Jewish Publication Society of America, 1947.

Greenberg, Joel. "Yeshayahu Leibowitz, 91, Iconoclastic Israeli Thinker." *New York Times* (August 19, 1994), http://www.nytimes.com/1994/08/19/obituaries/yeshayahu-leibowitz-91-iconoclastic-israeli-thinker.html [Last viewed December 9, 2015].

Greenberg, Uri Zvi, trans. Neta Stahl. "One Truth and Not Two." In "Jesus and the Pharisees Through the Eyes of Two Hebrew Writers: A Contrarian Perspective." *Hebrew Studies*, Vol. 56, No. 1 (December 11, 2015).

Grey, Edward, Viscount Grey of Fallodon. *Twenty-Five Years 1892–1916.* New York: Frederick A. Stokes Company, 1925.

Groenberg, Gershom. *The Accidental Empire: Israel and the Birth of the Settlements, 1967–1977.* New York: Henry Holt, 2006.

Grosbard, Ofer. *Menachem Begin: The Absent Leader.* Haifa: Strategic Research and Policy Center, National Defense College, IDF, 2007.

Guggenheim, Alan, and Adam Guggenheim. "Doomed from the Start." *Naval History*, Vol. 18, No. 1 (February 2004).

Halachmi, Benjamin Beit. *Despair and Deliverance: Private Salvation in Contemporary Israel.* Albany: State University of New York Press, 1992.

Halevi, Efraim. "Introduction." In *The Millions That Changed the Middle East: Immigrants from the Former USSR*, ed. Lily Galili and Roman Bronfman, http://matarbooks.co.il/printbook.php?book=1808&nav=4 [Last viewed December 7, 2015] [In Hebrew].

Halevi, Yossi Klein. *Like Dreamers: The Story of the Israeli Paratroopers Who Reunited Jerusalem and Divided a Nation.* New York: HarperCollins, 2013.

Halkin, Hillel. *Jabotinsky: A Life.* New Haven and London: Yale University Press, 2014.

Hartman, Ben. "'Gov't' Failed Gaza Evacuees." *Jerusalem Post* (June 16, 2010), http://www.jpost.com/Israel/Govt-failed-Gaza-evacuees [Last viewed December 9, 2015].

Hasson, Nir. "Jerusalem Neighborhood to Name Streets in Honor of Mizrahi Black Panthers." *Ha'aretz* (June 14, 2011), http://www.haaretz.com/jerusalem-neighborhood-to-name-streets-in-honor-of-mizrahi-black-panthers-1.369313 [Last viewed: March 23, 2016].

Hazaz, Haim. *The Sermon and Other Stories.* Jerusalem: Toby Press, 2005.

Hazony, Yoram. *The Jewish State: The Struggle for Israel's Soul.* New York: Basic Books, 2000.

Heller, Aron. "Western Europe Jewish Migration to Israel Hits All-Time High." *Associated Press* (January 14, 2016), http://bigstory.ap.org/article/164bbc1445aa42fc883ee85e4439523a/western-europe-jewish-migration-israel-hits-all-time-high [Last viewed March 23, 2016].

Helm, Sarah. "Yemeni Jews Describe Their Holocaust: Sarah Helm in Yehud Reports on Claims That Israelis Stole 4,500 Children from Immigrants." *Independent* (October 23, 2011), http://www.independent.co.uk/news/world/yemeni-jews-describe-their-holocaust-sarah-helm-in-yehud-reports-on-claims-that-israelis-stole-4500-children-from-immigrants-1370515.html [Last viewed December 8, 2015].

Hersh, Seymour. *The Samson Option: Israel's Nuclear Arsenal and America's Foreign Policy.* New York: Random House, 1991.

Hertzberg, Arthur. *The Zionist Idea.* Philadelphia: Jewish Publication Society, 1997.

Herzl, Theodor. *Old New Land.* Princeton, NJ: Markus Wiener Publishers, 1997.

———, trans. I. M. Lask. *The Jewish State.* Tel Aviv: M. Newman Publishing House, 1954.

Hess, Moses. *The Revival of Israel: Rome and Jerusalem, the Last Nationalist Questions.* Lincoln: University of Nebraska Press, 1995.

Hitler, Adolf. *Mein Kampf.* Boring, OR: CPA Book Publisher, 2000.

Hoffman, Bruce. *Anonymous Soldiers: The Struggle for Israel: 1917–1947.* New York: Alfred A. Knopf, 2015.

Hoffman, Gil Stern. "Dov Lipman to Direct WZO Department." *Jerusalem Post* (October 12, 2015), http://www.jpost.com/Israel-News/Politics-And-Diplomacy/Dov-Lipman-to-head-WZO-department-437000.

The Holy Bible (King James Version). Cambridge Edition, 1769.

Holtzman, Avner. "A New Truth from the Land of Israel: On the New Self Awareness in Second Aliyah Literature." In *The Second Aliyah: Studies,* ed. Israel Bartel. Jerusalem: Yad Yitzhak Ben-Zvi, 1997. [In Hebrew].

"Human Rights Actions." *Human Rights Voices,* http://www.humanrightsvoices.org/EYEontheUN/priorities/actions/body/?ua=1&ya=1&sa=1&tp=1 [Last viewed January 10, 2016].

Hurwitz, Zvi Harry. *Begin: His Life, Words, and Deeds.* Jerusalem: Gefen Publishing, 2004.

iCenter, "The Story of a Vote: Nov. 29, 1947." *iCenter* (November 1,

2012), http://www.theicenter.org/voice/story-vote-nov-29-1947 [Last viewed May 1, 2016].

IDF Spokesman and Israel Police. "Gaza Strip Evacuation." Israel Ministry of Foreign Affairs (August 17, 2005), http://www.mfa.gov.il/mfa/pressroom/2005/pages/start%20of%20gaza%20strip%20evacuation%2017-aug-2005.aspx [Last viewed January 10, 2016].

Inbari, Assaf. *HaBaita*. Tel Aviv: Yediyot Sefarim, 2009. [Translations by Daniel Gordis].

Isaacson, Walter. *Einstein: His Life and Universe*. New York: Simon & Schuster Paperbacks, 2007.

"Israel's Declaration of Independence 1948." *Avalon Project*, http://avalon.law.yale.edu/20th_century/israel.asp [Last viewed December 7, 2015].

"Israel's Haredi Population: Progress and Challenges." Myers-JDC-Brookdale (October 2015), http://brookdale.jdc.org.il/_Uploads/dbsAttachedFiles/Israels-Haredi-Population-2015–10-FINAL.pdf [Last viewed December 9, 2015].

"Israel's Illusion." *New York Times* (June 9, 1981), http://www.nytimes.com/1981/06/09/opinion/israel-s-illusion.html [Last viewed December 8, 2015].

"Israel Turns 68 with 8.5 Million People, 10 Times More Than in 1948." *Times of Israel* (May 9, 2016), http://www.timesofisrael.com/israel-turns-68-with-8-5-million-people-10-times-more-than-in-1948/.

Jabotinsky, Ze'ev (Vladimir). "The Basis of the Betarian Viewpoint Consists of One Idea: The Jewish State: The Ideology of Betar." World Zionist Organization, http://www.wzo.org.il/index.php?dir=site&page=articles&op=item&cs=3360&langpage=eng&category=3122&mode=print [Last viewed December 7, 2015].

——. "The Iron Wall." *Jewish Virtual Library*, http://www.jewishvirtuallibrary.org/jsource/Zionism/ironwall.html [Last viewed December 7, 2015].

Jacoby, Jeff. "Would Rabin Have Pulled the Plug on a 'Peace Process' That Failed?" *Boston Globe* (October 22, 2015), http://www.bostonglobe.com/opinion/2015/10/22/would-rabin-have-pulled-plug-peace-process-that-failed/fgHF1Y8bkh7leSbtgHfleL/story.html [Last viewed December 9, 2015].

Jewish Agency. "BeBayit BeYachad: Shiputz Mo'adon Olim Be-Beit Brodsky." http://www.jewishagency.org/he/blog/7606/article/11706 [Last viewed December 7, 2015] [In Hebrew].

Johnson, Paul. *A History of the Jews.* New York: HarperPerennial, 1988.

JTA. "Israel to Vote Today in First National Elections; Campaign Reaches High Peak." (January 25, 1949), http://www.jta.org/1949/01/25/archive/israel-to-vote-today-in-first-national-elections-campaign-reaches-high-peak [Last viewed December 7, 2015].

———. "Of Weizmann's Address Opening Session of Israeli Constituent Assembly." (February 15, 1949), http://www.jta.org/1949/02/15/archive/of-chaim-weizmanns-address-opening-session-of-israeli-constituent-assembly [Last viewed December 7, 2015].

Judis, John B. "Seeds of Doubt: Harry Truman's Concerns About Israel and Palestine Were Prescient—And Forgotten." *New Republic* (January 16, 2014), http://www.newrepublic.com/article/116215/was-harry-truman-zionist.

Kanafani, Ghassan. *Palestine's Children: Returning to Haifa and Other Stories.* Boulder, CO: Lynne Rienner, 2000.

Kark, Ruth. "Changing Patterns of Landownership in Nineteenth-Century Palestine: The European Influence." *Journal of Historical Geography,* Vol. 10, No. 4 (1984).

Katz, Shmuel. *Lone Wolf: A Biography of Vladimir (Ze'ev) Jabotinsky.* Fort Lee, NJ: Barricade Books, 1995.

Kaya, Furkan. "Minority Policies of Turkey and Wealth Tax of 1942." Yeditepe University (February 12, 2014), http://mpra.ub.uni-muenchen.de/53617/1/MPRA_paper_53617.pdf.

Kedar, Nir. "Ben-Gurion's Mamlakhtiyut: Etymological and Theoretical Roots." *Israel Studies,* Vol. 7, No. 3 (Fall 2002).

Kellner, Vered. "Longings and Disappointments: A Voter in Exile in New York." *Ha'aretz* (January 18, 2003), http://www.haaretz.com/misc/iphone-article/longings-and-disappointments-a-voter-in-exile-in-new-york.premium-1.494743 [Last viewed December 7, 2015].

Kemp, Richard. "The U.N.'s Gaza Report Is Flawed and Dangerous." *New York Times* (June 25, 2015), (http://www.nytimes.com/2015/06/26/opinion/the-uns-gaza-report-is-flawed-and-dangerous.html.

Kershner, Isabel. "Israel to Phase Out Religious Exemptions." *New York Times* (March 12, 2014), http://www.nytimes.com/2014/03/13/world/middleeast/israel-restricts-exemptions-from-military-service.html?_r=0 [Last viewed December 8, 2015].

"The Khartoum Resolutions." Ministry of Foreign Affairs of Israel

(September 1, 1967), http://www.mfa.gov.il/mfa/foreignpolicy/
peace/guide/pages/the%20khartoum%20resolutions.aspx   [Last
viewed December 8, 2015].

Khoury, Jack. "Israeli Arabs Mark Fifteenth Anniversary of October 2000
Riots." *Ha'aretz* (January 10, 2015), http://www.haaretz.com/israel
-news/.premium-1.678344 [Last viewed December 9, 2015].

King James Bible Online, 2016. http://www.kingjamesbibleonline.org.

"Kissinger and Ismail Conduct Secret Meetings." *Center for Israel Education*, http://israeled.org/kissinger-ismail-conduct-secret-meetings/
[Last viewed December 8, 2015].

Kissinger, Henry, and George P. Shultz. "The Iran Deal and Its Consequences." *Wall Street Journal* (April 7, 2015), http://www.wsj
.com/articles/the-iran-deal-and-its-consequences-1428447582 [Last
viewed December 9, 2015].

Kraft, Joseph. "For Begin, the End? He Should Be Voted Out for Raid
That Further Isolates Israel." *Los Angeles Times* (June 11, 1981).

Kramer, Martin. "Fouad Ajami Goes to Israel." *Mosaic* (January 8,
2015),   http://mosaicmagazine.com/observation/2015/01/fouad
-ajami-goes-to-israel/ [Last viewed March 23, 2016].

———. "What Happened at Lydda." *Mosaic*, (July 1, 2014), http://
mosaicmagazine.com/essay/2014/07/what-happened-at-lydda/
[Last viewed December 7, 2015].

Krauthammer, Charles. "At Last, Zion." *Jewish Ideas Daily* (September 21, 2012), http://www.jewishideasdaily.com/5057/features/at
-last-zion/ [Last viewed March 23, 2016].

Lam, Amira. "Peres Recalls Declaration of Independence: We Didn't
Have Time to Celebrate." *Ynetnews.com* (December 21, 2014),
http://www.ynetnews.com/articles/0,7340,L-4606090,00.html
[Last viewed May 1, 2016].

Lanchin, Mike. "SS *St Louis*: The Ship of Jewish Refugees Nobody
Wanted." *BBC World Service* (May 13, 2014), http://www.bbc.com/
news/magazine-27373131 [Last viewed December 7, 2015].

Landau, David. *Arik: The Life of Ariel Sharon*. New York: Alfred A.
Knopf, 2013.

Lapid, Yair, trans. Evan Fallenberg. *Memories After My Death: The Joseph
(Tommy) Lapid Story*. London: Elliott & Thompson Limited, 2011.

Lapidot, Yehuda, trans. Chaya Galai. "The *Altalena* Affair." *Etzel*, http://
www.etzel.org.il/english/ac20.htm [Last viewed December 7, 2015].

Lapin, Yaakov. "Katsav Entering Prison: 'You're Burying a Man Alive.'" *Jerusalem Post* (December 8, 2011), http://www.jpost.com/National-News/Katsav-entering-prison-Youre-burying-a-man-alive [Last viewed March 23, 2016].

Laqueur, Walter. *A History of Zionism*. New York: Schocken Books, 1976.

Lavy, George. *Germany and Israel: Moral Debt and National Interest*. London: Frank Cass, 1996.

Lazaroff, Tovah. "2012 Settler Population Grew Almost Three Times as Fast as National Rate." *Jerusalem Post* (September 7, 2013), http://www.jpost.com/National-News/2012-West-Bank-settler-population-growing-almost-three-times-as-fast-as-national-rate-326309 [Last viewed December 8, 2015].

Lelchuk, Alan, and Gershon Shaked. *8 Great Hebrew Short Novels*. New Milford, CT: Toby Press, 2012.

Lenhoff, Howard M., and Jerry L. Weaver. *Black Jews, Jews, and Other Heroes: How Grassroots Activism Led to the Rescue of the Ethiopian Jews*. Jerusalem: Gefen Publishing House, 2007.

Levy, Yagil. *The Hierarchy of Military Death*. Open University of Israel (Lisbon, April 14–19, 2009), https://ecpr.eu/Filestore/PaperProposal/2cfd87af-cab2–4374-b84d-eb03fbbc3cd1.pdf [Last viewed May 1, 2016].

Lichtblau, Eric. "Surviving the Nazis, Only to Be Jailed by America." *New York Times* (February 7, 2015), http://www.nytimes.com/2015/02/08/sunday-review/surviving-the-nazis-only-to-be-jailed-by-america.html [Last viewed December 7, 2015].

Lipstadt, Deborah E. *The Eichmann Trial*. New York: Knopf Doubleday, 2011.

Lis, Jonathan, and Yarden Skop. "Israel Election Updates Yesh Atid to Announce Openly Gay Candidate." *Ha'aretz* (January 26, 2015), http://www.haaretz.com/israel-news/elections/1.639040 [Last viewed December 9, 2015].

Little, Douglas. *American Orientalism: The United States and the Middle East Since 1945*. London: I. B. Tauris, 2002.

Lord, Amnon. "Intelligence Failure or Paralysis." *Jewish Political Studies Review*, Vol. 24, No. 3–4 (Fall 2012).

Makovsky, David. "The Silent Strike: How Israel Bombed a Syrian Nuclear Installation and Kept It Secret." *New Yorker* (September 17, 2012), http://www.newyorker.com/magazine/2012/09/17/the-silent-strike [Last viewed January 10, 2016].

————. *Churchill's Promised Land: Zionism and Statecraft*. New Haven: Yale University Press, 2007.

Man, Nadav. "1st IDF Parade from Behind the Lens." *Ynet news.com* (December 13, 2008), http://www.ynetnews.com/articles/0,7340,L-3637748,00.html [Last viewed December 7, 2015].

Mapu, Abraham, trans. Joseph Marymount. *The Love of Zion & Other Writings*. Israel: Toby Press, 2006.

"The Massive Immigration." Jewish Agency website, http://www.jewishagency.org/he/historical-aliyah/content/22097 [Last viewed December 10, 2015] [In Hebrew].

McCullough, David. *Truman*. New York: Simon & Schuster, 1993.

Meir, Golda. *My Life*. New York: Dell Publishing, 1975.

Meir-Glitzenstein, Esther. "Operation Magic Carpet: Constructing the Myth of the Magical Immigration of Yemenite Jews to Israel." *Israel Studies*. Vol. 16, No. 3 (Fall 2011).

Melman, Yossi. "Jews, Just Like Arabs, Hid Weapons in Immoral Places." *Ha'aretz* (January 27, 2011), http://www.haaretz.com/print-edition/features/jews-just-like-arabs-hid-weapons-in-immoral-places-1.339432.

Mendes-Flohr, Paul, and Yehuda Reinharz. *The Jew in the Modern World: A Documentary History,* 2nd ed. Oxford: Oxford University Press, 1995.

"Menendez Delivers Remarks on Iran Nuclear Deal at Seton Hall University's School of Diplomacy and International Relations." Bob Menendez for New Jersey (August 18, 2015), http://www.menendez.senate.gov/news-and-events/press/menendez-delivers-remarks-on-iran-nuclear-deal-at-seton-hall-universitys-school-of-diplomacy-and-international-relations [Last viewed January 10, 2016].

"Middle East: A Sabbath of Terror." *Time* (March 20, 1978), http://www.time.com/time/magazine/article/0,9171,919454,00.html.

Mikics, David. "Holocaust Pulp Fiction." *Tablet* (April 19, 2012), http://www.tabletmag.com/jewish-arts-and-culture/books/97160/ka-tzetnik [Last viewed March 23, 2015]

Miller, J. Maxwell, and John H. Hayes. *A History of Ancient Israel and Judah*. Louisville, KY: Westminster John Knox Press, 2006.

Mintz, Alan. "Kishinev and the Twentieth Century." *Prooftests*, Vol. 25, No. 1–2. (Winter/Spring 2005)

Mirsky, Yehudah. "What Is a Nation-State For?" *Marginalia* (March 11, 2015), http://marginalia.lareviewofbooks.org/nation-state-yehudah-mirsky/ [Last viewed May 1, 2016].

———. *Rav Kook: Mystic in a Time of Revolution.* New Haven: Yale University Press, 2014.

Mizrahi World Movement. "The First Ever Israeli Elections." http://mizrachi.org/the-first-ever-israeli-elections/ [Last viewed December 7, 2015].

Morris, Benny. "Exposing Abbas." *National Interest* (May 19, 2011), http://nationalinterest.org/commentary/exposing-abbas-5335 [Last viewed December 9, 2015].

———."The Historiography of Deir Yassin." *Journal of Israeli History: Politics, Society, Culture,* Vol. 24, No. 1 (August 2006).

———. "Peace? No Chance." *Guardian* (February 21, 2002), http://www.theguardian.com/world/2002/feb/21/israel2 [Last viewed January 10, 2016].

———. "Zionism's 'Black Boxes'." *Mosaic* (July 13, 2014), http://mosaicmagazine.com/response/2014/07/zionisms-black-boxes/ [Last viewed December 7, 2015].

———. *1948: The First Arab-Israeli War.* New Haven and London: Yale University Press, 2008.

———. *Israel's Border Wars 1949–1956: Arab Infiltration, Israeli Retaliation, and the Countdown to the Suez War.* Oxford: Oxford University Press, 1993.

———. *One State, Two States: Resolving the Israel/Palestine Conflict.* New Haven: Yale University Press, 2010.

———. *Righteous Victims: A History of the Zionist-Arab Conflict, 1881–2001.* New York: Vintage Books, 2001.

———. *The Road to Jerusalem: Glubb Pasha, Palestine, and the Jews.* London: I. B. Tauris, 2003.

"Moving Ceremony Marks Reburial of Herzl's Remains; Israeli Cabinet in Full Attendance," *Jewish Telegraphic Agency* (August 18, 1949), http://www.jta.org/1949/08/18/archive/moving-ceremony-marks-reburial-of-herzls-remains-israeli-cabinet-in-full-attendance.

Muravchik, Joshua. "Muslims and Terror: The Real Story." *Commentary* (February 1, 2015), https://www.commentarymagazine.com/articles/muslims-and-terror-the-real-story-1/ [Last viewed December 9, 2015].

Nadler, Alan. "Piety and Politics: The Case of the Satmar Rebbe." *Judaism*, Vol. 31 (1982).

Navoth, Michal. "Israel's Relationship with the UN Human Rights Council: Is There Hope for Change?" *Institute for Contemporary Affairs*, No. 601 (May–June 2014), http://jcpa.org/article/israels-relationship-un-human-rights-council/ [Last viewed January 10, 2016].

Nordau, Max. "Jewry of Muscle." In *The Jew in the Modern World: A Documentary History*, 2nd ed., edited by Paul Mendes-Flohr and Yehuda Reinharz. Oxford: Oxford University Press, 1995.

Oren, Amir. "CIA Report on Yom Kippur War: Israel Had Nuclear Arsenal." *Ha'aretz* (February 13, 2013), http://www.haaretz.com/news/diplomacy-defense/cia-report-on-yom-kippur-war-israel-had-nuclear-arsenal.premium-1.501101 [Last viewed December 8, 2015].

Oren, Michael B. "Did Israel Want the Six Day War?" *Azure*, No. 7 (Spring 5759/1999).

———. "The Second War of Independence." *Azure*, No. 27 (Winter 5767/2006).

———. *Ally: My Journey Across the American-Israeli Divide*. New York: Random House, 2015.

———. *Power, Faith, and Fantasy: America in the Middle East, 1776 to the Present*. New York: W. W. Norton, 2007.

———. *Six Days of War: June 1967 and the Making of the Modern Middle East*. Oxford: Oxford University Press, 2002.

Oz, Amos, trans. Nicholas de Lange. *A Tale of Love and Darkness*. Orlando: Harcourt, 2004.

Pappe, Ilan. "A Post-Zionist Critique of Israel and the Palestinians, Part II: The Media." in *Journal of Palestine Studies* (Spring 1997), pp. 37–43, cited in Michael Oren, "Did Israel Want the Six Day War? *Azure*, No. 7 (Spring 5759/1999), p. 48.

Parker, Richard Bordeaux, ed. *The October War: A Retrospective*. Gainsville: University Press of Florida, 2001.

Patai, Raphael. *The Jews of Hungary: History, Culture, Psychology*. Detroit: Wayne State University Press, 1996.

Patterson, David. "Introduction." In *The Love of Zion & Other Writings*, ed. Abraham Mapu, trans. Joseph Marymount. Israel: Toby Press, 2006.

Penkower, Monty Noam. "The Kishinev Pogrom of 1903." *Modern Judaism*, Vol. 24, No. 3 (2004).

Peres, Shimon, in conversation with David Landau. *Ben-Gurion: A Political Life*. New York: Schocken Books, 2011.

Persico, Tomer. "The Privatization of Religion and the Sanctification of the Nation: A History of the Collapse of Zionist Collectivism." *Akdamut*, No. 30 (February 2015).

Pianko, Noam. *Zionism and the Roads Not Taken: Rawidowicz, Kaplan, Kohn*. Bloomington: Indiana University Press, 2010.

Piper, Franciszek. "Gas Chambers and Crematoria." Jerusalem: Yad Vashem: The Holocaust Martyrs' and Heroes' Remembrance Authority, 2008.

Pitot, Geneviève, trans. Donna Edouard. *The Story of the Jewish Detainees in Mauritius 1940–1945*. Lanham, MD: Rowman and Littlefield, 1998.

"Planet Auschwitz." Testimony of Yehiel De-Nur at Eichmann trial, https://www.youtube.com/watch?v=o0T9tZiKYl4 [Last viewed May 1, 2016].

"PM Says Iran's Chief of Staff Vowed Sunday to Eliminate Israel." *Times of Israel* (May 21, 2012), http://www.timesofisrael.com/pm-says-irans-chief-of-staff-vowed-sunday-to-eliminate-israel/ [Last viewed December 9, 2015].

Porat, Dina. *The Blue and the Yellow Stars of David: The Zionist Leadership in Palestine and the Holocaust, 1939–1945*. Cambridge and London: Harvard University Press, 1990.

Power, Samantha. *Remarks at the Israel Middle East Model United Nations Conference on "Building a More Model UN."* Transcript (February 15, 2016), http://usun.state.gov/remarks/7138 [Last viewed March 23, 2016].

Quandt, William B. *Peace Process: American Diplomacy and the Arab-Israeli Conflict Since 1967*. Washington, DC: Brookings Institution, 2005.

Rabinovich, Abraham. *The Yom Kippur War: The Epic Encounter That Transformed the Middle East*. New York: Schocken Books, 2004.

Rabinowitz, Dan. "October 2000, Revisited." *Ha'aretz* (October 19, 2004), http://www.haaretz.com/print-edition/opinion/october-2000-revisited-1.137855 [Last viewed December 9, 2015].

Raviv, Dan, and Yossi Melman. *Spies Against Armageddon: The Mossad and the Intelligence Community*. Israel: Yediot Ahronoth Books, 2012.

Regev, Motti, and Edwin Seroussi. *Popular Music and National Culture in Israel*. Berkeley: University of California Press, 2004.

Reinfeld, Moshe. "State Commission: Missing Yemenite Babies Not Kidnapped." *Ha'aretz Service* (November 4, 2001), http://www .haaretz.com/news/state-commission-missing-yemenite-babies -not-kidnapped-1.73778 [Last viewed December 8, 2015].

Rosenberg, Yair. "Watch Orthodox Rabbi Benny Lau's Powerful Denunciation of Homophobia Justified in the Name of God." *Tablet* (August 3, 2015), http://www.tabletmag.com/scroll/192649/ watch-orthodox-rabbi-benny-laus-powerful-denunciation-of -homophobia-justified-in-the-name-of-god [Last viewed December 9, 2015].

Roskies, David G., ed. *The Literature of Destruction: Jewish Responses to Catastrophe*. Philadelphia: Jewish Publication Society, 1988.

Ross, Dennis. *Doomed to Succeed: The U.S.-Israel Relationships from Truman to Obama*. New York: Farrar, Straus and Giroux, 2015.

Rovner, Adam. *In the Shadows of Zion: Promised Lands Before Israel*. New York: New York University Press, 2014.

Sachar, Howard M. *A History of Israel: From the Rise of Zionism to Our Time*. New York: Alfred A. Knopf, 1979.

Samuel, Maurice, trans. *The New Palestine*, Vol. 8, No. 13 (March 27, 1925). Reproduced by Hebrew University in 2015 as commemorative issue. Copy on file with author.

Scheindlin, Raymond P. *A Short History of the Jewish People: From Legendary Times to Modern Statehood*. Oxford and New York: Oxford University Press, 2000.

Schiff, Zeev. *A History of the Israeli Army: 1874 to the Present*. London: Macmillan, 1985.

Schneer, Jonathan. *The Balfour Declaration: The Origins of the Arab-Israeli Conflict*. New York: Random House Trade Paperbacks, 2012.

Schwartzwald, Jack L. *Nine Lives of Israel: A Nation's History Through the Lives of Its Foremost Leaders*. Jefferson, NC: McFarland, 2012.

Segev, Tom. "In Letter, Naomi Shemer Admitted Lifting 'Jerusalem of Gold' Tune." *Ha'aretz* (May 5, 2005), http://www.haaretz.com/ news/in-letter-naomi-shemer-admitted-lifting-jerusalem-of-gold -tune-1.157851 [Last viewed December 8, 2015].

———, trans. Haim Watzman. *One Palestine, Complete: Jews and Arabs Under the British Mandate*. New York: Little, Brown, 2000.

———, trans. Haim Watzman. *The Seventh Million: The Israelis and the Holocaust*. New York: Henry Holt, 1991.

————, trans. Jessica Cohen. *1967: Israel, the War, and the Year That Transformed the Middle East*. New York: Henry Holt, 2005.

Seltzer, Robert M. *Jewish People, Jewish Thought: The Jewish Experience in History*. New York: Macmillan Publishing, 1980.

Senor, Dan, and Saul Singer. *Start-Up Nation: The Story of Israel's Economic Miracle*. New York: Twelve, 2012.

Shaked, Malka. *I'll Play You Forever: The Bible in Modern Hebrew Poetry*. Tel Aviv: Yediot Achronot, 2005.

Shalev, Ben. "Zohar Argov's Flower That Launched a Million Cassettes." *Ha'aretz* (May 4, 2012), http://www.haaretz.com/weekend/week-s-end/zohar-argov-s-flower-that-launched-a-million-cassettes-1.428235 [Last viewed December 8, 2015].

Shalev, Chemi. "Moshe Dayan's Enduring Gaza Eulogy: This Is the Fate of Our Generation." *Ha'aretz* (July 20, 2014), http://www.haaretz.com/blogs/west-of-eden/.premium-1.606258 [Last viewed December 8, 2015].

————. "Sharon's Gaza Disengagement Was a Necessary Act of Self-Preservation." *Ha'aretz* (July 29, 2015), http://www.haaretz.com/israel-news/.premium-1.667443 [Last viewed December 9, 2015].

Shapira, Anita, trans. Anthony Berris. *Ben-Gurion: Father of Modern Israel*. New Haven and London: Yale University Press, 2014.

————. *Israel: A History*. Waltham, MA: Brandeis University Press, 2012.

Sharon, Jeremy. "'Torat Hamelech' Authors Will Not Be Indicted." *Jerusalem Post* (May 28, 2012), http://www.jpost.com/National-News/A-G-Torat-Hamelech-authors-will-not-be-indicted [Last viewed December 9, 2015].

Shavit, Ari. *My Promised Land: The Triumph and Tragedy of Israel*. New York: Spiegel & Grau, 2013.

————. "Survival of the Fittest? An Interview with Benny Morris." *Ha'aretz* (January 8, 2004), http://www.haaretz.com/survival-of-the-fittest-1.61345 [Last viewed December 7, 2015].

Shavit, Yaacov, and Jehuda Reinharz. *Glorious, Accursed Europe*. Waltham, MA: Brandeis University Press, 2010.

Shilon, Avi, trans. Danielle Zilberberg and Yoram Sharett. *Menachem Begin: A Life*. New Haven and London: Yale University Press, 2007.

Shimoni, Gideon. *The Zionist Ideology*. Waltham, MA: Brandeis University Press, 1995.

Shindler, Colin. "Zionist History's Murder Mystery." *Jewish Chronicle Online* (June 16, 2013), http://www.thejc.com/comment-and-debate/comment/108596/zionist-historys-murder-mystery [Last viewed December 7, 2015].

———. *A History of Modern Israel,* 2nd ed. New York: Cambridge University Press, 2013.

"Shmuel Gonen, 73, An Ex-Israeli General." *New York Times* (October 2, 1991), http://www.nytimes.com/1991/10/02/obituaries/shmuel-gonen-73-an-ex-israeli-general.html [Last viewed December 8, 2015].

Shragai, Nadav. "The Legend of Ambushed Palmach Squad '35.'" *Ha'aretz* (April 27, 2009), http://www.haaretz.com/the-legend-of-ambushed-palmach-squad-35-1.274876.

Shtull-Trauring, Asaf. "Hebrew University Climbs to 57th Place on Global Ranking List." *Ha'aretz* (August 18, 2011), http://www.haaretz.com/print-edition/news/hebrew-university-climbs-to-57th-place-on-global-ranking-list-1.379203 [Last viewed November 20, 2011].

Siegel, Seth M. *Let There Be Water: Israel's Solution for a Water-Starved World.* New York: Thomas Dunne Books, 2015.

———. "50 Years Later, National Water Carrier Still an Inspiration." *Ynetnews.com* (September 6, 2014), http://www.ynetnews.com/articles/0,7340,L-4528200,00.html [Last viewed May 1, 2016].

Silver, Abba Hillel, Moshe Shertok, and Chaim Weizmann. "Before the United Nations: October 1947." Copy on file with the author.

Silver, Eric. *Begin: The Haunted Prophet.* New York: Random House, 1984.

Siniver, Asaf. *Abba Eban: A Biography.* New York and London: Overlook Duckworth, 2015.

Slater, Robert. *Rabin: 20 Years After.* Israel: KIP Kotarim International Publishing, 2015.

———. *Warrior Statesman: The Life of Moshe Dayan.* New York: St. Martin's Press, 1991.

Solnit, Rebecca. "Easy Chair: The War of the World." *Harper's Magazine* (February 2015).

Spiegel, Nina S. *Embodying Hebrew Culture.* Detroit: Wayne State University Press, 2013.

Steinberg, Jessica. "TV Show 'Shtisel' Subtly Changes Ultra-Orthodox Perceptions." *Times of Israel* (January 13, 2016), http://www.times

ofisrael.com/tv-show-shtisel-subtly-changes-ultra-orthodox
-perceptions/ [Last viewed March 23, 2016].

Tekumah. [Hebrew] *Rebirth: The First Fifty Years.* An Israeli television series, Channel 1, first broadcast 1998.

Temko, Ned. *To Win or to Die: A Personal Portrait of Menachem Begin.* New York: William Morrow, 1987.

Teveth, Shabtai. *Ben Gurion's Spy: The Story of the Political Scandal That Shaped Modern Israel.* New York: Columbia University Press, 1996.

Traubman, Tamara. "A Mystery That Defies Solution." *Ha'aretz* (November 5, 2001), http://www.haaretz.com/print-edition/news/a-mystery -that-defies-solution-1.73913 [Last viewed December 8, 2015].

Troen, S. Ilan. *Imagining Zion: Dreams, Designs, and Realities in a Century of Jewish Settlement.* New Haven and London: Yale University Press, 2003.

Troy, Gil. "Happy Birthday, Mr. Kissinger." *Tablet* (May 23, 2013), http:// www.tabletmag.com/jewish-news-and-politics/132819/happy-birthday -mr-kissinger#xCoSwz6BrWoHxhzI.99 [Last viewed December 8, 2015].

———. *Moynihan's Moment: America's Fight Against Zionism as Racism.* Oxford: Oxford University Press, 2013.

Tuchman, Barbara. "Israel: Land of Unlimited Impossibilities." In *Practicing History.* New York: Ballantine Books, 1981.

Twain, Mark. "Concerning the Jews." *Harper's Magazine,* Vol. 99 (March 1898).

Tzahor, Ze'ev. "Chaim Arlosoroff and His Attitude Toward the Rise of Nazism." *Jewish Social Studies,* Vol. 46, No. 3–4 (Summer–Autumn 1984).

UN Refugee Agency. "The State of the World's Refugees 2000: Fifty Years of Humanitarian Action" (January 1, 2000), http://www .unhcr.org/3ebf9bab0.pdf [Last viewed December 7, 2015].

"United Nations Security Council Resolution 487 (1981)." United Nations, http://www.un.org/documents/ga/res/36/a36r027.htm [Last viewed December 8, 2015].

Weinberg, David M. "Yitzhak Rabin Was 'Close to Stopping the Oslo Process.'" *Jerusalem Post* (October 17, 2013), http://www.jpost .com/Opinion/Columnists/Yitzhak-Rabin-was-close-to-stopping -the-Oslo-process-329064 [Last viewed March 23, 2016].

Winer, Stuart. "Uproar as Ethiopia-Born MK Denied Chance to Give Blood." *Times of Israel* (December 11, 2013), http://www.timesofisrael .com/uproar-as-ethiopian-mk-denied-chance-to-give-blood/ [Last viewed December 9, 2015].

Ya'alon, Moshe. *The Longer Shorter Way*. Tel Aviv: Yedioth Ahronoth Books and Chemed Books, 2007.

Yizhar, S., trans. Nicolas de Lange and Yaacob Dweck. *Khirbet Khizeh: A Novel*. New York: Farrar, Straus and Giroux, 2014.

Yosef, Eitan Bar. "The Last Crusade? British Propaganda and the Palestine Campaign, 1917–18." *Journal of Contemporary History,* Vol. 36, No. 1. (January 2001).

Zeret, Elad. "Kastner's Killer: I Would Never Have Shot Him Today." *Ynetnews.com* (October 29, 2014), http://www.ynetnews.com/articles/0,7340,L-4585767,00.html [Last viewed December 8, 2015].

Zipperstein, Steven J. *Elusive Prophet: Ahad Ha'am and the Origins of Zionism*. Berkeley: University of California Press, 1993.

INDEX